THE OXFORD HANDBOOK OF

FREEDOM OF SPEECH

THE OXFORD HANDBOOK OF

FREEDOM OF SPEECH

Edited by
ADRIENNE STONE
and
FREDERICK SCHAUER

Great Clarendon Street, Oxford, OX2 6DP,
United Kingdom

Oxford University Press is a department of the University of Oxford.
It furthers the University's objective of excellence in research, scholarship,
and education by publishing worldwide. Oxford is a registered trade mark of
Oxford University Press in the UK and in certain other countries

© Oxford University Press (Chapters 1–29) 2021
© Introduction Adrienne Stone and Frederick Schauer 2021

The moral rights of the authors have been asserted

First published 2021
First published in paperback 2024

All rights reserved. No part of this publication may be reproduced, stored in
a retrieval system, or transmitted, in any form or by any means, without the
prior permission in writing of Oxford University Press, or as expressly permitted
by law, by licence or under terms agreed with the appropriate reprographics
rights organization. Enquiries concerning reproduction outside the scope of the
above should be sent to the Rights Department, Oxford University Press, at the
address above

You must not circulate this work in any other form
and you must impose this same condition on any acquirer

Published in the United States of America by Oxford University Press
198 Madison Avenue, New York, NY 10016, United States of America

British Library Cataloguing in Publication Data
Data available

Library of Congress Cataloging in Publication Data
Data available

ISBN 978–0–19–882758–0 (Hbk.)
ISBN 978–0–19–893354–0 (Pbk.)

Links to third party websites are provided by Oxford in good faith and
for information only. Oxford disclaims any responsibility for the materials
contained in any third party website referenced in this work.

Contents

List of Abbreviations — viii
About the Contributors — ix
Introduction — xi

PART I THE IDEA OF FREEDOM OF SPEECH: HISTORY, RATIONALES, AND CONCEPTS

History:

1. Mill on the Liberty of Thought and Discussion — 3
   CHRISTOPHER MACLEOD

2. The Classic Arguments for Free Speech 1644–1927 — 20
   VINCENT BLASI

Rationales:

3. The Truth Justification for Freedom of Speech — 44
   WILLIAM P MARSHALL

4. Autonomy and Free Speech — 61
   CATRIONA MACKENZIE AND DENISE MEYERSON

5. Freedom of Expression and Democracy — 82
   ASHUTOSH BHAGWAT AND JAMES WEINSTEIN

6. Freedom of Speech and Human Dignity — 106
   DIETER GRIMM

Perspectives:

7. Economic Perspectives on Free Speech — 118
   DANIEL HEMEL

8. Freedom of Speech and Public Reason — 137
   WOJCIECH SADURSKI

PART II FREEDOM OF SPEECH AS A LEGAL PRINCIPLE

9. What is Speech? The Question of Coverage — 159
   Frederick Schauer

10. Proportionality and Limitations on Freedom of Speech — 173
    Grégoire Webber

11. Freedom of Speech in International law — 193
    Michael Hamilton

12. The Structure of a Free Speech Right — 213
    Stephen Gardbaum

13. Positive Free Speech: A Democratic Freedom — 231
    Andrew T Kenyon

14. Speaking Back — 249
    Katharine Gelber

PART III CONTROVERSIES AND CONTEXTS

15. Defamation Law, *Sullivan*, and the Shape of Free Speech — 269
    Andrew T Kenyon

16. Privacy and Speech — 292
    Ioanna Tourkochoriti

17. Free Speech and Elections — 312
    Joo-Cheong Tham and KD Ewing

18. When Is Speech That Causes Unlawful Conduct Protected by Freedom of Speech? The Case of the First Amendment? — 331
    Geoffrey R Stone

19. The Internet and Social Media — 350
    Gregory P Magarian

20. Parades, Picketing, and Demonstrations — 369
    Timothy Zick

21. Insult of Public Officials　389
　　Christoph Bezemek

22. Freedom of Expression in the Workplace　410
　　Cynthia Estlund

23. Music and Art　431
　　Mark Tushnet

24. Free Speech and Commercial Advertising　444
　　Frederick Schauer

25. Hate Speech　455
　　Alon Harel

26. Pornography　477
　　Caroline West

27. Religious Speech　499
　　Gautam Bhatia

28. Glorifying Censorship? Anti-Terror Law, Speech and Online Regulation　518
　　Eliza Bechtold and Gavin Phillipson

29. Freedom of Media　542
　　Dieter Grimm

Index　556

LIST OF ABBREVIATIONS

ACHR	American Convention on Human Rights
ACLU	American Civil Liberties Union
AEA	American Economics Association
CERD	Committee on the Elimination of Racial Discrimination
CJEU	Court of Justice of the European Union
CPI	Committee for Public Information (USA)
CRC	Convention on the Rights to the Child
CRPD	Convention on the Rights of Persons with Disabilities
ECHR	European Convention on Human Rights
ECtHR	European Court of Human Rights
EHRR	European Human Rights Reports
ECJ	European Court of Justice
EWCA	England and Wales Court of Appeal
EWHC	High Court of England and Wales
ICCPR	International Covenant on Civil and Political Rights
ICERD	International Convention on the Elimination of All Forms of Racial Discrimination
ICJ	International Commission of Jurists
ICRMW	International Convention on the Protection of the Rights of All Migrant Workers and Members of Their Families
IPSO	Independent Press Standards Organisation
NLRA	National Labor Relations Act (USA)
OHCHR	Office of the High Commissioner for Human Rights
UDHR	Universal Declaration of Human Rights
UNGA	United Nations General Assembly
UNCHR	United Nations Commission on Human Rights
UNHCHR	Office of the High Commissioner for Human Rights
UNHCR	United Nations High Commissioner for Refugees
UNHRC	United Nations Human Rights Committee
UNTS	United Nations Treaty Series

About the Contributors

Eliza Bechtold Doctoral Candidate, Durham Law School, Durham, United Kingdom.

Christoph Bezemek Professor, Institute of Public Law and Political Science, University of Graz, Graz, Austria.

Ashutosh Bhagwat Martin Luther King, Jr Professor of Law and Boochever and Bird Endowed Chair for the Study and Teaching of Freedom and Equality, UC Davis School of Law, Davis, United States.

Gautam Bhatia Advocate, New Delhi, India.

Vincent Blasi Corliss Lamont Professor of Civil Liberties, Columbia Law School, New York, United States.

Cynthia Estlund Catherine A. Rein Professor of Law, NYU Law School, New York, United States.

KD Ewing Professor of Public Law, Dickson Poon School of Law, King's College London, United Kingdom.

Stephen Gardbaum Stephen Yeazell Endowed Chair in Law, UCLA School of Law, Los Angeles, United States.

Katharine Gelber Professor of Politics and Public Policy, University of Queensland, Brisbane, Australia.

Dieter Grimm Professor, Institute for Advanced Study (*Wissenschaftskolleg zu Berlin*), Berlin, Germany.

Michael Hamilton Senior Lecturer in Public Protest Law, School of Law, University of East Anglia, Norwich, United Kingdom.

Alon Harel Phillip P Mizock and Estelle Mizock Chair in Administrative and Criminal Law, Hebrew University of Jerusalem, Israel.

Daniel Hemel Professor of Law, Ronald H. Coase Research Scholar, University of Chicago Law School, United States.

Andrew T Kenyon Professor of Law, Melbourne Law School, Australia.

Catriona MacKenzie Professor, Macquarie University, Sydney, Australia.

Christopher Macleod Senior Lecturer, University of Lancaster, United Kingdom.

Gregory P Magarian Thomas and Karole Green Professor of Law, Washington University School of Law, St. Louis, United States.

William P Marshall William Rand Kenan, Jr Distinguished Professor of Law, University of North Carolina, Chapel Hill, United States.

Denise Meyerson Professor of Law, Macquarie Law School, Sydney, Australia.

Gavin Phillipson Professor of Public Law and Human Rights, University of Bristol Law School, Bristol, United Kingdom.

Wojciech Sadurski Challis Professor of Jurisprudence, The University of Sydney, Australia.

Frederick Schauer David and Mary Harrison Distinguished Professor of Law, University of Virginia, Charlottesville, United States.

Adrienne Stone Redmond Barry Distinguished Professor, Melbourne Law School, Melbourne, Australia.

Geoffrey R Stone Edward H. Levi Distinguished Service Professor of Law, University of Chicago Law School, United States.

Joo-Cheong Tham Professor, Melbourne Law School, Australia.

Ioanna Tourkochoriti Lecturer above the Bar, School of Law, National University of Ireland, Galway, Ireland.

Mark Tushnet William Nelson Cromwell Professor of Law, Emeritus, Harvard Law School, Cambridge, United States.

Grégoire Webber Canada Research Chair in Public Law and Philosophy of Law, Queen's University, Kingston, Canada.

James Weinstein Dan Cracchiolo Chair in Constitutional Law, Sandra Day O'Connor College of Law, Arizona State University, Phoenix, United States.

Caroline West Senior Lecturer, University of Sydney, Australia.

Timothy Zick John Marshall Professor of Government and Citizenship and Cabell Research Professor, William & Mary Law School, Williamsburg, United States.

INTRODUCTION

ADRIENNE STONE AND FREDERICK SCHAUER

FREEDOM of speech is a central commitment of political liberalism, a principle of positive constitutional law in virtually all modern constitutions and a principle of international human rights law.[1] Although among the most widely agreed upon and celebrated legal and constitutional principles of modern times, it is also the source of enduring and intense disagreement. We cannot fail to notice, moreover, that this Handbook is to be published at a time of some controversy about the power of freedom of speech in the face of new threats to democracy[2] and the challenges of the digital economy.[3] At worst, freedom of speech might even be part of the problem—a principle weaponized against the ideals from which it sprang.[4]

In this tumultuous context, this Handbook provides a comprehensive exploration of freedom of speech both as a political idea and as a legal principle. It is arranged in three parts: The chapters in Part I focus on freedom of speech as a political idea and upon the ideas and rationales that underlie it; the chapters in Part II focus on distinctive features of freedom of speech as a legal principle. In Part III the Handbook, the chapters focus on a range of controversies that have arisen in constitutional systems throughout the world and which illustrate and elaborate upon the general themes of Parts I and II.

---

[1] Freedom of speech is used here interchangeably with 'freedom of expression', though on the relationship between these concepts, see Frederick Schauer 'What is Speech? The Question of Coverage' Chapter 9 in this volume.

[2] Mark Graber, Sanford Levinson, and Mark Tushnet, (eds), *Constitutional Democracy in Crisis?* (OUP, 2018).

[3] Tim Wu, 'Is the First Amendment Obsolete?' (2018) 117 *Mich L Rev* 547, 568.

[4] *Janus v AFSCME, Council 31*, 138 S Ct 2448, 3501 (2018). See also Cynthia Estlund, 'Freedom of Expression in the Workplace', Chapter 22 in this volume.

A. Fundamental Questions and Perspectives

Part I begins with the most fundamental questions about the nature of freedom of speech: its history and rationales. Although a form of freedom of speech was evident in ancient times,[5] it is Enlightenment thinking that is usually credited with the decisive influence on modern conceptions.[6] Its influence is especially well documented by scholars of the First Amendment to the Constitution of the United States. In Chapter 2, Vincent Blasi, in a subtle exploration of the classic arguments for freedom of speech, traces the first comprehensive argument for freedom of speech as a limiting principle of government to John Milton's *Areopagitica*, a polemic against censorship by a requirement of prior licensing in which Milton develops an argument for the pursuit of truth through exposure to false and heretical ideas rather than the passive reception of orthodoxy.[7]

Despite Milton's belief in the advancement of understanding through free inquiry, he was far from liberal in the modern sense of that term and he did not, for instance, extend the tolerance he advocated to Catholic religious texts. The most famous and influential exposition of a liberal theory of freedom of speech is found in the work of John Stuart Mill.[8] Mill's argument for freedom of speech, commonly understood as based on freedom of speech as a facilitator of the search for truth and knowledge,[9] is central to Chapters 1 and 3. In Chapter 1, Christopher Macleod reminds us of the precise nature of Mill's claim. Three especially important points come to the fore. First, Mill's argument turns on the fallibility of human knowledge and his belief in the consequent value in subjecting ideas to contradiction. Second, while in constitutional law the focus has been on interference with freedom of speech by the state, Mill was as much concerned with 'moral reproach' that arises from social intolerance and social pressure. Finally, by virtue of its focus on the pursuit of truth, the Millian argument is focused on discussion rather than expression more broadly and therefore has little obvious application to non-propositional expression found in instrumental music and abstract art. (A theme later taken up by others,[10] including Mark Tushnet who, in Chapter 23, explores the

---

[5] DM Carter, 'Citizen Attribute, Negative Right: A Conceptual Difference between Ancient and Modern Ideas of Freedom of Speech' in Ineke Sluiter and Ralph Rosen (eds), *Free Speech in Classical Antiquity* (Brill 2004).

[6] Elizabeth Powers (ed), *Freedom of Speech: The History of an Idea* (Bucknell UP 2011).

[7] John Milton, *Areopagitica: A Speech for the Liberty of Unlicensed Printing, to the Parliament of England* (JC Suffolk ed, University Tutorial P 1968).

[8] John Stuart Mill, *On Liberty* (David Spitz ed, WW Norton 1975).

[9] An alternative understanding of Mill sees *On Liberty* as less about the search for truth and more about the development of certain virtues of intellectual character. See Vincent Blasi, 'Shouting "Fire!" in a Theater and Vilifying Corn Dealers' (2011) 39 *Cap U L Rev* 535.

[10] See also Frederick Schauer, 'What is "Speech"? The Question of Coverage', Chapter 9 in this volume.

problem of incorporating music and art into a theory of freedom of speech without also including a far wider range of human activities.)

The complexities of the truth justification for freedom of speech are further explored by William Marshall in Chapter 3. Marshall identifies its many flaws: the implausibility of the claim that freedom of speech is a mechanism for producing truth; the problems of public irrationality and apathy in a 'post-truth' age; and, most fundamentally, the difficulties in identifying the normative appeal of truth itself, especially in circumstances in which it causes harm. Abandoning these traditional arguments for truth, Marshall appeals to truth as an ideal serving a narrative function 'akin to the role played by myth in religion'.[11]

The argument from truth is one of three prominent lines of thought evident in an extensive philosophical literature on freedom of expression. Each of these lines of argument are explored in chapters in Part I. A second line of argument relies on the connection between freedom of speech and autonomy. Freedom of speech is said to protect (or to be integral to) individual autonomy by allowing individuals to form their own opinions about their beliefs and actions or by enabling 'self-development'; or because respecting freedom of speech accords (or is constitutive of) dignity, equal concern and respect due to all individuals. In Chapter 4, Catriona Mackenzie and Denise Meyerson explore the autonomy argument generally, and in Chapter 6, Dieter Grimm explores the argument from dignity.

The third line of argument, perhaps the most widely influential in the constitutional law of freedom of speech, relies upon the connection between freedom of speech and democratic self-government. Ashutosh Bhagwat and James Weinstein explore the argument from democracy in Chapter 5.

These three lines of argument—something of a 'classic trio' of justifications for freedom of speech—are the usual starting point of philosophical inquiry. But each gives rise to complex problems. Some are common to each rationale. In an echo of some arguments made against the truth rationale, arguments from autonomy are criticized for their failure to focus on the conditions necessary for the realization of autonomy. This line of thought has been especially prominent in feminist analysis of freedom of speech. In their chapter, Mackenzie and Meyerson explore a number of ways in which the problem has been addressed, from Susan Brison's forthright critique of the autonomy justification for permitting hate speech[12] and for failing adequately to distinguish autonomous speech from non-speech forms of autonomy,[13] to Susan Williams's idea of relational autonomy.[14]

---

[11] William P Marshall, 'The Truth Justification for Freedom of Speech', Chapter 3 in this volume, p. 57.
[12] See Catriona Mackenzie and Denise Meyerson, 'Autonomy and Free Speech', Chapter 4 in this volume, p. 78.
[13] Susan Brison, ' The Autonomy Defense of Free Speech' (1998) 108 *Ethics* 312.
[14] See Catriona Mackenzie and Denise Meyerson, 'Autonomy and Free Speech', Chapter 4 in this volume, p. 74. See also Catriona Mackenzie and Natalie Stoljar (eds), *Relational Autonomy: Feminist Perspectives on Autonomy, Agency and the Social Self* (OUP 2000).

Another kind of challenge for these arguments arises from the complexity of the ideas that underscore each rationale. This emerges clearly in Bhagwat and Weinstein's chapter on the democracy justification. As they show, it is well recognized that freedom of speech performs an essential informing function, enabling the people to vote and participate in public discourse, and informs representatives of the views of the people. In addition, free speech also serves a legitimating function because law's legitimacy requires that the people are free to take part in the public deliberations through which public opinion, and ultimately laws, are formed. Distinctively, Bhagwat and Weinstein take the legitimating function of freedom of speech to be crucial not just to the legal system as a whole but also to the legitimacy of *individual laws* and posit that laws banning hate speech may render other laws (such as anti-discrimination laws) illegitimate.

Equally, however, Bhagwat and Weinstein show that the nature of a right of freedom of speech will depend upon which conception of democracy, among the multiple and competing conceptions, dominates. For instance, where democracy is representative rather than direct, or where it prizes public deliberation over the aggregation of pre-existing interests, greater emphasis will be placed on public discourse. In such democracies, freedom of speech is likely to cover a broader range of public discussion beyond that required for the process of voting and law making.[15]

An important distinction, which illuminates matters taken up in later parts of the book, lies in the distinction between relatively thick (or substantive) understandings of democracies over relatively thin, proceduralist accounts. Of these two conceptions, the thicker idea of democracy provides a basis for more extensive limits on freedom of speech. Where democracy is taken to be instrumental to certain ends, freedom of speech can be limited where it makes little contribution to (or even frustrates) such ends. At this point, the long debate about the regulation of hate speech enters the picture again. Substantive conceptions of democracy (which usually entail that a democratic polity will 'demonstrate tolerance, mutual respect, and an embrace of diversity') provides a foundation for arguments that 'the state not only need not tolerate, but to the contrary has a positive obligation to suppress hate speech'[16] (a matter of which Weinstein and Bhagwat are evidently sceptical).

The idea that democracy is instrumental to a more fundamental value is evident in Dieter Grimm's chapter 'Freedom of Speech and Human Dignity'. Writing from within the German constitutional tradition, in which dignity is a foundational value receiving explicit constitutional protection, Grimm writes:[17]

> We do not have freedom of speech for democracy's sake, but we have democracy because it is the form of political rule best compatible with the dignity and autonomy of the individual.

---

[15] Ashutosh Bhagwat and James Weinstein, 'Freedom of Expression and Democracy', Chapter 5 in this volume.

[16] Ibid p. 102.

[17] Dieter Grimm, 'Freedom of Speech and Human Dignity', Chapter 6 in this volume, p. 110.

The dignity-based conception of freedom of speech requires that the principle extends well beyond political speech. Speech is valuable because it allows humans to form social relationships and develop their personality—matters integral to human dignity. However, dignitarian arguments also justify limits on freedom of speech where that speech violates human dignity. Thus Grimm shows how dignity may furnish an argument for the regulation of hate speech where that speech:[18]

> attempts to deny human beings individual personhood, to strip them from all rights (or from the right to have rights), to classify certain individuals as such or because of their group membership as life not being worth lived, to claim that by their behaviour they have forfeited any claim to respect.

Dignity's role as both a justification for freedom of speech and for limiting it, points to a more general dynamic. Where freedom of speech is taken to be instrumental to a more fundamental value, it will usually be the case that the underlying value—equality, autonomy, dignity—will in some circumstances be deployed as an argument for freedom of speech and in others in support of a limitation. This 'double-sidedness' of freedom of speech is a particularly perplexing feature of free speech argumentation.[19] It means, as Alon Harel shows in his chapter on hate speech and as Gautam Bhatia shows in his chapter on religious speech, that many arguments about freedom of speech are not a defence of a liberal ideal against illiberalism.[20] Rather, many free speech arguments occur within liberalism and their resolution depends upon a quite precise rendering of the relationship between freedom of speech and its underlying values.

As the chapters so far mentioned demonstrate, there is a rich philosophical literature about freedom of speech. A final contribution in this vein from Wojciech Sadurski shows the power of philosophical argument to illuminate even most seemingly technical aspects of free speech.[21] The chapter explores the salience of the Rawlsian idea of public reason for freedom of speech. Sadurski argues that the idea helps explain the focus in free speech law in a number of countries on the distinction between content-based and content-neutral laws (and relatedly on viewpoint-based and viewpoint-neutral laws). Public reason analysis explains this focus, and reveals as potentially illegitimate laws based on reasons that are non-endorsable by reasonable persons to whom they apply.

Contributions from other disciplines to scholarship on freedom of speech have been more limited. In an important exception to this trend, Daniel Hemel, in Chapter 7, explores the potential for economic analysis to illuminate freedom of speech. Information economics, he argues, has the potential to explain failures in the 'marketplace of ideas'.

---

[18] Ibid p. 114.
[19] Adrienne Stone, 'Viewpoint Discrimination, Hate Speech Laws, and the Double-Sided Nature of Freedom of Speech' (2017) 32 *Const Comment* 687.
[20] Alon Harel, 'Hate Speech', Chapter 25 in this volume; Gautam Bhatia 'Religious Speech', Chapter 27 in this volume.
[21] Wojciech Sadurski, 'Freedom of Speech and Public Reason', Chapter 8 in this volume.

Just as information asymmetry in the market for goods and services allows low-quality goods and services to drive high-quality goods and services out of the marketplace, there is reason to think that 'bad speech' will tend to drive out the 'good'. For good information to compete in the market, readers and listeners must be able to tell the difference between good and bad information—an idea with particular resonance in the age of 'fake news', and with potential implications for the design of free speech laws.[22]

B. Freedom of Speech as a Legal Idea

Part II of the volume turns from general questions about the nature of and justifications for freedom of speech to an examination of pervasive issues that arise with particular clarity when freedom of speech is applied as a legal principle.

The focus of most of these chapters is on freedom of speech as a principle of constitutional law, which in turn provides the basis for an individual to challenge the law. However, there are many ways in which a free speech principle might operate in law: it may guide the interpretation of statutes and other instruments; in common law systems at least, it may influence the development of case law; and it is a principle of international law (as canvassed by Michael Hamilton in Chapter 11).

Conceived at a high level of generality, the framework for the determination of legal free speech claims is remarkably similar across a wide range of legal systems. As Stephen Gardbaum shows in his close but broadly comparative analysis in Chapter 12, the nature and extent of a free speech right depends upon a number of legal components: (1) the legal source of the right (in common law, statute or a constitution) and the force of the right having regard to how it is enforced, and whether and how it can be superseded; (2) the subject of the right (citizens, natural or legal persons); (3) the scope of the right; (4) the kind of obligation it imposes on others (a negative prohibition or a positive obligation); (5) who is bound to respect a right of freedom of expression and against whom the right may be asserted; and (6) whether and how a free speech right might be limited.[23]

The first two chapters in Part II take up two of these elements in detail. Tracing the distinction in free speech law between 'coverage' and 'protection' influentially illuminated in his work, Schauer, in Chapter 9, addresses the question acts or behaviour a principle of freedom of speech applies.[24]

This question of coverage (or in Gardbaum's terms 'scope') can be invisible in legal analysis especially if it is abundantly clear that the activity concerned is 'speech' within the accepted meaning of the word or if techniques of legal interpretation (text, history, and precedent, for instance) provide a ready answer. But, as Schauer shows, in many

---

[22] Daniel Hemel, 'Economic Perspectives on Free Speech', Chapter 7 in this volume.
[23] Stephen Gardbaum, 'The Structure of a Free Speech Right', Chapter 12 in this volume.
[24] Frederick Schauer, 'What is "Speech"? The Question of Coverage', Chapter 9 in this volume.

cases neither speech nor the common alternative 'expression' adequately capture the activity to which the principle applies. The only coherent way to approach the question of coverage is by reference to the underlying rationale or rationales for freedom of speech. In this light, the question of 'coverage' turns out to be highly revealing of some fundamental features of freedom of speech, namely that it is a complex ideal resting on multiple justifications.

The question of 'protection' (which corresponds to Gardbaum's final component, whether and to what extent the free speech right may be limited) goes to the weight or strength of the protection from regulation conferred on that which is covered. In the context of constitutional law, it is reflected in legal doctrines formulated by courts. The protection question brings to the fore the much-noted 'US exceptionalism' with respect to freedom of speech in constitutional law. As is well known, First Amendment law is characterized by a conceptual or categorial approach that applies relatively specific, rule-like limitations, as compared with the more flexible approach of 'structured proportionality' that dominates the rest of the world.

The relative merits of these approaches are the subject of an enormous literature in which proportionality analysis is usually lauded for its flexibility and context-sensitivity, as well as the transparency it purportedly brings to judicial reasoning. Some of its more influential expositions—including the seminal work of Robert Alexy—make the even more ambitious claim that proportionality is necessary or inevitable[25] or that it frees courts of difficult and contested decisions.[26] In Chapter 10, 'Proportionality and Limitations on Freedom of Speech', Grégoire Webber mounts a critique of these claims on behalf of proportionality, and a defence of approaches that treat freedom of speech as absolute, at least in the sense as not subject to exception within its scope.

In Chapter 13, 'Positive Free Speech: A Democratic Freedom', Andrew Kenyon then takes up Gardbaum's fourth component, the kind of obligations imposed, arguing that an effective free speech right must necessarily be conceived as including positive obligations on the state.

The final chapter in Part II, 'Speaking Back', turns to the question of remedies and responses. In it, Katharine Gelber interrogates the common claim that the remedy for falsehoods and other forms of 'bad speech' is 'more speech, not enforced silence'.[27] Applied indiscriminately, the idea of 'speaking back' is 'fanciful at best and harmful at worst' but Gelber defends it in some contexts, especially if—echoing Kenyon's chapter— freedom of speech is conceived of as requiring the state to empower 'speaking back'.[28]

The notion of state-backed 'speaking back' is picked up, again, in Caroline West's chapter on pornography. If certain pornography perpetuates or legitimates harmful sexist messages, West sees a role for state-backed 'speaking back'; specifically, public education aimed at countering harmful sexist messaging. But, she cautions, there are also

---

[25] Robert Alexy, *A Theory of Constitutional Rights* (Julian Rivers tr, OUP 2002) 66–9.
[26] David Beatty, *The Ultimate Rule of Law* (OUP 2004).
[27] *Whitney v California*, 274 US 357 (1927) 377.
[28] Katharine Gelber, 'Speaking Back', Chapter 14 in this volume, p. 262.

reasons to doubt its likely effectiveness. Harmful effects of pornography on its consumers may not be fully 'mentally intermediated', and so not amenable to rational revision in response to counter-speech.[29]

C. Contexts and Controversies

The chapters in Part III focus on particular contexts and controversies that have proved especially important and interesting for the application of free speech principles. The chapters are all rich with insights on the particular controversies they cover, and the themes explored in the first two parts. For example, question of 'coverage' is addressed in particular contexts by Frederick Schauer's chapter on commercial advertising,[30] Mark Tushnet's chapter on art,[31] Caroline West's chapter on pornography,[32] and Alon Harel's chapter on hate speech.[33]

Similarly, the democracy justification is revisited and elaborated upon in chapters by Joo-Cheong Tham and Keith Ewing on elections,[34] Andrew Kenyon on defamation of public officials,[35] Christoph Bezemek on public insult,[36] and Timothy Zick on parades, picketing, and demonstrations.[37] It is also addressed in Cynthia Estlund's chapter on the workplace, which explores the implications for democratic government of employment-based limitations on freedom of speech.[38]

These chapters are complemented by a pair of chapters that consider the challenges and complications arising from the nature of mass communication in the traditional media[39] and the digital economy.[40]

The 'double-sidedness' of freedom of speech is revisited in a group of chapters which focuses on the particular harms that may be caused by speech. Geoffrey Stone revisits the question of speech causing unlawful conduct,[41] a general theme picked upon in the

---

[29] Caroline West, 'Pornography', Chapter 26 in this volume, p. 497.
[30] Frederick Schauer, 'Free Speech and Commercial Advertising', Chapter 24 in this volume.
[31] Mark Tushnet, 'Music and Art', Chapter 23 in this volume.
[32] Caroline West, 'Pornography', Chapter 26 in this volume.
[33] Alon Harel, 'Hate Speech', Chapter 25 in this volume.
[34] Joo-Cheong Tham and Keith Ewing, 'Free Speech and Elections', Chapter 17 in this volume.
[35] Andrew T Kenyon, 'Defamation Law, *Sullivan*, and the Shape of Free Speech', Chapter 15 in this volume.
[36] Christoph Bezemek, 'Insult of Public Officials, Chapter 21 in this volume.
[37] Timothy Zick 'Parades, Picketing, and Demonstrations', Chapter 20 in this volume.
[38] Cynthia Estlund 'Freedom of Expression in the Workplace', Chapter 22 in this volume.
[39] Dieter Grimm, 'Freedom of Media', Chapter 29 in this volume.
[40] Gregory P Magarian, 'The Internet and Social Media', Chapter 19 in this volume.
[41] Geoffrey R Stone, 'When is Speech That Causes Unlawful Conduct Protected byFreedom of Speech? The Case of the First Amendment', Chapter 18 in this volume.

contemporary context of terrorism by Eliza Bechtold and Gavin Phillipson.[42] Alon Harel's chapter on hate speech,[43] Gautam Bhatia's chapter on religious speech,[44] Caroline West's chapter on pornography,[45] and Ioanna Tourkochoriti's chapter on privacy[46] focus on harms of a different kind which implicate other fundamental rights like dignity, equality, religious freedom, and privacy.

Among these chapters, First Amendment exceptionalism is evident again. As these chapters show, First Amendment law has had enormous influence on the development of free speech law globally, reflecting the comparatively long history of judicial review of the First Amendment, and the volume of case law and secondary literature it has produced. But as these chapters also show, many substantive aspects of First Amendment law are unique and, on questions as diverse as electoral funding, advocacy of illegality,[47] commercial advertising,[48] defamation and hate speech,[49] most democracies have taken a different path.[50]

The intellectual influence but substantive exceptionalism of First Amendment law is especially evident in chapters by Andrew Kenyon, Christoph Bezemek, and Joo-Cheong Tham and Keith Ewing. Each of these chapters takes an iconic First Amendment case and shows both how it illuminates freedom of speech *and* how it has been departed from elsewhere. Andrew Kenyon places *New York Times v Sullivan*[51] in the context of defamation law generally, noting how courts in other countries have been influenced by and yet departed from its approach. The exceptionalism of *Sullivan*, he argues, depends both on a relatively thin conception of the value of reputation and on a particular understanding of the idea of public debate. Christoph Bezemek takes the closely related question of 'fighting words' and the US Supreme Court's decision in *Chaplinsky v New Hampshire*[52] as his centrepiece for a discussion of public insult. *Chaplinsky* is, of course, something of an 'orphan' in the First Amendment canon.[53] It is tempting to think that while its 'fighting words' exception has withered in the United States, it had found a home in Europe where insult laws are widely accepted both by the European Court of Human Rights (ECtHR) and in domestic jurisdictions. But Bezemek shows that the

---

[42] Eliza Bechtold and Gavin Phillipson, 'Glorifying Censorship? Anti-Terror Law, Speech, and Online Regulation', Chapter 28 in this volume.
[43] Alon Harel, 'Hate Speech', Chapter 25 in this volume.
[44] Gautam Bhatia, 'Religious Speech', Chapter 27 in this volume.
[45] Caroline West, 'Pornography', Chapter 26 in this volume.
[46] Ioanna Tourkochoriti, 'Privacy and Speech', Chapter 16 in this volume.
[47] Eliza Bechtold and Gavin Phillipson, 'Glorifying Censorship? Anti-Terror Law, Speech and Online Regulation', Chapter 28 in this volume.
[48] Frederick Schauer, 'Free Speech and Commercial Advertising', Chapter 24 in this volume.
[49] Alon Harel, 'Hate Speech', Chapter 25 in this volume.
[50] Frederick Schauer, 'The Exceptional First Amendment' in Michael Ignatieff (ed), *American Exceptionalism and Human Rights* (Princeton UP 2005) 29.
[51] *New York Times v Sullivan*, 376 US 254 (1964).
[52] *Chaplinsky v New Hampshire*, 315 US 568, 570 (1942).
[53] The Supreme Court has never since upheld a conviction on the basis of the 'fighting words' exception that *Chaplinsky* apparently establishes. See Erwin Chemerinsky, *The First Amendment* (Wolters Kluwer 2018) 159.

approach of the ECtHR is structurally different, turning not on a narrowly defined categorical exception but upon case-by-case proportionality analysis of a kind that the US Supreme Court would eschew. Turning to the closely related question of insult to public officials (also discussed by Kenyon), Bezemek focuses again on structural differences in doctrine. Expanding his focus to include the Inter-American Court of Human Rights and the African Court on Human and Peoples' Rights, he shows that each proceeds on a rather different conception of 'public figure'.

Joo-Cheong Tham and Keith Ewing, in the most critical of these three chapters, take *Citizens United v Federal Electoral Commission*[54] as the centrepiece of their critique of First Amendment law. They identify the First Amendment's core non-redistributive principle as based on a uniquely US mistrust of government regulation of speech and laissez-faire attitude to the distorting power of private wealth. The European social-democratic model, by contrast, is premised on equality as a foundation of a just electoral system and, because the state is viewed less negatively, permits more government intervention in pursuit of that equality.

Their critique introduces a second theme: the problems that that arise from the exercise of private power. Classically, freedom of speech is conceived of as a negative right that operates to restrain government power, leaving private relations untouched. But, as Cynthia Estlund shows, unrestrained power of employers to interfere with the speech rights of employees would make public discourse impossible. Similarly, an unrestrained power to regulate speech activity on private property would prevent the collective action necessary for civic engagement that is central to 'cultural identification, acts of resistance, and . . . political contention in a democracy'.[55] In Estlund's chapter on the workplace, and Zick's chapter on parades, picketing, and demonstrations, the assessment of First Amendment law is somewhat hopeful. Estlund traces the way that US courts have, over the last century, carved out exceptions to the rights of employers to respect employees' freedom of speech, and detects a strand of 'neo-republican thought' in First Amendment law, sensitive to the dominating power of employers.[56] Timothy Zick shows how the US Supreme Court, relying on the concept of the 'public forum', built an 'expressive topography', a doctrinal categorization of public places that limits powers of regulation in these spaces.[57]

Nonetheless, Estlund concludes that the protection of freedom of speech in the workplace remains normatively deficient. Indeed the 'weaponization critique' mentioned at the outset, and pervasive in the commentary on the protection of commercial advertising, is traceable, at least in that language, to Justice Kagan's dissent in a labour law case, *Janus v AFSCME,* in which the majority held that requiring public sector employees to

---

[54] *Citizens United v Federal Electoral Commission*, 558 US 310 (2010).
[55] Timothy Zick 'Parades, Picketing, and Demonstrations', Chapter 20 in this volume, p. 369.
[56] Cynthia Estlund 'Freedom of Expression in the Workplace', Chapter 22 in this volume, p. 413.
[57] Timothy Zick 'Parades, Picketing and Demonstrations', Chapter 20 in this volume, p. 376.

pay union dues was invalid on First Amendment 'compelled speech' grounds.[58] Turning to public forums, the exclusion of private property has always meant that some places (privately-owned airports, shopping centres, malls, and plazas) where citizens seek to gather for free speech purposes may be excluded from the public forum doctrine. But the problem is much exacerbated by the increasing privatization of public space.

Outside First Amendment law, attitudes towards private power are quite different and the problems posed by private actors restricting freedom of speech or distorting public discourse can be dealt with in a more straightforward fashion. Three features of free speech law are especially pertinent to this difference. First, as Ioanna Tourkochoriti explains in her chapter on privacy, other systems of law (in her chapter—Germany and France) allow for the 'horizontal' application of free speech rights against private individuals.[59] By comparison, the 'verticalist' position usually taken to be exemplified by the First Amendment, applies free speech rights only against the state, reflecting an assumption that threats to freedom of expression are characterized as arising principally or only from the state. The line between these two positions can be blurry and may be less important in practice if there is a sufficiently capacious 'state action' doctrine.[60] The distinction between horizontal and vertical applications of rights, however, is indicative of a markedly different understanding of the role of constitutional rights. Second, in most other legal systems, the mistrust of government that characterizes First Amendment law is moderated and the state is more likely to be regarded as a positive actor in pursuit of legitimate goals.[61] This moderation of mistrust of government gives governments greater scope to address harms caused by private actors, notably on matters like hate speech and electoral funding.

Finally, in some systems, the problem of private power is addressed through positive obligations imposed upon the state. In his chapter on media,[62] Dieter Grimm explains Germany's broadcast jurisprudence as a means to address the problems of private power in public discourse. Under the German Basic Law, the German state is under a 'double obligation'. It must not unduly interfere with the freedom of media, but it is also required to act to protect the media against attempts of private actors that may lead to distortion of public discourse or dysfunction within the media.

---

[58] *Janus v AFSCME, Council 31*, 138 S Ct 2448, 2501 (2018) (Kagan J, dissenting).

[59] But see also Constitution of South Africa: 4 February 1997 ('South African Constitution'), s 8(2); Constitution of Colombia: 4 July 1991 ('Colombian Constitution'), art 86; Constitution of Ireland: 29 December 1937 (as amended to 1 October 2013) ('Irish Constitution'), s 40(3), and *Meskell v CIE* [1973] IR 121.

[60] There is also a third position—'indirect horizontal action'—which allows for the invocation of constitutional rights in private actions under the general law, see Stephen Gardbaum, 'The Structure of a Free Speech Right', Chapter 12 in this volume, p. 224.

[61] As in Canada, see Adrienne Stone, 'Canadian Constitutional Law of Freedom of Expression', in Richard Albert and David R Cameron (eds), *Canada in the World: Comparative Perspectives on the Canadian Constitution* (CUP 2017).

[62] Dieter Grimm, 'Freedom of Media', Chapter 29 in this volume.

D. The Changing Context

Grimm's chapter introduces our final theme: the changing nature and significance of the forums in which speech occurs. The most compelling development is the rise of the digital economy, which radically changes the dynamics of freedom of speech. The Internet is the subject of Gregory Magarian's chapter,[63] although the many complications posed by the Internet as a speech forum are explored in other chapters, including those on pornography, hate speech, media freedom, and international law.

As Magarian shows, the Internet offers huge opportunities for realizing the social benefits of freedom of speech—making powerful contributions to political movements and promoting art, science, and commerce—but by the same token this new medium amplifies the possibilities for harm and poses a distinct set of challenges.

For example, the ease of communication and vast increase in the quantity of available information has led to the breakdown of the traditional media and the 'gatekeeping' function they performed. That, combined with anonymity and the highly manipulable nature of digital imagery, makes it very difficult to assess the credibility of information before us. Ordinary citizens can disguise themselves as credible news sources; political operatives and agents of foreign governments can be made to look like ordinary citizens; images and even video can be faked. The result is a torrent of low-quality information, much of it worthless or worse, deliberately spread to serve disruptive and nefarious interests, foreign and domestic. Such speech may proliferate more readily, rapidly, and to a wider audience, amplifying its potential harm.

These challenges run especially deep because the shape of a solution is very unclear. The devolved and transnational architecture of the Internet poses real barriers to regulation even pursuant to horizontal and positive conceptions of freedom of speech. The problem of the Internet will require creative regulatory solutions and to which constitutional rights of freedom of speech will need to adapt.[64] At the same time, creative and novel regulatory solutions to harmful online speech may also have unintended adverse consequences. As Bechtold and Phillipson observe in their chapter, there is a risk that regulations aimed at swiftly and cost-effectively stemming the proliferation of harmful material online can be excessively broad and speech-restrictive, shift the burden of regulation onto transnational corporations, and lack adequate safeguards, scrutiny, and attention to rights.[65]

This leads us to a closing reflection on the changing nature of the subject of this volume. It is barely more than a century since the US Supreme Court began seriously to expound free speech norms; only seventy years since the end of World War II inspired

---

[63] Gregory P Magarian, 'The Internet and Social Media', Chapter 19 in this volume.

[64] See Jack Balkin, 'Free Speech Is a Triangle' (2012) 118 *Colum L Rev* 2011; see also Tim Wu, 'Is the First Amendment Obsolete?' (2018) 117 *Mich L Rev* 547. 568.

[65] Eliza Bechtold and Gavin Phillipson, 'Glorifying Censorship? Anti-Terror Law, Speech, and Online Regulation', Chapter 28 in this volume.

the global rise of human rights, and only thirty years since democratic constitutionalism—and with it constitutional rights of freedom of speech—became a truly global phenomenon. Yet in this time, the nature of public discourse has transformed radically. Today, vast swathes of ordinary human communication occur in previously unrecognizable ways.

Freedom of speech will be a treasured norm at least for as long as democracies persist, but beyond that simple fact, perhaps all that can be counted upon is that the fundamental and difficult questions which are the subject of this volume, and these chapters, will remain a source of contestation in law and politics.

E. With Thanks

Fittingly, given freedom of speech's transnational reach, this volume was a transnational effort and was both enabled—and at times challenged—by communication across the Internet. As editors, we express our thanks to the authors for their commitment to this project; their willingness to revise chapters during the editing process and to keep to the necessary word limit. We are delighted to have brought such a talented group of scholars together in these pages.

Adrienne Stone wishes to thank colleagues at Melbourne Law School in the Centre for Comparative Constitutional Studies and the Laureate Program on Comparative Constitutional Law for their assistance. Aftab Hussain and Gabrielle Dalsasso in their respective roles as Centre Administrator and Project Manager for the Laureate Program ensured the smooth running of other aspects of academic life, freeing time to work on this volume. Four talented and hardworking research assistants—Joshua Quinn-Watson, Colette Mintz, Anne Carter, and Gary Hansell—performed important research and editorial tasks that greatly improved the Handbook. Their work and Adrienne Stone's contribution was generously supported by the Australian Research Council through an Australian Laureate Fellowship.

We are finally very grateful to Oxford University Press and its editorial staff for initiating the project and for their expertise and patience through all stages of its production. We are proud and delighted to have made a contribution to the very fine Handbook series.

PART I

THE IDEA OF FREEDOM OF SPEECH: HISTORY, RATIONALES, AND CONCEPTS

CHAPTER 1

MILL ON THE LIBERTY OF THOUGHT AND DISCUSSION

Christopher Macleod

Chapter two of John Stuart Mill's *On Liberty*—'On the Liberty of Thought and Discussion'—is the best-known defence of free speech in the philosophical canon.[1] Familiarity has certainly not bred contempt: the chapter continues to be cited approvingly in both the academic literature and in judicial decisions, and the broad line of thought embodied in the text has been internalized as part of liberal society's self-understanding. Yet perhaps exactly because of its success, that text has itself in many ways become over-familiar. As a result, it has become easy to lose sight of the details of the arguments Mill offers, as well as their grounds and consequences. I wish, in this chapter, to offer a reconstruction of Mill's case for 'Liberty of Thought and Discussion' which focuses on various aspects of that argument which may be easily forgotten; I hope that doing so will not only provide a useful refresher on the specifics of Mill's own argument, but will also serve implicitly to highlight some of the distance between Mill's argument and current accounts of free speech.

I begin, in Section 1.1, by suggesting that Mill's argument in chapter two of *On Liberty* is a distinctively *epistemic* argument, and one which relies on a specific conception of man's cognitive nature and the character of human knowledge. There is, I claim, a strong connection between what I term Mill's Freedom of Discussion Principle and the way in which human beings come to know the world. In Section 1.2 I attempt to identify quite what Mill means to *rule out* by his argument—what, in short, freedom of discussion is freedom *from*—and quite what he means to *rule in*. I turn, finally, in Section 1.3, to consider the relation between the Freedom of Discussion Principle and its better known (though perhaps not much better understood) sibling, the Harm Principle, and the conditions under which these principles are applicable.

---

[1] JS Mill, 'On Liberty' in *The Collected Works of John Stuart Mill* (University of Toronto Press and Routledge 1963–91) (*Collected Works*) vol XVIII, 228–59.

1.1 Man's Cognitive Nature and the Epistemic Case for Freedom of Discussion

Mill's argument for freedom of discussion draws on his conception of human beings and their place in the world. Human beings are, Mill claims, wholly part of the natural order—as such, the human mind, as well as body, is entirely governed according to the laws uncovered by scientific investigation. This vision of the mind as operating according to natural laws leads to a view under which our only means of interaction with the world is *causal* interaction. Insofar as we are able to come to know the world, Mill claims, we can do so only by being receptive to the world causally. As such, the possibility of substantive a priori knowledge is precluded, for all receptivity to the world takes place *via* the senses.[2]

Our engagement with the world, to put this another way, is *sensible*. We can perhaps imagine beings capable of knowing elements of the world by direct and unmediated insight. Such creatures would know how things are without *being affected*. But we are not them. We could know the world by acts of pure reflection only 'if we could know a priori that we must have been created capable of conceiving whatever is capable of existing: that the universe of thought and that of reality, the Microcosm and the Macrocosm (as they once were called) must have been framed in complete correspondence'. '[A]n assumption more destitute of evidence could scarcely be made', however.[3] There is, for us, 'no knowledge cognizable by the mind's inward light'.[4] As natural beings, our knowledge of how things are has at its foundation modes of interaction with the world which are themselves wholly natural.

As well as being *sensible*, our engagement with the world is also *discursive*.[5] Thinking is conducted, Mill is clear, through and by the application of concepts—or, in terminology he prefers, 'general names'.[6] Our knowledge takes the form of understanding that *things are in a certain way*. A manner of engaging with the world which did not enable us to think of objects as possessing qualities 'would not enable us to make a single assertion respecting them'.[7] The claim that an object has a quality, however, is a relational claim: that *this* object is similar in some way to *other objects*. 'The only meaning of predicating a quality at all, is to affirm a resemblance'.[8] For us, such resemblances are not themselves

---

[2] See John Skorupski, *John Stuart Mill* (Routledge 1989) 5–43 for a useful overview of Mill's naturalistic approach to philosophy, and 376–83 for its connection to his account of free speech.

[3] JS Mill, 'An Examination of Sir William Hamilton's Philosophy' in *Collected Works*, vol IX, 68.

[4] JS Mill, 'Coleridge' in *Collected Works*, vol X, 125.

[5] I draw loosely on the terminology of Henry E Allison's *Kant's Transcendental Idealism: An Interpretation and Defense* (rev edn, Yale UP 2004) 77ff. There are of course clear and crucial differences in Mill and Kant's conception of the human intellect, though these should not be allowed to mask instructive parallels, which have often been overlooked.

[6] Mill, 'An Examination' (n 3) 315–19.

[7] JS Mill, 'Notes on Analysis' in *Collected Works*, vol XXXI, 142.   [8] Ibid 143.

sensed between objects, but involve thinking *about* what is delivered by sensation. Knowledge of the world, that is to say, involves sensation, but also interpretation.[9]

1.1.1 Fallibility, Evidence, and Judgment

It is in this context that we must understand Mill's claim that '[a]ll silencing of opinion is an assumption of infallibility'.[10] As Piers Turner has pointed out, Mill's claim is not that one must explicitly represent oneself as infallible in order to *actually* silence opinion, but rather that the only conditions under which one could be *justified* in silencing opinion are those of infallibility.[11] This is, Mill claims, because '[c]omplete liberty of contradicting and disproving opinion, is the very condition which justifies us in assuming its truth . . . on no other terms, can a being with human faculties have any rational assurance of being right'.[12]

That our engagement with the world is *sensible* means that human beings are fallible in the following sense: there is no evidence-base E_1 that could be acquired to support conclusion c such that E_1 could not in principle be extended into E_2 such that E_2 supports not-c. For this reason, in order to achieve knowledge of how things are, we must consider the *whole* of our own evidence-base in order to draw warranted conclusions—not merely part. Beings with faculties such as our own are subject to conflicting and countervailing evidence from the senses, and as such, ignoring part of the evidence can be misleading. Someone who concludes from the sound of tweeting that *there is a bird close by* while ignoring that they can also see a nearby radio with an active on-light is not warranted in their belief—though that person could have been warranted in their belief, had the *only* piece of evidence in their possession been the sound of a bird, or indeed had they *taken into account* the countervailing evidence but judged it on balance unpersuasive.

As regards one's own evidence, this sensible fallibility rules out a certain kind of evidentiary *silencing* which might otherwise seem tempting. Where we have reached a conclusion and have confidence in our warrant for that conclusion, we might be tempted to simply think that the force of existing countervailing evidence is reduced to nil—and

---

[9] That our knowledge is achieved *sensibly* and *discursively* perhaps admits of exception at the foundational level in Mill's view. *That I am having a coloured sensation* might be known immediately, not causally by a sensation delivered *from* that sensation; similarly, of two red sensations, *that these sensations are similar*, might be known without the application of concepts, but directly. See Mill, 'A System of Logic Ratiocinative and Inductive' in *Collected Works*, vol VII, 6–9, 70–2. And, Mill indicates, some simple and unstable forms of thought (and therefore perhaps knowledge) may be possible without linguistic, i.e. conceptual, resources. Ibid 19; Mill 'An Examination' (n 3) 311ff. Nevertheless, all knowledge more complex than this must be sensible and discursive, Mill holds—and I will confine my attention, for the purposes of a treatment of free speech concerning public claims, to such knowledge.

[10] Mill, 'On Liberty' (n 1) 229.

[11] See Piers Noris Turner, 'Authority, Progress, and the "Assumption of Infallibility" in *On Liberty*' (2013) 51 *J Hist Phil* 93.

[12] Mill, 'On Liberty' (n 1) 231.

that, as such, going forward, we can ignore such evidence, on the grounds that it is misleading. This would be a mistake, however, as can be seen by noting that the same portion of the initial evidence which would be regarded as *misleading* when outweighed by a competing set of evidence supporting some conclusion c, could be considered *supportive* when complemented by further evidence of not-c. The same considerations, of course, apply equally to newly acquired evidence: to disregard or silence such evidence because it conflicts with conclusions already drawn ignores the fact that our reasoning from evidence is always defeasible: 'There is the greatest difference between presuming an opinion to be true, because, with every opportunity for contesting it, it has not been refuted, and assuming its truth for the purpose of not permitting its refutation'.[13]

Taken at a social level, the link between consideration of the entirety of our evidence-base and robust norms of free discussion is clear. The features of the sensible intellect which make it necessary to consider all of one's *own* evidence—not merely part—also make it necessary to listen to the evidence offered by *others*. For however much supporting evidence any person may possess for a given belief, others may possess countervailing evidence which, on balance, outweighs it. If we are to have confidence in our beliefs, it must be on the basis that we have not neglected any evidence possessed by others. As such, a society committed to truth must be prepared to hear evidence openly—that is, to be governed by norms of free discussion.

An even more fundamental link between the need for norms of free discussion and our ability to have confidence in our beliefs, however, derives from the *discursivity* of our interaction with the world. Our sensible fallibility has its origins in the fact that evidence, when taken in part, can prove misleading. But we are also subject to discursive fallibility: even if, *per impossibile*, one could be confident that there was no more relevant experience to be had on a given matter, the question would still remain as to how to *interpret* the experience one *has* had in terms of claims about the world. Human beings learn about the world, Mill notes, by 'discussion and experience. Not by experience alone. There must be discussion, to show how experience is to be interpreted . . . Very few facts are able to tell their own story, without comments to bring out their meaning'.[14]

No interpretation of experience, Mill holds, is *self*-validating: there is a gap between the interpretation any individual *does* draw and the interpretation that would be *rational*, and as such we do not think that all interpretations are equally warranted. As beings that know the world only through the interpretation of experience, therefore, we are in need of a way of knowing whether the interpretation which we draw is a valid one. But such validation cannot itself be found purely *in* experience—as, for instance, the feeling of assurance, or the impression of correctness—for such an experience would itself simply amount to one more thing in need of interpretation and confirmation. To take any interpretation as confirmed *subjectively*, that is to say, amounts to 'denying the existence of any outwards standard, the conformity of an opinion to which constitutes its truth'—of

---

[13] Ibid.   [14] Ibid.

taking 'opinions [as] their own proof, and feelings [as] their own justification'.[15] The problem is a deep one: given that the authorization of interpretation is not encountered in experience, from where can it come?

Mill claims that the only test on our *own* judgments about the validity of an interpretation can be the judgments of *others*.[16] For beings such as ourselves, no escape from human interpretation is possible—but comparison of one interpretation with another can provide a route to assurance that is not merely subjective. I can have confidence that my interpretation is objectively warranted only insofar as I believe other independent agents would also converge upon that same interpretation. That my interpretation finds confirmation in the judgment of others should increase my confidence that I am genuinely warranted in my belief—as should its endurance in the face of ongoing free consideration of emerging alternatives. Discussion, in which experience is shared and interpretations are freely compared and contrasted, then, is a condition of our coming to take any of our beliefs as justified. Norms of free discussion provide the only context in which we can gain critical distance upon our own interpretations—without such a context, we can have no rational assurance, but only psychological conviction: 'To refuse a hearing to an opinion, because they are sure that it is false, is to assume that their certainty is the same thing as absolute certainty'.[17]

Mill's repeated reference to how *human beings* can come to know the world should remind us that his argument advances from substantive commitments about the nature of our intellect and the forms of knowledge and objectivity *we* are capable of:

> The beliefs which we have most warrant for, have no safeguard to rest on, but a standing invitation to the whole world to prove them unfounded. If the challenge is not accepted, or is accepted and the attempt fails, we are far enough from certainty still; but we have done the best that the existing state of human reason admits of . . . This is the amount of certainty attainable by a fallible being, and this the sole way of attaining it.[18]

If our contact with the world was immediate and non-causal, countervailing evidence with regards to evidence might not be possible; if our experience was self-interpreting, there would be no distinction between subjective confidence and objective warrant.

---

[15] Mill, 'A System of Logic' (n 9) 229; JS Mill, 'Letter to Gomperz' in *Collected Works*, vol XIV, 134.

[16] Mill struggles with this issue at various points in his philosophy. See JS Mill, 'Utilitarianism' in *Collected Works*, vol X, 206–7, in which Mill suggests judgments can be disciplined by, and tested against, *principles*; and Mill, 'A System of Logic' (n 9) 564, in which he notes that '[t]here is no appeal from the human faculties generally, but there is an appeal from one human faculty to another; from the judging faculty, to those which take cognizance of fact, the faculties of sense and consciousness'. Such mechanisms might be useful, but cannot provide an ultimately stable resting point—for of course the confidence that one is correctly *applying* principles, or correctly *judging* that the deliverances of independent faculties coincide, is itself merely delivered as the *experience* of confidence. Ultimately we must take the grounds that *warrant* such confidence to be grounded in something beyond the subject itself. See, in this connection, Ludwig Wittgenstein, *Philosophical Investigations* (GEM Anscombe tr, Basil Blackwell 1953) s 202; Saul A Kripke, *Wittgenstein on Rules and Private Language* (Harvard UP 1982) 89ff.

[17] Mill, 'On Liberty' (n 1) 232.   [18] Ibid 232.

(Indeed, Mill claims, the intuitionist model of coming to know amounts to the claim that we have exactly such a form of knowledge. Intuiting *how things are* purportedly involves unmediated knowledge of the world which does not require interpretation and cannot be overturned by further evidence.) Freedom of discussion would, for such beings, be redundant—or, at least, redundant from a distinctively epistemic perspective. But for humans—creatures for whom evidence may always be misleading because it is partial, and for whom objectivity of interpretation is only possible in dialogue with others—maintaining conditions of free discussion is pivotal to achieving knowledge.

1.1.2 Engagement with Falsehoods and Partial Truths

The argument from human fallibility is self-standing, and suffices on its own to establish what we might term the Freedom of Discussion Principle: that there should be no interference with the discussion of any opinion. For without unrestricted discussion, we cannot be confident that we have considered all of the available evidence or that our interpretation of the evidence is sound—and hence, we cannot take our beliefs to be justified. This argument, however, is bolstered by two further arguments. Whereas the first division of chapter two attempts to show that an opinion should not be suppressed because it may be true, the second and third divisions attempt to show that even if an opinion *is* false, or even if it is merely *part* of the truth, it should still be heard.

Mill's argument that even beliefs which are false should be heard draws on a quite specific conception of knowledge, based on observations about 'the way in which truth ought to be held by human beings'.[19] Knowledge *that* something is the case, Mill claims, involves certain practical abilities—knowledge *how* to do certain things—which are hard to maintain except in a context in which true beliefs are forced to defend themselves against false beliefs.[20] Far from it being epistemically deleterious to have falsehoods aired and engaged with, then, it is epistemically *useful* to have falsehoods articulated 'in earnest' by those who 'do their very utmost for them'.[21]

Knowledge, Mill claims, involves the ability to account for one's belief in terms of reasons: *justification* of a proposition consists not in an extra piece of information to be acquired, but a capacity made explicit in the social process of giving account to others for one's belief. Without the ability to successfully articulate the 'grounds for one's own opinion', a belief is not properly considered knowledge, 'but one superstition the more, accidentally clinging to the words which enunciate a truth'.[22] As Mill conceives the process, however, being able to offer reasons for one's belief—to explain why one believes

---

[19] Ibid 244.
[20] Though the early essay *On Genius* differs from *On Liberty* in emphasis—most notably, in placing a model of autonomous, rather than dialectical, discovery at its knowledge—it is nevertheless telling that it endorses a model of knowledge which involves *ability*. Knowledge is a 'something to be done', rather than to be *had*; it is not passive, but a 'power': see JS Mill, 'On Genius' in *Collected Works*, vol I, 336.
[21] Mill, 'On Liberty' (n 1) 245. [22] Ibid 244.

this rather than *that*—involves being able to 'refute the reasons on the opposite side'.²³ In order to qualify as knowing a proposition, that is to say, we must be able to show 'why that other theory cannot be the true one: and until this is shown, and until we know how it is shown, we do not understand the grounds of our opinion'.²⁴ As a result, 'he who knows only his own side of the case knows little of that'.²⁵ *Hearing, understanding*, and *arguing against* false beliefs helps to maintain our ability to provide justification for our own true beliefs.

At an even more basic level, however, the discussion of false beliefs is also the primary mechanism for us to clarify the *meaning* of true beliefs:

> [N]ot only the grounds of the opinion are forgotten in the absence of discussion, but too often the meaning of the opinion itself . . . Instead of a vivid conception and a living belief, there remain only a few phrases retained by rote; or, if any part, the shell and husk only of the meaning is retained, the finer essence being lost.²⁶

In a context in which beliefs are accepted without resistance, there is no need for active *thinking* about those beliefs, and we ourselves can too easily pass over their semantic import. In the absence of discussion and defence, that is to say, we can lose sight of the commitments—theoretical and practical—that are involved in *having* any given belief. We lose the ability in those circumstances to connect our knowledge to its implications for further belief and action—the mirror image of losing the ability to connect our knowledge to its grounds. In such circumstances, beliefs are held only nominally, 'without being ever realized in the imagination, the feelings, or the understanding'.²⁷

Lack of discussion of false beliefs, then, can lead to the loss of our ability to connect our true beliefs within a network of related beliefs and actions—in these circumstances a belief is 'held as a dead dogma, not a living truth'.²⁸ As such, open discussion and debate, in which falsehoods are 'fully, frequently, and fearlessly discussed', is epistemically useful.²⁹ It is also useful because it improves our chances of reaching the *whole*, rather than a merely *partial*, truth.

When two deeply held claims are in conflict, it is sometimes the case, Mill notes, that one claim is true and the other false: 'But there is a commoner case than either of these; when the conflicting doctrines, instead of being one true and the other false, share the truth between them'.³⁰ Mill offers examples of partial truths which help us to better understand the thought. Admirers of the eighteenth century, Mill claims, observe that *civilization leads to an improvement in the lives of individuals*. That is true—but only part of the truth, and can be misleading unless combined with an acknowledgement of the Rousseauian insight that some aspects of civilization are 'enervating and demoralizing'.³¹ The conservative is quite correct that *stability is necessary for a functioning state*—but

---

²³ Ibid 245. ²⁴ Ibid 244. ²⁵ Ibid 245. ²⁶ Ibid 247. ²⁷ Ibid.
²⁸ Ibid 243. ²⁹ Ibid. ³⁰ Ibid 252. ³¹ Ibid 253.

that point is deceptive if not combined with the liberal observation that progress is a condition which enables stability.[32]

Individuals, Mill thinks, are constitutionally liable to fall into the trap of mistaking the portion of the truth that *they* possess for the *whole* of the truth about a given matter. The experience of any person is necessarily limited—'clever & intelligent men hardly ever err from [seeing what is not], but no powers of mind are any protection against the evils arising from imperfect and partial views of what is real'[33]—and we display a tendency towards epistemic conceit:

> In general, man's capacity of putting himself into the position of another man, and identifying himself with that man's feelings and modes of thinking, when these are any way different from his own, is extremely limited. Most men, in consequence, regard the feelings and ideas excited in men of an opposite character to themselves, by objects which excite no such feelings in *them*, as monstrous and unnatural; or at least, radically wrong, and meriting no kind of consideration or allowance, either in reasoning or in conduct . . . Hence we have hundreds of systems founded on the partial views of one-sided minds.[34]

The best correction for such tendencies, Mill suggests, is open discussion, for it is in discussion that we encounter alternative perspectives and beliefs which, though contrary to are our own, are held just as deeply: 'The long or extensive prevalence of any opinion as a presumption that it [is] not altogether a fallacy; that to its first authors at least, it was the result of a struggle to express in words something which had a reality to them.'[35] The fact that some claim is held by thoughtful individuals, stands as evidence that there is *something* to it: that it must be accommodated as *part* of the truth. Achieving the whole truth on important matters, therefore, 'is so much a question of the reconciling and combining of opposites, that very few have minds sufficiently capacious and impartial to make the adjustment with an approach to correctness, and it has to be made by the rough process of a struggle between combatants fighting under hostile banners'. Unless two sides of the truth are 'expressed with equal freedom, and enforced and defended with equal talent and energy, there is no chance of both elements obtaining their due'.[36]

---

[32] Ibid; see also JS Mill, 'Considerations' in *Collected Works*, vol XIX, 383–9. Mill's most telling example of someone who possessed only *part* of the truth, however, is Jeremy Bentham. Bentham was correct, Mill observes, to note that *individuals are motivated by pursuit of utility*—but limited experience 'furnished him with an unusually slender stock of premises', which resulted in his overlooking other truths about human beings. This, Mill claims, did not make Bentham's premises false, but rather just incomplete—only 'half of the truth': see JS Mill, 'Bentham' in *Collected Works*, vol X, 93. See also Mill's comments on Auguste Comte and James Mill: JS Mill, 'Autobiography' in *Collected Works*, vol I, 164–5; JS Mill, 'Auguste Comte and Positivism' in *Collected Works*, vol X, 313.
[33] JS Mill, 'Letter to d'Eichthal' in *Collected Works*, vol XII, 42.
[34] JS Mill, 'Smart's Outline of Sematology [1]' in *Collected Works*, vol XXIII, 426.
[35] Mill, An Examination (n 3) 120.   [36] Mill, 'On Liberty' (n 1) 254.

1.1.3 Value of Truth

The case for freedom of discussion in chapter two of *On Liberty*, then, has three parts, and takes the following structure.

For any opinion φ,

[1, argument from fallibility]: φ might be true, and so should be not be supressed,[37]

[2, argument from improved justification/understanding]: φ might be false, but should not be suppressed, for its airing can contribute to a better justification and understanding of the truth,[38]

[3, argument from whole truth]: φ might be partially-true, but should not be suppressed, for its airing can help us achieve the whole truth.[39]

Therefore: there should be no interference with the discussion of any opinion φ. [Freedom of Discussion Principle]

It is easy to overlook the fundamentally different character of argument deployed in sections 1, 2 and 3. As noted above, the argument from fallibility is itself sufficient to establish the conclusion, whereas the arguments from improved justification/understanding and whole truth merely bolster the overall case. The first identifies *a condition for the possibility of knowledge*, whereas the other two point out *conditions which better facilitate the acquisition of knowledge*. Mill is not always clear about this difference, and the combination of arguments in chapter two of *On Liberty* often causes him to oscillate between language which stresses the strict necessity of free discussion, and language which merely points out its edifying effects, for knowledge.

Despite this distinction, it bears emphasis that the arguments share something important. They are *epistemic* arguments, appealing only to *the value of knowledge*—and not to any 'abstract right'[40]—in mounting the case for free discussion of opinion. The value of knowledge is itself all but taken for granted throughout the argument, however, receiving almost no defence as part of the argument. *Almost* no defence, but not *entirely* no defence—for Mill does advert to an argument for the value of truth when considering the suggestion that one might insulate an opinion from criticism not on the grounds of its truth, but on the grounds that it is too socially useful to dispense with.

Mill rejects that suggestion. To insulate an opinion of the grounds of its usefulness, he claims, one would at least need to be in a position to claim that the opinion in question is useful. To be in a position to make *this* claim, however, would involve opening the issue up for debate, for '[t]here is the same need of an infallible judge of opinions to decide an opinion to be noxious, as to decide it to be false, unless the opinion condemned has full opportunity of defending itself'.[41] And having this debate about a view's usefulness without entering into a substantive debate about the truth of the opinion itself would be impossible, because '[t]he truth of an opinion is part of its utility'.[42]

---

[37] Ibid 229–43. [38] Ibid 243–52. [39] Ibid 252–7.
[40] Ibid 224. [41] Ibid 223.
[42] Ibid 223; JS Mill, 'Utility of Religion' in *Collected Works*, vol X, 405.

The details of that argument need not concern us here, for what is primarily of interest for our purposes is the link Mill draws between *truth* and *utility*. As is well known, Mill claims in his moral philosophy 'that happiness is desirable, and the only thing desirable, as an end'.[43] The status of utility as the 'ultimate principle of teleology', does not mean that human beings do not have other ends—but only that those ends are themselves justified by their place in securing human happiness: 'I do not mean to assert that the promotion of happiness should be itself the end of all actions, or even of all rules of action. It is the justification, and ought to be the controller, of all ends, but is not itself the sole end'.[44] That Mill holds that the truth of an opinion is *part of its utility* shows how the orientation towards truth of Mill's argument in chapter two of *On Liberty* fits within his broader axiological commitments. Truth, in the form of *knowledge*, is the proximate end of enquiry and discussion—the end assumed valuable by that practice and regulating its norms. This end is in turn justified by its relation to the overarching end of human life: happiness.[45]

1.2 The Scope of Freedom of Discussion

Mill claims, then, that there should be no interference with the discussion of any opinion. So stated, however, the injunction is hard to interpret—for how demanding it will turn out to be depends greatly on how widely or narrowly *interference* and *discussion of opinion* are to be understood. I wish in this section, therefore, to clarify the scope of Mill's claim: put simply, what he means to limit by his Freedom of Discussion Principle, and what he means to protect.

As is generally well known, Mill's concern is not merely with interference by the *state*, but also by *society at large*. While Mill certainly takes seriously the possibility of governmental intrusion into individuals' lives, his primary focus in *On Liberty* is the newly emerging threat to liberty which arises as a result of democratic mass society—the social pressures made possible by egalitarian social structures and *mores*. Informal mechanisms of control possible in such societies are, he argues, just as insidious as legislative or executive action—and, indeed, can often be more so, given that they are capable of 'penetrating much more deeply into the details of life, and enslaving the soul itself':[46]

> Society can and does execute its own mandates . . . Protection, therefore, against the tyranny of the magistrate is not enough; there needs protection also against the tyranny of the prevailing opinion and feeling; against the tendency of society to impose, by other means than civil penalties, its own ideas and practices as rules of conduct on those who dissent from them.[47]

---

[43] Mill, 'Utilitarianism' (n 16) 234.   [44] Mill, 'A System of Logic' (n 9) 951–2.
[45] See Christopher Macleod, 'Mill on the Primary of Practical Reason' (2018) 78 *Analysis* 630.
[46] Mill, 'On Liberty' (n 1) 220.   [47] Ibid.

Mill's prohibition on interference with discussion applies as equally to social as to state interference—it applies to individuals attempting to censor by the use of stigma, as well as by the use of law.[48] '[T]o control the expression of opinion ... I deny the right of the people to exercise such coercion, either by themselves or by their government. The power itself is illegitimate'.[49] We might reasonably ask, however: what *counts* as an instance of the people exercising such interference? Mill does not offer an explicit answer to this question. The outer-boundaries of such interference are usefully marked by those reactions Mill *does not* count as interference, however.

Mill is clear that we are entitled to form opinions about others on the basis of their conduct and views, and to act on those opinions—this is not interference with *their* liberty, but merely a legitimate exercise of *our own* liberty: 'Though doing no wrong to any one, a person may so act as to compel us to judge him, and feel to him, as a fool, or as a being of an inferior order ... We have a right, also, in various ways, to act upon our unfavourable opinion of any one, not to the oppression of his individuality, but in the exercise of ours'.[50] Indeed, we are entitled to attempt to persuade a person, that is, not to express certain views—'remonstrating with him, or reasoning with him, or persuading him, or entreating him'[51]—or simply to avoid someone if we see fit: 'We are not bound, for example, to seek his society; we have a right to avoid it ... for we have a right to choose the society most acceptable to us. We have a right, and it may be our duty, to caution others against him, if we think his example or conversation likely to have a pernicious effect on those with whom he associates'.[52]

Such responses—'[a]dvice, instruction, persuasion, and avoidance by other people'[53]—do not amount to coercive interference with an agent, as they do not attempt to change their action by 'compelling' or 'visiting him with an evil'.[54] We can stray into the terrain of interference, however, if such acts constitute a threat of censure. And when we react with feelings of 'anger or resentment', we *do* visit the agent with an evil. As such, we coercively interfere in the permissible expression of ideas. We are not entitled to react with 'moral reprobation' to those who express ideas with whom we disagree, and we are not entitled to treat them as 'an enemy of society'. Indeed, though we are permitted to avoid those who engage in what we regard as distasteful expression, we are not entitled to 'parade our avoidance'.[55]

The distinction is a difficult one to draw precisely. It permits one to form an estimate of another's expressed opinion, but not to be judgmental—to withdraw from an individual personally if one sees fit, but not to withdraw our recognition of that person as a member with full standing in our moral community. Wherever the line lies between these categories of reaction, though, the resulting prohibition on interference will clearly be an exacting one. For Mill's claim is that we should not react to an agent's expressed opinion by public-facing reproach—that we should remain, in a word, *civil*—and this involves

---

[48] As Vincent Blasi notes, this is one key way in which Mill's argument differs from that of his most famous predecessors. See Chapter 2 of this volume, p. 20-4, 30.
[49] Mill, 'On Liberty' (n 1) 229.   [50] Ibid 278.   [51] Ibid 224.
[52] Ibid 278.   [53] Ibid.   [54] Ibid 224.   [55] Ibid 278-9.

taking an open attitude towards those whose opinions we think false, distasteful, or even immoral. As he himself puts it, individuals are 'to be allowed to say what they have got to say, & not be abused for their opinions so long as they *do* nothing wrong'.[56] They are 'to be judged by their actions ... & not by their speculative opinions'.[57]

Mill's notion of 'interference', then, is expansive—and, as such, much is ruled out as impermissible in response to discussion. What constitutes 'discussion', though, is perhaps surprisingly narrow. Recall that Mill's case for free discussion is *epistemic*, and argues from the claim that an opinion φ might be *true*, *false*, or *partially-true* to the claim that φ should be freely discussed. Because the argument is explicitly premised on contributions to discussion being either true, false, or partially-true, it is important to note that it is applicable only to statements which are *truth-apt*: capable of being evaluated in terms of truth. Moral and political claims, of course, are capable of truth or falsity—even when we do not know whether a proposition about *what we ought to do* is true or false, we know that it is the sort of claim which *admits* of being true or false—and are therefore protected by Mill's Freedom of Discussion Principle. Scientific claims are also truth-apt, as are broader claims about how things *are*, *were*, or *will be*, and so are similarly protected. All such propositions are capable of being affirmed, as well as being denied or merely entertained, and as such can form part of discussion.

Because the argument in chapter two of *On Liberty* only offers a case for protecting the assertion of truth-apt propositions as a contribution to discussion, however, the conclusion it establishes is significantly more restricted than that which those who advocate for 'freedom of speech' in the twenty-first century usually intend. We might note, for instance, that *jokes* are not truth-apt. It makes little sense to ask whether a joke is *true* or *false*. It can, to be sure, be witty or unamusing—penetrating or wide-of-the-mark—but it cannot be evaluated in terms of *truth*. The case Mill offers for the Freedom of Discussion, appealing to the truth-aptitude of opinions, does not speak to the case. Similarly, insofar as we hold that they cannot be persuasively characterized as capable of truth or falsity in anything other than a metaphorical sense, it cannot speak to the case of poetry or literature, painting or music.[58] Neither can one evaluate acts of protest or

---

[56] JS Mill, 'Letter to Lambert' in *Collected Works*, vol XVI, 1492 (my emphasis).

[57] Ibid 1479.

[58] Of course, this is not to deny that some artworks, religious symbols, jokes, and so on, can be used to persuade or to convey a message. But this is a feature that belongs only to some expressive acts and objects—it is clear that for example, an average landscape painting does not communicate any meaning—and such usage does not imply that works themselves *make a claim*. (It is of little use to note that an artwork can be *taken* by individuals to make a claim about the world—or indeed that an individual author can *intend* to make a claim *via* any expressive act—for such criteria threaten to trivialize the notion of meaningfulness by implying that *anything* can possess *any* meaning.) In the absence of tightly disciplined norms governing interpretation, commitment, and disagreement, expressive acts and objects cannot constitute moves in a discussion—and we cannot evaluate them as true or false.

support—the burning of a flag, or the wearing of a religious symbol—in terms of its truth or falsity.[59]

Discussion, then, has a technical meaning in Mill's work: freedom of discussion does not amount to freedom of expression. As such, many cases which are often argued in First Amendment terms to be covered by the *right to free speech* simply fall outside the scope of Mill's argument. Of course, this does not mean that Mill intends that such acts should receive no protection. Rather, it only means that Mill's arguments for the *freedom of discussion* do not offer them protection. Telling jokes, painting, and wearing religious symbols may well receive protection in Mill's work, but we have to look beyond the free speech arguments of chapter two of *On Liberty*—to the arguments of chapters three, four and five—to find its source. Such protections will have little to do with the epistemic case Mill makes for free discussion, but rather the utility of allowing people to develop their personality as they see fit, and pursue without interference any action which does not directly harm others.

Are *all* assertions of truth-apt claims protected by the Freedom of Discussion Principle? Mill's answer is complicated, but provides for clear cases in which the assertion of truth-apt claims is not permitted, and can be legitimately subject to interference:

> [O]pinions lose their immunity, when the circumstances in which they are expressed are such as to constitute their expression a positive instigation to some mischievous act. An opinion that corn-dealers are starvers of the poor, or that private property is robbery, ought to be unmolested when simply circulated through the press, but may justly incur punishment when delivered orally to an excited mob assembled before the house of a corn-dealer, or when handed about among the same mob in the form of a placard.[60]

The opinion that corn-dealers are starvers of the poor is not, in virtue of its *content*, proscribed. Assertion of the belief does not *itself* warrant interference—but interference can be warranted in certain contexts, when, for instance the assertion amounts to an *instigation to violence*. So, too, Mill notes that *the invasion of privacy* warrants interference, even when it takes place merely by the expression of truth-apt propositions:

> Mr. O'Connell goes farther than we are able to follow him, when he proposes that in all cases of private libel, truth should be a justification . . . But we would not permit the press to impute, even truly, acts, however discreditable, which are in their nature private . . . The proper tribunal for the cognizance of private immoralities, in so far as any censorship can be advantageously exercised over them by opinion at all, is the opinion of a person's friends and connexions.[61]

---

[59] I discuss this further in Christopher Macleod 'Truth, Discussion, and Free Speech in *On Liberty* II' *Utilitas* (forthcoming).
[60] Mill, 'On Liberty' (n 1) 260.
[61] JS Mill, 'Mr O'Connell's Bill for the Liberty of the Press' in *Collected Works*, vol VI, 165.

There is good reason to think that interference is also warranted in other cases of the assertion of truth-apt claims—for instance, in the case of *violation of copyright*.[62]

What is often missed, however, is that the range of cases in which interference with the assertion of a truth-apt proposition is permissible is far wider than such *legally actionable* instances of speech. Given that Mill's notion of interference is a broad one—broad enough to include *moral reproach* as interference—he must, for instance, endorse interference in cases of *lying*. While he would not advocate *legal* intervention as an expedient sanction in cases of individual lying—unless, presumably, that lie takes place in a context in which it qualifies as perjury—informal mechanisms of interference such as anger and resentment are entirely appropriate, because, as he repeatedly notes, lying is morally wrong.[63] That a lie takes the form of the assertion of a truth-apt proposition does not make it permissible, and does not oblige us to tolerate it as simply a contribution to discussion which permits its refutation.

The Freedom of Discussion Principle, we might note, is most plausible where discussion is portrayed as taking place solely within the space of reasons. Where volunteering a proposition is imagined to give rise only to disembodied reflection upon a claim, little can seem objectionable about the Freedom of Discussion Principle—for its consequences are seen only as moves of reason occasioned by acts of free thought. For human beings, however, discussion cannot take place solely in the space of reasons. (Though discussion in the seminar room can often seem to offer that ideal.) Because speech must take place within the causal order, it cannot only be the volunteering of a proposition, but must take on other aspects also, depending on its causal antecedents and consequences.

What may be accurately described as *asserting a proposition* might also, because one speaks too loudly, be described as *bursting one's interlocutor's eardrums*—and under the latter description might clearly be subject to interference. (It can seem tempting to distance the effects of the assertion by saying that bursting one's interlocutor's eardrums is merely the *effect* of the action—but in an important sense, it simply *is* the action, under an alternative description.[64]) Similarly, what might be *the assertion of a proposition* might also be *an instigation to violence, an invasion of privacy, a lie*, and so on. Because *all* actions in the causal world are subject to multiple descriptions, no action can be *only* a contribution to discussion. If the Freedom of Discussion Principle protects assertions in one of their aspects, but all assertions must also take on an additional aspect which may render them unprotected, how are we to know whether any *given* assertion is liable for warranted interference? To answer this, we must turn to Mill's discussion of the Harm Principle.

---

[62] See, for instance, Mill's comments on Appleton's proposals for international copyright: JS Mill, 'Letter to Rae' in *Collected Works*, vol XVII, 1853.

[63] See, eg, Mill, 'Utilitarianism' (n 16) 223, and Mill, 'Bentham' (n 32) 112.

[64] See Donald Davidson 'Actions, Reasons and Causes' in *Essays on Actions and Events* (OUP 1980) 4–5.

1.3 The Harm Principle and the Freedom of Discussion Principle

In chapter one of *On Liberty*, Mill articulates the central purpose of his essay as a whole:

> The object of this Essay is to assert one very simple principle, as entitled to govern absolutely the dealings of society with the individual in the way of compulsion and control, whether the means used be physical force in the form of legal penalties, or the moral coercion of public opinion. That principle is, that the sole end for which mankind are warranted, individually or collectively in interfering with the liberty of action of any of their number, is self-protection. That the only purpose for which power can be rightfully exercised over any member of a civilized community, against his will, is to prevent harm to others.[65]

The principle he specifies here has become known as the Harm Principle. A central question for the purpose of our discussion is how that principle relates to the one outlined in this chapter: how the Harm Principle, articulated in chapter one of *On Liberty*, is connected to the Freedom of Discussion of Principle, defended in chapter two.

There are three apparent options. Firstly, the Freedom of Discussion Principle might simply be *an instance* of the Harm Principle. That there should be no interference with the discussion of any opinion might be strictly implied by the fact that the only reason for interference *tout court* is harm to others. Secondly, the principles could be entirely independent of one another, offering guidance in different areas of life. Each might be a valid principle with self-standing normative force confined to its own domain. Thirdly, the principles could be independent, and speak to some of the same areas of life. Both could have force, but the principles might be in need of reconciliation in some way.

There is some support for each option. That the Freedom of Discussion Principle should be taken simply as *an instance* of the Harm Principle is certainly suggested by the fact that Mill seems to give the Harm Principle priority in *On Liberty* as the '*one* very simple principle' which the work seeks to assert.[66] Indeed, Mill seems to confirm in his *Autobiography* that *On Liberty* is dedicated to defending a *single* principle, rather than *multiple* principles, describing the work as 'a kind of philosophic text-book of a single truth'.[67] Viewing the principle defended in chapter two as a corollary to the Harm Principle would, additionally, make sense of Mill's claim that that chapter is 'a single branch' of his 'general thesis'.[68]

Nevertheless, there is a serious obstacle to interpreting the Freedom of Discussion Principle as merely an application of the Harm Principle. For nowhere in his defence of the Freedom of Discussion Principle does Mill even *mention* the Harm Principle—the

---

[65] Mill, 'On Liberty' (n 1) 223.   [66] Ibid (my emphasis).
[67] Mill, 'Autobiography' (n 32) 259.   [68] Mill, 'On Liberty' (n 1) 227.

notion of harm plays no role whatsoever in the argument of chapter two. As the materials were certainly at hand, we might have expected Mill to offer the following derivation in chapter two:

> [1, Harm Principle]: the only reason we are warranted in interfering in an action is to prevent harm to others.
> [2, No Harm in Discussion Claim]: discussion never causes harm,
> Therefore: there should be no interference with discussion. [Freedom of Discussion Principle]

Mill pointedly does *not* make this argument, however. He appeals, instead, to the epistemic argument outlined above. It is hard to believe, given its obviousness, that Mill's eschewal of the argument is accidental, or a matter of oversight—all the more so, because it would have lent greater unity to *On Liberty* as a whole. As such, it is impossible to resist the conclusion that Mill rejected the argument—either because he thought it unsound on the grounds of the No Harm in Discussion Claim, or because he thought it missed something important.[69]

Treating the Harm Principle and Freedom of Discussion Principle as independent of one another, but each restricted to their own domain, leads to other problems. As we have seen, as causal creatures, it is not possible to identify actions which are *only* 'discussion'—all actions are capable of being described in multiple ways. If the principles are to be treated as applicable to different domains, then, a detailed account is needed of to which acts of discussion the Freedom of Discussion Principle applies, and to which the Harm Principle applies.[70] (We can, no doubt, *define* discussion as that to which only the Freedom of Discussion Principle applies by fiat—but the task of determining the extension of the Freedom of Discussion Principle will remain. What is needed is a *non-circular* account.)

We are unlikely to be able to derive such an account a priori. While appealing to participants' intention to contribute to debate might seem to promise a way to isolate actions as accountable only to the Freedom of Discussion Principle, it would be absurd to claim that an action can escape appeal to the Harm Principle simply because it was intended, *however unreasonably*, as a contribution to debate. And while we might be able to offer a socio-historical account of domains in which free speech *has* been privileged as absolute—contexts in which it has been taken for granted that the causing of harm is either impossible, or is an unacceptable ground for interfering in discussion—what is needed is a *justification* for cordoning off such areas for treatment solely by the Freedom of Discussion Principle. Mill never offers such an account, and it is hard to imagine what one which does justice to the conditions of public entry we think appropriate for discursive areas in the modern world would look like. Entry into spaces for

---

[69] See, however, Daniel Jacobson, 'Mill on Freedom of Speech' in Christopher Macleod and Dale E Miller, *A Companion to Mill* (Wiley Blackwell 2017) 440–53 for a recent defence of this view.

[70] As Vincent Blasi puts it, this strategy will involve making sure 'the operative category "thought and discussion" is carefully delineated': see Chapter 2 in this volume, p. 32. As will be seen, I am less optimistic about achieving such a delineation than he is.

discussion, we might say, should not depend on a willingness to suffer whatever harms occur therein without any call for redress.

We are left, therefore, with an account according to which the authority of the Freedom of Speech Principle and Harm Principle each possess independent force, but in which their jurisdiction overlaps. How, then, are we to understand their interaction? Given Mill's clear preparedness to appeal to the Harm Principle for cases in which discussion amounts to for example incitement, it would be implausible to claim that Mill thinks that the Freedom of Discussion Principle trumps the Harm Principle in any case in which both apply—that where an action is describable *in merely one way* as discussion, the question of interference is settled ultimately by appeal to the Freedom of Discussion Principle rather than the Harm Principle. Rather, Mill's preparedness to countenance interference in some actions describable as discussion when those actions are harmful suggests that the application of the Harm Principle constrains the application of the Freedom of Discussion Principle.

The nature of that constraint, however, should be carefully understood. The Harm Principle, of course, offers a *necessary*, and not a *sufficient*, condition for interference. That an action harms another does not imply that we *should* interfere with that action, but rather opens up the possibility of *considering* interference which would otherwise be ruled out: '[I]t must by no means be supposed, because damage, or probability of damage, to the interests of others, can alone justify the interference of society, that therefore it always does justify such interference.'[71] Where it is not ruled out by the Harm Principle, judgments about interference must be made on the basis of prudential considerations: whether interference will, on balance and taking into account long term effects, be positive, and what form of interference (formal or informal) will lead to the *best* results. This applies as much to actions which can be described as discussion as to other forms of action.

Where the assertion of a proposition is also an action which causes harm—as we might think of assertions which amount to invasions of privacy, incitement, and so on—interference, therefore, is an option. Nonetheless, the Freedom of Discussion Principle retains force, providing independent considerations that count, albeit non-decisively, against such interference. The Freedom of Discussion Principle, to put this another way, provides extra reasons which must be taken into account in calculating whether interference is warranted *all things considered*—and as such the bar for interference in such cases is raised. That norms of free discussion are a necessary condition for the possibility of knowledge and facilitate the discovery of truth means that the cost of interference in discussion is non-trivial, and indeed can be extremely high. But that does not mean that interference cannot be warranted in any case whatsoever.[72] As Mill is clear, 'rules of conduct cannot be so framed as to require no exceptions'.[73] This applies as much to the Freedom of Discussion Principle as to any other rule.

---

[71] Mill, 'On Liberty' (n 1) 292.
[72] See Jonathan Riley, 'J.S. Mill's Doctrine of Freedom of Expression' (2005) 17 *Utilitas* 147 for a quite different interpretation of Mill's argument, which nevertheless, I think, reaches the same conclusion.
[73] Mill, 'Utilitarianism' (n 16) 225.

CHAPTER 2

THE CLASSIC ARGUMENTS FOR FREE SPEECH 1644–1927

VINCENT BLASI

2.1 JOHN MILTON

As ideals, free thought and free speech have roots in accounts by the historians Herodotus and Thucydides explaining the distinctiveness of fifth-century Athens,[1] in the Socratic search for philosophic clarity and appreciation of the limits of understanding,[2] in Euripides' celebration of political participation[3] and Aristotle's recognition of the power of public opinion,[4] in the efforts of Renaissance humanists such as Petrarch and Erasmus to liberate moral reasoning from scholastic formalism,[5] in Machiavelli's counsels of prudential rule,[6] in notions of free conscience and inquisitive duty introduced by the Protestant Reformation,[7] and in the scientific method's systematization of open-ended

---

[1] See J Peter Euben, 'The Battle of Salamis and the Origins of Political Theory' in J Peter Euben (ed), *Corrupting Youth: Political Education, Democratic Culture and Political Theory* (Princeton UP 1977) 74–85.

[2] See Plato 'The Apology' in RE Allen (tr), *The Dialogues of Plato*, vol 1 (Yale UP 1984) 61–104.

[3] See Arlene W Saxonhouse, *Free Speech and Democracy in Ancient Athens* (CUP 2006) 20–1, 131–4.

[4] See RG Mulgan, *Aristotle's Political Theory: An Introduction for Students of Political Theory* (Clarendon P 1977) 104–5.

[5] See Johan Huizinga, *Erasmus and the Age of Reformation* (Princeton UP 1984) 106–7; 'Changing Assumptions in Later Renaissance Culture' in William J Bouwsma, *A Usable Past: Essays in European Cultural History* (U of California P 1990) 74–92; Alister E McGrath, *Reformation Thought: An Introduction* (3rd edn, Blackwell 2000) 35–41, 69.

[6] Niccolò Machiavelli, *Discourses on Livy* (Harvey C Mansfield and Nathan Tarcov tr, U Chicago P 1966) 23–4.

[7] See Diarmaid MacCulloch, *The Reformation: Europe's House Divided, 1490–1700* (Allen Lane 2003) 70–87, 584–91.

knowledge seeking. However, for conceiving of the freedoms of speech and press as fundamental limiting principles of governance, the earliest argument that continues to be read today is John Milton's *Areopagitica* of 1644.[8] In that polemic, the great poet of *Paradise Lost* marshals a dizzying array of reasons and characterizations extolling bold individual inquiry and dynamic collective understanding.

Concerned about royalist propaganda and religious radicalism during the English Civil War, parliament instituted a requirement that all writings be approved before publication. This mimicking of the Crown censorship regime that had been in place for over a century-and-a-half distressed Milton, despite his otherwise strong support for the parliamentary side. He took up his pen and published a signed protest without getting approval, in proud defiance of the licensing requirement. He named it after an essay by an ancient Athenian critic of government.[9]

Milton's argument is audience-centred and deeply dependent on assumptions regarding the nature of religious belief and the responsibilities of citizens in a republic. Perhaps the most important idea he develops is that passive understanding in deference to custom or authority is a dereliction of duty. In this regard, heresy as conventionally understood to mean deviation from community orthodoxy, embracing ideas commonly thought to be false, is not a legitimate basis for regulation. Punishing heresy so conceived, he asserts, saps inquisitive energy, encourages shallow understanding, and presupposes a static 'possession' rather than an active, adaptive 'living' of truths. Milton's memorable phrase capturing this point is that one must not be a 'heretic in the truth', forming beliefs 'only because his pastor says so, or the Assembly so determines, without knowing other reason'.[10] That kind of passivity in citizens of a republic is irresponsible, Milton claims, and also contrary to scripture, where Truth is likened 'to a streaming fountain; if her waters flow not in a perpetual progression, they sicken into a muddy pool of conformity and tradition'.[11]

Even though he was convinced that there are objective religious and political truths—Milton was no relativist, pluralist, or sceptic—he maintained that appreciating and living those truths requires 'scouting into the regions of sin and falsity'.[12] 'I cannot praise', he says, 'a fugitive and cloistered virtue, unexercised and unbreathed, that never sallies out and sees her adversary'.[13] Anticipating a theme he would develop years later in *Paradise Lost*, he comments on the inseparability of good and evil after the Fall, leading to 'that doom which Adam fell into of knowing good and evil, that is of knowing good by evil'.[14] Part of the reason to expose oneself to falsehood and evil is to learn how to resist temptation. Throughout the tract, character development constitutes one of the chief benefits of enabling readers to confront unsettling ideas.

Proponents of licensing at the time were inclined to regulate speech in large part so as to preserve order towards the ends of military effectiveness in the Civil War and successful

---

[8] John Milton, *Areopagitica and other Prose Works* (first published 1927, Dover P 2016).
[9] See Eric Nelson, '"True Liberty": Isocrates and Milton's *Areopagitica*' (2001) 40 *Milton Stud* 201.
[10] Milton (n 8) 29.   [11] Ibid.   [12] Ibid 20.   [13] Ibid.   [14] Ibid.

completion of the Reformation. Urgency called for regulation. But Milton argues that the apparent disorder that so troubled the would-be licensers of writing is actually part of the divine design for effectuating the Reformation. 'Where there is much desire to learn, there of necessity will be much arguing, much writing, many opinions, for opinion in good men is but knowledge in the making'.[15] Dynamism in understanding is God's will. 'We cannot pitch our tent here', he tells his readers. A 'perpetual progression' of inquiry is the key to God's order, and also to the humanly constructed order of republican government.[16] Urgency requires freedom.

A modern reader is likely to find the *Areopagitica* deficient for its lack of detailed consideration of the harms that free speech can cause, even as Milton concedes at the outset that speech can 'spring up armed men'[17] and even as he briefly examines how evil ideas can cause 'infection', 'temptation', and 'distraction'.[18] But a probing examination of harm would be out of place in the tract. The essence of his case against licensing is not that false and evil ideas are inconsequential, but rather that the good that follows from letting audiences confront those ideas dwarfs the harm they cause. For he asserts that free inquiry is more than a good to be balanced against the costs it generates. For him, free inquiry is elemental. It is constitutive of Milton's twin causes of republicanism and Reformation. Both projects are utterly dependent on persons who are capable of thinking for themselves, and on an environment that encourages such thinking. Such persons and such an environment are not likely to flourish in a regime of comprehensive licensing, he warns.

Milton's prioritization of independent thought is the fulcrum of his argument. Without such a prioritization, the argument crumbles. The importance he attached to independent thought coheres with what he took to be a profound religious duty of highly personal inquiry. But even in his age and religious milieu, Milton's sense of what that duty entailed was exceptional. Few of his readers, then or now, could be expected to share it or to match the time and effort Milton devoted throughout his life to independent scriptural exegesis. That is why it is important to appreciate that his commitment to republican government also informed his prioritization of independent thought. At the outset, he specifies that his tract will address 'the discovery that might be yet further made both in religious and civil wisdom'.[19] In his lifetime, he was best known for having written the most widely-read polemics justifying the killing of a king (several were in Latin and read throughout Europe). When his side eventually lost out in the struggle over monarchy, Milton's high profile as the theorist of regicide made him a candidate for the scaffold. His republican credentials were central to his being.

His republicanism no less than his Protestantism may help to explain the feature of *Areopagitica* that most troubles modern readers: his refusal to extend the freedom for which he argues to would-be readers of Roman Catholic writings. If readers need to 'scout into the regions of sin and falsity' so as to know good by confronting evil, shouldn't they have access to the most sophisticated and widely-embraced alternative to Milton's

---

[15] Ibid 30.   [16] Ibid 29.   [17] Ibid 14.   [18] Ibid 20–4.   [19] Ibid 14.

religious world-view? So far as personal religious inquiry is concerned, the answer seems obvious. But when Milton says 'I mean not tolerated popery', his frame of reference is not that of an inquiring individual.[20] Catholicism, he complains, 'extirpates all religious and civil supremacies, so itself should be extirpate'.[21] His readers in 1644 could not have missed the intended allusion to the papal practice at the time of issuing formal interdicts instructing Catholics not to accept the authority of specified civil rulers. The most notorious of those interdicts during the early seventeenth century was issued in 1606 against the Venetian republic. The Catholic monk who sympathetically chronicled the Venetian resistance to that interdict, Fra Paolo Sarpi, became a celebrity among English republicans, much admired by Milton and cited with acclaim in *Areopagitica*.[22] Clearly, Milton considered the Catholic Counter-Reformation to be not simply an alternative theology but an existential threat to English republicanism.

Milton's republican and Protestant emphasis on character development and the collective energy of inquiry raises the question whether he has anything to say about methods of regulating speech that are less comprehensive and indiscriminately distrustful of writers and their audiences than is true of licensing. Criminal prosecution is selective and based on harms caused. So is the awarding of civil damages. Injunctions can be triggered by threats as well as past transgressions, but they too are selective. While in *Areopagitica* Milton, like a good lawyer,[23] argues the case at hand and leaves broader implications to be teased out by readers, his key claim that exposure to falsity helps audiences better to understand truth has purchase even against selective methods of regulating speech. All such methods, after all, are designed not only to punish and compensate but also to deter the speech that Milton believes has value despite its falsity and capacity to harm. Depending on the magnitude of their deterrence effects, such regulatory methods fall within the scope of Milton's arguments.

Even though the reasons Milton advances for treating free printing as a transcendent good apply to all efforts to prevent or punish speech, two aspects of his case against licensing warrant emphasis in considering how much his analysis can contribute to the resolution of free speech disputes in the modern world, where the comprehensive licensing of speech is for the most part a thing of the past. First, he relies heavily on a futility argument. Books and pamphlets already in print cannot be recalled. Those of foreign origin are certain to be smuggled into the commonwealth. Unlicensed writings of local origin will circulate underground. The inevitable evasions 'will make us all both ridiculous and weary, and yet frustrate'.[24] Attempting to control the thought of a nation by the exercise of bureaucratic authority is like 'the exploit of that gallant man who thought to pound up the crows by shutting his park gate'.[25] Second, the power to license will be exercised to settle scores, cut corners, and curry favour. Persons capable of

---

[20] Ibid 36.   [21] Ibid.
[22] See William J Bouwsma, *Venice and the Defense of Republican Liberty: Renaissance Values in the Age of the Counter Reformation* (U California P 1968); Barbara K Lewalski, *The Life of John Milton: A Critical Biography* (Blackwell 2000) 107.
[23] His brother Christopher was just that, and later a distinguished judge.   [24] Milton (n 8) 23.
[25] Ibid 21.

judging writings in a discerning, fair-minded manner will not be drawn to the assignment. His futility and corruption arguments invoke hard-headed practicality, as befits an admirer of Machiavelli. The futility and corruption calculus needs to be specific to each method of regulation. It seems likely that licensing is particularly prone to futility and corruption. Nevertheless, Milton's point can be read to be more fundamental: whatever the method chosen, in practice if not necessarily in theory, the quest for a disciplined, disinterested, measured, rational system for controlling ideas is chimerical. The centre cannot hold.

Reading Milton with an eye to his usefulness 375 years later is an inquiry he would have welcomed. He would be nobody's favourite in a humility contest; he saw himself as writing for the ages. Even as he tried to influence the parliament of 1644, he built his argument on the claims of posterity. He has succeeded better with posterity than he did with the parliament. The Licensing Order was not repealed. When the Stuart monarchy was restored in 1660, the licensing of books and pamphlets was ratcheted up with a vengeance. However, by the fiftieth anniversary of the *Areopagitica*, in the wake of the Glorious Revolution of 1689, comprehensive licensing was abolished in England, never to be reinstated. At the time of the passage of the First Amendment, there was much uncertainty and indeterminacy about its coverage and strength of protection, but all parties agreed that its minimal meaning was that the comprehensive licensing of pamphlets, newspapers, and books was categorically disallowed.

Milton's delayed impact is fitting. His judgment about the transcendent benefits of free thought and writing derived in no small measure from his belief that many of those benefits would be realized by future generations. As he put it in *Areopagitica*: 'a good book is the precious lifeblood of a master spirit, embalmed and treasured up on purpose for a life beyond life'.[26] Whether he would have said the same about a good pamphlet is not clear, but there can be no doubt that Milton's singular polemic against licensing has outlived him.

2.2 JAMES MADISON

The strangest phenomenon in the sociology of knowledge about the freedom of speech is that there exists a subtle, profound, extended essay on the subject by the principal author of the First Amendment which has attracted very few efforts at systematic interpretation and critique. This is all the more surprising because the author, James Madison, many of whose other reflections on the requisites of enduring republican government are widely studied and debated, had much to say about the role of public opinion as a crucial element in the creation of political authority and the preservation of rights. Currently, Madison scholarship is experiencing a major breakthrough in

---

[26] Ibid 14.

resurrecting his emphasis on public opinion, but that excellent work for the most part has not focused on what Madison wrote about the First Amendment.[27]

Madison's occasion for addressing in print the meaning of the First Amendment was the passage of the Sedition Act of 1798. Undoubtedly motivated by a desire to intimidate and incapacitate newspapers expected to support Thomas Jefferson in the presidential election two years hence, that statute made it a crime to publish any 'false, scandalous, and malicious writing' against 'the government of the United States, or the President of the United States, or either house of the Congress'. (At the time, Jefferson was Vice-President; it was no accident that the law omitted making it a crime to criticize the occupant of that office.) The statute specified that the requisite malice could be established by a finding that the defendant intended 'to excite' against the object of his criticism the 'hatred of the good people of the United States' or 'to stir up sedition'. In application, the falsity requirement routinely was found to be satisfied by determining that the defendant's opinionated characterizations and conjectures were unfounded; getting hard facts wrong was not a precondition for conviction. (Representative Matthew Lyon of Vermont, for example, was convicted and sentenced to four months in prison for writing that John Adams was engaged in 'a continual grasp for power, in an unbounded thirst for ridiculous pomp, foolish adulation, and selfish avarice'.[28]) Madison collaborated with Jefferson to draft resolutions challenging the constitutionality of the law, which were then passed by the Virginia and Kentucky legislatures and sent to the legislatures of all the other states. The disappointing response to those resolutions prompted Madison to write a lengthy, anonymous *Report on the Virginia Resolutions*, spelling out why the Sedition Act was unconstitutional. Part of that *Report* is a detailed account of how the Act violates the First Amendment. In the intervening eight years since its ratification, no one had published such a thorough and probing analysis of the Amendment.

Madison begins by discussing the inapplicability of the English common law regarding freedom of the press, the different theories of sovereignty in England and the United States, the traditions of criticism of public officials in the two countries, and the concerns that prompted the decision to amend the Constitution by adding the Bill of Rights. Then he announces that his acute, informative observations regarding these matters serve merely as a prologue to his controlling line of argument:

> But the question does not turn either on the wisdom of the Constitution or on the policy which gave rise to its particular organization. It turns on the actual meaning of the instrument.[29]

---

[27] See, eg, Lance Banning, *The Sacred Fire of Liberty: James Madison and the Founding of the Federal Republic* (Cornell UP 1995); Colleen A Sheehan, *James Madison and the Spirit of Republican Self-Government* (CUP 2009); Jeremy D Bailey, *James Madison and Constitutional Imperfection* (CUP 2015); Jack N Rakove, *A Politician Thinking: The Creative Mind of James Madison* (U Oklahoma P 2017).

[28] Anthony Lewis, *Make No Law: The Sullivan Case and the First Amendment* (Random House 1991) 63.

[29] James Madison, 'Report on the Alien and Sedition Acts' in James Madison, *Writings* (Library of America 1999) 651.

In this way, Madison presents as what we now call a 'textualist'. Read the document to discover meaning. However, his reading of the document marks him as a special kind of textualist. For he reads the First Amendment not in isolation but rather as an integral part of the Constitution viewed as a (textual) whole. This should not be surprising because when Madison first introduced to the House of Representatives his proposed amendments relating to religious liberty, freedom of the press, trial by jury and other rights, he urged that they be integrated into the pre-existing sections of the Constitution.

To his mind, the key to finding the 'actual meaning' of the First Amendment, or any other part of the Constitution, was to understand the structures and relationships, the assumptions and the functions, that are discernible from reading the text of the Constitution as an integrated whole establishing a republican form of government based on the principle of popular sovereignty. Textual enactment rather than philosophic wisdom or political intention must determine interpretation, but what is enacted is the full text, not its elements in isolation.

One feature of his comprehensive textualism is how he formulates the rights he takes to be violated by the Sedition Act of 1798. Madison discusses at length in the *Virginia Report* not only 'the freedom of the press' but also the 'right of freely examining public characters and measures', the right 'of free communication among the people' concerning public characters and measures, and the 'right of electing the members of the government'. The last three do not appear in the First Amendment or anywhere else in the Constitution as denominated rights as such, but Madison finds them to be enacted by the structure of accountability specified by the constitutional text. Interestingly, he does not discuss 'the freedom of speech' as a general right not limited to communication concerning public characters and measures.

He describes the rights-generating structure of accountability as follows:

1. The Constitution supposes that the President, the Congress, and each of its Houses, may not discharge their trusts . . . Hence all are made responsible to their constituents, at the returning periods of elections . . .
2. Should it happen, as the Constitution supposes it may happen, that either of these branches of the government may not have duly discharged its trust, it is natural and proper, that, according to the cause and degree of their faults, they should be brought into contempt or disrepute, and incur the hatred of the people.
3. Whether it has, in any case, happened that the proceedings of either or all of those branches evince such a violation of duty as to justify a contempt, a disrepute, or a hatred among the people, can only be determined by a free examination thereof, and a free communication among the people thereon.
4. Whenever it may have actually happened that proceedings of this sort are chargeable on all or either of the branches of the government, it is the duty, as well as the right, of intelligent and faithful citizens to discuss and promulgate

them freely—as well as to control them by the censorship of the public opinion, as to promote a remedy according the rules of the Constitution.³⁰

Madison then argues that this structure of accountability informed by government and citizen duties is undermined when officials seeking re-election are immunized by law from public scrutiny and criticism more than are their challengers:

> ... [T]he right of electing the members of the government constitutes more particularly the essence of a free and responsible government. The value and efficacy of this right depends on the knowledge of the comparative merits and demerits of the candidates for public trust, and on the equal freedom, consequently, of examining and discussing these merits and demerits of the candidates respectively.³¹

The Sedition Act of 1798, he maintains convincingly, was designed to achieve an electoral asymmetry advantageous to incumbents so far as exposure to critical scrutiny is concerned.

Following Locke and many other seventeenth- and eighteenth-century writers whose works he devoured, Madison believed in natural rights. Like Locke, he thought that individuals unable to protect their rights in the state of nature join together in civil society for the purpose of collectively safeguarding their rights, and to this end create governments that take the form of constitutional regimes. The civil society stage of this process—the instituting of regimes and, when they fail, the withdrawal of authority from them, typically by revolution—is central to notions of limited government, justifiable revolution, and the authority of public opinion which were the driving ideas of Madison's political life.³² When he speaks of such rights as freedom of the press and the right of freely examining public characters and measures, he cannot be saying they are natural rights in the sense of entitlements in the state of nature bestowed by the Creator and capable of being exercised while leaving 'to everyone else the like advantage'.³³ But neither can he be saying they are merely the creation of a particular constitutional regime. Such rights are for him fundamental—'secured' by the Constitution rather than brought into existence by it—because they enable the people in civil society to do their work of creating and withdrawing political authority. Madison scholar Gary Rosen labels these rights incident to civil society 'intermediate rights'.³⁴ I prefer the term 'constituting rights'. Whatever they are called, they play a large role in Madison's thought.

---

³⁰ Ibid 652.   ³¹ Ibid 655.
³² See Ralph Ketcham, *James Madison: A Biography* (UP Virginia 1990) 293–302.
³³ 'Property' in James Madison, *Writings* (Library of America 1999). In this important essay, Madison asserts that 'a man has a property in his opinions and the free communication of them' subject to his 'like advantage' for 'everyone else' condition. Thus, 'having one's say' might be a natural right, but not 'getting one's way' via competitive persuasion or superior communicative projection. His state of nature does not have political mobilization, printing presses, or miscreant officials. In Madison's scheme, entitlements relating to competition do not come into existence until the formation of civil society.
³⁴ Gary Rosen, *American Compact: James Madison and the Problem of Founding* (UP Kansas 1999) 20–1.

Madison believed that freedom of the press and the right of freely examining public characters and measures are constituting rights integral to a system of accountability that reaches back all the way to civil society itself. And because of the accountability of all regimes to civil society, he insisted on reading the Constitution in structural and functional terms, as a servant of civil society so to speak, beholden to a higher authority and properly to be interpreted with reference to how that higher authority, 'the people', is best served by the constitutional regime. This method of interpretation was on display three years after ratification of the First Amendment when Madison spoke in the House of Representatives in opposition to a proposed resolution condemning certain political societies whose anti-government polemics were thought to have encouraged a violent tax rebellion. Rather than invoke a freestanding right of freedom of speech, he said: '[i]f we advert to the nature of republican government, we shall find that the censorial power is in the people over the government, and not in the government over the people'.[35] Notably, this statement was quoted by the Supreme Court in its landmark opinion in *New York Times v Sullivan*, which decreed the rejection of seditious libel to be 'the central meaning of the First Amendment'.[36]

True to his comprehensive approach to understanding rights and powers, when Madison introduced his draft for a bill of rights, he urged (unsuccessfully) that the Constitution be amended to affirm

> That all power is originally vested in and consequently derived from the people . . . That the people have an indubitable, unalienable, and indefeasible right to reform and change their government whenever it be found adverse or inadequate to the purposes of its institution.[37]

The 'freedom of the press', the 'remedial right' of 'electing the members of the government' with 'equal freedom' to scrutinize the candidates, and the 'right of freely examining public characters and measures, and of free communication among the people thereon', Madison viewed as all derivative from the yet more fundamental right of people in civil society 'to reform and change their government'.[38] He was not only the father of a constitution but also the child of a revolution.

2.3 JOHN STUART MILL

Almost certainly the most widely-read of the classic arguments for free speech is that developed by John Stuart Mill in his *Essay On Liberty*, first published in 1859 and never out-of-print since then.[39] In the second chapter, entitled 'Of the Liberty of Thought and

---

[35] 4 *Annals of Cong.* 934 (1794). [36] *New York Times v Sullivan*, 376 US 254, 273, 275 (1964).
[37] 1 *Annals of Cong.* 451 (Joseph Gales, ed. 1789).
[38] James Madison, 'Report on the Virginia Resolutions' (1883) 43 *Niles' Weekly Register* 18, 19.
[39] John Stuart Mill, *Utilitarianism and On Liberty* (Mary Warnock ed, 2nd ed, Blackwell 2003) 88.

Discussion', Mill examines the value of free thought and discussion under three different assumptions: (1) that the received opinions which are being challenged by the speech at issue are false; (2) that the received opinions are true; and (3) that 'the conflicting doctrines, instead of one being true and the other false, share the truth between them; and the non-conforming opinion is needed to supply the remainder of the truth, of which the received doctrine embodies only a part'.[40] He offers powerful reasons why unregulated thought and discussion is of great value under each of the three assumptions.

So far as the possible falsity of received opinion is concerned, his argument turns on human fallibility. History is replete with instances of ideas that were held to be true by almost everyone, including the wisest persons of the place and time, but which no serious person now thinks are correct. Mill goes so far as to say that:

> the source of everything respectable in man, either as an intellectual or a moral being, [is that] his errors are corrigible. He is capable of rectifying his mistakes by discussion and experience.[41]

Because fallibility is endemic at every level of society, '[c]omplete liberty of contradicting and disproving our opinion is the very condition which justifies us in assuming its truth for purposes of acting'.[42]

When a received opinion is in fact true (his second assumption), there is great value in permitting it to be challenged so that it will be held as a 'living truth' rather than a 'dead dogma'.[43] Persons in possession of true opinions must know the best that can be said against those opinions. Ideally, the objections must be confronted 'in their most plausible and persuasive form' as developed by 'persons who actually believe them'.[44] Without such exposure to forceful challenge, believers will fail to achieve a 'lively apprehension of the truth', an understanding that 'may penetrate the feelings and acquire a real mastery over the conduct'.[45] For 'both teachers and learners go to sleep at their post as soon as there is no enemy in the field'.[46]

Mill's third assumption, 'when the conflicting doctrines ... share the truth between them', he takes to be the most common situation. For the 'standing antagonisms of practical life', such as those between order and progress, co-operation and competition, sociality and individuality, or liberty and discipline, 'it is in great measure the opposition of the other that keeps each within the limits of reason and sanity'.[47]

Like Milton before him, Mill's argument is audience-centred, devoted to the enhancement of collective understanding over time, and much concerned with the deadening effect of persons uncritically following custom in forming their beliefs. Like Milton, Mill argues that how persons hold their beliefs—actively, independently, and by engaging opposing ideas rather than passively—is very important to developing the individual character of members of the community. Like Milton, Mill seeks an energetic environment

---

[40] Ibid 122–3.   [41] Ibid 102.   [42] Ibid.   [43] Ibid 114.   [44] Ibid 116.
[45] Ibid 118.   [46] Ibid 120.   [47] Ibid 121–4.

of inquiry and debate within which individual beliefs are formed. Like Milton, Mill singles out paternalism for special contempt. However, unlike Milton, Mill accords no role to divine providence in ensuring the eventual triumph of truth over falsity and good over evil. Rather, he maintains that the 'real advantage which truth has' is that it can be rediscovered when circumstances are favourable to its acceptance.[48] Unlike Milton, Mill regards informal social punishment of persons with unpopular beliefs to be a greater threat to collective progress in understanding than is posed by the exercise of governmental power to censor. This focus on private punishment of dissenters may be Mill's most distinctive contribution.

Chapter two of *On Liberty* is preceded by a chapter in which Mill introduces his famous Harm Principle: 'the only purpose for which power can be rightfully exercised over any member of a civilized community, against his will, is to prevent harm to others'.[49] Later in the Essay he specifies that although harm to others is a necessary condition for limiting liberty it is not always a sufficient condition. That depends on whether the harm outweighs the benefit. Chapter two is succeeded by a chapter entitled 'On Individuality, As One of the Elements of Well-Being', in which Mill sketches a character ideal of the strong-minded, engaged, fearless, independent person who serves society by contributing to the creation of a diverse, energetic environment and abundant opportunities for various experiments in living. One of the great challenges in reading *On Liberty* is to figure out how, if at all, chapters one, two, and three hang together.

So far as speech is concerned, it is not hard to appreciate how Mill's character ideal in chapter three might serve the truth-seeking project that is the subject of chapter two. Inquisitive, assertive, courageous, resilient individuals are needed to generate the clash of opinions, including novel opinions, upon which progress in understanding depends. Such persons also are best able to stand up to the social pressures that Mill identifies as the greatest threat to independent thinking.

But how does Mill's Harm Principle of chapter one fit with his argument in chapter two regarding the transcendent social value of free thought and discussion? What should we make of the fact that in chapter two Mill never once discusses the harm that might follow from thought and discussion? The entire chapter is devoted to exploring only the benefits of those two activities. Moreover, at the end of chapter one, right after he introduces his Harm Principle, Mill says that the 'appropriate region of human liberty' comprises 'absolute freedom of opinion and sentiment on all subjects' as well as a comparable 'liberty of expressing and publishing opinions'.[50] This 'absolute' freedom, he specifies, does not govern the 'liberty of tastes and pursuits' or the liberty of 'combination among individuals', both of which liberties are bounded by the qualification 'so long as what we do does not harm [others]'.[51] No such qualification is appended to the 'liberty of expressing and publishing opinions'. Is the liberty of thought and discussion (including both freedom of opinion and sentiment and the liberty of expressing and

---

[48] Ibid 109.   [49] Ibid 94.   [50] Ibid 96.   [51] Ibid 97.

publishing opinions) different from the other liberties in being exempt from the Harm Principle? If so, why?

At the beginning of chapter three, the chapter about 'individuality', Mill offers an example—really two examples—which help to explain how his Harm Principle relates to his detailed account in chapter two of the various ways that an unqualified liberty of thought and discussion contributes to progress in understanding. He posits two instances of criticism of corn-dealers, whose practices affecting the price of bread were the subject in Mill's day of intense public controversy. One critic expresses the opinion that 'corn dealers are starvers of the poor' to 'an excited mob assembled before the house of a corn dealer'. The other critic publishes the identical opinion 'simply circulated through the press'.[52] Mill states that the speech of the critic addressing the excited mob can be punished but that the critic publishing his harsh opinion of corn-dealers in the press cannot. Why the difference? He does not invoke the differential probability of harm in the two situations, for he never examines how probable is the harm that might follow from publishing the harsh opinion in the press. Instead, Mill says that the on-site critic speaking to the assembled mob is engaging in a 'positive instigation to some mischievous act', something he does not say about the critic speaking through the press.[53] Is the way he differentiates these two examples, protecting one critic and not the other when both are saying the same thing, consistent with Mill's earlier embrace of the 'absolute' liberty of 'expressing and publishing opinions'? Are the examples consistent with his analysis in chapter two regarding the overriding value of the liberty of thought and discussion? Is the different treatment of the two examples consistent with his Harm Principle?

Mill says in chapter one of *On Liberty* 'I regard utility as the ultimate appeal on all ethical questions; but it must be utility in the largest sense, grounded on the permanent interests of man as a progressive being'.[54] All utilitarians, even 'progressive' utilitarians, are committed to comparing the pleasure and pain generated by the acts and activities they are evaluating. By definition, they count the costs. Thus, harm matters. Always. So why not for the harsh critic of corn-dealers publishing his opinion in the press? How can the freedom to express an opinion 'on all subjects' possibly be 'absolute' for a utilitarian committed to counting the cost? The answer to this question lies, I believe, in the distinction, long familiar to students of utilitarian ethics, between 'rule utilitarianism' and 'act utilitarianism'.[55]

The unit of reference for comparing the benefits and costs of communicative acts is not a given. The unit of reference can be a discrete act viewed in isolation. Or it can be a congeries of discrete acts that are similar enough to be considered together and evaluated categorically as an 'activity'. The unit of reference inevitably affects, indeed it can determine, how the balance of benefit and cost comes out. In chapter two, Mill fails to discuss the harms that can follow from particular instances of thought and discussion because he maintains that the general category he denominates 'thought and discussion' on balance

---

[52] Ibid 131.   [53] Ibid.   [54] Ibid 95.
[55] See Dale E Miller, *J. S. Mill: Moral, Social and Political Thought* (Polity 2010) 71–8.

generates more good than harm. Because of that categorical judgment, each particular instance of thought and discussion is not evaluated in terms of either benefit or harm but rather receives 'absolute' protection. A thinker like Mill, who places so much emphasis on progress through knowledge and reflection on experience, might stand ready to make such a categorical judgment of net utility. A thinker like Mill, who perceives individual character to be the most vital source of progress, might think that, when considered categorically, thought and discussion is so integral to character building that no amount of harm flowing from discussion can outweigh that elemental benefit.[56]

But that kind of categorical rule-utilitarian conclusion is defensible only if the operative category 'thought and discussion' is carefully delineated. The claim that the benefits outweigh the harms categorically would be implausible if the category were defined expansively to include uses of words or images that make no claim to enhance understanding by means of appealing to the judgment and sensibilities of members of the audience. Words and images serve various functions, not all of which entail or implicate 'thought' and 'discussion' as Mill employs those terms. It is no accident that all the arguments he summons in chapter two are about truth-seeking rather than self-expression, incitement, intimidation, bonding, or transmitting information for purposes other than advancing public knowledge.

In that regard, 'positive instigation to some mischievous act' is simply not 'thought and discussion'. To engage in such instigation is to exercise one's liberty, but it is not to engage in an activity about which we can say that the good categorically outweighs the harm. As such, the speech can be regulated when in the circumstances its probable harm outweighs its probable good. Particularistic act-utilitarian evaluation is needed.[57] Not so for the critic offering a harsh general opinion about corn-dealers via the press. That is chapter two 'thought and discussion' covered by Mill's categorical rule-utilitarian balancing judgment finding net utility in the overall activity. The Harm Principle is still applied, but at a higher level of generality than is appropriate for evaluating instances of positive instigation.

Many questions remain, even if this analysis explains why Mill does not discuss harm in chapter two and why he selectively ignores his Harm Principle when denominating at the end of chapter one the various liberties he is about to examine. We need to know Mill's criteria for differentiating thought and discussion from other endeavours involving words and images. We need to know how he computes the act-utilitarian benefits and harms that are generated by communications that do not qualify as thought and discussion. We need to know whether a regulation that is 'partial' in the sense of restricting the time, the manner, or the place of the discussion while leaving open ample alternative means to carry on the inquiry amounts to a violation of the 'absolute protection'

---

[56] The classic account of Mill's rule-utilitarianism is JO Urmson, 'The Interpretation of the Moral Philosophy of J.S. Mill' (1953) 3 *Phil Q* 33.

[57] It is unclear whether Mill should be considered an act-utilitarian or a rule-utilitarian. See Stephen Darwall, *Philosophical Ethics* (Westview P 1998) 127–38; Henry R West, *Mill's Utilitarianism: A Reader's Guide* (Continuum 2017) 10–11, 63–5. I believe that Mill employs both forms of utilitarianism in *On Liberty*.

for thought and discussion that Mill finds requisite. More fundamentally, we need to know whether we should accept at face value Mill's claim that he really is defending the liberty of thought and discussion on utilitarian grounds rather than, as several of his most sophisticated and admiring interpreters maintain, on the basis of what amounts to an autonomy argument.[58]

There are loose ends and unanswered questions aplenty in *On Liberty* but also much that is memorable. Mill's ambition in seeking to understand the freedom of thought and discussion in the context of the full range of liberties that might warrant special protection amounts to a lasting contribution in its own right. Important components of his legacy include his unrelenting emphasis on personal character as an engine of social progress and his recognition of the threat posed to individuality by informal private punishment. Perhaps Isaiah Berlin best captured the Essay's impact:

> [M]ost of his arguments can be turned against him; certainly none is conclusive, or such as would convince a determined or unsympathetic opponent . . . Nevertheless, the inner citadel—the central thesis—has stood the test. It may need elaboration or qualification, but it is still the clearest, most candid, persuasive, and moving exposition of the point of view of those who desire an open and tolerant society. The reason for this is not merely the honesty of Mill's mind, or the moral and intellectual charm of his prose, but the fact that he is saying something true and important about some of the most fundamental characteristics and aspirations of human beings . . .
> He was the teacher of a generation, of a nation, but still no more than a teacher. . . . He was not original, yet he transformed the structure of the human knowledge of his age.[59]

If history is a guide, Mill's compelling exploration will continue to fascinate, frustrate, and inspire students of the freedom of speech for generations to come.

2.4 LEARNED HAND

In the earliest judicial opinion on the subject that continues to be studied in law schools and discussed in the academic literature, the celebrated federal judge Learned Hand conceives of the freedom of speech as a majority-creating procedure rather than an individual right. He maintains that collective self-criticism is the essential precondition that gives the phenomenon of consent of the governed its authority to coerce compliance.

---

[58] See, eg, George Kateb, 'A Reading of *On Liberty*' in David Bromwich and George Kateb (eds), *On Liberty: John Stuart Mill* (Yale UP 2003) 28, 39, 46, 47, 49–53; Fred R Berger, *Happiness, Justice & Freedom: The Moral and Political Philosophy of John Stuart Mill* (U California P 1984) 232–53; CL Ten, *Mill On Liberty* (OUP 1980) 76–78, 83–5; cf Alan Ryan, *J.S. Mill* (Routledge 1974) 133.

[59] 'John Stuart Mill and the Ends of Life' in Isaiah Berlin, *Four Essays on Liberty* (OUP 1969) 173, 201, 205.

Hand's premise is that only laws passed and public opinion generated in the face of what he terms 'hostile criticism' can claim to embody the will of a governing majority.

In *Masses Publishing Company v Patten*,[60] one of the first judicial interpretations of the Espionage Act of 1917, he read the statute to prohibit only a statement that tells a person 'it is his interest or his duty' to violate the law. Political advocacy, however critical and intemperate, that falls short of invoking a duty or interest to break the law is 'part of that public opinion which is the final source of government in a democratic state'.[61] In Hand's understanding of 'the normal assumption of democratic government', the 'suppression of hostile criticism does not turn upon the justice of its substance or the decency or propriety of its temper'.[62] Neither does it turn on the predicted consequences of the speech. The anti-war advocacy under review in the *Masses* case involved sharp accusations that World War I was being fought to serve the class interests of economic elites. The issue of the magazine in dispute included admiring portraits of draft resisters. Hand characterized such speech as of a sort that might 'enervate public feeling at home', 'encourage the success of the enemies of the United States abroad', and 'promote a mutinous and insubordinate temper among the troops'.[63] However, because the speech amounted to political agitation rather than 'direct incitement to violent resistance', it qualified as hostile criticism that serves the democratic function of forging majority will.[64]

In a later opinion and in letters to Justice Oliver Wendell Holmes and the Harvard law professor Zechariah Chafee, Hand elaborated on his proposed legal test.[65] He reiterated his statement in *Masses* that he would make controlling not the literal meaning of the words used by the speaker but the message conveyed. He said that Mark Anthony would not escape punishment by his demagogic technique of literally admonishing against rioting to avenge Caesar's murder while unmistakably conveying the opposite message to his plebeian listeners.

In his subsequent explanations of his *Masses* opinion, Hand gave two reasons why legal liability should be a function of the meaning conveyed by the speaker's words rather than either the predicted consequences of the speech or the speaker's illicit intent. First, the meaning conveyed by the speech is what matters most in determining whether it contributes to the hostile criticism that serves the process of constituting a legitimate governing majority. In this view, it is the value of the speech that is the most important variable in deciding whether it is protected. Second, a test that turns on what the speaker actually said rather than what he risked causing or intended can take the form of 'a qualitative formula, hard, conventional, difficult to evade'. A legal standard of that type, Hand surmised, 'might be made to serve just a little to withhold the torrents of passion to which I suspect democracies will be found more subject than for example the whig

---

[60] *Masses Publishing Company v Patten*, 244 F 535 (1917).
[61] Ibid 540.   [62] Ibid.   [63] Ibid 539.   [64] Ibid 540.
[65] See *United States v Nearing* 252 F 223 (1918); Gerald Gunther, 'Learned Hand and the Origins of Modern First Amendment Doctrine: Some Fragments of History' (1975) 27 *Stan L Rev* 719.

autocracy of the 18th century'.⁶⁶ 'I think it is precisely at those times,' he wrote Chafee, 'when alone the freedom of speech becomes important as an institution'.⁶⁷

The two reasons are interrelated in that if the project is to secure a minimum of speech without which legitimate authority cannot be constituted, there is much to be said for a doctrinal safe harbour protecting the requisite speech unqualifiedly. A test that turns on predicted consequences or speaker intent is not well suited to providing such a safe harbour. Those phenomena are difficult to observe, measure, and prove. To identify them, a factfinder ordinarily must rely on speculation, inference, extrapolation, and generalization. What meaning a particular writing or speech conveys to its audience will not always be self-evident—interpretation and judgment cannot be eliminated from the process of applying a speech-protective standard—but the space for erratic or prejudicial assessment is smaller when the operative phenomenon is the actual meaning conveyed by a particular statement rather than its predicted consequences or the speaker's intent.

Hand's preference for a qualitative distinction between protected and unprotected speech was not driven solely by these practical concerns about the efficacy of a safe harbour and the risk of inconsistent, biased application. He considered the distinction between the direct advocacy of law violation and speech falling short of such advocacy to be fundamental as a matter of democratic theory, as this passage in a letter to Zechariah Chafee makes clear:

> [A]ny State which professes to be controlled by public opinion cannot take sides against any opinion except that which must express itself in the violation of law. On the contrary, it must regard all other expression of opinion as tolerable, if not good. As soon as it does not, it inevitably assumes that one opinion may control in spite of what might become an opposite opinion.⁶⁸

The commitment not to become 'a State based upon some opinion, as against any opinion which may get itself accepted' Hand considered to be 'indubitably the presupposition of democratic states, however little they have lived up to it'.⁶⁹ In this respect, adherence to the principle of majority rule is a dynamic process, evincing a concern about inchoate, incipient, and potential majorities no less than current ones.

For Hand, both the justification for protecting controversial speech and the limits to that protection depend on categorical judgments regarding which kinds of speech as a general matter serve the democratic function of creating a governing majority. But Hand was no formalist. He recognized that words and images are deployed to serve a multiplicity of functions, many of which have nothing to do with contributing to the hostile criticism that enables and legitimates majority rule. Speech serving such extraneous functions he considered not to fall within the domain of the freedom of speech.

---

⁶⁶ Letter from Learned Hand to Zechariah Chafee, Jr (2 January 1921) in Gunther (n 65) 769, 770.
⁶⁷ Ibid.
⁶⁸ Letter from Learned Hand to Zechariah Chafee, Jr (8 January 1920) in Gunther (n 65) 764, 765.
⁶⁹ Ibid.

One characteristically trenchant sentence making this point in his *Masses* opinion reveals how central it was to his analysis:

> Words are not only the keys of persuasion, but the triggers of action, and those which have no purport but to counsel the violation of law cannot by any latitude of interpretation be a part of that public opinion which is the final source of government in a democratic state.[70]

Hand derived his preferred limit to the freedom of speech from the same source from which he derived his justification for that freedom: the requisites of majority rule. In a letter to Eliot Richardson, written more than thirty years after he wrote the *Masses* opinion, Hand defended his refusal to ascribe democratic value to speech that counsels law violation:

> My reasons may sound didactic and too generalized; but here they are. Every society which promulgates a law means that it shall be obeyed until it is changed, and any society which lays down means by which its laws can be changed makes those means exclusive . . . If so, how in God's name can an incitement to do what will be unlawful if done, be itself lawful? How do words differ from any other way of bringing about an event?[71]

Majorities must be forged and sustained by surviving hostile criticism, and so must their laws, but the authority thereby created is brought into existence in order to govern, if necessary by deploying the resources of the state to enforce compliance. This is the other side of the coin of democratic function.

Those who understand the freedom of speech in these terms might reasonably disagree about which types of dissenting speech are fundamentally inconsistent with recognition of the authority of majority will, and in that respect not part of the very process that makes that freedom essential. At one extreme, some might conclude that the act of flag burning so diminishes the principal symbol of sovereignty as to compromise majority rule. At the other extreme, some might think that only the explicit and specific counselling of violence, perhaps only violence already planned in some detail and designed to be employed on a large scale, sufficiently contradicts majority rule as to fall outside the project of generating political authority by means of hostile criticism. The advocacy of non-violent civil disobedience to be undertaken openly, with willing submission to punishment, for the purpose of reforming the law—Dr Martin Luther King's definition of the concept[72]—might readily be considered part of the process of identifying majority will, particularly in the context of massive denial of the right to vote.

---

[70] *Masses* (n 60) 540.

[71] Letter from Learned Hand to Eliot Richardson (29 January 1952) in Constance Jordan (ed), *Reason and Imagination: The Selected Correspondence of Learned Hand 1897–1961* (OUP 2013) 311.

[72] See 'Letter from Birmingham Jail' in Martin Luther King, Jr, *Why We Can't Wait* (New American Library 1964) 85, 95.

There is nothing inevitable about where Hand drew the line. What is most significant about his analysis in the *Masses* case are the considerations he took to be relevant in determining the boundary between protected and unprotected speech, considerations that derive from the notion of freedom of speech as a majoritarian procedure.

2.5 OLIVER WENDELL HOLMES, JR.

The prominence of Justice Oliver Wendell Holmes, Jr in the history of American legal thought derives in no small measure from his characteristically terse but eloquent opinions about the freedom of speech. The irony is that it took the quick-witted Holmes seventy-eight years to overcome his instinctive rights scepticism and appreciate how robust constitutional protection for dissenting speakers can be justified.

His starting point was a proudly deflationary understanding of truth and rights. He liked to define 'truth' as 'the majority vote of that nation that could lick all others'.[73] A 'right' Holmes considered nothing more than a 'prophecy ... that the public force will be brought to bear on those who do things said to contravene it'.[74] What justifies rights is 'the fighting will of the subject to maintain them . . . A dog will fight for his bone'.[75] Energy and force are what interested him, not rationality, process, or human dignity.

Some students of Holmes believe that his harrowing experience as a Civil War soldier left him preoccupied with forces beyond individual control.[76] He was wounded three times, twice nearly mortally. During triage on the battlefield at Antietam, the first attending surgeon classified Holmes among the badly wounded not worth trying to save, but a medic demurred and had him moved to a farmhouse for treatment.[77] His less serious third wound, a heel injury suffered near Fredericksburg, probably saved his life. It required a few months' convalescence back in Boston. This prevented Captain Holmes from joining his regiment at the Battle of Gettysburg, where on the third day the Twentieth Massachusetts was stationed on Cemetery Ridge at the very apex of Pickett's Charge. That day, two-thirds of the officer corps of the Twentieth died.[78]

Not surprisingly, given this background, during his twenty years as a state Supreme Court justice in Massachusetts and for his first fifteen years on the Supreme Court, Holmes consistently ruled against free speech claims.[79] This pattern persisted into the

---

[73] Oliver Wendell Holmes, 'Natural Law' (1918) 32 *Harv L Rev* 40, 40.   [74] Ibid 42.
[75] Ibid.
[76] See, eg, Louis Menand, *The Metaphysical Club* (Farrar, Straus and Giroux 2001) 65–9.
[77] See Liva Baker, *The Justice from Beacon Hill: The Life and Times of Oliver Wendell Holmes* (Harper Collins 1991) 132–3.
[78] See George A Bruce, *The Twentieth Regiment of Massachusetts Volunteer Infantry 1861–1865* (Houghton, Mifflin 1906) 292–8.
[79] See, eg, *McAuliffe v Mayor of New Bedford*, 29 NE 517 (Mass 1892); *Commonwealth v Davis*, 39 NE 113 (Mass 1895); *Patterson v Colorado* 205 US 454 (1907); *Fox v Washington*, 236 US 273 (1915).

spring of 1919 in cases involving prosecutions of various speakers for statements critical of US participation in World War I and the accompanying draft.[80]

Then, in November of 1919, Holmes unexpectedly dissented from a decision upholding convictions of five Russian immigrants under the Espionage Act of 1918 for distributing pamphlets criticizing President Wilson's dispatch of US troops to Russia to aid forces fighting against the Bolsheviks.[81] When circulated, his proposed dissenting opinion so disturbed his colleagues in the majority that a delegation of them visited his home to implore him not to publish it.[82] Happily for posterity, the old soldier held his ground and resisted their entreaties. And so the most quoted paragraph ever written about the freedom of speech entered the US Reports.

Holmes begins that paragraph, the peroration of his dissent in *Abrams v United States*, by conceding the rational logic of persecution:

> If you have no doubt of your premises or your power and want a certain result with all your heart you naturally express your wishes in law and sweep away all opposition. To allow opposition by speech seems to indicate that you think the speech impotent, as when a man says that he has squared the circle, or that you do not care whole-heartedly for the result, or that you doubt either your power or your premises.[83]

Then, true to his observation forty years earlier in his book *The Common Law*[84] that 'the life of the law has not been logic; it has been experience', Holmes shifts gears:

> But when men have realized that time has upset many fighting faiths, they may come to believe even more than they believe the very foundations of their own conduct that the ultimate good desired is better reached by free trade in ideas—that the best test of truth is the power of the thought to get itself accepted in the competition of the market, and that truth is the only ground upon which their wishes safely can be carried out.[85]

By framing the issue in terms of how best 'safely' to achieve the 'ultimate good desired', Holmes finds his answer in the dynamic character of human understanding, a premise not only of the common law but also, in his view, of the constitutional regime. Far from being a repository of enduring principles, even the Constitution itself

---

[80] See *Schenck v United States*, 249 US 47 (1919); *Frohwerk v United States*, 249 US 204 (1919); *Debs v United States*, 249 US 211 (1919).

[81] See *Abrams v United States*, 250 US 616, 629 (1919). For a riveting account of Holmes's change of mind, see Thomas Healy, *The Great Dissent: How Oliver Wendell Holmes Changed His Mind and Changed the History of Speech in America* (Henry Holt 2013).

[82] See Sheldon M Novick, 'The Unrevised Holmes and Freedom of Expression' [1991] *Sup Ct Rev* 303, 343.

[83] *Abrams* (n 81) 630.   [84] Oliver Wendell Holmes, Jr, *The Common Law* (Little, Brown 1881) 1.

[85] *Abrams* (n 81).

is an experiment, as all life is an experiment. Every year if not every day we have to wager our salvation upon some prophecy based upon imperfect knowledge.[86]

If epistemic humility and adaptability sustained by the continuous competition of ideas is 'the only ground' upon which the people's 'wishes safely can be carried out', the freedom of speech takes on a special significance that sets it apart from other claims of right:

> While that experiment is part of our system I think that we should be eternally vigilant against attempts to check the expression of opinions that we loathe and believe to be fraught with death, unless they so imminently threaten immediate interference with the lawful and pressing purposes of the law that an immediate check is required to save the country.[87]

This distinctive significance had escaped Holmes's notice in his earlier free speech opinions. The change of attitude was not fleeting. As Holmes would put the matter in another memorable dissent ten years later:

> [I]f there is any principle of the Constitution that more imperatively calls for attachment than any other it is the principle of free thought—not free thought for those who agree with us but freedom for the thought that we hate.[88]

Why exactly did Holmes believe that 'the best test of truth is the power of the thought to get itself accepted in the competition of the market'?[89] The place to start in trying to answer this question, I submit, is Holmes's oft-proclaimed interest in the work of Charles Darwin. *The Origin of Species* came out when he was a Harvard undergraduate. It had an electrifying effect on the campus, and Holmes was in the middle of that. Later, when he returned home from the Civil War, Holmes joined a high-powered discussion group—other participants included William James and Charles Sanders Peirce—which self-mockingly called itself The Metaphysical Club. Its leader, Chauncey Wright, a thinker Holmes admired, corresponded with and visited Darwin, who considered Wright's command of evolutionary theory to be remarkable. Scientific method was frequently discussed by the group.[90]

Someone who brings a Darwinian perspective to the topic of market ordering is likely to be impressed by the way markets force adaptation to changing conditions. This includes attitudinal adaptation, which can be encouraged by having a plethora of points of view on offer. Adaptation also involves weeding out the fallacious and the obsolete. Holmes once explained his late-arriving regard for the freedom of speech in terms of

---

[86] Ibid.   [87] Ibid.
[88] *United States v Schwimmer*, 279 US 644, 653 (1929) (Holmes J, dissenting).
[89] *Abrams* (n 81).
[90] See Edward H Madden, *Chauncey Wright and the Foundations of Pragmatism* (U Washington P 1963) 28; Menand (n 76) 209–10, 216–17; Morton White, *Science and Sentiment in America: Philosophical Thought from Jonathon Edwards to John Dewey* (OUP 1972) 124–5.

such weeding out: 'in the main I am for aeration of all effervescing convictions—there is no way so quick for letting them get flat'.[91] Adaptation frequently demands the redirection of inquisitive energy, a corrective that can be stimulated by competition over ideas. Ordinarily, adaptation requires persons to overcome the forces of custom and inertia. By the way it can excite the passions and energize the will, sometimes even by the anger it generates, free speech can serve as a countervailing force. As with natural selection in biological evolution, adaptive change in the realm of ideas occurs mostly in populations rather than individuals, as demographic developments, most significantly generational turnover, change the mix and new arrivals with different priorities deriving from different experiences exert influence enabled by the relative openness of market ordering.

So far as the freedom of speech is concerned, Holmes is best known for three formulations: (1) his clear-and-present danger test; (2) his limiting example of falsely shouting 'Fire!' in a theatre and causing a panic; and (3) the marketplace-of-ideas metaphor. Each formulation—the proposed doctrinal standard, the limit case, the suggestive metaphor—is about the role that time plays in human events. When exercising his rare gift for minting aphorisms, Holmes repeatedly spoke about time: 'time has upset many fighting faiths';[92] 'property, friendship, and truth have a common root in time';[93] 'leave the correction of evil counsels to time'.[94] The point of his book *The Common Law* is that legal doctrine is all about evolution and adaptation.

Holmes came to value the freedom of speech largely for its capacity over time to generate new ways of thinking, discredit obsolete ideas, and alter priorities of inquiry. Those long-term consequences are what he had in mind when he pronounced the competition of the market to be the best test of truth. Characteristically, he saw the freedom of speech not as a source of individual understanding, assertion, or identity but rather a force—a force for collective adaptation.

2.6 LOUIS BRANDEIS

Justice Louis Brandeis understood the freedom of speech to be an individual liberty important as such but especially important for its contribution to democratic character.

Brandeis's concurring opinion in *Whitney v California*[95] decided in 1927, contains his most intellectually ambitious account of the freedom of speech. The four-paragraph segment of the opinion in which Brandeis spells out his general philosophy regarding free speech begins with a cascade of assertions regarding the beliefs of 'those who won our independence', beliefs that have a suspicious congruence with those we know

---

[91] Letter from Oliver Wendell Holmes, Jr to Harold J Laski (12 May 1919).
[92] *Abrams* (n 81) 630 (Holmes J, dissenting).
[93] Holmes (n 73) 40.
[94] *Abrams* (n 81) 630 (Holmes J, dissenting).
[95] *Whitney v California*, 274 US 357 (1927).

Brandeis held. Right away, a complex, interactive relationship between individual liberty and collective well-being is suggested:

> Those who won our independence believed that the final end of the state was to make men free to develop their faculties, and that in its government the deliberative forces should prevail over the arbitrary. They valued liberty both as an end and as a means. They believed liberty to be the secret of happiness and courage to be the secret of liberty. They believed that freedom to think as you will and to speak as you think are means indispensable to the discovery and spread of political truth.[96]

It may help in trying to interpret Brandeis to know that his observation about liberty being the secret of happiness and courage the secret of liberty was lifted from the Funeral Oration of Pericles, as rendered by Thucydides in his *History of the Peloponnesian War*.[97] Pericles attributed Athens' military success to the courage, awareness, and inventiveness that Athenians possessed as a result of their stimulating culture, which offered many opportunities for personal initiative and civic responsibility. His basic point was that individual, civic, and military flourishing are interconnected.[98]

In this regard, it is also noteworthy that throughout his *Whitney* opinion Brandeis seems unable to mention liberty without instantly invoking what it leads to: deliberative forces prevailing over arbitrary forces, happiness, the discovery and spread of political truth. The list grows as the paragraph progresses:

> [Those who won our independence] knew that order cannot be secured merely through fear of punishment for its infraction; that it is hazardous to discourage thought, hope and imagination; that fear breeds repression; that repression breeds hate; that hate menaces stable government; that the path of safety lies in the opportunity to discuss freely supposed grievances and proposed remedies; and that the fitting remedy for evil counsels is good ones. Believing in the power of reason as applied through public discussion, they eschewed silence coerced by law—the argument of force in its worst form.[99]

Order, stable government, the path of safety, the fitting remedy, non-arbitrary resolution of differences—this is a catalogue of the most important goods that governments are instituted to provide, and they all flow from the freedom of speech, according to Brandeis.

Not only individual rights but also civic duties are part of this complex web of relationships:

---

[96] Ibid 375 (Brandeis J, concurring).
[97] See Philippa Strum, *Louis D. Brandeis: Justice for the People* (Harvard UP 1984) 237–8.
[98] Every law clerk and extended relative of Brandeis was urged by him to read Alfred Zimmern's book, *The Greek Commonwealth*, a celebration of fifth-century Athens, the central chapter of which is about the Funeral Oration: ibid, 242; see Alfred E Zimmern, *The Greek Commonwealth: Politics and Economics in Fifth-Century Athens* (5th ed, OUP 1931).
[99] *Whitney* (n 95) 375.

> Those who won our independence believed . . . [t]hat the greatest menace to freedom is an inert people; that public discussion is a political duty; and that this should be a fundamental principle of the American government.[100]

Brandeis viewed the freedom of speech as generated in significant part by duties. Rights and goods that others think of as protecting individual choice or personal space—privacy, economic security, entrepreneurial opportunity, leisure time—Brandeis prioritized for their contribution to the discharge of the duties of citizenship. For him freedom was serious business.

Further evidence of this seriousness can be gleaned from the paragraphs that follow Brandeis's account of 'the final end of the state'. They are mostly about civic character, something that was much discussed in ancient Athens and Rome, as well as during the American founding, less so in Brandeis's time or today. In uncharacteristically soaring prose, first he proclaims:

> Fear of serious injury cannot alone justify suppression of free speech and assembly. Men feared witches and burnt women. It is the function of speech to free men from the bondage of irrational fears.[101]

Then he comments on the character of the founding generation:

> Those who won our independence by revolution were not cowards. They did not fear political change. They did not exalt order at the cost of liberty.[102]

Next, he explains how the clear-and-present-danger test that he and Holmes had earlier embraced is best understood not as a standard marking the threshold of rational regulatory prediction of harm but rather the point when strong character cannot save the situation for lack of time:

> To courageous, self-reliant men, with confidence in the power of free and fearless reasoning applied through the processes of popular government, no danger flowing from speech can be deemed clear and present, unless the incidence of the evil apprehended is so imminent that it may befall before there is opportunity for full discussion.[103]

In short, the freedom of speech is a remedy as much as a right, or rather a right that can best be justified and demarcated by appreciating its role in preserving civic order, identity, and aspiration:

> If there be time to expose through discussion the falsehood and fallacies, to avert the evil by the processes of education, the remedy to be applied is more speech, not

---

[100] Ibid.   [101] Ibid 376.   [102] Ibid 377.   [103] Ibid.

enforced silence. Only an emergency can justify repression. Such must be the rule if authority is to be reconciled with freedom.[104]

The key to understanding Brandeis, I think, is to realize that when he uses the term 'reconciled' in this passage he means 'integrated into' rather than 'traded off against'. Like the ancient Greeks and the American Founders, he believed that government based on popular sovereignty depends most of all on the character of its people. Character is a public good, arguably the most precious. Not only does civic courage—the courage of the citizenry to confront unwelcome challenges, the courage to sustain commitment in the face of difficulty or disappointment—constitute the strongest check against evil ideas, it provides the energy of reform and aspiration. For all its dangers and excesses, free discussion is an indispensable ingredient of civic courage.

Brandeis insisted that the liberties deserving of special constitutional recognition are not threats to political and public order but rather *components* of such order. He came to that insistence not only by learning what he could from ancient and modern history, but also, and much more importantly, by spending most of his life tirelessly contending with various forces of political entrenchment and corruption. Brandeis's integration of individual liberty and majority rule embodied his credo that experience and responsibility are the best teachers. He valued the freedom of speech mainly for its function of broadening public understanding of and engagement with 'supposed grievances and proposed remedies'.[105] He considered fact- and experience-driven independent judgment about public issues to be crucial for legislators, administrators, reformers, and other democratic actors, not least ordinary persons occupying 'the most important office' in the land, the office of citizen.[106] In this and many other respects, Brandeis viewed the freedom of speech as intimately bound up with the responsibilities of citizenship.

---

[104] Ibid.   [105] *Whitney* (n 95) 375 (Brandeis J, concurring).
[106] See Strum (n 98) 66.

CHAPTER 3

THE TRUTH JUSTIFICATION FOR FREEDOM OF SPEECH

WILLIAM P MARSHALL

3.1 INTRODUCTION

WHY protect freedom of speech? Some contend that freedom of speech is essential to self-government. The citizenry must have access to information in order to exercise the franchise intelligently and hold their elected representatives accountable.[1] Others argue that freedom of speech must be defended because it is a central aspect of personal autonomy and self-realization.[2] Some, particularly in the international community, defend freedom of speech as an essential aspect of individual dignity.[3]

The oldest rationale offered in support of freedom of speech, however, is the 'search for truth' justification. According to this rationale, protecting freedom of speech creates a marketplace of ideas in which truth ultimately prevails over falsity. Speech therefore must not be restricted, because to do so would inhibit this search for truth.

Despite its long-standing pedigree, however, the truth justification has been under sustained attack from a number of directions, so much so that at least one commentator has described it as being 'on the wane'.[4] Further, and perhaps relatedly, the idea of truth itself also seems to have become a concept with less and less currency in an increasingly

---

[1] Alexander Meiklejohn, *Free Speech and Its Relation to Self-Government* (Harper & Brothers 1948).
[2] C Edwin Baker, 'Scope of the First Amendment Freedom of Speech' (1978) 25 *UCLA L Rev* 964; Martin Redish, 'The Value of Free Speech' (1982) 130 *U Pa L Rev* 591.
[3] Guy E Carmi, 'Dignity Versus Liberty: The Two Western Cultures of Free Speech' (2008) 26 *BU Int'l LJ* 277, 290.
[4] Alexander Tsesis, 'Balancing Free Speech' (2016) 96 *BU L Rev* 1, 8.

polarized world. That some would still consider the search for truth to be a primary justification for freedom of expression might be considered by others as hopelessly misguided and naïve.

The truth justification, however, has its defenders.[5] The concept of truth has long held sway over the human imagination, and the explanatory power of truth as a guide for human conduct continues to resonate. The question of whether the truth justification remains a valid rationale for supporting freedom of speech is, therefore, an open inquiry.

This chapter examines the search for truth rationale as a freedom of speech justification. Section 3.1 provides the necessary background. It first presents brief accounts of how the truth justification developed, how it has been applied in US First Amendment jurisprudence, and how it has been accepted (or more accurately, not accepted) in legal systems outside the United States. Section 3.2 canvasses the reasons that have been advanced in defence of the truth justification and the attacks raised against its validity. Section 3.3 discusses another possible explanation in support of the truth justification—that the search for truth provides a valuable narrative for human existence, even if the goal of discovering truth is unlikely to be realized.

One caveat before proceeding: an initial difficulty in investigating the search for truth rationale is that the meaning of 'truth' as it is used in the free speech context is often not clear. At times, 'truth' seems to refer to the truth claims that arise in 'normative, religious, ideological, and political disagreements'.[6] As we shall see, this is the type of truth that writers such as John Milton and Oliver Wendell Holmes Jr. appear to be referring to in their seminal works setting forth the truth justification. For lack of a better word, I will refer to truth in this sense as 'transcendent' truth.

At other times, the search for truth refers to basic questions of fact—questions like how many calories are there in a donut, how high is Mount Everest, or how much is two times two? Sometimes such facts may be highly contested, such as claims that the world is getting hotter or that smoking causes cancer, or the size of the crowd at the Washington Mall during a political protest or presidential inauguration. But they involve facts nonetheless. I will refer to these sorts of truths as 'factual' truths. As we shall see, the considerations both for, and against, the truth justification may vary depending upon the type of truth discussed.

---

[5] William P Marshall, 'In Defense of the Search for Truth as a First Amendment Justification' (1995) 30 *Ga L Rev* 1; Eugene Volokh, 'In Defense of the Marketplace of Ideas/Search for Truth as a Theory of Free Speech Protection' (2011) 97 *Va L Rev* 595; Brian C Murchison, 'Speech and the Truth-Seeking Value' (2015) 39 *Colum J L & Arts* 55.

[6] Frederick Schauer, 'Facts and the First Amendment' (2010) 57 *UCLA L Rev* 897.

3.2 Background

3.2.1 The Origins of the Truth Justification

The truth justification first appeared in US freedom of speech jurisprudence in Holmes's dissent in the case of *Abrams v United States*.[7] In that case, Justice Holmes famously wrote:

> Persecution for the expression of opinions seems to me perfectly logical. If you have no doubt of your premises or your power, and want a certain result with all your heart, you naturally express your wishes in law, and sweep away all opposition. To allow opposition by speech seems to indicate that you think the speech impotent, as when a man says that he has squared the circle, or that you do not care wholeheartedly for the result, or that you doubt either your power or your premises. But when men have realized that time has upset many fighting faiths, they may come to believe even more than they believe the very foundations of their own conduct that the ultimate good desired is better reached by free trade in ideas—that the best test of truth is the power of the thought to get itself accepted in the competition of the market, and that truth is the only ground upon which their wishes safely can be carried out. That, at any rate, is the theory of our Constitution.

Holmes, however, was not writing on a blank slate. John Stuart Mill related the search for truth to freedom of expression in *On Liberty* in 1859.[8] Mill, in turn, was influenced by John Milton, who pioneered the idea that freedom of speech would lead to truth in his *Areopagitica*. As Milton wrote:

> And though all the winds of doctrine were let loose to play upon the earth, so Truth be in the field, we do injuriously, by licensing and prohibiting, to misdoubt her strength. Let her and Falsehood grapple; who ever knew Truth put to the worse, in a free and open encounter?[9]

Nor was Holmes the first to bring the concept of the search for truth as a justification for individual freedom to the Americas. In 1777, Thomas Jefferson raised the truth battling falsehood metaphor in the context of freedom of religion in his Bill for Establishing Religious Freedom:

---

[7] *Abrams v United States*, 250 US 616 (1919).
[8] John Stuart Mill, *On Liberty* (Michael B Mathias ed, Pearson Longman 2007).
[9] John Milton, 'Areopagitica' in Merritt Y Hughes (ed), *John Milton, Complete Poems and Major Prose* (Macmillan 1957) 720.

Truth is great, and will prevail if left to herself, that she is the proper and sufficient antagonist to error, and has nothing to fear from the conflict, unless by human interposition disarmed of her natural weapons free argument and debate, errors ceasing to be dangerous when it is permitted freely to contradict them.[10]

Holmes was, however, the first to introduce the truth justification into US constitutional law, and its effects have been enduring. As Joseph Blocher observed, Holmes's dissent in *Abrams*, 'conceptualized the purpose of free speech so powerfully that [it] revolutionized not just First Amendment doctrine, but popular and academic understanding of free speech'.[11]

3.2.2 The Truth Justification and Freedom of Speech Doctrine in the United States

The words in Holmes's dissent have now echoed through more than one hundred years of freedom of speech decisions. However, perhaps even more pronounced than its rhetorical reverberations has been its substantive impact on the case law. Based in significant part on the truth justification and its marketplace of ideas metaphor, the US Supreme Court has fashioned an expansive freedom of speech jurisprudence under which few restrictions on free speech are upheld. In the last few years alone, the US Supreme Court has relied on freedom of speech principles to strike down restrictions on depictions of animal abuse,[12] violent video games,[13] speech that causes emotional harm,[14] and speech provided by crisis centres to pregnant women.[15] Increasingly, it seems, the Court has found that there is little outside of the free speech ambit.

It would be inaccurate, however, to assert that the current US free speech jurisprudence inevitably followed from the Holmes dissent. Rather, the truth justification could have been used as a vehicle to limit freedom of speech as well as to enhance it. After all, if the reason to protect speech is that it aids in the search for truth, then presumably speech that does not aid in that search would be outside free speech parameters. Milton, for example, excluded the espousal of Catholicism from free speech protections because he denied 'even the possibility that genuine truth might be lurking in Catholic theology'.[16] To Milton, speech that did not lead to truth could be excluded from free speech protections.

---

[10] Thomas Jefferson, 'A Bill for Establishing Religious Freedom' in Julian P Boyd (ed), *The Papers of Thomas Jefferson* (Princeton UP 1950) vol 2, 545.
[11] Joseph Blocher, 'Institutions in the Marketplace of Ideas' (2008) 57 *Duke LJ* 821, 823.
[12] *United States v Stevens*, 559 US 460 (2010).
[13] *Brown v Entertainment Merchants Ass'n*, 564 US 786 (2011).
[14] *Snyder v Phelps*, 562 US 443 (2011).
[15] *Nat'l Inst of Family and Life Advocates v Becerra*, 138 S Ct 2361 (2018).
[16] Vincent Blasi, 'A Reader's Guide to John Milton's *Areopagitica*, the Foundational Essay of the First Amendment Tradition' (2018) *Sup Ct Rev* 273.

The US Supreme Court at one point also hinted that it might adopt such an approach. In *Chaplinsky v New Hampshire*, decided in the 1940s, the Court stated that there were certain classes of speech such as 'the lewd and obscene, the profane, the libelous, and the insulting or "fighting" words [which might be permissibly regulated because they were] *of such slight social value as a step to truth* that any benefit that may be derived from them [was] clearly outweighed by the social interest in order and morality'.[17] Like Milton, the *Chaplinsky* Court appeared ready to qualitatively evaluate which types of speech furthered the truth-seeking function.

In later cases, however, the Court veered away from this approach, studiously avoiding passing qualitative judgment on what types of speech facilitate the search for truth and what types of speech do not. Instead, the Court left the decision of what is valuable for the search for truth to the market to decide and not to the courts or a regulatory body. Accordingly, under this approach, the value of speech is solely in the eye of the beholder, or in marketplace terms, the 'consumer'. As the Court famously stated in *Cohen v California*, 'one man's vulgarity is another's lyric'.[18]

This reluctance to engage in qualitative analysis regarding the truth value of certain categories of speech is what has led the Court to construct a markedly robust free speech jurisprudence. For example, under this approach the Court has rigorously required that restrictions on speech must be 'content-neutral' so that governments cannot 'interfere' with the open marketplace by admitting some viewpoints and topics to the exclusion of others.[19] This means that even minor regulations, such as those which set forth the length of time certain signs can be displayed on public property, are subject to exacting judicial scrutiny.[20]

The marketplace approach also led the Court to protect speech that many would find harmful and/or dangerous. Under current doctrine, for example, incitement of lawless action is protected almost up to the moment when violence begins. The state may not 'forbid or proscribe advocacy of the use of force or of law violation except where such advocacy is directed to inciting or producing imminent lawless action and is likely to incite or produce such action'.[21] Additionally, the search for truth has also provided the basis for Supreme Court decisions that have seriously curtailed the extent that libel,[22] and profane speech,[23] can be restricted, even though both categories were deemed to be among the forms of speech that were explicitly referenced by the *Chaplinsky* opinion as being of only slight value in the search for truth. The truth justification has also been instrumental to the Court in striking down regulations of commercial speech,[24] and it has provided the framework from which prohibitions on hate speech have been invalidated.[25] The Court has even used the search for truth rationale to invalidate a law that prohibited deliberate and intentional falsity. In striking down the so-called 'stolen

---

[17] *Chaplinsky v State of New Hampshire*, 315 US 568 (1942).
[18] *Cohen v California*, 403 US 15, 25 (1971).
[19] *Reed v Town of Gilbert*, 135 S Ct 2218, 2233 (2015). [20] Ibid.
[21] *Brandenburg v Ohio*, 395 US 444 (1969). [22] *New York Times v Sullivan*, 376 US 254 (1964).
[23] *Cohen* (n 18). [24] *44 Liquormart, Inc v Rhode Island*, 517 US 484 (1996).
[25] *Doe v University of Michigan*, 721 F Supp 852 (ED Mich 1989).

valour' provision that forbade falsely representing oneself as having received any US military decoration or medal, the Court in *Alvarez v United States* stated, '[t]ruth needs neither handcuffs nor a badge for its vindication'.[26]

Finally, the Court has relied on the truth rationale to expand freedom of speech to more than an individual right. In the context of speech by corporations,[27] for example, the Court ruled that whether speech is protected is not based upon the speaker's rights but upon the notion that ideas entering the marketplace will facilitate the search for truth no matter what their source. Accordingly, based on this reasoning, the Court in *Citizens United v FEC* struck down limits on corporate campaign expenditures, even though it did not hold that corporations are entities with free speech rights.[28]

3.2.3 The Truth Justification Outside the United States

Perhaps, in part, because US free speech jurisprudence has been seen as too expansive,[29] the truth justification has not enjoyed much traction outside the United States. International human rights law, for example, treats human dignity as the foundational value for human rights, including for freedom of speech. The Universal Declaration of Human Rights (UDHR) proclaims that 'recognition of the inherent dignity and of the equal and inalienable rights of all members of the human family is the foundation of freedom, justice and peace in the world'.[30] The European Convention on Human Rights (ECHR) makes clear that freedom of expression is a fundamental but limited right, allowing for restrictions that 'are necessary in a democratic society' for purposes of protecting 'health or morals', 'the prevention of disorder', and 'the rights of others'.[31]

Most individual countries, as well, do not recognize the truth justification. The United Kingdom, for example, in addition to signing on to the ECHR, centres its protection for freedom of speech on the value of promoting democracy.[32] Australia, although it does not have a specific constitutional provision governing freedom of speech, has found an implied freedom of political communication stemming from the form of representative government established by the Constitution.[33] Similar to the UK, Australian courts have identified the primary purpose of freedom of speech to be preserving the conditions necessary for self-government. Accordingly, speech that does not contribute to this end falls outside of the freedom of speech protection.[34]

---

[26] *United States v Alvarez*, 567 US 709 (2012).
[27] *First National Bank of Boston v Bellotti*, 435 US 765 (1978).
[28] *Citizens United v FEC*, 558 US 310 (2010).
[29] Lorraine Eisenstate Weinrib, 'Hate Promotion in a Free and Democratic Society: *R v Keegstra*' (1991) 36 *McGill LJ* 1416.
[30] UDHR (adopted 10 December 1948) UNGA Res 217 A(III), art 1.
[31] Convention for the Protection of Human Rights and Fundamental Freedoms (ECHR), art 10.
[32] Jeffrey A Brauch, 'The Margin of Appreciation and the Jurisprudence of the European Court of Human Rights: Threat to the Rule of Law' (2005) 11 *Colum J Eur L* 113.
[33] *Australian Capital Television v Commonwealth* (1992) 177 CLR 106.
[34] *Lange v Australian Broadcasting Corporation* (1997) 189 CLR 520.

Some countries actually do acknowledge the truth justification. Yet even in those countries, the truth justification appears subordinate to other values. For example, though Canada and South Africa at times nod in the direction of the truth rationale, both countries allow the regulation of certain kinds of hate speech in a way the United States does not because of concerns for other overriding interests—Canada out of a commitment to equality and multiculturalism,[35] South Africa in the interests of equality and human dignity.[36] The Canadian approach, in this respect, is particularly notable. Although Canada nominally allows hate speech defendants to argue their speech contributes to the search for truth, the defence can be rejected on grounds that there is a high degree of certainty that such speech is erroneous, and thus without value in the search for truth.[37]

Germany may be the most interesting case. Although for the most part German law replicates the UDHR in setting forth human dignity as the paramount value,[38] it does have one notable exception. Germany does not allow the restriction of artistic, research, and scientific expression, suggesting that in at least those areas it finds the truth justification to be paramount.[39] That example aside, however, the consensus outside the United States is that the position that truth is the foundational value for freedom of speech is essentially misguided.

3.3 Appraising the Truth Justification

3.3.1 The Arguments in Defence of the Truth Justification

The initial case in support of the truth justification is straightforward. After all, if transcendent truth exists, its importance is, by definition, virtually ultimate, and its importance in guiding human behaviour potentially absolute.[40] The realization of truth, accordingly, may be the highest goal to which humanity can aspire. Transcendent truth questions are also unavoidable. Even assertions that absolute truth does not exist, or that if it does exist, it is unintelligible to human powers of understanding, are themselves truth claims.

The case for the search for factual truth is equally compelling. Being able to separate truth from falsity is necessary for basic human decision-making. Knowing that opioids are dangerously addictive, for example, will inform a person's decision about whether to

---

[35] *R v Keegstra* [1990] 3 SCR 697.
[36] *Islamic Unity Convention v Independent Broadcasting Authority and Others* 2002 (4) SA 294.
[37] *Keegstra* (n 35).
[38] Aernout Nieuwenhuis, 'Freedom of Speech: USA vs Germany and Europe' (2000) 18 *NQHR* 195.
[39] Edward J Eberle, 'Articles Public Discourse in Contemporary Germany' (1997) 47 *Case W Res L Rev* 797.
[40] John M Finnis, 'Skepticism, Self-Refutation and the Good of Truth' in PMS Hacker and J Raz (eds), *Law, Morality and Society: Essays in Honour of HLA Hart* (Clarendon P 1977) 247, 250; Michael Gelven, *Truth and Existence: A Philosophical Inquiry* (Pennsylvania State UP 1990).

use them and a doctor's decision about whether they should prescribe them. Similarly, factual truths are also critical for communal decisions. Public bodies must know the facts underlying competing policy choices so that they can 'make sufficiently well-informed judgments and decisions concerning the most suitable disposition of the public interest'.[41] Knowledge that opioids are dangerously addictive, for example, will inform political entities so that they can intelligently consider whether to take remedial measures.

The argument in support of the truth justification is also buttressed by the fact that truth (both transcendent and factual) has long held pre-eminent importance in Western philosophy and theology. Socrates believed the value of truth to be greater than the value of life.[42] Plato described truth as the purest form of knowledge.[43] Christian theology asserted that 'Truth ... is great and stronger than all else', and that 'the Truth will make you free'.[44] Enlightenment thought placed truth at the centre of human inquiry. John Locke, for example, described truth-seeking as 'the most elevated faculty of the soul'.[45] Even Friedrich Nietzsche, whose work was singularly powerful in deconstructing human understanding and reason, maintained that truth was the highest philosophical concern.[46] The truth justification therefore comfortably fits within a deep-rooted intellectual tradition.

Further, and relatedly, truth-seeking has also long been seen as an aspect of virtue. Truth denotes open-mindedness rather than retrenchment. It requires humility in the sense that it reflects the 'recognition that there are facts and truth over which we cannot hope to exercise direct or immediate control'.[47] Further, the search for truth also produces individual perseverance. While for some, searching for truth reveals constraints that limit what we can achieve, for others searching for and committing to an individual truth may reveal that societal constraints do not limit their endeavour. The perceived virtue of the truth-seeker, moreover, applies to both those who seek factual truth and those who seek transcendent truth. The scientist and the scholar, as well as the philosopher and the theologian, are admired because of their commitment to the pursuit of truth.[48]

Finally, the search for truth justification is strongly supported by what might be considered a negative consideration: it disempowers the state. By keeping the avenues to truth open, the truth justification prevents the state from appropriating claims of truth for its own purposes and imposing its own orthodoxy. As Professor Thomas Emerson

---

[41] Murchison (n 5) 73.
[42] Plato, 'Apology' in Benjamin Jowett (tr), *The Dialogues of Plato* (Encyclopedia Britannica 1952).
[43] Plato, *The Republic of Plato* (Francis Cornford tr, Clarendon P 1941).
[44] *The Apocrypha of the Old Testament* '1: Esdras 4:35' (Bruce Metzger ed, rev edn, OUP 1977).
[45] John Locke, *An Essay Concerning Human Understanding* (Maurice William Cranston ed, Collier Books 1965) 23.
[46] Peter Berkowitz, 'On the Laws Governing Free Spirits and Philosophers of the Future: A Response to Nonet's "What is Positive Law?"' (1990) 100 *Yale LJ* 701, 715 (citing Friedrich Nietzsche, *Beyond Good and Evil* (Walter Kaufmann tr, Vintage Books 1966)).
[47] Murchison (n 5) 82, quoting Henry Frankfurt, *On Truth* (Knopf 2006) 100.
[48] Daniel A Farber and Suzanna Sherry, 'The 200,000 Cards of Dimitri Yurasov: Further Reflections on Scholarship and Truth' (1994) 46 *Stan L Rev* 647, 648.

noted: '[t]he effort to coerce belief ... is the hallmark of a feudal or totalitarian society'.[49] It is this concern with government imposed orthodoxy that motivated John Milton in *Areopagitica*, and echoes of this rationale also resonate in US case law. For example, in a case examining the right of the Jehovah's Witnesses to refuse to salute the flag and say the Pledge of Allegiance, the Court stated: 'If there is any fixed star in our constitutional constellation, it is that no official, high or petty, can prescribe which shall be orthodox in politics, nationalism, religion, or other matters of opinion'.[50]

The concern with preventing the state from imposing belief and orthodoxy has more obvious application to assertions of transcendent truth of the type addressed by Milton, than to assertions of factual truth. After all, statements that the Holocaust did not occur or that a candidate for office earned a military medal arguably do not help the cause of truth if those statements are false. As Senator Daniel Patrick Moynihan stated, '[e]veryone is entitled to his own opinion, but not to his own facts'.[51]

Nevertheless, there are reasons why it might be problematic to allow the state to proscribe factual falsity. First, and most importantly, it would invest the government with enormous power to limit expression. As the Supreme Court explained in *Alvarez*:

> Permitting the government to decree [lying about earning a military medal] to be a criminal offense, whether shouted from the rooftops or made in a barely audible whisper, would endorse government authority to compile a list of subjects about which false statements are punishable. That governmental power has no clear limiting principle. Our constitutional tradition stands against the idea that we need [an Orwellian] Ministry of Truth ... Were the Court to hold that the interest in truthful discourse alone is sufficient to sustain a ban on speech, absent any evidence that the speech was used to gain a material advantage, it would give government a broad censorial power unprecedented in this Court's cases or in our constitutional tradition.[52]

Second, as the *Alvarez* Court went on to explain, allowing the state to proscribe falsity may also chill the speech of persons who are not completely sure of the verity of their statements or who are concerned about the possible costs in defending against a prosecution, even when they are sure of their accounts. Outlawing falsity, in short, may also work to curb the dissemination of truth.

Third, some 'facts' can change. The medical community, for example, long accepted the 'fact' that antioxidants like those naturally found in red wine 'are recognized to be good for health'.[53] Later studies now suggest that consuming even moderate amounts of

---

[49] Thomas I Emerson, *The System of Freedom of Expression* (Random House 1970) 21.
[50] *West Virginia State Board of Education v Barnette*, 319 US 624, 642 (1943).
[51] Daniel Patrick Moynihan, *Daniel Patrick Moynihan: A Portrait in Letters of an American Visionary* (Steven R Weisman ed, PublicAffairs 2010).
[52] Alvarez (n 26) [723], citing George Orwell, *Nineteen Eighty-Four* (1949; Centennial 2003).
[53] Raffaella Aversa and others, 'One Can Slow Down the Aging through Antioxidants' (2016) 9 *Am J Engineering and Applied Sci* 1112, 1112.

alcohol is unhealthy.[54] Future research may still lead to different conclusions. Determining that something is a 'fact', in short, is not always the end of the inquiry. After all, as Frederick Schauer points out, it was once a settled 'fact' that the world was flat.[55]

In sum, the negative case in support of the truth justification is a particularly strong one. As Schauer notes, '[t]he reason for preferring the marketplace of ideas to the selection of truth by government may be less the proven ability of the former than it is the often evidenced inability of the latter'.[56]

3.3.2 The Arguments in Opposition to the Truth Justification

As demonstrated in the previous section, the arguments in support of the truth justification are varied and substantial. As this section will show, the same can also be said with respect to the attacks on the truth rationale. Yet there is a significant difference. While the arguments *defending* the truth justification's application to both transcendent and factual truth largely overlap, that is not the case with respect to the arguments *attacking* the truth justification. In this regard, there is a substantial difference in the arguments relating to the two types of truths. Accordingly, the remainder of this section is divided into two parts—one addressing the attacks on transcendent truth as a free speech justification and one focusing on the attacks on factual truth.

3.3.2.1 *Transcendent Truth*

A first critique of the search for transcendent truth as a justification for freedom of speech relates to the value of truth itself. Postmodern thought does not accept that truth exists, or if it does exist, that it is intelligible to human understanding.[57] The belief that humanity can realize truth is a relic of religious thought and/or a product of the Enlightenment that has long faded into philosophical obsolescence.[58] Religious truths are now seen as only products of individual belief and not insights into a greater reality.[59] The optimism of the Enlightenment that the powers of reason could lead humanity to a knowledge of truth has been thoroughly discredited; the belief that human reason could uncover transcendent truth has been exposed as just that—a belief.[60] There is no truth to be found.

A second line of attack on the truth justification comes from the other side—the possibility that truth does exist and is accessible. As some theorists have noted, truth and

---

[54] Angela Wood and others, 'Risk Thresholds for Alcohol Consumption: Combined Analysis of Individual-Participant Data for 599 912 Current Drinkers in 83 Prospective Studies' (2018) 391 *The Lancet* 1513.
[55] Frederick Schauer, 'Free Speech, the Search for Truth, and the Problem of Collective Knowledge' (2017) 70 *SMU L Rev* 231, 236.
[56] Frederick F Schauer, *Free Speech: A Philosophical Enquiry* (CUP 1982) 34.
[57] C Edwin Baker, 'Scope of the First Amendment Freedom of Speech' (1978) 25 *UCLA L Rev* 964, 965.
[58] Marshall (n 5) 2–3.   [59] Ibid 3.
[60] Carl L Becker, *The Heavenly City of the Eighteenth-Century Philosophers* (Yale UP 1932) 74.

freedom are in tension. A person who knows transcendent truth presumably does not have the freedom to reject it. They would be bound by the ultimate order. Thus, ironically, it is the absence of the knowledge of universal truth that grants the freedom to the individual to seek their own truth. This is why, as Leonard Levy once explained, freedom of speech could not become a civil liberty 'until the truth of [human] opinions, especially their religious opinions, was regarded as relative rather than absolute'.[61]

A third, and related concern, is that playing with truth is a dangerous game. In the *Abrams* passage quoted at the outset of this chapter, Justice Holmes pointed out that certainty of belief is what at times leads to the suppression of competing ideas. As he stated, 'If you have no doubt of your premises or your power, and want a certain result with all your heart, you naturally express your wishes in law, and sweep away all opposition'.[62] This passage recognizes that if someone believes their search has succeeded and they have found truth, their next logical step is not protecting the freedom of speech of others. More likely, it would be a reason (or at least a motivation) for them to take action to quell the dissent.

Fourth, the value of transcendent truth as providing a justification for freedom of speech might also be rejected because concerns of universal truth are too far removed from daily life. Freedom of speech obviously is not only of philosophical concern. It has immense practical implications for real-world problems including democratic governance and social relations. Constructing a system of freedom of expression around transcendent truth may divert its understanding from more pragmatic purposes.[63]

Finally, the use of transcendent truth as providing a justification for freedom of speech might also be problematic because the concept is arguably theistically-laden. Richard Rorty, for example, characterizes the idea of transcendent truth as essentially a 'God surrogate'.[64] If so, placing the search for transcendent truth at the centre of freedom of speech would appear to endorse one world-view (theism) as being the most worthy of human pursuits. As such, it would contain a normative judgment about human conduct that a full commitment to the individual's freedom to choose their own values would appear to deny.[65]

3.3.2.2 *Factual Truth*

The attacks on the truth justification with respect to factual truth may be even more severe than the attacks with respect to transcendent truth. For example, numerous arguments have been advanced questioning the validity of the marketplace of ideas metaphor—that factual truth will prevail over falsity in a free and open encounter as the marketplace of

---

[61] Leonard W Levy, *Legacy of Suppression: Freedom of Speech and Press in Early American History* (Belknap P of Harvard UP 1960) 95.

[62] *Abrams* (n 7) 630.

[63] Richard Rorty, 'To the Sunlit Uplands', London Review of Books (31 October 2002), reviewing Bernard Williams, *Truth and Truthfulness: An Essay in Genealogy* (Princeton UP 2002); Murchison (n 5) 70–1, citing Michael P Lynch, 'Democracy as a Space of Reasons' in Jeremy Elkins and Andrew Norris (eds), *Truth and Democracy* (U Pennsylvania P 2012) 115.

[64] Murchison (n 5) 70, quoting Richard Rorty and Pascal Engel, *What's the Use of Truth?* (William McCuaig tr, Columbia UP 2007) 40.

[65] Murchison (n 5).

ideas. First, as some have contended, to the extent that the truth justification relies on something akin to an economic theory of the marketplace, it is on shaky ground. In the words of one writer, 'the market is an imperfect and frequently malfunctioning machine and the costs of exchange add friction to its gears'.[66] There is no reason, in short, to assume the marketplace of ideas will be able to overcome the transaction costs and the other types of barriers that impair other markets. Marketplaces of ideas, like other markets, seldom achieve optimum results.

Second, as others have noted, truth may not prevail in the marketplace of ideas because access to the market is profoundly unequal. Those with greater resources are able to disseminate their position in a manner in which those without similar resources cannot.[67] Those with the greater resources can use their market domination to better 'sell' their ideas and convince the 'consumer' to adopt their versions of what is true. Meanwhile, those who do not have the resources to enter the market can be frozen out, despite the verity of their assertions.[68]

Third, the marketplace assumes that participants are rational—yet, as advertisers well know, the form of the message can have as much, if not more, influence over the purchaser's choice than the truth of the message in question.[69] Better products, after all, do not always prevail over better-advertised products.[70]

Fourth, even aside from the possibilities of market failure, the marketplace may not be the best arbiter of truth. Consensus that something is true does not make it true. As Robert Post argues, '[t]he purpose of fostering a marketplace of ideas is an implausible goal of First Amendment doctrine because new knowledge cannot be created without the concomitant power to judge ideas as true or false, as better or worse'. Accordingly, as Post sees it, the marketplace of ideas must be complemented by oversight and judgment, as when scientific journals and universities make qualitative decisions regarding the merits of scientific studies and academic research.[71]

Fifth, even if factual truth was able to somehow emerge from the marketplace, it is not at all clear that consumers are interested in buying the product. As Lee McIntyre has pointed out, we currently live in a 'post-truth' world, defined as one in which 'objective facts are less influential in shaping public opinion than appeals to emotion and personal belief'.[72] In such a world, many of us are more interested in acting on what our emotions desire than what we might actually know to be true.[73] This is not a trivial concern. If a system of freedom of speech is to be constructed around a foundational principle, that principle should have some normative attraction.

---

[66] Blocher (n 11) 826.
[67] *Animal Defenders International v United Kingdom* (2013) 57 EHRR 21.
[68] Alexander Tsesis, 'Free Speech Constitutionalism' [2015] *U Ill L Rev* 1015.
[69] *Irwin Toy Ltd v Quebec (AG)* [1989] 1 SCR 927.
[70] Steven Shiffrin, 'First Amendment and Economic Regulation: Away from a General Theory of the First Amendment' (1983–4) 78 *Nw U L Rev* 1212.
[71] Robert Post, 'Participatory Democracy and Free Speech' (2011) 97 *Va L Rev* 477.
[72] Lee C McIntyre, *Post-Truth* (MIT P 2018) 5.
[73] Jonathan D Varat, 'Truth, Courage, and Other Human Dispositions: Reflections on Falsehoods and the First Amendment' (2018) 71 *Okla L Rev* 35, 55.

Further, the problems with the truth justification as it applies to factual truth may actually run deeper than just the weaknesses identified within the marketplace metaphor. To begin with, factual truth, unlike transcendent truth, is not necessarily an end in itself. While the realization of transcendent truth would be, by definition, of ultimate significance, the same cannot be so readily asserted about factual truth. Rather, some explanation is needed to defend why factual truth should be considered to have primacy over other values.

To be sure, the belief that factual truth has pre-eminent value has traditionally been thought to be 'self-evident'.[74] Yet the value of knowing a fact for its own sake is questionable. Why is knowing a fact to be true of value unless that knowledge is to be applied for some other use? Proceeding along these lines, Frederick Schauer has argued that factual truth should not be considered an end in itself. Rather, according to Schauer, it should be considered as having only 'instrumental' value in the pursuit of some 'deeper good'.[75]

The implication of this understanding for freedom of speech is significant. If the value of factual truth is contingent on how well it serves a larger purpose, then whether individuals should be free to speak those truths would also be contingent on how well that speech furthers the underlying goal. This depends on two questions: what is the deeper good and what is the fact in question? For example, if the deeper good is deemed to be promoting happiness, then speech that causes serious emotional harm might not be worthy of protection—even if the speech in question is true. Or if the deeper good is deemed to be social stability, then highly socially disruptive speech might also be found to be outside the bounds of what freedom of speech protects—even if that speech is true.

Certainly, this approach still leaves some major work to be done. One has to identify the 'deeper good' around which instrumental values are to be evaluated.[76] But no matter what good is seen to have primacy, the larger point in Schauer's critique is that there is no obvious reason to continue to keep factual truth on its pre-eminent perch.

This leads to a related point. Some factual truths are harmful.[77] The dissemination of highly personal revelations about an individual can cause serious emotional and economic harm. The 'truth' that a journalist or intelligence agent is working undercover can threaten their life. The release of information about how to make a chemical weapon can lead to mass destruction. Publishing trade secrets can destroy the value of a product. A freedom of speech regime that makes truth the foundational value, therefore, may not only be problematic on the theoretical ground that the value of truth is more properly viewed as instrumental than as an end in itself. It may also be problematic because it allows for the protection of speech that inflicts real-world harms. Not all factual truths are unmitigated goods.[78]

---

[74] Frederick Schauer, 'Reflections on the Value of Truth' (1991) 41 *Case W Res L Rev* 699, 706.
[75] Ibid.   [76] Ibid 707.
[77] Rebecca L Brown, 'The Harm Principle and Free Speech' (2016) 89 *S Cal L Rev* 953.
[78] Conversely, some factual lies are not unmitigated evils: Alan K Chen and Justin Marceau, 'Developing a Taxonomy of Lies Under the First Amendment' (2018) 89 *U Colo L Rev* 655.

3.4 Evaluating the Truth Justification: Truth as Narrative

As we have seen thus far, the literal case in favour of the truth justification for freedom of speech is weaker than one might expect given the strengths of the attacks. There is little reason to believe that freedom of speech will lead us to the realization of transcendent truth which, if it exists at all, is likely beyond the ken of human understanding. Nor is their reason to believe freedom of speech will reliably lead us to the discovery of factual truths. The marketplace of ideas is a flawed mechanism for distinguishing between truth and falsity; and even aside from that, the value of factual truth may lie more in its instrumental role in allowing individuals and society to achieve more foundational goods, such as happiness or social stability, than as an end in itself.

The truth justification fares better as a rationale to disempower government from deciding what is true and what is not. Governments, after all, are not likely to use the power to be an arbiter of truth to their own disadvantage. And the Orwellian risk that government will abuse its power to appropriate truth for its own purposes may alone be enough to support the truth justification.

Yet the truth justification arguably stands on something greater than increasing knowledge or restricting the power of government. Justice Holmes, whose *Abrams* dissent began this chapter, once famously remarked, '[w]e live by symbols';[79] and it is in those terms where we can begin to examine another critical aspect of the truth justification—its value as a symbol of human aspiration. The question then becomes whether the search for truth provides a sufficiently compelling narrative for guiding human conduct so as to justify freedom of speech.

When viewed in this manner, truth does not have to account for factual or even transcendent verity. Rather it represents, as John Milton might see it, 'a transcendent ideal toward which all good men should strive'.[80] This is the meaning of truth to which Blaise Pascal refers when he declares, '[w]e make an idol of truth itself'.[81]

The significance of truth in this sense is akin to the role played by myth in religion. It purports to provide the type of sustaining vision that societies have 'found necessary to point to and preserve as centrally valid for their entire existence'.[82] As such, to repeat, the authority of the truth justification does not depend on whether freedom of speech actually leads to truth discovery. It depends instead upon whether the truth justification successfully serves the narrative function.

---

[79] Oliver Wendell Holmes Jr, *Collected Legal Papers* (Harcourt, Brace & Howe 1920) 270.
[80] David Cole, 'Agon at Agora: Creative Misreadings in the First Amendment Tradition' (1996) 95 *Yale LJ* 857, 876 (describing Milton's understanding of truth).
[81] Blaise Pascal, *Pascal's Pensées* (WF Trotter tr, EP Dutton 1958) 582.
[82] Kees Bolle, 'Myth' in Mircea Eliade and others (eds), *Encyclopedia of Religion* (Macmillan 1987) vol 10, 262–3.

The arguments that it does so are considerable. To begin with, as noted previously, the search for truth has traditionally been at the heart of philosophical and theological inquiry and its pursuit a hallmark of personal virtue. This is no accident. Seeking truth is intrinsic to human nature. As Michael Perry writes, 'an essential characteristic of human beings is their need for, and their capacity to pursue and achieve, an ever better understanding of reality'.[83]

That need is even more profound when the subject is transcendent truth. Questions surrounding transcendent truth are particularly compelling because they address existential concerns about life's meaning, purpose, and consequence and thereby respond to humanity's deepest curiosities and anxieties.[84] Further, even though transcendent truth may be beyond human understanding (if it exists at all), its possibility adds imperative to the narrative.[85] After all, if truth does exist, it is, by definition, of ultimate importance and its authority potentially absolute in setting forth standards to guide human behaviour.[86] There is little wonder, then, why the narrative of transcendent truth has had such hold over the human imagination.[87]

This is not to say that defending the truth justification as a narrative rather than as a literal search for truth is without its weaknesses. First, it does not overcome the objection that the project is still ultimately an exercise in futility. The myth of Sisyphus may teach us about the importance of reaching for a summit and the nobility of those who try, but Sisyphus himself was relegated to pushing a boulder up a hill for all of eternity.[88]

Second, it might be contended that the narrative defence of the truth justification, if it works at all, applies only to transcendent truth. There is merit in this objection as well. After all, there is something qualitatively different in a narrative in which the individual is seeking the meaning of the cosmos than one in which they are trying to ascertain how many miles there are between Oxford and Cambridge.

At the same time, removing the search for factual truth from the narrative is problematic. To begin with, although some factual truth investigations may be trivial, others hold a gravity that approaches that of transcendent truth. Consider, for example, the narratives surrounding the research into DNA or the scientific inquiry into the origin of the universe. Indeed, the line between factual and transcendent truth is not always clear, as the origins of the universe example suggests.

The more significant problem, however, is that the authority and attraction of the truth narrative may be weakened if it is subject to qualification. Certainly, the rhetorical power of Milton's *Areopagitica* or Holmes's *Abrams* dissent would have been lost if they

---

[83] Michael J Perry, 'Freedom of Expression: An Essay on Theory and Doctrine' (1983) 78 *Nw U L Rev* 1137, 1155.

[84] Peter L Berger, *The Sacred Canopy: Elements of a Sociological Theory of Religion* (Anchor Books 1967) 56.

[85] Rudolf Otto, *The Idea of the Holy* (John W Harvey tr, 2nd edn, OUP 1950) 12–19.

[86] Pascal (n 81) para 343.

[87] See, eg, Erwin R Goodenough, *The Psychology of Religious Experiences* (Basic Books 1965) 8–14.

[88] Albert Camus, *The Myth of Sisyphus* (Justin O'Brien tr, Hamish Hamilton 1955).

had had to pause and specify that the idealization of truth refers to some kinds of truths but not to others. Therefore, it may be that if the rhetorical power of the truth narrative is to be maintained, factual truths need be included in its parameters.

Third, the truth narrative might be critiqued for too readily protecting harmful speech, as some argue has been the case in US First Amendment law.[89] Yet, as alluded to previously, endorsing the truth justification does not require applying it expansively in the manner of US jurisprudence. As we have seen, Canada adheres to the truth rationale but allows restrictions on hate speech on the grounds that such utterances are almost certainly not true.[90] Similarly, as discussed earlier, even the US Supreme Court once suggested in the *Chaplinsky* case that weeding out speech that does not meaningfully aid in the search for truth from free speech protections could be permissible.[91] It was only when the Court abandoned that approach that US speech jurisprudence became as expansive as it did.

Additionally, and somewhat ironically, culling certain types of speech from free speech protections may actually serve to further the truth narrative. To the extent that the purpose in removing certain kinds of speech from free speech protections is explained as intended to promote the search for truth, it reinforces the primacy of the truth narrative by emphasizing a central qualitative concern at the heart of the free speech right. That lesson has been lost in a jurisprudence that suggests that all speech is equal;[92] or that one person's vulgarity is another person's lyric.[93]

No doubt, this is risky business. It explicitly lets the government in the door to make qualitative determinations as to what types of speech further the truth-seeking interest. It therefore undermines what we have already concluded is one of the strongest arguments supporting the truth justification—restricting government power. The question is how to draw the balance or whether it is even possible to draw the balance at all.

That said, the truth justification—despite its flaws—fares well in comparison to the other theories that have been advanced to support the commitment to freedom of speech. Its ambition is higher than the self-governance rationale in that it suggests that the value of freedom is more than just political. It is less self-absorbed than the autonomy and self-realization rationales because it suggests there is more to freedom than pursuing self-interest. It is more open than the dignity rationale because it suggests there is freedom to move beyond a pre-encumbered self.[94] Finally, and unlike any of its competing rationales, the truth justification reflects a humility that there is at least the possibility of a reality that is greater than the individual.

Whether any, or all of this, is persuasive in defending the truth justification from its many critiques is undoubtedly contestable. But there is one last question to be

---

[89] Brown (n 77).   [90] *Keegstra* (n 35).   [91] *Chaplinsky* (n 17).
[92] *Chicago Police Dept v Mosley*, 408 US 92 (1971).   [93] *Cohen* (n 18).
[94] Michael J Sandel, 'Religious Liberty: Freedom of Conscience or Freedom of Choice' (1989) *Utah L Rev* 597, 611.

asked in evaluating the truth justification: What would freedom of speech be without it? The question is not hypothetical. As some observers have noted, we have already moved into a 'post-truth' world where truth has become 'irrelevant', where what a person desires to be true is the only truth that matters, and where there are no normative distinctions between truth and lies.[95] Before abandoning the truth justification entirely, it is worthwhile considering whether moving towards post-truth is a step in the right direction.

---

[95] McIntyre (n 72) 5.

CHAPTER 4

AUTONOMY AND FREE SPEECH

CATRIONA MACKENZIE AND DENISE MEYERSON

The traditional justifications for freedom of speech fall into two broad categories, depending on whether freedom of speech is thought to serve societal interests, such as truth and democracy, or individual interests, such as autonomy.[1] This chapter focuses on the relationship between autonomy and freedom of speech. As will emerge, there is no single theoretical account of this relationship. The complexity of the subject matter is due to several factors.

First, autonomy is a contested concept and there are rival conceptions of the concept. These rival conceptions are connected to different conceptions of the nature of the self, and different views about the nature, scope, and limits of individual freedom. For instance, some theorists associate autonomy with a realm of negative liberty, while others defend a thicker, substantive conception of autonomy as the valuable capacity to live one's life according to values that are in some sense authentic or 'one's own'—a capacity that may be more or less realized, depending on the extent to which social and political conditions are an impediment to living an autonomous life. Secondly, there is more than one way in which autonomy can play a role in arguments for free speech. Free speech can be justified by reference to the state's obligation to treat citizens as autonomous or respect their autonomy, but autonomy can also be seen as a goal to which free speech makes an instrumental contribution—for instance, by fostering the development of our mental capacities. Thirdly, respecting and advancing autonomy are not mutually exclusive and, apart from libertarians such as Nozick, most people would agree that the state has a mixture of negative and positive duties—duties to respect autonomy (ie, not to impair it), to protect autonomy (ie, to take measures which prevent private parties from impairing autonomy), and to promote autonomy (by providing the environment

---

[1] Frederick Schauer, *Free Speech: A Philosophical Enquiry* (CUP 1982) 47–8.

necessary for developing it).² At the same time, it is clear that these duties can compete in particular circumstances. Hate speech, for instance, involves autonomous choice on the part of speakers and willing listeners, but it damages the substantive autonomy of its targets. The state will need to resolve these conflicts between competing autonomy claims (and the different conceptions of autonomy on which they rest), but there is more than one way to approach this issue.

One possible view is that none of the state's duties automatically takes priority over any other when they come into conflict. If this account of the state's duties is accepted, on which autonomy is equally shield and sword, it will be necessary to consider the effects of speech on the autonomy interests of all affected parties, and whether speech should be protected or restricted in particular circumstances will depend on the relative strength of the competing autonomy claims. This account implies that the value of autonomy is 'double-sided', to use a term of Adrienne Stone's, being capable of being wielded both for and against freedom of speech.³

The other possible view is that it is worse for the state to infringe autonomy than to fail to provide the conditions for autonomy or prevent other actors from infringing autonomy. If this view is accepted, on which the state is more responsible for harming people than failing to benefit them, the state's negative duty to respect autonomy will trump its positive duty to advance autonomy, and it will be impermissible for the state to put its positive duties ahead of its negative duties. On this view, the state is never faced with a choice between fulfilling its negative duty of non-interference and its positive obligation to aid. On the contrary, it is entirely precluded from balancing autonomy losses against autonomy gains when regulating speech, and the fact that restrictions on speech might increase autonomy overall will be of no consequence. Thus, the state will be obliged to give priority to respecting the liberty claims of speakers and willing audiences, and the value of autonomy will point in one direction only—that of protecting speech.⁴

We will explore these themes in what follows. We will begin with broadly liberty-based understandings of the concept of autonomy, focusing on some influential accounts which associate autonomy (1) either with our capacity to judge the worth of different views for ourselves or (2) with non-violent, non-coercive, self-expressive choices. These conceptions of autonomy are generally coupled at the political level with the view that the state is under a non-negotiable, negative obligation not to impair autonomy—an obligation that disables it from pursuing goals that would otherwise be

---

² This taxonomy is drawn from human rights law, in terms of which states have obligations to respect human rights, to protect individuals against human rights abuses, and to fulfil human rights by taking action to facilitate their enjoyment. The human rights approach is influenced by the conceptual framework developed by Henry Shue in *Basic Rights: Subsistence, Affluence, and US Foreign Policy* (2nd edn, Princeton UP 1996).

³ Adrienne Stone, 'Viewpoint Discrimination, Hate Speech Laws, and the Double-Sided Nature of Freedom of Speech' (2017) 32 *Const Comment* 687, 688–9.

⁴ Philippa Foot argues for the priority of negative over positive duties in 'Killing and Letting Die' in Philippa Foot, *Moral Dilemmas and Other Topics in Moral Philosophy* (Clarendon P 2002) 78. See generally Judith Lichtenberg, 'Negative Duties, Positive Duties and the "New Harms"' (2010) 120 *Ethics* 557, for discussion of the distinction between negative and positive duties.

desirable, including the promotion of substantive autonomy. This combination of views requires very stringent protections for speech, rendering almost all content regulation impermissible. On this approach, autonomy serves to protect us from the government, not from other citizens. It provides speakers and audiences with a 'shield against the policeman',[5] preventing the state from suppressing speech because of the harm caused by its meaning or message, except in circumstances of compelling necessity,[6] such as when a speaker attempts to incite a mob.

We will then turn to conceptions of autonomy that highlight the relational and social preconditions for autonomy. While these conceptions emphasize the value of individual autonomy and seek to delineate the complex capacities that underpin it, they also focus on the role of social relationships in enabling the development and ongoing exercise of these capacities. This shift in focus yields fresh perspectives on why speech is critical for autonomy and hence why free speech generally deserves protection. It also yields a somewhat different view about state obligations with respect to autonomy. By contrast with the liberty-based conceptions, relational conceptions hold that the state has positive duties to promote the autonomy of all citizens and that these duties sometimes trump the negative liberty of individual citizens. Relational conceptions are thus more likely to be willing to support some forms of regulatory control over 'speech systems'[7], as well as some forms of content regulation, on a case-by-case basis, for example with respect to hate speech.

4.1 Mental Autonomy and Freedom of Speech

Some free speech theorists see autonomy as involving sovereignty over our own minds—an autonomy that permits us, as Frederick Schauer says, the final choice as to what to believe and how to act, even though we might be punished for our choices.[8] Ronald Dworkin relies on this notion of autonomy when he says that morally responsible people 'insist on making up their own minds about what is good or bad in life or in politics, or what is true and false in matters of justice or faith'.[9] Thomas Nagel talks in similar terms of 'the sovereignty of each person's reason over his own beliefs and values';[10] Charles Fried talks of our status as 'rational sovereigns', who cannot 'cede to

---

[5] Owen Fiss, 'Free Speech and Social Structure' (1986) 71 *Iowa L Rev* 1405, 1423.
[6] Ronald Dworkin, *Freedom's Law: The Moral Reading of the American Constitution* (Harvard UP 1996) ch 9, 218.
[7] The term 'speech systems' is taken from Susan Williams, *Truth, Autonomy, and Speech: Feminist Theory and the First Amendment* (New York UP 2004). We will discuss Williams's narrative and relational conception of autonomy and its implications for freedom of speech later in the chapter.
[8] Schauer (n 1) 68.   [9] See Dworkin (n 6) ch 8, 200.
[10] Thomas Nagel, 'Personal Rights and Public Space' (1995) 24 *Phil & Pub Aff* 83, 96.

the state the authority to limit [our] use of [our] rational powers';[11] and Thomas Scanlon says that agents who regard themselves as autonomous regard themselves as sovereign in deciding what to believe and what to do.[12] According to Scanlon, '[a]n autonomous person cannot accept without independent consideration the judgment of others as to what he should believe or what he should do'.[13]

When this view about the nature of autonomy is combined at the political level with the view that respect for citizens' autonomy is a side-constraint on the exercise of state power, the effect is powerfully speech protective, disabling the state from restricting speech in an effort to prevent people from being exposed to views which might lead them to behave in harmful ways. Scanlon provides the most sustained defence of this approach in his influential early article, 'A Theory of Freedom of Expression'. Although Scanlon later reconsidered some of his claims, it is his initial position that is of most interest here.

Scanlon's starting point is the Kantian idea that 'a legitimate government is one whose authority citizens can recognize while still regarding themselves as equal, autonomous, rational agents'.[14] This places government under an obligation not to impair autonomy, even in the pursuit of objectives that would otherwise be desirable. As noted above, Scanlon believes that regarding oneself as autonomous involves regarding oneself as sovereign in deciding what to believe and how to act. Scanlon also argues that to regard agents as autonomous is to regard them as responsible for their own beliefs.[15] Thus if rational individuals are persuaded by speech to cause harm, we should hold them responsible for their harmful acts, not the speaker. To hold the speaker responsible would ignore the autonomy of the listeners.

This combination of views leads Scanlon to a very strong freedom of speech principle, which he calls the 'Millian principle'. The Millian principle states that the government has no authority to restrict any category of speech (whether, for instance, political, artistic, or commercial) on account of certain of its harmful consequences. The harms in question are: (1) the harm of an audience coming to have false beliefs and (2) harmful acts performed as a result of speech, where the connection consists merely in the fact that the speech led the audience to believe that the acts are worth performing.[16] In Scanlon's view, these kinds of harm should have no weight at all in considering whether legal restrictions on speech are justifiable, since autonomous agents would not agree to the government protecting them from harm by depriving them of the grounds for making an independent judgment as to what to believe and as to whether to obey the law.[17] If they were to concede to the state the authority to control speech for these reasons, they would not be able to defend the grounds of their beliefs 'as not obviously skewed or otherwise suspect'.[18]

[11] Charles Fried, 'The New First Amendment Jurisprudence: A Threat to Liberty' (1992) 59 *U Chi L Rev* 225, 233.
[12] Thomas Scanlon, 'A Theory of Freedom of Expression' (1972) 1 *Phil & Pub Aff* 204, 215.
[13] Ibid 216. [14] Ibid 214. [15] Ibid 212. [16] Ibid 213. [17] Ibid 217–18.
[18] Ibid 218.

For Scanlon, the only exceptions to the Millian principle are trivial, such as punishing speech which causes people to perform harmful acts in situations in which they are temporarily incapable of rational deliberation, such as a false shout of 'fire' in a crowded theatre. Apart from momentary and uncontroversial measures of this kind, which do not prevent people from making up their own minds about some question, Scanlon thinks that virtually all content-based restrictions on speech are incompatible with the premise that citizens are autonomous. They therefore amount to an illegitimate exercise of power.[19]

Some of the consequences of the Millian principle are, however, implausible, as Scanlon came to recognize. For instance, its blanket hostility to content-based restrictions of speech implies that laws against false or deceptive advertising are impermissible—a view with which almost everyone would disagree.[20] In addition to coming to believe that the Millian principle is too sweeping, Scanlon also came to reject his justification for it, namely, that the idea of autonomy functions as an absolute constraint on the exercise of state power. In his reconsideration of these issues, he argues that the idea of citizens as autonomous, rational agents should not be employed as a constraint on the harms that can justify restrictions on freedom of speech, saying that it can sometimes be more important to prevent harmful changes in belief and behaviour caused by speech than to 'enhance our decision-making capacity'.[21] At the same time, Scanlon continues to defend a theory of free speech which is autonomy-based,[22] in the sense that he believes that the reason to protect freedom of speech is that it protects and advances important interests in substantive autonomy—not only of audiences in deciding what to believe and what reasons to act on, but also of speakers who seek to communicate and express their values to others, and bystanders or members of the general public who benefit from living in a society that enjoys freedom of speech.[23]

Scanlon's later, intuitionistic approach is less protective of speech than his earlier absolutist approach, since he is now willing to weigh autonomy in the sense of a good to be promoted against the harmful changes in belief and behaviour caused by speech. This presumably includes not only harms to the audience (as in the false and deceptive advertising case) but also harms to the broader public when audiences are convinced to accept dangerous opinions. Furthermore, as part of this case-by-case, weighing exercise, Scanlon emphasizes that the degree to which autonomy interests are threatened by content-based restrictions on speech can vary, depending on what kind of speech is involved, and the degree to which there are 'reasonably clear and objective criteria of truth' in the area.[24] Thus Scanlon argues that when it comes to political issues, individuals' substantive autonomy interests as speakers and audiences are substantial.

[19] Ibid 220.
[20] Thomas Scanlon, 'Freedom of Expression and Categories of Expression' (1979) 40 *U Pitt L Rev* 519, 532.
[21] Ibid 533.
[22] Thomas Scanlon, 'Comment on Baker's Autonomy and Free Speech' (2011) 27 *Const Comment* 319, 320.
[23] Ibid 319–20.   [24] Scanlon, 'Freedom of Expression' (n 20) 541.

Furthermore, there is a high likelihood that governments permitted to restrict political speech on the ground that it is false would do so in a partisan way that would damage these interests. By contrast, laws that restrict false advertising are of less (though not no) concern from the perspective of autonomy, because the interests of sellers and consumers are generally not as important as interests in political speech, and there is also less reason to believe that the power to restrict false advertising would be abused in ways that would threaten these interests.[25] In his re-examination of his earlier views, Scanlon also suggests that autonomy might in some cases be 'better advanced' by shielding ourselves from certain influences.[26] He claims, for instance, that audience interests in receiving information can be enhanced by restrictions on false and misleading advertising that increase the reliability of information.[27]

David Strauss also invokes the value of autonomy to defend a principle which is similar to Scanlon's Millian principle but not, according to him, susceptible to the objections that led Scanlon to give up the Millian principle. Strauss's principle—which he calls the 'persuasion principle'—states that the government may not suppress speech on the ground that the speech is likely to persuade those who hear it to cause harm.[28] Strauss argues that the reason why it is wrong for governments to violate the persuasion principle is the same reason which explains why it is wrong to lie to someone in order to influence their behaviour: both infringe autonomy, which Strauss understands as mental autonomy or control over one's reasoning processes. Thus, Strauss claims that if A lies to B in order to influence B's thought or behaviour, A disrespects B, and uses B as a tool or instrument of A's will. This kind of manipulative lie is a way of exerting control over B's thought processes and therefore violates B's autonomy.[29] Denying people access to information or views for the purpose of influencing their behaviour is likewise a way of attempting to control their thought processes and a violation of their autonomy.[30] Strauss writes: '[w]hen the government violates the persuasion principle, it has determined that people will, to a degree, pursue its—the government's—objectives, instead of their own'.[31] It is engaging in a form of 'thought control'.[32]

Strauss goes on to argue that the persuasion principle does not forbid restricting speech which seeks to precipitate an 'ill-considered reaction', of which false statements of fact are the clearest example.[33] This is because, according to Strauss, 'persuade' is not synonymous with 'induce': speech persuades when 'it induces action through a process that a rational person would value'.[34] Thus, action induced by false statements of fact cannot be described as 'persuasion', since a rational person would not want to act on such statements. Strauss also says that restrictions on false statements of fact do not deny the audience's autonomy because the restrictions are not manipulative. According to Strauss, since rational people

---

[25] Scanlon, 'Comment on Baker's Autonomy' (n 22) 322–3; Thomas Scanlon, *The Difficulty of Tolerance: Essays in Political Philosophy* (CUP 2003) ch 8, 162–3.
[26] Scanlon, 'Freedom of Expression' (n 20) 534.
[27] Scanlon, 'Comment on Baker's Autonomy' (n 22) 324.
[28] David Strauss, 'Persuasion, Autonomy, and Freedom of Expression' (1991) 91 Colum L Rev 334, 334.
[29] Ibid 354–5.   [30] Ibid 355–6.   [31] Ibid 356.   [32] Ibid 360.
[33] Ibid 335–7.   [34] Ibid 335.

would not want to act on the basis of false information, when the government prevents them from doing so 'it does not manipulate their mental processes to serve the government's ends', but rather 'enables those processes to function as they should, to promote the ends of the listener'.[35] Strauss concludes that the persuasion principle is able to explain why restrictions on false statements of fact are permissible, and is therefore superior to Scanlon's Millian principle, which rules out all restrictions on the grounds that speech will lead to false beliefs and harmful acts as incompatible with autonomy, whether or not the speech in question leads to this result through persuasion.[36]

Although Strauss's approach permits more restrictions on speech than the Millian principle, these restrictions are not extensive. Strauss thinks it is permissible for the government to restrict speech which conveys false statements of fact, but not speech which engages in more subtle forms of manipulation of our thought processes, such as tendentious and one-sided speech. The question, however, is whether it is possible to draw a bright-line distinction of this kind: if false statements of fact can be restricted because they do not seek to persuade, and restricting them does not impair autonomy, why should it not be permissible to restrict more subtly manipulative speech for the same reasons? After all, rational persons would not want to act on such speech, and restrictions on it would not appear to impair their autonomy, since it would not be a matter of the government denying people access to ideas in order to control their behaviour. As speech of this kind is ubiquitous, Strauss's persuasion principle seems to permit extensive restrictions on speech, not stringent protections for it.

Strauss notes that it would be impossible to tell when we have a system of expression free of manipulation, in light of the existence of counter-speech correcting the distortions, the fact that listeners can often overcome distortions themselves, and the fact that governmental interventions ostensibly justified by the need to correct private manipulation might be a way for the government manipulatively to substitute distortions it favours.[37] However, although these claims may be plausible, they do not provide a principled way of distinguishing between false statements of fact and more subtle forms of manipulative speech. Instead, Strauss's points suggest that we should draw the line at false statements of fact for pragmatic reasons: although restrictions on more subtle forms of manipulative speech do not necessarily infringe the autonomy of audiences, once given this power the government might abuse it for the purposes of 'thought control'.

4.2 Choice Autonomy, Self-expression, and Freedom of Speech

In his early work, Scanlon was concerned with the way in which respect for autonomy constrains the reasons for which the state may legitimately restrict speech. Edwin Baker's influential defence of free speech starts from similar premises about the connection

---

[35] Ibid 357. [36] Ibid 356, n 62. [37] Ibid 369.

between the legitimacy of the legal order and respect for the autonomy that the state must attribute to citizens who are expected to obey its laws. However, as Scanlon observes, Baker's understanding of the requirement of respect goes further than merely ruling out 'thought control'.[38] This is because Baker is primarily concerned with the state's obligations to respect the conduct of speakers, not with the exercise of the capacity to make up one's own mind. Thus, where Scanlon's Millian principle and Strauss's persuasion principle are concerned with the autonomy of audiences, Baker's aim is to protect the liberty of speakers wishing to express their own values free of government interference.

As Baker explains, he is concerned with speech's source in the self, rather than its communicative aspect.[39] He thinks that to engage voluntarily in a speech act is to engage in self-expression or self-definition as a means to self-fulfilment or self-realization.[40] He gives the example of a war protestor who explains that 'when she chants "Stop This War Now" ... [she] chants to define herself publicly, partly to define herself to herself, as in opposition to the war'.[41] Baker describes self-expressive or value-expressive choices of this kind as exercises of 'formal autonomy', by which he means our authority or right to make decisions about ourselves, provided that we do not interfere with another person's similar authority or right.[42] Formal autonomy is therefore synonymous with liberty,[43] understood as non-violent, non-coercive, expressive activity.[44]

Baker distinguishes formal autonomy from the 'actual capacity and opportunities to lead the best, most meaningful, self-directed life possible',[45] which he describes as a matter of 'substantive autonomy', and the enjoyment of which is a matter of degree, depending on such matters as material and psychological resources and other natural and social conditions.[46] Although Baker thinks that the state should promote substantive autonomy, he also thinks that pursuit of this goal should not be at the expense of formal autonomy,[47] because the legitimacy of a legal order depends on viewing citizens as 'agents with proper claims to self-determination as well as having their interest in self-realization'.[48] Thus respect for formal autonomy operates as a side-constraint on laws, constraining the means by which government can pursue even good ends.[49] Baker concludes that expressive exercises of formal autonomy warrant virtually absolute protection from and respect by the state,[50] while noting that '[l]aw's respect for formal autonomy of one person never denies respect for the formal autonomy ... of another',[51] so that there is no possibility of the state having to balance conflicting obligations in this area.

---

[38] Scanlon 'Comment on Baker's Autonomy' (n 22) 321.
[39] C Edwin Baker, *Human Liberty and Freedom of Speech* (OUP 1989) 52.   [40] Ibid 47–51.
[41] Ibid 53.   [42] C Edwin Baker, 'Autonomy and Free Speech' (2011) 27 *Const Comment* 251, 254.
[43] Ibid 254, n 8.   [44] Baker, *Human Liberty and Freedom of Speech* (n 39) 47.
[45] C Edwin Baker, 'Autonomy and Hate Speech' in Ivan Hare and James Weinstein (eds), *Extreme Speech and Democracy* (OUP 2009) 143.
[46] Baker, 'Autonomy and Free Speech' (n 42) 253.
[47] Baker, 'Autonomy and Hate Speech' (n 45) 143.
[48] Baker, 'Autonomy and Free Speech' (n 42) 265.   [49] Ibid 253–4.   [50] Ibid 254.
[51] Baker, 'Autonomy and Hate Speech' (n 45) 142.

The implication of Baker's account is that we have the right to use speech to develop and express ourselves in a way that corresponds with our values, no matter what these values are.[52] We are therefore entitled to use speech to persuade or provide information, even if its expressive content causes harm to listeners and third parties, including by undermining their substantive autonomy, since the harm results from 'mental assimilation of the intended meaning that the speaker honestly expressed'.[53] Since speech operates through the mind of the recipient, the recipient has the choice to reject the message.[54] Thus, Baker concludes that it is illegitimate for the state to restrict speech on the ground that it might persuade the recipient to adopt false beliefs or engage in harmful conduct.

By contrast, Baker argues that when speech causes harm not by an exercise of formal autonomy but by undermining the will of others (ie, by failing to respect *their* formal autonomy), the state can legitimately restrict the speech.[55] For instance, speech used in an attempt to commit a crime (eg, the leader of a group of bank robbers ordering another member to shoot); speech which is used to coerce others (eg, blackmail or the use of threats to gain control over another person); and manipulative lies can legitimately be prohibited.[56] Baker insists, however, that speech 'cannot normally be viewed as improperly interfering with a listener's or third party's proper realm of decision-making authority',[57] and that when the formal autonomy of others is not infringed, speakers should be at liberty to express their views, no matter how offensive or harmful their content, and even if they damage the substantive autonomy of others.[58] Thus, Baker thinks that prohibitions on racist speech are generally impermissible, except in special contexts, such as where an employee has given up their right to act autonomously in order to discharge the requirements of their position.[59]

One attraction of autonomy-based theories is the breadth of the protection they provide for speech. For instance, they have no difficulty in explaining why art should be protected as free speech, since restrictions on art clearly threaten the liberty of artists. By contrast, theories which justify free speech by reference to democratic values or the importance of discovering the truth struggle to explain why artistic discourse should be protected. Baker's theory is, however, atypically narrow in one respect, since he argues that commercial speech deserves no protection (not merely reduced protection). He comes to this conclusion because his theory focuses exclusively on the autonomy interests of speakers and because he believes that the speech of market participants has nothing to do with individual freedom or choice. In his view, commercial speech is dictated by the imperative to make money and is not used as a means of self-expression or

---

[52] Baker, *Human Liberty and Freedom of Speech* (n 39) 59.
[53] Baker, 'Autonomy and Free Speech' (n 42) 259. [54] Ibid 255.
[55] Baker, *Human Liberty and Freedom of Speech* (n 39) 59.
[56] Ibid 59–60; Baker, 'Autonomy and Free Speech' (n 42) 256.
[57] Baker, *Human Liberty and Freedom of Speech* (n 39) 59.
[58] Baker, 'Autonomy and Free Speech' (n 42) 254.
[59] Baker, 'Autonomy and Hate Speech' (n 45) 143.

self-realization.⁶⁰ These claims have generally been found implausible. Even if we focus only on speakers, it is clear that speech undertaken out of a desire to make money can amount to self-expression, as many artistic endeavours attest.⁶¹ Furthermore, once one attends to the autonomy interests of audiences (in this case, the interests of consumers in receiving information from advertising), it becomes even more difficult to accept that restrictions on commercial speech pose no threat to autonomy.⁶²

Baker argues that it is a virtue of his speakers' liberty theory that it provides a ready explanation of why compelled speech amounts to an infringement of freedom of speech. In this regard, Baker refers approvingly to the US case of *West Virginia State Board of Education v Barnette*, in which the Supreme Court held that a regulation requiring public school children to salute the US flag violated the First Amendment, even though the children were not prevented from criticizing the flag salute and were free to contribute to public debate on the matter. The Court said that what was at stake was 'a right of self-determination in matters that touch individual opinion and personal attitude',⁶³ and that the regulation invaded 'the sphere of intellect and spirit which it is the purpose of the First Amendment ... to reserve from all official control'.⁶⁴ Baker describes the decision as 'the poster child of autonomy theory',⁶⁵ since it recognized the 'child's liberty, her claim to autonomy, and ... her dissent'.⁶⁶ Likewise, Baker argues that the Supreme Court was concerned with individual autonomy when it struck down a New Hampshire law which compelled cars to bear licence plates displaying the motto 'Live Free or Die', with the Court holding that 'the right to speak and the right to refrain from speaking are complementary components of the broader concept of "individual freedom of mind"'.⁶⁷

One prominent line of argument against Baker's theory, arising out of the fact that speech is merely one kind of self-expressive conduct, has been put forward by Schauer. As Schauer points out, there are many non-communicative activities, such as how one chooses to dress, that amount to acts of self-expression and facilitate self-realization.⁶⁸ Yet, as Schauer says, most people do not believe that expressive activity, even non-violent, non-coercive expressive activity, deserves the special immunity from government regulation which speech deserves. But if this view is correct, and there is no general liberty to engage in non-violent, non-coercive expressive activity, a theory which does not tell us why speech is distinguishable from or more valuable than other forms of expressive activity is not capable of generating robust protections for speech. As Schauer puts it, 'if freedom of speech is an instance of a liberty to engage in any

---

⁶⁰ Baker, 'Autonomy and Free Speech' (n 42) 272–4.
⁶¹ Martin H Redish, 'The Value of Free Speech' (1982) 130 *U Penn L Rev* 591, 621.
⁶² Scanlon, 'Comment on Baker's Autonomy' (n 22) 323–4.
⁶³ *West Virginia State Board of Education v Barnette*, 319 US 624, 631 (1943).   ⁶⁴ Ibid 642.
⁶⁵ Baker, 'Autonomy and Free Speech' (n 42) 270.
⁶⁶ C Edwin Baker, 'Is Democracy a Sound Basis for a Free Speech Principle?' (2011) 97 *Va L Rev* 515, 527.
⁶⁷ *Wooley v Maynard*, 430 US 705, 714 (1977).   ⁶⁸ Schauer (n 1) 52.

non-violent act, then a failure to recognize that liberty extinguishes freedom of speech *pro tanto*'.[69]

Although Schauer is right that seeing speech as merely an instance of a broader category holds it hostage to difficulties that may be associated with protecting the broader category, it is possible to turn Schauer's argument on its head. Instead of accepting the prevailing view that it is relatively easy for the state to justify interferences with expressive activity, which diminishes the protection for speech if speech is merely one form of expressive activity, one could reject the prevailing view, arguing that all non-violent expressive activity, including speech, deserves robust protection from governmental interference. In other words, instead of 'levelling down' the protection conferred on speech, one could 'level up' the protection conferred on the broader class of expressive activity. In fact, it seems that Baker is attracted to the latter view, because he says that he is sympathetic to a broader libertarian principle in terms of which the state should respect our personal liberty, especially our self-expressive choices, provided that they do not invade the personal liberty of others or infringe their formal autonomy.[70]

One final comment is that Baker's theory may face the same problems as Strauss's: once it has been acknowledged that the government may restrict coercive speech, there may be no clear way to confine the kinds of speech which can be restricted to a narrow class of cases, such as threats. As Richard H Fallon points out, 'coercion' is a vague and value-laden concept. For instance, it can be argued that at least some forms of racist speech, such as face-to-face racist insults, are coercive, since their targets are typically too intimidated to respond.[71] If this is correct, it would follow that insults should not be protected in terms of Baker's own autonomy-based framework. Baker resists this expansion of the concept of 'coercion', saying that 'meaningful limits on government's authority to restrict speech will require a narrow, precise and defensible concept of coercion that is clearly distinguished from the broader notion of harm'.[72] However, this response can be criticized for putting the cart before the horse: it tailors the concept of coercion to a desired outcome—limiting the government's authority to restrict speech—when the real question is whether Baker is correct in thinking that racist insults are not coercive.

The autonomy-based justifications discussed so far focus on the autonomy of the individual speaker or hearer but pay little attention to the background social conditions required for the development of capacities for autonomy. This individualistic focus has been criticized by feminist free speech theorists, including Susan Williams and Susan Brison, who propose that relational conceptions of autonomy can help to reframe conceptions of freedom of speech.[73] We will discuss the views of Williams and Brison shortly, but we will begin by considering Seana Shiffrin's 'thinker-based' approach to

---

[69] Ibid 9. [70] Baker, 'Autonomy and Free Speech' (n 42) 256–8.
[71] Richard H Fallon, 'Two Senses of Autonomy' (1994) 46 *Stan L Rev* 875, 881–2, 889.
[72] Baker, *Human Liberty and Freedom of Speech* (n 39) 56.
[73] Williams (n 7); Susan J Brison, 'The Autonomy Defense of Free Speech' (1998) 108 *Ethics* 312; Susan J Brison, 'Relational Autonomy and Freedom of Expression' in Catriona Mackenzie and Natalie Stoljar (eds), *Relational Autonomy: Feminist Perspectives on Autonomy, Agency and the Social Self* (OUP 2000) 280.

freedom of speech, which articulates what might be thought of as an intermediate position between the liberal accounts discussed so far and the feminist, relational views of Williams and Brison.[74]

4.3 Freedom of Thought and Freedom of Speech

Shiffrin's 'thinker-based' approach explains the importance of freedom of speech in terms of its central role in enabling freedom of thought. Shiffrin's account is similar in some respects to the mental autonomy views discussed earlier, including Scanlon's. However, Shiffrin's view draws attention to the critical role of social relationships in the development of the capacities required for freedom of thought. In this respect, her view points in the direction of a free speech defence which is more in tune with relational conceptions of autonomy.

Shiffrin's 'thinker-based' view is a normative, ideal theory of freedom of speech, as opposed to a theory which takes current free speech practices as foundational. Its central claim is that the right to freedom of speech is grounded in 'the individual agent's interest in the protection of the free development and operation of her mind'.[75] Shiffrin argues that each human agent has an interest in developing their capacities for moral agency, and practical and theoretical thought, forming true beliefs both about themselves and the social and natural environment with which they interact, and exercising their imagination. Additionally, each human agent has an interest in developing a distinctive perspective, personality, and sense of themselves as a separate individual, and in doing so authentically, which is to say by 'forming thoughts, beliefs, practical judgments, intentions and other mental contents on the basis of reasons, perceptions and reactions through processes that, in the main and over the long term, are independent of distortive influences'.[76]

These interests, Shiffrin argues, can only be realized through social interaction and social relationships. To become a distinctive self and a moral agent, to come to know and respect oneself requires ongoing interaction with and recognition by others. In other words, social interaction is a causally necessary ongoing precondition for the development of individuality, moral agency, and the capacities for freedom of thought. Shiffrin's defence of the value of speech, and especially freedom of speech, is grounded in this claim about the necessity of social interaction for individual intellectual and moral agency. Speech is the primary medium through which we communicate the contents of our minds with others, come to understand others' minds and perspectives, and thereby

---

[74] Seana Valentine Shiffrin, 'A Thinker-Based Approach to Freedom of Speech' (2011) 27 *Const Comment* 283.
[75] Ibid 287.   [76] Ibid 290.

acquire knowledge of ourselves, other people, and the environment. Moreover, speech should not be understood simply as a matter of making public through linguistic or other forms of representation contents that are already fully formed in the mind. Rather, speech also makes possible new forms of thought, while knowledge of ourselves and our environment requires access, through linguistic and other forms of representational media, to 'others' insights and beliefs, as well as their reactions and evaluative responses to our beliefs'.[77] Speech, communication, and social interaction are in fact so critical, Shiffrin argues, that being deprived of them—for example, in situations of solitary confinement—can lead to significant mental and emotional deterioration, loss of grip on reality, hallucinations, paranoia, and sometimes psychosis. To forbid or impose substantial restrictions on free expression, while 'not tantamount to solitary confinement . . . lies on a spectrum with it: it is to institute a sort of solitary confinement . . . within one's own mind'.[78]

Shiffrin argues that because of the importance of freedom of speech for our development and proper functioning as thinkers, no distinction should be drawn between political speech and many other forms of speech or communicative representation, including religious speech, literary and artistic representation, music, and private speech and discourse. Thus while she calls for strong protections for 'political speech and, in particular, for incendiary speech and other forms of dissent', she rejects the idea that there is any lexical hierarchy of value between political speech and these other forms of speech and representation.[79] Shiffrin concurs with Baker, however, in thinking that 'non-press, business corporate, and commercial speech'[80] is frequently driven by the profit motive, although she thinks Baker over-generalizes in saying that commercial speech is never a manifestation of individual choice. Nevertheless, her view is that these forms of speech generally do not 'facilitate and, indeed tend to discourage the authentic expression of individuals' judgment'.[81] For this reason, they should not enjoy the same kind of protections as other forms of speech.

Shiffrin argues that an important advantage of her thinker-based approach, compared with speaker- and listener-based approaches, is that it provides a more comprehensive explanation of the wrongfulness of thought control or attempts at thought control. Scanlon's Millian principle explains what is objectionable about regulation which aims to prevent listeners from hearing certain views because they might form 'false beliefs and practical judgments as *consequences* of expression'.[82] However, listener-based views cannot explain what is objectionable about other forms of thought control, such as 'regulations or government activity aimed at instilling beliefs, attitudes, or reasons through compulsion, subliminal manipulation, and other efforts to circumvent rational deliberation'.[83] The thinker-based view, by contrast, which highlights our interests in forming thoughts, beliefs, practical judgments, intentions, and other mental contents free from distorting influences, can explain what is objectionable about this kind of interference.

---

[77] Ibid 293. [78] Ibid 294. [79] Ibid 285. [80] Ibid 297. [81] Ibid 296.
[82] Ibid 300. [83] Ibid.

Shiffrin also argues that her approach gives a better account of the problems with compelled speech than speaker-oriented approaches, such as Baker's. She cites the case of *West Virginia State Board of Education v Barnette*, discussed above, and argues that if it is clear that the pledge of allegiance is compelled, and if the speaker is free to disavow the pledge, it seems a strain to say their speaker-based interests are restricted. The thinker-based view helps to clarify that the problem with a compelled pledge is rather the way it attempts to influence people, subliminally and coercively, to identify with the message embodied in the pledge. Thus:

> Compelled speech of this kind, threatens (or at least aims) to interfere with free thinking processes of the speaker/listener and to influence mental content in ways and through methods that are illicit: nontransparent, via repetition, and through coercive manipulations of a character virtue, namely that of sincerity.[84]

Another advantage of her theory, Shiffrin suggests, is that its emphasis on the importance for knowledge and idea formation of communicative interaction, mutual collaboration, and mutual influence highlights the connection between freedom of speech and freedom of association. It also highlights the important role of speech, in comparison with its wordless expressive counterparts, in enabling us to know and communicate with others. In this sense, speech is special because 'it is a uniquely specific mechanism for the transmission of mental contents and their discussion, evaluation, development and refinement'.[85]

Shiffrin's response to the challenge posed by Schauer, concerning what makes speech special, is thus that it facilitates, in uniquely specific and precise ways, the core interests of autonomous agents to understand themselves and others, to co-operate with one another, to investigate and understand the world, and to exercise human moral agency.[86]

4.4 Relational Autonomy and Freedom of Speech

Susan Williams has articulated a distinctive and original response to Schauer's challenge in the course of developing a relational and narrative autonomy theory of free speech.[87] Williams argues that First Amendment jurisprudence has been limited by its reliance on a liberal conception of autonomy that is excessively individualistic and overly focused on choice. This conception of autonomy has been criticized by feminist theorists for failing to attend to the relational and social dimensions of autonomy.[88] These theorists argue

---

[84] Ibid 302. [85] Ibid 306. [86] Ibid 305. [87] Williams (n 7).
[88] See, eg, Catriona Mackenzie and Natalie Stoljar (eds), *Relational Autonomy: Feminist Perspectives on Autonomy, Agency and the Social Self* (OUP 2000); Jennifer Nedelsky, 'Reconceiving Autonomy: Sources, Thoughts and Possibilities' (1989) 1 *Yale J L & Feminism* 7.

that autonomy should be reconceptualized as relational for several reasons. First, the rational, volitional and imaginative capacities necessary for autonomy are causally enabled or constrained by an individual's social relationships and social environment. Second, our individual identities are socially constituted; that is, they are shaped and constrained by social relationships and the social, linguistic, and cultural environments in which we are embedded. Third, the reasons, values, ideals, and commitments that frame our choices emerge out of specific social contexts and the norms and practices that characterize those contexts. In addition, feminist theorists have drawn attention to the detrimental effects of social inequality, disadvantage, and oppression on the development and exercise of autonomy.

Williams's narrative theory of autonomy builds on the central insights of relational autonomy theory. She argues that the exercise of autonomy is focused not on choice but on acts of interpretation and narration through which we construct our individual identities, take ownership of our actions and choices, and make sense of our lives. Autonomy on this view is 'neither a pre-existing condition to be assumed for all persons, nor is it an end-state that can be taken for granted once achieved'.[89] Rather, it is an ongoing activity or process of interpretation, narration, self-construction, and meaning-making. This activity of self-reflection and narration is creative and involves a range of rational, imaginative, and interpersonal capacities. Crucially, it is an inherently dialogical and relational activity. Our individual narratives are interwoven with the narratives of particular others as well as the narratives of the social and cultural groups to which we belong. It is only through dialogical interaction with such others that we can understand ourselves, because our narratives are constructed using culturally given and available materials. Further, the linguistic, cognitive, emotional, and imaginative capacities necessary for narrative autonomy are developed and sustained through social relationships and broader social and institutional structures, including the law.

A narrative, relational model of autonomy focuses attention on the social conditions required to develop and exercise the capacities for autonomy. It also draws attention to the impairing effects of social exclusion on the autonomy of individuals and social groups with limited access to educational and other social resources and to the means of social and political participation. Williams therefore highlights the connections between her model of autonomy and discursive, deliberative (rather than aggregative) models of democracy. Aggregative models, paired with liberty-based models of autonomy, represent the value of democracy primarily in defensive terms, as protecting us 'from incursions on our freedom by the government'. In contrast, discursive models, paired with relational models of autonomy, understand the value of democracy in constructive terms, as providing 'the opportunity for all citizens to participate in the political relationships that constitute one form of autonomy'.[90]

How does this conception of autonomy help address the challenge of explaining why speech is so critical for autonomy? Williams's answer to this question involves three main claims. First, if autonomy is understood as the activity of meaning-making

---

[89] Williams (n 7) 130.   [90] Ibid 170.

through narration ('formulating, expressing, and reinterpreting one's story'),[91] then speech plays a distinctive role in autonomy that cannot be assimilated with other forms of activity. Speech acts, through which a speaker intends to convey meaning to a potential audience—as well as some other activities of symbolic meaning-making (eg, flag burning, demonstrations, sit-ins)—are central to the development and exercise of narrative autonomy and as such deserve protection.[92]

According to Williams, protection should not be understood simply as a negative liberty right, nor should its focus be on individual speech acts only. Williams' second and very important claim is that a relational approach to autonomy requires us also to focus attention on the health and good functioning of the matrix of social systems of speech; that is, whether such speech systems provide the conditions necessary for developing and exercising citizens' capacities for narrative autonomy. While many background social structures and institutions (eg, economic, political, legal) play an important role in shaping the resources and opportunities available to citizens for developing these capacities, speech systems are among the most important. Speech systems include 'the educational system, the mass media, the internet, political campaigns, the system of government funding for artistic speech, the rules governing the use of public fora and other government property for speech purposes'.[93] These systems 'control whether or not one gets to speak, the conditions under which one speaks, and what one is allowed to say, and they thereby directly affect the opportunity for speech to function as an exercise of autonomy'.[94] Whereas Baker argues that it is not legitimate for the state to promote citizens' substantive autonomy if this conflicts with its negative duties to protect formal autonomy, William argues that a relational approach to autonomy shifts the focus of free speech jurisprudence 'from the individual speaker or listener to the social structures and practices that support speech on a large scale'.[95] Referring back to the taxonomy introduced at the outset, what this means in effect is that the state's duty to promote citizens' autonomy requires that it exercise regulatory oversight of the matrix of speech systems, and that this duty may sometimes trump negative duties of non-interference.

Williams illustrates the implications of this view with reference to debates between autonomy and democracy free speech theorists concerning campaign finance reform. Autonomy-based theories have blocked campaign finance reform on three main grounds: violation of speaker's autonomy; violation of listener's autonomy; and violation of liberal neutrality. The first autonomy-based objection is that such reform would sacrifice the speaker's (campaign contributor's) autonomy in order to achieve the goal of equality.[96] Williams argues in response that campaign contributions are not exercises of narrative autonomy, and therefore not protected speech, but rather practical contributions to the outcome of elections. More importantly, the speaker's autonomy interests are not the only relevant consideration, and the issue should not be framed in terms of

---

[91] Ibid 204.   [92] Ibid 199–202.   [93] Ibid 222.
[94] Ibid 209.   [95] Ibid 210.
[96] Williams cites as an example of this objection the Supreme Court's opinion in *Buckley v Valeo*, 424 US 1, 48–9 (1976).

whether speakers have a right to be left alone to distribute campaign funds as they see fit. Rather, the autonomy interests of other citizens must also be taken into account, in particular whether unrestrained spending unjustly harms less wealthy citizens by reducing their ability to set the agenda and participate in political dialogue. Thus, a narrative, relational approach to autonomy 'highlights the limits of the speaker's autonomy claims and the importance of potential autonomy concerns of other parties'.[97]

The second autonomy-based objection to campaign finance reform is that it would involve paternalistic government manipulation of the information that listeners receive. Scanlon's and Strauss's listener-based theories, discussed earlier, rule out this kind of paternalistic manipulation on grounds of autonomy. Williams concurs that the state has no right to suppress speech that may cause listeners to behave in ways that the government may wish to prevent. However, she argues that since the government is always in the business of allocating social resources in ways that impact autonomy, it is neither paternalistic nor illegitimate 'for the government to seek to restructure the use and allocation of social resources' so as to promote citizens' autonomy.[98] Indeed in the case of campaign finance reform, if the aim of such reform is to reduce inequalities in participation and promote the narrative autonomy of a larger number of citizens, 'then the government has a legitimate, even compelling, interest in assuring that systems of speech provide adequate opportunities for the exercise of that autonomy'.[99]

The third objection appeals to the idea of liberal neutrality (that the state should refrain from imposing substantive standards on public debate) and the priority of government's negative duties to suggest that it is illegitimate for government to intrude into speech systems, even if the aim of doing so is the positive aim of trying to improve them.[100] Williams' response is to question the idea of neutrality and the idea that there is a clear-cut distinction between negative and positive state duties. She points out that the choices of private actors (eg campaign contributors) are not '"natural and inevitable", but a direct product of government regulation and support',[101] and that the 'government has always already acted, if only to set up the underlying property and contract regimes that generate speech opportunities'.[102] Even under current First Amendment law, the possibility exists that a speaker can in effect call upon the government to guarantee access to private property for purposes of speech in certain circumstances. Government regulation of speech systems, she insists, is therefore inevitable and unavoidable. The issue is not whether or not speech systems should be regulated, but how to ensure that such regulation does not involve an abuse of government power. However, Williams thinks that if the aim of regulation is to reallocate social resources in order to increase the opportunities for more citizens to participate in political dialogue, thereby promoting narrative autonomy, it is not clear why we should regard this as an abuse of power.

Williams's third answer to the question of how a narrative conception of autonomy helps to address the challenge of explaining why speech is so critical for autonomy

---

[97] Williams (n 7) 214. [98] Ibid 215. [99] Ibid 216.
[100] Ibid 217. [101] Ibid 218. [102] Ibid 219.

focuses on the relationship between autonomy and democratic participation.[103] Political participation, she claims, is central to the exercise of narrative autonomy because the opportunity to participate in political discourse is 'central to the construction of identity and the social relations in which it operates', and 'speech is the primary means of such participation'.[104] Politics is important for autonomy because autonomy depends on the way the political process distributes resources and freedoms. Williams does not, however, want to draw a sharp distinction between political and non-political speech, nor does she think that only political speech deserves protection. Other categories of speech which also create the social conditions for autonomy (eg, artistic expression and even commercial speech) also deserve protection.

In sum, then, Williams's answer to the challenge posed by Schauer is that:

> Speech is the primary mechanism through which we exercise narrative autonomy; speech systems are an essential component in providing opportunities for that exercise and in promoting the development of the capacities for autonomy; and speech is the central democratic activity in the discursive model of democracy that grows out of a relational view of autonomy.[105]

Free speech law should therefore be focused on 'practical questions about how the legal system supports, or fails to support, the role of speech in promoting narrative autonomy'.[106]

Unlike Shiffrin and Williams, Brison's primary concern is not to explain the value of speech and freedom of speech for autonomy. It is rather to take issue with the way the autonomy defence of free speech has been used to counter attempts to regulate hate speech. Brison defines hate speech as:

> speech that vilifies individuals or groups on the basis of characteristics such as race, sex, ethnicity, religion, and sexual orientation and that (1) directly assaults its target(s), (2) creates a hostile environment, or (3) is a kind of group libel.[107]

In 'The Autonomy Defense of Free Speech', she distinguishes five different philosophical accounts of autonomy used in the free speech literature: Isaiah Berlin's account of autonomy as negative liberty; Dworkin's account of autonomy as moral independence; Scanlon's earlier Millian principle, which conceives of autonomy as a side-constraint on government interference; Scanlon's later account of autonomy as rational self-legislation; and Baker's and Redish's account of autonomy as self-realization.[108] She argues that none is satisfactory as an account of autonomy and that none explains why hate speech should be protected.

---

[103] Williams's discussion of this issue builds on work by Cass Sunstein on the role of speech in discursive democracy. See Cass Sunstein, *Democracy and the Problem of Free Speech* (Free P 1993).
[104] Williams (n 7) 225.   [105] Ibid 242.   [106] Ibid.
[107] Brison, 'Relational Autonomy and Freedom of Expression' (n 73) 281.
[108] Brison, 'The Autonomy Defense of Free Speech' (n 73) 312–39.

It is beyond the scope of our concerns in this chapter to discuss and evaluate Brison's critique of these five accounts of autonomy. Of more relevance to our concerns is Brison's discussion in a later article of relational approaches to autonomy and their implications for debates about the regulation of hate speech.[109] Brison argues that an agent's autonomy depends crucially on her social environment and relations with others, in three main ways.[110] First, as Williams also argues, the development and exercise of the capacities or competences necessary for autonomy are causally dependent on the character of a person's social relationships and broader social environment. Second, drawing on Joseph Raz's theory of autonomy and Amartya Sen's capabilities theory,[111] Brison argues that autonomy requires the availability in the agent's social environment of an adequate array of *significant* options to yield an adequate capability set. Third, as the phenomenon of adaptive preference formation reveals, autonomy depends on a person's '*ability to recognize* significant options as options *for her* . . . and this also depends on others'.[112]

While access to others' speech is important to all three ways in which our autonomy is relational or social, Brison argues that this relational view does not support an argument in favour of unregulated hate speech. To the contrary, unregulated hate speech can undermine autonomy by diminishing agents' capability sets. Referring back to her definition of hate speech, she argues that assaultive speech can trigger strong and often automatic emotional responses 'akin to a slap in the face', such as fear, rage, humiliation, and disorientation—responses that can interfere with reasoning capacities and the ability to think autonomously.[113] Moreover, 'hate speech that creates a hostile environment can diminish someone's capability set by affecting her self-esteem, her views about her options, her beliefs about her abilities, and the formation of her preferences'.[114] Further, hate speech that constitutes group libel or defamation, such as racist speech or depictions that entrench harmful stereotypes, can diminish the opportunities available to individual members of targeted social groups by affecting others' beliefs, attitudes, and behaviour towards them. Thus, Brison concludes:

> We need to look at the autonomy-enhancing and the autonomy-undermining effects of such speech—on the speakers, audiences, bystanders, and targets—on a case-by-case basis, to determine whether regulating it would promote or undercut autonomy.[115]

The Canadian case of *R v Keegstra*,[116] which upheld the constitutionality of a provision in the Canadian Criminal Code criminalizing hate speech, provides a good example of the balancing approach which Brison recommends. The Supreme Court of Canada conceded that the challenged provision infringes the right of free expression because it seeks

---

[109] Brison, 'Relational Autonomy and Freedom of Expression' (n 73) 280–99.   [110] Ibid 283–6.
[111] Joseph Raz, *The Morality of Freedom* (OUP 1986); Amartya Sen, *Inequality Reexamined* (Harvard UP 1992).
[112] Brison, 'Relational Autonomy and Freedom of Expression' (n 73) 285 (emphasis in original).
[113] Ibid 286.   [114] Ibid.   [115] Ibid 293.   [116] *R v Keegstra* [1990] 3 SCR 697.

to suppress ideas. It found, however, that the infringement is justifiable, on the ground that hate speech undermines the very values that free speech is intended to protect.[117] In relation to the value of autonomy specifically, which the Court understood as 'the ability to gain self-fulfilment by developing and articulating thoughts and ideas as [individuals] see fit',[118] the Court acknowledged that prohibiting hate speech impairs the autonomy of speakers. It said, however, that autonomy stems in large part from identifying with the cultural and religious groups to which individuals belong,[119] and observed that hate speech views 'as execrable the process of individual self-development and human flourishing among all members of society'.[120] The Court concluded that hate speech is only weakly connected with the value of autonomy (and the other values underlying freedom of expression) and that its suppression is therefore not a serious infringement of freedom of expression.[121] Indeed, the Court went further, suggesting that the best way for the state to encourage the values central to freedom of expression is to suppress hate speech.[122] In effect, because the Court understood autonomy to be a value underpinning the right to free expression, not the source of a negative duty constraining the exercise of state power, it was able to weigh the autonomy claims on both sides, finding that restrictions on hate speech are not merely permissible but morally required in order to serve autonomy.

4.5 Conclusion

This chapter has examined a variety of autonomy-based justifications for the importance of speech and especially of freedom of speech. The differences between these justifications relate not only to the different conceptions of autonomy that underpin them, but also to their different responses to the problem of competing autonomy interests. It is plausible to think that the state should respect, protect, and promote the autonomy of everyone—speakers, listeners, thinkers, bystanders, and members of the public at large. Enhancing the autonomy of some might, however, require restricting the speech of others. The issue which divides different theorists concerns how conflicts of this kind should be resolved: should the state balance the interests of everyone whose autonomy is at stake, so as to maximize autonomy overall, or should it concern itself only with the autonomy interests of speakers and listeners? The liberty-based conceptions of autonomy outlined in this chapter prioritize the interests of speakers and listeners, and hold that the primary obligation of the state is the negative duty not to interfere with the autonomy of individual speakers and listeners. As such, these views support very stringent free speech protections. By contrast, the relational conceptions of autonomy discussed above hold that the negative liberty interests of individual speakers and hearers should be balanced against the positive duties of the state to promote the social conditions necessary for the development and exercise of autonomy by all citizens.

[117] Ibid 741.   [118] Ibid 763.   [119] Ibid.   [120] Ibid.
[121] Ibid 787.   [122] Ibid 764.

According to these views, in some contexts, the state has an obligation to prioritize these positive duties, using regulatory mechanisms to enable the political participation of citizens with less access to power and resources, or to impose content-based restrictions on some kinds of speech, such as hate speech. Thus, while both liberty-based and relational conceptions of autonomy support freedom of speech, their different answers to the connected questions of whose autonomy interests are relevant, and whether autonomy losses should be balanced against autonomy gains, will yield different views about the scope and limits of state regulation when it comes to contentious issues such as campaign finance and hate speech.

CHAPTER 5

FREEDOM OF EXPRESSION AND DEMOCRACY

ASHUTOSH BHAGWAT AND JAMES WEINSTEIN

5.1 INTRODUCTION

THIS chapter examines the relationship between freedom of expression and democracy from both a historical and a theoretical perspective. As used in this chapter, the term 'freedom of expression' includes free speech, freedom of the press, the right to petition government, and freedom of political association.

Even before democratic forms of government took root in the modern world[1] in the late eighteenth century, proponents of popular government had long offered democratic justifications for freedom of expression. During the English Civil War in the middle of the seventeenth century, the Levellers, a group of Puritans who advocated expansive manhood suffrage,[2] invoked popular sovereignty as a reason for freedom of expression on public matters.[3] In 1670, the Jewish-Dutch philosopher Baruch Spinoza reasoned that because in a 'democratic state' every collective decision is open to revision in case the people 'should find a better course', it follows that everyone should be 'allowed to

---

[1] Though it would be anachronistic to consider the practice as conferring a right, citizens in democratic ancient Athens were encouraged to engage in parrhesia, or 'frank talk', when speaking in the assembly: Arlene W Saxenhouse, *Free Speech and Democracy in Ancient Athens* (CUP 2006). As the fate of Socrates reveals, however, such frank talk was riskier outside the assembly.

[2] Michael Kent Curtis, 'In Pursuit of Liberty: The Levellers and the American Bill of Rights' (1991) 8 *Const Comment* 359, 372.

[3] Michael Kent Curtis, *Free Speech, The People's Darling Privilege* (Duke UP 2000) 25.

think what they wish and to say what they think'.[4] In the 1720s, reflecting the Radical English Whig argument in favour of popular rather than parliamentary sovereignty, John Trenchard and Thomas Gordon, writing as Cato, defended a robust right to criticize public officials.[5] Cato's essays were enormously influential in the American colonies when first published. They continued to be widely read in America when, at the end of the eighteenth century, Americans adopted a constitution whose opening words, 'We the People', established a government based on popular sovereignty, and which shortly thereafter was amended to protect freedom of expression.

The first part of the chapter demonstrates that freedom of political expression is a necessary component of democracy. It then describes two core functions of such expression: an informing one and a legitimating one. Finally, this chapter examines the concept of 'democracy', noting the ways in which democracies vary among themselves, as well as the implications of those variations for freedom of expression.

5.2 The Essential Connection between Freedom of Expression and Democracy

Democracy literally means 'rule by the people', combining the Greek words demos ('the people') and kratein ('to rule').[6] Contemporary democracies come in many varieties, each coloured by its particular culture and history. Despite these differences, a common denominator of all contemporary democracies is a practical, if not always formal, commitment to popular sovereignty—a state of affairs in which the people exercise ultimate control over their government. Another basic precept of every contemporary democracy is formal political equality of every citizen. A necessary component of each of these two basic democratic norms is freedom of political expression. Though largely overlapping, the expression inherent in these two basic democratic norms have some distinct features.

---

[4] Benedict De Spinoza, *Theological-Political Treatise* (Jonathan Israel ed, CUP 2007) 257, 259.

[5] David Rabban, 'The Ahistorical Historian: Leonard Levy on Freedom of Expression in Early American History' (1985) 37 *Stan L Rev* 795, 823–8. In a 1742 essay, David Hume defended freedom of the press in terms of Great Britain's 'mixed' monarchical and republican form of government. See David Hume, 'Of Liberty of the Press' in *Essays Moral, Political and Literary* (5 Founders' Constitution, Amendment I (Speech and Press)) <http://press-pubs.uchicago.edu/founders/documents/amendI_speechs2.html> accessed 29 December 2018.

[6] Until the end of the eighteenth century, the term 'democracy' meant what we would today call 'direct democracy': Barry Holden, *Understanding Liberal Democracy* (2nd edn, Harvester Wheatsheaf 1993). At that time, the preferred word for systems characterized by democratic representation and divided powers was 'republic': see, eg, The Federalist No 10 (James Madison) ('A republic, by which I mean a government in which the scheme of representation takes place').

5.2.1 Political Expression as a Necessary Component of Popular Sovereignty

Popular sovereignty requires that 'ultimate political power resides in the population at large, that the people as a body are sovereign, and that they, either directly or through their elected representatives in a significant sense actually control the operation of government'.[7] The most obvious and direct way that the people exercise control over their government is through voting, either by electing representatives, or by directly voting on laws or policies through ballot measures such as referenda, initiatives, and recall.[8] Because the right to vote is so crucial to popular control of government, a society entirely lacking the franchise is plainly not a democracy. The directness of this control, however, tends to obscure a less direct, yet equally essential, prerequisite of modern democracy: the right of the people to speak freely about collective decisions within the purview of the people's ultimate sovereignty, that is, on matters of public concern.

As James Madison recognized more than two centuries ago, because '[t]he people, not the government, possess the absolute sovereignty',[9] it follows that the 'censorial power is in the people over the government and not in the government over the people'.[10] Or as more recently explained in an opinion of the House of Lords, then the highest court in the United Kingdom:

> Modern democratic government means government of the people by the people for the people. But there can be no government by the people if they are ignorant of the issues to be resolved, the arguments for and against different solutions and the facts underlying those arguments.[11]

---

[7] Frederick Schauer, *Free Speech: A Philosophical Inquiry* (CUP 1982) 36. Chapter 3 of that book, 'The argument from democracy', is an invaluable source for understanding the relationship between free speech and democracy. For another excellent treatment of the subject, see Eric Barendt, *Freedom of Speech* (2nd edn, OUP 2005) 18–23. For a discussion of democracy as the core principle of contemporary First Amendment doctrine, see Robert Post, 'Participatory Democracy and Free Speech' (2011) 97 *Va L Rev* 477; James Weinstein, 'Participatory Democracy as the Central Value of American Free Speech Doctrine' (2011) 97 *Va L Rev* 491, 498.

[8] There are very few contemporary jurisdictions that are entirely direct democracies of the type that existed in ancient Athens: Bruno S Frey, Marcel Kucher, and Alois Stutzer, 'Outcome, Process and Power in Direct Democracy' (2001) 107 *Pub Choice* 271, 271. Rather, mechanisms of direct democracy such as initiatives and referenda frequently operate within representative democracies that commonly exist today.

[9] 'Report on the Virginia Resolutions' in Jonathan Elliot (ed), *Debates in the Several State Conventions on the Adoption of the Federal Constitution* (2nd edn, Lenox Hill 1836) vol 4, 569–70.

[10] 4 *Annals of Cong.* 934 (1794).

[11] *R v Shayler* [2002] UKHL 11, [2003] 1 AC 247 [21] (Lord Bingham). Similarly, the US Supreme Court has explained that '[t]he maintenance of the opportunity for free political discussion [is] to the end that government may be responsive to the will of the people' (*Stromberg v California*, 283 US 359, 369 (1931)). See also *Roth v US*, 354 US 476, 484 (1957) ('The protection given speech and press was fashioned to assure unfettered interchange of ideas for the bringing about of political and social changes desired by the people.'); *Faber v Hungary* App no 40721/08 (ECtHR, 24 July 2012) ('Freedom of expression, as secured in para 1 of art 10, constitutes one of the essential foundations of a democratic society').

Thus, like the franchise, 'the principle of freedom of speech springs from the necessities of the program of self-government'.[12]

5.2.1.1 *The Crucial Role of Public Opinion*

The primary mechanism through which freedom of expression in a democracy controls government is public opinion.[13] As Madison observed in a 1791 essay on the subject, '[p]ublic opinion sets bounds to every government, and is the real sovereign in every free one'.[14] It is an important link in what James Wilson, another framer of the US Constitution, called the 'chain of communication between the people, and those, to whom they committed the exercise of the powers of government'.[15] In a representative democracy, public opinion not only influences who is elected to govern, but also influences the decisions made by these representatives between elections. For while elections are 'an intermittent mechanism', public opinion is 'constantly active'.[16] When the people directly make laws or policy through ballot measures rather than indirectly through their representatives, public opinion will tend to have a correspondingly greater direct effect on the outcome.

The right of the people to speak freely on matters of public concern is, in turn, essential to the formation of the public opinion by which the people control the government. This is because government propaganda and statements by government officials also affect public opinion. If the people cannot freely express their views on public matters, then public opinion will largely reflect the views of government officials and thus be an ineffective means of popular control of government.

As Madison's statement about public opinion demonstrates, even in the early stages of the development of modern democracy some leading political figures thought public opinion was a potentially important mechanism by which the people in a democracy could—and should—control their government.[17] With the advent of methods of communication 'such as the telegraph, the newspaper, and the fast mail' that made early forms of mass media possible, the roles of public opinion and an active citizenry in democracy were cemented.[18] By the middle of the twentieth century, with the

---

[12] Alexander Meiklejohn, *Free Speech and Its Relation to Self-Government* (Harper Brothers 1948) 26.

[13] For a comprehensive discussion of the relationship between free speech, public opinion, and US democracy, see Robert Post, *Citizens Divided: Campaign Finance Reform and the Constitution* (Harvard UP 2014) 7–43. The discussion in this chapter of the role of public opinion in a democracy draws substantially from this work, especially the sources it quotes.

[14] James Madison, 'Public Opinion' *National Gazette* (19 December 1791) in William T Hutchinson and others (eds), *Papers of James Madison* (U Virginia P 1983) vol 14.

[15] James Wilson and Thomas McKean, *Commentaries on the Constitution of the United States of America* (J Debrett 1792) 30–1.

[16] James Bryce, *The American Commonwealth* (Macmillan 1888) vol 3.

[17] In contrast, other key figures in the early US Republic, including George Washington and Alexander Hamilton, were considerably more sceptical about the importance, indeed even the propriety, of public opinion, as well as of an active citizenry more generally, in a representative democracy. Ultimately, however, the Madisonian view prevailed. See Ashutosh Bhagwat, 'The Democratic First Amendment' (2016) 110 *Nw U L Rev* 1097, 1119–23.

[18] Charles Horton Cooley, *Social Organization: A Study of the Larger Mind* (Charles Scribner's Sons 1910) 85.

development of modern mass media such as radio, television, and film, Hans Kelsen could proclaim that the discussion about proposed laws and policies takes place 'not only in parliament, but also, and foremost, at political meetings, in newspapers, books, and other vehicles of public opinion'.[19] And by the end of the century, the advent of the Internet and social media further increased the power of public opinion as a source of popular control of the government.

It has been aptly observed that '[a] democracy without public opinion is a contradiction in terms'.[20] In light of the essential relationship between freedom of political expression and public opinion, a democracy without such a political freedom is similarly an oxymoron. Precisely how much freedom of political expression must exist in a society before it can properly be referred to as a democracy is perhaps not susceptible to a precise answer. But this should not obscure the fact that at some point governmental prohibition of this freedom renders the government non-democratic.

5.2.1.2 Judicial Decisions Deriving a Right of Free Speech from a Commitment to Popular Sovereignty

Supporting the view that free speech is a necessary component of democracy, courts in several jurisdictions lacking an express provision protecting freedom of expression have derived such a freedom from their nation's commitment to popular sovereignty. In a noted 1992 decision, the High Court of Australia (the highest court in Australia's legal system) found freedom of political expression to be necessary to the system of representative government established by those provisions of the Australian Constitution creating a parliament elected by popular vote.[21] Because representatives are not only chosen by the people 'but exercise their legislative and executive powers as representatives of the people', representatives are 'accountable to the people' and have 'a responsibility' to take account of the views of those on whose behalf they act.[22] 'Indispensable' to such accountability and responsibility

> is freedom of communication, at least in relation to public affairs and political discussion. Only by exercising that freedom can the citizen communicate his or her views on the wide range of matters that may call for, or are relevant to, political action or decision. Only by exercising that freedom can the citizen criticize government decisions and actions, seek to bring about change, call for action where none has been taken and in this way influence the elected representatives . . . [In addition] elected representatives have a responsibility not only to ascertain the views of the electorate but also to explain and account for their decisions and actions in government and to inform the people so that they may make informed judgments on relevant matters. Absent such a freedom of communication, representative government would fail to achieve its purpose, namely, government by the people through their elected representatives.[23]

---

[19] Hans Kelsen, *A General Theory of Law and State* (Anders Wedberg tr, Harvard UP 1945) 287–8.
[20] Ibid.   [21] *Australian Capital Television Pty Ltd v Commonwealth* (1992) 177 CLR 106, 137.
[22] Ibid 138.
[23] Ibid 138–9.

Similarly, the Supreme Court of Israel found a right to freedom of expression implicit in Israel's commitment to popular sovereignty.[24] Likewise, the Canadian Supreme Court has observed that even before the right to freedom of expression was enshrined as a fundamental freedom in the Canadian Charter, 'freedom of speech and expression had been recognized as an essential feature of Canadian parliamentary democracy'.[25]

5.2.1.3 *The Argument that Freedom of Expression is Not a Necessary Component of Popular Sovereignty*

Because it can hardly be denied that freedom of political expression is an indispensable means by which the people in contemporary democracies control their government, the argument against the view that such expression is a necessary component of popular sovereignty is of a different order, invoking a supposed 'paradox of power'.[26] As pithily summarized by Frederick Schauer:

> If the people collectively are in fact the sovereign, and if that sovereign has the unlimited powers normally associated with sovereignty, the acceptance of this view of democracy compels acceptance of the power of the sovereign to restrict the liberty of speech just as the sovereign may restrict any other liberty.[27]

But there is no true paradox here. For if the people exercise their sovereignty to abolish a truly necessary component of popular control of their government, they have by definition abolished popular sovereignty and hence democracy. Suppose that the people in a democratic society adopt a constitution that abolishes its popularly elected legislature and executive and installs a populist demagogue as dictator for life with unlimited power to rule by decree.[28] Despite its origins in an exercise of popular sovereignty, moving forward this system of government cannot be properly referred to as a democracy. Now suppose instead that the people retain a popularly elected legislature and executive, but amend the constitution to prohibit anyone from publicly criticizing government officials or urging their defeat in an election. If, as is argued above, freedom of political expression is, like voting, an indispensable means by which people control their government, then so long as this speech ban remains part of the constitution and is actually enforced, this system of government is also not a democracy.

It might be argued that because voting for representatives is a more direct way that people control their government than is political expression, the franchise is a more important component of popular sovereignty than is the basic right of political expression.

---

[24] HCJ 73/53, *Kol Ha'am Company Limited v Minister of the Interior* (1953) 7 PD 871 in *Selected Judgment of the Supreme Court of Israel: 1948–1953* (Supreme Court of Israel 1948) vol 1, 90.
[25] *Retail, Wholesale and Department Store Union, Local 580 v Dolphin Delivery Ltd* [1986] 2 SCR 573.
[26] Schauer (n 7) 40.   [27] Ibid.
[28] Karl Popper notes that Plato in his criticism of democracy and his story of the rise of the tyrant implicitly raised the issue of the people in a democracy restricting future exercises of their sovereignty. See Karl R Popper, *The Open Society and Its Enemies, Part I: The Spell of Plato* (Princeton UP 1950) vol 1, 122.

But even if this is true, it would not undercut the claim that freedom of political expression is a necessary component of popular sovereignty. An engine may be more important than wheels to making an automobile run, but wheels are nonetheless a necessary component of an automobile.[29]

5.2.2 Political Expression as a Necessary Component of Formal Political Equality

A basic precept of Enlightenment philosophy is that each person is of equal moral worth.[30] What precisely this precept requires of government has long been and remains highly contested. Despite the continuing debate about various important details, there is now, however, a clear consensus among contemporary democracies that respect for the equal moral worth of each individual requires at least *formal* political equality.[31] This commitment includes a formal (or procedural) right to equal participation in the political process.[32] As Robert Dahl has explained: 'The democratic process is generally believed to be justified on the ground that people are entitled to participate as political equals in making binding decisions, enforced by the state, on matters that have important consequences for their individual and collective interest'.[33]

As with popular sovereignty, the most apparent manifestation of this commitment to political equality is voting. This commitment is reflected in the universal adult suffrage

---

[29] It is important to distinguish the proposition that freedom of expression is a necessary component of popular sovereignty and hence of democracy, from whether *judicial enforcement* of this freedom is similarly essential to democracy. The role of judicial enforcement in assuring effective freedom of expression in a given society is a large and difficult topic beyond the scope of this chapter. Suffice it to say that the inability of the judiciary to declare an act of the legislature void because it contravenes freedom of expression does not automatically render a society undemocratic if political norms are sufficiently strong to ensure that freedom of expression is not unduly restricted. This is demonstrated, for instance, by the British constitutional arrangement in which courts have never possessed the power to declare an act of parliament void, on free speech or any other grounds.

[30] Immanuel Kant, *The Metaphysics of Morals* (first published 1797, Mary Gregor tr, CUP 1991); John Locke, *Second Treatise of Government,* (CB Macpherson ed, Hackett Publishing 1980) ch 2, ss 4, 6, 8, 9, and 52. See also the statement of Thomas Rainboro during the 1647 Putney debates: 'Really I think that the poorest he that is in England has a life to live as the richest he; and therefore truly, Sir, I think it's clear, that every man that is to live under a government ought first by his own consent to put himself under that government': Robert A Licht (ed), *Old Rights and New* (American Enterprise Institute 1993) 54.

[31] Formal political equality prohibits the government from treating people differently with regard to characteristics deemed irrelevant to one's status as a citizen such as race, sex, and wealth. Substantive political equality requires the government to take measures to equalize citizens' political power, including in some situations redistribution of resources necessary towards this end. In contrast to the universal commitment to formal political equality among contemporary democracies, no such consensus exists regarding substantive equality.

[32] Schauer (n 7) 41, 62–3.

[33] Robert A Dahl, *Controlling Nuclear Weapons: Democracy versus Guardianship* (Syracuse UP 1985) 5. See also Schauer (n 7) 44 ('[e]qual participation by all people in the process of government is even more fundamental to the ideal of self-government than is the idea of majority power').

practised in every contemporary democracy.[34] Just as crucially, however, formal political equality also includes the right of every person to contribute to public opinion by freely expressing their views on matters of public concern.[35] For this reason, the expression protected by this right is vitally connected to the formation of public opinion and as such overlaps to a considerable extent with the freedom of expression derived from popular sovereignty. There are, however, some significant differences in the nature and scope of freedom of expression inherent in these two basic democratic precepts.

The political expression inherent in popular sovereignty primarily promotes the informing function of freedom of expression discussed in detail in Section 5.3.1, below. As such, it primarily vindicates audience interests, especially by assuring that the electorate has access to information and perspectives needed 'to vote wise decisions'.[36] In contrast, the right of freedom of expression derived from formal equality primarily vindicates speaker interests. It does so by assuring individuals the free and equal opportunity to try to persuade others about the proper determination of society's collective decisions.[37] In addition to any potential persuasive effect, such expression serves 'to confirm [the speaker's] standing as a responsible agent in, rather than a passive victim of, collective action'.[38] As discussed in detail in Section 5.3.2, below, vindication of these important speaker interests promotes the crucial legitimation function of democracy.

Because of its speaker orientation, the right to freedom of expression inherent in formal political equality is somewhat broader in scope than is the freedom of expression that is a necessary component of popular sovereignty. Because the primary function of the latter is informational, '[w]hat is essential is not that everyone shall speak, but everything worth saying shall be said'.[39] The right of freedom of expression derived from formal political equality also includes the expression of information and ideas through which speakers try to influence public opinion. But because this right in addition includes expression by which speakers confirm their 'standing as a responsible agent[s] in, rather than a passive victim of, collective action', it also protects the right of speakers to have their 'say'[40] on matters of public concern, even if in doing so they do not supply the audience with useful information or perspectives. As discussed in Section 5.3.2,

---

[34] Ludvig Beckman, 'Who Should Vote? Conceptualizing Universal Suffrage in Studies of Democracy' (2007) 15 *Democratization* 29, 29. The right to equal political participation is also reflected in the basic understanding that everyone should be entitled to cast the same number of votes (usually one) for a representative or a ballot proposition.

[35] Because it is a component of formal rather than of substantive political equality, this right does not obligate government to equalize resources through which individuals seek to influence public opinion or to guarantee equal access to the media to express one's views on matter of public concern. This right, however, does not, in principle at least, forbid such remedies.

[36] Meiklejohn (n 12) 26.

[37] This does not mean, however, that access to information and perspectives on matters of public concern is not important to the right of equal participation. See Section 5.3.1, below.

[38] Ronald Dworkin, 'Foreword' in Ivan Hare and James Weinstein (eds), *Extreme Speech and Democracy* (OUP 2009) vii.

[39] Meiklejohn (n 12) 26.

[40] C Edwin Baker, 'Autonomy and Free Speech' (2011) 27 *Const Comment* 251, 263.

below, this arguably includes expression whose content is primarily emotional rather than cognitive, such as the use of profanity in public discourse.

Finally, but crucially, a right of freedom of political expression based in formal equality provides a stronger guarantee of equal treatment of speakers engaged in political speech than does a right derived from popular sovereignty. For instance, it is not obvious that a law banning the use of loud speakers in political demonstrations on public streets adjacent to medical facilities but providing an exception for anti-abortion protestors would deprive the electorate of valuable information or perspectives. Such an unequal law, however, would manifestly violate the rights of those who support abortion rights who want to use loudspeakers in protests in front of medical facilities.

5.3 Two Core Democratic Functions of Freedom of Expression

As will be explored in detail in the next section, the strength and scope of speech protection in a given democracy is a product of the emphasis each society places on various forms of democracy (as well, of course, on free speech values other than democratic ones). Despite this variation, however, in every contemporary democracy freedom of expression promotes two key democratic purposes reflecting the shared commitment to popular sovereignty and formal political equality: an informed citizenry and political legitimacy.

5.3.1 The Informing Function

The importance of the informing function of freedom of expression to contemporary democracy is underscored by Article 10 of the European Convention of Human Rights (ECHR), which provides that freedom of expression shall include freedom 'to receive and impart information and ideas without interference by public authority'. This crucial democratic free speech function can usefully be divided into three categories: (1) expression that informs the electorate so that the people can 'vote wise decisions';[41] (2) expression that informs speakers so that they can knowledgably participate in public discourse; and (3) expression that informs representatives of the views of the electorate. The representative informing function has already been discussed in Section 5.2.1.1. This section, then, will focus on the other two democratic informing functions of freedom of expression.

The necessity of freedom of expression for an informed electorate is among the most often invoked justifications for freedom of expression, democratic or otherwise. It is the

---

[41] Meiklejohn (n 12) 26.

central theme, for instance, of Alexander Meiklejohn's enormously influential book, *Free Speech and its Relationship to Self-Government*.[42] Focusing on the First Amendment to the US Constitution but in terms that apply equally to any contemporary democracy, Meiklejohn explains that the purpose of the constitutional protection of free speech

> is to give every voting member of the body politic the fullest possible participation in the understanding of those problems with which the citizens of a self-governing society must deal. When a free man is voting, it is not enough that the truth is known by someone else, by some scholar or administrator or legislator. The voters must have it, all of them ... That is why no idea, no opinion, no doubt, no belief, no counterbelief, nor relevant information, may be kept from them.[43]

In the same vein, the High Court of Australia has emphasized the function of freedom of expression to assure 'access to the people to relevant information about the functioning of government ... and about the policies of political parties and candidates for election'.[44]

As exemplified by the above quotation from Meiklejohn, discussion of the democratic informing function of freedom of expression is usually audience centred, focusing on the importance of such expression to informed voting. Although not frequently emphasized, there is, however, another democratic informing function of free speech that promotes speaker interests. One reason people participate in the discussion of matters of public concern is to try to persuade others of their views. While it is regrettably true that uninformed speakers are often persuasive, in many settings being well informed on a subject amplifies a speaker's persuasive power. For this reason, laws that interfere with citizens' ability to become informed on matters of public concern interfere not only with the ability of voters to participate in the political process but also with speakers' participatory interests. Crucially, any regulation that *selectively* interferes with the expression of particular ideas or perspectives infringes the fundamental precept of *equal* political participation discussed above.[45]

Finally, any discussion of the democratic informing function of freedom of expression would be remiss if it did not note the special role played by the institutional press. Before the rise of social media, the institutional press was for many citizens in democratic societies the principal source of information and perspectives on matters of public concern. Although no longer enjoying this virtual information-providing monopoly, the institutional press remains the primary entity that engages in investigative journalism

---

[42] Ibid.   [43] Ibid 88–9.
[44] *Lange v Australian Broadcasting Corporation* (1997) 189 CLR 520, 560.
[45] Schauer (n 7) 41 ('If everyone is to participate equally, then everyone must have the information necessary to make participation meaningful'). As Meiklejohn famously observed, 'equality of status in the field of ideas lies deep in the very foundations of the self-governing process': Meiklejohn (n 12) 26. Although Meiklejohn was, per usual, focusing on audience interests as it relates to well-informed voting, this observation also applies to the interest of speakers to participate equally in 'the self-governing process'. In any event, this statement anticipated and influenced contemporary First Amendment doctrine's intense hostility towards viewpoint discrimination. See, eg, *Rosenberger v University of Virginia*, 515 US 819, 829 (1995).

exposing government corruption and malfeasance. In this way, the institutional press remains crucial to the informing function of freedom of expression.[46]

5.3.2 The Legitimating Function

Another core democratic function performed by freedom of expression is the promotion of political legitimacy. Although not as frequently emphasized, this function is arguably as important to democracy as is the informing function.[47]

Political legitimacy refers to the conditions that entitle a political entity to govern, and in particular, to use coercion to enforce its laws.[48] Additionally, indeed some would say correlatively,[49] it refers to the conditions that create an obligation for people to obey the laws of a political entity. Political legitimacy has both a descriptive and normative sense. Descriptively, the term refers to the people's belief that the political entity asserting authority over them has a right to do so. In addition, it refers to their belief that they have an obligation to obey the laws enacted by this entity.[50] Normatively, political legitimacy usually refers to 'the conditions permitting the political state to justifiably demand obedience from its citizens, and thus to impose its laws on those who refuse to obey'.[51]

With respect to normative legitimacy, democracy provides the best available answer to the age-old problem of justifying the use of force against free and autonomous people to make them obey a law with which they can reasonably disagree. There may well be no completely satisfactory justification for the use of such force. However, the opportunity to participate as an equal in the political process discussed in Section 5.2.2, above, goes a long way towards justifying what would otherwise be the immoral use of coercion to enforce the law. As C Edwin Baker explains: because '[a] democratic process "equally" respects people as properly having a "say" in the rules they live under', democracy is

---

[46] An important topic, but one beyond the scope of this chapter, is governmental regulation of expression justified as enhancing the informing function of freedom of expression and whether such regulations are consistent with democratic or other free speech norms.

[47] The topic of freedom of expression and political legitimacy is explored at length in 'Symposium: Hate Speech and Legitimacy' (2017) 32 *Const Comment* 527.

[48] Christopher H Wellman, 'Liberalism, Samaritanism, and Political Legitimacy' (1996) 25 *Phil & Pub Aff* 211, 211–12.

[49] See, eg, A John Simmons, 'Justification and Legitimacy' (1999) 109 *Ethics* 739, 746 (arguing that 'state legitimacy is the logical correlate of various obligations, including subjects' political obligations'); Michael Huemer, *The Problem of Political Authority* (Palgrave Macmillan 2012) 12–14. Cf Rolf Sartorius, 'Political Authority and Political Obligation' (1981) 67 *Va L Rev* 3, 4 (concluding that 'those in political power may often correctly claim a moral right to rule but that those under their power may not, under any philosophically interesting conditions, be said to have a correlative moral obligation to obey the law').

[50] Descriptive legitimacy is often referred to as 'sociological' legitimacy.

[51] Frederick Schauer, 'Does Freedom of Speech Increase Obedience to Law' (2017) 32 *Const Comment* 661, 662.

'arguably the best that can be done ... for justifying the legitimacy of the legal order'.[52] With respect to descriptive legitimacy, empirical studies suggest that 'an opportunity to take part in [a] decision-making process',[53] in which citizens are able 'to present their views'[54] and are treated with 'dignity and respect',[55] increases the participants' feeling that they 'ought to obey the law',[56] including laws with which they disagree.[57]

A manifestly crucial way that citizens have a 'say' in the rules they live under is through voting for representatives or by directly determining these rules through voting on ballot measures such as referenda. Equal voting rights are thus unquestionably a vital means for promoting the legitimacy of a governing entity. Conversely, denying the right to vote to a particular person, or to a group of people, would, without exceedingly strong justification, violate the fundamental democratic precept of formal political equality discussed in Section 5.2.2, above. Such disenfranchisement can thus have grave implications for political legitimacy in both its descriptive and normative sense.[58]

Freedom of political expression is another important way in which people can have a 'say' in the rules they live under. As discussed in Section 5.2.1.1, above, public opinion controls the actions of elected officials between elections. '[A] necessary condition for citizens to identify with public opinion is the guarantee that all can freely participate in the public deliberations by which public opinion is formed'.[59] By the same token, speech *restrictions* can undermine the legitimacy of a legal system. Like selective restrictions on voting, unless justified by extremely weighty reasons, rules forbidding the expression of particular viewpoints or perspectives on matters of public concern violate the basic democratic commitment to formal equality by selectively denying citizens their fundamental interest in equal political participation. To the extent that such censorship prevents people from expressing what they believe is best for society, it is insulting; insofar as the speech restriction impairs their ability to promote or protect their own self-interest, it is fundamentally unfair. For these reasons, viewpoint-discriminatory

---

[52] Baker (n 40) 263. See also Robert Post, 'Democracy, Popular Sovereignty, and Judicial Review' (1998) 86 *Cal L Rev* 429, 434 ('Finding it implausible to postulate [as did Rousseau] that the particular wills of individuals can be determinably identified with the specific enactments of the state, [modern] critics have suggested that democratic self-government requires that the particular will of individuals be connected instead to the *system* by which these enactments are created').

[53] Tom R Tyler, *Why People Obey the Law* (2nd edn, Princeton UP 2006) 163. See also Tom R Tyler, 'Multiculturalism and the Willingness of Citizens to Defer to Law and to Legal Authorities' (2000) 25 *L & Soc Inquiry* 983, 995–6, 1007.

[54] Tyler, *Why People Obey the Law* (n 53) 147.   [55] Ibid 178.

[56] Ibid 161–2. Additionally, these studies find that people's increased belief in their having an obligation to obey the law results in their voluntary compliance with the law. Ibid 4, 27, 57, 62, 66. Conversely, '[i]f people have an experience not characterized by fair procedures, their later compliance will be based less strongly on the legitimacy of the legal authorities'. Ibid 172.

[57] Ibid 64.

[58] Indeed, a strong case could be made that the long-standing practice of disenfranchising African-Americans in various jurisdiction in the United States until the latter part of the twentieth century rendered the legal system in these jurisdictions illegitimate as to these disenfranchised citizens.

[59] Post (n 52) 434.

restrictions tend to undermine the legitimacy of the legal system in both its normative and descriptive sense.

Descriptively, at least some of those who were legally prevented from expressing their views will be less likely to feel that the political entity that imposed the restriction has the right to assert authority over them or that they have an obligation to obey the entity's laws. Normatively, this censorship tends to undermine the moral justification that this entity has to use coercion to enforce its laws against dissenters.

While laws prohibiting the expression of particular viewpoints on matters of public concern are especially damaging to political legitimacy, they are not the only type of speech restrictions that can undermine legitimacy. At least in its descriptive sense, legitimacy might be compromised by viewpoint-neutral laws banning only offensive *forms* of expression, such as the use of profanity, bigoted epithets, or the burning of a national flag. As the US Supreme Court explained in upholding the First Amendment right of an anti-war protestor to appear in public wearing a jacket bearing the message 'Fuck the Draft', 'words are often chosen as much for their emotive as their cognitive force'.[60] For those speakers for whom the emotive force of public expression is at least as important as the cognitive, such a ban may seem unjustifiably censorious. As a result, such restrictions may diminish their belief that their government has a right to assert authority over them as well as weaken their sense of political obligation to obey the law.[61]

Discussion of the legitimation function of free speech usually focuses on the effect of free speech and its restriction on the legitimacy of the legal *system*. But freedom of political expression, and its restriction, can also affect the legitimacy of *individual laws* within a legal system.[62] Even the most egregious speech restriction likely to be enacted in a mature and stable democracy, while diminishing the legal system's legitimacy 'reservoir',[63] would not likely cause catastrophic damage to that nation's political legitimacy. In contrast, an isolated speech restriction might even in a mature and stable democracy have a ruinous effect on the legitimacy of an individual law about which there can be reasonable disagreement.[64] Applications of hate speech bans and public order act provisions to criticism of homosexuality provide an example of the potential of speech restrictions to destroy the legitimacy of certain applications of individual laws.

Recently, there has been a debate in many democratic jurisdictions as to propriety of expanding anti-discrimination laws to forbid discrimination on the basis of sexual orientation in places of public accommodation, and if so whether to allow religious exemptions. This controversy involves a clash of important individual interests. On the

---

[60] *Cohen v California*, 403 US 15, 22 (1971).

[61] In contrast, viewpoint-neutral bans on such vituperation will not substantially damage normative legitimacy. It has been forcefully argued that bans on such vituperation do not significantly interfere with a speakers' ability to express the 'propositional content' of their views: Jeremy Waldron, 'Conditions of Legitimacy of Legitimacy: A Response to James Weinstein' (2017) 32 *Const Comment* 697. If this view is correct, then such speech restrictions would, at most, only minimally compromise the normative legitimating function of freedom of expression.

[62] James Weinstein, 'Hate Speech Bans, Democracy and Political Legitimacy' (2017) 32 *Const Comment* 527.

[63] Robert A Dahl, *Polyarchy: Participation and Opposition* (Yale UP 1971) 148–9.

[64] Weinstein (n 62) 566–74. For a criticism of this view, see Waldron (n 61) 707–12.

one hand, such an extension would protect the interests of homosexual persons by assuring them access to goods and services in places of public accommodation.[65] On the other hand, the application of such laws to some religious proprietors would substantially burden their sincerely held religious beliefs.[66] Moreover, unlike, say, laws prohibiting murder, arson, and mayhem, such an extension of a jurisdiction's anti-discrimination measures is one about which there can be reasonable disagreement, especially as regards their application in ways that burden religious belief. In many democratic countries, however, people have been arrested, tried, and even convicted for publicly proclaiming that homosexuality is immoral or disordered.[67] In these jurisdictions, therefore, some citizens, including those whose interests would be directly affected by the law, were precluded from freely expressing their authentic views in opposition to the expanded anti-discrimination measure.

Descriptively, the inability of these dissenters to have their 'say' about the propriety of the law might well have for many of them destroyed any belief that the jurisdiction has any right to apply this law to them and, similarly, obliterated any obligation that they may have felt to obey the law. Normatively, these speech restrictions may have rendered immoral what would have otherwise been the appropriate use of coercion to enforce these laws against dissenters. Conversely, the opportunity of dissenters to freely present their authentic views for opposing a law reinforces the morality of using coercion to make them comply with laws with which they can reasonably disagree.

5.4 Forms of Democracy and Their Implications for Free Expression

This section examines more closely the meaning of the word 'democracy'. Democracy is, after all, a capacious term. It has been practised in many different forms over the centuries, and even in the modern world varies significantly even among fully democratic nations. And these differences have implications for the extent and nature of the protections these nations must and do provide for free expression.

One very common way to approach differences is to identify specific, defined 'models' of democracy and their natures.[68] Rather than taking this somewhat rigid approach,

---

[65] *Bull v Hull* [2013] UKSC 73, [2018] 1 WLR 3741, [5].
[66] Ibid. See also *Lee v Ashers Baking Co*, [2018] UKSC 49, [2018] 3 WLR 1294.
[67] Weinstein (n 62) 555–61 (discussing, eg, a preacher fined under the UK public order act for displaying a placard in a public square proclaiming that homosexuality is immoral; the conviction and fine, overturned on appeal, of a French politician for saying that that homosexual behaviour was a threat to humanity and 'morally inferior' to heterosexuality; and the unsuccessful criminal prosecution of a Catholic bishop in Belgium for stating that homosexuality is a 'blockage in normal psychological development, rendering [homosexuals] abnormal').
[68] See, eg, Jürgen Habermas, 'Three Normative Models of Democracy' (1994) 1 *Constellations* 1; David Held, *Models of Democracy* (3rd edn, Stanford UP 2006).

however, this section instead identifies four different axes along which democracies differ: direct versus representative democracy; pluralist versus deliberative democracy; substantive versus proceduralist democracy; and libertarian versus militant democracy. Different political systems of course exist in different places along each axis.

5.4.1 Direct/Participatory Versus Representative Democracy

The oldest, and probably most significant axis upon which democracies vary is between democracies in which citizens directly make binding decisions, called direct democracies (or sometimes participatory democracies because citizens participate in the decision-making process), and democracies where power is wielded by the people's elected representatives. The ancient democracies of the Greek city-states, notably Athens, were direct democracies. In the modern era, direct democracy of that form, with citizens meeting in person, discussing issues, and then voting, survives only in a few small jurisdictions such as the town meetings still held in the New England region of the United States.[69] The reason for the decline of direct, face-to-face democracy is of course the enormous increase in the physical size and populations of modern nations and their significant subdivisions, making physical meetings impossible. It should be noted, however, that as the Internet becomes ubiquitous and more complex, there remains the possibility that large-scale, virtual direct democracy could have a resurgence.

Currently, however, the dominant form of direct democracy is not the town meeting, but rather ballot measures such as initiative and recall. Such ballot measures do not typically constitute the entire decision-making apparatus of modern democracies, but rather complement representative government to a greater or lesser degree. In the United States, there are no mechanisms of direct democracy at the national level; but ballot measures play a very significant role in the governance of many state and local governments, including notably in the largest state, California. In Europe, nations vary significantly in the degree to which they supplement representative government with direct democracy, from a very significant or even primary role in Switzerland, to a far lesser role in larger democracies. But even the largest, most traditionally representative democracies of Europe sometimes turn to direct democratic mechanisms, as illustrated by the Brexit referendum of 2016 in the United Kingdom and the referenda on the proposed European Constitution held in France and the Netherlands in 2005.

Nevertheless, there can be no doubt that the dominant form of democracy in the modern world is representative democracy. Every major democratic nation in the world allocates primary legislative and executive authority to representatives of the people, and requires regular elections to select those representatives. Representative democra-

---

[69] Alexander Meiklejohn, who as noted earlier was the leading US theorist of the relationship between free speech and democracy, was much enamoured of the New England town meeting and used it as his fundamental model of democracy. See Alexander Meiklejohn, *Political Freedom: The Constitutional Powers of the People* (OUP 1965) 24.

cies, however, vary widely in their forms of democracy, including along the axes discussed below and one distinction—presidential versus parliamentary democracy—which is not addressed here.

What, then, are the implications of the direct/representative axis for free expression? Potentially they are quite significant. For starters, in a pure, direct democracy of the Athenian/New England mode it might be that only very limited free expression rights would be required outside of the assembly (though admittedly, this is a largely hypothetical point since in the modern world, the few such democracies that exist are embedded within broader representative democracies). Within the assembly, of course, strong rights of free expression would be essential or the entire deliberative process of decision-making that direct democracy relies upon would be eviscerated. The analogy here is to the parliamentary privilege of free speech recognized in the English Bill of Rights of 1689,[70] and in the Speech and Debate Clause of Article I of the US Constitution.[71] Outside of the meeting, however, it is not clear to what extent pure direct democracy, as opposed to ballot measures, requires strong protections for free expression. Presumably, the opportunity to participate directly in decision-making would vindicate the legitimization interest fully, so long as all citizens are given the opportunity to participate fully in the debate.[72] Speech outside of, and in-between, formal democratic meetings does advance the informing function to some extent, but given the opportunity to inform the electorate *during* the meeting, the need for general public discourse in a direct democracy is at the least reduced. In practice, however, since modern direct democracies are universally situated within broader representative democracies, speech outside meetings must of course be protected in order to enable participation in that broader democracy.

When one turns to the relationship between free expression and direct democracy via ballot measures, the story becomes more complex. At first cut, there would seem to be no difference between such direct democracy and representative democracy vis-à-vis free speech. In both instances, presumably strong protection for free expression (and association and assembly) is essential, since it is through public discourse that citizens will become informed about the issues. And in both instances the opportunity to participate in public discourse will promote legitimacy in both its descriptive and normative sense. There is, however, one important difference between ballot initiative democracy and representative democracy. In a representative democracy, as noted earlier, a substantial role of free expression is to permit citizens to express their views *to their*

---

[70] Bill of Rights 1689 ('the freedom of speech and debates or proceedings in Parliament ought not to be impeached or questioned in any court or place out of Parliament').

[71] US Const art I, § 6 ('for any Speech or Debate in either House, they [Senators and Representatives] shall not be questioned in any other Place').

[72] This last caveat indicates that Alexander Meiklejohn was wrong when he famously stated, regarding debate in direct democracies, that '[w]hat is essential is not that everyone shall speak, but that everything worth saying shall be said'. Meiklejohn (n 12) 26. While his statement might be true if one focuses only on the informational function as Meiklejohn does, it ignores the significance of the legitimization function, which for reasons noted earlier requires citizens to be able to participate in public discourse, not just to vote.

representatives, either directly to them or through the formation of public opinion, between elections. And similarly, an important role of free expression (especially in the form of a free press) in such democracies is to oversee and check representatives. Both of these functions, however, are irrelevant in a direct democracy, even of the ballot measure variety. One obvious illustration of this point is that one of the core, expressive freedoms protected in the First Amendment to the US Constitution—the right 'to petition the Government for a redress of grievances'[73]—has little relevance to ballot measures. So even in a direct democracy through ballot measures, the scope of needed protection for free expression is somewhat narrower than in representative democracies.

5.4.2 Pluralist versus Deliberative Democracy

Aside from the distinction between direct and representative democracies, modern democratic theory also draws a distinction between pluralist (or liberal) democracies, and deliberative (sometimes called republican) democracies. Unlike the direct/representative axis, the distinction between pluralist and deliberative democracies does not focus so much on the actual mechanisms of democratic decision-making as on the ways in which citizens interact within broader democratic cultures. And here too, the distinctions drawn are better understood as an axis along which different systems vary rather than as sharply defined categories. Nevertheless, the differences between pluralist and deliberative approaches to democracy have important implications for freedom of expression.

Let us begin with pluralism. The pluralist vision of democracy is most associated with the US political scientist Robert Dahl[74] (though it can be traced back to James Madison's 1787 discussion of factions in Federalist No 10). It envisions the democratic process as a series of contests between distinct interest groups seeking to control state power and obtain benefits from the state. Policy is advanced, and stability is achieved, through a process by which government officials mediate between interest groups to form working majorities. Individuals themselves influence policy through their membership in interest groups, but because no particular interest group is ever likely to represent a majority, compromise and co-operation lie at the heart of the pluralist vision of democratic politics.

Pluralism is a form of democracy because it is in part through democratic mechanisms such as elections and political parties that interest groups seek to influence government officials—though pluralist theory tends to emphasize informal means of obtaining responsiveness and accountability at least as much as formal democratic processes. Furthermore, precisely because individual citizens' interests are defended and advanced

---

[73] US Const amend I.
[74] Robert A Dahl, *A Preface to Democratic Theory* (U Chicago P 1956); Robert A Dahl, *Who Governs? Democracy and Power in an American City* (Yale UP 1961); Robert A Dahl, *Democracy and Its Critics* (Yale UP 1989).

by organized interest groups, pluralism permits a democracy to consist of many inactive or disengaged citizens who nonetheless may be said to indirectly participate in the polity.

Finally, and perhaps most importantly, pluralism presumes that pre-existing private preferences are in place, and the job of democratic politics is to combine those disparate preferences into a coherent policy. In this sense, pluralism envisions citizens as actors in, but not as the subjects of, democratic politics. Citizens have desires, express those desires through interest groups, and seek to obtain policies from the state which advance those preferences.

The primary modern alternative to the pluralist model of democracy is deliberative democracy, the leading modern theorist of which is the German philosopher and sociologist Jürgen Habermas.[75] Other leading proponents of deliberative democracy include the US legal scholar Cass Sunstein,[76] and the political scientist James Fishkin.[77] The crucial differences between deliberative and pluralist democracies lie in how citizens are seen to interact with one another and with the democratic system. First, and perhaps foremost, deliberative democracy does not take citizens' interests and preferences as given. Instead, citizens engage in dialogue and discourse with one another in order to shape and influence one another's preferences. As Sunstein puts it, the purpose of a system of deliberative democracy 'is to ensure discussion and debate among people who are genuinely different in their perspectives and position, in the interests of creating a process through which reflection will encourage the emergence of general truths'.[78] Just as citizens participate in and shape the deliberative process, so too they are shaped by that process.

The corollary of deliberative democracy's rejection of pre-existing preferences is its further rejection of pluralism's vision of the democratic process as simply combining or accommodating conflicting preferences. To the contrary, deliberative theories of democracy see political participation as a positive right and duty. And more significantly, through that process of participation citizens 'become aware of their dependence on one another' and develop 'the orientation to the common good'.[79] For this reason, deliberative democracy requires citizens to give reasons for their positions rather than simply express them as bald preferences. Public reasoning lies at the heart of deliberative democracy. Finally, it is highly significant that the deliberative discourse envisioned by deliberative democracy does not occur within the auspices of, or even in the shadow of, the state and public officials. It is rather a process for citizens, by which citizens construct the public will. Of course, in representative systems deliberation is not limited to citizens but must also occur among representatives to the legislative body; but nonetheless

---

[75] Habermas (n 68) 1. Habermas uses the terms 'liberal' and 'republican' democracy respectively instead of 'pluralist' and 'deliberative'.
[76] Cass R Sunstein, *Democracy and the Problem of Free Speech* (Free P 1995) ch 8.
[77] James S Fishkin, *Democracy and Deliberation: New Directions for Democratic Reform* (Yale UP 1991).
[78] Sunstein (n 76) 241.
[79] Habermas (n 68) 1.

citizens committed to the greater good are the core participants in deliberative democracies.

The differences between pluralist and deliberative approaches to democracy have important implications for freedom of expression. Both of course require some significant protections for free expression if they are to function. Pluralism, for example, cannot operate unless strong protection is provided to freedom of association, so that interest groups, the primary actors in pluralist democracies, can organize themselves. Pluralism also requires strong protection for expressive activities through which citizens and interest groups effectively advocate their preferences to government officials. Indeed, given the centrality of interest groups to pluralism, it would appear that pluralism requires the strongest level of protection be given to the speech of such groups, even over the speech of individuals.[80]

There are, however, limits to the sorts of protection of free expression that pluralism requires. Most importantly, because pluralism takes preferences as a given, it provides little support for protections for speech beyond the political sphere (such as literary or other cultural speech). And regarding associational rights, pluralism again suggests a relatively narrow right that protects associations that are involved in the process of interest-group politics, but not to other groups more focused on cultural or personal topics. Pluralism concerns itself with the organization of interest groups, and their ability to engage in a back-and-forth dialogue with each other and public officials, because these activities sit at the heart of pluralistic democracy. But beyond these processes, pluralism has little to say about free expression.

Deliberative democracy, on the other hand, necessarily requires protecting a far broader scope of freedom of expression and association. Deliberative democracy requires almost absolute protection for discourse among citizens, because that is the primary focus of such a system. And because democratic discourse is intended to shape preferences and values, not just aggregate them, the range of expression requiring protection is also far greater. It encompasses cultural, scientific, and other topics that are crucial to the formation of preferences and, ultimately, to the creation of the public will. Similarly, public discourse can occur in the broad public square, but also within the confines of a vast array of private associations touching on a vast array of subjects relevant to personal and political preferences, and to the character, of citizens.[81] Indeed, the interesting question is not whether deliberative democracy requires capacious protections for expressive activities and groups—it clearly does—it is whether within a system of deliberative democracy *any* restrictions on political, cultural, or scientific speech—beyond, of course, those necessary to prevent immediate and tangible social harm—are permissible. That question is explored further in the next section.

---

[80] For an argument to this effect, see Ashutosh Bhagwat, 'Associational Speech' (2011) 120 *Yale LJ* 978.
[81] Archon Fung, 'Associations and Democracy: Between Theories, Hopes, and Realities' (2003) 29 *Ann Rev Soc* 515, 524–6.

5.4.3 Substantive versus Proceduralist Democracy

Another axis along which democracies vary is the extent to which they emphasize specific substantive outcomes that they envision democratic processes must produce, as opposed to focusing mainly or only on democratic procedures, remaining agnostic to the policy outcomes those procedures result in. This distinction is relevant to all forms of democracy but it becomes most salient in discussions of deliberative democracy. And finally, the degree to which a democracy concludes that specific substantive outcomes such as permitting private discrimination based on race, sex, or sexual orientation are incontestable will influence the scope of protections it accords to free expression.

As Habermas points out, even within the broad camp of deliberative democracy, sharp differences exist regarding whether democracy mandates specific substantive outcomes. Many if not most theorists of deliberative democracy assume that proper and effective deliberation will produce a 'communitarian' outcome in which citizens are committed to a broadly accepted public good and to 'a concrete, substantively integrated ethical community'.[82] Habermas, on the other hand, defends a more proceduralist vision of deliberative democracy that he labels 'discourse theory'. Discourse theory accepts the existence of unbridgeable differences among citizens, and so rejects the inevitability of the communitarian consensus envisioned by what Habermas labels republican democracy theory.[83] In this sense, discourse theory resembles pluralist or liberal democracy. But Habermas insists that discourse theory differs from pluralism in that it does not see politics as simply the aggregation and reconciling of private preferences. Instead, it emphasizes dialogue and deliberation across differences—though given differences, some compromise is inevitable.

How might an orientation towards substantive versus proceduralist accounts of deliberative democracy influence attitudes towards freedom of expression? At an abstract level, substantive versions of democracy take a primarily instrumental view of free expression (and for that matter, democracy itself), as means for achieving the 'correct' deliberative ends: the discovery of the public good and its manifestation as public opinion. But these accounts do not value speech, or even deliberation, for its own sake. For that reason, as Robert Post points out, substantive communitarian (what he calls 'collective') approaches to democracy tend to permit a greater managerial role for the state in guiding deliberation and speech towards appropriate ends.[84] Proceduralist accounts, however, value discourse and deliberation for their own sakes, as the essence of democracy and as the means for legitimization of the state.[85] As such, and because of the lack of prescribed outcomes for deliberation, proceduralists would allow a substantially

---

[82] Habermas (n 68) 4. See also Robert Post, 'Meiklejohn's Mistake: Individual Autonomy and the Reform of Public Discourse' (1993) 64 *U Colo L Rev* 1109 (distinguishing between 'collectivist' approaches to democratic deliberation and approaches which emphasize 'autonomy').

[83] Habermas (n 68) 5, 7–8.

[84] Post (n 82) 1119–24.   [85] Habermas (n 68) 8–9; Post (n 82) 1115–16.

broader range of ethical and moral issues to enter into the deliberative process, and so into the scope of protected expression.

As a practical matter, in recent years the distinction between substantive and proceduralist accounts of democracy tend to manifest themselves in debates over, on the one hand, multiculturalism, and on the other hand, expression, which can be considered discriminatory or derogatory—or as more commonly labelled, hate speech. Most substantive accounts of democracy assume that the political process—whether it be pluralistic or deliberative—will result in a polity and policies which demonstrate tolerance, mutual respect, and an embrace of diversity. Only so, after all, can a common will emerge. The clear implication of this presumption is that speech which undermines this process by treating particular groups—racial and religious minorities, women, LGBT (lesbian, gay, bisexual, and transgender) individuals, or members of other historically marginalized groups—as outsiders not deserving of mutual respect has no place in a democracy. Such speech in no way advances the goals of either democratic deliberation or even democratic bargaining (in a pluralistic model), and so is deserving of no protection. To the contrary, by silencing voices and excluding victims' voices from the democratic process, such speech actively undermines democracy and prevents the achievement of consensus.[86] As such, an argument can be made that in a strongly substantive vision of democracy the state not only need not tolerate, but to the contrary has a positive obligation to suppress hate speech.

From a proceduralist perspective, the story is more complicated. Certainly a similar story can be told, that hate speech tends to exclude victims from the deliberative process, and so is inconsistent with even a proceduralist account of deliberative democracy.[87] But the countervailing argument is that unlike substantive accounts, a proceduralist account of democracy cannot assume any particular outcome of the deliberative process, including a tolerant one. To permit the suppression of speech that some might consider hateful poses a problem then for two separate reasons. First, such suppression imposes what Habermas calls 'an *ethical constriction* of *political discourse*' without resolving where the ethical standard comes from.[88] Relatedly, as noted above in Section 5.3.2, like any viewpoint-based speech restriction on public discourse, suppression of hate speech prevents certain speakers from free and equal participation in the political process, and thus can have a detrimental effect on political legitimacy.

---

[86] For arguments for banning hate speech based upon such a silencing effect, see Alexander Brown, 'Hate Speech Laws, Legitimacy and Precaution: A Reply to James Weinstein' (2017) 32 *Const Comment* 599, 610–17; Katharine Gelber, 'Hate Speech: Definitions & Empirical Evidence' (2017) 32 *Const Comment* 619, 620–6; Adrienne Stone, 'Viewpoint Discrimination, Hate Speech Laws, and the Double-Sided Nature of Freedom of Speech' (2017) 32 *Const Comment* 687, 688–95. For an argument that there is a 'paucity of evidence' that hate speech in public discourse (as opposed to speech in other settings) has such an effect, see James Weinstein, 'Viewpoint Discrimination, Hate Speech, and Political Legitimacy' (2017) 32 *Const Comment* 757–9.

[87] Jeremy Waldron, 'The Conditions of Legitimacy: A Response to James Weinstein' (2017) 32 *Const Comment* 697, 713–14.

[88] Habermas (n 68) 4 (emphasis in original).

Second, a willingness to suppress hate speech presumes a consensus, an existing public will regarding the exact content of unprotected expression—that is, it requires an agreed upon definition of what constitutes hate speech. But in fact, such a consensus does not exist and in a proceduralist account cannot necessarily be expected to emerge. Examples of disagreements over the nature of speech to be excluded from discourse include speech broadly condemning of homosexual conduct from a religious perspective, or speech attacking racial preferences for minorities in employment or education. Some would consider either or both of these forms of expressions hateful, while others would not. Absent a strong substantive account of what democracy entails, it is difficult to see how a system that permits the suppression of hate speech would not run a significant risk of unduly circumscribing the deliberative process that is the life blood of democracy in a proceduralist account. Many proceduralists are likely to conclude that that is too high price to pay, despite the troubling possibility that hate speech itself may interfere with meaningful deliberation.

5.4.4 Libertarian versus Militant Democracy

The final axis considered here along which democracies vary is the degree to which they tolerate speech and associations that are opposed to and threaten the very democratic structures that enable democratic self-governance. At one end of the spectrum are democracies, which we might label libertarian democracies, which provide very strong protections even for anti-democratic speech and associations until the point is reached where such speech or groups actually threaten imminent political violence. At the other end of this spectrum is a form of democracy that has been labelled militant democracy (or alternatively 'defensive democracy' or 'fighting democracy'). These are regimes which are willing to adopt restrictive and even illiberal measures, including notably restrictions on speech and association, which are deemed necessary to protect democracy itself not just from violent overthrow but also from non-violent subversion through originally democratic means (the exemplar of the latter being the rise to power of the Nazi Party in Germany in 1933 through the democratic process, which it then eliminated).[89] Since the very definitions of these forms of democracy turn on their willingness to restrict speech and association, this axis reveals radical disagreements among democratic nations about the relationship between speech, citizenship, and the state.

Libertarian democracies are characterized by a very high tolerance for speech and associations, such as fascist and communist speech and parties, which explicitly advocate and support the elimination or even the violent overthrow of democratic systems of government. The contemporary exemplar of such a democracy is the United States. Under US law, even speech which explicitly advocates the violent overthrow of democratic institutions or other forms of political violence may not be suppressed unless it

---

[89] Jan-Werner Müller, 'Militant Democracy' in Michael Rosenfeld and András Sajó (eds), *The Oxford Handbook of Comparative Constitutional Law* (OUP 2012).

can be proven that the speech 'is directed to inciting or producing *imminent* lawless action and is *likely* to incite or produce such action'.[90] In the same 1969 decision that announced this standard, the US Supreme Court indicated that the same level of protection was due to organizations and assemblies that advocated violent overthrow of democratic government.[91] Under this approach, which remains the law today, it is almost impossible to suppress speech or associations based on the mere advocacy or possibility of political violence. Instead, extremely likely, imminent violence is required—a standard almost impossible to satisfy if no actual violence occurs. And if such violence does occur, the need to prosecute *speech* is limited. The cost of tolerating speech advocating political violence is, of course, that it creates the risk of serious violence occurring.

At the other side of the axis, modern Germany is generally considered a strong example, among Western democracies at least, of militant democracy. The term 'militant democracy' was first articulated by the exiled German political scientist Karl Loewenstein in 1937, in response to the Nazi Party's overthrow of the German Weimar Republic.[92] The principle was adopted after World War II by the (then West) German Constitutional Court as an essential element of German democracy, and elements of militant democracy have also been incorporated into the constitutions of other European democracies, notably France and Spain.[93] And the embrace of militant democracy in these countries has not been merely rhetorical; it has led to extensive suppression of violent political parties and organizations by Germany and Spain.[94] Militant democracy, then, inevitably threatens to sacrifice potentially harmless expression in the name of social stability, just as libertarian democracy risks the converse.

5.5 CONCLUSION

This chapter has examined the relationship between free expression and democracy. Free expression, it has been shown, is an essential element of any system of democratic government, both because without free expression popular sovereignty would not be possible, and because restrictions on free expression undermine formal political equality among citizens. The chapter also examined two distinct functions that free expression plays in a democratic system of government: the informing function, which seeks to ensure that citizens have access to the information necessary to exercise their sovereign powers in an educated manner; and the legitimating function, by which citizens attribute legitimacy both to the system of government, and to specific laws, because they were able to participate in democratic discourse. Finally, the chapter surveyed various

---

[90] *Brandenburg v Ohio*, 395 US 444, 447 (1969) (emphasis added).   [91] Ibid 449, n 4.
[92] Karl Loewenstein, 'Militant Democracy and Fundamental Rights I' (1937) 31 *Am Pol Sci Rev* 417.
[93] Müller (n 89) 1254.
[94] Ibid 1258–60, 1263–4. See also Ian Cram, 'Constitutional Responses to Extremist Political Associations: *ETA, Batasuna* and Democratic Norms' (2008) 28 *Legal Stud* 68.

axes along which democracies vary among themselves, and explored the implications of those variations for protection of free expression.

It should be noted in closing, however, that while free expression is necessary for democracy, the actual protection of free expression required by democracy is limited. Certainly, democracy necessitates robust protection for discourse on political and policy matters, as well as on the actions and character of government officials. Furthermore, most forms of democracy also require protection for a broad range of cultural and scientific expression. But protection for many other forms of expression, such as commercial advertising and perhaps even music and abstract art, find little support in democratic theory. Justifications for protection of these forms of expression, if they are to be protected, must be found in theories of free speech other than democratic self-government.

CHAPTER 6

FREEDOM OF SPEECH AND HUMAN DIGNITY

DIETER GRIMM

6.1 SOME GENERAL REMARKS ON DIGNITY

FREEDOM of speech has been part of modern constitutionalism since its beginnings in the last quarter of the eighteenth century. Human dignity as a constitutional guarantee is new. It is a post–World War II element of constitutionalism. Apparently, it needed the atrocities of totalitarian systems like Hitler's Germany and Stalin's Soviet Union and the tremendous human costs of World War II to create the feeling that something more than a number of individual rights was necessary to protect the human being, a foundational norm on which the various rights could be grounded and from which they derived their meaning.

This need was satisfied by the concept of human dignity, first in the Universal Declaration of Human Rights (UDHR) of 1948, then in the post-war constitutions of the losers of World War II, most prominently in the German Basic Law of 1949, where dignity figures in article 1(1).[1] The provision reads: 'Human dignity shall be inviolable. To respect and to protect it shall be the duty of all state authority'. Meanwhile, reference to human dignity appears in almost all constitutions drafted in the last quarter of the twentieth century after nations had freed themselves from dictatorial, racist, and colonist regimes. Dignity marks the difference between older constitutions and those that reflect the totalitarian experience.

---

[1] *Basic Law for the Federal Republic of Germany*, 1949, art 1(1) ('German Basic Law'). For an account of some marginal forerunners, see Christopher McCrudden, 'Human Dignity and Judicial Interpretation of Human Rights' (2008) 19 *Eur J Int'l L* 655, 664.

But even in constitutional orders without a guarantee of dignity, it plays an important role as principle behind the enumerated rights and guidelines for their interpretation. Canada, a country without a totalitarian past, is an example. The Canadian Charter of Rights and Freedoms of 1982 does not feature dignity. However, the Canadian Supreme Court ruled in 1988 in *Morgentaler*: 'The idea of human dignity finds expression in almost every right and freedom guaranteed in the Charter'.[2] And again in 2000 in *Blencoe*: 'The Charter and the rights it guarantees are inextricably bound to concepts of human dignity'.[3]

The same is true for the first regional declaration of rights, the European Convention of Human Rights (ECHR).[4] Although enacted in 1950 in view of the totalitarian regimes and devastating wars in Europe, and citing the UDHR as a model, it does not contain a guarantee of human dignity. Dignity appears only in the preamble of Protocol 13 of 2002.[5] Nevertheless, the European Court of Human Rights (ECtHR) frequently refers to dignity. It is even regarded as 'the very essence of the Convention'.[6] Other regional human rights pacts mention dignity in the preamble; so too do the American, Arab, and African conventions or charters. In the Charter of the European Union it appears in Article 1, in a formulation evoking the German Basic Law.

The legal status of dignity varies from country to country. Aharon Barak distinguishes three forms of dignity: (1) dignity as a constitutional value, meaning that it is not part of the written constitution, but is recognized as a background assumption that guides the interpretation of enumerated rights; (2) dignity as a right; and (3) dignity as a framework right, also called a 'mother-right', which implies that there are 'daughter-rights'.[7] Occasionally, the framework right appears also as a principle from which more concrete rights may flow. This differs slightly from the usual distinction between right and principle, according to which a principle obliges government but does not entitle individuals (objective right), whereas a right entitles individuals (subjective right).

In some countries dignity is on the same level as other rights, whereas in others it enjoys a position on top of a hierarchy. In some countries, it is regarded as a relative right that can be limited in the interest of other rights or constitutional principles, in others it is regarded as an absolute right, which means that in a conflict with other rights or constitutionally-protected values, dignity always prevails. In some constitutions, such as the German Basic Law, human dignity is exempted from constitutional amendment because of its role in shaping the identity of the constitutional order. It cannot be abolished, although the wording may be changed as long as the essence is preserved.

The meaning of dignity is notoriously unclear,[8] more so than the meaning of traditional fundamental rights like freedom of speech, freedom of religion, freedom of

---

[2] *R v Morgentaler* [1988] 1 SCR 30.
[3] *Blencoe v British Columbia (Human Rights Commission)* [2000] 2 SCR 307.
[4] *Tyrer v United Kingdom* (1980) 2 EHRR 1.
[5] Convention for the Protection of Human Rights and Fundamental Freedoms (ECHR), Protocol 13.
[6] *Pretty v United Kingdom* (2002) 35 EHRR 1, [65].
[7] Aharon Barak, *Human Dignity* (CUP 2015) 103.
[8] See the extremely rich and thoughtful account by McCrudden (n 1) 697.

telecommunication, which are also regarded as more or less open-ended themselves. However, these rights refer to certain areas or institutions of social life, which exist independently of, but are shaped by, the law according to the principle of individual freedom. As point of reference, these areas or institutions delimit the scope of the right and facilitate the determination of the meaning of freedom in relation to the specific object of protection.

Dignity, to the contrary, has no such delimited scope and is not identical with freedom. Dignity is a quality attributed to every individual by law, which public authority has to respect wherever it enters into contact with individuals. But most constitutions lack any specification of what dignity means or what constitutes a violation of dignity. This explains the enhanced difficulty that dignity poses for constitutional interpretation, which, in turn, causes some authors to refrain from using dignity in legal reasoning. However, this does not help if dignity forms part of the text of the constitution, so that the judge cannot escape determining when it applies and what it means if it applies.

Various philosophical and theological theories claim to be at the bottom of dignity[9] and might therefore help to clarify its legal meaning. However, unless there is clear evidence that the constitution-makers adopted a certain concept, no direct path leads from an extra-legal theory to the legal term. With the incorporation into a legal text, the notion is disconnected from its extra-legal sources and gains an independent existence. This does not mean that the extra-legal concepts are without any informational value for legal interpretation. Constitutions and constitutional concepts are not made out of the blue. But in most cases it will be doubtful which concept was in the mind of whom, and in which of its perhaps many understandings.

To ascertain the meaning of dignity as a legal norm, it seems more promising to find out why the notion appeared at a certain historical moment and under certain historical conditions in the text of the constitution although, as a philosophical or religious notion, it had existed long before.[10] In particular, the post-totalitarian origin allows some general assumptions, at least in countries where dignity appears in reaction to a totalitarian experience. Here, dignity marks the negation of the way dictatorial systems treated their subjects.

Dignity is then regarded as a property of human beings. It is not about the dignity of Germans or Brazilians. It is the dignity of all human beings. They enjoy dignity in their capacity as part of mankind, independently of race, colour, and gender, and also independently of physical and mental status, and so on. And they enjoy it independently of their way of life. Dignity is not earned by leading a good life and not forfeited by leading a bad life. It prohibits denying a human being individual personhood, or distinguishing between classes that are more and others that are less worthy.

In order to give a more concrete meaning to dignity, some courts start from the atrocities committed in the past, which prompted the constitutional recognition of dignity,

---

[9] See, eg, various contributions in Christopher McCrudden (ed), *Understanding Human Dignity* (OUP 2013) 59, 207, 289.
[10] See Dieter Grimm, 'Dignity in a Legal Context' in Christopher McCrudden (ed), *Understanding Human Dignity* (OUP 2013) 381.

and from there draw analogies to other acts that are of a similar nature and should therefore be regarded as incompatible with dignity. However, not all countries that recognize dignity as a constitutional value or right have a totalitarian past, and those which share such a past have undergone different experiences. The extermination of Jewish people differs from race discrimination in the form of apartheid, and this differs from the exploitation of the working class.

Moreover, in all countries, regardless of their past, dignity encounters new challenges, often created by scientific and technological progress like in biomedicine.[11] But also a number of means employed in the fight against terrorism raise questions of dignity. Laws permitting shooting down a captured airplane in order to save the people in the target are examples.[12] Courts have to deal with these problems. Thus, dignity is concretized over time and layers of consensus about its meaning facilitate the application of the concept. However, there is a universal consensus that treatments like slavery and torture are incompatible with dignity.[13]

Nevertheless, it would be rash to assume a universally shared consensus about the meaning of dignity. The more abstractly the content of dignity is described, the greater is the consensus, while the consensus becomes thinner and thinner on the level of concretization, which is, of course, the level where cases are decided by courts, especially if conflicts between dignity and other constitutionally-protected values have to be solved. Christopher McCrudden tries to cope with this problem by distinguishing between the concept of dignity, which is universally accepted, and the conceptions of dignity that vary greatly according to historical experience, cultural heritage, and legal systems.[14]

6.2 The Relationship between Dignity and Free Speech

With this contingency in mind, we can now ask how dignity relates to freedom of speech as a fundamental right. Some authors assume that every fundamental right has a dignity core so that also freedom of speech might be regarded as a concretization of dignity. As a general assumption, this seems to be exaggerated. Think of the Brazilian Constitution

---

[11] See Marion Albers 'Biotechnology and Human Dignity' in Dieter Grimm, Alexandra Kemmerer, and Christoph Möllers (eds), *Human Dignity in Context* (Hart 2018) 509; Tatjana Hörnle, 'How to Define Human Dignity, and the Resulting Implications for Biotechnology Dignity' in Dieter Grimm, Alexandra Kemmerer, and Christoph Möllers (eds), *Human Dignity in Context* (Hart 2018) 561.

[12] See the decision of the German Constitutional Court on the constitutionality of the Aviation Security Law: *Aviation Security Law Case* [2006] 115 BVerfGE 118.

[13] Convention Against Torture and Other Cruel, Inhuman or Degrading Treatment or Punishment (adopted 10 December 1984, entered into force 26 June 1987) 1465 UNTS 85; UDHR (adopted 10 December 1948) UNGA Res 217 A(III), art 4; International Covenant on Civil and Political Rights (adopted 16 December 1966, entered into force 23 March 1976) 999 UNTS 171 (ICCPR), art 8.

[14] McCrudden (n 1) 679, 712.

with its more than one hundred fundamental rights. It is very unlikely that each of them could have been derived from human dignity. But for a number of fundamental rights, most of the classical rights among them, this is true. Barak's idea of daughter-rights helps to clarify this. For him, rights are partly 'freestanding', partly a derivation of the mother-right dignity.[15]

Freedom of speech is among those rights that can be traced back to dignity, as explicitly observed by the South African Constitutional Court.[16] It seems difficult to imagine human dignity without a person's right to express ideas, beliefs, or interests, and to receive the expression of others and thus form opinions. The human being is a social being, and all social relations are based on communication. Speech is not the only form of communication, but the most important one. This does not mean, however, that freedom of speech is connected to dignity in all its ramifications. Justice Stevens's dissent in *Citizens United* is an example of this. He related individual speech to dignity, whereas he called corporate speech 'derivative speech' whose restriction would impinge no one's dignity in the least.[17]

On the other hand, some limitations of the scope of free speech become problematic if freedom of speech is related to dignity. One such limitation often flows from the assumption that the right to free speech finds its justification in democracy, an opinion widely held in the United States.[18] As a consequence, only political speech enjoys constitutional protection. But even if political speech is understood broadly, it remains an instrumentalization of freedom of speech in the interest of a supra-individual purpose and thus negates the dignity aspect of speech, which can but refer to the individual. The dignity aspect of speech finds its justification also and even foremost in the intrinsic worth and autonomy of the individual. It is not per se limited to democratic constitutions.[19]

This is not to deny the close relationship between freedom of speech and democracy. There is no democracy without freedom of speech and freedom of information. Rather, freedom of speech and information is constitutive for democracy, but freedom of speech does not derive its recognition as a fundamental right from democracy. We do not have freedom of speech for democracy's sake, but we have democracy because it is the form of political rule best compatible with the dignity and autonomy of the individual. As a consequence, freedom of speech cannot be limited to political speech.

Having been constitutionally recognized later than freedom of speech, dignity is often perceived as a justification of restrictions of free speech. But this would be one-sided. Since dignity in its capacity as a constitutional principle or a right emerged in order to serve as a foundation or unifying element of the various traditional fundamental rights,

---

[15] Barak (n 7) 156.

[16] *Khumalo v Holomisa* [2002] ZACC 12. See also Ronald Dworkin, *Taking Rights Seriously* (Harvard UP 1978) 266–78, 364–8; Jeremy Waldron, *The Harm in Hate Speech* (Harvard UP 2012) 139.

[17] *Citizens United v FEC*, 558 US 310 (2010).

[18] Beginning with Alexander Meiklejohn, *Free Speech and Its Relation to Self-Government* (Lawbook Exchange 1948).

[19] Regarding justifications of freedom of speech, see Eric Barendt, *Freedom of Speech* (2nd edn, OUP 2005) 6.

it is not only negatively but also positively connected with rights.[20] It is sword and shield, as Daly says. By 'sword' she means 'insisting on the right to express oneself freely and the right to information to make such expression meaningful'.[21] 'Shield', in turn, is explained as 'protecting against defamatory and other harmful speech'.[22] McCrudden calls dignity a 'metric common' to both sides of the conflict.[23]

In its positive relation, dignity re-enforces freedom of speech. Re-enforcement may occur in a double capacity. In jurisdictions with a constitutional guarantee of free speech, dignity may function as an additional safeguard against limitations of speech, which would affect the dignity core of free speech, but has not found recognition in the text of the constitution. In countries without a guarantee of free speech, dignity may generate a minimum guarantee of free speech. This is the case, for instance, in Israel, where the rudimentary constitution contains a guarantee of dignity, but not of free speech. The Israeli Supreme Court found freedom of speech to a certain extent inherent in dignity.[24]

On the other hand, it may also occur that dignity limits freedom of speech. As speech has the ability to harm other rights or constitutionally guaranteed values, it cannot be excluded that occasionally the harm will amount to an encroachment on a person's dignity. This would, for instance, be the case if speech humiliates or demeans persons, classifies them as inferior because of race, colour, gender, religious belief, and so on.[25] If in cases like these the law contains no limits to the right to free speech, limitations may be derived either directly or mediated through legislation that is constitutionally mandated from the principle of dignity.

The twofold dimension of dignity vis-à-vis freedom of speech can even be observed in the United States, where the role of dignity in constitutional jurisprudence is less salient than in countries with more recent constitutions and where First Amendment rights enjoy a privileged status.[26] In *Cohen v California*, where the Supreme Court upheld Cohen's right to wear a jacket with the inscription 'Fuck the Draft', Justice Harlan expressed 'the belief that no other approach would comport with the premise of individual dignity and choice upon which our political system rests'. On the other hand, the Court has ruled that defamation laws are 'directed to the worthy objective of ensuring the "essential dignity and worth of every human being"'.[27]

Whenever legislation protecting dignity exists, there is no longer a need to resort to dignity directly. The more precise norm applies (*lex specialis derogate legi generali*).

---

[20] Ibid 15, 31; Dworkin (n 16); McCrudden (n 1) 702.
[21] Erin Daly, *Dignity Rights* (U Penn P 2013) 95.   [22] Ibid.   [23] McCrudden (n 1) 719.
[24] HCJ 10203/03 *HaMifkad HaLeumi v Attorney General* (2008) IsrLR 402; CA 105/92 *Re'em Ltd v The Municipality of Nazerath-Illit* (2003) IsrSC 47(5) 189; LCrimA 8295/02 *Biton v Sultan* (2005) IsrSC 59(6) 554.
[25] But see the decision of the Australian High Court in *Clubb v Edwards* (2019) 93 ALJR 448, where dignity is invoked for a much lesser purpose, namely to protect persons against political messages that third persons 'force upon' them.
[26] See Gerald L Neuman, 'Human Dignity in United States Constitutional Law' in Dieter Simon and Manfred Weiss (eds), *Zur Autonomie des Individuums* (Liber Amicorum Spiros Simitis 2000) 249.
[27] *Cohen v California*, 403 US 15 (1971).

Dignity remains in the background and gains an immediate role only if legislation should prove to be insufficient to protect dignity, for example if new threats to dignity arise. This might be the case for violations of dignity on the Internet, for which legal rules are frequently lacking. In any case, dignity continues to exercise its indirect influence as a guideline for interpretation of ordinary law. As a matter of fact, it is more frequently used in this mode than as a directly applicable criterion.

This means that dignity will usually come in a subsidiary or complementary role. It can play this role in two ways. On the one hand, it may intervene if speech is not at all or not sufficiently protected in a given constitution, but dignity is like in Israel. On the other hand, it can come in when the possibility to protect persons against certain exercises of free speech is lacking or insufficient in positive law. In these cases, dignity serves as a remedy of last resort to either permit or forbid speech, depending on where such a serious lack of positive recognition exists that it affects dignity.

What happens if dignity enters into conflict with freedom of speech? The answer depends on the recognition or rejection of a hierarchy among the two rights. Three constellations are imaginable: dignity enjoys a hierarchical status; freedom of speech enjoys a hierarchical status; or both rights rank on the same level. If a hierarchy among the rights is recognized, the answer depends on whether one of the rights is considered as absolute. This is true for dignity in the German legal system, whereas in the US legal system freedom of speech is seen in a preferred yet not absolute position.

Germany's understanding of dignity as absolute right is based on the language of Article 1 of the German Basic Law.[28] According to the provision, human dignity is *'unantastbar'*, literally 'untouchable' but usually translated as 'inviolable', the German synonym being *'unverletzlich'*. *'Unantastbar'* is used only in connection with dignity, whereas *'unverletzlich'* is used several times in connection with other fundamental rights. This difference is levelled by translating both words as 'inviolable'. German jurisprudence assumes that the choice of different terms indicates that there must be a difference in substance and concludes that *'unantastbar'* has to be understood as absolute.

'Absolute' means, first, that no limitation of dignity is permitted. Every legal act, be it legislative or other, which undertakes to limit or infringe dignity is unconstitutional. It also means that dignity is not submitted to balancing, because balancing would imply the possibility that dignity has to cede. If dignity enters into a conflict with another fundamental right, dignity always prevails. Freedom of speech is no exception. It is but relatively protected. A right that is subject to balancing cannot maintain its absolute status.

However, the absolute character of dignity can be upheld only if the scope of dignity is construed narrowly. If construed broadly, the absolute character would bring about untenable results. Only gross and outrageous attacks on the personhood of human beings fall within the scope of dignity, while other offences are left to the many fundamental rights ranking below dignity. Also, it means that dignity does not protect behaviour and action, as every action can harm other rights or values. Dignity protects the

---

[28] See Grimm (n 10).

individual only against being treated by others in a way incompatible with the guarantee.

Finally, the two-tier approach that has become usual in handling fundamental rights cases does not apply. According to this approach, it is necessary to distinguish between infringement and violation of a fundamental right. As rights may be limited by law or pursuant to law, not every infringement constitutes a violation. The first question to be asked is therefore whether a certain state act constitutes an infringement, that is, affects the right negatively. The second question is whether the infringement is justified or prohibited by the constitution. If dignity is regarded as absolute right, this distinction is of no use. Every infringement is a violation.

In the United States, where dignity is absent in the Bill of Rights, the status of free speech as a preferred right leads to a presumption that, in a conflict between freedom of speech and other constitutionally-protected rights or interests, freedom of speech prevails. But this presumption can be refuted. It is strong if the core of freedom of speech is affected, namely political speech. It is less strong if a limitation concerns but the periphery of the right, for example commercial speech. In legal systems without any hierarchy, no such assumption exists.

In both cases, conflicts between freedom of speech and dignity have to be resolved by some sort of balancing, provided that dignity is not regarded as absolute right.[29] The United States try to handle this problem by distinguishing different degrees of scrutiny. If strict scrutiny applies, the right that has been limited by law has a good chance to prevail. Since freedom of speech is regarded as a preferred right, strict scrutiny usually applies in conflicts with other rights, at least if the core of free speech is affected, that is, in cases of political speech, democracy being considered the justification or at least an important justification for the constitutional recognition of freedom of speech.

In most other parts of the world, conflicts between fundamental rights are handled according to the principle of proportionality. The principle operates in a four-step analysis. Step 1 requires a legitimate purpose for every law restricting a fundamental right. In step 2, the question asked is whether the law that limits a right is at all capable of reaching its purpose; in step 3 whether the purpose could be reached as effectively by applying a less restrictive means. Step 4 is the balancing step. Questions to be asked are, on the side of the right that is limited by law, whether the core or the periphery is affected and how intense the effect is; on the side of the law, how important the purpose that the law pursues is and what the law contributes to promote the purpose. If this has been accurately ascertained the balancing takes place.

---

[29] See Nils Teifke, 'Balancing Human Dignity: Human Dignity as Principle and as a Constitutional Right' in Dieter Grimm, Alexandra Kemmerer, and Christoph Möllers (eds), *Human Dignity in Context* (Hart 2018) 225.

6.3 SOME REFLECTIONS ON HARD CASES

The hardest cases of conflict between freedom of speech and dignity are probably hate speech and pornographic expression.[30] Hate speech is defined in Article 20(2) of the International Covenant on Civil and Political Rights (ICCPR) as 'any advocacy of national, racial, or religious hatred that constitutes incitement to discrimination, hostility, or violence'. However understood, hate speech leaves us with the problem of distinguishing it from criticism of certain national or ethnic groups, races, believers, and so on, and from disapproval of beliefs, attitudes, practices of such groups. Is dignity helpful in drawing the line between criticism and hatred?

The problem is, of course, the various connotations of dignity in different jurisdictions. However, if one refers to the anti-totalitarian origins of dignity as a constitutional principle or right, one may perhaps say that all attempts to deny human beings individual personhood, to strip them from all rights (or from the right to have rights), to classify certain individuals as such or because of their group membership as life not being worth lived, to claim that by their behaviour they have forfeited any claim to respect, constitute violations of dignity and as such furnish grounds to prohibit speech, even independently of whether they create an imminent danger to the persons affected.

There are, of course, thicker notions of dignity that comprise social norms of civility of certain communities, but such norms may be derived as well from more specific rights like guarantees of personal honour, reputation, or privacy. The differences in recognition of such values as limits to free speech between the United States and Europe are well known. Robert Post attributes them to different degrees of heterogeneity of the US and the European societies and to a different trust in public discourse to tolerate even sharpest disputes, so that for the United States, only an imminent danger of violence would justify a limitation of speech, whereas in Europe a much smaller degree of causality is required.[31]

Treatment can happen by physical acts, but it can also happen by speech acts. If others persistently speak about persons or groups in a way that violates norms which protect their dignity, the victims find themselves not only demeaned but threatened. They cannot exclude that speech will create a climate in which action becomes likely. Holocaust denial may serve as an example. Germany (and other states as well) made it a crime and the German Constitutional Court held, in a widely discussed ruling, that this was compatible with freedom of speech.[32]

---

[30] See Ivan Hare and James Weinstein (eds), *Extreme Speech and Democracy* (OUP 2009); Barendt (n 19) 352.
[31] See Robert Post, 'Hate Speech' in Ivan Hare and James Weinstein (eds), *Extreme Speech and Democracy* (OUP 2009) 123.
[32] *Holocaust Denial Case* [1994] 90 BVerfGE 241; Dieter Grimm, 'The Holocaust Denial Decision of the Federal Constitutional Court of Germany' in Ivan Hare and James Weinstein (eds), *Extreme Speech and Democracy* (OUP 2009) 557.

In the reasoning of the Court, dignity played a role. The Court found that, in the light of the persecution and extermination of Jews in Germany during the Nazi rule, Holocaust denial poses a threat to the Jews who are living in Germany today. The historical experience of the Holocaust has become part of their identity. Its denial is an attack on their specific claim to recognition and to their dignity. This recognition is a guarantee against a repetition of the historical discrimination. If it were legal to deny the Holocaust, the Jewish inhabitants of Germany might have reason to believe that their right to recognition and dignity is no longer safe.

This reasoning shows that decisive for the outcome was not the assumption that the Holocaust had been 'the evil as such', as David Fraser assumes,[33] but a concrete evaluation of what Holocaust denial still means in Germany more than seventy years after the events. It is the German responsibility for these events that explains the ruling of the Court. It is a German justification of the criminalization that cannot be generalized. Nowhere do the reasons for including dignity in the Basic Law and giving it a particular strong position appear more clearly than in this case.

However, the criminalization of Holocaust denial is not limited to Germany or countries whose government or parts of the population collaborated with the Nazi occupiers. It is therefore remarkable that the ECtHR had no objection against punishing the Holocaust denial also in European countries other than Germany. Although this Court routinely emphasizes the importance of freedom of speech, it found that any justification of a pro-Nazi policy is not covered by Article 10 of the Convention. It regarded Holocaust denial as a misuse of Convention rights in the sense of Article 17.[34]

But also the Supreme Court of Canada, a country totally unaffected by the Nazi atrocities, held in *Keegstra* that Holocaust denial created harm so serious that a prohibition was justified.[35] Chief Justice Dickson saw two sorts of injury caused by hate speech like Holocaust denial: harm to the members of the targeted group and harm for society at large. Regarding the first harm, dignity played a role. The Chief Justice wrote: 'A person's sense of human dignity and belonging to the community at large is closely linked to the concern and respect accorded to the group to which he or she belongs . . . The derision, hostility and abuse encouraged by hate propaganda therefore have a severely negative impact on the individual's sense of self-worth and acceptance'.[36]

Justice McLachlin in her dissent agreed that the legislative goal of protecting individual dignity is of a substantive nature and that dignity is adversely affected by the propagation of hateful sentiment. 'The evil of hate propaganda is beyond doubt. It inflicts pain and indignity upon individual members of the group in question'.[37] However, in comparing the harm caused to dignity with the loss for freedom of speech, she could not see how the criminalization would foster this value: 'It is far from clear that the legislature

---

[33] David Fraser, '"On the Internet, Nobody Knows You're a Nazi"': Some Comparative Legal Aspects of Holocaust Denial on the WWW' in Ivan Hare and James Weinstein (eds), *Extreme Speech and Democracy* (OUP 2009) 511.
[34] *Garaudy v France* App no 65831/01 (ECHR, 24 June 2003).
[35] *R v Keegstra* [1990] 3 SCR 697.   [36] Ibid 746.   [37] Ibid 812.

does not promote the case of hate-mongering extremists more than it discourages the spread of hate propaganda'.[38] Framed like this, the arguments remind more of step 2 than of step 4 of the proportionality test.

While hate speech is speech, pornography is not necessarily speech. A number of jurisdictions distinguish between speech and conduct. This excludes some phenomena from the protection of free speech, but certainly not all.[39] It may exclude the sexual activities themselves, but not their presentation in 'words, writings and pictures'.[40] Even a narrow definition of speech leaves enough candidates for protection. Some constitutions distinguish between freedom of speech and of art. But this does not eliminate the problem, it only shifts part of it to another provision of the constitution.[41]

Thus, the unavoidable question is in what way pornography could specifically violate human dignity (and not other rights like physical integrity, honour, privacy). The answer is not as easy as in the case of hate speech. Different from pornography, hate speech has a clear target whose dignity might be affected: the person or group against which it instigates hatred. Who is the target of pornography and which harm does it inflict on persons or society at large if it were not prohibited? The Canadian Supreme Court struggled with this question when it had to review the punishment of a dealer of hard-core pornography, prohibited by the obscenity provision of section 163 of the *Criminal Code*.[42]

The Court saw itself confronted with 'one of the most difficult and controversial of contemporary issues, that of determining whether, and to what extent, Parliament may legitimately criminalize obscenity'.[43] As a restriction of free speech, section 163 was justifiable only if it had a legitimate purpose and met the requirements of the proportionality test. The Court refused to recognize 'the morals or the fabric of society' as a legitimate purpose. Instead, it drew an analogy to its decision in *Keegstra*[44] and regarded obscenity, which 'degrades and dehumanizes', as analogous to hate propaganda: obscene materials 'run against the principles of equality and dignity of all human beings'.[45]

According to the Court, the harm that consisted in treatment 'degrading and dehumanizing' would be caused directly or indirectly to 'individuals, groups such as women and children, and consequently to society as a whole'.[46] As far as dignity is the criterion against which section 163 had to be measured, 'women and children' may be affected. As persons, they are bearers of dignity, whereas 'society as a whole' is not a bearer of dignity. There may be other legitimate purposes that would justify a criminalization of obscenity in the interest of society as a whole, but not dignity.

The clearest case insofar as target and harm are concerned seems to be the abuse of children and its presentation in pictures. The act that is depicted will be criminalized in almost all jurisdictions. The ban on dissemination of pictures portraying the criminal act can rather easily be justified because the profit from selling the pictures is an important incentive for abuse. Usually, there will be no need to justify the ban on such pictures

---

[38] Ibid 864. [39] See Barendt (n 19) 78.
[40] See the definition of the scope in German Basic Law, art 5.
[41] See Caroline West, 'Pornography', Chapter 6 in this volume. [42] *R v Butler* [1992] 1 SCR 452.
[43] Ibid 460. [44] Ibid 498; see also n 36. [45] Ibid 479. [46] Ibid 509.

by resorting to dignity. Dignity might come in only if a prohibition is lacking so that the duty to protect dignity might apply if such a duty is recognized by the laws of a country.[47] The same is true for women if they were forced to endure the sexual acts or did not know that the activity was recorded and the pictures were sold.

But what about images of sexual behaviour among adults, which degrades and dehumanizes the woman but did not happen against her will? This raises the question as to whether dignity may be waived. It is, of course, not limited to problems of pornography. There is little doubt that the bearers of rights can waive their rights. Rights protect freedom, and freedom implies the right not to use one's rights. This applies also to speech. One may agree not to tell something or not to publish certain pictures. But what about dignity? Does the consent of the woman to a certain degrading or dehumanizing treatment exclude a violation of her dignity (*voluntas non fit iniuria*)?

If dignity is a right like all other rights, one would probably conclude that it can be waived. However, if dignity is regarded as a particularly precious or even absolute right, a violation of which is an attack not only on the target but on mankind, a waiver may seem inadmissible. Regarding peep shows, the German administrative courts drew this consequence from the absolute character of dignity, and the French Conseil d'État adopted the same attitude in the famous dwarf-throwing case and found the support of the European Human Rights Commission, which dismissed the complaint of the dwarf.[48]

---

[47] For the duty to protect, see Dieter Grimm, 'The Protective Function of the State' in Georg Nolte (ed), *European and US Constitutionalism* (CUP 2005) 137.
[48] See *Decisions of the Bundesverwaltungsgericht* (Vol 64) 274; Conseil d'État, requ. Nos. 136–720 and 173–578 (1985); *Wackenheim v France* App no 29961/96 (Commission Decision, 16 October 1996).

CHAPTER 7

ECONOMIC PERSPECTIVES ON FREE SPEECH

DANIEL HEMEL

The metaphor of a 'marketplace of ideas' has long pervaded discussions of free speech in and beyond the United States.[1] For early scholars of law and economics (L&E), the similarities and differences between the metaphorical marketplace for ideas and literal markets for goods and services were subjects of much attention. Aaron Director—the University of Chicago law professor who helped to found the L&E movement but rarely reduced his own ideas to writing—devoted one of his few published papers to the contrast between the laissez-faire approach to speech and command-and-control regulation of other markets in the mid-twentieth-century United States.[2] Ronald Coase, Director's colleague at Chicago, and ultimately a Nobel laureate, took up the topic of free speech several times over the course of his long career[3] and—like Director—questioned the justifications for differential regulatory treatment of the 'market for goods' and the 'market for ideas'. Richard Posner, the intellectual successor to Coase and Director, grappled with the subject in the first edition of his field-defining 1973 book *Economic Analysis of Law* and in subsequent editions,[4] as well as in later lectures, articles, and monographs.[5]

---

[1] Stanley Ingber, 'The Marketplace of Ideas: A Legitimizing Myth' [1984] *Duke LJ* 1.
[2] Aaron Director, 'The Parity of the Economic Market Place' (1964) 7 *JL & Econ* 1.
[3] RH Coase, 'The Federal Communications Commission' (1959) 2 *JL & Econ* 1; RH Coase, 'The Market for Goods and the Market for Ideas' (1974) 64 *Am Econ R* 384; RH Coase, 'Advertising and Free Speech' (1977) 6 *J Legal Stud* 1.
[4] Richard A Posner, *Economic Analysis of Law* (1st edn, Little, Brown 1973); Richard A Posner, *Economic Analysis of Law* (9th edn, Wolters Kluwer 2014).
[5] Richard A Posner, 'Free Speech in an Economic Perspective' (1986) 20 *Suffolk U L Rev* 1; Richard A Posner, 'Richard T Ely Lecture: The Law and Economics Movement' (1987) 77 *Am Econ Rev* 1; Richard A Posner, *Frontiers of Legal Theory* (Harvard UP 2004) 62–94.

More recently, however, while the L&E movement has flourished, economic analysis of free speech has lagged. Although L&E has branched out from its traditional emphasis on private law to topics such as criminal law, judicial behaviour, and agency structure, free speech has faded from its focus. Free-speech-related papers are a rare sight at the largest L&E conferences[6] and in the pages of the most prestigious L&E journals, and the empirical turn in L&E scholarship has largely overlooked free speech as a subject.

The leanness of the L&E literature on free speech should not be understood to imply that economics has little to say on the topic. Perhaps most significantly, the 'new information economics',[7] for which George Akerlof, Michael Spence, and Joseph Stiglitz won the Nobel prize in 2001, carries profound implications for free speech—implications noted by a handful of legal scholars[8] but not exhaustively explored. The new information economics challenges the faith in free markets reflected in the writings and thinking of early L&E scholars, and—though less directly—the faith in a free marketplace of ideas reflected in much of US First Amendment jurisprudence. It suggests that under certain circumstances, the regulation of speech not only can protect individuals and societies from speech-related harms but also can promote speech itself.

This chapter provides an introduction to the economic analysis of free speech,[9] with special attention to the new information economics perspective. Section 7.1 critically summarizes the small L&E literature on free speech. Section 7.2 offers an overview of the new information economics. Section 7.3 applies insights from the new information economics to free speech subjects.

---

[6] The 2019 annual meeting of the American Law and Economics Association, for example, featured 186 papers on a wide range of subjects ranging from corporate law (21 papers) to contract law, criminal law, and tax law (12 each), but only one paper on a free speech topic (by the author of this chapter).

[7] Joseph E Stiglitz, 'Information and Economic Analysis: A Perspective' (1985) 95 *Econ J* 21, 34.

[8] See Albert Breton and Ronald Wintrobe, 'Freedom of Speech vs. Efficient Regulation in Markets for Ideas' (1992) 17 *J Econ Behav & Org* 217; Jean-Michel G Josselin and Alain Marciano, 'Freedom of Speech in a Constitutional Political Economy Perspective' (2002) 29 *J of Econ Stud* 324; Cass R Sunstein, 'Informing America: Risk, Disclosure, and the First Amendment' (1992) 20 *Fla St U L Rev* 653; and Rebecca Tushnet, 'It Depends on What the Meaning of "False" Is: Falsity and Misleadingness in Commercial Speech Doctrine' (2007) 41 *Loy L Rev* 227.

[9] In a recent book, Judge Guido Calabresi—who introduced this author as a student to the L&E approach—develops a distinction between 'Economic Analysis of Law' and 'Law and Economics'. The former 'uses economic theory to analyze the legal world'; the latter 'begins with an agnostic acceptance of the world as it is' and 'then looks to whether economic theory can explain that world, that reality'. Guido Calabresi, *The Future of Law and Economics: Essays in Reform and Recollection* (Yale UP 2016) 2–3. In the economic analysis of law, as Henry Smith puts it, 'the methodological traffic is all one way—from economics to law'. Henry E Smith, 'Complexity and the Cathedral: Making Law and Economics More Calabresian' (2019) 48 *Eur J L & Econ* 44, 45. Calabresi's call for two-way methodological travel is well taken, and this chapter seeks to highlight ways in which economic analysis and free speech law can inform each other. The chapter does not, however, adhere to Calabresi's nomenclatural distinction between 'economic analysis of law' and 'law and economics', as many of the arguments and ideas considered here straddle the line that Calabresi draws.

7.1 THE ECONOMIC ANALYSIS OF FREE SPEECH: A CRITICAL REVIEW

7.1.1 The Early Years

Economic analysis of free speech arguably started with Adam Smith's *Wealth of Nations* in 1776,[10] but the modern L&E movement's engagement with the subject began in the wake of World War II, with Aaron Director's 'The Parity of the Economic Market Place'. That paper, presented at the University of Chicago Law School in 1953 and reprinted in the *Journal of Law & Economics* eleven years later, set the course for much of the L&E literature on free speech that would follow.

Director's approach to the subject of free speech starkly contrasts with the increasingly formal and empirical thrust of L&E scholarship today. 'Bearing in mind the danger of generalization without empirical investigation', Director writes, 'it may nevertheless be asserted with some confidence that among intellectuals there is an inverse correlation between the appreciation of the merits of civil liberty—including freedom of speech—and the merits of economic freedom'. Director continues: 'Lacking empirical data for this generalization, I must resort to intellectual pride as partial proof'. Director then seeks to explain the dichotomy between the intellectual class's attitude towards free speech—'the only area where laissez faire is still respectable'—and its embrace of government intervention into markets for goods and services.[11]

Director quickly sets aside one possible explanation: that the freedom of speech is enshrined in the First Amendment while immunity from economic regulation is nowhere codified in the US Constitution. The 'preference' for free speech over free markets, he says, 'goes beyond' such 'constitutional considerations'. Director then offers two additional explanations for the contrast. The first focuses on the self-regard of intellectuals. 'Everyone tends to magnify the importance of his own occupation and to minimize that of his neighbor', Director writes. Intellectuals, he hypothesizes, have elevated their own occupation (speech, broadly defined) over the trades and businesses plied by others (producing and selling goods and services). The second explanation, according to Director, is the 'undue importance attached to discussion as a method of solving problems'. In Director's view, ordinary people rely on economic arrangements to address the principal problems in their lives more than on politics. Market exchange thus merits at least the same status as political speech.[12]

A striking aspect of Director's essay is that there is almost nothing in it that the contemporary legal economist would recognize as economic analysis. There is no examination of supply and demand or of prices or incentives. It is an exercise in normative

---

[10] On the role of speech in Smith's *Wealth of Nations*, see Andreas Kalyvas and Ira Katznelson, 'The Rhetoric of the Market: Adam Smith on Recognition, Speech, and Exchange' (2001) 63 *Rev Pol* 549.
[11] Director (n 2) 5.   [12] Ibid 5–9.

political theory without even the appearance of social science. Nonetheless, Director makes an important intellectual move that guides later L&E analysis of free speech. By breaking down the distinction between the marketplace of ideas and markets for goods and services, Director nudges later L&E scholars towards applying the tools they use in the economic analysis of traditional markets to the study of speech.

Following Director's first foray, other important figures in the L&E movement took up the subject of free speech as well. The British-born Coase, who had written a monograph on the British broadcasting monopoly before moving to the United States, came to consider free-speech-related questions in his study of the US Federal Communications Commission (FCC) published in the *Journal of Law & Economics* in 1959. While that article is best known for Coase's proposal to allocate radio frequencies by auction, the article also includes an extensive discussion of the free-speech implications of the FCC's then-existing licensing regime. 'The situation in the American broadcasting industry is not essentially different in character from that which would be found if a commission appointed by the federal government had the task of selecting those who were to be allowed to publish newspapers and periodicals in each city, town, and village of the United States', Coase observes. 'A proposal to do this would, of course, be rejected out of hand as inconsistent with the doctrine of freedom of the press.'[13]

Unlike Director's 1953 paper, Coase's 1959 article is very much an economic analysis—though without many of the technical accoutrements that one might expect to find in much L&E scholarship today. The economic analysis and the free speech analysis are, however, split. The overall structure of Coase's argument is as follows: (1) A discretionary licensing regime is not necessary to allocate scarce spectrum resources among competing claimants; and (2) given that discretionary licensing is not necessary, the free-speech constraints imposed by the then-current regime are difficult to justify. The first step of that argument entails an economic analysis of the price mechanism as a solution to the problem of scarcity; the second step requires little engagement with economics at all. Coase's 1959 article thus illustrates the potential utility of applying economic analysis to free speech-related issues, but not the power of economic analysis of speech itself.

Coase returned to the subject of free speech in a 1973 address to the American Economics Association (AEA).[14] The address traversed much of the same terrain as Director's 1953 paper (crediting Director throughout). Coase concludes:

> We have to decide whether the government is as incompetent as is generally assumed in the market for ideas, in which case we would want to decrease government intervention in the market for goods, or whether it is as efficient as it is generally assumed to be in the market for goods, in which case we would want to increase government regulation in the market for ideas.[15]

---

[13] Coase, 'The Federal Communications Commission' (n 3) 7.
[14] Coase, 'The Market for Goods and the Market for Ideas' (n 3).   [15] Ibid 390.

Concerned that his remarks had been misinterpreted as an argument for greater regulation of speech, Coase elaborated on his AEA address in an article in the *Journal of Legal Studies* three years later.[16] While again questioning the notion that freedom of speech outranks freedom of economic exchange in the hierarchy of values, Coase emphasizes that his argument does not depend on relative rankings: '[E]ven if the market for ideas were more important, it does not follow that the two markets should be treated differently'. If we assume that government intervention in the market of ideas would be bad, and therefore that the market of ideas—because of its importance—ought to be shielded from intervention, 'why deny the same advantages to those whose welfare depends on the lesser market, the market for goods'? And if we think 'that the government is competent to regulate and is so motivated to do so properly, with the result that regulation enables the market to work better', then why not extend that benefit to the market for ideas as well? Coase does not hide his own view as to which of these two alternatives—greater government regulation of the marketplace of ideas or less government regulation of markets for goods and services—is preferable: '[T]hat regulation makes things worse or, at the best, makes very little difference, seems to be the usual finding of studies which have been made in areas ranging from agriculture to zoning, with many examples in between.'[17]

Coase's central insight—that parallel arguments apply to the regulation of economic markets and speech—resonates more than four decades later. His analysis, however, yields relatively few concrete implications for free speech jurisprudence. Coase believed that some 'balancing' of speakers' interests against the general welfare was 'inevitable'—and desirable. Near the end of his essay, he writes:

> [I]t is reasonable that First Amendment freedoms should be curtailed when they impair the enjoyment of life (privacy), inflict great damage on others (slander and libel), are disturbing (loudness), destroy incentives to carry out useful work (copyright), create dangers for society (sedition and national security), or are offensive and corrupting (obscenity).[18]

He does not, though, say much more on how judges should balance the conflicting interests of speakers and society in any of these areas.

7.1.2 Posner and the *Dennis* Formula

Just as Coase was returning to the subject of free speech in the 1970s, one of Coase's colleagues at the University of Chicago Law School, Richard Posner, was developing his own 'economic model' of free speech. Posner included a short chapter on free speech in the first edition of his influential volume *Economic Analysis of Law* in 1973 and expanded upon it in subsequent editions. Posner further fleshed out his model in a pair of lectures

---

[16] Coase, 'Advertising and Free Speech' (n 3). [17] Ibid 4–5. [18] Ibid 32.

in 1986—one at Brown University and one at Suffolk University—which formed the basis of an article in the latter institution's law review.[19] By that time, Posner was himself a federal judge on the US Court of Appeals for the Seventh Circuit.

In that article, Posner proposes to 'give the free-speech icon an acid bath of economics'.[20] From an opinion by his own judicial hero, Learned Hand, who served on the federal bench for more than a half-century, Posner derives the '*Dennis* formula' (so named for the case, *United States v Dennis*, in which Hand supposedly intimated its elements). As stated by Posner, the formula instructs courts to permit the regulation of speech if and only if:

$$V + E < P \times L(1 + i)^n,$$

where V is the value to society of suppressed information, E represents the 'legal-error costs incurred in trying to distinguish the information that society desires to suppress from valuable information', P is the probability of harm if the speech in question is not suppressed, and $L(1 + i)^n$ is the loss to society from allowing the harmful speech, discounted to present value at the prevailing interest rate i.[21] Posner then applies this formula to questions ranging from defamation to obscenity to copyright law's fair-use doctrine.

Posner's formula has spawned many pages of critical commentary, including an insightful 1988 note by then-law student (now law professor) Peter Hammer.[22] Hammer observes that Posner's algebraic formula amounts to a complicated statement of a straightforward proposition—'that a restriction on speech should be upheld if the benefits of suppressing the speech outweigh the costs'. In Hammer's view, this 'cost-benefit statement is true by definition' once 'one accepts . . . that speech is not an absolute value'. Put differently: 'It is little different from saying that the judge should always make the correct decision'.[23] Michael Rushton, writing nearly two decades later, makes a similar point. Posner's formula, Rushton remarks, simply states that judges should uphold speech restrictions if and only if the 'cost of suppressing expression' is less than 'the probable cost of allowing the expression'. In Rushton's view, '[t]he inequality offers nothing very controversial'.[24]

Upon further inspection, however, Posner's formula reveals itself to be much more than a tautology—and far from an uncontroversial statement. Posner, Hammer, and Rushton all assume that once one rejects the premise that free speech is an absolute right (ie, once one recognizes that there will be some cases in which the freedom of speech ought to be abridged), the obvious alternative is to uphold speech restrictions if, by the judge's own lights, the benefits of suppressing speech outweigh the costs. That is a plausible position, but it is not the only plausible position. A middle ground between free speech absolutism and the cost-benefit standard embodied in Posner's *Dennis* formula

---

[19] Posner, 'Free Speech in an Economic Perspective' (n 5).   [20] Ibid 7.   [21] Ibid 8.
[22] Peter J Hammer, 'Note: Free Speech and the "Acid Bath": An Evaluation and Critique of Judge Richard Posner's Economic Interpretation of the First Amendment' (1988) 87 *Mich L Rev* 499.
[23] Ibid 510.
[24] Michael Rushton, 'Economic Analysis of Freedom of Expression' (2005) 21 *Ga St U L Rev* 693, 709.

is 'weighted balancing'—essentially, cost-benefit analysis with a 'heavy thumb on the scale' in the speaker's favour.[25] 'Weighted balancing' might be used to 'smoke out' improper legislative motives[26] or to honour a constitutional commitment to free speech 'without imposing ... a straitjacket that disables government from responding to serious problems'.[27] In algebraic terms, the weighted balancing approach would suggest that courts should uphold speech restrictions only if $V + E <<< P \times L(1 + i)^n$, or—in English—if the costs of suppressing speech are significantly less than the expected benefits. The 'strict scrutiny' doctrine in US First Amendment law—whereby a speech restriction will survive judicial review only if it is narrowly tailored to achieve a compelling government interest and does so by the least restrictive means possible—arguably reflects this 'weighted balancing' view.[28] So-called 'intermediate scrutiny'—which requires an important government interest and a substantial relationship between the speech restriction and that interest—is arguably another type of weighted balancing, though with a somewhat lighter weight.

The mirror-image position is plausible as well. The fact that a legislature has enacted a speech restriction presumably reflects its own calculation that the benefits of suppressing speech exceed the costs. One might argue that a court should displace the legislature's judgment only if it is quite sure that the legislature is wrong—that is, only if, in the court's view, $V + E >>> P \times L(1 + i)^n$. 'Rational basis' review in US constitutional law arguably reflects this latter version of weighted balancing: there is a heavy thumb on the scale in favour of a provision's constitutionality, and a court will strike down a statute only when the balance tips overwhelmingly against the legislature. Interestingly, while the US Supreme Court applies strict scrutiny, intermediate scrutiny, and rational basis to speech restrictions of different varieties, US free speech law never allows judges to engage in the unweighted cost-benefit analysis that Posner advocates.

Importantly, Posner's perspective on free speech and the economic perspective on free speech should not be seen as one and the same. As Rushton notes, '[t]he essence of Posner's approach is *balance*'—weighing the benefits of speech suppression against its costs.[29] Balancing, however, is not the only prescription that one might derive from economic analysis. Categorical rules (eg, an absolute prohibition on viewpoint discrimination) may enhance welfare overall even if they sometimes produce peculiar results.[30] Posner's perspective is '*an* economic perspective' but certainly not the only economic perspective on the subject.

---

[25] Adam Winkler, 'Fatal in Theory and Strict in Fact: An Empirical Analysis of Strict Scrutiny in Federal Courts' (2006) 59 *Vand L Rev* 793, 803.
[26] Ibid 805.   [27] Ibid 803.
[28] Richard H Fallon Jr, 'Strict Judicial Scrutiny' (2007) 54 *UCLA L Rev* 1267, 1306–8.
[29] Rushton (n 24) 715–16.
[30] See, eg, Louis Kaplow, 'Rules Versus Standards: An Economic Analysis' (1992) 42 *Duke LJ* 557.

7.1.3 After the 'Acid Bath'

Posner's 1986 article is not the last effort at an economically informed framework for free speech analysis. Daniel Farber's widely cited 1991 *Harvard Law Review* article attempts a similarly general economic theory of free speech.[31] Farber succinctly summarizes his theory in a single paragraph:

> [B]ecause information is a public good, it is likely to be undervalued by both the market and the political system. Individuals have an incentive to 'free ride' because they can enjoy the benefits of public goods without helping to produce those goods. Consequently, neither market demand nor political incentives fully capture the social value of public goods such as information. Our polity responds to this undervaluation of information by providing special constitutional protection for information-related activities. This simple insight explains a surprising amount of First Amendment doctrine.[32]

In contrast to accounts of free speech that 'celebrate the Romantic ideals of self-expression and self-realization', Farber characterizes his account as a 'very *un*romantic understanding of the First Amendment's protection of free speech'.[33] His 'economic theory of free speech places no special intrinsic value on self-expression',[34] though it often lands in the same place as theories that do.

Farber's analysis, while illuminating in important respects, also poses a number of puzzles. He perceptively observes that, in a free market, the output of information will likely fall below the socially optimal level because the producer of information cannot collect payments from all who benefit from it. The unresolved question, though, is why the public good attributes of information should lead to less rather than more regulation. As Kathleen Sullivan notes in response to Farber's argument: 'Public goods are precisely those that the government does not leave to markets but produces or subsidizes itself'.[35] Governments do not respond to the public-good aspect of national defence by deregulating it; they respond by providing it. The public good aspect of free speech would, likewise, justify government funding for speech rather than a laissez-faire approach. Yet sometimes free speech doctrine leads to *restrictions* on free speech subsidies—a perverse outcome if the problem that free speech protection seeks to solve is, as Farber posits, information undersupply. Farber himself acknowledges the apparent paradox.[36] Sometimes courts strike down government subsidies because the government has selectively subsidized speech advocating certain viewpoints but not others.[37] In such cases, the legislature may 'respond[] by eliminating the subsidy

---

[31] Daniel A Farber, 'Free Speech Without Romance: Public Choice and the First Amendment' (1991) 105 *Harv L Rev* 554.
[32] Ibid 555.   [33] Ibid.   [34] Ibid 582.
[35] Kathleen M Sullivan, 'Free Speech and Unfree Markets' (1995) 42 *UCLA L Rev* 949, 960.
[36] Farber (n 31) 572.
[37] See, eg, *Legal Services Corp v Velazquez*, 531 US 533 (2001).

altogether', likely leading to a 'lower level of information' than if free speech doctrine had not intervened.[38]

Comparison of information to other public goods further underscores the peculiarity of the First Amendment's laissez-faire approach if information production is the underlying goal. Vaccines against infectious diseases such as measles are clear public goods. The US Food and Drug Administration heavily regulates vaccines so that individuals can have confidence in their safety. We take the opposite approach to political speech—which, according to Farber, is a public good as well—even though regulation might give individuals greater confidence in the truth value of political information. In other cases, governments boost the production of public goods through mandates: homeowners must shovel the sidewalks outside their homes in a snowstorm, motorists must turn on their headlights at night, and so on. Yet explicit speech mandates often run afoul of the First Amendment compelled speech doctrine in the United States.

While Farber's essay aims to arrive at a general theory of free speech protection through economic analysis, several other writers in the L&E tradition have sought to apply economic insights to a number of specific free speech-related issues, including desecration laws, hate speech laws, and libel and slander laws. Eric Rasmusen and Eric Posner both analyse laws against desecration from an economic perspective. Rasmusen observes that laws against desecration—such as flag-burning bans—address the negative 'mental externalities' that symbol desecrators impose upon symbol venerators. He adds that allowing desecration will reduce incentives to create and maintain new symbols. For these reasons, he concludes that US Supreme Court decisions striking down flag-burning bans were mistaken.[39] Eric Posner offers a contrasting view. He notes that laws mandating flag veneration may reduce the value of the signal that veneration sends, because everyone (regardless of patriotism) must venerate the flag. Alternatively, a law punishing flag desecration may enhance the value of desecration as a commitment mechanism for members of a 'deviant subcommunity' because desecrators—by breaking the law—'reduce the value of their opportunities outside their group' and 'thus enhance their trustworthiness within the group'. Given the 'complexity of predicting the effect of a flag-burning ban on behavior and beliefs', Posner expresses scepticism towards the 'claim that a law against flag burning would have any predictable effect that would be socially desirable'.[40]

Other important work in the economic analysis of free speech has focused on hate speech laws. Dhammika Dharmapala and Richard McAdams take up that subject, beginning from the assumption that perpetrators of hate crimes seek esteem from others who share their world-view. Speech can convey information about what actions will generate esteem. Restrictions on hate speech can reduce the availability of information about which actions will be esteem-generating. Dharmapala and McAdams consider several ways in which this uncertainty may affect the behaviour of potential perpetrators. For example, if potential perpetrators are risk-averse, then uncertainty about the

---

[38] Farber (n 31) 572.

[39] Eric Rasmusen, 'The Economics of Desecration: Flag Burning and Related Activities' (1998) 27 J Legal Stud 245.

[40] Eric A Posner, 'Symbols, Signals, and Social Norms in Politics and the Law' (1998) 27 J Legal Stud 765, 780–1.

amount of esteem associated with hate crime commission will reduce the incentive to commit such crimes in the first place. This might strengthen the case for laws against hate speech, though the authors emphasize that their model 'highlights only one factor that fits within a comprehensive cost-benefit analysis of speech regulation'.[41]

A number of scholars have analysed the tort of defamation (ie, libel and slander) from an economic perspective, including Nuno Garoupa,[42] Oren Bar-Gill and Assaf Hamdani,[43] David Acheson and Ansgar Wohlschlegel,[44] Yonathan Arbel, and Murat Mungan,[45] and this author with Ariel Porat.[46] All these authors note that liability can have a 'chilling effect' on true speech because potential speakers will worry about the litigation costs of potential lawsuits as well as the prospects that fallible courts will hold them liable. Bar-Gill and Hamdani emphasize that defamation liability also encourages publishers to invest more heavily in verifying factual statements. Arbel and Mungan, as well as Porat and I, highlight the effect of defamation liability on listeners' beliefs. When talk is cheap—when there is no liability for false statements—then audiences may ascribe less credibility to the statements they hear and read. Arbel and Mungan argue that the effect of liability on audiences undermines the case for defamation law, because defamation law—rather than protecting the victims of defamation—'*amplifies* the pernicious effect of false allegations'.[47] Porat and I acknowledge that defamation law potentially amplifies harms to victims but also emphasize that defamation law also can facilitate communication by enhancing the credibility of speech. (Section 7.3 returns to this subject.)

The emergence of behavioural economics opens up new frontiers for economic analysis of free speech law. Christine Jolls, Cass Sunstein, and Richard Thaler briefly consider the subject of prior restraints on speech in their field-defining 1998 article laying out a 'behavioral approach to law and economics'. Jolls and her co-authors hypothesize that court orders generate 'endowment effects', causing the party that obtains the order to attach a particularly high value to the entitlement conferred. The judicial hostility to prior restraints, Jolls and her co-authors suggest, can be justified as an effort to prevent prosecutors from experiencing an endowment effect after they obtain an injunction against speech. If such injunctions were allowed, prosecutors might place excessive value on enforcing those injunctions even if subsequent information suggested that the

---

[41] Dhammika Dharmapala and Richard H McAdams, 'Words That Kill? An Economic Model of the Influence of Speech on Behavior (with Particular Reference to Hate Speech)' (2005) 34 *J Legal Stud* 93, 132.

[42] Nuno Garoupa, 'Dishonesty and Libel Law: The Economics of the "Chilling" Effect' (1999) 155 *J of Inst & Theo Econ* 284; Nuno Garoupa, 'The Economics of Political Dishonesty and Defamation' (1999) 19 *Intl R L & Econ* 167.

[43] Oren Bar-Gill and Assaf Hamdani, 'Optimal Liability for Libel' (2003) 2 *Contr Econ Anal & Pol'y* 1.

[44] David J Acheson and Ansgar Wohlschlegel, 'The Economics of Weaponized Defamation Lawsuits' (2018) 47 *Sw L Rev* 335.

[45] Yonathan A Arbel and Murat Mungan, 'The Case Against Strict Defamation Laws' (2019) U of Alabama Legal Studies Research Paper No 3311527 <https://ssrn.com/abstract=3311527> accessed 3 November 2019.

[46] Daniel Hemel and Ariel Porat, 'Free Speech and Cheap Talk' (2019) 11 *J Legal Anal* 46.

[47] Arbel and Mungan (n 45) 6.

enjoined speech ought not be criminalized.[48] More recently, Jolls analyses visual elements in legally required communications—such as graphic warning labels on cigarette packages—through a behavioural lens.[49]

The rise of behaviouralism is one—but not the only—'revolution' in economics that has occurred since the early days of L&E. The 'new information economics', discussed presently, is another discipline-redefining development. As the next two sections will seek to show, the implications of the new information economics for the study of free speech are particularly far-reaching.[50]

7.2 THE NEW INFORMATION ECONOMICS

The 'new information economics' is not exactly new anymore. It began, by most accounts, a half-century ago with George Akerlof's 1970 article 'The Market for "Lemons": Quality Uncertainty and the Market Mechanism'.[51] Akerlof argues that under conditions of information asymmetry, low-quality goods can drive high-quality goods out of the marketplace. In these cases, either government intervention or private intervention can increase welfare. He illustrates this point with an extended example involving second-hand automobiles. Akerlof imagines that used-car owners know whether their vehicles are bad cars ('lemons') or good cars (which later literature refers to as 'peaches'). Buyers, however, have no way of knowing whether any given car is a 'lemon' or a 'peach'. They therefore are willing to pay a price reflecting the average quality of used cars on the market—higher than the price of a lemon, but less than the price of a peach. Lemon-owners are very willing to sell their bad cars for that price, but peach-owners are unwilling to sell their well-maintained cars for substantially less than they are worth.

---

[48] Christine Jolls, Cass R Sunstein, and Richard Thaler, 'A Behavioral Approach to Law and Economics' (1998) 50 *Stan L Rev* 1471, 1497–8, 1517.

[49] Christine Jolls, 'Debiasing Through Law and the First Amendment' (2015) 67 *Stan L Rev* 1411. For another perspective on free speech informed by behavioral economics, see Paul Horwitz, 'Free Speech as Risk Analysis: Heuristics, Biases, and Institutions in the First Amendment' (2003) 76 *Temp L Rev* 1, 26–48.

[50] Other contributions to the economic analysis of free speech include Clifford G Holderness, Michael C Jensen, and William H Meckling, 'The Logic of the First Amendment' (2000) Harvard Business School NOM Unit Working Paper No 00–01 <https://papers.ssrn.com/sol3/papers.cfm?abstract_id=215468> accessed 3 November 2019; and Fred S McChesney, 'A Positive Regulatory Theory of the First Amendment' (1988) 20 *Conn L Rev* 355. For another review of the economic literature on free speech, see Hugo M Mialon and Paul H Rubin, 'The Economics of the Bill of Rights' (2008) 10 *Am L & Econ Rev* 1, 6–15. For an economically informed analysis of the social (rather than legal) regulation of speech, see Glenn C Loury, 'Self-Censorship in Public Discourse: A Theory of "Political Correctness" and Related Phenomena' (1994) 6 *Ration & Soc'y* 428.

[51] George A Akerlof, 'The Market for "Lemons": Quality Uncertainty and the Market Mechanism' (1970) 84 *Q J Econ* 488.

Ultimately, the only used cars on the market will be the lemons. That is, '[t]he "bad" cars tend to drive out the good'.[52]

Akerlof refers to this phenomenon as 'adverse selection' and notes examples in markets for insurance, labour, and credit. He then identifies a number of institutions that can counteract the effects of quality uncertainty. Guarantees are one example. A seller may, for example, warrant that a car is a peach and be held liable for damages if it turns out not to be. Another example is reputation. 'Brand names', he observes, 'give the consumer a means of retaliation if quality does not meet expectations', as 'the consumer will then curtail future purchases'. A third is licensing (or certification). A licence to practice medicine or law—or a professional degree from a prestigious institution—operates as a certification of proficiency. Akerlof notes that '[t]he high school diploma, the baccalaureate degree, the Ph.D., even the Nobel Prize, to some degree, serve thus function of certification' as well.[53]

Tens of thousands of later papers in economics and other fields cite and build on Akerlof's elegant model. Of particular note, Michael Spence's 1973 essay on 'signalling' posits that educational degrees can serve to distinguish high-quality job applicants ('peaches') from low-quality applicants ('lemons') if the cost of a degree is negatively correlated with productivity (ie, if it is cheaper for a high-quality applicant than for a low-quality applicant to earn a degree).[54] Joseph Stiglitz, among others, has identified 'screening' as an alternative to 'signalling'.[55] An employer may, for example, 'screen' potential employees by offering contingent contracts that require an employee to pay a fine if it turns out that they have overstated their ability. Stiglitz notes that such screening occurs 'in a slightly modified form' relatively routinely: 'Individuals accept low wages while they prove themselves; the low wages today are compensated for by high wages later if they do prove themselves', and '[i]f they do not, the difference between the low wages and what they could have obtained elsewhere acts as a fine'.[56] The difference between 'signalling' and 'screening' is that signals are transmitted by the better-informed party (in Spence's case, the employee who knows that they are highly productive and obtain a degree to show it) while screens are set by the less-informed party (in Stiglitz's case, the employer who seeks to distinguish high-quality and low-quality workers).[57]

Despite the large and growing literature inspired by Akerlof's initial article, one passage in 'The Market for "Lemons"' has gone almost entirely unexplored. Akerlof notes that under conditions of asymmetric information, governmental or private institutions can intervene to enhance welfare. He then writes: 'By nature, however, these institutions are nonatomistic, and therefore concentrations of power—with ill consequences of their

---

[52] Ibid 489.   [53] Ibid 499–500.
[54] Michael Spence, 'Job Market Signaling' (1973) 87 *Q J Econ* 355.
[55] Joseph E Stiglitz, 'The Theory of "Screening" Education, and the Distribution of Income' (1975) 65 *Am Econ R* 283.
[56] Ibid 292.
[57] See John G Riley, 'Silver Signals: Twenty-Five Years of Screening and Signaling' (2001) 39 *J Econ Lit* 432, 443–4.

own—can develop'.[58] Only a few subsequent papers—and none in mainline economics journals—have sought to make sense of this remark.[59]

Competition is 'atomistic' when markets are characterized by large numbers of small sellers who lack market power. Akerlof appears to be saying that the institutions that can resolve adverse selection problems necessarily *will* have market power. In the used-car context, CarMax buys up old vehicles and stakes its reputation on its claims about quality. In the licensing context, JD and MD degrees signal proficiency only because not everyone can get one—or, at least, not everyone can get one from an accredited medical school or law school. The Liaison Committee on Medical Education and the American Bar Association are near-monopolies in the US medical and law school contexts. Warranties—which are another way for sellers to address information asymmetries—do not depend upon private-sector monopolies or oligopolies, but they do depend upon courts. We can think of courts as monopolists (or, perhaps more accurately, oligopolists[60]) in the market for warranty enforcement. In all of these contexts, the solution to the adverse selection problem results in the aggregation of power in the hands of institutions that are sheltered from market competition. The implications of these power concentrations in the speech context will be considered below.

7.3 ON LIBERTY AND LEMONS

The canonical papers by Akerlof, Spence, and Stiglitz all focus on information asymmetries in markets for goods and services. Their insights apply equally, though, to information asymmetries in the market for information itself. We might imagine speakers as 'sellers' and listeners as 'buyers', with falsehoods as 'lemons' and truths as 'peaches'. In general (though not always), truths are more expensive to produce than falsehoods.[61]

---

[58] Akerlof (n 51) 488.

[59] See Glenn Fox, 'Asymmetric Information and Market Failure: A Market Process Perspective' [2016] J of Prices & Markets 11 <http://pricesandmarkets.org/wp-content/uploads/2016/11/Asymmetric-Information-and-Market-Failure-A-Market-Process-Perspective-by-Fox.pdf> accessed 3 November 2019; Mark Steckbeck and Peter Boettke, 'Turning Lemons into Lemonade: Entrepreneurial Solutions to Adverse Selection Problems in E-Commerce' in Jack Birner and Pierre Garrouste (eds), *Markets, Information and Communication: Austrian Perspectives on the Internet Economy* (Routledge 2003).

[60] Not only is there interjurisdictional competition among courts, but there is also competition between courts and private-sector arbitrators. The 'market for lemons' problem reappears in the market for arbitration services, where parties rely on the reputations of individual arbitrators and certification by bodies such as the American Association of Arbitration and the International Centre for Dispute Resolution.

[61] The costs of producing 'truths' are sometimes monetary and sometimes psychic. For example, a truth producer may have to incur the psychic costs of conveying information that clashes with their own values or world-view. A producer of falsehoods, by contrast, can avoid that cost by always saying what they find ideologically congenial.

Listeners, we also generally assume, prefer truths.[62] Listeners, though, cannot easily distinguish truths from falsehoods themselves. (If listeners already knew what was true and what was false, then speech would carry no informational value.) As the share of speech that is false rises, listeners will be willing to pay less for it (note that 'payment' here can refer to monetary payments such as magazine and newspaper subscriptions or to payments that take other forms, such as political support or esteem). Truth-tellers, then, will be less willing to bear the high cost of producing truth given the low price. Bad speech will tend to drive out the good.

The previous paragraph's dystopian view of information markets is, to be sure, heavily stylized. We may today live in an ocean of 'fake news', but truth has not vanished from the earth. (Nor, for that matter, have high-quality used cars.) Starting from the stylized model, though, helps us identify the institutions that address information asymmetries in familiar information markets. Each of the institutions that Akerlof mentions—warranties, reputation, and licensing/certification—have analogues in the speech context.

7.3.1 Warranties and Liability

Warranties in information markets take several forms. Occasionally, a speaker will explicitly warrant that their statement is true and promise to pay a sum certain to anyone who proves them wrong. The canonical example is *Carlill v Carbolic Smoke Ball Co*, in which the manufacturer of a 'smoke ball' averred that its product could prevent viral infections and promised to pay £100 to anyone who used it as directed and contracted a cold or the flu afterwards. One Ms Carlill did so, caught the flu, and sued. The court held that the manufacturer's 'prove-me-wrong' offer was a valid offer which Ms Carlill accepted, resulting in an enforceable contract.[63] A well-known US analogue is *James v*

---

[62] Writing nearly three decades ago, David Strauss thought it a 'fair generalization that no rational person ever wants to act on the basis of a false statement of fact'—or, at least, any exceptions to this generalization 'seem too unusual and peripheral to implicate the basic institutional structure governing freedom of expression'. David Strauss, 'Persuasion, Autonomy, and Freedom of Expression' (1991) 91 *Colum L Rev* 334, 336 and n 77. Subsequent years have led many to doubt that claim. See, eg, Michiko Kakutani, *The Death of Truth: Notes on Falsehoods in the Age of Trump* (Tim Duggan Books 2018). Experimental evidence suggests that substantial numbers of individuals do seek out truth and update their beliefs accordingly, though results are heavily context-dependent. See, eg, Geoffrey L Cohen, Joshua Aronson, and Claude M Steele, 'When Beliefs Yield to Evidence: Reducing Biased Evaluation by Affirming the Self' (2000) 26 *Pers & Soc Psychol Bull* 1151; Lisa Farman and others, 'Finding the Truth in Politics: An Empirical Validation of the Epistemic Political Efficacy Concept' (2018) 26 *Atlantic J Comm* 1; Raymond James Pingree, Dominique Brossard, and Douglas M McLeod, 'Effects of Journalistic Adjudication on Factual Beliefs, News Evaluations, Information Seeking, and Epistemic Political Efficacy' (2014) 17 *Mass Comm & Soc'y* 615; and Axel Westerwick, Steven B Kleinman, and Silvia Knobloch-Westerwick, 'Turn a Blind Eye If You Care: Impacts of Attitude Consistency, Importance, and Credibility on Seeking of Political Information and Implications for Attitudes' (2013) 63 *J of Comm* 432. In any event, the empirical claim that 'listeners prefer truths' is likely not essential to the case for greater speech regulation. If the claim turns out to be false, then the idea that an unbridled marketplace of ideas will bring truths to the top seems suspect from the start.

[63] *Carlill v Carbolic Smoke Ball Co* [1893] 1 QB 256.

Turilli, in which Rudy Turilli, the operator of a museum devoted to bank and train robber Jesse James, claimed that the outlaw had lived with him in a house in Missouri until the 1950s. (James, by all other accounts, died in a shootout in 1882.) Turilli offered a $10,000 reward to anyone who could prove his claim wrong. James's daughter-in-law and grandchildren accepted the offer, established the falsity of Turilli's assertion, and sought to collect the reward. A Missouri court ordered him to pay.[64]

While the 'smoke ball' case and the Jesse James case are not the only examples, 'prove-me-wrong' offers remain relatively rare. In some cases, courts have refused to enforce them.[65] Daniel O'Gorman argues that prove-me-wrong offers 'are usually not supported by consideration and are therefore typically not enforceable as a unilateral contract'.[66] The US Court of Appeals for the Eleventh Circuit recently considered a defence lawyer's $1 million prove-me-wrong offer to anyone who could show that his client could have travelled from Atlanta's Hartsfield-Jackson airport to a murder scene as quickly as the prosecution's timeline alleged. A law student tried to take up the offer and recorded himself making the journey within the prosecution's twenty-eight-minute time frame. The court refused to enforce the warranty. 'The exaggerated amount of "a million dollars"—the common choice of movie villains and schoolyard wagerers alike—indicates that this was hyperbole', the court said.[67]

Aside from explicit prove-me-wrong offers, another way that speakers effectively 'warrant' the truth of their statements is by speaking against a background of defamation liability. When defamation liability potentially applies, a speaker's reputation-damaging statement about another operates as a warranty that the statement is true and binds the speaker to pay damages if it turns out not to be. Defamation liability can thus enhance the credibility of speech, which then may boost the price that listeners are willing to pay and encourage more true information to be generated. Ariel Porat and I have termed this the 'warming effect' of defamation, in contrast to the better known 'chilling effect'. Defamation law's 'chilling' and 'warming' effects cut in opposite directions, and the net effect of defamation on the quantity of speech is therefore ambiguous. Porat and I conclude that US Supreme Court case law on defamation—which, in the name of free speech, significantly limits the scope of liability—may be counter-productive if the goal of the First Amendment's free speech clause is to facilitate speech.[68]

Warranties and liability do not, importantly, avoid Akerlof's concerns regarding 'concentrations of power' produced by institutional solutions to asymmetric information. Instead, they vest courts with the concentrated power to decide what statements are true and false for purposes of prove-me-wrong offers and defamation. 'Ill consequences' will follow, as Akerlof warns, if courts are biased against particular viewpoints. As we shall soon see, though, the alternatives to judicial speech regulation will entail power concentrations of a different sort.

---

[64] *James v Turilli*, 473 S W 2d 757 (1971).
[65] See, eg, *Cudahy Junior Chamber of Commerce v Quirk*, 165 N W 2d 116 (1969).
[66] Daniel P O'Gorman, '"Prove Me Wrong" Cases and Consideration Theory' (2015) 23 *George Mason L Rev* 125, 125.
[67] *Kolodziej v Mason*, 774 F 3d 736, 741 (2014).
[68] Hemel and Porat (n 46) 66–72.

7.3.2 Reputation

Reputation is, as noted by Akerlof, an alternative institution for addressing quality uncertainty. It is perhaps the mechanism most often used for quality assurance in the marketplace for information and ideas. We in the United States rely on the *New York Times*, the *New Yorker*, and National Public Radio to provide accurate information about national and world events. We trust the *New England Journal of Medicine* for health information and *Consumer Reports* for product information. Each of these institutions stakes its reputational capital on the information that it publishes. We trust these institutions because we believe they have implemented rigorous verification processes and because they have a lot to lose if they get facts wrong.

Reliance on private-sector institutions with high reputational capital poses problems of its own. Sometimes, the institutions in which we place our trust fail to live up to their reputations for accuracy. Consider, for example, the *New York Times*' publication of what its editors later described as 'misinformation' regarding the development of weapons of mass destruction by Iraqi dictator Saddam Hussein.[69] Apart from inaccuracies (which are inevitable in at least some instances, even if the Iraq weapons-of-mass-destruction one was not), reliance on high-reputation institutions results in the 'concentrations of power' of which Akerlof warned. The publisher and editors of the *New York Times*—and their counterparts at other high-reputation institutions—exert enormous influence over intelligent discourse and informed thought. Even if the people who occupy these roles are for the most part talented and well-meaning, we may nonetheless be concerned about the control over information markets exercised by individuals who are neither democratically elected nor broadly representative of the backgrounds, viewpoints, and concerns of the general population.

The discussion here highlights the trade-off between liability and reputation in information markets. Liability—whether in the form of warranty enforcement or defamation law—allocates authority to courts to distinguish fact from fiction. Reliance on reputation makes institutions with high reputational capital the arbiters of truth. The trade-off is, as Akerlof emphasizes, ultimately unavoidable when consumers (whether of goods and services or of information and ideas) cannot readily ascertain quality.

7.3.3 Licensing and Certification

Licensing and certification are the last set of institutional responses to the 'market for lemons' problem that Akerlof considers, and here too, there are information market analogues. Journalism degrees might be thought of as certificates of truth-seeking proficiency, though at least in the United States, journalism degrees have not come to play the same certification role that the JD, MBA, and MD do in law, business, and medicine (respectively). Journalism awards such as the Pulitzer Prize serve an ex post certification

---

[69] Editorial, 'From the Editors; The Times and Iraq' *New York Times* (New York, 26 May 2004) 10.

function. The FCC's 'fairness doctrine' formerly required radio and television stations—as a condition for their licences—to provide accurate coverage of opposing views,[70] though the commission later concluded that 'the fairness doctrine chills speech' and therefore abandoned it in 1987.[71]

Licensing and certification play larger roles in some other information markets. Since December 2017, the Independent Press Standards Organisation (IPSO) in the United Kingdom has maintained an optional licensing system for newspapers and magazines. IPSO members must adhere to an 'Editor's Code', which sets forth standards related to accuracy and respect for personal privacy. Individuals can complain to IPSO about inaccurate reports, privacy invasions, and other code violations. If IPSO finds that a member publication has violated the Editor's Code, it can require the publication to print a correction and impose a fine of up to £1 million. (The kitemark can thus be understood as both a certification and as a warranty.) Publications that are members of IPSO can carry the organization's 'kitemark', a symbol that denotes adherence to the code. IPSO has sought to educate the British public about the meaning of the kitemark through advertisements with slogans such as 'FAKE NEWS NOT WELCOME WHERE YOU SEE THIS MARK'.[72]

Most newspapers and magazines in the UK have signed up to the IPSO certification regime. Illustrating the substitutability between reputation and other institutions for addressing quality uncertainty, however, the *Guardian*, *Independent*, and *Financial Times*—three of the British newspapers with the highest reputational capital—have opted not to join.[73] A sympathetic understanding of these newspapers' choices is that they believe they can overcome the 'market for lemons' problem on the basis of their reputational stores without the additional credibility that IPSO membership potentially brings. A more cynical view is that they see IPSO's kitemarking system as a threat to their own oligopolistic power in the market for trustworthy news.

7.3.4 Signalling and Screening

The emergent state of affairs in the UK—with most publications making use of certification and a handful resting on reputation—can be analysed in 'signalling' and 'screening' terms. A regime of opt-in liability potentially can 'screen' speakers who know more about their own type than the regulator does. The IPSO system in the UK is binary (opt-in or opt-out), but we also could imagine multiple levels of liability, with speakers who

---

[70] See *Red Lion Broadcasting Co v Federal Communications Commission*, 395 US 367 (1969).

[71] *Syracuse Peace Council v Federal Communications Commission*, 2 FCC Rcd 5043, 5057 (1987).

[72] Charlotte Tobitt, 'Press Regulator IPSO Launches Newspaper Ad Campaign To Say "Fake News Is Not Welcome" in Its Members' Publications', *Press Gazette* (London, 30 April 2018) <https://www.pressgazette.co.uk/press-regulator-ipso-launches-newspaper-ad-campaign-to-say-fake-news-is-not-welcome-in-its-members-publications> accessed 3 November 2019.

[73] IPSO, 'Complaints' (IPSO, 2018) <https://www.ipso.co.uk/faqs/complaints> accessed 20 October 2019.

know themselves to be more accurate opting for higher liability levels. Each level would be associated with a mark or other designation that serves as a 'signal' of quality. Ideally, the system would result in what the new information economics describes as a 'separating equilibrium': the highest quality speakers ('peaches') would opt into the highest level of liability; the lowest quality speakers ('lemons') would opt for the lowest level; and speakers of the intermediate quality type (call them 'melons') would opt for more liability than the lemons but less than the peaches.

Signalling and screening efforts do not always result in separating equilibria, however. Speakers of different types may opt for the same level of liability—a phenomenon known in the literature as a 'pooling equilibrium'. For example, purveyors of 'fake news' as well as high-reputation speakers both might opt out of the regulatory regime—the former because they are worried about liability, the latter because they think they can convey information credibly without the boost from certification. High-reputation speakers might even have an incentive to disrupt separating equilibria because effective signalling and screening may erode the value of reputational capital.

The potential role of law as a facilitator for signalling and screening in markets for information is a subject that merits additional investigation, and the discussion here is exploratory rather than exhaustive. The key points are (1) that one size needs to fit all,[74] (2) that multiple liability levels with an option for speakers to choose among them might have information revelation benefits, and (3) that designing a menu of liability options that produces a separating equilibrium among speakers will require much thought—and perhaps a certain amount of trial and error as well. Such a system could go some way towards deconcentrating power in the market for information, as both courts (or as in IPSO's case, an industry self-regulatory organization) and high-reputation private institutions that remain outside the regulatory regime will be competing power centres. Truly atomistic competition in the marketplace of ideas, though, likely remains an impossibility, as Akerlof foresaw from the outset.

7.4 Conclusion

The L&E literature on free speech has, for the most part, seen law as an obstacle to a robust market for information and ideas. L&E scholars have not advocated a completely laissez-faire approach to speech, but they generally have characterized the trade-off as between more speech, on the one hand, and legal protection against speech-related harms, on the other. Richard Posner's *Dennis* formula and Daniel Farber's celebration of the First Amendment as a subsidy for speech exemplify this perspective.

---

[74] Breton and Wintrobe say that 'the *same* set of regulations' must 'be consistently applied to all statements' in 'any ideas market': Breton and Wintrobe (n 8) 220. The discussion here (and the experience in the UK) illustrates that this is indeed not the case.

The new information economics suggests a different view. Knowledge asymmetries between producers and consumers make the market for information and ideas potentially a 'market for lemons'. Law can address that asymmetry—for example, by imposing liability on purveyors of falsehoods—but at the cost of courts turning into arbiters of truth. The alternative is for law to recede and reputation to play a more prominent role, though only at the cost of concentrating power in high-reputation private-sector institutions. Perhaps the best that law can do is to offer different options to different speakers, permitting some to rely on their own reputational capital while allowing others to enjoy the enhanced credibility that liability brings. A system that gives speakers the opportunity of *un*free speech—that is, the option to engage in talk that is not cheap—may, in the end, do more to promote a robust marketplace for information and ideas than a system in which all speech is free.

CHAPTER 8

FREEDOM OF SPEECH AND PUBLIC REASON

WOJCIECH SADURSKI

THE idea of Public Reason rests upon a view that the legitimacy of laws is crucially dependent upon the sort of *reasons* provided for these laws—and not only those 'provided', but also demonstrable, as the most likely purposes pursued by the law-maker.[1] These publicly admissible reasons confer legitimacy upon legal decisions. The idea is more recognizable in its negative articulation, as a reason-constraining conception of legitimacy: certain motives which trigger the law, and which are not reasonably acceptable to all—for instance because they are sectarian, or based on prejudice, hatred, or self-interest of the law-makers—taint the law as illegitimate. More specifically, in the interpretation advanced by John Rawls, only those reasons which are reasonably endorsable by all those to whom they apply may qualify as properly public, or in a negative and more modest formulation, only those reasons which cannot be reasonably rejected by those to whom they are addressed will qualify.

This general idea naturally can be, and was, subjected to various criticisms,[2] but for the purposes of my argument in this chapter I will assume that the conception of public reason is both morally attractive and workable—that we can plausibly distinguish between legislative motives which are rationally acceptable to all reasonable persons, and those motives that are 'sectarian', that is, reasonably rejected by some to whom the laws in question apply. I will also assume that legislative motives are a proper proxy for legislative reasons or purposes, even though this assumption may be questioned. If it seems that I am assuming *arguendo* too much, I can only point to my other work where I

---

[1] See John Rawls, *Political Liberalism* (Columbia UP 1993) 212–54; John Rawls, 'The Idea of Public Reason Revisited' in *The Law of Peoples* (Harvard UP 1999) 129–80; Charles Larmore, 'Public Reason' in Samuel Freeman (ed), *The Cambridge Companion to Rawls* (CUP 2003).

[2] See Ronald Dworkin, *Justice in Robes* (Harvard UP 2006) 252–4; Jeremy Waldron, 'Public Reason and "Justification" in the Courtroom' (2017) 1 *JL, Phil & Cult* 107.

have undertaken to rebut these and some other objections to the doctrine of public reason,[3] as well as other philosophical and legal defences of this idea.[4]

Can we find traces of this ideal in legal arguments, by legislators, judges, and scholars, about freedom of speech? The salience of motive-oriented scrutiny, which resonates with the idea of public reason, is clearly visible in the field of freedom of speech where, some time ago, it was observed that:

> for free speech problems regarding the exchange of ideas, the challenging party establishes a first amendment violation by showing that the decisionmaker's action was *motivated* solely by ideological considerations likely to compromise the rights to acquire information or ideas, or subtly to influence the party's beliefs.[5]

More generally, Elena Kagan argued in her wide-ranging article that 'First Amendment law, as developed by the Supreme Court over the past several decades, has as its primary though unstated object the discovery of *improper governmental motives*. The doctrine comprises a series of tools to flush out illicit motives and to invalidate actions infected with it'.[6] This chapter will trace the connections between some persuasive doctrines of freedom of expression and will attempt to specify and make more explicit the 'improper governmental motives', hinted at by Professor Kagan (as she then was), which contaminate a regulation of speech. It will be shown, in particular, that the requirements of viewpoint neutrality of regulations resonate with the fundamental principles of public reason.

8.1 Speech, Harm, and Viewpoint

Speech may harm people, and speech regulation that is motivated by the elimination or reduction of harms is compatible with the demands of public reason. But the regulation of speech may also be based on a hostility towards the ideas expressed or a willingness to screen out some information or opinion from the public domain regardless of whether it is harmful. These motives for the suppression of speech are prima facie illegitimate; they are incompatible with public reason because they would not be endorsable by the holders of those opinions or information. Much of the debate in the United States about—and the difficulty raised by—a proper role for government in regulating speech

---

[3] See Wojciech Sadurski, 'Reason of State and Public Reason' (2014) 27 *Ratio Juris* 21; Wojciech Sadurski, 'The Idea of Public Reason Re-Revisited: Common Good and Respect for Persons' (2014) 2 *Rivista del filosofia del diritto* 377.

[4] See, eg, Samuel Freeman, 'Public Reason and Political Justifications' (2004) 72 *Fordham L Rev* 2021; Ronald C Den Otter, *Judicial Review in an Age of Moral Pluralism* (CUP 2009) 200–30; Micah Schwartzman, 'The Sincerity of Public Reason' (2011) 19 *J Pol Phil* 375.

[5] John Donovan, 'Unconstitutional Motivation Analysis and the First Amendment: The Further Demise of a "Wise and Ancient Doctrine"' (1983) 33 *Case W Res L Rev* 271, 291–2 (emphasis added).

[6] Elena Kagan, 'Private Speech, Public Purpose: The Role of Governmental Motive in First Amendment Doctrine' (1996) 63 *U Chi L Rev* 413, 414 (emphasis added).

centres on a distinction between harm-based and hostility-based restrictions of speech. The line between both types of motivation can be 'exceedingly fine',[7] but in principle this distinction (corresponding, as it does, to public reason-compatible and public reason-incompatible motives) explains much about the First Amendment speech jurisprudence. This line marks a difference between 'government censorship' and 'legitimate, reasonable, neutral justifications' (based on prohibiting 'special harms')[8] of speech regulation.

This is where the motive for restrictions acquires crucial importance. The general principle governing the US First Amendment jurisprudence (and as will be shown, also outside the United States) may be formulated as follows: restrictions that express a viewpoint that is preferred (or, conversely, disliked) by the government should be subjected to very strong scrutiny, with an implication of their likely invalidation. In contrast, restrictions that are viewpoint-neutral, and which do not discriminate among different viewpoints, may be subject to more lenient scrutiny because there is little reason for suspicion that they result from improper governmental motives. The latter restrictions are sometimes presented as content-based rather than viewpoint-based, which is imprecise: I will return to this point below.

But first I wish to consider the relationship between harm-based restrictions of speech (which, presumptively, are perfectly unimpeachable from the point of view of public reason) and content-based restrictions that are based upon hostility to the point of view, which prima facie appear incompatible with public reason.[9] Is this a distinction with a difference? Consider an example of a restriction which would command quasi-universal endorsement even by the most radical libertarians: that of child pornography. A proponent of a viewpoint-based theory (a theory which presumptively prohibits viewpoint restrictions) may say: this restriction is perfectly compatible with my theory because it is targeted at a very special kind of harm rather than a viewpoint. That is, it is not a 'viewpoint' (which might be articulated as the opinion that exploiting children for sexual purposes is acceptable) which is the target of the restriction but the real harm done to children. A proponent of viewpoint-based theory may cite Geoffrey Stone's formula that 'the government may not restrict expression *simply* because it disagrees with the speaker's views',[10] and maintain that, in the case of child pornography the restriction is imposed not *simply* because of the disagreement with a pornographer's perspective. Rather, it just so happens that pursuing the aim of prevention of a great harm coincides with the effect of restricting the viewpoints which are supportive of the harm. The primary aim, the

---

[7] Ibid 422, n 27.
[8] For this distinction, framed in these words, see *RAV v City of St Paul*, 505 US 377, 434 (1992) (Stevens J, concurring).
[9] See further Wojciech Sadurski, *Freedom of Speech and Its Limits* (Kluwer Academic Publishers 1999) 58–72.
[10] Geoffrey R Stone, 'Content Regulation and the First Amendment' (1983) 15 *Wm & Mary L Rev* 189, 227 (emphasis added, citations omitted).

argument *may* go, is to avoid harm, and '[t]hat aim might dwarf, or *even be unaccompanied by*, any bias toward the point of view expressed'.[11]

The italicized words in this quote from Steven Shiffrin indicate a theoretical problem: can we really envisage a harm-oriented regulation of speech completely 'unaccompanied by' any dislike of the point of view expressed? At a minimum, there will always be a 'point of view' that the harm claimed by the law-maker is insignificant, or is not harm at all. But this articulation of the harm-viewpoint connection renders it trivial: we can always concoct a 'point of view' parallel to the task of harm reduction. When, for instance, a regulator wants to minimize an obvious harm arising from false or misleading advertisements by lawyers without targeting all other advertisements (an obvious content-based regulation),[12] we can always attribute it to a 'viewpoint' that the harms of false advertising by this professional group are of special character. However, this attribution is not interesting, because this 'viewpoint' description does not add anything to the harm language.

What is more interesting and important, for our purposes, is the *opposite* situation: can we imagine viewpoint-oriented restrictions *unaccompanied* by the targeting of harm? Some believe that we cannot. Laurence Tribe, for instance, suggested that '*[a]ll* viewpoint-based regulations are targeted at some supposed harm, whether it be linked to an unsettling ideology like 'Communism or Nazism or to socially shunned practices like adultery'.[13] And if any putative viewpoint-based restriction in fact collapses into harm reduction, the idea that viewpoint-based restrictions reveal illicit motivations is in trouble.

However, the very fact that we can identify content-based speech regulations which are fundamentally harm-oriented, with a minor viewpoint ingredient, *is* significant for the application of the idea of public reason in constitutional law: such laws will not, normally, lend themselves to the search for illicit motives. Whether we encounter an opposite scenario—a viewpoint-oriented restriction which is harm-insensitive—may therefore be less important for the theory of public reason. Even if we answer the question in the negative, there will still be room for public reason, at least in certifying public reason-compatibility of harm-oriented speech regulations. Perhaps we can say this: viewpoint-based restrictions which look harm-insensitive occur when there is a significant disagreement as to whether a given act of speech is indeed harmful, and even if there is a consensus about its harmfulness, there is disagreement about the gravity of harm and whether it prevails over the harms of restrictions. When, however, there is a high degree of consensus about the harmfulness of speech and about its gravity which is likely to easily prevail over the harm of costs of restrictions (as in the case of prohibition of child pornography), we do not need to reach the viewpoint-related argument. It is redundant; it does not add anything to the argument that the gravity of harm of speech

---

[11] Steven H Shiffrin, *The First Amendment, Democracy, and Romance* (Harvard UP 1990) 18 (emphasis added, citations omitted).

[12] See *Bates v State Bar of Arizona*, 433 US 350 (1977).

[13] Laurence H Tribe, *American Constitutional Law* (2nd edn, Foundation P 1988) 925 (emphasis in original).

prevails over the harm of regulation. This is particularly visible in the case of so-called 'fighting words', defined as 'those [words] which by their very utterance inflict injury or tend to incite an immediate breach of the peace'.[14] The articulation of a 'viewpoint' targeted by a legislator does not add anything to our firm and widely shared views about the harm arising from verbal assaults captured by this concept. When, however, there is a degree of disagreement and uncertainty about the harm of speech and about its weighing and balancing with the harm of regulation (for example, in regulating defamation of public officials, hate speech or milder forms of pornography), the viewpoint-oriented analysis acquires a real bite. A viewpoint-characterization of a regulation may therefore be parasitic on the fact that the assessment of harm in question is controversial.

8.2 Content, Subject Matter, and Viewpoint

It is necessary now to draw a distinction between content-based (as a broader notion) and viewpoint-based (as a narrower notion) restrictions. These two notions are sometimes used interchangeably, and the very idea of a viewpoint-based approach is sometimes captured by the concept of 'content-based' restrictions. In one of the most oft-quoted phrases in the First Amendment canon, Justice Marshall said: 'above all else, the First Amendment means that the government has no power to restrict expression because of its message, its ideas, its subject matter, or its content'.[15] And to reinforce the impression that he really *meant* it, he added: '[a]ny restriction on expressive activity because of its content would completely undercut the "profound national commitment to the principle that debate on public issues should be uninhibited, robust, and wide open"'.[16] But this is an obvious overstatement, which cannot be taken seriously either as an account of First Amendment law or as a normative proposition. Regarding the first point (descriptive), if Marshall's statement were to be taken at face value, it would, for instance, completely undermine the legally established (and perfectly reasonable) idea of a hierarchy of categories of speech which call for varying degrees of legal protection under the US First Amendment: think, for instance, of standards of protection for political speech[17] and for commercial speech,[18] not to mention malicious defamation of non-public figures[19] or obscene speech.[20] In addition, Marshall's propositions are formulated in a categorical mode ('*no* power', '*any* restriction', '*completely* undercut') while,

---

[14] *Chaplinsky v New Hampshire*, 315 US 568, 572 (1942).
[15] *Police Department of Chicago v Mosley*, 408 US 92, 95 (1972).
[16] Ibid 96, quoting *New York Times v Sullivan*, 376 US 254, 270 (1964).
[17] See, eg, *Whitney v California*, 274 US 357 (1927).
[18] See, eg, *44 Liquormart v Rhode Island*, 517 US 484 (1996).
[19] See, eg, *Gertz v Robert Welch Inc*, 418 US 323 (1974).
[20] See, eg, *Miller v California*, 413 US 15 (1973).

under the First Amendment authoritative doctrine, a prohibition on content restrictions is only presumptive and can be overridden under a sufficiently high standard of scrutiny. What Marshall presents as an absolute prohibition is merely a manner of describing a very exacting scrutiny of governmental regulation of speech. Second, Marshall's statement is not attractive as a normative proposition: a law which would attach equal importance (and provide equal protection) to a graphic depiction of sexual intercourse as to a political speech in an election campaign would be morally unappealing.

To be sure, one can appreciate the reasons for a position according to which *any* differentiation of restriction based on the substance of speech is objectionable. The principle that 'a court should not attempt to differentiate or allow the state to differentiate the value of particular messages'[21] can, at first blush, claim support from powerful libertarian arguments. The risk of entrusting an authoritative body with the power of assigning different value to different categories of speech, even before they consider the harm of specific speech, is manifest. But a demand for a uniform standard is unrealistic. Even in the United States, which may be seen as a paragon of a strongly libertarian approach to the protection of speech, 'it is clear that some speech may be regulated not merely because it is harmful but also because the government need not, for that category of expression, meet the ordinary, highly protective standards for regulating speech'.[22] Most importantly, uniform levels of scrutiny could be, ironically, damaging to the general system of protection of speech.[23] Dispensing with a hierarchy of categories of speech which call for varying degrees of legal protection would, more likely than not, result in a lowering of speech protection across the board. As Justice Blackmun observed, '[i]f all expressive activity must be accorded the same protection, that protection would be scant'.[24] As an illustration of this effect, consider a *Harvard Law Review* note about the Supreme Court's 1990 decision on child pornography in *Osborne v Ohio*.[25] The majority applied a standard of 'intermediate scrutiny' but failed to classify expressly that the speech in question was of 'low value'. This failure, according to the (anonymous) authors of the Review Note, could 'erode the protection of "core" speech as well'.[26] As the Note further suggested, '[b]ecause *Osborne* did not openly endorse the "low-value" approach, lower courts might conclude that child pornography is core speech and that *Osborne* is an example of a relaxed strict scrutiny analysis'.[27] As a result, '[c]ourts could view *Osborne* as generally relaxing the strict scrutiny requirements that the government have a compelling interest in order to regulate protected speech'.[28]

From my point of view in this chapter, Marshall's dictum that 'the government has no power to restrict expression because of its message, its ideas, its subject matter, or its

---

[21] Archibald Cox, 'The Supreme Court, 1979 Term: Foreword: Freedom of Expression in Burger Court' (1980) 94 *Harv L Rev* 1, 28.
[22] Cass R Sunstein, *Democracy and the Problem of Free Speech* (Free Press 1993) 124.
[23] See Sadurski (n 9) 41–3.   [24] *RAV* (n 8) 415 (Blackmun J, concurring).
[25] *Osborne v Ohio* 495 US 103 (1990).
[26] Note, 'The Supreme Court, Leading Cases' (1990) 104 *Harv L Rev* 129, 245.
[27] Ibid (citations omitted).   [28] Ibid.

content' is additionally misleading because it merges, unhelpfully, subject-matter based and viewpoint-based approaches. For the sake of clarity, and consistently with accepted definitions, I will be using these two different notions as belonging to a broader class of 'content-based' restrictions, and contrast them with 'content-neutral' ones. It has been widely accepted that the latter restrictions (viewpoint-based) are more pernicious, and should be regarded with more suspicion than the former (subject-matter based). As Justice Stevens observed in his concurrence in the famous 'cross-burning case',

> As we have long recognized, subject-matter regulations generally do not raise the same concerns of government censorship and the distortion of public discourse presented by viewpoint regulations. Thus, in upholding subject-matter regulations we have carefully noted that viewpoint-based discrimination was not implicated'.[29]

The question is, how to explain this difference?

Before attempting to answer the question, it is worth noting that something like the idea of 'viewpoint neutrality' is present in the protection of freedom of speech in other legal systems, even if a different terminology is used. In Germany, for instance, an idea very similar to the rule of viewpoint neutrality has been articulated by the Federal Constitutional Court when interpreting the constitutional requirement that any legal limitation of (inter alia) constitutional freedom of speech[30] must be contained in the 'provisions of general laws'.[31] The requirement of generality has been seen, in a 2009 decision of the Court,[32] as meaning that 'the legal interest in question [which justifies the restriction] must be protected per se, without regard to a specific opinion ... and that links to content must therefore be neutral with regard to the various political currents and ideologies'.[33] Elsewhere in the same judgment, the Court defined the 'generality' of the laws as meaning that 'they prove to be consistent and abstractly thought in terms of the legal interest and are designed *regardless of views* which are found to be held in specific instances'.[34]

What is perhaps ironic is that the Court undertook to elaborate its understanding of viewpoint neutrality in a decision which *upheld* constitutionality of a law which was definitely *not* viewpoint-neutral: a 2005 amendment to the Criminal Code which makes it a punishable crime to approve of, glorify, or justify National Socialist rule of arbitrary force. But the Court made it clear that its approval for this law was a clear exception to the 'generality' requirement, or, as it put it, 'an exception to the ban on the special legislation for opinion-related laws'.[35] The exception, the Court stressed, was justified on the basis of 'the unique nature of the crimes committed under the historical National Socialist rule of arbitrary force and the resultant responsibility for the Federal Republic of Germany'.[36] But, the exception aside, the Court's understanding of 'generality' bears

---

[29] *RAV* (n 8) 434 (Stevens J, concurring).
[30] *Basic Law for the Republic of Germany*, 1949, art 5(1).   [31] Ibid, art 5(2).
[32] 'Wunsiedel' [2009] 1 BvR 2150/08; BVerfGE 124, 300.   [33] Ibid [33].
[34] Ibid [35] (emphasis added).   [35] Ibid [41].
[36] Ibid [45].

strong resemblance to the US-style viewpoint neutrality. Further, and importantly for our purposes, the Court explicitly links the issue of generality (viewpoint neutrality) with legislative purposes/intentions for the law to be general, in a requisite sense:

> their *purpose* may not aim to ensure that protective measures are taken towards impacts of specific expressions of opinion that remain purely intellectual. The *intention* of preventing statements with content that is damaging or dangerous in their conceptual consequence rescinds the principle of freedom of opinion itself and is illegitimate.[37]

Another legal system in which an idea similar to 'viewpoint neutrality' has appeared is New Zealand. In a comment on a decision of the High Court about a swastika display on a residential house,[38] legal scholar Bede Harris used terms identical to the 'viewpoint neutrality' discourse in criticizing the judgment. While agreeing with the outcome (the Court upheld a ban on swastikas), Harris claimed that a similar conclusion could have been reached 'on considerations of time and place', and without any regard to the content or the viewpoint of the expression. 'The issue of viewpoint neutrality is central to freedom of expression, yet was not addressed in the judgment', Harris deplored, and added: 'The result was a decision which, by restricting the ambit of permissible expression to what conforms to prevailing notions of ideological acceptability, quietly legitimated viewpoint censorship'.[39] Regardless of the merits of this argument concerning that particular court judgment, it is clear that by using a harsh notion of 'viewpoint censorship', the author endorsed a position of strong distaste towards regulating speech based on the viewpoint it expresses.

The distinction between viewpoint neutrality and subject-matter neutrality makes good sense if we adopt a template of *motive*-oriented approach to freedom of speech jurisprudence. It is of course not the case that subject-matter regulations do not implicate a motive scrutiny, or even that they necessarily implicate motive scrutiny to a lesser degree than viewpoint regulations. But in real life, viewpoint regulations seem to evoke improper motivations more urgently and obviously than subject-matter motivations. Geoffrey Stone captured this difference well, saying that 'the probability that an improper motivation has tainted a decision to restrict expression is far greater when the restriction is directed at a particular idea, viewpoint . . . than when it is content-neutral'[40] (note, incidentally, an unfortunate tendency to contrast the viewpoint approach and *content* neutrality as if these two options exhausted the possibilities, thus leaving subject-matter restrictions outside the dichotomy). The main point I am making here is that, within a subset of content regulations, viewpoint regulations implicate and reveal *different* motivations than subject-matter regulations do, and that this more invidious

---

[37] Ibid [49] (emphasis added).   [38] *Zdrahal v Wellington City Council* [1995] 1 NZLR 700.
[39] Bede Harris, 'Viewpoint Neutrality and Freedom of Expression in New Zealand' (1996) 8 *Otago L Rev* 515, 537–8.
[40] Stone (n 10) 230.

character of the motivations triggering viewpoint regulations explains our higher degree of hostility towards viewpoint- than subject-matter regulations.

Before suggesting an underlying distinction in defects of both types of regulations, let me go back to Justice Marshall's opinion in *Mosley*. Soon after making an extravagant claim about the absolute impermissibility of any content-based regulations, Marshall went on to say: 'necessarily ... government may not grant the use of a forum to people whose views it finds acceptable, but deny use to those wishing *to express less favored* or more controversial views. And it may not select *which issues are worth discussing or debating* in public facilities'.[41] This statement clearly belongs to the vexed and excessively complicated 'public forum' doctrine, which it will be prudent to stay away from in this chapter, but for our purposes we may treat Marshall's statement as a helpful characterization of the difference between viewpoint-based restrictions (in the first sentence of the quoted passage) and subject-matter ones (in the second sentence). For Marshall, both are equally reprehensible from a constitutional point of view, but we do not need to endorse this implication. It is not particularly hard to reconstruct a possible defect in governmental motivation for the first type of restriction: it is an official dislike (or its opposite, official preference) for a particular viewpoint, ideology, or opinion. As Geoffrey Stone put it, referring to a famous formula by Alexander Meiklejohn, 'by effectively excising a specific message from public debate, [a viewpoint discriminatory law] mutilates "the thinking process of the community"'.[42] So the main deplorable result of such laws is that they skew public debate, rather than they limit or impoverish public discourse.

To be sure, the 'skewing of public debate' may occur also as a result of arguably content-neutral regulations. As Martin Redish suggests, such regulations also may have a differential impact upon the competing views in a particular controversy: 'Individuals who have heard one side of an issue may well be precluded from learning the other by content-neutral restrictions ... While such regulations do not focus upon the expression of a single opinion, or impede expression of the same viewpoint at all times, *erratic and unpredictable distortion of the marketplace* is no less a distortion'.[43] But the italicized words indicate what is wrong about Redish's argument. When a restriction limits public expression in a content-neutral manner, the pattern of distortion is largely 'erratic and unpredictable'. It may just be an unfortunate case that a viewpoint A is hit harder than a viewpoint B. But if such a disproportionate impact is by and large random, and if it could not be anticipated, much less intended, then it is perhaps deplorable but not unfair. There are, however, circumstances in which the legislators and judges *do* have a way of anticipating which viewpoints will be disadvantaged and which will be favoured. If they then tailor a visibly content-neutral restriction in order to achieve a specific result which favours one side of the controversy, then it will be an example of indirect viewpoint discrimination. Consider a restriction on leafleting, supported officially by arguments

---

[41] *Mosley* (n 15) 96 (emphasis added).
[42] Stone (n 10) 198, quoting Alexander Meiklejohn, *Political Freedom: The Constitutional Powers of the People* (Harper 1960) 27.
[43] Martin H Redish, 'The Content Distinction in First Amendment Analysis' (1981) 34 *Stan L Rev* 113, 131 (emphasis added).

about reducing litter. It may look like a content-neutral restriction (all leaflets are prohibited, regardless of content) but it may in fact operate as an indirect viewpoint discrimination because one party to a particular controversy may lack the resources to propagate their cause by other means, and this financial disadvantage may well correlate with a particular ideology. So when we contemplate cases of viewpoint discrimination, it is proper to include in this category also indirect discrimination. Just as with the concept of discrimination simpliciter, the recognition of indirect discrimination does not undermine a distinction between discriminatory and neutral regulations.[44]

Just as it is important to insist on a clear line to be drawn between viewpoint-based and content-neutral restrictions, so it is important to draw a principled line, within a broader category of content-based regulations, between those which are subject-matter based and those which are viewpoint-based. This was the main question raised by *Rosenberger v University of Virginia*,[45] and different answers to the question of whether the university's denial of funding for a religious student newspaper was a subject-matter regulation or a viewpoint-based regulation were determinative of the outcome. The majority believed the latter, and largely on this ground decided that the denial of funds was a violation of the First Amendment.[46] Writing the opinion of the Court, Justice Kennedy tends to blur the distinction between both types of regulation ('the distinction is not a precise one'[47]), but in the end concludes that 'viewpoint discrimination is the proper way to interpret the university's objection to [the student newspaper]' because the university did not 'exclude religion as a subject matter' but rather 'select[ed] for disfavored treatment those student journalistic efforts with religious editorial viewpoints'.[48] This sounds like an ad-hoc judgment. Without inquiring into the likely *motives* for the denial of funds, Justice Kennedy does not tell us why to interpret the restriction as based on a religious viewpoint as contrasted to a restriction based on religion as a subject matter of the newspaper. Consider, for a moment, an analogy between restrictions on religious expression (as was the case in *Rosenberger*) with restrictions on *political* expression. When a restriction does not specify any particular political view as affected by a regulation, a restriction on political speech, per se, seems to be better characterized as subject-matter based than viewpoint-based. And, incidentally, *this* is how the US Supreme Court characterized the exclusion of political speech from various fora as consistent with the First Amendment. For example, it upheld a municipal public transport system ban upon political advertising on its trains, a ban on entry by political speakers into a military base, and an exclusion of political speech from a charity drive in a federal workplace.[49] In all these cases, the outcome was due to the characterization of political

---

[44] More on indirect viewpoint discrimination, see Sadurski (n 9) 167–73.
[45] *Rosenberger v University of Virginia*, 515 US 819 (1995).
[46] The case implicated both the free speech and religion clause of the First Amendment, and here I focus only on the former.
[47] Ibid 831.   [48] Ibid.
[49] See *Lehman v City of Shaker Heights*, 418 US 298 (1974) (public transport); *Greer v Spock*, 424 US 828 (1976) (military base); *Cornelius v NAACP Legal Defense & Ed. Fund*, 473 US 788 (1985) (charity drive).

speech as a subject matter rather than a viewpoint. Why, then, would 'religion' describe a viewpoint? As a result of such a characterization, political speech would receive lower protection than religious speech.

The point I want to make is that the distinction is not unstable but rather that it can be intelligibly drawn only if we compare the *evil captured* by the 'subject-matter regulation' category with that described by 'viewpoint regulation', and this will inevitably lead us to an enquiry about legislative motives. And this is the burden of Justice Souter's argument in that section of his dissent in *Rosenberger* which addresses the free speech clause of the First Amendment. He emphasizes that the relevant inquiry is 'not merely whether the University bases its funding decisions on subject-matter of student speech' but rather whether the university is 'impermissibly distinguishing among competing viewpoints'.[50] These are, for him (as for the argument pressed in the present chapter) two distinctive questions. Further, he states (echoing an earlier judgment of the Court) that in distinguishing between the two types of regulation '"the government's purpose is the controlling consideration"'.[51] This resonates with the argument that the two types of regulations correspond to distinctive governmental motives, or purposes, both of which are prima facie objectionable, but differently so.

As far as the motive behind viewpoint-based restrictions is concerned, it can be discerned from the evil that such restrictions produce: we infer here, as so often in the law, from effects to motives/purposes. As Justice Souter says in his dissent, 'the prohibition on viewpoint discrimination serves that important purpose of the Free Speech Clause, which is to bar the government from skewing public debate'.[52] As we have already seen, the 'skewing of public debate' by the authorities is an evil which can be properly targeted by legal principles protecting speech. Justice Souter helpfully states the obvious: '[i]t is precisely this element of taking sides in a public debate that identifies viewpoint discrimination and makes it the most pernicious of all distinctions based on content'.[53] Governmental partisanship is thus the main sin targeted by the principle of viewpoint neutrality. Partisanship (favouritism) and intolerance (official dislike) are two sides of the same coin.

8.3 Intolerance and Paternalism in Regulations of Speech

If intolerance is a proper word to describe the attitude behind viewpoint-based regulation, what is a likely and at the same time reprehensible motivation for a second defect, namely a government's selection of issues worth discussing and debating, and by implication, issues not worth discussing in public (hence, subject-matter regulation)? Let me

---

[50] *Rosenberger* (n 45) 893 (Souter J, dissenting).
[51] Ibid 894, quoting *Ward v Rock Against Racism*, 491 US 781, 791 (1989).   [52] Ibid 894.
[53] Ibid 895.

anticipate my conclusions before I develop the argument: the likely motive behind such a preference or reprobation for an entire subject matter is the one of paternalism, and the sort of paternalism which is implicated in subject-matter restrictions is likely to be *less* objectionable than the sort of intolerance for a point of view discernible in viewpoint regulation. This explains a lesser antipathy towards subject-matter based restrictions than towards viewpoint regulations.

In terms of *effects*, the distinction between two types of governmental intervention is clear but normatively non-conclusive: subject-matter interventions impoverish public debate by removing a particular issue from the agenda while viewpoint regulations skew the debate in a particular direction, favoured by the government. Both these effects may be deplored as cases of governmental 'censorship' but they work differently, and it is plausible that the effects of agenda-narrowing are more acceptable than the effects of privileging a particular viewpoint. Suppose a public university A refuses to fund any student media activities (a student newspaper, for instance) having as their object a discussion of religious issues, from whatever perspective, whereas university B refuses funding only to pro-religious (or only atheistic) groups.[54] The latter effect *may be* seen to be more reprehensible because the debate has been biased in a direction expected by the rule-maker, the university B. But is this a convincing position? After all, the impoverishment of the debate in terms of subject removal by university A may also have devastating effects on public discourse. And there may be something instantly paradoxical about accepting the legitimate power of the public body to *entirely* remove a particular subject from the forum, but not to prohibit only some viewpoints while maintaining others intact: doesn't the greater power include the lesser? So, we really need to reconstruct the most likely *motives* of official action in both scenarios to appreciate the different status of both types of restrictions.

To return to our example of a public university refusing any funding to a student group which intends to discuss religious issues (university A), a condition of the grant will be that religion will not be on the agenda. What reasons for targeting the whole subject matter might the university have? To make our thinking sharper, we must exclude, for the sake of argument, indirect viewpoint discrimination; we must assume that we have accounted for a situation where the subject is a proxy for a viewpoint. And we need to bracket purely legal (institutional) arguments, to the effect that a constitutional provision in a given legal system, as authoritatively interpreted by courts, permits subject-matter but not viewpoint-based regulations of speech. We need to find the likely moral or political arguments because what we search for is not a purely formal characterization of the official action but the best, or the most likely, *justification* of such action.

In my view, the most likely (though not necessarily the only) justification for a subject-matter regulation in our imaginary university A will be a view that discussing religion is, at least under some circumstances and in some settings (such as those relevant to university funding), not good for the discussants themselves. For instance, it may be divisive, bring or amplify antagonisms within the student body, divert students'

---

[54] This example roughly corresponds to the facts of *Rosenberger* (n 45).

attention from more pressing issues or from their studies, and so on. Now each of these rationales may sound silly (and probably they *are* silly, to some extent), but they are not outright absurd, and they are not inconceivable as rationales for the regulation. In fact, they seem to me to be the most plausible explanation for such an action. (Someone may phrase the alleged damage in institutional terms, as a damage to the institution as a whole, but surely such an argument would boil down, at least in large part, to the argument about damage to students). And this is, of course, a paternalistic argument par excellence: intervention in an action for the benefit of willing, adult participants, against their avowed preferences.

As we know, no regulation is based on a single rationale, and we can think of some other, non-paternalistic motivations for the prohibition in our example. The university, for instance, may fear public disorder on the campus arising out of religious antagonisms. More generally, issue suppression may be often seen as a condition of an orderly and constructive debate. As Justice Stevens once noted, '[a]s is true of many other aspects of liberty, some forms of orderly regulation actually promote freedom more than would a state of total anarchy'.[55] 'Gag rules', a phenomenon defined and analysed by Stephen Holmes, are often a device for making a debate orderly, and indeed, for making it possible. As Holmes nicely puts it, 'strategic self-censorship seems to be an almost universally employed technique of self-management and self-rule'.[56] So what matters for the characterization of a regulation as paternalistic (and for the normative implications of such characterization) is *which* of the rationales is dominant. The public order rationales seem to me to be clearly secondary, pretextual, and largely disingenuous, because these effects are relatively easy to control and cabin without interfering with speech. In contrast, paternalistic concerns are not as easily addressed without minimizing the likelihood of discussions about religion on the campus, and a refusal of funding seems like a reasonable means to that end.

To see that paternalistic motivations are the likely, though not the only, triggers of many subject-matter restrictions, consider a landmark decision of 1992 from the High Court of Australia. The Court struck down, as contrary to an implied constitutional right of freedom of political communication, a legislative provision that prohibited the broadcasting of paid political advertisements during an election campaign and instead attempted to impose upon broadcasters a duty to provide free time to political parties according to a complex formula.[57] One of the two dissenting judges, Brennan J, reconstructed (approvingly) the legislative aims behind the regulation as the 'minimising of the risk of corruption of the Parliament and the reduction of an untoward advantage of wealth in the formation of political opinion'.[58] Unlike the majority, Brennan J found the restrictions in question to be 'comfortably proportionate' to those important objects, the

---

[55] *Consolidated Edison Co v Public Service Comm'n*, 447 US 530, 546 (1980) (Stevens J, concurring, citations omitted).
[56] Stephen Holmes, 'Gag Rules or the Politics of Omission' in Jon Elster and Rune Slagstad (eds), *Constitutionalism and Democracy* (CUP 1988) 57.
[57] *Australian Capital Television Pty Ltd v Commonwealth* (1992) 177 CLR 106. [58] Ibid 156.

achievement of which would 'go far to ensuring an open and equal democracy'.[59] He then expressed the application of the proportionality principle in this context as follows: 'a law may validly restrict a freedom of communication about political or economic matters' where it serves 'some other legitimate interest and it must be proportionate to the interest to be served'.[60]

Brennan J characterized the regulation in question clearly in terms of subject-matter restrictions though *sans le mot*. This is, admittedly, only one way of characterizing the restriction at stake; another would be to say, using the US constitutional language, that it is a 'time, place, and manner' type of restriction. It applied only to paid advertisements in broadcast media; other, equally 'political' contents, were beyond the regulation's scope. As Brennan J observed: 'All news, current affairs and talk-back programmes are unaffected by the restrictions. The print media are unaffected. The other methods of disseminating political views such as public meetings, door knocks and the distribution of handbills are unaffected.'[61] This is all true. However, it is equally true that within the content-neutral category of 'paid advertisements on broadcast media', the regulation used a subject-matter distinction between political and all other advertisement. So, for our purposes it is clearly a subject-matter regulation.

In the course of his argument, Brennan J explains why such a restriction does not raise serious problems: '[t]elevision advertising is brief, its brevity tends to trivialise the subject; it cannot deal in any depth with the complex issues of government. Its appeal is therefore directed more to the emotions than to the intellect'.[62] He then goes on to summarize some empirical studies and parliamentary reports, both in Australia and in the United States, which show the distorting and generally negative impact of political advertising. While he acknowledges that 'the formation of political judgment is not solely an intellectual exercise', he nevertheless would grant the parliament an authority 'to make a low assessment of the contribution made by electronic advertising to the formation of political judgment'.[63]

Now this opinion clearly smacks of paternalism. While not stated explicitly, one way of understanding Brennan J's message is that it is actually *bad* for citizens to form their political judgments based on TV advertisements. They risk having their rationality distorted, and have their 'prejudices, fears and uncertainties' reinforced, as a result of 'the repetition of catchwords until they attain truth by familiarity'.[64] Admittedly, this is not the only reading of Brennan J's argument (another may be through a collective harm to democracy), and not the only argument in *defence* of the provisions under scrutiny (the main one is to reduce the chief impediment in political participation).[65] But it is *a* plausible argument: people who want to form their electoral choices in a rational and responsible manner are actually harmed (the argument goes) when exposed to political advertising. They may be also harmed by being exposed to any *other* advertising, of course, but this other harm does not register for the purposes of the argument in which a right is defined as freedom of *political* communication (with no right of free

[59] Ibid 161. [60] Ibid 150. [61] Ibid 160. [62] Ibid. [63] Ibid 161.
[64] Ibid. [65] Ibid 155.

communication per se asserted, as is the case in the Australian constitutional system). It therefore shows, as my broader argument in this context suggests, that paternalistic motivation is a likely ingredient of many subject-matter restrictions on speech.

8.4 Is Intolerance Worse (Less Public Reason-Compatible) than Paternalism?

An obvious question at this point is: what difference does it make whether a regulation is based on intolerance (as is the case in viewpoint-based restrictions) or on paternalism (as is the case in subject-matter based regulations)? Put bluntly, why is paternalism *less bad* than intolerance, so that the difference can properly explain the different degree of scrutiny of viewpoint-based and subject-matter based regulations, and their associated motivations? The best explanation must show that paternalism, at least of the sort likely to underlie subject-matter regulations, is a less objectionable moral position than an official intolerance of a particular opinion, as discernible in viewpoint-based regulations. And this will be the burden of the argument below.

First, however, it is important to realize that both positions, paternalism and intolerance, are significantly *different* from each other. Paternalism is not intolerance: it would be a misnomer to characterize an action of removing a particular subject matter from public debate as 'intolerance' towards a particular topic. Indeed, it is hard to understand how a rational person may 'dislike' an issue (as opposed to disliking a particular 'take' on an issue). One may of course dislike the very fact that a particular issue is debated but this is just an *effect* of a motive which still needs to be established; it is merely an announcement rather than a rationale for one's desire of subject removal. One may, for instance, dislike the fact of discussing electoral politics in the workplace or in army barracks, but it must be an attitude based on some further reasons which are not captured by the concept of intolerance or dislike.

Also vice versa, intolerance is not paternalism: when we are objecting to a particular viewpoint, and believe that it should be suppressed, rarely do we articulate such an objection on the basis of concern for those who share and express that viewpoint. Suppose that someone advances the principle that the majority's dislike of an opinion is a sufficient ground to warrant a prohibition of that opinion. There is nothing paternalistic about such a principle because paternalism occurs when someone's liberty is restricted on the basis of an argument about *that person's* good. However, protecting the majority against offence restricts the speaker's liberty for the alleged benefit of the hearer—*another person* who, it is urged, wants to be protected against the unpleasant sensation of being offended.

We may generalize the last point. It is not plausible to believe that viewpoint-based restrictions can be based on paternalistic motives, that is, upon a genuine concern for the speakers rather than the hearers. If expressing a view is seen as harmful to the speaker (a condition of paternalistic intervention) then it may be for one of the following three reasons: (1) because the law-makers believe that acting upon a given view will be harmful to the speakers; (2) because they believe that the view is so immoral that the very act of expressing it causes a self-inflicted moral harm; or (3) in order to protect the speaker against a violent reaction by a hostile audience. As far as (1) is concerned, such motivation seems irrational. We may well protect persons from self-inflicted harms by prohibiting an action (for instance, driving without a seat belt) but not by prohibiting an expression of support for an action. Restrictions on expressions of a particular view in order to prevent harm resulting from acting upon that view may be rational only insofar as we want to protect the *hearers* (who, as we fear, may be persuaded to take a harmful course) but not the speakers. It is therefore not paternalistic. As far as (2) is concerned, the motivation in this case is not genuinely paternalistic but moralistic. To say that we may prevent self-inflicted 'moral harm' is a manner of speaking that an expression which is considered immoral can be prohibited. This is because the only sense that can be given to a notion of self-inflicted 'moral harm' is that the person failed to meet what we consider to be proper moral standards.[66] Only (3) is a genuine paternalistic motive. This, however, seems to apply to exceptional and rare circumstances only, as we may think of a great number of viewpoint-based restrictions where the motive of protecting the speakers against violent response is highly unlikely. And while paternalistic arguments *may* support restrictions on unpopular expressions, it is a widely accepted principle, in particular in the US, that a hostile audience per se should not motivate a restriction on speech, the argument being that such a restriction would amount to a 'heckler's veto' on an unpopular view.[67] So probably the most likely (even if exceptional) paternalistic support for viewpoint restrictions lacks sufficient legal traction; it is rejected not because it is paternalistic but because its adoption endangers the system of protection of unpopular speech.

So far I have argued that, typically, viewpoint restrictions are based on legislative motivations which may be characterized as intolerance, while subject-matter restrictions are based on paternalism, and that the distinction is intelligible. It is time now to address a question: what does it matter? Since viewpoint restrictions are normally (and properly) viewed as more problematic than subject-matter restrictions, and the former should trigger a more searching scrutiny than the latter, the argument must be made that paternalism is a less reprehensible attitude for legislators to take than intolerance.

I am not claiming of course that paternalism is a non-objectionable, much less that it is a benign moral position. There may be some paternalistic restrictions which are intolerable, and on the other hand, there may be intolerance-based restrictions which are so mild as to be justifiable. So in abstract terms, it is difficult to argue that paternalism, as such, is less objectionable than intolerance. As Frederick Schauer urged, '[i]f the first amendment is in fact designed in theory to protect discussion over a wide area, a

---

[66] See Joel Feinberg, *The Moral Limits of the Criminal Law* (OUP 1984) vol 1, 65–70.
[67] See *Skokie v National Socialist Party of America*, 373 NE2d 21 (1978).

subject matter restriction is no more justifiable than a viewpoint restriction'.[68] According to Schauer, similar theoretical underpinnings of the free speech principle to those which support hostility to viewpoint distinctions also argue against subject-matter regulations. Likewise, the Supreme Court once announced that '[t]he First Amendment's hostility to content-based regulation extends not only to restrictions on particular viewpoints, but also to prohibition of public discussion of an entire topic'.[69]

One can see why, in abstract terms, paternalism in the sphere of speech can be seen as anathema to free society. The central values which underlie freedom of speech, discussed at length elsewhere in this volume—individual autonomy and self-fulfilment ('people will perceive their own best interests if only they are well enough informed'[70]) as well as democratic self-government ('the people in our democracy are entrusted with the responsibility for judging and evaluating the relative merits of conflicting arguments'[71])—are the very values which are endangered by paternalistic intervention which assumes that, at times, people are *not* the best judges of their interests. Restraining people for their own good is incompatible with the values of autonomy, self-fulfilment, and self-government which support a robust system of protection of freedom of speech.

But in the context of freedom of speech restrictions on a subject matter, some instances of paternalism may be compatible with (and under a stronger argument, even mandated by) the values of respect for individuals. This is for the reasons which were pressed in HLA Hart's restatement of Mill's harm principle: the anti-paternalistic zeal of Mill was based on his belief in the individual rationality and knowledge which is unpersuasive today. 'Mill carried his protests against paternalism to lengths that may now appear fantastic',[72] Hart famously asserted. There is no denying that often paternalism in the area of freedom of speech may be deeply offensive; for instance, to argue about limiting some information because it will merely upset the hearers is incompatible with the fundamental dignity of the hearers as mature individuals who can make their own judgment about the speech to which they are exposed. But paternalism endorsed as a solution to collective action problems, or to dilemmas resulting from imperfect knowledge or defective preference formation, need not be always offensive to the dignity of individuals. This is, more generally, the case when the removal of a subject matter is considered good for the audience members *for reasons other than their alleged incapacity to evaluate information.*

Consider again the already used example of religious debates in the university. Whatever reasons there may be for the university's refusal to fund a religious discussion (university *A* in our example), distrust of the audience based on suspicion that they will

---

[68] Frederick Schauer, 'Categories and the First Amendment: A Play in Three Acts' (1981) 34 *Vand L Rev* 265, 285.
[69] *Consolidated Edison* (n 55) 537.
[70] *Virginia Pharmacy Board v Virginia Consumer Council*, 425 US 748, 770 (1976).
[71] *First National Bank of Boston v Bellotti*, 435 US 765, 791 (1978) (citations omitted).
[72] HLA Hart, *Law, Liberty, and Morality* (Stanford UP 1963) 32.

not be able to properly evaluate the information is unlikely to figure among them. This would be a truly reprehensible rationale, but the imaginary university's decision to deny funding would very unlikely stem from *that* paternalistic motive. Rather, the more likely argument would be that it would create extra divisiveness which is not good for participants.[73] To be sure, it is still a paternalistic intervention, but it is not as objectionable as if it were based on distrust in their good judgment. It is paternalistic in the broad sense of the word (because it is an unwanted intervention based on the perceived good of the person), but it is not paternalistic in the *offensive* meaning of the word, where individuals' actual preferences are displaced by the regulator. In the religion-on-campus example, the good of avoiding divisiveness may be recognized by the individuals themselves, even if they do not have sufficient motivations to pursue it, not knowing how others will behave.

An act which imposes constraints upon a person's liberty for their own good, but which can be recognized by that person as necessary in order to achieve the goal espoused by that person, is not 'paternalistic' in a stronger, more objectionable sense. Rather it is the sort of paternalism which imposes constraints upon individual action in order to produce a collective good or to avoid a collective harm, and as such seems to resonate with a proper understanding of public reason. Or, to put it somewhat differently, it consists of the foreclosure of certain individual actions which, if taken by many, would make everybody or nearly everybody worse-off, and which people have an incentive to take unless assured that others will also abstain from an action producing sub-optimal collective results.

This variety of paternalism, resulting from an attempt to solve the Prisoner's Dilemma just described, has been recognized as not exactly fitting the usual warnings against forcing people for their own good.[74] In a genuine Prisoner's Dilemma, foreclosure of one avenue of action is a condition for the attainment of the optimal solution for every participant. In the absence of such a foreclosure (in our example, a restriction on a subject matter) a suboptimal result will be attained. It is therefore very likely that most of those whose freedom is restricted by a regulation would recognize that they are better off by virtue of a universal compliance with the rule. So while the constraint is paternalistic in a broad sense of the word (because it restricts the choices open to individuals based on their own good), its motivation is not paternalistic because it does not depend on the argument that those people cannot recognize what is really good for them. Instead, it gives effect to their actual choices which can be implemented only when there is mutual compliance enforced by a legal constraint.

What criteria may be used to distinguish between an objectionable and a tolerable paternalism? The yardstick should be surely whether a limitation of freedom (here, freedom of speech) for the sake of the agent themselves gives effect to a fundamental

---

[73] In fact the fear of divisiveness had been occasionally cited by the US Supreme Court as a major rationale for the Establishment Clause of the First Amendment: see *Lemon v Kurtzman*, 403 US 602, 622 (1971).

[74] See, eg, Cass R Sunstein, 'Legal Interference with Private Preferences' (1986) 53 *U Chi L Rev* 1129, 1140–5.

disrespect for their own sincerely held values. As Isaiah Berlin had suggested a long time ago, what is wrong with paternalism is that it is 'an insult to my conception of myself as a human being, determined to make my own life in accordance with my own (not necessarily rational or benevolent) purposes'.[75] But not every version of paternalism *sensu largo* (which occurs whenever a person's liberty is restricted for their own benefit) is at the same time such an objectionable paternalism *sensu stricto*, which expresses the sort of insult that Berlin was writing about. If a paternalistic (*sensu largo*) suppression of the subject matter from a particular forum follows correctly a calculus about the costs of an unrestricted forum to the participants in the forum themselves, there is no necessary objectionable paternalistic defect in it. Hence, no actual values espoused by the participants are being overridden; it is not the case of Big Brother telling them, 'You may like to discuss this matter but we will not allow you because it is not good for you'. Instead, we are forced to behave in accordance with the values which we actually espouse but which we tend to disregard sometimes in our conduct.

8.5 Conclusion

In this chapter, I have tried to apply a philosophical template of public reason to a typically legal issue: what motivations for speech restrictions render the restriction legitimate under the public reason criterion, and what motivations taint the law as illegitimate, because they are non-endorsable by reasonable persons to whom they apply. Traces of this pattern of argument, I suggested, can be found in several legal systems: in the United States, Germany, New Zealand, and Australia, when they grapple with constitutionality of restrictions on freedom of speech, and choose the motive path (rather than the effects path) of scrutiny. The most typical pattern of argument, I further suggested, is the one which disfavours content-oriented restrictions, as compared to content-neutral restrictions. This distinction offers attractive avenues of argument when it is viewed in the context of legislative motives, and how they fare under a general principle of public reason.

Moving along this avenue, I sought to establish that viewpoint restrictions and subject-matter restrictions (two subcategories of a broader genus of content-based restrictions of freedom of speech) correspond to two perceived wrongful motivations in regulating speech: intolerance and paternalism. The fact that these two types of regulation are (plausibly) viewed as triggering unequal levels of scrutiny can be best explained by the fact that these two moral defects of motivations are of unequal moral weight: paternalism (at least in the forms likely to inform subject-matter regulation) is less objectionable than intolerance, and that it is more acceptable if we adopt a general benchmark of public reason to evaluate restrictions on constitutional

---

[75] Isaiah Berlin, *Four Essays on Liberty* (OUP 1969) 157.

rights. This provides a normative explanation for the broader idea that often the law of freedom of speech is aimed at ferreting out improper motivations for regulation.

At times, however, we focus entirely and exclusively on the *effect* of harm rather than improper *motives*. When the harm is produced instantly by the very fact of uttering certain words, as in 'fighting words', the language of wrongful motives is redundant; harm prevention is a sufficient justification for the restriction of speech. But it is not devastating to a motive-based theory such as the theory of public reason because these are 'easy cases' in which the distinctiveness of speech compared to non-speech disappears, and they often do not even register in our thinking as restrictions on freedom of speech.

PART II

FREEDOM OF SPEECH AS A LEGAL PRINCIPLE

CHAPTER 9

WHAT IS SPEECH? THE QUESTION OF COVERAGE

FREDERICK SCHAUER

9.1 Labelling the Right

As the title of this Handbook demonstrates, the traditional English-language label for the rights discussed throughout this work is 'freedom of speech'. And although some notion of what we now think of as freedom of speech can be identified as early as sixth-century BC Athens, the English-language origins of the phrase 'freedom of speech' date to the late fifteenth or early sixteenth century, and then became crystallized in the (English) Bill of Rights of 1689. In this bill of rights, however, the phrase 'freedom of speech' referred narrowly and specifically to the immunity of members of parliament from sanctions for what they said—spoke—on the floor of parliament and not to anything more comprehensive. Only thereafter did the phrase take on anything resembling its more modern meaning. This shift can be traced roughly to the early eighteenth century, and from then on the phrase appears to have departed from its original parliamentary-immunity moorings, with 'freedom of speech' becoming more commonly understood as referring to a right of citizens and not just to an immunity of members of parliament.[1]

Importantly, this broader conception of the right of (some) citizens to speak freely (on some topics, in some places) without fear of (some) sanctions came into wide usage throughout the British Empire, and thus the phrase 'freedom of speech' found its way

---

[1] On the early history of the phrase 'freedom of speech', and its relation to changes in the underlying principle it denoted, see Leonard W Levy, *Emergence of a Free Press* (OUP 1985) 3–6. See also Zechariah Chafee, Jr, *Three Human Rights in the Constitution of 1787* (U Kansas P 1956) 4–89; Harold Hulme, 'The Winning of Freedom of Speech by the House of Commons'(1956) 61 *Am Hist Rev* 825; Robert J Reinstein and Harvey A Silverglate, 'Legislative Privilege and the Separation of Powers'(1973) 86 *Harv L Rev* 1113, 1122–35.

into common parlance, judicial decisions, political discourse, and the constitutions of some of the North American colonies, as with the Pennsylvania constitution of 1776, which provided in its Article XII that 'the people have a right to freedom of speech, and of writing, and publishing their sentiments; therefore the freedom of the press ought not to be restrained'. By the time we get to 1791, the phrase had become widely used, and it was this phrase that was enshrined into the First Amendment to the Constitution of the United States, providing that 'Congress shall make no law…abridging the freedom of speech, or of the press; or the right of the people peaceably to assemble, and to petition the Government for a redress of grievances'.[2]

Although the phrase 'freedom of speech' is now widespread, especially in countries with an English heritage, there has developed a concern that tying the freedom to the word 'speech' is too narrow. Even if we understand 'speech' to include the written (and printed) word as well as words that are spoken, perhaps contrary to eighteenth-century usage, it is still the case that limiting the freedom of speech to words or language, whether spoken or written or printed, remains seriously under-inclusive. Most liberal democracies, after all, now understand the right to include a wide range of symbolic and communicative but non-linguistic forms of public speaking and public protest, including marching, picketing, parading, sign-carrying, armband-wearing, flag-waving, flag-burning, effigy-burning, and much more of this non-linguistic character,[3] none of which activities would be described as 'speech' in the ordinary English-language sense of that word.

In response to the potential narrowness of the word 'speech', the drafters of many modern constitutions and human rights documents have replaced it with 'expression'—a word that appears capacious enough to include various forms of non-linguistic communication, as with the examples noted in the previous paragraph. And thus we see the 'freedom of expression' protected in article 5 of the German Basic Law,[4] in Article 10 of

---

[2] Interestingly, what became the First Amendment was first approved by the US Congress as the third amendment to the original (1787) constitution, and thus as the third amendment contained in the original proposed bill of rights. The first two proposed amendments failed to be ratified by the requisite number of states, however, and thus the original bill of rights of twelve amendments became a bill of rights of ten amendments, and the original third amendment became what is now the first. Although the First Amendment reads literally as a restraint on 'Congress,' it is now well-accepted that the First Amendment applies not only to other branches and officers of the national government, but also to the states and their officials. See *Gitlow v New York*, 268 US 652 (1925); *Fiske v Kansas*, 274 US 380 (1927); Adam Winkler, 'Free Speech Federalism' (2009) 108 *Mich L Rev* 153.

[3] See further Zick, Chapter 20 in this volume.

[4] The terminological issue is somewhat more complex in the case of Germany. The version of article 5 in the original German contains no title, but the authorized and official English translation of article 5 captions it as 'Freedom of Expression.' The text of the article provides that: 'Every person shall have the right freely to express and disseminate his opinions in speech, writing, and pictures and to inform himself without hindrance from generally accessible sources.' Basic Law for the Federal Republic of Germany, 1949, art 5. The article then goes on to protect freedom of the press, freedom of reporting, freedom of art, freedom of scholarship, and freedom of research and teaching.

the European Convention on Human Rights (ECHR),[5] in Article 19 of the Universal Declaration of Human Rights (UDHR),[6] in section 2 of the Canadian Charter of Rights and Freedoms,[7] in many other legal instruments and human rights documents, and in most of the contemporary international and philosophical literature on the topic.[8]

Yet although the problem with describing the right as a right to 'freedom of speech' may be misleadingly narrow, describing it as 'freedom of expression' may be misleadingly broad. It is true that speaking, writing, printing, protesting, demonstrating, photographing, and much else are all forms of expression, but it is also possible to express one's self in non-communicative ways. Many people express themselves in terms of how they dress, where they live, what they choose as a profession, what avocations they pursue, and much else. Moreover, it is consistent with how we understand the meaning of 'expression' for me to say that I expressed my anger by kicking the chair, or expressed my disappointment by crying, or expressed my frustration by putting aside the frustrating task and having a drink.[9] In cases like these we express ourselves in countless ways, but we do not speak, and we do not communicate in any way. As a result, there is some risk that describing the right as a right to 'freedom of expression' will fall prey to this ambiguity, leading 'freedom of expression' to become synonymous with, or collapse into, a more general conception of personal liberty or personal freedom or personal autonomy in all of liberty's (or freedom's, or autonomy's) countless forms.[10] When such an understanding prevails, we have lost the sense that the freedom under discussion is in some way distinct, or special, or to be differentiated from simply freedom of action or personal autonomy.[11]

---

[5] 'Everyone has the right to freedom of expression. This right shall include freedom to hold opinions and to receive and impart information and ideas without interference by public authority and regardless of frontiers': Convention for the Protection of Human Rights and Fundamental Freedoms (ECHR), art 10. The freedoms of association and assembly, as well as the freedoms of thought and conscience, are dealt with in separate articles.

[6] 'Everyone has the right to freedom of opinion and expression; this right includes freedom to hold opinions without interference and to seek, receive, and impart information and ideas through any media and regardless of frontiers'. UDHR (adopted 10 December 1948) UNGA Res 217 A(III), art. 19.

[7] 'Everyone has [the right to] . . . freedom of thought, belief, opinion and expression, including freedom of the press and other media of communication'. Canadian Charter of Rights and Freedoms, s 2. See Richard Moon, *The Constitutional Protection of Freedom of Expression* (U Toronto P 2000).

[8] See, for example, Larry Alexander, *Is There a Right to Freedom of Expression?* (CUP 2005); Jeremy Harris Lipschutz, *Free Expression in the Age of the Internet: Social and Legal Boundaries* (Westview P 1999); Mark Tushnet, *Advanced Introduction to Freedom of Expression* (Edward Elgar 2018); WJ Waluchow (ed), *Free Expression: Essays in Law and Philosophy* (OUP 1994); Thomas Scanlon, 'A Theory of Freedom of Expression' (1972) 1 *Phil & Pub Aff* 204. Earlier, see Thomas I Emerson, *The System of Freedom of Expression* (Random House 1970).

[9] See Frederick Schauer, *Free Speech: A Philosophical Enquiry* (CUP 1982) 47–72.

[10] On the distinction between freedom as personal liberty and freedom of speech more narrowly understood, see Frederick Schauer, 'On the Relation Between Chapters One and Two of John Stuart Mill's *On Liberty*' (2010) 39 *Cap U L Rev* 571.

[11] Among theorists who seek to ground a right to freedom of speech in larger conceptions of personal autonomy, the most straightforward recognition of the problem described in the text is in Seana Valentine Shiffrin, *Speech Matters: On Lying, Morality, and the Law* (Princeton UP 2014) 79–114.

Implicitly recognizing these terminological issues of under- and over-inclusiveness, it has become increasingly common to refer to the right in question as the 'freedom of communication'.[12] This shift in terminology does address the problems of the under-inclusiveness of 'speech' and the over-inclusiveness of 'expression', but at the same time the shift exposes a larger and more important problem, one that goes beyond mere labelling. Specifically, the various attempts to find the right label for this right expose what we can call the problem of *coverage*, and it is to that which we now turn.

9.2 ON THE COVERAGE OF THE RIGHT TO FREEDOM OF SPEECH

The problem that even the label 'freedom of communication' reveals is that a vast number of acts that might count as 'speech', 'expression', or even 'communication' as a matter of ordinary language appear to have nothing at all to do with any sensible understanding of what the right at issue is all about. Consider, for example, the communications that are involved in making a contract, or writing a will. The terms of a contract or of a will are plainly 'speech' if the word 'speech' includes writing, and those terms are even more plainly acts of communication. But no sensible understanding of a political, moral, legal, or constitutional right to freedom of communication would suggest that the law regulating the validity of contracts or wills, or providing for their enforcement, is subject to limitations from the right to freedom of speech. Or consider the ordinary criminal law, ordinary in the sense of non-public and non-political (or ideological) criminal acts.[13] If one sibling suggests to another sibling that they kill their father and then divide the inheritance, and if the recipient of this communication then proceeds to kill the father as a result of this communication, it is scarcely imaginable that principles of freedom of speech would preclude (or even be relevant to) liability as an accessory, as an aider or abettor, or as a co-conspirator, for the sibling who proposed the act.

Other examples come quickly to mind. Inaccurate instructions accompanying a dangerous product (a chainsaw, for example, or a drug with perilous side effects) typically produce legal liability for any ensuing injuries or harms, but a free speech defence in a lawsuit seeking redress would be universally rejected as laughable. And so too with navigation charts that failed to include hazardous rocks lying just beneath the surface of the sea. Or consider competing business leaders who discuss with each other their proposed

---

[12] See, for example, Tom Campbell and Wojciech Sadurski (eds), *Freedom of Communication* (Dartmouth 1994).

[13] For a comprehensive analysis of the arguable tension between a free speech principle and the numerous ways in which long-standing, well-accepted, and non-controversial principles of the criminal law often impose liability for various verbal acts, see Kent Greenawalt, *Speech, Crime, and the Uses of Language* (OUP 1989), expanded from Kent Greenawalt, 'Speech and Crime' (1980) 5 *Am B Found Res J* 645. See also Note, 'Rehabilitating the Performative' (2007) 120 *Harv L Rev* 2200.

prices, with the aim of ensuring that neither undercuts the other. Countries vary with how seriously they take such price-fixing, with some (such as the United States) treating it as a major felony and others (such as the United Kingdom) viewing it as a crime, but of much lesser magnitude. But in no country would a freedom of speech defence to legal action under the fair competition laws be taken seriously, even though the business leaders did nothing other than communicate factually accurate information.

Such examples emphasize what United States Supreme Court Justice Oliver Wendell Holmes, Jr, observed a century ago—that the freedom of speech protected by the First Amendment 'cannot have been, and obviously was not intended to give immunity for every possible use of language'.[14] And if we accept what seemed obvious to Holmes one hundred years ago and still seems obvious now, we must confront the ubiquitous but often invisible question of *coverage*—just what acts or what forms of behaviour, whether by speakers (or writers) or by those who would restrict those acts, implicate the idea of freedom of speech at the outset? Just what actions by communicators or restrictors make the free speech principle even relevant? This is the question of coverage, and the fact that it is often either assumed or ignored does not make it any less important.

We can approach the question of coverage by stepping back from issues specific to freedom of speech. And thus we observe, questions of rights and of freedom of speech aside, that any rule will apply to some acts but not others. The sign on the motorway limiting speed to 100kph does not apply to other roads, just as the old jurisprudential chestnut of 'No Vehicles in the Park'[15] does not limit vehicular use in other places. Nor does that rule have anything to say about musical instruments, alcoholic beverages, or the countless other things that people might wish to bring into the park. And so it is with rights, which themselves function as rules. Rights to equality, which are rights against some forms of inequality, do not encompass rights against burdens universally imposed. A right to state-appointed counsel in criminal cases does not extend to civil actions under private law. And a positive right to health care, as exists in some jurisdictions, is not a positive right to housing or education.

These banal examples make clear that much the same applies to a right to freedom of speech. Although we are interested, in the final analysis, in whether some act winds up being or not being protected against state interference,[16] we do not even get to that question until we first determine whether something is a free speech issue at all. As in the

---

[11] *Frohwerk v United States*, 249 US 204, 206 (1919). For analysis and commentary on the case, with a focus on this phrase, see Frederick Schauer, 'Every Possible Use of Language?' in Lee C Bollinger and Geoffrey R Stone (eds), *The Free Speech Century* (OUP 2019) 33–47.

[15] Originally from HLA Hart, 'Positivism and the Separation of Law and Morals' (1958) 71 *Harv L Rev* 593, 606–15.

[16] The text describes the issues in terms of the right to freedom of speech in its most traditional sense—as a negative right against interference by the state. But the point would be applicable as well to freedom of speech as a claim-right of some sort against private interference, and to freedom of speech as a positive right to state (or, again, private) support for some forms of speaking or writing.

United States (under the Second Amendment to the Constitution[17]), I may have a right to possess a firearm, but that right is not a right to speak, just as the right to freedom of speech is not the right to possess a firearm. They are different rights to different things, and they cover different forms of behaviour. This differentiation among rights makes it clear that all rights do not cover all acts, and the same holds true even when we are distinguishing rights from non-right based considerations of policy, or utility, or anything else. The basic point is that rights, like rules, are limited in scope. The scope of a right is its *coverage*, and the question of coverage is the question whether some act triggers whatever forms of analysis, or whatever degree of protection, is understood as applicable to the acts covered by the right.

Questions of coverage are often invisible, because the name of a right commonly tells us a great deal about the acts that the right covers. A right to engage in public prayer, say, is a right whose coverage is limited, but the question of coverage can almost be read off the name of the right, because we know what public prayer is and what it is not. So too, perhaps, with the aforesaid right to possess a firearm. But when we turn to freedom of speech, or freedom of expression, or freedom of communication, things are not so straightforward, as noted above, precisely because the name of the right tells us little about the activities that the right covers. Because so much of what any of these terms encompass is not even plausibly related to what the right is all about, attempting to ascertain the coverage of the right to freedom of speech turns into a far more complex task.

The divergence between the ordinary meaning of the name of the right and the activities that the right covers necessitates looking elsewhere for answers to the question of coverage. And if we think of this as a legal question in the strict sense, then the answer to the question of coverage implicates the full range of questions and complications about legal, statutory, and constitutional interpretation. Thus, if the protection of some right appears in a constitution, answering the question about what activities the right covers will require taking a position on just how the canonical and authoritative words in a constitution should be interpreted. Should they be interpreted in a flexible or adaptable way, as US views about a 'living constitution'[18] or Canadian ones about a 'living tree'[19] approach would suggest? Or, instead, should the words creating or guaranteeing the right be understood and interpreted according to the goals, purposes, motives, and

---

[17] On the highly controversial willingness of the US Supreme Court to give that right a robust interpretation, see *District of Columbia v Heller*, 554 US 570 (2008); *McDonald v City of Chicago*, 561 US 742 (2010).

[18] See David A Strauss, *The Living Constitution* (OUP 2010).

[19] The metaphor comes originally from *Edwards v Attorney General for Canada* [1930] AC 124 (PC), 136, and is defended at length in, inter alia, WJ Waluchow, *A Common Law Theory of Judicial Review: The Living Tree* (CUP 2007); WJ Waluchow, 'Democracy and the Living Tree Constitution' (2011) 59 *Drake L Rev* 1001. See also Bradley W Miller, 'Origin Myth: The Persons Case, the Living Tree, and the New Originalism' in Grant Huscroft and Bradley W Miller (eds), *The Challenge of Originalism: Theories of Constitutional Interpretation* (CUP 2011) 120–46.

intentions of those who enacted the document containing the right in the first instance?[20] Or should those words be understood and interpreted now as those words would have been publicly understood at the time they were authoritatively put into the relevant document?[21] And so on.[22]

Obviously, neither this Handbook nor this chapter in particular is the place to explore the full topic of the interpretation of constitutions or other authoritative legal texts. But even if we put the intricacies of legal interpretation aside, we remain concerned with just what acts or types of acts the right to freedom of speech covers. And to respond to this concern, it is necessary to determine just what a principle of free speech, as a distinct principle, is understood to do. We will necessarily be interested in this question if we have adopted a flexible or purpose-oriented view of legal interpretation of an authoritative text, or if free speech decision-making in a common law context makes assessment and reassessment of the purpose of some legal principle inevitable, or even if we are talking about freedom of speech not as a matter of positive law but instead as a philosophical or political question. In any of these contexts, the question of the coverage of the right persists, and is at least somewhat distinct from the question of how to interpret an authoritative legal text.

When the question of coverage is detached from the question of legal or constitutional interpretation, the coverage of the right will even more obviously be dependent on the underlying purpose that the right is thought to serve. And this is not to suggest a necessarily teleological or pragmatic perspective. It is to say only that the coverage of any right is thus dependent on the underlying *point* of that right, and thus the coverage of the right to free speech, or the principle of free speech, is similarly dependent on the underlying point of the principle and of the right that emanates from it.

Consider, for example, the view that the point of the right to freedom of speech is closely connected with democratic decision-making and with the importance of speech and discussion to public deliberation about matters of public policy and public importance. The details of this justification, often associated with the US political theorist

---

[20] See Larry Alexander, 'Simple-Minded Originalism' in Grant Huscroft and Bradley W Miller (eds), *The Challenge of Originalism: Theories of Constitutional Interpretation* (CUP 2011) 87–96; Larry Alexander, 'Telepathic Law' (2010) 27 *Const Comment* 139; Robert H Bork, 'The Original Understanding' in Susan J Brison and Walter Sinnott-Armstrong (eds), *Contemporary Perspectives on Constitutional Interpretation* (Westview P 1993) 48–67.

[21] This is a reference to so-called original public meaning originalism. See Randy E Barnett, *Restoring the Lost Constitution: The Presumption of Liberty* (rev edn, Princeton UP 2013); Antonin Scalia, *A Matter of Interpretation: Federal Courts and the Law* (Princeton UP 1997); Keith Whittington, *Constitutional Interpretation: Textual Meaning, Original Intent, and Judicial Review* (UP Kansas 1999).

[22] See Jeffrey Goldsworthy (ed), *Interpreting Constitutions: A Comparative Study* (OUP 2006).

Alexander Meiklejohn,[23] need not derail us here, but the basic idea as it relates to the question of coverage is that this justification would support coverage of a wide range of speech relating to policy or political matters, or related questions of public importance that are the subject of public deliberation, but would only with difficulty apply to literary or artistic or even scientific utterances. The point of the right to freedom of speech being largely about democratic deliberation, the coverage of the right emerging from this justification would be defined by and limited by the nature of the justification.[24]

By way of comparison, consider the view that a regime of freedom of speech derives its value from the unrestricted speech's contribution to the search for truth and the exposure of error. This argument from truth, with its origins in Milton's *Areopagtica*[25] and its most prominent embodiment in John Stuart Mill's *On Liberty*,[26] while arguably also supporting the notion of a search for political or policy truth, would appear to support a broader coverage for the right than a more narrowly focused political or democratic justification.[27] Not all truths are the truths of politics or policy, and many non-political or non-policy truths—scientific truths, historical truths, and other truths about the empirical world, for example—are at best only remotely relevant to the kinds of justifications that the political or Meiklejohnian explanation of the special value of freedom of speech would support. If the point of a free speech principle is to facilitate the process of discovering truth, exposing error, and increasing knowledge in general,

---

[23] See 'Free Speech and its Relation to Self-Government' in Alexander Meiklejohn, *Political Freedom: The Constitutional Powers of the People* (OUP 1965) pt 1; Alexander Meiklejohn, 'The First Amendment is an Absolute' [1961] *Sup Ct Rev* 245. Applications and elaboration of Meiklejohn's political deliberation view of the central point of freedom of speech include Lillian BeVier, 'The First Amendment and Political Speech: An Inquiry into the Substance and Limits of Principle' (1978) 30 *Stan L Rev* 299; Robert Bork, 'Neutral Principles and Some First Amendment Problems' (1971) 47 *Ind LJ* 1; Frank Morrow, 'Speech, Expression, and the Constitution' (1975) 85 *Ethics* 235. When the High Court of Australia found a right to political expression in the Constitution of Australia (which contains no enumeration of rights), it did so largely on what the court understood to be a necessary connection between freedom of political speech and democracy itself: *Australian Capital Television Pty Ltd v Commonwealth* (1992) 177 CLR 106. For discussion and analysis, see Michael Chesterman, *Freedom of Speech in Australian Law: A Delicate Plant* (Ashgate 2000).

[24] Meiklejohn himself, whose basic ideas were first put forward in the 1940s, eventually came to resist the idea that the right was so constricted, as did some of his sympathetic followers. Harry Kalven, Jr, 'The New York Times Case: A Note on the "Central Meaning of the First Amendment"' [1964] *Sup Ct Rev* 191; Alexander Meiklejohn, 'The Balancing of Self-Preservation Against Political Freedom' (1961) 49 *Cal L Rev* 4. But however true it is that non-political art and non-political literature might be in some way relevant to public political deliberation and decision-making, stretching the right in this way seems to lose the bite of Meiklejohn's basic insight. See further Weinstein and Bhagwat, Chapter 5 in this volume.

[25] John Milton, *Areopagitica: A Speech for the Liberty of Unlicensed Printing, to the Parliament of England* (JC Suffolk ed, University Tutorial P 1968). On *Areopagitica*'s relevance to contemporary freedom of speech controversies, see 'Milton's Areopagitica and the Modern First Amendment' in Vincent Blasi, *Ideas of the First Amendment* (2nd edn, West P 2012) 101–7. See also Blasi, Chapter 2 in this volume.

[26] John Stuart Mill, *On Liberty* (David Spitz ed, WW Norton 1975). See also Macleod, Chapter 1 in this volume.

[27] See also Marshall, Chapter 3 in this volume.

then communications fostering this goal would appear to be covered, and so too would official actions aimed at interfering with this process.[28]

Consider then those justifications sounding in liberty, autonomy, self-expression, self-realization, and associated virtues.[29] Starting from this family of justifications, it would be plausible to conclude that the coverage of the emergent right is both broader and narrower than it would be under either of the argument from democracy or the argument from truth. The coverage would seemingly be broader because a principal focus on the autonomy or self-expression of the speaker (or writer) would include a range of self-expressive artistic or emotive acts whose communicative context is minimal. But precisely because autonomy appears to be an individual or personal virtue, the coverage of a right so justified would not appear to include speech by corporations or other collective business entities, however much that speech might produce social goods of knowledge acquisition, error exposure, or political deliberation.[30] Similarly, if the value of free speech lies principally in how it enables our minds and thoughts to be illuminated by the minds and thoughts of others, as Seana Shiffrin influentially argues,[31] then intentional falsity—lying—would not, as Shiffrin insists, even come within the scope of the free speech principle at all.

The foregoing paragraphs have done little more than skim some of the surfaces of some of the more prominent traditional arguments underlying a principle of freedom of speech. The point in this chapter is not to deal comprehensively with the topic of free speech justifications.[32] And thus the preceding paragraphs are only designed to illustrate, non-exhaustively, that the coverage of the free speech principle is necessarily dependent on the point of there being such a principle, and as a result the coverage of a right to free speech will be determined by the underlying justifications for the right in the first instance.

There is no reason, of course, why the justification for a right to freedom of speech need be as singular as the foregoing discussion might have suggested. The right to freedom of speech may well be multiply justified, serving a collection of different goals and purposes. Indeed, the brief survey just offered of several of the most prominent

---

[28] As alluded to in the closing phrase in the text, an important issue is whether a free speech principle is activated—covered—by the nature of the activity being restricted or instead by the nature and motivation of the restriction itself. Although it is typical to think of a free speech principle's coverage in terms of the activities—speech, communication, and so on—of the agent putatively being regulated, and alternative view would locate coverage in the existence of certain impermissible actions or motivations on the part of the restricting agent, most commonly government. See Alexander (n 8); Larry Alexander, 'The Misconceived Search for the Meaning of "Speech" in Freedom of Speech' (2015) 5 Open J Phil 39.

[29] See, eg, C Edwin Baker, *Human Liberty and Freedom of Speech* (OUP 1989); Ronald Dworkin, *Taking Rights Seriously* (Duckworth 1977) 184–205; Ronald Dworkin, *A Matter of Principle* (1986 Harvard UP) ch 17; David AJ Richards, 'Free Speech and Obscenity Law: Toward a Moral Theory of the First Amendment' (1974) 123 U Pa L Rev 45. See also Mackenzie and Meyerson, Chapter 4 in this volume.

[30] As explicitly argued in C Edwin Baker, 'Scope of the First Amendment Freedom of Speech' (1978) 25 UCLA L Rev 964.

[31] Shiffrin (n 11) ch 3.

[32] See the chapters in Part I of this volume.

justifications omits others of importance, including the value of dissent,[33] the virtues of tolerance,[34] and various others. And so if what we call 'freedom of speech' has multiple justifications or multiple points, then the coverage of the right will include the behaviours, whether by communicators or by restricters, covered by any of the justifications. But the central claim remains that the coverage of the right to freedom of speech, just like the coverage of any other right, will be a function of the underlying purposes or background justifications for the right.

The possibility that the right to freedom of speech may have multiple justifications invites consideration of a related issue, the question whether we are talking about only one right when we talk about 'freedom of speech'. Thus, if we contemplate the range of issues commonly associated with the right to freedom of speech, we find ourselves with an extensive list of issues, controversies, and problems. Accordingly, and even apart from questions about the distinction between policies and rights,[35] there is commonly thought, at least in most liberal democracies, to be a right (of indeterminate scope) of citizens to speak out on matters of public importance without fear of official punishment; a right of artists and writers to create in the face of efforts to suppress their creations on grounds of offensiveness, indecency, or obscenity;[36] a right of academics and other researchers to teach, write, and investigate free of official pressure or accepted orthodoxy; a right of people not to be forced to say or write things that are inconsistent with their own consciences or their own personal beliefs; and so on. This list is not intended to be exhaustive. Instead, it illuminates a larger issue—that what is commonly summarized as 'freedom of speech' or 'freedom of expression' or 'freedom of communication' may be the encompassing label for what are in fact multiple rights. There is no reason to suppose that this must be so, but nor is there any reason to suppose that it cannot be so. 'Freedom of speech' is a label, and whether it is a label for one unitary right or multiple distinct (but possibly overlapping in extension) rights is not something that can be determined by looking at the label alone.

9.3 On the Distinction between Coverage and Protection

The point of stressing the idea of coverage is to highlight the important distinction between the coverage of a right and the protection that the right offers. When some act is covered by a principle of freedom of speech, it means that the question whether that act will be considered permissible or not must be measured against criteria incorporating

---

[33] See, eg, Steven H Shiffrin, *Dissent, Injustice, and the Meanings of America* (Princeton UP 1999).
[34] See Lee C Bollinger, *The Tolerant Society: Freedom of Speech and Extremist Speech in America* (OUP 1986).
[35] See Ronald Dworkin, *Law's Empire* (Belknap P 1986).
[36] See Tushnet, Chapter 23 in this volume.

the values of freedom of speech. But measuring a putative restriction of speech against criteria informed by a free speech principle does not necessarily produce the conclusion that the speech will be protected. Recognizing that conduct—speech, to oversimplify— covered by a free speech principle will not necessarily wind up being protected shows that the question of coverage is different from the question of (ultimate) protection, and it is the theoretical and practical difference between coverage and protection that explains its importance.

The distinction between coverage and protection is most apparent in jurisdictions and contexts in which coverage by a right explicitly generates a distinct and heightened degree of scrutiny, whether judicial or political, for rights-infringing acts. And this is perhaps most apparent in US law. In the structure of US constitutional law, governmental restrictions on conduct in general, when no constitutionally-protected right is implicated, need meet only the extraordinary minimal requirements typically described as 'rational basis'.[37] That minimal standard of justification is raised, however, when conduct covered by the First Amendment's protection of freedom of speech is implicated. In some contexts the standard of justification is such that the government must show a 'clear and present danger',[38] in others a 'compelling interest',[39] and for other restrictions—such as those dealing with defamation[40] or obscenity,[41] for example—still other standards apply. All of these standards, however, have in common that they hold a restricting government to a higher burden of justification than would be required were the restricting government seeking to restrict behaviour not covered by the right to freedom of speech. Consequently, and apart from which exact formulation is applicable in which context, the basic idea is that restrictions satisfying the rational basis standard may well wind up not satisfying the heightened standard of justification applicable to covered behaviour. As a result, some behaviour that is *covered* by a free speech right will wind up, by virtue of the heightened justification applicable to covered speech, being also *protected* by that right, even though the conduct would not be so protected were it not within the coverage of the right. Conversely, on occasion—albeit only rarely in the highly speech-protective US law—the heightened standard will in fact be met. In some instances there may actually be a compelling interest, or actually be a clear and present

---

[37] See, eg, *Ferguson v Skrupa*, 372 US 726 (1963); *Williamson v Lee Optical of Oklahoma, Inc*, 348 US 483 (1955).

[38] The now-ubiquitous phrase stems from Justice Oliver Wendell Holmes, Jr's opinion for the Supreme Court in *Schenck v United States*, 249 US 47 (1919), but the standard it represents has been superseded, in the context of advocacy of unlawful or violent conduct, by the even more stringent standard in *Brandenburg v Ohio*, 395 US 444 (1969). Although the matter is unclear, it appears that 'clear and present danger' is still the standard to be applied when government seeks to restrict a speaker or an entire event for fear of violence stemming from the existence of a so-called hostile audience. See *Terminiello v Chicago*, 337 US 1 (1949).

[39] See *New York v Ferber*, 458 US 747 (1982).

[40] See *New York Times Co v Sullivan*, 376 US 254 (1964) (First Amendment-inspired standard of 'actual malice' required in defamation cases brought by public officials); *Curtis Publishing Co v Butts*, 388 US 130 (1967) (same for actions brought by 'public figures' who are not public officials).

[41] *Miller v California*, 413 US 15 (1973) (setting forth a First Amendment-inspired standard for the determination of obscenity).

danger. In such cases, behaviour that is in fact covered by a right to free speech will nevertheless wind up being unprotected. Determining that behaviour is covered by the free speech right is only the first step in the analysis. It is the step that determines at the outset whether the free speech principle is even applicable. But even if the free speech principle or a right to free speech is applicable, it is the second step that determines, in light of applicable free speech-influenced criteria, whether the conduct is indeed protected against restriction.

It is often thought the method of analysis just described is more or less peculiar to the United States, and that the *proportionality* analysis much more common elsewhere[42] has little or no use for an alleged (or, pejoratively, 'formalistic') distinction between coverage and protection.[43] On closer analysis, however, it appears that this is not so.

The fundamental method of proportionality analysis is the determination by the adjudicator that the extent of some restriction on some right or interest is no more than proportional to the deprivation produced by the restriction. But at this point we can ask 'proportional to what'?, here the inescapable nature of the question of coverage becomes apparent. If we are not talking about rights at all, including a right to free speech, then proportionality analysis still requires an assessment of, as Matthias Jestaedt puts it, the 'value of the interest'.[44] But if the value of a free speech interest has no greater weight than any other value, and especially the value of liberty or freedom *simpliciter*, then we simply do not have what can properly be called a right. If, however, the interest in freedom of speech has greater weight, even if we do not label this interest as a 'right', then it is still necessary to determine whether in some particular instance this 'greater weight' is activated. And making that determination is, in different language, simply a determination of coverage. If the interest involved in the writings that constitute a contract is no greater than any other commercial or contractual interest, then there is no additional weight simply because writings are involved, which is but an alternative way of saying that a principle of free speech, which would provide added weight, is not implicated, or that a principle of free speech, even if recognized, does not cover the matter. But if, by contrast, we are assessing, in a proportionality analysis, the weight of an interest in, say,

---

[42] See, among a much larger volume of works, Robert Alexy, *A Theory of Constitutional Rights* (Julian Rivers tr, OUP 2002); Aharon Barak, *Proportionality: Constitutional Rights and Their Limitations* (CUP 2012); Jacco Bomhoff, *Balancing Constitutional Rights: The Origins and Meanings of Postwar Legal Discourse* (CUP 2013); Moshe Cohen-Eliya and Iddo Porat, *Proportionality and Constitutional Culture* (CUP 2013); Vicki C Jackson and Mark Tushnet (eds), *Proportionality: New Frontiers, New Challenges* (CUP 2017); Matthias Klatt (ed), *Institutionalized Reason: The Jurisprudence of Robert Alexy* (OUP 2012) 152–271; George Letsas, *A Theory of Interpretation of the European Convention on Human Rights* (OUP 2007); Katharine G Young, *Constituting Economic and Social Rights* (OUP 2012) 120–9; Gráinne de Búrca, 'The Principle of Proportionality and its Application in EC Law' (2013) 13 *YB Eur L* 105; Vicki C Jackson, 'Constitutional Law in an Age of Proportionality' (2015) 124 *Yale LJ* 3094. In the specific context of freedom of speech, see Moon (n 7) 32–75; Adrienne Stone, 'Proportionality and Its Alternatives' (2020) 48 *Fed L Rev* 1; see also Webber, Chapter 10 in this volume.

[43] See Jamal Greene, 'Foreword: Rights as Trumps?' (2018) 132 *Harv L Rev* 28; Lorraine Weinrib, 'Comment' in Georg Nolte (ed), *European and US Constitutionalism* (CUP 2005) 70–4.

[44] Matthias Jestaedt, 'The Doctrine of Balancing: Its Strengths and Weaknesses' in Matthias Klatt (ed), *Institutionalized Reason: The Jurisprudence of Robert Alexy* (OUP 2012) 152, 155.

protesting against government corruption, or an interest in creating a work of art, then recognizing the special value of freedom of speech will provide more value, in Jaestaedt's terms, than would an interest not *covered* the interest in freedom of speech. In other words, any method of analysis that requires assessing the value of the interest that is restricted is a method that will give more weight to some interests than others. In a regime that does not recognize the special or added weight of a free speech interest, we might conclude that there simply is no free speech principle at work in that regime. But if free speech is to be limited, and if the limitation is assessed in terms of whether the limitation is proportional to the free speech interest, then the first inquiry must be whether a free speech interest is implicated at all, and this, in different terms, is the question of coverage.

The same conclusion follows even more easily if we understand freedom of speech as a *right*, even assuming that proportionality analysis is the appropriate approach. Once again, the first determination must be whether the right is implicated at all, at least if the same restriction that might be permissibly proportional in the case of a non-right will be impermissibly out of proportion if the restriction is on a right. If there is no difference, then the right, as a descriptive matter, does not exist. But if some restrictions that might be permissibly proportional for a non-right are impermissibly out of proportion as restrictions on rights, then it is necessary to determine at the outset whether this is indeed a restriction on the right, and that, in different terms, is the question of coverage.

Many of the claims of difference between proportionality and other forms of analysis[45] appear premised on the idea that in forms of analysis other than proportionality a determination of coverage necessarily produces a conclusion of protection—that is, that rights are necessarily absolute, such that determining coverage determines protection. But once we recognize that rights need not be absolute, and can do at least some work simply by raising the threshold necessary to justify a restriction, then it turns out not only that the alleged distinction between proportionality and other approaches dissolves, but also that the initial determination of coverage is as important for one as it is for the other.

9.4 Conclusion

Beneath the language and complexities of the question of coverage, and apart from the misleading question, 'what is speech?', is a much simpler question that is necessarily the first question always to be asked—'is this a free speech dispute?'. The question of coverage is this question. At times the answer will be determined by an authoritative text. At times it will be answered by examining the underlying point of a distinct and weighty principle of free speech. And at times the answer will be so obviously 'yes'

---

[45] As with those made in the references in n 43.

or 'no' that we may not even recognize that the question is there. But the question, whether explicit or implicit, is always there. Labelling the question as the question of coverage, and distinguishing between coverage and protection, brings to the surface a component that is necessarily part of addressing any free speech issue and any free speech dispute.

CHAPTER 10

PROPORTIONALITY AND LIMITATIONS ON FREEDOM OF SPEECH

GRÉGOIRE WEBBER*

10.1 INTRODUCTION

'NOTHING is more certain in modern society', Chief Justice Vinson wrote in the First Amendment case of *Dennis v United States* (1951), 'than the principle that *there are no absolutes*'.[1] That conviction was affirmed and developed in Justice Frankfurter's concurring opinion, according to which '[t]he demands of free speech in a democratic society, as well as the interest in national security, are better served by candid and informed weighing of the competing interests'.[2] Today, the confidence with which it is asserted that freedom of expression is not absolute and that competing interests are to be weighed and balanced in adjudicating free expression claims is even more resolute. With the qualification that First Amendment doctrine has evolved in directions that take some distance from the transparent weighing of competing interests,[3] apex courts on all five continents adjudicate freedom of expression claims by denying that the freedom is absolute and by employing the principle of proportionality and its all-important balancing test.

---

* For comments on drafts, I thank the Handbook editors, Ben Ewing, Stephen Gardbaum, Grant Huscroft, Bradley Miller, Geoff Sigalet, Jean Thomas, Leah Trueblood, Sabine Tsuruda, Francisco Urbina, Ashwini Vasanthakumar, and Jacob Weinrib. I thank Don Couturier for editorial assistance.

[1] *Dennis v United States* (1951), 341 US 494 (1951) 508 (emphasis added).   [2] Ibid 524–5.
[3] But see Vicki C Jackson, 'Constitutional Law in an Age of Proportionality' (2015) 124 *Yale LJ* 3094. See also Paul Yowell, 'Proportionality in United States Constitutional Law' in Liora Lazarus, Christopher McCrudden, and Nigel Bowles (eds), *Reasoning Rights: Comparative Judicial Engagement* (Hart 2014).

It repays to return to the debates surrounding the US Supreme Court's embrace of balancing under the First Amendment in the 1950s and 1960s, not least to encounter two features of those debates that are muted or absent from the corresponding embrace of proportionality in apex courts today: judicial dissent and academic criticism. Unlike the ready embrace of proportionality among the judiciary in Europe, the Commonwealth, and beyond—itself encouraged by widespread academic consensus that proportionality and balancing are inevitable because inherent to the very adjudication of rights claims—balancing under the First Amendment was subject to pertinacious criticism within the US Court and academy. Justice Black, with the support of Justice Douglas, dissented not only in result but also in method from the defining cases during the near two-decade lifespan of First Amendment balancing. Justice Black referred to 'the dangerous constitutional doctrine of "balancing"',[4] which 'permits constitutionally protected rights to be *"balanced" away* whenever a majority of the Court thinks that a State might have interest sufficient to justify abridgment of those freedoms'.[5] Under balancing, the First Amendment's injunction that 'Congress shall make no law...abridging the freedom of speech' was translated into 'little more than an admonition to Congress'.[6] That admonition, feared Justice Black, would itself be 'at the mercy of a case-by-case, day-by-day majority of this Court', such that the American people could no longer 'rely for their freedom on the Constitution's commands', but rather must seek 'the grace of this Court on an individual basis'.[7] In the light of the results in defining First Amendment balancing cases like *Dennis*,[8] *Barenblatt* (1959),[9] and *Konigsberg* (1961),[10] Justice Black was free to conclude that the grace of the Court was not a generous gift.

What support Justice Black failed to secure on the Court he found in the academy. With some exceptions,[11] scholars sided with Justice Black against the balancing majority. The academic criticisms formulated in the 1960s and developed in Aleinikoff's masterful retrospective in 1987 anticipated near all of the challenges that would surface again when proportionality assumed its status as *the* doctrine for resolving freedom of expression cases elsewhere in the world.[12] Balancing was said to attempt to 'measure the unmeasurable' and 'compare the incomparable',[13] to weaken the constitutional status of the First Amendment's 'thunderous "Thou shalt not abridge" into a quavering "Abridge if you must, but try to keep it reasonable"',[14] to abandon reverence and respect for the constitution by undertaking reasoning that 'goes on *next to* the Constitution',[15] and to

---

[4] *Communist Party of the United States v Subversive Activities Control Board*, 367 US 1 (1961) 164.
[5] *Konigsberg v State Bar of California*, 366 US 36 (1961) 61 (emphasis added).
[6] *Dennis* (n 1) 580.
[7] *Beauharnais v Illinois*, 343 US 250 (1952) 274–5.   [8] *Dennis* (n 1).
[9] *Barenblatt v United States*, 360 US 109 (1959).   [10] *Konigsberg* (n 5).
[11] See, eg, Wallace Mendelson, 'On the Meaning of the First Amendment: Absolutes in the Balance' (1962) 50 *Cal L Rev* 821.
[12] T Alexander Aleinikoff, 'Constitutional Law in the Age of Balancing' (1987) 96 *Yale LJ* 943.
[13] Laurent B Frantz, 'Is the First Amendment Law? A Reply to Professor Mendelson' (1963) 51 *Cal L Rev* 729, 748.
[14] Laurent B Frantz, 'The First Amendment in the Balance' (1962) 71 *Yale LJ* 1424, 1449.
[15] Aleinikoff (n 12) 989.

afford freedom of expression 'little, if any, more' protection than it would have received had the First Amendment 'never been adopted'.[16] There were other criticisms, some of which we will return to below, but one bears special mention: balancing's chilling effect on speech. It was said that the 'attitude toward freedom of speech which encouraged uninhibited discussion' required confidence in assertions like: 'You have a right to say it. This is a free country'. That assertion required one to be able to conclude that 'the right to speak is so clear that there is no substantial danger that doing so might result in prosecution', a conclusion foreclosed if, true to balancing, all that one can say with some measure of confidence is that 'the right to speak out will probably be upheld by the Supreme Court upon a weighing of all relevant factors'.[17] Given this chilling effect on speech, only a hero or a fool would be emboldened to speak truth to power in a climate unfavourable to dissent.

By the mid-1960s, it was said that '[s]o much has been written on the subject' that we have been told 'more about balancing than we wanted to know', even if, after all that had been said, there nonetheless remained 'some uncertainty about what the very term means'.[18] Today, much more has been said and the principle of proportionality has been adopted the world over as the favoured method for resolving free expression claims. Perhaps as a result, it may be thought that there is less uncertainty about what proportionality and balancing mean and require. In this chapter, I review the depth of judicial and scholarly consensus respecting the principle of proportionality and offer an expository and critical account of proportionality analysis. I aim to introduce readers to different understandings of proportionality, showing how the judicial and scholarly consensus is only surface deep. Of course, the fact of disagreement between and within jurisdictions need not deny that the principle of proportionality has merit. But it does put in doubt the confident claims by some proponents that proportionality is 'essential', 'indispensable', and 'unavoidable'[19] and that, when it comes to rights, it 'is all and only about proportionality'.[20] As I also aim to show, the lack of consensus is no great surprise, for much of proportionality analysis lacks direction.

To explore these thoughts, and to demonstrate how much of the US debates from the 1950s and 1960s remain apposite today, I begin by exploring the appeal of proportionality and balancing for the adjudication of freedom of expression claims and then review proportionality's four evaluations. I conclude by revisiting the idea with which this chapter begins: that freedom of expression cannot be absolute. It is an idea that is oft-repeated, but one that, I aim to show in brief, is based on a mistaken premise.

---

[16] Frantz, 'The First Amendment in the Balance' (n 14) 1443.
[17] Ibid.
[18] Kenneth L Karst, 'The First Amendment and Harry Kalven' (1965) 13 *UCLA L Rev* 1, 22.
[19] David Beatty, *The Ultimate Rule of Law* (OUP 2004) 162; Matthias Klatt and Moritz Meister, *Constitutional Structure of Proportionality* (OUP 2012) 1; Robert Alexy, *A Theory of Constitutional Rights* (OUP 2002) 48–9, 57, 74.
[20] Beatty (n 19) 170.

10.2 Freedom of Expression and Contested Questions

What was the appeal of balancing in the US Supreme Court in the 1950s and 1960s? And what is the appeal of proportionality in European, Commonwealth, and other courts today? To think through the answers to these questions, one may position oneself in the role of a judge invited to evaluate the injunction that 'Congress shall make no law...abridging the freedom of speech' or the guarantee that 'Everyone has freedom of expression'. How should a judge relate that injunction or that guarantee to the contested and controversial claims of free expression? When confronted with a claim that freedom of expression awards the claimant the right to deny the Holocaust, to spend during an election campaign, to defame a public figure, to refuse to pledge one's allegiance, or to incite violence, what is a judge to do?

With few exceptions,[21] guarantees of freedom of expression are singularly unhelpful in guiding a judge to the resolution of contested and controversial claims. They make no explicit reference to libel and slander, blasphemy, commercial advertising, election advertising, censorship, publication bans, state secrets, fraudulent misrepresentation, or the range of other expression-related claims that will animate disputes before courts. Guarantees of free expression leave the resolution of these disputes to another day.[22]

To the judge confronting contested and controversial questions, assertions like the following cast more shadow than light: 'the Bill of Rights means what it says';[23] 'The phrase "Congress shall make no law" is composed of plain words, easily understood';[24] 'no law abridging... mean[s] *no law abridging*';[25] 'The First Amendment is an absolute'.[26] When it is added by the authors of assertions like these that, of course, the freedom of speech or expression 'does not establish "an unlimited right to talk"',[27] one imagines many a judge thinking that something has gone wrong in the minds of those insisting that the guarantee of freedom of expression is clear, absolute, and yet not as encompassing as its 'plain words, easily understood' would suggest. And, indeed, the balancing majority on the US Supreme Court certainly thought that advocates of these assertions were engaging in rhetorical sleight of hand. Justice Harlan rejected the thought that the scope of protection could be 'gathered solely from a literal reading of the First

---

[21] Exceptions include specifications of what is included within and what is excluded from the guarantee. For eg, the International Covenant on Civil and Political Rights (ICCPR) specifies, at Article 19(2), that freedom of expression 'shall include' the right to 'receive' information and, at Article 20(1), requires that '[a]ny propaganda for war shall be prohibited by law'.

[22] I explore this feature of bills of rights in Grégoire Webber, *The Negotiable Constitution: On the Limitation of Rights* (CUP 2009) 1–12, 160–73.

[23] *Barenblatt* (n 9) 143–4 (Black J).

[24] Hugo L Black, 'The Bill of Rights' (1960) 35 *NYU L Rev* 865, 874.

[25] *Smith v California*, 361 US 147, 157 (1959) (Black J).

[26] Alexander Meiklejohn, 'The First Amendment is an Absolute' [1961] *Sup Ct Rev* 245.

[27] Ibid 261.

Amendment'.²⁸ He attributed to 'absolutists' like Justice Black a belief in 'an unlimited license to talk', which 'cannot be reconciled with the law relating to libel, slander, misrepresentation, obscenity, perjury, false advertising, solicitation of crime, complicity by encouragement, conspiracy, and the like'.²⁹ For Justice Frankfurter, the 'absolutists' advocated 'dogmas too inflexible for the non-Euclidean problems to be solved' and employed 'a sonorous formula which is in fact only a euphemistic disguise for an unresolved conflict'.³⁰ In short, the view that the First Amendment is an absolute was taken to lead to 'absurd, undesirable, and self-contradictory consequences'.³¹

For defenders of an absolute understanding of the First Amendment, this judicial criticism amounted to 'substitut[ing] caricature for refutation'.³² Academic proponents of Justice Black's position distanced themselves from his suggestion that the First Amendment's words were clear without more, but sought to furnish that 'more' in a manner that stayed true to the unforgiving nature of the Amendment's injunction against congressional abridgement. They sought to articulate the scope of the First Amendment such that, once defined, the constitutional guarantee would be absolute and not subject to a balancing of competing interests. All participants in the First Amendment debates agreed that the constitution did not protect 'an unlimited license to talk'. No one dissented from Justice Holmes' conclusion, articulated long before the balancing debate took flight, that the First Amendment 'cannot have been, and obviously was not, intended to give immunity for every possible use of language'.³³

US scholars promoting an absolute conception of the First Amendment coalesced around self-government and political speech as the markers of the right's boundaries,³⁴ even as they disagreed on how much speech would be within or beyond those markers. Some would have restricted the scope to 'speech that is explicitly political', meaning 'criticisms of public officials and policies, proposals for the adoption or repeal of legislation or constitutional provisions and speech addressed to the conduct of any governmental unit in the country'.³⁵ Others would have included all speech favourable to the responsible exercise of self-government, which would include the 'many forms of thought and expression within the range of human communications from which the voter derives...knowledge, intelligence, sensitivity to human values'.³⁶ Among those forms that 'must suffer no abridgement' were included 'education, in all its phases'; the 'achievements of philosophy and the sciences'; 'literature and the arts'; and 'public discussions of public issues'.³⁷ Then as now, one is tempted to wonder just how discriminating a marker 'self-government' could prove itself to be.

In contrast to these attempts to articulate an unabridgable boundary for the First Amendment by reference to a principle ('self government') or a category of speech ('explicitly political'), a different strategy was favoured by a majority of the US Supreme

---

²⁸ *Konigsberg* (n 5) 49. ²⁹ Ibid. ³⁰ *Dennis* (n 1) 525, 519.
³¹ Frantz, 'The First Amendment in the Balance' (n 14) 1435. ³² Meiklejohn (n 26) 248.
³³ *Frohwerk v United States*, 249 US 204 (1919) 206.
³⁴ See Meiklejohn (n 26); Frantz, 'First Amendment in the Balance' (n 14) 1449, n 105; Robert H Bork, 'Neutral Principles and Some First Amendment Problems' (1971) 47 *Ind LJ* 1.
³⁵ Bork (n 34) 29. ³⁶ Meiklejohn (n 26) 244. ³⁷ Ibid 244–5.

Court. Instead of concluding that Congress has acted unlawfully if it 'infringe[s] constitutionally protected rights', Justice Frankfurter would instead affirm that such infringement would be but 'one of the points of reference from which analysis must begin'; it would be 'the condition for', not 'the conclusion of, constitutional decision'.[38] This strategy freed the Court from the need to settle on a theory of the First Amendment—a theory that would leave enough speech in, but only enough as to maintain an unforgiving injunction against congressional abridgement. Justice Frankfurter's approach to the First Amendment allowed more speech to be included within the constitution's scope because the conclusion that such speech had been abridged only triggered the need for further constitutional analysis. It was thought to be a 'liberating technique', freeing the Court from the challenges confronting Justice Black and the other absolutists.[39]

A similar interpretive strategy is now favoured by courts confronting the guarantee of freedom of expression. The Supreme Court of Canada has concluded that '*all* content of expression irrespective of the meaning or message sought to be conveyed' is guaranteed, making exception only for violence and threats of violence.[40] Similarly, the European Court of Human Rights (ECtHR), in interpreting the scope of the Article 10 guarantee that 'Everyone has the right to freedom of expression', affirms that it extends 'not only to "information" or "ideas" that are favourably received or regarded as inoffensive or as a matter of indifference, but also to those that offend, shock or disturb the State or any sector of the population'.[41] Textbook writers conclude that, under the interpretation favoured by the European Court, the Convention protects '[a]ll forms of expression ... through any medium'[42] and that 'speech through almost every known expressive medium, and with almost any content falls within the scope' of the Convention.[43]

The strategy to include (near) all expression within the scope of freedom of expression might appear to contradict the one premise of debate that secures ready agreement: that freedom of expression does not include 'an unlimited license to talk'. How can judges endorse that premise *and* allow into the scope of freedom of expression all talk? The answer has been sketched above: the abridgement of an unlimited licence to talk is not conclusive of the unlawfulness of the abridgement. What is conclusive is the further reasoning that such abridgement triggers: balancing (in the United States of the 1950s and 1960s) or proportionality (elsewhere today).

Whereas the US Supreme Court had no textual basis to qualify a First Amendment 'abridgement' with recourse to balancing, European, Commonwealth, and other courts

---

[38] *Communist Party* (n 4) 90–1.

[39] Charles Fried, 'Two Concepts of Interests: Some Reflections on the Supreme Court's Balancing Test' (1963) 76 Harv L Rev 755, 755.

[40] *Reference re ss. 193 and 195.1(1)(c) of the Criminal Code* [1990] 1 SCR 1123, 1181. See also *Irwin Toy v Quebec* [1989] 1 SCR 927.

[41] See *Handyside v United Kingdom* (1979–80) 1 EHRR 737 [48].

[42] Bernadette Rainey, Elizabeth Wicks, and Clare Ovey, *Jacobs, White, and Ovey: The European Convention on Human Rights* (7th edn, OUP 2017) 483–4.

[43] Anthony Lester and Pushpinder Saini, 'Article 10: Freedom of Expression' in Lord Lester, Lord David Pannick, and Javan Herberg (eds), *Human Rights Law and Practice* (3rd edn, LexisNexis 2009) 483 (citations omitted).

have grounded their appeals to proportionality by reference to 'limitation clauses'. For example, Article 10 of the European Convention on Human Rights (ECHR) affirms not only, in its first paragraph, that 'Everyone has the right to freedom of expression', but also the right's 'limitation' in its second paragraph, which provides that the exercise of the freedom 'may be subject to such formalities, conditions, restrictions or penalties as are prescribed by law and are necessary in a democratic society'. Other rights and freedoms in the ECHR are similarly paired with a similarly worded second paragraph.[44] In turn, other bills of rights, like the Canadian Charter and the New Zealand Bill of Rights Act, contain a single, overarching limitation clause applicable to all rights and freedoms, which are 'subject only to such reasonable limits prescribed by law as can be demonstrably justified in a free and democratic society'.[45] Although the words 'proportionality' or 'balancing' do not appear in these limitation clauses, courts quickly concluded that what is 'necessary in a democratic society' or 'justified in a free and democratic society' is to be evaluated by recourse to proportionality, such that 'every "formality", "condition", "restriction" or "penalty" ... must be proportionate to the legitimate aim pursued'.[46] Indeed, so settled had the view become that limitation clauses call for proportionality analysis that the limitation clause in the 1996 South African Bill of Rights codified much of the proportionality analysis common across European and Commonwealth courts[47] and the limitation clause in the 2012 Charter of Fundamental Rights of the European Union made express reference to 'the principle of proportionality'.[48]

What then is the principle of proportionality? Allowing for differences across jurisdictions and scholarly interpretations—differences we return to below—a leading formulation is the one given by the Supreme Court of Canada:

(1) The objective, 'which the measures responsible for a limit on a...right or freedom are designed to serve', must 'relate to concerns which are pressing and substantial in a free and democratic society' (the 'legitimate aim' or 'objective' requirement);
(2) 'The measures adopted must be...rationally connected to the objective' (the 'rational connection' or 'suitability' requirement);
(3) 'The means...should impair "as little as possible" the right or freedom in question' (the 'minimal impairment' or 'necessity' requirement); and
(4) 'There must be a proportionality between the effects of the measures which are responsible for limiting the...right or freedom, and the objective which has been identified as of "sufficient importance"' (the 'balancing' or 'proportionality *stricto sensu*' requirement).[49]

---

[44] ECHR, Arts 8(2), 9(2), 11(2).
[45] Canadian Charter of Rights and Freedoms, s 1; New Zealand Bill of Rights Act 1990, s 5.
[46] *Handyside* (n 41) [48].   [47] Constitution of South Africa, s 36(1).
[48] 2012/C 326/02, Article 52(1). For a comparative review of limitation clauses, see Webber, *Negotiable Constitution* (n 22) 59–65.
[49] *R v Oakes* [1986] 1 SCR 103 [69]–[70].

Before exploring these four evaluations in the following sections, let us pause and ask: where does all of this leave us respecting freedom of expression and contested and controversial claims? We find ourselves in a rather simple place. The first question confronting a judge will be to inquire whether the contested claim falls within the scope of freedom of expression. With few exceptions, the answer will be: yes, it does. Given that a positive conclusion at this stage is but a threshold and not a final conclusion, courts have generally favoured an expansive reading of the scope of freedom of expression. The conclusion that *this* contested claim of expression falls within the scope of the guarantee triggers recourse to the principle of proportionality. The 'abridgement of' (to use the US idiom) or 'infringement of' or 'interference with' (to use the favoured European and Commonwealth idioms) freedom of expression is *not* unlawful, at least not without more. The 'more' is the proportionality evaluation. And so, the *proportionate* abridgement, interference, or infringement of freedom of expression is not unconstitutional— only the *disproportionate* abridgement, interference, or infringement is. And because proportionality is the measure of what is justified, courts and scholars speak of a *justified* (because proportionate) or *unjustified* (because disproportionate) abridgement, interference, or infringement of freedom of expression. As aptly put by Stephen Gardbaum in his Handbook chapter, 'what you have by virtue of having a free speech...right is a right against disproportionate' infringement.[50]

10.3 Legitimate Aim (Objective)

The first inquiry under the principle of proportionality relates to the objective pursued by the legislature in infringing freedom of expression. In other words: why has the legislature adopted the infringing measure? Although not explicitly a question for the court in the US balancing decades, it was a silent premise insofar as the identification of an 'interest' that competes with the freedom of speech interest required the Court to articulate the reasons why speech was being abridged. The competing objectives-qua-interests in the defining First Amendment cases of the 1950s and 1960s included 'public order'[51] and 'national security'[52] and, less concisely and more specifically, 'the interest of the Congress in demanding disclosures from an unwilling witness'[53] and 'the State's interest in having lawyers who are devoted to the law in its broadest sense'.[54] Today, courts have generally taken their cue from the more economical formulations in the second paragraph of Article 10 of the ECHR, which outlines objectives including: national security, public safety, the prevention of disorder or crime, the protection of health or morals,

---

[50] Stephen Gardbaum, 'The Structure of a Free Speech Right', Chapter 12 in this volume, p. 228.
[51] *American Communications Association v Douds*, 339 US 382 (1950) 399–400.
[52] *Dennis* (n 1) 525, 547.
[53] *Barenblatt* (n 9) 126–7.
[54] *Konigsberg* (n 5) 52.

and the protection of the reputation or rights of others. On this, there is broad consensus, but it does not extend to two other matters for decision under this proportionality inquiry.

First: the standard against which the objective should be evaluated. In the Supreme Court of Canada's formulation, the objective must be 'pressing and substantial in a free and democratic society'.[55] In the UK's final court of appeal, it is said that the objective must be 'sufficiently important to justify limiting a fundamental right'.[56] For the High Court of Australia, the purpose of the law must be 'legitimate',[57] a view generally shared by academic proponents and critics of the principle of proportionality.[58] For Aharon Barak, former President of the Supreme Court of Israel, the purpose must be 'proper', meaning that it 'suits the values of the society in a constitutional democracy'.[59] And for Robert Alexy, chief interpreter of the case law of the German Federal Constitutional Court, the objective should be a principle, but the threshold for recognition as a principle is low to non-existent.[60] At the level of formulation, it appears that an objective has different thresholds of importance to meet depending on court and scholar—ranging from non-existent to 'proper' to 'legitimate' to 'sufficiently important' to 'pressing and substantial'.

Second: how 'abstractly' to formulate the objective. Consider this example. In evaluating the proportionality of legislative measures that banned tobacco advertising, restricted the use of tobacco company trademarks, and imposed a mandatory package warning on tobacco products, the Supreme Court of Canada was divided on how to cast the legislative objective. For some members of the Court, the measures had, as their objective, to 'protect[] public health from the detrimental effects of tobacco consumption' or, more specifically, 'to protect public health by reducing the number of inducements for Canadians to consume tobacco'.[61] For other members of the Court, however, this 'overstate[d] the objective', as proportionality analysis requires the judge to narrow the search for the objective to the 'infringing measure, since it is the infringing measure and nothing else which is sought to be justified'.[62] What, then, was said to be the objective of the advertising ban and trademark usage restrictions? This: 'to prevent people in Canada from being persuaded by advertising and promotion to use tobacco products'.[63]

---

[55] *Oakes* (n 49) [69].

[56] See *R (Daly) v Secretary of State for the Home Department* [2001] UKHL 26 and *Huang v Secretary of State for the Home Department* [2007] UKHL 11.

[57] See *McCloy v New South Wales* (2015) 257 CLR 178, 193–4. In the High Court's interpretation of the freedom of political communication, 'legitimate' is said to refer to: 'compatible with the maintenance of the constitutionally prescribed system of representative government'.

[58] See Francisco Urbina, *A Critique of Proportionality and Balancing* (CUP 2017) 5; Yowell (n 3); Kai Möller, 'Proportionality and Rights Inflation' in Grant Huscroft, Bradley W Miller, and Grégoire Webber (eds), *Proportionality and the Rule of Law: Rights, Justification, Reasoning* (CUP 2014) 156.

[59] For the spread of proportionality, see Aharon Barak, *Proportionality: Constitutional Rights and Their Limitations* (CUP 2012) 246.

[60] Alexy (n 19) 61. Alexy gives the example of the 'principle of racial segregation'.

[61] *RJR-Macdonald v Canada* [1995] 3 SCR 199, [61], [65]–[66].

[62] Ibid [144].

[63] Ibid.

In turn, the objective of the mandatory package warning was held to be 'to discourage people who see the package from tobacco use'.[64] Which version of the objective is called for by the principle of proportionality? How 'abstract' is too abstract? How 'narrow' is narrow enough?[65]

These are challenging questions and they invite reflection on the relationship of an objective to its means, reflections that disclose that the questions escape ready answers. In a plan of action, all but the first and last steps in a chain of means-to-objectives are *both* means *and* objectives. The narrower objectives—to prevent people from being persuaded by advertising and promotion to use tobacco products and to discourage people who see the package from tobacco use—are very plausibly the immediate objectives of the measures in the chain of reasoning animating the regulation of tobacco products. In other words, banning tobacco advertising was judged by parliament to be a *means to* the objective of preventing people from being persuaded by advertising. But one is compelled to ask *why* parliament would seek to pursue this objective? To answer that question, one turns to the wider objective favoured by other members of the Court: to protect public health from the detrimental effects of tobacco consumption. From the perspective of *that* objective, the narrower objective is not an objective but a means to the broader objective's realization. Indeed, banning tobacco advertising *and* preventing people from being persuaded by advertising are *both* means to the broader objective of protecting public health from the detrimental effects of tobacco consumption. Even this broader objective is not basic or ultimate, however; it, too, answers to the question why—it is a means to a more basic objective, that of being healthy. Although there are many instrumental reasons to be healthy, human health has a good claim to be a basic reason for action, an ultimate objective in the chain of reasoning. Indeed, that final, organizing objective—being healthy—gives sense to and unites the series of means-and-objectives into a whole, a plan for action. From that organizing objective's point of view, all subsidiary objectives are means to its realization.

What light does this shed on the disagreement between members of the Court in relation to the objective of the contested tobacco measures? The immediate objective favoured by some members of the Court and the more general objective favoured by other members both have claim to be the measures' objective. But both are also means, not objectives, when considered from the point of view of the ultimate objective on which parliament acted: human health. The principle of proportionality's instruction to identify the measures' objective, without more, does not assist one in choosing where along the chain of means-to-objectives to stop. The matter is not only of theoretical interest. Different objectives ('to prevent people from being persuaded by advertising' vs human health) will rank higher or lower against thresholds like 'pressing and substantial'. And, as we now turn to see, proportionality's next two evaluations are heavily guided by the formulation of the objective.

---

[64] Ibid.
[65] For judicial consideration of this problem, see *Monis v The Queen* (2013) 249 CLR 92 (High Court of Australia).

10.4 Rational Connection (Suitability)

The next inquiry under the principle of proportionality is often cast as requiring that the measures be suitable for the objective. In one favoured formulation, it is said that the measures 'must be rationally connected to the objective'.[66] On this idea, there is broad consensus. On closer inspection, however, it appears that there are two different inquiries under the umbrella idea of 'rational connection'. For some, like the high courts in the UK and Canada, the inquiry is whether the measures are 'designed' or 'carefully designed to achieve the objective'.[67] For others, like the former President of Israel's Supreme Court, the 'requirement is that the means used by the limiting law can realize or advance the underlying purpose of that law'[68] or, to put the point more precisely, whether the means 'effectively further the government's end'.[69] For Alexy, suitability is part of an investigation into what is 'factually possible', and his key words to describe the relationship between means and ends—'bringing about' and 'promoting'—suggest an investigation into effects.[70]

What do these different inquiries suggest? They point to different measures of suitability: one looks to policy design, the other to the scheme's effectiveness. To return to our tobacco regulations, consider how a court is to conclude whether the contested measures are rationally connected to the objective of protecting public health (or one of the more narrowly formulated objectives). Should the court inquire into the policy design of the scheme, interrogating whether there are good reasons for pursuing an objective in this way? That was the position favoured by some members of the Court, who relied on a number of 'common sense observations', including that 'Canadian tobacco companies would [not] spend over 75 million dollars every year on advertising if they did not know that advertising increases the consumption of their product'.[71] It was therefore sound for parliament to design its scheme in this way. For other members of the Court, however, some evidence that these measures really do serve these objectives *in practice* was required. In the absence of sufficient evidence, a majority of the Court denied that there was 'any causal connection between the objective of decreasing tobacco consumption and the absolute prohibition on the use of a tobacco trade mark on articles other than tobacco products', concluding that there was 'no causal connection based on direct evidence' and no 'causal connection based in logic or reason'.[72] It was thought 'hard to imagine how the presence of a tobacco logo on a cigarette lighter, for example, would increase [tobacco] consumption'.[73] (Others may find it less hard.)

---

[66] *Oakes* (n 49). [67] See *Huang* (n 56); *Oakes* (n 49). [68] Barak (n 59) 303.
[69] Yowell (n 3) 88. [70] Alexy (n 19) 68–9.
[71] *RJR-Macdonald* (n 61) [84]–[87]. In other judgments, the Court speaks of 'reasonable risk of harm' or a 'reasonable apprehension' of harm: *R v Sharpe* [2001] 1 SCR 45.
[72] *RJR-Macdonald* (n 61) [159].
[73] Ibid.

On this reading of rational connect, and in those jurisdictions where the proportionality analysis puts the onus of argument and of proof on government, counsel will need to show not only that the legislature had before it an evidentiary record to support its policy design and, more generally, had good reasons for designing its legislative scheme in this way, but *also* that there is empirical evidence to support the legislature's scheme in practice.

10.5 Minimal Impairment (Necessity or Least Restrictive Means)

We turn, now, to the third inquiry, namely whether, in the words of the South African limitation clause, there are 'less restrictive means to achieve the purpose'.[74] The consensus idea is that, if the objective may be pursued by means that would be less restrictive of freedom of expression, *those* means should be used rather than the means being challenged. In the words of the UK courts, the 'means used to impair the right or freedom' should be 'no more than is necessary to accomplish the objective'.[75] Formulated from the point of view of freedom of expression, it is said by the Supreme Court of Canada that the means 'should impair "as little as possible" the right or freedom in question',[76] a view shared by proponent and critic of proportionality alike.[77]

On its face, this appears to be a fairly straightforward inquiry. However, it reveals itself to be ambiguous in what it asks of courts. The question whether it is *necessary* to abridge freedom of expression invites one to consider alternative ways in which one could pursue the objective, to compare the alternatives as abridging the freedom more or less, and then to locate the challenged measure in comparison to the others. But how is one to decide what counts as an alternative? Is the inquiry technical or moral?[78] At a minimum, alternatives must be 'suitable' or 'rationally connected' to the objective, but that recalls the different readings of *that* requirement. Compounding these uncertainties is the lack of consensus over how one evaluates whether an alternative 'pursues the objective'. For some, only those alternative measures that pursue the objective *as effectively as* the contested measures qualify for consideration.[79] This technical inquiry purports to be able to measure the effectiveness of alternatives and to rule out of consideration those alternatives that, whatever their other merits, are less effective in

---

[74] Constitution of South Africa, s 36(1)(e).   [75] *Huang* (n 56).   [76] *Oakes* (n 49).
[77] See Barak (n 59) 317; Urbina (n 58) 5; Yowell (n 3) 88.
[78] See Bradley W Miller 'Proportionality's Blind Spot: "Neutrality" and Political Philosophy' in Grant Huscroft, Bradley W Miller, and Grégoire Webber (eds), *Proportionality and the Rule of Law: Rights, Justification, Reasoning* (CUP 2014) 375–80.
[79] See, eg, Alexy (n 19) 68; Möller (n 58) 156.

pursuing the objective. For others, however, measures that pursue the objective to some threshold degree, even if they do so less effectively, will qualify for consideration if they are less impairing of freedom of expression. On this understanding, there can be a trade-off between effectiveness and free expression, such that an alternative should count, despite being less effective, if it ranks better against freedom of expression. This evaluation is not a technical evaluation of the effectiveness of means-to-ends, but rather a moral evaluation of more or less effectiveness in exchange for less or more freedom of expression. It invites moral evaluation as to how much 'cost' to the objective's pursuit is acceptable before some alternative fails to count among live alternatives. The range of alternatives against which to evaluate the challenged measures will differ depending on one's understanding of 'necessity'.

Now consider how one is to compare different alternatives as impairing freedom of expression more or less. The tobacco regulations banning all forms of tobacco advertisement again illustrate the problem well. Members of the Supreme Court accepted that tobacco advertisement could be categorized into lifestyle advertising (which seeks to increase market share) and brand preference and informational advertising (which seeks to inform the consumer about available products). How should one compare and rank a measure that prohibits only lifestyle advertising against a measure that prohibits *both* lifestyle *and* informational advertising? Is one 'less' and the other 'more' impairing of freedom of expression? When confronted with questions like these, courts have been quick to conclude that the former measure is less impairing. But why? Is it because less expression is captured and therefore more freedom of expression is protected? That could suggest that more expression, *just as such*, is better for freedom of expression, a proposition that would require some defending against ready counter-examples like deception, fraud, manipulation, and verbal abuse, all of which are instances of 'expression' but not obviously better for 'freedom of expression'. Is it, instead, because more persons can express themselves? This could suggest that more expression by more players, *just as such*, is better for freedom of expression, a proposition that would also require some defending against ready counter-examples, like the infinite number of possible corporate players (like tobacco manufacturers) whose collective voices could dominate the marketplace of ideas. Although words can be counted and persons can be counted, that is not what an inquiry into the minimal impairment of freedom of expression purports to evaluate. Some work is required to show that *freedom of expression* is more or less impaired by a more or less expansive ban on tobacco advertisement, work that, on its face, is not done merely by pointing to more (or less) expression, just as such, or more (or fewer) persons expressing themselves, just as such. It seems that the evaluation here required into freedom of expression is precisely the sort of evaluation that was eschewed in concluding that (near) all expression should be included within freedom of expression. It was thought that a clear-minded proportionality analysis could help judges avoid such hard questions. On closer inspection, the hard questions are stubborn in their persistence.

10.6 Overall Balance (Proportionality Stricto Sensu)

The final inquiry under the principle of proportionality is balancing and it is here that US debates from times past most naturally find their present-day home. In the US debates, it was broadly accepted that 'interests' were in the balance. (The capacious boundaries of 'interest' caution against reading too much into that broad acceptance.) Today, there seems to be no obvious agreement as to what is to be balanced. The Supreme Court of Canada, for example, began by affirming that the balance would be between 'the effects of the measures... and the objective',[80] but then added that the balance would also be between the 'actual salutary effects of impugned legislation' and 'its deleterious effects',[81] and now sometimes drops the objective altogether from consideration.[82] In the UK, the evaluation is said to be between 'the interests of society and those of individuals and groups'.[83] Australia appears to favour the early Canadian position, in calling for a 'balance between the importance of the purpose served by the restrictive measure and the extent of the restriction it imposes on the freedom'.[84] The former President of the Supreme Court of Israel directs one to a 'proper relation... between the benefits gained by fulfilling the purpose and the harm caused to the constitutional right from obtaining that purpose'.[85] In turn, Alexy reads the German Federal Constitutional Court as comparing 'the degree of non-satisfaction of, or detriment to, one principle' as against another.[86] Other scholars invite a comparison between the objective and the effects of the measures or between the burden on individual interests and the value of the government's objective or between competing values or, again, between 'the benefits of infringing the protected interests' and 'the loss incurred with regard to the infringed interest'.[87] Some speak in utilitarian or consequentialist terms.[88]

The present-day candidates under balancing are far more numerous than the 'interests' of the US debates. Yet, the addition of effects, objectives, principles, values, benefits, burdens, intensities of interference, gains, and costs has offered no gain in answering or avoiding the challenges to balancing that were identified in the 1950s and 1960s. So let us simplify the discussion by referring to 'interests', a simplification that assists in showing how dated criticisms on numbers, characterization, formulation, outcome, and comparison all persist.

---

[80] *Oakes* (n 49) [70].   [81] *Dagenais v Canadian Broadcasting Corp* [1994] 3 SCR 835, 888.
[82] See, eg, *R v KRJ* 2016 SCC 31.   [83] *Huang* (n 56).   [84] *McCloy* (n 57) [3].
[85] Barak (n 59) 340.   [86] Alexy (n 19) 102.
[87] See, eg, Urbina (n 58) 5; Yowell (n 3) 88; Möller (n 58) 167; Klatt and Meister (n 19) 1. The quotation is from Mattias Kumm, 'Who is Afraid of the Total Constitution?' (2006) 7 *German LJ* 341, 348.
[88] Julian Rivers, 'Proportionality and Variable Intensity of Review' (2006) 65 *Cambridge LJ* 174, 181. See also Mattias Kumm, 'Political Liberalism and the Structure of Rights: On the Place and Limits of the Proportionality Requirement' in George Pavlakos (ed), *Law, Rights and Discourse: The Legal Philosophy of Robert Alexy* (Hart 2007) 131, 153.

The number of interests. One criticism queries which interests are to be included in the balance. Kumm reports a settled view among proponents when he says that 'proportionality analysis taken seriously means that *all relevant considerations* must be taken into account'.[89] And yet, as Aleinikoff concluded in his review of US cases, 'the Court never makes a full inventory of the relevant interests'.[90] This conclusion, which holds true today, suggests that '[t]aking balancing seriously would seem to demand the kind of investigation of the world that courts are unable or unwilling to undertake'.[91] Indeed, a favoured simplification of the balancing of interests employed by courts is to delegate to the parties which interests are to count: the individual's as put forward in argument by claimant's counsel and 'the public's' or 'the community's' or 'society's' as put forward by government counsel. In practice, 'courts make no serious effort to place the interests of non-parties on the scale'.[92] Indeed, should a judge look beyond the parties before the court, they would confront the question that has frustrated every attempt at balancing *all* relevant interests: the question of demarcation. Should the interests of persons *here* and *now* count? Or the interests of those beyond the court's jurisdiction? Or the interests of persons that *may come to be* in future? In the foreseeable future? The indeterminate future? Even putting some of these worries aside, what can justify restricting the search for interests to *two*—one individual, one governmental? This simplification of great constitutional debates surrounding freedom of expression should be unacceptable to any 'conscientious balancer',[93] and yet neither judicial nor academic proponents have demonstrated how balancing can accommodate a third or fourth or however many other interests.

The characterization of interests. Another criticism of balancing targets the favoured and common characterization of one of the competing interests as 'individual' and the other as 'public' or 'social' or 'governmental'. The artifice of this simplification was noted by US commentators. Consider the refusal of a witness to answer questions put to him by a congressional committee on alleged communist activities. The witness's 'interest' might be cast as an interest 'to withhold the information' *or* 'to protect his reputation and employability' *or* 'to protect the friends whom the Committee will require him to identify' *or* 'to choose his ideas and associates without governmental supervision' *or* 'to behave as his conscience dictates' *or* 'to vindicate the first amendment' *or* 'to vindicate freedom of speech' *or* 'to vindicate freedom in general'.[94] On the other side of the balance, the 'government's' interest may be characterized as the interest of a committee member to have her questions answered *or* 'the Committee's interest in verifying [the witness'] testimony' *or* the Committee's interest in 'unobstructed freedom in determining what it ought to investigate' *or* 'to vindicate its own authority, or that of the Congress' *or* 'the public interest in having legislation based on full information' *or* 'the national interest in being fully informed on the nature and extent of communist activities' *or* 'the nation's (or democracy's, or humanity's) interest in the fight against communism (or

---

[89] Kumm, 'Political Liberalism and the Structure of Rights' (n 88) 151 (emphasis added).
[90] Aleinikoff (n 12) 977. [91] Ibid 978. [92] Ibid (emphasis in original, citations omitted).
[93] Ibid 979.
[94] Frantz, 'Is the First Amendment Law? (n 13) 747. Frantz is reflecting on the facts in *Barenblatt* (n 9).

against tyranny in general)'.[95] Putting aside the different levels of generality among these different formulations of the competing 'interests', it becomes obvious that several of the 'individual's' interests are more and less 'individual' and several of the 'government's' interests are others more or less 'public' or 'social'.

The conscientious judge will ask: how should the interests be characterized? The 'individual' interest in protecting one's friends may fare differently against the 'governmental' interest in fighting tyranny, as opposed to the 'governmental' interest in having this committee member get their way in having their questions answered. In turn, the 'governmental' interest—no matter how it is cast—may struggle against an 'individual' interest in 'vindicating freedom'. The different possible characterizations of the interests suggested for US commentators that it will be 'very difficult' for a judge to 'identify the "interests" without predetermining the result'.[96] It is a view shared today by senior members of the judiciary in other jurisdictions.[97] In the half-century since these objections were raised in the United States, we have come no further in answering the challenge. Instead, we appear to be in the same place that Frantz left us in saying that, when it comes to characterizing the competing interests: 'Anyone can do it. And anyone can reverse it just as easily by the opposite process'.[98]

The formulation of interests. The problems with balancing do not end with the number or characterization of competing interests. They extend to how concretely or abstractly they are to be formulated. To return to the example of our congressional questioning, the competing interests can be formulated in a very concrete, case-specific way as—

> the interest of the committee in having this particular piece of information from this particular witness on this particular occasion, balanced against the interest of this particular witness on this occasion in withholding this same item

or more abstractly as—

> the interest of the legislative branch of government, through its committees, in forming itself and perhaps the public about matters it deems relevant to the possible exercise or nonexercise of its functions as balanced against the interest of individuals generally in pursuing their political and intellectual lives free from all official inquiry

or somewhere in between as—

> the interest of the committee in pursuing a particular investigation according to its own best judgment, balanced against the interest of the witness in withholding information about certain sorts of associations.[99]

---

[95] Ibid. [96] Ibid.
[97] See Jonathan Sumption, 'Judicial and Political Decision-Making: The Uncertain Boundary' (2011) 16 *Jud Rev* 301, 306; Lord Justice Elias, 'Are Judges Becoming Too Political?' (2014) 3 *Cambridge J Int'l Comp L* 1, 26.
[98] Frantz, 'Is the First Amendment Law?' (n 13) 747.
[99] Fried (n 39) 758.

Now, for Fried, it would be 'begging the question to purport to balance some highly generalized and obviously crucial interest...against some rather particular and narrowly conceived claim', which is doubtless true. However, as he recognized, this truth does not help a court in answering 'the really difficult question, which is at what level of generality should it consider *both* claims'.[100]

The outcome of balancing. The question of formulation is related to the question of outcome: what is decided by a balancing of competing interests? Is the exercise ad hoc and case-specific or is it directed to help inform the scope and meaning of freedom of expression for future cases? A survey of the case law in Europe and the Commonwealth discloses no firm commitment. For example, the ECtHR has concluded that Holocaust denial is, categorically, denied freedom of expression protection under the ECHR.[101] (The basis for this conclusion is open to different readings.[102]) However, when it came to evaluating a denial of the Armenian genocide against freedom of expression, the European Court took a more case-specific view, noting that 'the context in which [the statements] were made was not marked by heightened tensions or special historical overtones in Switzerland' and that 'the statements cannot be regarded as affecting the dignity of members of the Armenian community to the point of requiring a criminal law response in Switzerland'.[103] Holocaust denial is categorically excluded from freedom of expression. Full stop. Denial of the Armenian genocide is protected by the Convention *in Switzerland* given *present-day* circumstances. Why the difference? We are not told.

For some, the distinction between categorical, definitional balancing, on the one hand, and ad hoc, case-specific balancing, on the other, is a false one.[104] As Aleinikoff perceptively put it, '[n]ew situations present new interests and different weights for old interests', such that balancing can be definitional 'only if the Court wants to stop thinking about the question'.[105] The Supreme Court of Canada has decided that it should not stop thinking about the question and has invited even inferior courts to overturn its constitutional precedents if a new balance is called for.[106]

The comparability of interests. Once the judge has identified all relevant interests, characterized them, formulated them, and taken a view whether to resolve one case or to establish a new rule for future cases, the judge must then award weight to the interests and compare them. The challenge here put by critiques is that of incommensurability, described as 'possibly the most underestimated challenge to proportionality reasoning'.[107] Incommensurability is not a new challenge, but it is one that takes on renewed relevance when present-day balancing is no longer said to be between interests (which at least *sound* commensurable), but between benefits and burdens and principles

---

[100] Ibid 763. See also Aleinikoff (n 12) 948.
[101] See *Garaudy v France* App no 65831/01 (ECHR, 24 June 2003) 23.
[102] One line of reasoning relies on the Article 17 prohibition of abuse of rights: see ibid. Another relies on the limitation clause in Article 10(2): see *Perincek v Switzerland* (2016) 63 EHRR 6 [103]–[115].
[103] *Perincek* (n 102) [280].
[104] For a critical review, see Grégoire Webber, 'Proportionality and Absolute Rights' in Vicki C Jackson and Mark Tushnet (eds), *Proportionality: New Frontiers, New Challenges* (CUP 2017) 75.
[105] Aleinikoff (n 12) 980–1.
[106] See *Canada v Bedford* 2013 SCC 72 [42] and *Carter v Canada* 2015 SCC 5 [44].
[107] Urbina (n 58) 39.

and objectives and effects and harms and values and degrees of interference, all of which call for an undisclosed common denominator in order to be commensurated.

There have been some attempts to identify a criterion for comparison—such as Alexy's reference to the 'importance for the constitution' or Barak's appeal to 'marginal social importance'—but these attempts have been dismissed as achieving no more than repackaging under a single label 'considerations that are themselves incommensurable'.[108] On the whole, defenders of balancing appear to favour one of two strategies for insisting that balancing really is possible notwithstanding the incommensurability challenge. The first is to decry that if the incommensurability challenge is correct, then there is 'no possibility of rational choice' between the competing interests (or benefits, burdens, harms, and so on) and, therefore, reasoning is without compass and irrational.[109] The *reductio ad absurdum* strategy fails for lack of imagination. The world of reasoning is greater than measure, weight, and comparison. Where incommensurability holds, it rules out *certain* forms of practical reasoning, most notably the technical weighing and comparing of alternative courses of action which, when assessed, may reveal one course of action to be superior to all of the others. However, incommensurability does not rule out *all* forms of practical reasoning. It is an altogether remarkable assertion to suggest that the only form of reasoning in human affairs is one that denies that one has choice between unranked alternatives, that denies that our world reveals 'a surplus of valuations, not a single metric' for comparing and ranking different courses of action,[110] and that denies that one can act according to reason in exercising true choice between alternatives. Incommensurability does not 'paralyze deliberation and action' *just because* technical 'rational choice' reasoning is ruled out.[111] Reason is fully engaged in providing the parameters for making a decision, but reason leaves to the author of the decision a *choice*—a *free* choice guided, but not determined by reason.

A second strategy for insisting that balancing is possible notwithstanding the incommensurability challenge is to deny any appeal to measurement and weights and comparisons and, instead, to suggest that balancing talk is metaphorical. What is truly balanced are reasons, as when one says that one is balancing the reasons for and against a course of action. This strategy reveals a shift in how some proponents understand balancing,[112] a shift that is fundamentally different than, if not also fundamentally incompatible with, the understanding of balancing that animated US debates and that has animated much case law and scholarship since.

---

[108] Barak (n 59) 349; Robert Alexy, 'On Balancing and Subsumption' (2003) 16 *Ratio Juris* 433, 442; Timothy Endicott, 'Proportionality and Incommensurability' in Grant Huscroft, Bradley W Miller, and Grégoire Webber (eds), *Proportionality and the Rule of Law: Rights, Justification, Reasoning* (CUP 2014) 318.

[109] See, eg, Virgílio Afonso da Silva, 'Comparing the Incommensurable: Constitutional Principles, Balancing and Rational Decision' (2011) 31 *Oxford J Legal Stud* 273, 295.

[110] Webber, *Negotiable Constitution* (n 22) 97.

[111] Richard Ekins, 'Legislating Proportionately' in Grant Huscroft, Bradley W Miller, and Grégoire Webber (eds), *Proportionality and the Rule of Law* (CUP 2014) 349, 354.

[112] These two conceptions are traced with great care in Urbina (n 58).

Leaving aside the question whether the judicial forum has the institutional capacity for 'unconstrained moral reasoning',[113] this shift appears to turn the principle of proportionality on its head. First, academic proponents of balancing-as-moral-reasoning appear not to have taken seriously the possibility that sound practical reasoning may quite rightly *reject* the principle of proportionality and its denial of the priority of rights.[114] Second, the recourse to moral reasoning helps to reveal one aspect of moral thought that the principle of proportionality altogether fails to highlight: an inquiry into whether the *means* are illegitimate.[115] This omission is all the more surprising given that the principle of proportionality begins its analysis by asking whether the legislature's *aim* is legitimate. Questions of legitimacy in moral thought are quite rightly put to both ends and means and yet the legitimacy of means seems to factor into the principle of proportionality only in an instrumentalist frame, as when one judges that unsuitable or ineffective means are 'illegitimate' because instrumentally deficient for the pursuit of some aim or end.

10.7 Conclusion

Let us return to the question raised earlier in this chapter: where does all of this leave us respecting freedom of expression and contested and controversial claims? The 'rather simple place' that proportionality promised now appears somewhat less simple. If it is the case that, having walked down the path charted by Justice Frankfurter and others, we express discomfort with the idea that freedom of expression awards a right-holder 'an entitlement to have her claim evaluated under the proportionality framework, and nothing more',[116] we have reason to revisit the path not taken.

The path not taken was the absolutist conception of the First Amendment favoured by Justice Black and his academic supporters. What conception of freedom of expression is communicated by the idea of 'absolute'? In Frantz's audit of different possible meanings, he rejected two as distractions. A first distraction takes 'absolute' to mean 'without limits'. No one, not even the absolutists, thought freedom of speech 'infinite in scope' and everyone, including the absolutists, thought it in need of definition, a definition that, by the very nature of definitions, sets limits. A second, related distraction takes 'absolute' to mean 'not open to exceptions'. This is the conception of 'absolute' that, for Frantz, seemed to animate the anti-absolutists insofar as they took freedom of speech to be defined as 'each individual's right to say anything he pleases, on any subject, at any time, in any manner he pleases, and regardless of the circumstances'. Because *this* understanding of freedom of expression must be subject to exceptions, it was said that the

---

[113] Ibid, ch 6.
[114] See Grégoire Webber, 'On the Loss of Rights' in Grant Huscroft, Bradley W Miller, and Grégoire Webber (eds), *Proportionality and the Rule of Law: Rights, Justification, Reasoning* (CUP 2014).
[115] I credit Urbina (n 58) 37, 140 with making this point explicitly.
[116] Jud Mathews and Alec Stone Sweet, 'All Things in Proportion? American Rights Review and the Problem of Balancing' (2011) 60 *Emory LJ* 797, 809.

freedom is therefore not absolute.[117] Yet, as reviewed above, no absolutist adhered to this understanding of freedom of expression and, so, no absolutist would have accepted that this argument undermined the freedom's claim to be absolute.

For Frantz, there was a third understanding of 'absolute': 'mandatory', meaning that *once* the meaning and scope of the First Amendment have been determined, the constitutional guarantee is 'obligatory'.[118] On this understanding, once expression falls within the meaning and scope of freedom of expression, that concludes the constitutional question. This account of 'absolute' sidestepped near all of the objections put to the absolutists. As Frantz would recount, the objections would begin with the premise that 'the first amendment cannot be "absolute" in the sense of unlimited in scope' (a premise that was universally shared), but conclude with the claim that 'it cannot be "absolute" in the sense of unconditionally obligatory within its proper scope'. That simply did not follow. And yet, despite the *non sequitur*, the 'confidence with which it can be asserted that scope and obligation are indistinguishable is sometimes astonishing'.[119]

With the distinction between scope and obligation firmly in view, the hard work of articulating the scope and meaning of freedom of expression can begin. It is work that will not be completed by searching out for only one principle or only one category of speech to set the markers for scope and meaning, as was attempted by some absolutists in the 1950s and 1960s. The task will be much more complex.[120] But there is no alternative to complex tasks in this or any area of law. As our review of proportionality has suggested, the promise of proportionality's liberating technique is a false promise. But it was a false promise itself based on a false understanding: that there was no alternative to proportionality because freedom of expression cannot be absolute. Perhaps it can.[121] And perhaps it can be guaranteed in a manner that will give one who is neither fool nor hero the confidence to speak truth to power because assertions like 'You have a right to say it—this is a free country' will mean what they say.

---

[117] Frantz, 'Is the First Amendment Law?' (n 13) 750.   [118] Ibid 752.
[119] Frantz, 'The First Amendment in the Balance' (n 14) 1436.
[120] That complexity is explored in Grégoire Webber and others, *Legislated Rights* (CUP 2018).
[121] I have argued that all rights, once specified, are absolute. See, eg, Webber, *The Negotiable Constitution* (n 22) 141–6; Webber 'Proportionality and Absolute Rights' (n 104).

CHAPTER 11

FREEDOM OF SPEECH IN INTERNATIONAL LAW

MICHAEL HAMILTON

11.1 INTRODUCTION

IN 2004, three Holocaust survivors obtained an injunction against the animal rights group, *People for the Ethical Treatment of Animals (PETA) Deutschland*. The injunction prohibited the launch of a poster campaign that drew graphic parallels between animal cruelty and human suffering in Nazi concentration camps. PETA were unsuccessful in challenging the restrictions imposed—not only in the German Federal Constitutional Court but also before the European Court of Human Rights (ECtHR).[1] PETA's case, however, foregrounds two important background questions that are central to this chapter's inquiry into whether international law affords an *effective* right to freedom of speech. These two questions ask, respectively, to what extent the protection of freedom of expression ought to be contextually determined, and whether the changing nature of the 'marketplace of ideas' suggests a need to revisit long established threshold principles of speech protection.

The first question conjures themes of relativism, subsidiarity, and the corresponding potential for variable application of free speech standards: might speech protected against restriction in one country or at a certain time legitimately be restricted in a different setting?[2] In *PETA Deutschland*, the ECtHR deferred to the domestic authorities, recognizing Germany's particular 'historical and social context'.[3] This reasoning underscores the importance, when reading international cases, of disentangling substantive reasoning (concerning the scope of the free speech right and the weight placed upon countervailing

---

[1] See *PETA Deutschland v Germany* App no 43481/09 (ECHR, 8 November 2012).
[2] Eg, *Perinçek v Switzerland* App no 27510/08 (ECHR, 15 October 2015) [242]–[248], [280]. See also *Fáber v Hungary* App no 40721/08 (ECHR, 24 July 2012) [58].
[3] *PETA Deutschland* (n 1) [48]–[51], but note also the Concurring Opinion of Judge Zupančič, joined by Judge Spielmann, rejecting the relativism implied in the Court's judgment.

interests) from reasoning pertaining to the inherently limited (subsidiary) role of international courts.[4] International treaty protections are commonly described as providing merely a 'floor' rather than a 'ceiling' of rights protection,[5] and the doctrine of subsidiarity often renders the outcomes of international free speech cases unreliable as a guide to the principles established or engaged. *PETA Deutschland* ultimately suggests a rather limited contribution for international law—focused less on ensuring an effective right to freedom of speech than on curbing merely the worst excesses of state interference.

Secondly, the *PETA Deutschland* case also raises a different kind of structural question—one concerning the nature of the contemporary media landscape. PETA's lawyers argued that, because of 'sensory overload through commercials and advertisements', the applicant was 'dependent on gaining attention for its cause in drastic ways'.[6] While not specifically addressed by the court, this line of argument underscores the ways in which technological developments have fundamentally changed the nature of the 'marketplace of ideas'. Speakers today are able to both reach and construct audiences previously unimaginable.[7] Moreover, they compete in an intensely competitive 'marketplace of attention',[8] where audiences are algorithmically induced and where there are endless possibilities for 'consumerist manipulation'.[9] It is also a marketplace in which 'disinformation' can seemingly flourish and where less visible forms of regulation and restriction emerge—ranging from censorship by privately owned social media platforms to government subsidization of media outlets.[10]

This chapter seeks to map the broad contours of the right to freedom of speech as it has evolved in international law, principally under Article 19(2) of the 1996 International Covenant on Civil and Political Rights (ICCPR or 'the Covenant').[11] Any speech protective principles deriving from the international jurisprudence are qualified by the background factors flagged above—the contextual contingency of the value of speech, the inherently limited reach of international scrutiny, the changing nature of the marketplace, and emerging forms of censorship (particularly by private actors). The following section outlines the key human rights treaty protections for freedom of speech, before further exploring the scope of the right (including what different forms of speech qualify for protection under Article 19(2) of the ICCPR, the freedom to seek and receive

---

[4] See further, George Letsas, 'Two Concepts of the Margin of Appreciation' (2006) 26 *Oxford J Legal Stud* 705; Dominic McGoldrick, 'A Defence of the Margin of Appreciation and an Argument for Its application by the Human Rights Committee' (2016) 65 *Int'l & Comp LQ* 21.

[5] Eg, Zechariah Chafee, Jr, 'Some Problems of the Draft International Covenant on Human Rights' (1951) 95 *Proc Am Phil Soc'y* 471, 481–2.

[6] *PETA Deutschland* (n 1) [31]. For further examples, see Rita C Hubbard, 'Shock Advertising: The Benetton Case' (1993) 16 *Stud Pop Cult* 39.

[7] Eg, *Perinçek* (n 2) [246]: 'at present, especially with the use of electronic means of communication, no message may be regarded as purely local'.

[8] James Webster, *The Marketplace of Attention* (MIT Press 2014).

[9] See, eg, András Sajó, *Constitutional Sentiments* (Yale UP 2011) 210–11.

[10] In this regard, UNHRC, 'General Comment 34—Article 19: Freedom of Opinion and Expression' (12 September 2011) UN Doc CCPR/C/GC/34 [10] (General Comment 34) [41] cautions against soft forms of compulsion or influence—particularly in relation to awarding government subsidies to media outlets.

[11] ICCPR (adopted 16 December 1966, entered into force 23 March 1976) 999 UNTS 171. Also, Article 19 of the non-binding UDHR (adopted 10 December 1948) UNGA Res 217 A(III).

information, and the special protections afforded to journalists and others who perform similar watchdog functions). In turning then to examine the permissible grounds for speech restriction, the chapter highlights two contested categories of speech (namely, incitement to hatred and glorification of terrorism) where international law not only concedes the low value of such speech, but specifically mandates its prohibition in domestic law. States that introduce broadly framed speech restrictions may claim to be acting in satisfaction of this prohibitory requirement. In consequence, as the chapter concludes, the intensity of any ensuing international scrutiny will inevitably be substantially reduced.

11.2 Treaty Protections for Freedom of Speech

Article 19(2) of the ICCPR proclaims that 'Everyone shall have the right to freedom of expression'.[12] It is notable that the debates that occurred during the drafting of Article 19(2)[13] foreshadow many of the controversies that today beset the right to freedom of speech—'fake news',[14] populist propaganda,[15] anonymous speech,[16] attacks on religion[17] and unauthorized disclosures of official information.[18]

---

[12] The recognized guide to the Covenant's travaux préparatoires is Marc J Bossuyt, *Guide to the 'Travaux Préparatoires' of the International Covenant on Civil and Political Rights* (Martinus Nijhoff 1987). Key commentaries include: Tarlach McGonagle and Yvonne Donders (eds), *The United Nations and Freedom of Expression and Information: Critical Perspectives* (CUP 2015); Sarah Joseph and Melissa Castan, *The International Covenant on Civil and Political Rights: Cases, Materials and Commentary* (3rd edn, OUP 2014) ch 18; Manfred Nowak, *UN Covenant on Civil and Political Rights: CCPR Commentary* (2nd rev edn, NP Engel 2005).

[13] Bossuyt (n 12) 381. Contemporaneous accounts include: Chafee (n 5); John B Whitton, 'The UN Conference on Freedom of Information and the Movement against International Propaganda' (1949) 43 *Am J Int'l L* 73; Erwin D Canham, 'International Freedom of Information' (1949) 14 *L & Contemp Probl* 584, 591–2.

[14] Bossuyt (n 12) 387; Tarlach McGonagle, '"Fake News": False Fears or Real Concerns?' (2017) 35 *Netherlands Q Hum Rts* 203, 205–6. See further, European Commission Directorate-General for Communication Networks, Content and Technology, *A Multi-Dimensional Approach to Disinformation: Report of the Independent High Level Group on Fake News and Online Disinformation* (March 2018) <http://ec.europa.eu/newsroom/dae/document.cfm?doc_id=50271> accessed 15 November 2018.

[15] UNCHR, Fifth Session 10 June 1949, 'Summary Record of the One Hundred and Twenty-Third Meeting' (14 June 1949) UN Doc E/CN.4/SR 123, 4 (Mr Pavlov of the Union of Soviet Socialist Republics debating ICCPR draft art 21—now ICCPR art 20(2)).

[16] Brazil proposed an amendment to para 1 on the right to freedom of information inserting 'Anonymity is not permitted', but it was recognized that this might 'prevent the use of pen names' and 'anonymity might at times be necessary to protect the author'. See Bossuyt (n 12) 379–80.

[17] India, for example, sought to add 'attacks on founders of religions' to the list of grounds for limiting freedom of speech. See Bossuyt (n 12) 395.

[18] The United Kingdom, for example, sought to add a further limitation ground: 'for the protection of official information from unauthorized disclosure'. UNGA, 'Draft International Covenants on Human Rights—United Kingdom of Great Britain and Northern Ireland: Amendments to Article 19 of the Draft Covenant on Civil and Political Rights' (13 October 1961) UN Doc A/C.3/L.924.

Mirroring the wording of Article 19(2) of the ICCPR, Article 13 of the Convention on the Rights to the Child (CRC)[19] and Article 13 of the International Convention on the Protection of the Rights of All Migrant Workers and Members of Their Families (ICRMW)[20] expressly extend the same right to children, and to migrant workers and their families, respectively.[21] Article 21 of the Convention on the Rights of Persons with Disabilities (CRPD) further sets out a number of measures which States Parties 'shall' take to ensure that persons with disabilities can exercise the right to freedom of expression 'on an equal basis with others and through all forms of communication of their choice'.[22]

The next section focuses upon what lies at the core of the right to freedom of speech in international law. A key source in this regard is the UNHRC's 'General Comment 34'[23]—adopted in 2011 following a two-year drafting process.[24] General Comment 34 distills key principles from the Committee's free speech jurisprudence and Concluding Observations on State Reports. It underscores the fundamental value of free speech as both an individual and societal good—'indispensable... for the full development of the person' and 'essential for any society'.[25] The Committee has further described the right to freedom of expression as a 'cornerstone' of any free and democratic society, emphasizing that citizens must be able to 'criticize or openly and publicly evaluate their Governments without fear of interference or punishment'.[26] In addition, since both direct and indirect restrictions on speech can have profoundly damaging consequences for both political participation[27] and civic space,[28] freedom of speech is commonly viewed as an enabling (or 'multiplier') right—making the enjoyment of other rights possible.[29]

---

[19] CRC adopted 20 November 1989, entered into force 2 September 1990: 1577 UNTS 3.

[20] ICRMW adopted 18 December 1990, entered into force 1 July 2003: 220 UNTS 3.

[21] In addition, CRC art 12 provides that 'States Parties shall assure to the child who is capable of forming his or her own views the right to express those views freely in all matters affecting the child'. In differentiating between the obligations arising from Articles 12 and 13 CRC, see UNCRC, 'General Comment 12—The Right of the Child to be Heard' (20 July 2009) UN Doc CRC/C/GC/12, [81].

[22] UNGA Res 61/106 (2007) UN Doc A/RES/61/106, Annex (CRPD).

[23] General Comment 34 (n 10). See further, Michael O'Flaherty, 'Freedom of Expression: Article 19 of the International Covenant on Civil and Political Rights and the Human Rights Committee's General Comment No. 34' (2012) 12 *Hum Rts L Rev* 627, 646.

[24] Between March 2009 and July 2011. See O'Flaherty (n 23) 645.

[25] General Comment 34 (n 10) [2].

[26] UNHRC, *Views: Communication No 1128/2002* (29 March 2005) UN Doc CCPR/C/83/D/1128/2002 (*de Morais v Angola*) [6.8].

[27] General Comment 34 (n 10) [13] replicates (verbatim) the wording of UNHRC, 'General Comment—Article 25: The Right to Participate in Public Affairs, Voting Rights and the Right of Equal Access to Public Service' (12 July 1996) UN Doc CCPR/C/21/Rev.1/Add.7 (General Comment 25) [25].

[28] See, eg, UNHRC, 'Concluding Observations on the Fifth Periodic Report of Sudan' (19 November 2018) UN Doc CCPR/C/SDN/CO/5, [45].

[29] See, eg, the preamble to UNCHR Res 45 (1993) UN Doc E/CN.4/RES/1993/45; Dominic McGoldrick, *The Human Rights Committee: Its Role in the Development of the International Covenant on Civil and Political Rights* (Clarendon P 1994) 461.

11.3 THE SCOPE OF THE RIGHT TO FREEDOM OF SPEECH

The right to freedom of speech under Article 19(2) of the ICCPR spans a wide range of speech in terms of both content and form. Article 19(1) also confers absolute protection on 'the right to hold opinions without interference', but this limb of Article 19 is beyond the scope of this chapter—except to note, as stated in General Comment 34, that this 'necessarily includes freedom *not to express* one's opinion'.[30]

The UNHRC has emphasized the importance of expression that 'relates to political discourse, commentary on one's own and on public affairs and the discussion of human rights'.[31] This privileged status of political speech (insofar as it can be distinguished from private or non-political speech)[32] has resulted in strong protections for political dissent—including criticism of incumbent politicians and calls for election boycotts.[33] In one case, the Belarusian authorities attempted to argue that the imposition of an administrative sanction for calling on others to boycott elections was necessary to protect voters from intimidation. While the UNHRC agreed that intimidation and coercion of voters ought to be prohibited,[34] the Committee emphasized that 'intimidation and coercion must be distinguished from encouraging voters to boycott an election'.[35] Sir Nigel Rodley's concurring opinion went even further, emphasizing that 'in any system it must always be possible for a person to advocate non-cooperation with an electoral exercise whose legitimacy that person may wish to challenge'.

As General Comment 34 confirms, the right to freedom of speech 'embraces even expression that may be regarded as deeply offensive'[36]—even to those who hold religious beliefs. General Comment 34 emphasizes that: '[p]rohibitions of displays of lack of respect for a religion or other belief system, including blasphemy laws, are incompatible with the Covenant'.[37] Somewhat more equivocally, the Strasbourg court has often

---

[30] General Comment 34 (n 10) [10] (emphasis added).
[31] UNHRC, Views: Communication No 2627/2015 (7 November 2017) UN Doc CCPR/C/121/D/2627/2015 (*Reyes and others v Chile*), [7.3], citing General Comment 34 (n 10) [11].
[32] See, eg, C Edwin Baker, *Human Liberty and Freedom of Speech* (OUP 1989) 34–6; Cass Sunstein, *Democracy and the Problem of Free Speech* (Free P 1993) 130; Sajó (n 9) 210–11. See also the dissenting opinion of Judge Wojtyczek in *Baka v Hungary* App no 20261/12 (ECHR, 23 June 2016) [6], [8].
[33] General Comment 34 (n 10) [28]. UNHRC, Views: Communication No 2076/2011 (29 October 2015) UN Doc CCPR/C/124/D/2266 (*Derzhavtsev v Belarus*) [8.4] and [8.7].
[34] Recognizing the right to vote under ICCPR art 25(b) and General Comment 25 (n 27) [11].
[35] UNHRC, Views: Communication No 927/2000 (8 July 2004) UN Doc CCPR/C/81/D/927/2000 (*Svetik v Belarus*) [7.3].
[36] General Comment 34 (n 10) [11], citing UNHRC, Views: Communication No 736/97 (18 October 2000) UN Doc CCPR/C/70/D/736/1997 (*Ross v Canada*); *Handyside v UK* App no 5493/72 (ECHR, 7 December 1976) [49], famously holding that freedom of speech is applicable to information and ideas 'that offend, shock or disturb the State or any sector of the population'.
[37] General Comment 34 (n 10) [48]. See also Sejal Parmar, 'Uprooting "Defamation of Religions" and Planting a New Approach to Freedom of Expression at the United Nations', in Tarlach McGonagle and Yvonne Donders (eds), *The United Nations and Freedom of Expression and Information: Critical Perspectives* (CUP 2015) 373.

noted that speakers have a 'duty to avoid as far as possible...expression that is, in regard to objects of veneration, gratuitously offensive'.[38]

The UNHRC has also been emphatic that Article 19(2) extends to commercial speech. The case of *Ballantyne and others v Canada* involved a challenge by three English-speaking business owners to the prohibition of English language commercial advertising in Quebec. The Committee held that freedom of speech 'should not be confined to means of political, cultural or artistic expression',[39] but rather 'must be interpreted as encompassing every form of subjective ideas and opinions capable of transmission to others...of news and information, of commercial expression and advertising, of works of art etc'.[40]

As noted at the outset of this chapter, international law is also necessarily concerned with the structural conditions of the speech marketplace. As such, 'issues relating to the registration and/or re-registration of the mass media fall within the scope of the right to freedom of expression'.[41] States have an obligation 'to encourage an independent and diverse media'[42]—in particular, by avoiding the imposition of onerous licensing conditions and fees on broadcast media, and by ensuring that licensing criteria are reasonable and objective, clear, transparent, and non-discriminatory.[43]

Of course, speech monopolies can also arise in other institutions beyond the corporate media world. These include institutions that play a role in the production of cultural and educational life—speech that (in Jack Balkin's words) creates the 'infrastructure or substrate' for political democracy.[44] Such speech has sometimes not been protected to the same degree as avowedly political speech. Consider, for example, the Seoul school teacher who, early in South Korea's transition towards democracy, wished to introduce a new national language book into the school curriculum.[45] He argued that the right to freedom of expression under Article 19, at a minimum, entitled him to have his textbook scrutinized for possible inclusion on the national curriculum.[46] The UNHRC disagreed—entirely sidestepping the author's argument that 'a curricular textbook was the only *effective* way of communicating his ideas'.[47] The Committee held that such a claim was inadmissible since it fell outside the scope of Article 19.[48] This exclusion from the protective scope of Article 19 might be read

---

[38] See *ES v Austria* App no 38450/12 (ECHR, 25 October 2018) [43], [52], and *Sekmadienis Ltd v Lithuania* App no 69317/14 (ECHR, 30 January 2018) [74]. Notably, *Sekmadienis* rejects the majoritarian premise of the Court's earlier judgment in *Otto-Preminger-Institut v Austria* App no 13470/87 (ECHR, 20 September 1994).

[39] Eg, UNHRC, *Views: Communication No 926/2000* (16 March 2004) UN Doc CCPR/C/80/D/926/2000 (*Hak-Chul Shin v Republic of Korea*) [7.2], recalling 'that Article 19(2) specifically refers to ideas imparted "in the form of art"'.

[40] UNHRC, *Views: Communications No 359/1989 and 385/1989* (31 March 1993) UN Doc CCPR/C/47/D/359/1989 (*Ballantyne v Canada*) [11.3]. See also UNHRC, *Views: Communication No 760/97* (25 July 2000) UN Doc CCPR/C/69/D/760/1996 (*Diergaardt v Namibia*). See also *Mouvement raëlien suisse v Switzerland* App no 16354/06 (ECHR, 13 July 2012) [61].

[41] UNHRC, *Views: Communication No 1334/2004* (19 March 2009) UN Doc CCPR/C/95/D/1334/2004(*Mavlonov and Sa'di v Uzbekistan*) [8.3].

[42] General Comment 34 (n 10) [14].

[43] UNHRC, *Views: Communication No 2205/2012* (27 October 2016) UN Doc CCPR/C/118/D/2205/2012 (*Agazade and Jafarov v Azerbaijan*) [7.4], citing General Comment 34 (n 10) [39].

[44] Jack M Balkin, 'Cultural Democracy and the First Amendment' (2016) 110 *Nw U L Rev* 1053, 1060.

[45] UNHRC, *Views: Communication No 693/1996* (28 July 2003) UN Doc CCPR/C/78/D/693/1996 (*Nam v Republic of Korea*).

[46] Ibid [10].   [47] Ibid [3] (emphasis added).   [48] Ibid [10].

as an example of the prioritization of a narrow conception of political speech, one that fails to sufficiently recognize Balkin's democratic 'substrate'.

11.3.1 Art-Mobs, Hunger-Strikes and Single-Person Protests

The scope of Article 19 does not end merely with the written or spoken word,[49] but covers a wide range of modes of expression from the maintenance of Internet archives[50] to 'art-mobs'.[51] Even hunger-strikes have not been excluded from the protective scope of the right.[52] Indeed, General Comment 34 refrains from singling out particular examples on the basis that Article 19 should remain open to *all* potential forms of speech.[53]

Some forms of speech, however, are more problematic. The UNHRC has found, for example, that politically motivated defacement of road signs—as part of a campaign urging bilingual (Breton and French) road signage—did not fall within the right to freedom of speech.[54] Complications have also arisen in terms of the interrelationship between freedom of speech under Article 19 of the ICCPR and freedom of assembly under Article 21—perhaps especially, in relation to single-person protests.[55] While the UNHRC has often properly emphasized the interdependence of expression and assembly,[56] it has frequently found concurrent violations of expression *and* assembly without adequately explaining the distinctiveness of these two rights (for example, as *lex specialis/lex generalis*).[57] The Committee's General Comment 37 (on the right of peaceful assembly) further clarifies the relationship between Articles 19 and 21.[58]

---

[49] General Comment 34 (n 10) [12].
[50] *Times Newspapers Ltd (Nos 1 and 2) v United Kingdom* Apps no 3002/03 and 23676/03 (ECHR, 10 March 2009) [27].
[51] UNHRC, *Views: Communication No 2137/2012* (21 October 2014) UN Doc CCPR/C112/D/2137/2012 (*Toregozhina v Kazakhstan*).
[52] UNHRC, *Views: Communication No 1014/2001* (6 August 2003) UN Doc CCPR/C/78/D/1014/2001(*Baban v Australia*) [6.7].
[53] O'Flaherty (n 23) 648, noting that the first draft of General Comment 34 (n 10) had expressly included within the scope of Article 19, the 'choice of clothing or the wearing or carrying of a religious or other symbol, and hunger strike'.
[54] UNHRC, *Views: Communication No 247/1988* (1 November 1991) UN Doc CCPR/C/43/D/347/1988 (*SG v France*) [5.2].
[55] Contrast, eg. UNHRC, *Views: Communication No 1157/2003* (17 July 2006) UN Doc CCPR/C/87/D/1157/2003 (*Coleman v Australia*) [6.4] with UNHRC, *Views: Communication No 1836/2008* (24 October 2012) UN Doc CCPR/C/106/D/1836/2008 (*Katsora v Belarus*) [6.4], [7.6].
[56] See, eg, UNHRC, *Views: Communication No 2029/2011* (10 October 2014) UN Doc CCPR/C/112/D/2029/2011 (*Praded v Belarus*) [7.3], citing General Comment 34 (n 10) [4].
[57] Concurrent violations of arts 19 and 21 were found, for example, in UNHRC, *Views: Communication No 2175/2012* (4 April 2018) UN Doc CCPR/C/122/D/2175/2012 (*Kim v Uzbekistan*) [13.7]–[13.10]. Cf the standard approach of the ECtHR: see, eg, *Lashmankin v Russia* App no 57818/09 (ECHR, 7 February 2017) [363].
[58] UNHRC, 'General Comment No. 37 (2020) on the right of peaceful assembly (article 21)' (17 September 2020) UN Doc CCPR/C/GC/37.

11.3.2 Freedom to Seek and Receive Information

Freedom of speech has been recognized as 'a necessary condition for the realization of the principles of transparency and accountability that are, in turn, essential for the promotion and protection of human rights'.[59] For example, the need to protect whistleblowers has been recognized.[60] The ECtHR has long confirmed that 'the signalling by an employee in the public sector of illegal conduct or wrong-doing in the workplace should, in certain circumstances, enjoy protection'[61] (though the UNHRC missed an opportunity to provide similar guarantees in the 2016 case of *Kerrouche v Algeria*).[62]

In wording that was agreed by the Third Committee of the UN General Assembly in 1961, the right to freedom of expression includes the 'freedom to seek, receive and impart information and ideas of all kinds, regardless of frontiers, either orally, in writing or in print, in the form of art, or through any other media of his choice'. Notably, during the drafting of Article 19, the word 'seek' was preferred by some members of the Third Committee over 'gather' because 'it implied the right of active inquiry', whereas ' "gather" was thought to connote 'passively accepting news provided by Governments or news agencies'. Other members argued that ' "seek" had come to imply unrestrained and often shameless probing into the affairs of others while "gather" … merely lacked the aggressive connotations of "seek" '.[63] This tension has been reflected in the evolving case law—particularly in distinguishing between a passive right to *receive* information (merely the corollary of others' freedom of expression), an active right to *seek* information, and a positive right of *access to* information.[64] As such, these rights have benefitted from a process of norm strengthening (or 'gradual clarification')[65] in international law.[66]

The ECtHR has also recognized the vital role of the Internet in disseminating information, noting 'its accessibility and its capacity to store and communicate vast amounts of

---

[59] General Comment 34 (n 10) [3], [18]–[19].

[60] UNHRC, 'Report of the United Nations High Commissioner for Human Rights on the Role of the Public Service as an Essential Component of Good Governance in the Promotion and Protection of Human Rights' (23 December 2013) UN Doc A/HRC/25/27, [17]: 'Provisions on whistle-blowing should include the existence of reporting mechanisms and legal protection for the whistle-blower'.

[61] See, eg, *Heinisch v Germany* App no 28274/08 (ECHR, 21 July 2011) [63].

[62] See UNHRC, *Views: Communication No 2128/2012* (3 November 2016) UN Doc CCPR/C/118/D/2128/2012 (*Kerrouche v Algeria*), individual opinion of Olivier de Frouville. See also Committee of Ministers of the Council of Europe, Recommendation CM/REC(2014)7 'Protection of Whistleblowers' (30 April 2014).

[63] UNGA, 'Draft International Covenants on Human Rights: Report of the Third Committee' (5 December 1961) UN Doc A/5000, [22]. See Bossuyt (n 12) 384.

[64] Cf the individual opinion of Gerald L Neuman (concurring) in UNHRC, *Views: Communication No 1470/2006* (28 March 2011) UN Doc CCPR/C/101/D/1470/2006 (*Toktakunov v Kyrgyzstan*).

[65] *Magyar Helsinki Bizottság v Hungary* App no 18030/11 (ECHR, 8 November 2016) [149].

[66] UNGA, 'Report of the Special Rapporteur on the Promotion and Protection of the Right to Freedom of Opinion and Expression' (4 September 2013) UN Doc A/68/362, [2], [76] (identifying a number of 'core principles'). See also *Marcel Claude Reyes v Chile*, Merits, Inter-American Court of Human Rights Series C No 151 (19 September 2006) [77] and *Magyar Helsinki Bizottság* (n 65) 126–70. Note, too, the Council of Europe Convention on Access to Official Documents (opened for signature, 18 June 2009) CETS 205.

information'.⁶⁷ Moreover, platforms that host user-generated speech have been regarded by the Court as uniquely valuable given their capacity to share 'political content ignored by the traditional media'.⁶⁸ While this undoubtedly represents a shift away from the privileging of mainstream or professional media, journalists are still properly accorded certain protections due to their contribution to public discourse. The functions and responsibilities of journalists—and those who perform similar roles—are addressed in the following section.

11.3.3 Special Protection for Journalists and Public Watchdogs

'Among the functions of the press are the creation of forums for public debate and the forming of public, or for that matter, individual opinion on matters of legitimate public concern'.⁶⁹ The UNHRC has noted that a journalist's main professional task is to inform society about issues of public interest—including where this reveals corruption and abuse of state power.⁷⁰

More generally, the proliferation of user-generated content and fragmentation of the media sector has meant that traditional media outlets no longer occupy the same privileged position in terms of political will formation as they once did. As such, it is increasingly difficult (and unhelpful) to attempt to draw bright-line distinctions between old and new media, or professional and citizen journalists.⁷¹ As the UNHRC has noted, 'the realization of these functions is not limited to the media or professional journalists, and ... can also be exercised by public associations or private individuals'.⁷² In this light, General Comment 34 acknowledges that 'there is now a global network for exchanging ideas and opinions that does not necessarily rely on the traditional mass media intermediaries' and urges states to 'take all necessary steps to foster the independence of these new media and to ensure access of individuals thereto'.⁷³

Status-driven categorizations of 'journalists' have thus given way to an emphasis on functional understandings of their role. In this regard, questions inevitably arise about extending to others the protections previously afforded only to mainstream journalists (bound by professional codes and ethical standards).⁷⁴ Insofar as this question has been

---

⁶⁷ *Times Newspapers Ltd (Nos 1 and 2)* (n 50) [27].
⁶⁸ *Cengiz v Turkey* Apps no 48226 and 14027/11 (ECHR, 1 December 2015) [52], also citing *Delfi AS v Estonia* App no 64569/09 (ECHR, 16 June 2015) [110]; *Tamiz v UK* App no 3877/14 (ECHR, 19 September 2017) [90].
⁶⁹ *Toktakunov* (n 64) [6.3].
⁷⁰ UNHRC, *Views: Communication No 2129/2012* (29 March 2016) UN Doc CCPR/C/116/D/2129/2012 (*Esergepov v Kazakhstan*) [11.9].
⁷¹ General Comment 34 (n 10) [44].
⁷² *Toktakunov* (n 64) [6.3], [7.4]. See also *Butkevich v Russia* App no 5865/07 (ECHR, 13 February 2018) [131].
⁷³ General Comment 34 (n 10) [15].
⁷⁴ See, eg, *Bladet Tromsø and Stensaas v Norway* App no 21980/93 (ECHR, 20 May 1999) [65]: those 'acting in good faith in order to provide accurate and reliable information in accordance with the ethics of journalism'.

addressed in international human rights jurisprudence, the ECtHR has recognized that 'the function of bloggers and popular users of the social media may be also assimilated to that of "public watchdogs" in so far as the protection afforded by Article 10 is concerned'.[75] Such protections have included the so-called 'journalistic purposes' derogation from data protection regulations,[76] which the Court of Justice of the European Union has emphasized must be interpreted to take account 'of the evolution and proliferation of methods of communication and the dissemination of information'.[77]

Journalistic protections have also included safeguards concerning the confidentiality of sources.[78] This is regarded as 'one of the basic conditions for press freedom', without which 'sources may be deterred from assisting the press in informing the public on matters of public interest' thereby undermining 'the vital public-watchdog role of the press'.[79] Indeed, a requirement to disclose sources will be incompatible with the right to freedom of speech 'unless it is justified by an overriding requirement in the public interest'.[80] In *Big Brother Watch v UK*[81]—an important 2018 case regarding the bulk interception by state intelligence services of data potentially involving confidential journalistic material—the Strasbourg Court found that the UK had violated the right to freedom of speech because there was nothing in the relevant Code of Practice 'circumscribing the intelligence services' power to search for confidential journalistic or other material'.[82] The Court also found that the regime for acquiring communications data from communication service providers (CSPs) violated Article 10 of the ECHR because, inter alia, there were 'no special provisions restricting access [to a journalist's communications data] to the purpose of combating "serious crime"'.[83]

Journalists have also enjoyed certain privileged rights of access (for example, to official press conferences). The UNHRC has stipulated that while State Parties *are* entitled to limit access to certain venues (in particular, to prevent obstruction of the work of elected bodies), any such accreditation scheme constitutes a *de facto* restriction of Article 19 rights and must not operate in an arbitrary manner. Moreover, '[t]he relevant criteria for the accreditation scheme should be specific, fair and reasonable, and their application should be transparent'.[84]

---

[75] *Magyar Helsinki Bizottság* (n 65) [168].

[76] Council Directive 95/46/EC of 24 October 1995 on the protection of individuals with regard to the processing of personal data and on the free movement of such data [1995] OJ L281/31.

[77] Case C-73/07 *Tietosuojavaltuutettu v Satakunnan Markkinapörssi Oy and Satamedia Oy* [2008] ECR I-09831, [60]. See also *Satakunnan Markkinapörssi Oy and Satamedia Oy v Finland* App no 931/13 (ECHR, 27 June 2017).

[78] For a summary of the Strasbourg Court's jurisprudence, see *Becker v Norway* App no 21272/12 (ECHR, 5 October 2017) [65]–[70]; Recommendation No. R(2000) 7 on the right of journalists not to disclose their sources of information, adopted by the Committee of Ministers of the Council of Europe on 8 March 2000.

[79] *Goodwin v United Kingdom* App no 17488/90 (ECHR, 27 March 1996) [39].

[80] *Sanoma Uitgevers BV v the Netherlands* App no 38224/03 (ECHR, 14 September 2010, GC) [51]; see also [44].

[81] *Big Brother Watch v United Kingdom* Apps no 58170/13, 62322/14 and 24960/15 (ECHR, 13 September 2018).

[82] Ibid [493].   [83] Ibid [499].

[84] UNHRC, *Views: Communication No 1985/2010* (24 July 2014) UN Doc CCPR/C/111/D/1985/2010 (*Koktish v Belarus*) [8.3].

Most sobering of all in relation to the protection of journalists is the fact that they often face risks to life because of their investigative work.[85] Grave risks also confront human rights defenders who, exercising their freedom of speech, have sought to assist or engage with international mechanisms of human rights protection but have subsequently then been subjected to reprisals.[86] A number of initiatives at the international and regional levels have focused on how international bodies should respond to such reprisals,[87] and how states can more effectively protect the safety of journalists given this backdrop of threatened and actual violence.[88]

11.4 Restrictions on Freedom of Speech in International Law

International law has recognized that measures should be taken to prevent the harms arising from certain types of speech—including hate speech (examined further below), forms of pornography[89] and speech that is harmful to children.[90] Any such restrictions must, however, be in compliance with Article 19(3) of the ICCPR, which reads as follows:

> The exercise of the rights provided for in paragraph 2 of this Article carries with it special duties and responsibilities. It may therefore be subject to certain restrictions, but these shall only be such as are provided by law and are necessary:
>
> (a) For respect of the rights or reputations of others;
>
> (b) For the protection of national security or of public order (*ordre public*), or of public health or morals.

---

[85] UNHRC, *Views: Communication No 2767/2016* (17 July 2018) UN Doc CCPR/C/123/D/2767/2016 (*Ribeiro (represented by Article 19) v Mexico*). See also UNHRC, *Views: Communication No 1353/2005* (19 March 2007) UN Doc CCPR/C/89/D/1353/2005 (*Njaru v Cameroon*).

[86] See, eg, UNGA, 'Report of the Special Rapporteur on Extrajudicial, Summary or Arbitrary Executions' (27 May 2009) UN Doc A/HRC/11/2. See also General Comment 34 (n 10) [23].

[87] See further, UNHCHR, 'The Role of Key UN Human Rights Mechanisms in Addressing Intimidation and Reprisals for Cooperation with the UN in the field of Human Rights' (Office of the High Commissioner for Human Rights) <www.ohchr.org/EN/Issues/Reprisals/Pages/RoleOfKeyUNHRMechanisms.aspx> accessed 10 April 2019.

[88] See, eg, International Federation of Journalists, *Draft International Convention on the Safety and Independence of Journalists and Other Media Professionals* (November 2017) <https://www.ifj.org/fileadmin/user_upload/Draft_Convention_Journalists_E.pdf> accessed 14 April 2019.

[89] See UNHRC, 'General Comment 28—Article 3: The Equality of Rights Between Men and Women' (29 March 2000) UN Doc CCPR/C/21/Rev.1/Add.10 (General Comment 28) [22]; UNGA Res 54/263 (25 May 2000) UN Doc A/RES/54/263 (Optional Protocol to the Convention on the Rights of the Child on the Sale of Children, Child Prostitution and Child Pornography), art 3(1)(c).

[90] CRC art 17. See also *Ross v Canada* (n 36) [11.6]; similar concerns are reflected in the text of ACHR art 13(4) and in the case law of the ECHR. See, eg, *Handyside* (n 36) and *Vejdeland v Sweden* App no 1813/07 (ECHR, 9 February 2012) [54]–[57].

The UNHRC has consistently emphasized that any restrictions on the exercise of the right to freedom of speech must 'meet a strict test of justification'.[91] Here, the burden of justification falls on the State Party to demonstrate the necessity of any restrictions imposed.[92] Speculative grounds will not suffice[93] and states 'must demonstrate in specific fashion the precise nature of the threat to any of the enumerated purposes'.[94] Moreover, Article 19(3) 'may never be invoked as a justification for the muzzling of any advocacy of multi-party democracy, democratic tenets and human rights',[95] and 'the relation between right and restriction and between norm and exception must not be reversed'.[96]

It is noteworthy that, unlike Article 19(3) of the ICCPR or Article 10(2) of the ECHR, Article 13(2) of the American Convention on Human Rights (ACHR) expressly prohibits 'prior censorship', allowing only for the 'subsequent imposition of liability'.[97] In this regard, the ECtHR has held that 'prior restraints are not necessarily incompatible with the Convention as a matter of principle. However, a legal framework is required, ensuring both tight control over the scope of bans and effective judicial review to prevent any abuse of power'.[98]

Once it is established that there has been an interference with the right to freedom of expression, it must be demonstrated that the interference was 'provided by law',[99] pursued one (or more) of the legitimate aims listed in Article 19(3), and was necessary and proportionate to achieving that purpose.[100] While space precludes an exploration here of the interpretation of each of the Article 19(3) aims, this final section summarily overviews the interpretation in international law of three grounds commonly relied upon to justify restrictions on freedom of speech—namely, the reputation or others, incitement to hatred, and national security. The last two grounds for restriction—incitement to hatred and national security—reveal something of the Janus-face of international human rights law: these are both areas in which *restrictions* on speech (rather than primarily its protection) are expressly mandated by international law. As the following sections demonstrate, the implementation of these proscriptions has in several countries undermined the protection of political speech (especially that which is critical of the state).

---

[91] UNHRC, *Views: Communication No 1022/2001* (20 October 2005) UN Doc CCPR/C/85/D/1022/2001 (*Velichkin v Belarus*) [7.3].

[92] See, eg, UNHRC, *Views: Communication No 2082/2011* (14 July 2016) UN Doc CCPR/C/117/D/2082/2011 (*Levinov v Belarus*) [8.3].

[93] *Reyes* (n 31) [7.5].   [94] *Hak-Chul Shin* (n 39) [7.2].   [95] General Comment 34 (n 10) [23].

[96] Ibid [21].

[97] With an exception in art 13(4) for the protection of children and adolescents in relation to public entertainment. See further, Marjan Ajevski, 'Freedom of Speech as Related to Journalists in the ECtHR, IACtHR and the Human Rights Committee: A Study of Fragmentation' (2014) 34 *Nordic J Hum Rts* 118, 121–3.

[98] See, eg, *Yildirim v Turkey* App no 3111/10 (ECHR, 18 December 2012) [64].

[99] General Comment 34 (n 10) [25]. ECHR art 10 instead uses the phrase 'prescribed by law'.

[100] Ibid [22], [34].

11.4.1 Respect for the Reputations of Others

Article 19(3)(a) permits restrictions to be imposed on the exercise of freedom of speech in order to ensure respect for the reputations of others,[101] notwithstanding the 'paramount importance, in a democratic society... of a free and uncensored press or other media'.[102] A higher tolerance threshold is expected of public figures who are ordinarily 'subject to criticism and opposition'.[103] The UNHRC has set out its approach when considering allegations of defamation, explaining that it 'takes account of the form and context of the expression at issue as well as the means of its dissemination and recalls that public interest in the subject matter of a criticism is a factor to be taken into account'.[104] The Committee has further observed that 'in circumstances of public debate in a democratic society, especially in the media, concerning figures in the political domain, the value placed by the Covenant upon uninhibited expression is particularly high'.[105] General Comment 34 emphasizes that defamation laws must not, in practice, stifle freedom of expression, and must contain adequate safeguards such as defences of truth and a public interest in the subject matter, and a malice requirement (at least in relation to comments about public figures).[106] Furthermore, states are under an obligation to enact legislation that enables 'everyone to be able to protect himself or herself effectively against any unlawful attacks that do occur and to have an effective remedy against those responsible'.[107]

11.4.2 Incitement to Hatred

Article 20 of the ICCPR singles out two forms of speech for express limitation. States are instructed to prohibit by law 'any propaganda for war'[108] and 'any advocacy of national,

---

[101] Interests which, in addition to ICCPR art 19(3), are protected under the ICCPR art 17 right to privacy.

[102] *De Morais* (n 26) [6.8]. [103] Ibid.

[104] UNHRC, Views: Communication No 1986/2010 (24 July 2014) UN Doc CCPR/C/111/D/1986/2010 (*Kozlov v Belarus*) [7.5]. See also *Medžlis Islamske Zajednice Brčko and Others v Bosnia and Herzegovina* App no 17224/11 (ECHR, 27 June 2017) [88].

[105] UNHRC, Views: Communication No 1180/2003 (31 October 2005) UN Doc CCPR/C/85/D/1180/2003 (*Bodrožic v Serbia and Montenegro*) [7.2].

[106] General Comment 34 (n 10) [47]. See, eg, UNHRC, Views: Communication No 1815/2008 (26 October 2011) UN Doc CCPR/C/103/D/1815/2008 (*Adonis v The Philippines*) [7.7].

[107] UNHRC, Views: Communication No 2430/2014 (19 July 2017) UN Doc CCPR/C/120/D/2430/2014 (*Allakulov v Uzbekistan*) [7.6], citing UNHRC, 'General Comment 16—Article 17: The Right to Respect of Privacy, Family, Home and Correspondence, and Protection of Honour and Reputation' (8 April 1988) UN Doc HRI/Gen/1/Rev.9 (General Comment 16) [11]. On the 'right to reply', see *Eker v Turkey* App no 24016/05 (ECHR, 24 October 2017) [45]–[46]; Felix Hempel, 'The Right of Reply under the European Convention on Human Rights: An Analysis of *Eker v Turkey*' (2018) 10 J Media L 17.

[108] ICCPR art 20(1). See, Michael Kearney, *The Prohibition of Propaganda for War in International Law* (OUP 2007). UNHRC, 'General Comment 36—Article 6: The Right to Life' (30 October 2018) UN Doc CCPR/C/GC/36, [59] provides that '[f]ailure to comply with these obligations... may also constitute a failure to take the necessary measures to protect the right to life under article 6'.

racial or religious hatred that constitutes incitement to discrimination, hostility or violence'.[109] In similar (but even more widely cast) terms, Article 4 of the International Convention on the Elimination of All Forms of Racial Discrimination (ICERD) obliges States Parties to declare as a punishable offence:

> all dissemination of ideas based on racial superiority or hatred, incitement to racial discrimination, as well as all acts of violence or incitement to such acts against any race or group of persons of another colour or ethnic origin, and also the provision of any assistance to racist activities, including the financing thereof.[110]

On ratifying ICERD, several states expressed reservations in respect of Article 4—most famously, the United States, which refused to accept any obligation to limit individual freedom of speech, expression, and association imposed by the Convention.

In terms of the intersection of Articles 19, 20(2) of the ICCPR and Article 4 of the ICERD, the UNHRC has emphasized that Article 20(2) of the ICCPR is narrowly crafted so as not to unduly infringe on other Covenant rights, particularly Article 19.[111] Moreover, the strict requirements of Article 19(3) must also be met where a restriction on speech might be justified under Article 20(2).[112] In addition, the CERD has recognized that, 'measures to monitor and combat racist speech should not be used as a pretext to curtail expression of protest at injustice, social discontent or opposition'.[113] Indeed, under Article 4 of the ICERD, 'the criminalization of forms of racist expression should be reserved for serious cases'.[114]

Prompted in part by the tide of hostility directed at migrants in many countries, a high-level initiative by the UN High Commissioner on Human Rights culminated in the adoption in October 2012 of the Rabat Plan of Action on the prohibition of advocacy of national, racial, or religious hatred that constitutes incitement to discrimination, hostility or violence.[115] Among many other legal and non-legal measures recommended in

---

[109] ICCPR art 20(2). Described by Nowak (n 12) 468 as 'an alien element in the system of the Covenant', and by Partsch as 'practically a fourth paragraph to Article 19': Karl Josef Partsch, 'Freedom of Conscience and Expression, and Political Freedoms' in Louis Henkin (ed), *The International Bill of Rights: The Covenant on Civil and Political Rights* (Columbia UP 1981) 227. Jeremy Waldron notes that it is an obligation which has 'bolstered' states in legislating against hate speech. Jeremy Waldron, 'Libel and Legitimacy' (Holmes Lectures, Harvard Law School, 5–7 October 2009) <https://www.law.nyu.edu/sites/default/files/ECM_PRO_063314.pdf> accessed 15 November 2018.

[110] See further, UNCERD, 'General Recommendation No 35—Combating Racist Hate Speech' (26 September 2013) UN Doc CERD/C/GC/35 (General Recommendation No 35) drawing on UNHRC 'Report of the United Nations High Commissioner for Human Rights on the Expert Workshops on the Prohibition of Incitement to National, Racial or Religious Hatred' (11 January 2013) UN Doc A/HRC/22/17/Add.4 ('Rabat Plan of Action').

[111] Eg, UNHRC, *Views: Communication No 2124/211* (14 July 2016) UN Doc CCPR/C/117/D/2124/2011 (*Rabbae, ABS and NA v The Netherlands*) [10.4].

[112] General Comment 34 (n 10) [26]. [113] General Recommendation No 35 (n 110) [20].

[114] Ibid [12].

[115] Rabat Plan of Action (n 110).

the Rabat Plan of Action,[116] it spells out the contextual factors that ought to be taken into account in qualifying incitement to hatred as an offence punishable by law. These are in turn reflected in CERD General Recommendation No 35, emphasizing that close attention must be given to (a) the content and form of speech, (b) the economic, social and political climate, (c) the position or status of the speaker, (d) the reach of the speech, and (e) the objectives of the speech. In terms of incitement, the intention of the speaker, and the imminence of the risk or likelihood that the conduct desired will result are also vital.[117] This list helpfully identifies the relevant contextual factors—though these factors do not substitute for the requirements of Article 19(3) and must instead be considered through that prism.

The CERD has asserted that '[t]he relationship between the proscription of racist hate speech and the flourishing of freedom of expression should be seen as complementary'.[118] Nonetheless, the tension between these provisions, and the potential for them to give rise to contrary interpretations, can be seen in respective treaty bodies' approaches to holocaust denial laws. The UNHRC's General Comment 34 states that laws penalizing 'the expression of opinions about historical facts are incompatible with the...freedom of opinion and expression',[119] whereas the CERD General Recommendation 35 specifically recommends 'that public denials or attempts to justify crimes of genocide and crimes against humanity, as defined by international law, should be declared as offences punishable by law, provided that they clearly constitute incitement to racial violence or hatred'.[120]

This 'push and pull' relationship is also borne out in the international hate speech jurisprudence. Essentially, two different types of challenge have arisen—those alleging a violation of free speech rights under Article 19 of the ICCPR and those brought by listeners alleging a violation of either Article 4 of the CERD or Article 20(2) of the ICCPR (the purported failure by states to sufficiently censor virulent forms of hate speech).[121] In the handful of 'hate speech' cases where a speaker has argued that restrictions have violated their Article 19 rights under the Covenant, the UNHRC has generally sided

---

[116] See Sejal Parmar, 'The Rabat Plan of Action: A Global Blueprint for Combating "Hate Speech"' (2014) 1 *Eur Hum Rts L Rev* 21.

[117] General Recommendation No 35 (n 110) [15], [16], drawing on the Rabat Plan of Action (n 110) [22].

[118] General Recommendation No 35 (n 110) [45].

[119] Ibid [49]. However, see also UNHRC, *Views: Communication No 550/1993* (8 November 1996) UN Doc CCPR/C/58/D/550/1993 (*Faurisson v France*) in which speech thought to strengthen anti-semitic feeling was held to have been legitimately restricted to uphold the Jewish communities' right to be protected from religious hatred. The Committee held that the rights or reputations of others ground may relate to 'a community as a whole'.

[120] General Recommendation No 35 (n 110) [10]. See also *Perinçek* (n 2).

[121] UNHRC, *Views: Communication No 1570/2007* (19 March 2009) UN Doc CCPR/C/95/D/1570/2007 (*Vassilari and others v Greece*). The justiciability of Article 20(2) ICCPR is still debated: see, *Rabbae* (n 111) [9.7], upholding the justiciability of art 20(2); cf the individual opinion (partly concurring and partly dissenting) of Committee members Yuval Shany and Sir Nigel Rodley, [6]–[8].

with the state authorities and upheld the speech restrictions imposed.[122] As Stefan Sottiaux has argued in relation to the ECtHR, justification of hate speech restrictions has sometimes involved 'bad-tendency' style reasoning which 'is simply too broad and vague' to protect an effective right to freedom of speech.[123]

In relation to the second type of challenge (audiences claiming that certain speech has violated their rights), the CERD held in *Jewish Community of Oslo and others v Norway*[124] that the acquittal of the leader of a far-right commemorative event in Askim, near Oslo had violated the rights of the authors—as members of the Jewish community—under Article 4 of the ICERD.[125] The UNHRC has, however, emphasized that the obligation to prosecute under Article 20(2) is an obligation of means, not of result.[126] As such, the failure to secure the conviction of Geert Wilders, founder of the right-wing Party for Freedom, for incitement to discrimination, violence and hatred did not violate Article 20(2), due in particular to the Dutch legislative framework and the detailed judgment of the trial court.[127]

Challenges have also arisen in relation to the reporting of hate speech by journalists. Here, the weight placed on the 'public watchdog' function of journalists has tended to result in their protection.[128] However, in a case involving publication by a newspaper of statements made by the president of the Chechen Republic in 2004 during the continuing conflict with Russia, the ECtHR urged 'particular caution' 'when consideration is being given to the publication of views of representatives of organisations which resort to violence against the state lest the media become a vehicle for the dissemination of "hate speech" and the promotion of violence'.[129] Judgments regarding the reporting of hate speech by others are instructive since they parallel current debates about the liabilities of social media platforms and internet service providers—who similarly claim that they are contributing to public discourse and informing the public about the existence of views which, as mere hosts, they do not themselves necessarily share.

The discussion of hate speech regulation here recalls the background factors with which this chapter began (there, in relation to the *PETA Deutschland* case)—the contextual contingency of speech protection, the limited reach of international scrutiny, and the changing nature of the speech marketplace. In this latter regard, the UNHRC, in Concluding Observations on State Reports, has raised concerns about the role of the internet and online forums in spreading hate speech.[130] More strikingly, the report of the independent international fact-finding mission on Myanmar (established by the

---

[122] UNHRC, *Views: Communication No 104/1981* (6 April 1983) UN Doc CPR/C/OP/2 (*JRT and the WG Party v Canada*) [8](b).

[123] Stefan Sottiaux, '"Bad Tendencies" in the ECtHR's "Hate Speech" Jurisprudence' (2001) *Eur Const L Rev* 40, especially 53 and 57. See, eg, *Féret v Belgium* App no 15614/07 (ECHR, 16 July 2009); *ES* (n 38) [52]–[55].

[124] UNHRC, *Views: Communication No 30/2003* (15 August 2005) UN Doc CERD/C/67D/30/2003 (*Jewish Community of Oslo and others v Norway*).

[125] Ibid [10.4].

[126] More generally, there is no right under the Covenant to see a person prosecuted. See, eg, *Vassilari* (n 121) [7.2].

[127] *Rabbae* (n 111).   [128] *Jersild v Denmark* App No 15890/89 (ECHR, 23 September 1994).

[129] *Dmitriyevskiy v Russia* App no 42168/06 (ECHR, 3 October 2017) [117].

[130] See, eg, UNHRC, 'Concluding Observations on the Fifth Periodic Report of Austria' (3 December 2015) UN Doc CCPR/C/AUT/CO/5, [15].

UN Human Rights Council in March 2017) emphasized the 'significant' role of social media in sharing 'dehumanizing and stigmatizing language against the Rohingya' and criticized Facebook's response as 'slow and ineffective'.[131] Since the 1994 Rwandan genocide, much has been written about the amplifying effect of popular media platforms in fostering the conditions for grave acts of violence.[132] Nonetheless, the centrality of social media platforms to the propagation of hatred (whether one favours protection or prohibition) presents a system challenge to international human rights law, hitherto concerned primarily with policing the voluntary undertakings of state actors.

11.4.3 National Security

As with hate speech, in addition to the obligation to prohibit 'any propaganda for war' under Article 20(1) of the ICCPR, international law has specifically required states to take concrete steps to prohibit incitement to terrorism. UN Security Council Resolution 1624[133] called upon states to prohibit incitement to commit terrorist acts, taking any 'measures as may be necessary and appropriate'.[134] Additional pronouncements by both the Council of Europe and the Council of the European Union have further urged states to criminalize intentional 'public provocation to commit a terrorist offence'.[135] In their wake, a report by the International Commission of Jurists lamented the fact that states had introduced a much wider range of offences such as '"apologia" or "praising", "glorification or indirect encouragement", "public justification", and the "promotion" of terrorist acts'.[136] Taking account of such developments, the UNHRC, in General Comment 34, specifically emphasized that:

> Such offences as 'encouragement of terrorism' and 'extremist activity' as well as offences of 'praising', 'glorifying', or 'justifying' terrorism, should be clearly defined to ensure that they do not lead to a disproportionate interference with freedom of expression.[137]

---

[131] UNHRC, 'Report of the Independent International Fact-Finding Mission on Myanmar' (12 September 2018) Un Doc A/HRC/39/64, [73].

[132] See, eg, Richard Ashby Wilson, *Incitement on Trial: Prosecuting International Speech Crimes* (CUP 2017) 16–17.

[133] UNSC Res 1624 (14 September 2005) UN Doc S/RES/1624.

[134] See also Yael Ronen, 'Incitement to Terrorist Acts and International Law' (2010) 23 *Leiden J Int'l L* 645, 648.

[135] Council of Europe Convention on the Prevention of Terrorism 2005, art 5; Council of the European Union Framework Decision on Combating Terrorism 2008.

[136] International Commission of Jurists, *Assessing Damage, Urging Action: Report of the Eminent Jurists Panel on Terrorism, Counter-terrorism and Human Rights* (ICJ 2009) <www.icj.org/wp-content/uploads/2012/04/Report-on-Terrorism-Counter-terrorism-and-Human-Rights-Eminent-Jurists-Panel-on-Terrorism-series-2009.pdf> accessed 15 November 2018. See also *Stomakhin v Russia* App no 52273/07 (ECHR, 9 May 2018) [117] and Dirk Voorhoof, 'No Overbroad Suppression of Extremist Opinions and "Hate Speech"' (*Strasbourg Observers*, 12 June 2018) <https://strasbourgobservers.com/2018/06/12/no-overbroad-suppression-of-extremist-opinions-and-hate-speech/> accessed 15 November 2018.

[137] General Comment 34 (n 10) [46] (citations omitted). See also The Representative on Freedom of the Media, *Joint Declarations of Representatives of Intergovernmental Bodies to Protect Free Media and Expression* (OSCE 2013) <https://www.osce.org/fom/99558> accessed 15 November 2018.

The UNHRC frequently raises concerns about the impact on freedom of speech of vaguely framed counter-terrorism measures in its Concluding Observations on State Reports.[138] However, it has addressed relatively few cases involving restrictions of speech imposed on national security grounds. While it has been prepared to challenge purported national security justifications advanced by a state,[139] the Committee has also been willing to defer to the judgment of the domestic courts where a modicum of due process has been demonstrated. For example, shortly after Uzbek authorities blamed Hizb ut-Tahrir for the February 1999 bombings in Tashkent (which killed sixteen and injured more than 120 people), two Uzbek nationals—both members of Hizb ut-Tahrir— were arrested and convicted of attempting to overturn the constitutional order. They had been discovered with written materials calling for the establishment of an Islamic State. The UNHRC noted that the Uzbek authorities were concerned with a perceived threat to national security and the Committee felt unable to conclude that the authors' sentences (each to 16 years' imprisonment) were incompatible with Article 19(3).[140] The Committee placed weight on both the apparent acceptance by the two individuals of the charges against them and on 'the careful steps...engaged in by the judicial process'.[141] This suggests that in the realm of national security—where sovereigntist sensitivities are especially acute—less intensive scrutiny of restrictions on speech might ensue where there is at least *some* evidence of domestic rule of law safeguards.

This too has been the approach of the ECtHR. While the Court recognized that the right to freedom of expression includes the right to challenge the constitutional order,[142] the Strasbourg institutions have often deferred to the national authorities' assessment of whether speech restrictions were 'necessary' in a bid to counter 'terrorism', affording a wide 'margin of appreciation' in this area.[143] However, four judgments of the Strasbourg court (two in the context of the post-2000 Chechen insurgency against Russian control of Chechnya, and two in the context of the 2016 attempted coup in Turkey) suggest a greater willingness to carefully scrutinize the necessity and proportionality of restrictions

---

[138] See, eg, UNHRC 'Concluding Observations on the Fifth Periodic Report of France' (17 August 2015) UN Doc CCPR/C/FRA/CO/5,[10]; UNHRC, 'Concluding Observations on the Initial Report of Bahrain' (15 November 2018) UN Doc CCPR/C/BHR/CO/1, [29].

[139] *Hak-Chul Shin* (n 39) [7.2].

[140] UNHRC, Views: Communication No 1233/2003 (31 March 2009) UN Doc CCPR/C/95/D/1233/2003 (*AK and AR v Uzbekistan*) [7.2].

[141] Ibid (and even though the authors argued, at [2.8], that their aim had merely been to acquire a deeper knowledge of Islam).

[142] 'It is of the essence of democracy to allow diverse political projects to be proposed and debated, even those that call into question the way a State is currently organised.' See, eg, *Socialist Party v Turkey* App no 21237/93 (ECHR, 25 May 1998) [47].

[143] See, eg, *Kern v Germany* App no 26870/04 (ECHR, 29 May 2007); *Leroy v France* App no 36109/03 (ECHR, 2 October 2008). See also *Purcell v Ireland* App no 15404/89 (Commission Decision, 15 April 1991); *Brind and Others v UK* App no 18714/91 (Commission Decision, 9 May 1994).

on 'terrorist speech'.[144] In the Turkish cases,[145] a third-party intervention by the UN Special Rapporteur on freedom of expression may have further emboldened the Court to find that the prosecution of two journalists, during a declared state of emergency, violated ECHR Article 10.[146] The Court, while recognizing that the attempted military coup *had* disclosed the existence of a 'public emergency threatening the life of the nation',[147] stated that 'the existence of a "public emergency threatening the life of the nation" must not serve as a pretext for limiting freedom of political debate, which is at the very core of the concept of a democratic society'.[148]

In like manner, in *Dmitriyevskiy v Russia*[149] and *Stomakhin v Russia*,[150] the Strasbourg court found a violation of ECHR Article 10 regarding the sentencing of a newspaper editor and journalist respectively—both of whom were charged with inciting extremist activities (supporting Chechen separatism) and in the case of *Stomakhin*, also with inciting hatred (virulently criticizing the Russian military). These cases are particularly interesting given the methodology employed by the Court—attempting to analyse and classify each of the impugned statements (as hate speech, glorification of violence, or legitimate political speech). While on the one hand this might signal a welcome intensification of scrutiny, Judge Keller, in her concurring opinion in *Stomakhin*, disagreed with the Court's 'rigid' approach and sought to 'caution the Court against the dangers of micro-managing the classification of statements'. Her concerns stemmed not only from disagreement with the Court's classifications, but also because she regarded such an approach as elevating the Court to 'a fourth-instance position', overreaching its subsidiary role.

11.5 Conclusion

The scope of the right to freedom of speech in international law is broad: notwithstanding the prioritization of 'political speech' (and some case law that might suggest weaker protection for cultural and educational speech), international law purports to offer principled protection for deeply offensive speech, commercial advertising, and (following General Comment 34) defamation of religion, as well as the developing freedom to access state-held information.

---

[144] A term used here simply to capture all forms of direct and indirect incitement (including 'glorification' and 'apology') associated with 'terrorism' however defined.

[145] *Altan v Turkey* App no 13237/17 (ECHR, 20 March 2018); *Alpay v Turkey* App no 16538/17 (ECHR, 20 March 2018).

[146] United Nations Special Rapporteur on the Promotion and Protection of the Right to Freedom of Opinion and Expression, 'Intervention in the European Court of Human Rights' (20 October 2017) <https://www.ohchr.org/Documents/Issues/Expression/AmicusFiling-ECHR-Turkey-UNSR.pdf> accessed 15 November 2018, [36].

[147] *Altan* (n 145) [93]; *Alpay* (n 145) [77].   [148] *Alpay* (n 145) [180]; *Altan* (n 145) [210].

[149] *Dmitriyevskiy* (n 129).   [150] *Stomakhin* (n 136).

International law is confronted with dilemmas similar to those arising in national courts in seeking to ensure an 'effective' right to freedom of speech. In particular, legal protections must keep pace with the changing nature of both 'the marketplace' (including media proliferation, user-generated content, audience saturation) and 'the press' (with a much wider range of individuals and civic organizations now undertaking the 'watchdog' role, once the preserve of professional journalists). In this regard, the classic paradigm of speech protections (*against* the State) must give way to a more complex matrix of responsibility which recognizes the important role of other stakeholders (such as Internet service providers and platform hosts). This, of course, creates particular challenges for international law given its state-centricity.

The state-centric nature of international law also limits the protection of speech in another way: the scrutiny of speech restrictions by international courts is inherently constrained by their subsidiary status. While in some areas (including defamation and political dissent) international law serves to buttress domestic speech protections, in others—most notably in countering both 'hate speech' and 'terrorist speech'—international law has itself arguably contributed to domestic protection deficits. It is important to recognize the compound role played by international law: it is not simply that it cedes the low value of such speech in normative terms, it is also that the latitude given to states in these areas inevitably takes root *within* the domestic legal framework—precisely where international law is least able to reassert human rights principles. It is in such circumstances that an effective right to freedom of speech is most at risk.

CHAPTER 12

THE STRUCTURE OF A FREE SPEECH RIGHT

STEPHEN GARDBAUM

Where free speech is recognized as a legal principle, what are the structural elements or components of a free speech right? What must a person establish in order to successfully claim they have a right to free speech or that it has been violated? Although, of course, the answer to this second question will vary among legal systems, the series of sub-questions that must be addressed to arrive at this answer is largely uniform and common across jurisdictions. This is because they collectively form the underlying structure of a free speech right. It is on this series of sub-questions that this chapter focuses: identifying and clarifying what they are; showing how they are both distinct from, but also sometimes interact with, each other; and illustrating how the range of possible and actual answers to each significantly impacts the nature and extent of 'substantive' free speech rights in a given legal order. Accordingly, what you have in virtue of being the holder of a free speech right can vary considerably depending on how these structural elements are combined.

In providing this overview of the structure of free speech as a legal principle, this chapter will introduce, analyse, and illustrate some variations among, the following six components. The first is the 'force' of a free speech right. This includes what type of legal right to free speech is formally recognized or at issue: for example, common law, statutory, or constitutional. This in turn helps to determine whether and how easily a free speech right can be legally superseded. Another aspect of force is whether and how the right is judicially enforceable. The second component is the 'subject' of free speech rights, or who are the rights-holders: for example, all persons within a jurisdiction or only citizens; legal persons including corporations or only natural persons? The third is the 'scope' of a free speech right: a right to say or do what exactly? Does it include falsehoods, hate speech, or baking a cake? The fourth, as a distinct structural element concerning content, addresses whether the right includes not only negative prohibitions on relevant others but also positive obligations, such as a duty to affirmatively protect the free speech of rights-holders from third-party threats? The fifth component is the 'object' of a free speech right: who are these 'relevant others' that are bound by the holder's rights? Against whom can the right be validly asserted? Finally, there is the 'limitation' of a free speech right. If the prior questions have all been answered to the effect that a free speech right *is* implicated and infringed in a particular situation, when, if ever, might there be a legally justified limitation of that right? Is the right an absolute bar or 'trump' against inconsistent action and, if not, what presumptive weight attaches to it? How, when, and why can the presumption be rebutted? Collectively, by constituting and expressing the underlying structure of the right to free speech, the answers to these six questions help to define the nature and extent of any particular such right in a given legal system.

12.1 THE FORCE OF A FREE SPEECH RIGHT

By the force of a free speech right, I am referring here to its status within the normative legal hierarchy and the nature and type of judicial enforceability it is afforded.[1] In terms of status, once free speech is recognized as a legal principle, as distinct from either a moral principle only or not being recognized as a valid norm at all, the next issue becomes what type of legal free speech right exists. In common law jurisdictions, free speech may be, and historically was, a right recognized by the common law. Thus, for example, the English common law has long affirmed a free speech right against prior restraint on publication.[2] As with all common law rights and liberties, free speech shares the general characteristics and normative status of this source of law, although what exactly these are, beyond the narrowly formalistic, has long been a source of controversy and disagreement, especially in common law jurisdictions lacking a codified constitution.[3] But the 'narrowly formalistic' are relatively easy to state. What the judges give, they may also take away, so that a common law free speech right can be developed by the courts over time, either expansively or restrictively. It also can be fully and completely

---

[1] These are not the only possible senses of the force of a free speech right, but they are the ones I focus on in this section. In Section 12.6 on limitations below, I look at another: the relative weight that a free speech right is granted when it is 'balanced' against other values that potentially can limit it. In drawing his helpful distinction between the coverage and protection of a right to freedom of expression, Fred Schauer includes some of these senses within the latter. See Frederick Schauer, *Free Speech: A Philosophical Enquiry* (CUP 1982) 91.

[2] See William Blackstone, *Commentaries on the Laws of England*, vol 4 (first published 1769) 151–2.

[3] For the long-standing but unorthodox view that the common law permits judges to invalidate statutes inconsistent with its fundamental rights and liberties, see *Dr Bonham's Case* (1610) 8 Co Rep 107a, 77 ER 638 (Coke CJ); *R (Jackson) v Attorney General* [2006] 1 AC 262; TRS Allan, *Constitutional Justice: A Liberal Theory of the Rule of Law* (OUP 2003).

abrogated by ordinary statute, although under both the common law principle of legality and a similar canon of construction, the statute must typically do so expressly.[4]

A free speech right may also be statutory in status, in whole or part, which generally entails that it can be modified upwards or downwards, or completely repealed, by subsequent statute. In recent years, judicial *dicta* and scholarly commentary have suggested that certain statutes may become both legally and politically entrenched,[5] although the extent of the former is usually limited to ousting the normal doctrine of implied repeal. More typically in modern legal systems, free speech has the higher status of a constitutional right, which at least in theory entrenches it against both such ordinary legislative repeal and judicial modification downwards. Here, the only formal legal means of superseding the right is via the constitutional amendment process, with its standard supermajority requirement of one sort or another. The final and highest legal status of a free speech right may be termed 'super-constitutional'. Here, the free speech right is protected even against the formal amendment process, either as requiring a special and higher supermajority for amendment or as being unamendable altogether. This in turn may be the result either of express textual provision to this effect[6] or judicial implication of a 'basic structure' doctrine that does not permit amendment of the central pillars of a constitution and includes free speech in them.[7] In sum, the different possible legal statuses that the right to free speech may be afforded determines how easily, as a formal matter, it can be superseded by other law.

A second dimension of force is the existence and extent of protection by means of judicial enforceability of the right. As we have just seen, where free speech has only common law or ordinary statute status, courts may play a more or less significant role in both developing and protecting the right. As the creators of the right, this is obvious and inevitable in the case of the common law, although it has also been argued by some 'common law constitutionalists' that judicial protection of fundamental common law rights, such

---

[4] The common law principle of legality means that fundamental common law rights may only be abrogated by express words or necessary implication on the part of the legislature. See *R v Secretary of State for the Home Department ex parte Simms* [2000] 2 AC 115 (Hoffman LJ). The canon of construction is that statutes in derogation of the common law will be narrowly construed. An example of such express statutory abrogation of a fundamental common law, speech-related right is the UK's Criminal Justice and Public Order Act 1994, which mostly abolished the historic right to remain silent during police questioning and trial.

[5] On legal entrenchment, it has been argued that 'constitutional statutes' are not subject to the normal doctrine of implied repeal by subsequent ones. See *Thoburn v Sunderland City Council* [2003] QB 151 (Laws LJ). On political entrenchment, see William N Eskridge, Jr and John Ferejohn, 'Super-Statutes' (2001) 50 *Duke LJ* 1215.

[6] For example, in South Africa, amending the Bill of Rights requires a two-thirds vote in both houses of the legislature, whereas the default amendment rule for most other parts of the Constitution is a two-thirds vote of the lower house (the National Assembly) only. See Constitution of the Republic of South Africa, No 108 of 1996 (1996) s 74. This phenomenon has been called 'tiered constitutionalism'. See Rosalind Dixon and David Landau, 'Tiered Constitutional Design' (2018) 86 *Geo Wash L Rev* 438. In the case of complete unamendability, the textual provision is usually referred to as an 'eternity clause'.

[7] The basic structure doctrine originated with the Indian Supreme Court in the landmark 1973 case of *Kesavananda Bharati v State of Kerala* (1973) 4 SCC 225, and subsequently spread to other countries in south Asia and elsewhere (eg Colombia).

as free speech, extends to invalidating contrary statutes.[8] Statutory free speech rights can also receive heightened judicial protection through various means of restrictively interpreting subsequent conflicting enactments.[9] But the role of courts and judicial enforceability is no less varied or consequential where free speech rights have constitutional, or even super-constitutional, status. Thus, a key issue is whether and how courts have the power to engage in constitutional review of statutes, in particular, that implicate free speech rights. Such rights can be part of a constitution's bill of rights, but that same constitution may deny to courts the power to question the validity of a statute, as in the Netherlands.[10] Or, it may grant the legislature the power to 'override' a judicial decision invalidating a statute for violating free speech, as in Canada.[11] A further variation, albeit in the context of statutory bills of rights, exists in the United Kingdom, the Australian Capital Territory and state of Victoria, where courts are granted the power to declare a statute inconsistent or incompatible with the protected rights, including freedom of speech, but the declaration has no legal effect on the continuing validity of the statute, which the legislature may or may not elect to amend or repeal.[12] Whether these 'weaker' forms of judicial review are in practice any less 'strong' than the more standard constitutional system in which legislatures are powerless to resolve the rights issue themselves in the face of a court decision is a matter of scholarly disagreement,[13] but for current purposes they may be.

12.2 The Subject of a Free Speech Right

The second structural element that helps to define the contours of a free speech right in any jurisdiction is the identity of the rights-holders. Assuming now the constitutional status of the right, the next question is who its beneficiaries are. Moving from broader to narrower answers, in principle these might be (1) all persons within the jurisdiction, including both natural and legal or juristic persons; (2) all natural persons or individuals;

---

[8] Allan (n 3).
[9] As, for example, with the New Zealand Bill of Rights Act 1990, which (in section 6) requires courts to interpret statutes consistently with rights wherever possible.
[10] Constitution of the Kingdom of the Netherlands, 2008, art 120.
[11] For a renewable five-year period. See Canadian Charter of Rights and Freedom 1982, s 33. In 1989, Quebec employed section 33 to override the right to freedom of expression under section 2(b) of the Charter in re-enacting its French-only commercial signs law, Bill 178, previously held unconstitutional by the Supreme Court of Canada.
[12] See Human Rights Act 1998, s 4; Human Rights Act 2004 (ACT), s 32; Charter of Human Rights and Responsibilities Act 2006 (Vic), s 32.
[13] See, eg, Aileen Kavanagh, 'What's So Weak About "Weak-Form Review": The Case of the UK Human Rights Act' (2015) 13 *Int'l J Const Law* 1008; Stephen Gardbaum, 'What's So Weak About "Weak-Form Review": A Reply to Aileen Kavanagh' (2015) 13 *Int'l J Const Law* 1040. It has also been argued that such 'formal mechanisms' as section 33 and the declaration of incompatibility are not necessary for 'weak-form' judicial review, which may exist where courts engage in a dialogic approach with legislatures, either by choice or necessity. See Po Jen Yap, *Constitutional Dialogue in Common Law Asia* (OUP 2015).

(3) all citizens, but only citizens; or (4) any given subset of the above, such as all female citizens or all individuals over the age of twenty-one. In addition, or alternatively, there might be a more particularized free speech right applying only to specific individuals or a group, such as the freedom of the press or academic freedom.

Although, especially in light of the well-known *Citizens United* case,[14] it is sometimes thought that affording free speech rights to corporations is unique to the United States, this is not the case. Indeed, whereas in the United States such 'constitutional corporate personhood' has been the (sometimes controversial) product of judicial implication from a text that simply refers to 'no law...abridging the freedom of speech' or depriving 'any person of life, liberty, or property',[15] several modern constitutions grant express protection to corporations as rights-holders. Thus, the German Basic Law states that '[t]he basic rights [which include freedom of speech] shall apply also to domestic juristic persons to the extent that the nature of such rights permits'.[16] The Final South African Constitution of 1996 borrows from this clause: 'A juristic person is entitled to the rights in the Bill of Rights to the extent required by the nature of the right and the nature of that juristic person'.[17] Both provisions exclude only such inherently individual rights as life, marriage, and bodily freedom,[18] but not freedom of speech. Any difference between the United States and such countries is *not* in bestowing free speech rights on corporations in the first place, but in either or both (1) the scope and content of the right, in particular the notion that free speech encompasses political donations and (2) the type and extent of countervailing values that might be taken to justify limitations on corporate free speech; that is, with respect to another structural element considered below.

Some constitutions distinguish between certain rights that are granted to all persons or individuals and others that are granted only to citizens. India and Colombia are reverse examples of this phenomenon. Thus, the Indian Constitution expressly limits the right to freedom of speech and expression (along with the other rights contained in article 19) to '[a]ll citizens', whereas several other fundamental rights, including the right to equality before the law and equal protection of the laws, to life or personal liberty, and freedom of religion, are granted to all persons.[19] The Supreme Court of India has confirmed the plain meaning of the text, that non-citizens of India, including corporations, are not beneficiaries of the right to freedom of speech.[20] By contrast, the Colombian

---

[14] *Citizens United v Federal Election Commission* 558 US 310 (2010).
[15] Moreover, the judicial implication long predates *Citizens United*. It arguably began in the 1819 case of *Trustees of Dartmouth College v Woodward* 17 US 518 (1819), in which the Court held that as a contract, a corporate charter was protected against impairment of obligation under art 1, s 10, and was clearly established in the 1888 case of *Pembira Consolidated Silver Mines and Milling Co v Pennsylvania* 125 US 181 (1888), in which the Court held that 'under the designation "person" there is no doubt that a private corporation is included [in the Fourteenth Amendment]'.
[16] Basic Law for the Republic of Germany, 1949, art 19(3).
[17] Constitution of the Republic of South Africa, s 7(4).
[18] On Germany, see David P Currie, *The Constitution of the Federal Republic of Germany* (U Chicago P 1994) 12.
[19] Constitution of India (1950) arts 14, 21, 25.
[20] *State Trading Corporation of India v Commercial Tax Officer* (1964) (4) SCR 99.

Constitution states that '[e]very individual is guaranteed the right to express and diffuse his/her thoughts and opinions',[21] whereas the separate rights 'to participate in the establishment, exercise, and control of political power' and 'to move about freely across the national territory' are expressly limited to Colombian citizens.[22] Indeed, in invalidating provisions of a presidential election law permitting campaign contributions by corporations, the Colombian Constitutional Court categorized such contributions as involving the right to political participation (and, by implication, not free speech), which is held only by citizens.[23]

In addition to the general category of rights-holder, there may also be more specific ones. The press is singled out as a particularly important free speech rights-holder in many legal systems, because of its distinctive role in tracking, publicizing, and revealing governmental activities as well as providing essential information and platforms for elections. Even though this does not necessarily mean the press is afforded greater free speech rights than ordinary rights-holders in order to protect these public functions, the general right is sometime expanded to take its special needs into account.[24] For somewhat similar reasons, members of a legislature *are* typically granted greater free speech rights, in terms of immunities, than ordinary persons or citizens.[25] The academic freedom enjoyed (only) by university teachers is also sometimes specially protected as part of freedom of speech in a constitution, as for example in article 5(3) of the German Basic Law and article 23 of the Japanese Constitution.[26]

12.3 THE SCOPE OF A FREE SPEECH RIGHT

Reverting to the general right to freedom of speech, what is included? What is it the right to say or do exactly? A chapter on the structure of a free speech right is not the place to go into detail about its substance, but falling within the scope of the right is obviously an essential structural element of any successful claim. To take a well-publicized recent example from the United States, the critical threshold issue for the baker's free speech claim in *Masterpiece Cakeshop v Colorado Civil Rights Commission*[27] was whether making a cake as a self-proclaimed 'cake artist' is an exercise of protected free speech, rather than straightforwardly regulable commercial activity.

---

[21] Constitution of Colombia (1991), art 20.   [22] art 24.

[23] Decision C-1153 of 2005, translated and discussed in Manuel José Cepeda Espinosa and David Landau, *Colombian Constitutional Law: Leading Cases* (OUP 2017) 130–2.

[24] As, for example, in the cases of defamation of public officials/figures and the media's protection of its sources.

[25] For example, the special privileges and immunities granted to legislators under article 71 of the Spanish, section 58 of the South African, and Article I, section 6 of the US, constitutions.

[26] See, eg, Constitution of Japan (3 November 1946) art 23 ('Art and science, research, and teaching shall be free. Freedom of teaching shall not release anyone from his allegiance to the constitution'); Basic Law for the Republic of Germany, art 5(3) ('Academic freedom is guaranteed').

[27] *Masterpiece Cakeshop v Colorado Civil Rights Commission*, 584 US _ (2018).

In some bills of rights, the scope of the right is stated in highly minimal and abstract ways—'no law...abridging the freedom of speech'[28] or 'the right to freedom of speech and expression'[29]—as if the meaning and coverage of these terms were settled and common knowledge, like the right to vote. But this of course is not the case as, unlike voting, there are almost endless possible forms, styles, and contents of 'speech' and 'expression'. What counts as an act of speech or expression (at least away from core instances) and which should be protected may be deeply contested, as are the functions and justifications of the right that might provide guidance for what is included. In other constitutions, there is a little more content, although nowhere is the coverage of the right fully and comprehensively resolved by the text. Thus, the freedom of expression granted by section 16(1) of the South African Constitution is stated to include freedom of the press and other media, freedom to receive and impart information or ideas, freedom of artistic creativity, and academic freedom and freedom of scientific research. Article 20 of the Colombian Constitution guarantees 'the freedom to express and diffuse one's thoughts and opinions, to transmit and receive information that is true and impartial, and to establish mass communications media'.

A few textual provisions on free speech partially delimit the scope of the right by specifying certain things falling outside it. One well-known example is section 16(2) of the South African Constitution, which states that the right to freedom of expression set out in subsection (1) 'does not extend to (a) propaganda for war; (b) incitement of imminent violence; or (c) advocacy of hatred that is based on race, ethnicity, gender or religion, and that constitutes incitement to cause harm'. Another similar provision is Article 20 of the International Covenant on Civil and Political Rights (ICCPR), which follows Article 19 on freedom of expression and states that: '[a]ny advocacy of national, racial or religious hatred that constitutes incitement to discrimination, hostility or violence shall be prohibited by law'. Its mandatory nature implies that such advocacy does not fall within the scope of the freedom of expression in the first place; it does not state the conditions for a permissible limitation of the right (these, in any event, are set out in Article 19(2)), but rather a statement of its boundaries. In the vast majority of cases, however, such provisions are lacking and the scope of the right must be judicially constructed.

Among the more contested boundary issues that, in the usual absence of much textual guidance, courts have had to resolve are whether falsehoods, political donations, the expression of 'subversive', extreme, or anti-democratic views, 'hate speech', and defamation of public officials/figures fall inside or outside the right to free speech. To some extent, they have been guided by one or more of the following: (1) general conceptions of a constitutional right, (2) perceived justifications or functions of free speech, and (3) the particular teleology of their own constitutional order.

Where the essential conception of a constitutional right is to require the government to reasonably justify the burdens it places on individuals in terms of public reasons, courts tend to take a liberal approach to the scope of a right and focus their attention and scrutiny of the proffered justification. Arguably, the Canadian Supreme Court has adopted this approach, as it has given an extremely broad definition to the 'freedom of

---

[28] US Constitution, amend XIV.   [29] Constitution of India, art 19(1).

thought, belief, opinion and expression' in section 2(b) of the Charter as 'any activity that conveys, or attempts to convey, meaning to the exception of acts of violence or threats of violence'.[30] By contrast, under the 'excluded reasons' or 'motivational' conception of rights, freedom of speech means the right not to have your speech restricted for impermissible, content-related reasons.[31]

To which of the three classic justifications or goals of free speech—truth-finding, individual autonomy, and democracy—a judge, court, or constitutional order adheres also has implications for the scope of the right. Thus, for example, the US Supreme Court's scepticism, at least outside the commercial context, towards the distinction between truth and falsity for First Amendment purposes[32] is explicable in significant part by the long-standing hold of the argument for freedom of expression, expressed by Mill and Holmes, founded on the fallibility of human judgment and the 'marketplace of ideas' as the 'best test of truth'.[33] Similarly, the claim of the baker to be engaged in artistic self-expression is more likely to be accepted under the individual autonomy argument for freedom of speech than the democracy argument, in which political speech is at the core.

Finally, the particular history and teleology of a constitutional order can also play a role in fashioning the contours of its free speech protections. Thus, the express exclusion of hate speech that incites harm from the scope of the right, along with many other provisions of the text, testify to the centrality of racial equality in post-apartheid South Africa. Similarly, the German Constitutional Court's interpretation of article 5 not to include protection for demonstrably false statements of fact[34] and its mistrust of the marketplace of ideas derive from the history of the Nazi regime's popularity, the Holocaust, and its denial. By contrast, the United States' faith in the same marketplace, rooted in its anti-governmental political culture, cannot be fully understood without its own history of revolution against a tyrannical king.

12.4 NEGATIVE AND POSITIVE FREE SPEECH RIGHTS

A related structural issue concerning the scope of a free speech right is whether the right is exclusively 'negative' in nature—that is, a right not to be regulated or interfered with when exercising the protected free speech—or also 'positive', a right to demand that

---

[30] *Irwin Toy Ltd v Quebec (AG)* [1989] 1 SCR 927.
[31] See Richard H Pildes, 'Avoiding Balancing: The Role of Exclusionary Reasons in Constitutional Law' (1994) 45 *Hastings LJ* 711; Daniel Halberstam, 'Desperately Seeking Europe: On Comparative Methodology and Conceptions of Rights' (2007) 5 *Int'l J Const L* 166.
[32] See, eg, *Gertz v Robert Welch, Inc*, 418 US 323 (1974) ('punishing [factual] error runs the risk of inducing a cautious and restrictive exercise [of free speech]').
[33] See *Abrams v United States*, 250 US 616, 630 (1919) (Holmes J, dissenting); *Gertz* (n 32) ('[h]owever pernicious an opinion may seem, we depend for its correction not on the conscience of judges and juries but on the competition of other ideas').
[34] *Holocaust Denial Case* [1994] 90 BVerfGE 241.

enjoyment of the protected free speech be ensured or protected.[35] Such a positive right may be that of the speaker, in terms of guaranteed communication or dissemination of one's ideas, or of the audience, the assurance of receiving (and not only imparting) information. From the perspective of those bound by the right rather than from that of the rights-holder, the same distinction can be expressed by asking whether the free speech right imposes a duty not to interfere only or also one to protect, ensure, or promote it.

Many older, more 'classically liberal' constitutions, as well as those of most (but not all) common law jurisdictions hue to the conception of constitutional rights generally, and free speech in particular, as a 'charter of negative rights'.[36] Thus, for example, in the United States, where the scope of the right to free speech is taken to include making financial contributions to political campaigns and candidates, the Supreme Court famously affirmed the exclusively negative nature of the right and its rejection of the positive conception (which, in this context, would emphasize the importance of meaningful access to effective means of political expression and information) in *Buckley v Valeo*.[37] According to the Court: 'The concept that government may restrict the speech of some [in] order to enhance the relative voice of others is wholly foreign to the First Amendment'.[38] This also underscores the deep connection between the negative/positive rights distinction and the differing normative emphases within comparative free speech law of the value of liberty versus equality. Similarly, in Australia, the High Court rejected a claim that the constitutional right to freedom of political communication entitled a candidate in a national election to media coverage.[39] To the contrary, the right only prohibits interference with, or regulation of, such coverage, including potentially the mandating of it.

Examples of positive free speech rights in other jurisdictions are also numerous, and tend to range from a general textual provision obliging the state not only to respect but also to protect and promote the rights contained in more modern bills of rights,[40] to more particular textual rights of reply in the media and to receive information.[41] They are also frequently the product of judicial implication. The European Court of Human Rights (ECtHR) has interpreted several of the rights in the 1950 European Convention on Human Rights (ECHR), including freedom of expression under Article 10, to have the positive dimension of obligating the forty-seven member states to protect individuals from deprivation of these rights by other individuals. In the case of Article 10, this is somewhat surprising because the text suggests only a negative prohibition: 'This right [to freedom of expression] shall include freedom to hold opinions and to receive and impart information and ideas *without interference by public authority* and

---

[35] To be sure, the distinction between negative and positive speech rights is not always clear-cut and there are boundary issues, mostly depending on whether the baseline is taken to be for or against the speech claim, such as the right to demonstrate on streets and in other public spaces.
[36] *Jackson v City of Joliet* 715 F2d 1200, 1203 (7th Cir, 1983), *cert denied*, 465 US 1049 (Posner J).
[37] *Buckley v Valeo*, 424 US 1 (1976).   [38] Ibid 48–9.
[39] *McClure v Australian Electoral Commission* [1999] HCA 31; (2017) 344 ALR 421.
[40] See, eg, Constitution of the Republic of South Africa, s 7(2).
[41] Both, for example, are contained in Constitution of Colombia, art 20.

regardless of frontiers'.[42] Nonetheless, since 2000, the Court has interpreted article 10 to impose an affirmative duty on government to protect the right from private threats.[43] A useful example is the 2001 case of *Özgür Gündem v Turkey*.[44] Here, the claimant newspaper alleged violations of both the Turkish government's positive obligation under Article 10 to protect its freedom of expression against acts of violence perpetrated by private parties and the negative duty of not itself interfering with this freedom through a series of searches and prosecutions of the newspaper's offices and staff. The ECtHR upheld both claims.

Similarly the German Constitutional Court has read a duty of protection (*Schutzpflichten*) into several of the rights contained in the Basic Law. This began with the right to freedom of expression under article 5, when famously in the 1961 *First Television Case*,[45] the Court held that the state had a constitutional duty to protect and preserve broadcasting freedom by ensuring the existence of 'balance, objectivity and reciprocal respect' in programming. Although it justified this decision on the basis of the unique 'spectrum scarcity' of broadcasting as compared with the press, more general media regulation to protect pluralism against ordinary monopolizing market forces was also later held to be constitutionally required not only in Germany, but also in France and Italy.[46] Subsequently, such duties were extended to other rights in the Basic Law, most controversially to impose a constitutional obligation on the state to protect the right to life of the foetus against its mother.[47] Other common positive speech rights, such as the right of reply to attacks in the media and the right to receive information, may not directly or necessarily impose constitutional duties on government, but nonetheless normally assume the existence (or creation) of a judicial or regulatory framework in which the rights are realized and enforced.

12.5 THE OBJECT OF A FREE SPEECH RIGHT

Once we know the identity of the free speech rights-holder and the content of the right that is held, the further structural question arises of who is bound to respect it. Who or what is burdened or constrained by the right? This question has two dimensions: (1) in federal systems, does a federal right to free speech bind only the national government or also state or provincial ones; (2) in all systems, does a right to free speech bind only government actors or also non-governmental or private ones? To what extent does it impact the private sphere? This first sub-question is far easier to answer than the second, at least in a full or complete manner, so we will start with it.

---

[42] art 10(1) ECHR (emphasis added).
[43] The key case was *Fuentes Bobo v Spain*, no 39293/98, judgment of 29 February 2000.
[44] *Özgür Gündem v Turkey* [2001] 31 EHRR 49.
[45] *First Television Case* [1961] 12 BVerfGE 205.
[46] See Eric Barendt, *Freedom of Speech* (2nd edn, OUP 2007) 67–71, 429–33.
[47] *First Abortion Case* [1975] 39 BVerfGE 1.

Some federal bills of rights containing the right to free speech apply only to the federal government of a country but not to the constituent state or provincial ones. In such systems, the bill of rights is part of the set of legal limits on federal authority and not a minimum national guarantee of rights. Examples include the Canadian Bill of Rights of 1960,[48] a still operative statute the significance of which was much reduced by passage of the subsequent constitutional and province-binding Charter of Rights and Freedoms in 1982,[49] and the US Bill of Rights, including the First Amendment, for the hundred-plus years prior to selective 'incorporation' against the states by the Fourteenth Amendment.[50] In Australia, a proposed national bill of rights in 2009 that was ultimately never enacted would have applied only against the federal government.[51] By contrast, the more common situation is for the bill of rights to be part of the supreme or fundamental law of the nation as a whole and so to bind the constituent political units as well as the federal government as a set of guaranteed minimum rights. This is the case, for example, in India, South Africa, Brazil, Mexico, and Germany.

The complexity of the second sub-question is belied by the seemingly simple and straightforward bifurcation between the 'vertical' and 'horizontal' effect of constitutional rights, including free speech. Rights with vertical effect apply only against the government whereas horizontal rights also apply against private actors. For several well-known reasons which need not be rehearsed here, most rights in most constitutions—whether more traditional civil and political rights or less traditional economic, social, cultural, and collective ones—are and have been vertical in nature, with at a maximum only a few exceptional ones being horizontal in application. Thus, for example, the sole exception in the US Constitution to its well-known 'state action doctrine' of vertical effect is the Thirteenth Amendment's ban on slavery and involuntary servitude 'anywhere in the United States', which applies both vertically and horizontally. The Supreme Court of India has consistently adhered to the general position that the Fundamental Rights contained in part III of the Constitution, including freedom of speech, apply only against the government and not against private individuals.[52] At the same time, it has recognized some exceptions, holding that the subject-less—although not expressly horizontal—provisions abolishing 'untouchability',[53] prohibiting human traffic and forced labour,[54] and prohibiting employment of children below fourteen years of age in

---

[48] SC 1960, c 44, s 1(d) contains the free speech provision.
[49] Section 2(b) contains 'freedom of thought, belief, opinion and expression, including freedom of the press and other media of communication'.
[50] The right to free speech was first 'incorporated' against the states by the 1925 case of *Gitlow v People of the State of New York*, 268 US 652 (1925).
[51] National Human Rights Consultation Committee, National Human Rights Consultation Report (2009) 363–4.
[52] *Zoroastrian Cooperative Housing Society v District Registrar* (2005) 5 SCC 632 ('The Fundamental Rights in Part III of the Constitution are normally enforced against State action or action by other authorities who may come within the provision of article 12 of the Constitution').
[53] art 17. [54] art 23.

factories, mines or other hazardous occupations[55] are 'plainly and indubitably enforceable against everyone'.[56]

By contrast, the general position under section 8(2) of the South African Constitution is that, in principle, all rights can have horizontal effect, depending on context.[57] In Colombia, article 86 of the Constitution permits *tutelas* or individual complaints for violations of constitutional rights to be brought against private actors when they are 'providing a public service or whose conduct may affect seriously the public interest, or in respect of whom the applicant may find himself/herself in a state of subordination or vulnerability'. The Constitutional Court has regularly allowed *tutelas* to be brought by those seeking to exercise their article 20 right to rectification against private media outlets.[58]

Although the vertical-horizontal distinction drawn in terms of who has constitutional duties to comply with a bill of rights remains a useful starting point, its binary nature significantly oversimplifies the reality. This is because constitutional rights may adversely impact and effectively regulate private actors even in systems that adhere to the basic vertical position. To take a well-known free speech example from Germany, in the landmark *Lüth* decision the Constitutional Court held that although the Basic Law's rights, including freedom of expression under article 5, apply only against the legislative, executive and judicial branches of government and not private persons like the plaintiff, a Nazi-era film director, it nonetheless overturned on free speech grounds an injunction awarded to him under the Civil Code by the lower court against the boycott of his new film organized by another citizen.[59]

Accordingly, a second distinction has been introduced that emphasizes this latter way in which constitutional rights may impact non-state actors: the distinction between their direct and *indirect* horizontal effect. 'Direct horizontal effect' is the position within the basic dichotomy in which constitutional rights bind private actors. Where it applies, individuals can be sued by their fellow citizens for violating their constitutional rights, as for example under the writ of *tutela* in Colombia or constitutional tort actions in Ireland.[60] By contrast, 'indirect horizontal effect' means that although constitutional rights do not directly regulate and impose duties on private actors, they may nonetheless impact and indirectly regulate them. What is 'indirect' in the concept is the effect of

---

[55] art 24.
[56] *People's Union for Democratic Rights v Union of India* (1982) 2 SCC 235. In addition are the textually horizontal article 15(2) against certain specified types of private discrimination and a small part of the broad modern understanding of the right to life under article 21.
[57] 'A provision of the Bill of Rights binds a natural or justice person if, and to the extent that, it is applicable, taking into account the nature of the right and the nature of any duty imposed by the right'. In practice, only relatively rarely has the South African Constitutional Court directly applied constitutional rights to private actors. One instance is *Governing Body of the Juma Musjid Primary School v Essay NO 2011* (8) BCLR 761 (CC) (private trust bound not to impair right to basic education under section 29 of the Constitution).
[58] See Cepeda Espinosa and Landau (n 23) 122.
[59] *Lüth* [1958] BVerfGE 7, 198.
[60] See, eg, *Hosford v John Murphy & Sons* [1987] IR 621.

a constitutional right on an individual, by comparison with the immediate, unmediated, or direct application under the fully horizontal position.

Indirect horizontality typically occurs in one of two general ways. The first is where (vertical) rights impose an affirmative constitutional duty on the government to protect individuals from certain actions by other private actors, as we saw in the previous section. Here, constitutional rights indirectly impact private individuals and entities by mandating that the government enact and enforce measures against certain of their conduct that is not itself directly regulated by the constitution. For example, in the ECtHR case *of Özgür Gündem v Turkey* discussed above, article 10 was held to require the Turkish government to protect the newspaper from the private violence to which it was being subjected, which would typically result in the perpetrators being prosecuted.

The second way is through the application of constitutional rights to private law, the rules that structure the legal relationships of individuals *inter se*. Indirect horizontal effect occurs via the impact of a bill of rights on the law that individuals invoke and rely on in civil disputes, thereby limiting what they can be authorized to do and which of their interests, choices, and actions may be protected by law. So whereas under direct horizontal effect, a bill of rights governs all *actions*, under indirect horizontal effect it governs all *laws*. By subjecting the provisions of private law to the requirements of a bill of rights, a constitutional system narrows the public–private gap in the scope of those rights.

This general technique, as well as the important point that indirect horizontal effect is perfectly consistent with taking a vertical position within the basic dichotomy, originated with the *Lüth* case from Germany mentioned above. Here, in overturning the lower court's damage award to the plaintiff, the Constitutional Court famously held that the rights contained in the Basic Law form 'an objective order of values' that must 'radiate' throughout the entire legal system, including in private litigation. Accordingly, private law must be compatible with these constitutional values and, if it cannot be interpreted consistently with them, is invalid.[61] Since the Civil Code, under which the plaintiff was suing for economic loss, has open-ended general clauses capable of accommodating the constitutional value of free expression, it must be interpreted and applied by the ordinary courts in a way that sufficiently takes it into account. A second example is the landmark US Supreme Court decision in *New York Times v Sullivan*, overturning a state court damage award and invalidating on free speech grounds part of the private law of defamation within a constitutional system well-known for its threshold 'state action' requirement.[62] As a result, the losing plaintiff was adversely affected by the First Amendment, which was deemed to govern his legal relations with the newspaper, even though he was not bound by its provisions.

---

[61] *Lüth* (n 59).   [62] *New York Times v Sullivan*, 376 US 254 (1964).

Indeed, here a further distinction has been suggested in the literature between 'strong' and 'weak' indirect horizontal effect.[63] The former is where all private law is fully and equally subject to a bill of rights, regardless of type (common law versus statute, or subject-matter) and the nature of the litigation in which it is relied upon (including 'purely private litigation' between individuals). By contrast, weak indirect horizontal effect means that some or all private law is not fully and equally subject to a bill of rights as compared with other types of government action. An example is the situation in Canada where the Charter of Rights and Freedoms does not apply to the common law at issue in private litigation—unlike a statute—although courts are supposed to take its values into account in developing the common law. This was decided in a case where a trade union claimed that its Charter right to freedom of expression was violated by an injunction granted to its target employer under the common law against secondary picketing.[64] By contrast, the common law at issue in private litigation in *New York Times* was fully and equally subject to the First Amendment (and held to violate it), and in the United States statutes and common law provisions would be treated identically. Of course, unlike the common law of defamation in *New York Times*, much ordinary general private law—torts, contracts, property—will easily pass constitutional muster under current substantive understandings of the First Amendment.

12.6 LIMITING A FREE SPEECH RIGHT

In practice (if not necessarily in theory), the dominant general conception of a constitutional free speech right, as with constitutionally rights generally, is that of an important prima facie legal claim that is nonetheless capable of being justifiably limited or overridden by certain conflicting public policy objectives. At least as it applies to the United States, this general conception has been referred to as constitutional rights as 'shields', in contrast to the peremptory or absolute conception of rights as 'trumps'.[65] It also contrasts, although less starkly, with a third conception of free speech and other constitutional rights as stating exclusionary reasons for government action.[66]

Within this dominant general conception, the weight of the presumption in favour of the rights claim varies somewhat from country to country and in some cases from right to right. It is sometimes claimed, for example, especially in the free speech context, that the United States has a more 'categorical' conception of rights in this sense, not because

---

[63] See Gavin Phillipson, 'The Human Rights Act, "Horizontal Effect" and the Common Law: a Bang or a Whimper?' (1999) 62 *Mod L Rev* 824, 830; Stephen Gardbaum, 'The "Horizontal Effect" of Constitutional Rights' (2003) 102 *Mich L Rev* 387, 435–7.

[64] *Retail, Wholesale and Dep't Store Union v Dolphin Delivery Ltd* [1986] 2 SCR 573.

[65] Frederick Schauer, 'A Comment on the Structure of Rights' (1993) 27 *Ga L Rev* 415, 423. On the absolute conception, see also Grégoire Webber, 'Proportionality and Limitations on Freedom of Speech', Chapter 10 of this volume.

[66] See Pildes (n 31); Halberstam (n 31).

rights are necessarily trumps but because they afford a larger shield; that is, a greater general presumptive weight in favour of a rights claim.

This general conception of a free speech or other constitutional right is typically operationalized and adjudicated through a two-step process. The first step consists of everything we have considered thus far in this chapter and determines whether a free speech right is implicated and has been infringed; that is, whether the prima facie claim has been established. The second step determines whether the infringement is nonetheless a justified one and asks whether the defendant has rebutted this prima facie case by satisfying the constitutional criteria for limited or overriding the right. The first step concerns the coverage of the right—its subject, object, and scope; the second step involves its protection: the weight of the right in the face of the strength and relevance of the public policy reasons for the infringement.[67]

The capacity of free speech and other rights to be justifiably limited in this way is standardly expressed in modern constitutional texts through one of two types of 'limitations clause': specific or general. The former are contained in the text's free speech provision itself, sometimes in a separate sub-paragraph, and contain customized wording relating to the justified limitation of the right. For example, article 19(2) of the Indian Constitution states that '[n]othing in sub-clause (a) of clause (1) [the free speech provisions] shall... prevent the State from making any law, in so far as such law imposes reasonable restrictions on the exercise of the right... in the interests of the security of the State, friendly relations with foreign States, public order, decency or morality, or in relation to contempt of court, defamation, or incitement to an offence'. Article 5(2) of the German Basic Law states that: 'These rights [to freedom of expression] find their limits in the provisions of general statutes, in statutory provisions for the protection of youth, and in the right to respect for personal honour'. Examples of general limitations clauses, which specify the uniform criteria for limiting all the rights in a bill of rights, are section 36 of the South African Constitution and section 1 of the Canadian Charter.[68] Free speech rights unqualified by either type of express limitation clause may still be subject to judicially implied limits, where they conflict with other protected rights or with certain public policy objectives. So, for example, the Colombian Constitutional Court has held that the textually unqualified right to freedom of expression and information may be justifiably limited where it conflicts with such other fundamental rights as the right to a good name or to privacy.[69] The US Supreme Court has never accepted Justice Hugo Black's absolutist, strict textualist position that 'no law abridging the freedom of

---

[67] Here again, I am referencing Fred Schauer's distinction. See Schauer (n 1).

[68] Section 36 of the Constitution of the Republic of South Africa states as follows: 'The rights in the Bill of Rights may be limited only in terms of law of general application to the extent that the limitation is reasonable and justifiable in an open and democratic society based on human dignity, equality and freedom, taking into account all relevant factors, including—(a) the nature of the right; (b) the importance of the purpose of the limitation; (c) the nature and extent of the limitation; (d) the relation between the limitation and its purpose; and (e) less restrictive means to achieve the purpose'. Section 1 of the Canadian Charter states its rights are guaranteed 'subject only to such reasonable limits prescribed by law as can be demonstrably justified in a free and democratic society'.

[69] Decision T-066 of 1998.

speech ... mean[s] no law abridging'.[70] And, having implied a right to freedom of political communication, the High Court of Australia has also implied certain limits to it.[71]

The second step of rights analysis and adjudication is widely and increasingly implemented by application of the principle of proportionality. Having its origins in German administrative law, proportionality began to be applied by the Federal Constitutional Court a few years after it came into being, in the late 1950s, and has spread over succeeding decades at rapid speed to the majority of domestic constitutional systems in all parts of the world, as well as to international human rights regimes.[72] As the dominant principle applying to all protected rights, it has become a sort of one-stop shop, a near-universal test for limiting rights. Increasingly, what you have by virtue of having a free speech, or any other, right is a right against disproportionate limitation.

The proportionality principle is operationalized through a sequenced three- or four-pronged test. Where the public policy objectives that are in principle capable of justifying the limitation of a free speech right are *not* specified in the relevant limitations clause, there is typically a threshold requirement to the effect that the (usually governmental) end or objective is 'sufficiently important' or 'pressing and substantial' in the circumstances to warrant overriding it.[73] The remaining three prongs focus on the means employed to promote this objective: (1) are they rationally related to it?; (2) are they necessary or the least restrictive of the right?; (3) even if so, do they nonetheless impose disproportionate burdens on the right relative to the objective?[74] This last prong is often referred to as proportionality in the strict sense (or *stricto sensu*), and requires balancing the relative weight of the right and the limitation in the particular circumstances. In this way, even though this same test (or minor variations on it) applies to limitations of all rights within a system, it does not necessarily involve a single weight attaching to all rights equally, as the final prong may take into account the relative importance of different constitutional rights, or the same right in different contexts. Such flexibility and focus on particular circumstances is often thought to be one of the distinguishing features (and, for some, benefits) of the principle of proportionality compared to a more 'categorical' approach to rights and their limits.

An example where the limitation of the right to free speech was held to be unjustified under the proportionality test is the South African case of *Johncom Media Investments Limited v M and Others*.[75] Here, the Constitutional Court found that the complete ban on publication of information emerging from divorce proceedings in order to protect

---

[70] *Smith v California*, 361 US 147 (1959) (Black J, concurring).

[71] See *Attorney-General (SA) v Corporation of the City of Adelaide* (2013) 249 CLR 1 (preventing obstruction in the use of a road is legitimate basis for limiting the right).

[72] Alec Stone Sweet and Jud Mathews, 'Proportionality, Balancing and Global Constitutionalism' (2008) 47 *Colum J Transnat'l L* 68. Starting with the European Court, several international human rights courts also apply a 'margin of appreciation', or degree of state discretion, towards the domestic decision they are effectively reviewing.

[73] These terms come from the Canadian case of *R v Oakes* [1986] 1 SCR 103.

[74] For a more detailed analysis of these four prongs, as well as the identification of some generally unacknowledged complexities in their application, see Chapter 10 (n 65) in this volume.

[75] *Johncom Media Investments Limited v M and Others* [2009] ZACC 5.

the privacy and dignity of the parties and their children under section 12 of the Divorce Act was not the least restrictive means of promoting these legitimate objectives, and so was a disproportionate and unconstitutional infringement of the right to freedom of expression. A converse example is the Canadian case of *R v Keegstra*,[76] in which the Supreme Court held that section 319(2) of the Criminal Code prohibiting the wilful promotion of hatred, other than in private conversation, towards any section of the public distinguished by colour, race, religion, or ethnic origin satisfied all four prongs of the proportionality test and so was a justified limitation on the right of expression under section 2(b) of the Charter.

An alternative second-step methodology for evaluating whether limits are justified is to have separate standards, or tiers, of review embodying differential weights and presumptions for different rights, or even for different types of laws implicating the same right, as generally in the United States. Thus, for example, whether 'strict scrutiny', 'intermediate scrutiny', or 'rational basis review', with their very different presumptions and likely outcomes, applies to the limitation of free speech rights under the First Amendment depends on the nature and type of the speech restriction. Under current doctrine, content-based (versus content-neutral) regulation and restriction of the right to free speech is subject to the highest tier of scrutiny, strict scrutiny, requiring that the government proves its measure was necessary for a compelling public interest. Only relatively rarely do restrictions on protected speech satisfy strict scrutiny, and generally less often than they pass the proportionality test. Again, where combined with a negative conception of the right to free speech, this effectively amounts to a stronger presumption in favour of liberty than where countervailing values, such as equality, are afforded greater scope at the second step of analysis. By contrast, content-neutral restrictions, such as time, place, and manner restrictions on speech, as well as any regulation of commercial speech, are subject to the lesser standard of intermediate scrutiny, which requires the measure in question to be substantially related to an important public interest. Finally, general laws with only incidental burdens on free speech—such as ordinary private tort and contract law, including employment-at-will—are subject to rational basis review requiring only reasonable relation to a legitimate public interest, which is difficult to fail. Accordingly, an American Keegstra[77] could perhaps be fired from his teaching job, but not criminally prosecuted, for using the classroom as a forum for indoctrinating students with his anti-semitic views.[78]

Although this alternative, tiers of review methodology is certainly more 'categorical' in the sense of the importance of putting things in the right box, the weight of a free speech claim varies considerably depending on into which one it is placed; the third category affords little protection compared to the first, and generally less than under proportionality. Moreover, it is widely acknowledged that this approach still requires courts to 'balance' rights against conflicting governmental interests, as under the final step of proportionality analysis. Indeed, much of the 'anti-balancing critique', judicial and

---

[76] *R v Keegstra* [1990] 3 SCR 697.   [77] Ibid.   [78] See Halberstam (n 31).

academic, originates in the United States.[79] So while it is uncontested that the United States employs neither the label nor the precise content of the proportionality test in its free speech jurisprudence, several scholars have argued that the differences between the two second-step methodologies are smaller and less significant than often assumed or claimed.[80]

Apart from the exclusionary reasons conception of free speech and other constitutional rights mentioned above,[81] which creates a binary of either prohibited or permissible reasons for government action and so has no conceptual space for justified limitations of rights, another alternative to both balancing methodologies is the specification theory of rights.[82] Under this account, free speech and most other textual constitutional rights are relatively abstract statements of principle and underdetermined with respect to their content in particular situations. As such, they are in need of further specification or delimitation, and this is really how the second-step process of what the conventional picture misconceives as limiting or overriding rights should be understood. The result is a bounded but absolute right.

---

[79] Most famously, Justice Black (n 70) and T Alexander Aleinikoff, 'Constitutional Law in the Age of Balancing' (1987) 95 *Yale LJ* 943.

[80] See Stephen Gardbaum, 'The Myth and the Reality of American Constitutional Exceptionalism' (2008) 107 *Mich L Rev* 391; Vicki C Jackson, 'Constitutional Law in an Age of Proportionality' (2015) 124 *Yale LJ* 3094.

[81] See n 31.

[82] Grégoire CN Webber, *The Negotiable Constitution: On the Limitation of Rights* (CUP 2009); John Oberdiek, 'Specifying Constitutional Rights' (2010) 27 *Const Comment* 231.

CHAPTER 13

POSITIVE FREE SPEECH: A DEMOCRATIC FREEDOM

ANDREW T KENYON

13.1 INTRODUCTION

FREE speech is classically understood as a negative liberty, something that limits state restrictions on speech. 'Freedom' is freedom from external restraint. Freedom is not thought to involve the state acting so much as the state not acting. What counts as an allowable restriction on the freedom and what counts as speech in the first place are typical points of debate in legal analysis. But within the debates, freedom is commonly understood in negative terms. This need not be the case. Freedom can be understood to have positive dimensions as well as negative. In simple terms, freedom of speech can be understood to involve the presence of supports for speech as well as the absence of restrictions on speech. The idea is far from unknown in free speech writing and doctrine but warrants further consideration. In negative approaches to free speech, a line is drawn between actions aimed at restricting speech and actions that establish underlying conditions affecting speech. While there are differences between those two types of action, it is not clear that only one type is relevant to communicative freedom.[1]

The state always acts in a myriad of ways that affect speech, but negative approaches to the freedom bracket out other actions affecting speech. Such actions simply do not register as questions of free speech. For example, does the state provide subsidies to certain forms of public communication, such as reduced taxes or charges that some jurisdictions have long applied to printed media? Is competition law applied in a particular manner to media and communications sectors, or are media businesses treated like

---

[1] I use terms such as free speech, freedom of expression, and communicative freedom interchangeably in this chapter, and communicative freedom is not used in the sense adopted by Jürgen Habermas: see, eg, Jürgen Habermas, *Between Facts and Norms: Contributions to a Discourse Theory of Law and Democracy* (William Rehg tr, Polity 1996) 119–20.

those selling toasters?[2] Does the state create and fund public media and, if so, in what manner? Are there legal requirements of transparency for media ownership and funding so that audiences can easily find information about the issues? What about the legal approach to demonstrations and the public resources that can be needed to support them, access to court information and other public information, protection of editorial freedom, and protection of journalists' safety?[3] Matters such as these can be analysed through free speech's positive dimensions: the freedom can be much broader than a negative liberty.[4]

In this chapter, I have a more specific focus. My interest lies in using a democratic free speech rationale to consider positive structural dimensions of the freedom.[5] While far from the only aspect of positive free speech, I think it offers a useful example of the freedom's positive dimensions. My focus is on legal conditions underlying public speech and their links to democratic constitutional arrangements. I begin with a few points of introduction, then provide an outline of the general approach before drawing brief comparisons with two well-known US approaches to free speech and media freedom.

Many points are left aside in this chapter, four of which are worth noting at the outset. First, similar ideas about positive freedom could be drawn from work on positive human rights or from analyses of political freedom. This could extend to an explanation of how Isaiah Berlin's famous exposition of positive and negative freedom has little relevance to free speech.[6] Among other matters, his argument is one against monism, but analyses of positive freedom are often pluralist. They are almost invariably so for positive free speech. In addition, Berlin's concern is not with structural, communicative supports for democracy, but with limits that must be applied to democracy to preserve individual freedom. He does not address whether democracy itself has other requirements, including communicative ones.

---

[2] In the 1980s, the head of the US regulator (the Federal Communications Commission) infamously referred to television as really just 'a toaster with pictures'; see, eg, Peter J Boyer, 'Under Fowler, FCC Treated TV as Commerce, *New York Times* (19 January 1987) 15.

[3] See, eg, Eric Barendt, *Freedom of Speech* (2nd edn, OUP 2005) 100–8; Herdís Thorgeirsdóttir, 'Journalism Worthy of the Name: An Affirmative Reading of Article 10 of the ECHR' (2004) 22 *Netherlands Q Hum Rts* 601; Tarlach McGonagle, 'Positive Obligations Concerning Freedom of Expression: Mere Potential or Real Power?' in Onur Andreotti (ed), *Journalism at Risk: Threats, Challenges and Perspectives* (Council of Europe 2015) 9; Sandra Fredman, *Comparative Human Rights Law* (OUP 2018) 349–53; Mark Tushnet, *Advanced Introduction to Freedom of Expression* (Edward Elgar 2018) 83–103.

[4] For an examination of free speech as potentially including much more than non-censorship (such as the provision of compulsory education, library and research funding, and non-elite public television) see Frederick Schauer, 'Hohfeld's First Amendment' (2008) 76 *Geo Wash L Rev* 914.

[5] My analysis here draws, in part, on a longer consideration of the issues: Andrew T Kenyon, *Democracy of Expression: Positive Free Speech and Law* (CUP, in press).

[6] Isaiah Berlin, *Two Concepts of Liberty: An Inaugural Lecture delivered before the University of Oxford on 31 October 1958* (Clarendon 1958). See also 'Introduction' in Isaiah Berlin, *Four Essays on Liberty* (OUP 1969) ix, in which Berlin further explains his approach.

Second, existing scholarship addressing free speech and its positive dimensions would repay examination to expand on what is said in this chapter.[7] Much of that work is focused on public speech in a mass media age, a focus that is also useful for my purposes. However, translating the analysis into the contemporary context remains a separate and important question. Clearly, public communication now differs from a generation ago, but public speech still has gatekeepers and questions of 'exposure diversity'—whether audiences are exposed to a diverse range of material—appear to be significant.[8] The short point to note here is that arguments remain plausible for 'structuring the social and technological conditions (such as search engine rankings, newsfeed algorithms, and content moderation systems) that lead people to the "ideas and experiences"' that are needed under democratic rationales for free speech.[9] Understanding free speech's positive dimensions is likely to assist in developing such arguments.

Third, suggesting that free speech is democratically important invites consideration of democracy. A common approach is to classify forms of democracy—republican, liberal, radical, and so forth—and suggest that each one makes different demands of free speech.[10] The approach is understandable when examining a particular democracy, but I think a democratic free speech analysis leads to a slightly different position. In each of the long-standing democracies with which I am concerned here,[11] the form that democracy takes can vary. This is true in terms of possible constitutional reform—a democracy could become more republican or less so—but it is also relevant to the interpretation of existing constitutional provisions. While recognizing problems in the realization of any given democracy, the point for my purposes is that the variety of ways in which

---

[7] See, eg, Jerome A Barron, 'Access to the Press: A New First Amendment Right' (1967) 80 *Harv L Rev* 1641; Thomas I Emerson, *The System of Freedom of Expression* (Random House 1970); Thomas I Emerson 'The Affirmative Side of the First Amendment' (1981) 15 *Ga L Rev* 795; Paul Chevigny, *More Speech: Dialogue Rights and Modern Liberty* (Temple UP 1988); Jack M Balkin, 'Some Realism about Pluralism: Legal Realist Approaches to the First Amendment' [1990] *Duke LJ* 375; Robert B Horwitz, 'The First Amendment Meets Some New Technologies: Broadcasting, Common Carriers, and Free Speech in the 1990s' (1991) 20 *Theory and Soc'y* 21; Owen Fiss, *The Irony of Free Speech* (Harvard UP 1996); Susan H Williams, *Truth, Autonomy, and Speech: Feminist Theory and the First Amendment* (NYU P 2004); Laura Stein, *Speech Rights in America: The First Amendment, Democracy, and the Media* (U Illinois P 2006); Stephen Breyer, *Active Liberty: Interpreting a Democratic Constitution* (OUP 2008); Marvin Ammori, 'First Amendment Architecture' [2012] *Wis L Rev* 1; Thomas Gibbons, 'Free Speech, Communication and the State' in Merris Amos, Jackie Harrison, and Lorna Woods (eds), *Freedom of Expression and the Media* (Martinus Nijhoff 2012) 19; Tarlach McGonagle, 'The State and Beyond: Activating (Non-)Media Voices' in Helena Sousa and others (eds), *Media Policy and Regulation: Activating Voices, Illuminating Silences* (U Minho 2013) 187; Victor Pickard, 'Towards a People's Internet: The Fight for Positive Freedoms in an Age of Corporate Libertarianism' in Maria Edström, Andrew T Kenyon, and Eva-Maria Svensson (eds), *Blurring the Lines: Market-Driven and Democracy-Driven Freedom of Expression* (Nordicom 2016); Mike Ananny, *Networked Press Freedom: Creating Infrastructures for a Public Right to Hear* (MIT P 2018).
[8] See, eg, Philip M Napoli, 'Exposure Diversity Reconsidered' (2011) 1 *J Inf Pol'y* 246; Natali Helberger, 'Exposure Diversity as a Policy Goal' (2012) 4 *J Media L* 65.
[9] Ananny (n 7) 38, referencing *Red Lion Broadcasting v FCC*, 395 US 367 (1969).
[10] See, eg, C Edwin Baker, *Media, Markets, and Democracy* (CUP 2002), ch 6, 'Different Democracies and Their Media', 129–53.
[11] In simple terms, North and Western European, North American, and similar contexts.

democracy can be pursued suggests something about democratic free speech. As Eric Heinze has argued in a different context, free speech has a 'distinct grounding in democratic public discourse'.[12] This grounding is separate from other common free speech rationales because of the way in which constitutions provide for their own reform. In effect, democratic constitutions 'present themselves as constituted through nothing *but* an ongoing process of public discourse... Within a democracy, public discourse is the constitution *of* the constitution'.[13] The result is that sustained plural public speech, of a form to allow republican, liberal, and other inflections of democracy to be imagined, argued for, or pursued, is required for a constitutional democracy to be substantially legitimate in terms of its communicative freedom. An explicitly elite democracy—one that does not imagine any meaningful role for wider public debate or participation—sits uneasily with this claim, but I am content to leave aside arguments that democracy should be elite-controlled. One result of the approach suggested here is that the challenge of legitimate democratic constitutional foundation is moved, in part at least, to public speech and the communicative freedom that underlies it.

Fourth, 'positive' and 'negative' are merely labels of convenience. There are many words that could be used for these dimensions of free speech. Other possibilities for the positive dimensions include active, affirmative, effective, and empowering.[14] Positive and negative are useful terms in part because of their use in studies of freedom outside law, even if what exactly is meant by positive differs across some analyses. While each dimension could at times be collapsed into its opposite, and whatever points might be made by challenging the positive–negative distinction itself, there appear to be 'two such families of conceptions of political freedom abroad'.[15] In relation to free speech, I would suggest they are not two *forms* of communicative freedom—positive and negative—but different *dimensions* of the freedom. The point of this chapter is to suggest that both dimensions are significant. Negative dimensions of free speech understandably gain much attention; they are clearly important. Positive dimensions of the freedom also warrant attention, certainly within democratic arguments for free speech which are so commonly made in law.[16]

While other labels could be used, it is worth highlighting two of the multiple ways in which 'positive' can be used in relation to free speech. Positive may concern *positive freedom*, the idea that freedom is not only a negative liberty but requires support or enablement. This links positive free speech with a particular quality of speech, not in the sense of high- or low-quality speech but in the sense of sustained plural public speech. The

---

[12] Eric Heinze, *Hate Speech and Democratic Citizenship* (OUP 2016) 9.

[13] Ibid 6 (emphasis in original).

[14] See, eg, Gibbons (n 7) 25, n 14 ('active'); Stein (n 7) ('defensive and empowering'). Some analyses resemble the positive–negative approach to free speech outlined in this chapter, without using the terminology: See, eg, Gautam Bhatia, *Offend, Shock, or Disturb: Free Speech under the Indian Constitution* (OUP 2016) ch 11, 'The Meaning of "Freedom"'.

[15] Charles Taylor, 'What's Wrong with Negative Liberty' in Alan Ryan (ed), *The Idea of Freedom: Essays in Honour of Isaiah Berlin* (OUP 1979) 175.

[16] Eg, Barendt (n 3) 20.

support for it could come in various ways from various actors, extending well beyond courts. Positive can also be used in terms of a *positive right*, typically a legal right enforced through courts. Constitutional rights are often understood in that way, and this chapter examines one court system acting to support positive free speech. But equivalent approaches to positive communicative freedom could be pursued by other actors: the quality of freedom is the primary concern not the actor. For readers who doubt that constitutional judges in a particular jurisdiction will act in support of positive free speech (or doubt that any action will be effective), considering how and why some courts act helps to understand what is involved in the first sense of positive free speech and to think about how it might be pursued, whether inside or outside courts.

After the above points of clarification, a brief outline of some of democratic free speech's positive dimensions can be offered.

13.2 Democratic Positive Free Speech

In a democratic context, one aim for public discourse is for *sustained plural public speech* involving diverse entities, missions, funding, and people, with substantial transparency for each of those elements.[17] This aim is supported by free speech. Valuing debate and diversity is commonplace in democratic rationales for free speech. For example, classic US Supreme Court statements underline the country's 'profound national commitment to the principle that debate on public issues should be uninhibited, robust, and wide-open'.[18] Further, as Sophie Boyron suggests of French free speech law, for a people 'to express its opinion in democratic elections ... it needs to be able to form an opinion first' which requires plural media containing diverse public speech.[19] I would reword her point a little as the need is continuous, not limited to the moment of an election. That is, for people to express opinions in, and *in-between*, democratic elections they need to form opinions, which requires sustained plural public speech. As this suggests, democratic free speech is, in important ways, a freedom of reception. It encompasses the democratic citizen as hearer.[20]

The aim is not just for endless diversity in speech, even if greater diversity has understandably been a focus in mass media analyses (especially when media access was severely limited). Rather, the aim is a structural diversity in support of broad and inclusive speech as well as sectoral speech. The aim is for media with a variety of operating models and funding bases, run by diverse staff, aimed at varied audiences (including wide audiences), and curating different, overlapping, and interacting public debate. It might well be understood as speech for a 'complex democracy', a point to

---

[17] Eg, Onora O'Neill, 'Practices of Toleration' in Judith Lichtenberg (ed), *Democracy and the Mass Media: A Collection of Essays* (CUP 1990) 155, 178.
[18] *New York Times v Sullivan*, 376 US 254, 270 (1964).
[19] Sophie Boyron, *The Constitution of France: A Contextual Analysis* (Hart 2013) 194.
[20] Morris Lipson, 'Autonomy and Democracy' (1995) 104 *Yale LJ* 2249, 2261.

which I return. The communication is 'sustained' across time, 'plural' in multiple senses, and it is 'public' in the way it forms smaller and larger publics, including publics of sectional debate as well as ones coming closer to society-wide debate.[21] In part, the approach resembles ideas about media pluralism. But, as the media models outlined below suggest, it goes further in terms of the range and styles of diversity, even than current European work on monitoring media pluralism.[22] And the approach differs from most analyses of media pluralism by placing questions of pluralism *within* free speech, not as a separate policy question that can be dealt with independently of communicative freedom.

Free speech supports the aim for sustained plural public speech through its two broad dimensions, negative and positive: the former can be identified as non-censorship, the latter as multiplicity of voice and viewpoint. These are two broad goals within common free speech rationales. As Judith Lichtenberg explains:

> The first we may call the *noninterference or no censorship principle:* One should not be prevented from thinking, speaking, reading, writing, or listening as one sees fit. The other I call *the multiplicity of voices principle:* The purposes of freedom of speech are realized when expression and diversity of expression flourish.[23]

Diverse, multiple voices are needed for free speech interests to be met. The requisite quality should not merely be assumed to exist in a market-based media system. While that point could be debated, here I merely note varied research supports the claim that 'the multiplicity of voices' does not arise spontaneously whenever restrictions on speech are limited.[24]

Models of media proposed by James Curran and Georgina Born can be used to illustrate the general ideas.[25] Curran's work, in particular, is notable for its use in legal scholarship.[26] His analysis suggests the need for a *diversity of media sectors*, with varied

---

[21] On speech forming publics see, eg, Andrew T Kenyon, 'What Conversation? Free Speech and Defamation Law' (2010) 73 Mod L Rev 697, 707–10; Michael Warner, *Publics and Counterpublics* (Zone 2002). See also Ananny (n 7) on the public-forming effects of digitally networked media.

[22] On the European Media Pluralism Monitor project see, eg, Peggy Valcke, Miklós Sükösd and Robert G Picard (eds), *Media Pluralism and Diversity: Concepts, Risks and Global Trends* (Palgrave Macmillan 2015); Elda Brogi and others, *Monitoring Media Pluralism in Europe: Application of the Media Pluralism Monitor 2016 in the European Union, Montenegro and Turkey* (European University Institute 2017).

[23] Judith Lichtenberg, 'Foundations and Limits of Freedom of the Press' in Judith Lichtenberg (ed), *Democracy and the Mass Media: A Collection of Essays* (CUP 1990) 102, 107.

[24] See, eg, Baker, *Media, Markets, and Democracy* (n 10); Toril Aalberg and James Curran (eds), *How Media Inform Democracy: A Comparative Approach* (Routledge 2012). See further Andrew T Kenyon, 'Assuming Free Speech' (2014) 77 Mod L Rev 379.

[25] See James Curran, *Media and Power* (Routledge 2002) 240–6; Georgina Born, 'Digitising Democracy' (2005) 76 (supp 1) Pol Q 102.

[26] See eg Baker, *Media, Markets, and Democracy* (n 10) 189–90; Rachel Craufurd Smith, *Broadcasting Law and Fundamental Rights* (Clarendon P 1997) 61; Thomas Gibbons, '"Fair Play to All Sides of the Truth": Controlling Media Distortions' (2009) 62 Curr Legal Probl 286, 314–15; Jacob Rowbottom, *Democracy Distorted: Wealth, Influence and Democratic Politics* (CUP 2010) 173–7.

staffing, missions, and funding across five media sectors: public, civic, professional, commercial, and social market. Born suggests the requirement for five forms of *diversity in terms of content and audiences*; namely, antagonistic opinions presented for wide debate, intercultural communication between groups and intracultural communication within groups, and communication for communities of interest that are territorially and non-territorially based. The aim is for media with different 'operating logics' providing varied, sectoral speech in addition to wider public communication.[27] The models offer a 'normative architecture' for communication under conditions of social diversity.[28] And they suggest what a media environment would contain under conditions of positive free speech in long-standing democracies. While US law has a 'profound national commitment' to 'uninhibited, robust, and wide-open' public debate, its structures of public speech appear to be lacking in these terms. There is not the variety of operating logics across media entities that could support a variety of approaches to accessing, producing, and publishing content and a variety of approaches to supporting public speech. The professed goal may be real, but US law tends to overlook the significance of positive dimensions of the freedom in supporting that goal.

As to positive free speech and law, an initial point is that the meaning of 'freedom' within free speech is determined less by constitutional provisions than by judicial interpretation.[29] Courts can and do recognize free speech's positive dimensions in some jurisdictions and some contexts. And they do so with constitutional texts that are open to varied readings. Texts that might be thought to describe free speech solely in negative terms can be found to contain positive as well as negative dimensions of the freedom. As noted above, a related matter is who acts in law about positive dimensions of free speech. For example, it might be regulators, executives, parliaments, or courts who do so. More plausibly, it might be a combination of such actors. But is the judicial role simply to review action taken by others? Courts may have a role to do more than that when other actors have not done enough in relation to free speech's positive dimensions. An example I come to soon suggests that courts could frame the possibilities and obligations for legislative, executive, and regulatory action, and that courts should do so because positive free speech is unlikely to be supported sufficiently if left only to other actors. Instead of being rare, the need for such judicial action may be central to the communicative requirements of democracy. Such an approach raises matters such as standing and access to courts, and the appointment, term, and background of constitutional judges, as highly significant for positive dimensions of free speech as a constitutional right.

There are many possible objections to the idea that courts should act in relation to positive dimensions of free speech. In some ways they mirror wider arguments on judicial review and democracy. Here, I largely leave the issues aside while noting that courts commonly rule on foundational aspects of democratic constitutions. Constitutions are not subject to unlimited rewriting or reinterpretation by executives or parliaments. Rather, courts rule on matters such as the division of powers between different arms of

---

[27] Kari Karppinen, *Rethinking Media Pluralism* (Fordham UP 2012) 79.   [28] Born (n 25) 116.
[29] See, eg, Barendt (n 3) 101.

government, electoral requirements, and the process of constitutional reform. If free speech has a similar constitutional quality, courts would have a similar role protecting its constitutional position. Suggesting courts may have a role does not ignore the institutional challenges and weaknesses they face: courts are commonly seen as not well suited to address polycentric problems and the wide range of factors that could be judged relevant to them. Other actors, however, also have real limitations in relation to communicative freedom and relying solely on them may be too problematic. Even so, there are important differences when courts act in relation to positive (as opposed to negative) free speech, related to the discretions which exist about positive dimensions of communicative freedom. I turn to that point after considering an example of judicial protection of positive free speech.

13.3 THE GERMAN FEDERAL CONSTITUTIONAL COURT

How might positive aspects of free speech be considered by a constitutional court? The German Federal Constitutional Court offers a long-standing example that is useful to consider here.[30] It is not the only example that could be used, but it is a well-developed one from a highly respected court.[31] I leave aside debates about the overall effectiveness of the court's approach to free speech.[32] My interest lies in aspects of the court's approach to the freedom and, just as importantly, the reasons the court offers for acting. They are reasons that appear to be significant in a host of long-standing constitutional democracies, but they are rarely addressed in many relevant jurisdictions.

---

[30] A classic English language analysis of the court is Donald P Kommers and Russell A Miller, *The Constitutional Jurisprudence of the Federal Republic of Germany* (3rd edn, Duke UP 2012).

[31] Other research notes jurisdictions such as Argentina, France, Italy, Japan, the Netherlands, Portugal, and Spain, where law's interpretation of the freedom 'compels the state to legally structure the broadcasting corporations in a particular way': Bernd Grzeszick, 'The "Serving" Freedom to Broadcast: Subjective versus Objective Dimensions of a Fundamental Right' in Hermann Pünder and Christian Waldhoff (eds), *Debates in German Public Law* (Hart 2014) 75, 90–3. There are also common law examples that take similar approaches, such as India: see, eg, Bhatia (n 14) 298, 300, noting Indian Supreme Court statements that the dangers of broadcast content being dominated means there must be 'a central agency representative of all sections of the society free from control both of the Government and the dominant influential sections of the society'.

[32] See, eg, Christopher Witteman, 'Constitutionalizing Communications: The German Constitutional Court's Jurisprudence of Communications Freedom' (2010) 33 *Hastings Int'l & Comp L Rev* 95; Thomas Gibbons and Peter Humphreys, *Audiovisual Regulation under Pressure: Comparative Cases from North America and Europe* (Routledge 2012); Christian Potschka, *Towards a Market in Broadcasting: Communications Policy in the UK and Germany* (Palgrave Macmillan 2012); Wolfgang Schulz, 'How to Control Informal Practices by Formal Law? The German Constitutional Court's Ruling on the Independence of the Public Service Broadcaster ZDF from the State' (2016) 7 *J Media L* 145; Greg Taylor, 'Diversity Within Government Broadcasters' in Georgios Gounalakis and Greg Taylor (eds), *Media Diversity Law: Australia and Germany Compared* (Peter Lang 2016) 221.

Across decisions spanning more than five decades, the Constitutional Court has set out detailed requirements for television broadcasting. The approach flows from the free speech provision in Article 5 of Germany's Basic Law and its protection for broadcasting freedom. The court through its interpretation of article 5 has been hugely influential domestically. It is not an exaggeration to describe the court as 'the most influential and determining factor in German media policymaking'.[33] German broadcasting 'has been ruled, at least partially, by [the court's] decisions'.[34]

One important reason for the court's significance is that it has interpreted article 5 as containing both positive and negative dimensions. For the court, democracy requires free public discourse to support individual and collective will formation which, in turn, requires a 'comprehensive freedom of communication' with 'active' as well as 'passive' dimensions.[35] These two dimensions are not explicit on the face of article 5, which is traditionally translated:

> Every person shall have the right freely to express and disseminate his opinions in speech, writing and pictures, and to inform himself without hindrance from generally accessible sources. Freedom of the press and freedom of reporting by means of broadcasts and films shall be guaranteed. There shall be no censorship.[36]

Even if the positive dimensions are not explicit, they are contained in the free speech and freedom of reporting of article 5. The constitutional purpose of free speech—and the broadcasting freedom that lies within article 5—is individual and collective opinion formation. That purpose requires the judicial evaluation of more than legal restrictions on speech. The freedom has an objective and social dimension. The freedom is more than negative.

The Constitutional Court has fashioned a broad freedom that protects a dual system of public and private broadcasting, with public broadcasting having the fundamental role. To meet the constitutional mandate for opinion formation, the service must be comprehensive in scope, available to the entire population, and contain substantial diversity of opinion.[37] Article 5 requires state action in pursuit of its goals: 'a positive order is necessary, which ensures…the variety of existing opinion is expressed…as widely and completely as possible'.[38] In this approach, broadcasting freedom is a state of affairs in which diversity in content is sought along with freedom from state and market control.

---

[33] Potschka (n 32) 7.

[34] Karen Arriaza Ibarra, 'Management and Organization of Public Service Media Companies: Basic Concepts Related to Efficiency and Failure in European Public Service Media, with Two Case Examples (Germany and Spain)' in Karen Arriaza Ibarra, Eva Nowak, and Raymond Kuhn (eds), *Public Service Media in Europe: A Comparative Approach* (Routledge 2015) 145, 155–6.

[35] Dieter Grimm, 'Freedom of Speech in a Globalized World' in Ivan Hare and James Weinstein (eds), *Extreme Speech and Democracy* (OUP 2009) 11.

[36] Basic Law for the Republic of Germany, 1949. Gender neutral translations also exist, see, eg Potschka (n 32) 161.

[37] *North Rhine-Westphalia Broadcasting Case* [1991] BVerfGE 83.

[38] *Third Broadcasting Case* [1981] BVerfGE 57.

The point I want to bring out here is *why* the court acts. It takes what I would call a precautionary approach in seeking to lessen commercial and political pressures on public broadcasting. There are two steps to the analysis. The first step is that free speech is of primary constitutional importance—it is 'absolutely basic' in the court's words. Even in Germany, where the Basic Law protects dignity as its fundamental value in article 1, speech has a foundational democratic role. As the court stated in its early *Lüth* decision:

> The basic right of freedom of opinion … is absolutely basic to a liberal-democratic constitutional order because it alone makes possible the constant intellectual exchange and contest among opinions that form the lifeblood of such an order; it is 'the matrix, the indispensable condition of nearly every other form of freedom'.[39]

The 'matrix' quotation comes from US Supreme Court Justice Benjamin Cardozo.[40] Its use alongside a French constitutional example underlines that the German court views free speech as having this importance in democratic constitutions generally.[41]

The second step underlying the court's precautionary approach is that speech is formative. Speech occurs within contexts of speech; speech is influenced by past speech. That means concentrations of power over public opinion are dangerous and difficult to address after they develop. Influences over public opinion cannot be avoided, that is not the aim, but they need to be diverse rather than concentrated. Domination by state or market is problematic. The court emphasizes that precautions are warranted: care must be taken to protect the comprehensive freedom of communication. This is because 'when emerging developments prove to be faulty, they can only be rescinded—if at all— to a certain degree and only with considerable difficulty'.[42] Speech requires protection prior to normal institutional political processes. It needs protection by the Constitutional Court, and this includes protection of the freedom's positive dimensions: 'precautions for the protection of journalistic diversity' are vital.[43] There is nothing about the idea that is necessarily limited to the German context; it is about individual and collective opinion formation within a democracy. Of course, the particular German constitutional context and path dependency is significant, but for present purposes that is bracketed as a separate matter. Rather, the example suggests it is possible for constitutional adjudication to recognize positive dimensions of free speech, despite the challenges to doing that seen in some other jurisdictions.[44] It is also worth noting that the need for diversity under article 5 is not ameliorated by the Internet. The Constitutional Court has continued its approach as recently as 2018, despite the dramatically different

---

[39] *Lüth* [1958] BVerfGE 7, 198. [40] *Palko v Connecticut*, 302 US 319, 327 (1937).
[41] The Federal Constitutional Court also quoted, at the same point, from article 11 of the French Declaration of the Rights of Man and of the Citizen 1789 (*Déclaration des Droits de l'Homme et du Citoyen*) which protects freedom of communication.
[42] *Third Broadcasting Case* (n 38). [43] *ZDF State Treaty Case* [2014] BVerfGE 136, [36].
[44] See, eg, Richard Moon for an assessment of this sort of limitation in Canadian law, emphasizing the tensions between a fuller understanding of free speech and the structure of Canadian constitutional adjudication: Richard Moon, *The Constitutional Protection of Freedom of Expression* (U Toronto P 2000).

context for public communication compared with its first broadcasting decision at the start of the 1960s.[45]

This precautionary aspect of the German approach means that neither executive nor legislature can be left to deal with broadcasting as a matter of policy entirely separate from the constitutional requirements of free speech. The free speech issues at stake mean the Constitutional Court sets out conditions the legislature must meet; conditions which, in turn, restrict the executive's room for action. The legislature cannot, for example, limit public broadcasting to its current technological basis.[46] That would breach the requirements of article 5. Neither can politicians choose to fund public broadcasting less than the amount required for a comprehensive service. The amount of funding is meant to be less a political decision than a constitutional imperative. Overall, the German court acts to protect structural aspects of the freedom. And, importantly, the court's position is that because structures affecting public communication also influence political processes, some of the architecture underlying public speech must be set *prior to* public debate and decisions by politicians.

Some readers, perhaps especially some from the common law tradition, might think this all sounds too foreign. While perhaps true in terms of whether similar legal change is likely in many jurisdictions soon, that remains a separate question to the logic suggested by this approach to free speech. And there are examples of common law analysis, even from US writers, which resemble it.[47]

For instance, Jack Balkin has written something similar in a 'realist' approach to communicative freedom in a mass media age. Free speech involves questions of substantive freedom, with the state 'always' being 'implicated in access to speech' because of the underlying influence of law.[48] He suggests that free speech where there is 'radically unequal economic power is not free speech at all'.[49] Balkin's aim for an 'effective' means of public communication leads him to suggest that some state funding of public media may be constitutionally required (not just permissible).[50] While he says such questions would generally be left to institutional politics—to legislation and other measures

---

[45] *Broadcasting Contribution Fee Case* [2018] 1 BvR 1675/16, 745/17, 836/17, 981/17. This decision held the residence-based (rather than equipment-based) levy used to fund public media in recent years to be substantially constitutional. While the focus was more on equality than broadcasting freedom, the court emphasized the importance of public service media in the contemporary communications environment and the continuing role of public media in protecting journalistic diversity: ibid [77]–[80] See, eg, Michael Wagner, 'German Constitutional Court Upholds PSM Funding Model While Highlighting PSM's Key Role in Digital Landscape' (2018) European Broadcasting Union Legal Case Note <https://www.ebu.ch/news/2018/07/german-constitutional-court-upholds-psm-funding-model-while-highlighting-psms-key-role-in-digital-landscape> accessed 20 April 2019.
[46] Eg, *North Rhine-Westphalia Broadcasting Case* (n 37), *Twelfth Broadcasting Judgment* [2007] BVerfGE 119.
[47] I discuss some further examples in Kenyon (n 24).
[48] Balkin (n 7) 411. I consider elsewhere Balkin's more recent writing, in which the issues addressed here are not discussed: see Kenyon (n 5).
[49] Balkin (n 7) 379.
[50] Ibid 412.

supporting positive free speech—he does see a role for courts. In fact, he suggests something with a family resemblance to the German approach. Balkin states:

> The point I am making is true of every affirmative liberty (such as education), and it is especially true of every negative liberty that turns out to be an affirmative liberty (like speech). Where affirmative liberties are at stake, *the most that courts can do is define a range of alternatives for the political branches to pick from, or direct the political branches to propose their own alternatives* and then accept them if they appear reasonably calculated to succeed.[51]

That is, in relation to free speech, the court would frame the obligation to act and the space in which to act.

The point captures something of Robert Alexy's distinction between legal *prohibitions* and legal *obligations*. Insofar as free speech is a liberty against the state—something that limits the state's ability to restrict speech—then *every* restriction on speech by the state must be evaluated. But free speech's positive dimensions take it beyond a bare liberty to include obligations for a certain 'state of affairs' to be pursued.[52] The obligations do not entail a precise set of actions but choosing some actions from many possibilities. Not every action that would support sustained plural public speech is necessary, nor is it possible to undertake every action concurrently. Positive dimensions of free speech involve discretion. However, as discussed at length in German law (and flagged independently by Balkin) the discretion is framed by law, and the obligation to act in pursuit of the freedom can be set out by courts.

All this suggests an approach in which a democratic commitment to free speech implies media of varied institutional form, internal organization, and economic base containing speech of diverse content and style, aimed at different ends, creating different and only partially overlapping publics, and supporting (among other things) individual and collective political decisions. That is, media something like a model drawn from the examples of Curran and Born noted briefly above. Public debate and parliamentary or executive action could reshape this 'architecture' to some degree, but the changes could not go beyond the constitutional requirements of free speech. Further, such a structure of public speech does not often arise unpromoted. Rather, it can be sought through deliberate state action, which can include court action. As US writer Susan Williams has noted:

> The great fear of government control over speech systems should not blind us to the fact that our present speech systems are also the product of government regulation… Surely we cannot believe ourselves better off, our autonomy better protected, by refusing to allow government to do—with conscious consideration and according to constitutional standards—what it has already done unconsciously.[53]

---

[51] Ibid 413 (emphasis added).
[52] Robert Alexy, *A Theory of Constitutional Rights* (Julian Rivers tr, OUP 2002) 330. Alexy uses the term 'state of affairs' when discussing the Basic Law's protection of broadcasting freedom.
[53] Williams (n 7) 221.

13.4 Post and State Control of Speech

The approach I have sketched above is one argument for legal protection of positive free speech to support sustained plural public speech. Given the summary quality of the sketch, it may be helpful to offer some comparisons with other free speech analyses. There are countless examples that could be considered. Here, I consider something of Robert Post's approach and then work by Edwin Baker.

Post sets out an explanation of existing First Amendment case law and demarcates an area of speech—public discourse—for special protection under US law. Public discourse is the 'communication constitutionally deemed necessary for formation of public opinion'.[54] The idea is used to explain US court decisions against government restrictions of speech. Restrictions are most suspect when they limit public discourse (rather than limiting other domains of speech). Government should not control public discourse's content; rather, people must be 'free to participate in the formation of public opinion' and, through that, free to influence government.[55] This process involves the formation of collective identity through public speech. But the fact that collective identity is invariably a matter of political debate in a plural society (like contemporary US society) means the boundaries of public discourse should be formed through public discourse; they should not be set by regulation. The requirement is that 'all possible objectives, all possible versions of national identity, be rendered problematic and open to inquiry' in public discourse.[56] At the least, the state cannot restrict public speech by, for example, requiring civility in public discourse.

The analysis is perceptive in relation to US constitutional law on negative free speech. But quite where it leaves state action aimed at supporting a 'multiplicity of voices' is less clear. I do not want to make too much of the point here: Post's interest lies in explaining US Supreme Court decisions, so it is unsurprising that he does not engage closely with matters that US case law rarely considers. Post also recognizes difficulties with assuming equality in public speech. As he notes, some people lack resources to 'participate in the formation of public opinion' and their views 'are systematically and persistently repudiated by the majority'.[57] The argument does not prohibit 'constructive interventions by an activist state', just interventions based on 'any particular conception of collective identity'.[58] Post suggests, for example, that:

---

[54] Robert C Post, *Democracy, Expertise and Academic Freedom: A First Amendment Jurisprudence for the Modern State* (Yale UP 2012) 15; see generally Robert C Post, *Constitutional Domains: Democracy, Community, Management* (Harvard UP 1995). Another writer that could clearly be considered within this general approach is James Weinstein: see, eg, James Weinstein, 'Participatory Democracy as the Central Value of American Free Speech Doctrine' (2011) 97 *Va L Rev* 491. Doing so may be useful because his analysis extends beyond the US First Amendment context addressed by Post.

[55] Robert C Post, 'Understanding the First Amendment' (2012) 87 *Wash L Rev* 549, 553.

[56] Robert C Post, 'Managing Deliberation: The Quandary of Democratic Dialogue' (1993) 103 *Ethics* 654, 662.

[57] Post, *Democracy, Expertise and Academic Freedom* (n 54) 18.

[58] Robert C Post, 'Subsidized Speech' (1996) 106 *Yale LJ* 151, 183 and n 169.

corporate domination of media outlets might perhaps be addressed by characterizing certain broadcast media as public functionaries and hence as subject to various forms of regulation that would otherwise be prohibited by the free speech tradition…Certainly it is compatible with the free speech tradition for the state to act positively to subsidize and thereby to supplement and improve public discourse.[59]

Equally, however, the argument does not *require* constructive interventions and it seems to fall back on ideas that an '*uncoerced domain* of public discourse'[60] exists or, at least, ascribes such a state of affairs. Descriptively, US law generally appears to assume that negative free speech is enough for its goal of uninhibited, robust, and wide-open debate. Normatively, however, I am not convinced. A common concern about the approach is captured by Jacob Rowbottom's succinct point that, while Post's analysis 'highlights the problem of granting…broad power to the state to fix the political agenda, a similar objection can be made if those with more economic resources determine the agenda'.[61]

Post has provided a detailed criticism of what might be understood as a positive analysis of free speech. In the article 'Equality and Autonomy in First Amendment Jurisprudence', he addresses the free speech writing of Owen Fiss, who was Post's mentor as a younger scholar and something of his 'ideal' law professor.[62] Fiss could generally be described as taking a positive approach to free speech, although it differs in several ways from the one set out in this chapter. The point I want to note here is that Post explicitly supports many of the criticisms of public speech, especially mass media speech,

---

[59] Robert C Post, 'Equality and Autonomy in First Amendment Jurisprudence' (1997) 95 *Mich L Rev* 1517, 1539, citing Robert C Post, 'Meiklejohn's Mistake: Individual Autonomy and the Reform of Public Discourse' (1993) 64 *U Colo L Rev* 1109, 1125–8; Post, 'Subsidized Speech' (n 58) 158–63, 176–94.
[60] Post 'Understanding the First Amendment' (n 55) 562 (emphasis added).
[61] Rowbottom (n 26) 51.
[62] Post, 'Equality and Autonomy in First Amendment Jurisprudence' (n 59). See also Post, 'Subsidized Speech' (n 58) 187–92 for a similar, briefer analysis of Fiss. Interestingly, Post (n 58) notes at 190:

> In fact, a constitutional standard mandating that decision rules for the allocation of [state] subsidies [for speech] be evaluated according to their effect on ensuring the quality of public discourse seems to me theoretically and constitutionally attractive. The only question that it raises…is how such an affirmative standard could institutionally be applied by courts. Decisions to disburse subsidies are always made in the context of scarcity, and they are highly polycentric…
>
> [The evaluation standard] would…have to be conceived as an aspirational goal toward which government officials should aim. From the perspective of a reviewing court, therefore, the standard would require judicial evaluation of whether the goal could have been better achieved through a different set of allocation rules. As this will always be the case, the adoption of Fiss's proposed standard would lead either to substantial judicial preemption of, or substantial judicial deference to, decision rules for allocating subsidies.

Again, there could be significant value in engaging with the German example (or with examples of other jurisdictions noted above, see n 31). Understanding free speech's positive dimensions as a matter of degree—as an aspirational goal in the quoted passage—is precisely the point and need not necessarily undermine a significant judicial role.

that underlie Fiss's argument.[63] In short, Post describes the United States as having a 'disgraceful structure of communication'.[64] And he does this despite his view that a state acting affirmatively in relation to speech risks undermining the individual autonomy required for democratic self-determination. Thus, he is not at all blind to the sorts of concerns that drive many analyses of positive free speech, but his response differs. One reason may be a different understanding of freedom, a different understanding of what is entailed in 'the state treat[ing] equally the self-determining agency of all persons'.[65] Post notes the issue, without exploring it at length, stating that:

> the argument that citizens should have sufficient access to public debate so as to ensure that public debate serves for them the function of reconciling individual and collective autonomy...is not only consistent with, it is actually entailed by, the free speech tradition. It is an argument that turns on the nature of liberty.[66]

Somewhat like Morris Lipson, who closely analysed Post's work in the mid-1990s,[67] I would suggest the question is less about the access of democratic citizens to public debate in terms of having *access to speak*. Rather, it encompasses their ability to access substantially diverse public debate, with access being understood in terms of *access to receive* such debate and subsequently deliberate (which then may also involve them speaking). In short, what public debate must be to serve self-determination is in part a question of freedom. Thus, one might agree with Post that citizenship 'presupposes the attribution of freedom',[68] but disagree as to what freedom entails.

A positive approach to free speech will include negative freedom, so it will agree with Post that the state should not *control* the content of public speech. German law does not understand its approach as meaning the state sets the political agenda in that way; rather, the law supports a structure in which broadcasting is said to be free of market and state control. The goal is to avoid domination by market and state. Of course, there are connections and influences between markets, governments, social groups, and public speech; they are inevitable.[69] Notably, the German approach arises from the same sorts of concerns for democratic legitimacy that Post addresses in relation to US law but, at base, it differs on what is required for freedom.

Like that example, the approach to positive free speech sketched in this chapter is concerned with individual and collective opinion formation; it is concerned with personal autonomy *and* collective self-government, to adapt terms more familiar within Post's analysis. But positive free speech understands such individual and collective self-determination within a democracy as *depending on* a multiplicity of voices that *in itself*

---

[63] Post, 'Equality and Autonomy in First Amendment Jurisprudence' (n 59) 1533.   [64] Ibid 1539.
[65] Ibid 1534.   [66] Ibid 1538 and n 41 (internal citation removed).   [67] Lipson (n 20).
[68] Post, 'Meiklejohn's Mistake' (n 59) 1131.
[69] On the importance of government and media connections, even under US First Amendment law, see, eg, Timothy E Cook, *Governing with the News: The News Media as a Political Institution* (2nd edn, U Chicago P 2005); Timothy E Cook (ed), *Freeing the Presses: The First Amendment in Action* (Louisiana State UP 2005).

requires state action, state action that in the German instance is prompted and limited by a constitutional court.

13.5 Baker, Democratic Media, and Courts

I noted above that sustained plural public speech might be understood as speech for a 'complex democracy', which is a phrase used by Baker in his analysis of media freedom. In many ways, his approach resembles the one set out in this chapter. His focus is democratic, the aim is for 'communicative power' to be widely distributed,[70] and he uses Curran's model of a mixed media system to illustrate what he has in mind. Baker states the 'ultimate beneficiary' of constitutional protection is 'the audience or the public'[71] and, in words resembling the point made by Boyron above, he argues that democracy requires people to have 'the capacity to form public opinion and then to have that public opinion influence and ultimately control public "will formation"—that is, government laws and policies'.[72]

There is, however, a difference of degree from this chapter. Baker argues that legislatures have responsibility for the structural underpinnings of public speech and that courts should largely be excluded. Judges should review the actions of legislatures sympathetically, and that is all. It is a perfectly understandable position in the context of First Amendment case law, at the time he wrote and probably even more so now. It may be the best approach pragmatically in the US context. However, it is interesting that Baker briefly notes other places, including Germany, where courts do act,[73] without examining the *reasons* given for such action and without considering what I have called the German court's precautionary approach. It is not that Baker suggests the dispersal of communicative power will be easily obtained, just that it should be pursued politically.[74] However, the dangers of leaving the issue to the political process alone is exactly why German constitutional law involves a more active approach by the Federal Constitutional Court. The court does not make all the choices, but it frames the obligations and areas of choice of other constitutional actors.

Baker does raise the general idea that democratic legitimacy might be *aided* by judicial review, not undermined by it. But he concludes that questions of media freedom are better left to 'legislative assessment' because of 'the legislature's greater sensitivity to

---

[70] C Edwin Baker, *Media Concentration and Democracy: Why Ownership Matters* (CUP 2007) 5–16.
[71] Ibid 127.   [72] Ibid 7.
[73] Ibid 125 and n 6, citing Barendt (n 3).
[74] A similar result can be seen where analyses doubt the suitability of judges—given their background and training—to decide such questions. See, eg, Joel Bakan, *Just Words: Constitutional Rights and Social Wrongs* (U Toronto P 1997) 103–12.

variable empirical factors'.⁷⁵ This means legislatures 'have the responsibility to make good faith judgments, embodied in law, about which aspects of the media require special, overt nurture'.⁷⁶ Given this is unlikely to occur, as he recognizes, it is unfortunate to leave aside reasons offered elsewhere for courts to act in support of diverse public speech. Baker suggests the media has 'unique influence' over public opinion about political matters, which can make 'political resistance' to what dominant media wants 'more difficult than resistance to the lobbying power of other economic monoliths'. And he recognizes that 'the economic interests of huge media conglomerates will largely control the policy debates and legal outcomes relating to media policy'.⁷⁷ Such problematic connections between media and politics underlie the German court's precautionary approach to media freedom. Baker comes to a similar position about desired media structures, but he does so without supporting action being taken by courts. For Baker, 'no democracy should risk the danger' of undemocratic dominance of public speech.⁷⁸ The precautionary approach would agree, but it differs on how that freedom can realistically be pursued.

Overall, Baker suggests that if US courts evaluated laws affecting media structure sympathetically, then legislation and regulation in support of media diversity would not be held invalid on First Amendment grounds. That may well be true but, if the First Amendment is said to support a communicatively legitimate democracy, then perhaps the First Amendment should be understood differently. If that is unlikely to occur, pragmatic arguments would lead to something like Baker's analysis of legislative and regulatory action. Positive dimensions of free speech can well be pursued by a host of actors;⁷⁹ avenues other than courts may in some contexts be the only plausible avenues to pursue. In some contexts, they may be best avenues to pursue. That, however, is separate from what ideas of democratic free speech would suggest.

13.6 CONCLUSION

Once free speech is understood to contain positive as well as negative dimensions, a host of issues arise about actors, choices, and actions in relation to the freedom. Here, I have considered some structural implications of positive free speech on what could be called the legal infrastructure of public speech. Obviously, public debate does not only need

---

⁷⁵ Baker, *Media Concentration and Democracy* (n 70) 148. Separate concerns may tell against judicial action in relation to positive free speech; namely, that substantial judicial roles can limit what North American writing often calls 'progressive' legal change.
⁷⁶ Ibid 138.   ⁷⁷ Baker, *Media Concentration and Democracy* (n 70) 49 (note omitted).
⁷⁸ Ibid 16 (emphasis in original).
⁷⁹ Eg, the US Freedom of Information Act 5 USC § 552 (1966) can be understood as 'a statutory grant of positive rights': Frederick Schauer, 'Positive Rights, Negative Rights, and the Right to Know' in David E Pozen and Michael Schudson (eds), *Troubling Transparency: The History and Future of Freedom of Information* (Columbia UP 2018) 34, 43.

free speech law. Public speech has a much richer social organization. Law is only part of 'the social infrastructure of public deliberation',[80] even if it is an important part.

In concluding, I want to note a cost of not considering positive dimensions of free speech. In *The Morality of Freedom*, Joseph Raz describes freedom as a collective good that requires 'positively encouraging the flourishing of a plurality of incompatible and competing pursuits, projects and relationships' to allow people to exercise autonomy.[81] While his approach lies outside many uses of negative and positive freedom, it can be analysed through that distinction.[82] The point I want to note comes from the end of his analysis and concerns the limitations of government. For Raz, the idea that state power is fallible and should not be trusted is 'both true and false'.[83] In short, limited government involves failure:

> [F]reedom from governmental action is based on the practical inability of governments to discharge their duty to serve the freedom of their subjects. And in most cases the result is that that freedom remains lacking. In most cases there is no other body nor any other social process which can achieve what government action fails to, that is the existence of a full capacity for autonomy to all members of a community.[84]

The claim that freedom mostly remains lacking under solely negative freedom—where there is not government action in support of its positive dimensions—appears to be equally significant for free speech. If public actors do not promote positive dimensions of communicative freedom, then those dimensions will often remain lacking. In some contexts, a negative 'freedom of imperfection'[85] may be the better option, but the failure it involves should be recognized. The corollary to this point is not that positive freedom should be understood as a freedom of perfection. Rather, positive free speech involves matters of degree and approximation, of optimization. Inevitably, the obligations for state action that arise from positive free speech involve many discretions—but not unbounded discretions—and there is never one perfect response. As Thomas Emerson suggests, only 'rough but practical' responses are possible for positive dimensions of free speech.[86] That should not be thought to make them any less important.

---

[80] Bernhard Peters, *Public Deliberation and Public Culture: The Writings of Bernhard Peters, 1993–2005* (Hartmut Wessler ed, Keith Tribe tr, Palgrave Macmillan 2008) 81.
[81] Joseph Raz, *The Morality of Freedom* (Clarendon P 1986) 425.
[82] See, eg, Katrin Flikschuh, *Freedom: Contemporary Liberal Perspectives* (Polity 2007) 141–66. See also Barendt (n 3) 34–5 for a brief consideration more directly concerned with free speech.
[83] Raz (n 81) 428.
[84] Ibid 428–9.   [85] Ibid 429.   [86] Emerson, *The System of Freedom* (n 7) 667.

CHAPTER 14

SPEAKING BACK

KATHARINE GELBER

One of the most enduring tropes within contemporary free speech scholarship, especially that informed by First Amendment jurisprudence, is the idea that the best remedy for speech with which one disagrees, or which one finds intolerable, is to engage in counter-speech, to speak back.[1] This principle has been central to First Amendment doctrine since Justice Louis Brandeis's now famous concurrence in *Whitney v California*,[2] in which he stated:

> deliberative forces should prevail over the arbitrary...freedom to speak as you think...[is a] means indispensable to the discovery and spread of political truth...public discussion is a political duty...If there be a time to expose through discussion the falsehood and fallacies, to avert the evil by the processes of education, the remedy to be applied is more speech, not enforced silence.

This view, that speech will expose lies and silence will not, and that engaging in more speech is educative and therefore the appropriate remedy to speech with which one disagrees, is attractive because it engages our senses of fair play and justice. It makes intuitive sense that engaging in more speech will do at least a better job of responding to disagreeable speech than silence or censorship could. Indeed, given some of the free speech challenges facing the globe today—including an allegedly 'post-truth'[3] political

---

[1] I use the terms 'counter speech' and 'speaking back' interchangeably in this chapter. I equate it with all communicatively expressive activities engaged in, in response to prior speech which one wishes to counter. It is not limited to the spoken and written word; for example, people with disabilities that render them incapable of, or of limited ability to engage in, speaking can be supported and assisted to engage in speech practices in other ways.
[2] *Whitney v California* 274 US 357 (1927) 377, cited in Cass R Sunstein, *Democracy and the Problem of Free Speech* (2nd edn, Free P 1995) 27.
[3] Defined as a political culture in which facts are ignored and treated as assertions, see Jane Suiter, 'Post-Truth Politics' (2016) 7 *Pol Insight* 25. See also Jason Hannon, 'Trolling Ourselves to Death? Social Media and Post-Truth Politics' (2018) 33 *Eur J Comm* 214.

era,[4] micro-agressions,[5] campus 'safe spaces',[6] de-platforming of controversial speakers,[7] public shaming,[8] emboldened hate speech by white supremacists,[9] athletes kneeling during the playing of their national anthem to protest police brutality,[10] and the vilification of migrants,[11] to name just a few—understanding the contours of counter-speech appears more important than it has ever been.

In this chapter, I will first investigate the idea of speaking back, showing its origins and connection with theories of freedom of speech. This will also show its ubiquity as an advocated remedy for 'bad' speech. I then interrogate some of the potential weaknesses of the concept. These include an implicit assumption that all who are exhorted to speak back have the same opportunity and capacity to do so, and that the idea of speaking back tends to be applied equally to all types of speech which can be found to be disagreeable. With a focus on the highly controversial example of 'hate speech', I show the contours of the debate around when it is, or may not be, appropriate to rely on speaking back as the preferred remedy to bad speech. This discussion shows that speaking back can, at times, be unrealistic and unfair. It can be unrealistic in so far as it rests on an assumption that speech takes place on a level playing field; that participants in public discourse may individually choose to engage in speaking back whenever they wish to do so. Yet this is evidently not the case. It can be unfair to the extent that it places the primary burden of bearing the costs of the difficult speech on its targets.

I move then to examine the effectiveness of speaking back as a remedy for bad speech. This is an interesting thing to do, since it is an endeavour rarely undertaken by those whose claimed preference is for more speech. The analysis shows that, paucity of evidence notwithstanding, there is evidence both that speaking back is difficult for the targets of some speech and that the effectiveness of speaking back is heavily dependent on

---

[4] For extensive discussion of 'fake news', see the symposium in (2017–18) 16 First Amendment Law Rev.

[5] Nick Haslam, 'The Trouble with "Microaggressions"' (*The Conversation*, 17 January 2017) <https://theconversation.com/the-trouble-with-microaggressions-71364> accessed 14 January 2019.

[6] Jeffrey Sachs, 'The "campus free speech crisis" is a myth: Here are the Facts' (*Washington Post*, 16 March 2018) <https://www.washingtonpost.com/news/monkey-cage/wp/2018/03/16/the-campus-free-speech-crisis-is-a-myth-here-are-the-facts/?noredirect=on&utm_term=.286f63eb9985> accessed 14 January 2019.

[7] See, eg, Camilla Turner, 'Universities which "no-platform" controversial speakers will face government intervention' (*Telegraph*, 3 May 2018) <https://www.telegraph.co.uk/education/2018/05/03/universities-no-platform-controversial-speakers-will-face-government/> accessed 14 January 2019.

[8] Jon Ronson, *So You've Been Publicly Shamed* (Riverhead Books 2015).

[9] Glenn Thrush and Maggie Haberman, 'Trump Gives White Supremacists an Unequivocal Boost' (*New York Times*, 15 August 2017) <https://www.nytimes.com/2017/08/15/us/politics/trump-charlottesville-white-nationalists.html> accessed 14 January 2019.

[10] John Branch, 'National Anthem Protests Sidelined by Ambiguity' (*New York Times*, 1 Jan 2018) <https://www.nytimes.com/2018/01/01/sports/nfl-national-anthem-protests.html> accessed 14 January 2019.

[11] Lizzie Dearden, 'UN Human Rights Chief Attacks Europe's "Chilling Indifference" to Refugees as 2017 Sees Record Deaths' (*Independent*, 8 March 2017) <https://www.independent.co.uk/news/world/europe/refugee-crisis-migrants-asylum-seekers-latest-un-zeid-hussein-human-rights-chilling-indifference-a7619301.html> accessed 14 January 2019.

the type of speech being addressed, and therefore the type of remedy for bad speech being sought.

In response to these weaknesses, I outline alternative conceptions of speaking back, including one that I have developed at length elsewhere.[12] These versions rest on a positive conception of freedom of speech that, I argue, overcomes some of the weaknesses of the narrower conception. Alternative conceptions of counter-speech suggest that effective speaking back requires that both it, and free speech, be thought of in positive, and not negative, terms. Speaking back is essential to participatory political discourse, and its realization requires more than the traditional negative conception of freedom of speech implies.

14.1 WHAT IS 'SPEAKING BACK'?

In their early, formative years children are exhorted to 'use your words' as a means of resolving disputes and differences with other children. They are taught to choose words over physical violence; indeed, this is one of the first lessons they are taught in the social environments of childcare, preschool, and school. Words are, of course, preferable to physical violence in modern democratic, liberal states as the chosen response to those with whom one disagrees. They assist in moving towards a resolution in which the strongest do not always or necessarily prevail. The adult version of the same idea is well-known—that the pen is mightier than the sword. It conveys the idea that expressing oneself is far preferable to resorting to violence to sort out differences. Counter-speech draws from this well-known idea, central to the operation of liberal democratic orders, that speech is the preferred means of settling disputes and disagreements.

Speech is, to this extent, an essentially social activity.[13] It is through speech that people are able to interact in complex ways with one another. Through that interaction, and related activities in tandem with others, people have constructed complex systems of governance, law and policy. They have created communities, societies, nations, culture, and international orders.

In matters to do with the body politic and democratic deliberation, the role of speech is crucial. This is because theories of democracy are entwined with notions of civic duty,

---

[12] Katharine Gelber, *Speaking Back: The Free Speech versus Hate Speech Debate* (John Benjamins 2002); Katharine Gelber, 'Reconceptualizing Counterspeech in Hate-Speech Policy (with a Focus on Australia)' in Michael Herz and Peter Molnar (eds), *The Content and Context of Hate Speech: Rethinking Regulation and Responses* (CUP 2012); Katharine Gelber, 'Speaking Back: The Likely Fate of Hate Speech Policy in the United States and Australia' in Ishani Maitra and Mary Kate McGowan (eds), *Speech and Harm: Controversies Over Free Speech* (OUP 2012).

[13] This was recognized by Hobbes, who stated that '*ratio*, now, is but *oratio*', cited in Hannah Dawson, 'Hobbes, Language and Philip Pettit' (2009) 22 Hobbes Stud 219, 225; see also Philip Pettit, *Made with Words: Hobbes on Language, Mind and Politics* (Princeton UP 2008). I am indebted to Susan Brison for this quotation.

and one of the duties of active citizens is to engage in public deliberation.[14] The quote from Justice Brandeis, reproduced in the introduction to this chapter, emphasizes the role of public deliberation in its depiction of a civic conception of free speech. In this account citizens have not only a right, but a duty, to engage in the speech essential to instantiating democratic governance, by holding government accountable, testing the truth of propositions put forward, and developing their own intellectual capacities and self-governance. These core arguments justify the protection of freedom of speech (the search for truth, self-realization, and the democratic argument, are discussed in Chapters 3, 4, and 5 of this volume). The related idea of a civic duty to speak remains at the core of free speech scholarship today. Cass Sunstein, for example, writes that, 'the free speech principle should be read in light of the commitment to democratic deliberation',[15] and Kevin Saunders that, '[a]ny advocate for democracy must also be an advocate for free expression; the latter is essential to the former'.[16]

Speaking back is an extension of the idea that engaging in speech is crucial in and for people's lives in these individual and collective ways. It is therefore a logical extension of the core arguments in defence of freedom of speech. It responds both to the social characteristics of speech and to the importance of its protection. In doing so, it suggests that the two objectives of protecting free speech and remedying bad speech need not, indeed ought not, be counterposed, but can be simultaneously advocated and achieved. This fulfils many mandates. It enables the social preference for speech over violence, and enhances speech's role in instantiating democracy. In being a non-restrictive response, it does not justify limiting free speech, which would violate the free speech principle, but instead seeks to enhance the quantum of speech that is occurring. Speaking back is a mechanism whereby alternative viewpoints can be aired, thus aiding in speech's deliberative and truth-seeking functions. Finally, speaking back assists in the self-development of the speaker who engages in speech as a result of speaking back. The idea of speaking back, then, permits the achievement of many components of free speech doctrine and its underpinning theories simultaneously. It is a powerful and evocative response to speech with which one disagrees.

This explains why it has been adopted and advocated so often in free speech debates on topics ranging from the risks of censorship, to the role of artwork, the right to protest, and more. For example, Article 19 argues that restrictions on free speech, the right to protest, and rights of association shrink opportunities for public debate, which in turn 'limits the freedom of all people to speak out to counter' hate speech.[17] Index on Censorship states that 'art really works for society, when it encourages debate, inspires

---

[14] Sunstein, *Democracy and the Problem of Free Speech* (n 2) 27–8.
[15] Cass R Sunstein, *Republic.com 2.0* (Princeton UP 2007) 177.
[16] Kevin W Saunders, *Free Expression and Democracy: A Comparative Analysis* (CUP 2017) 1.
[17] 'Tackling Hate: Action on UN Standards to Promotion Inclusion, Diversity and Pluralism' (*Article 19*, 14 March 2018) <https://www.article19.org/resources/tackling-hate-action-un-standards-promote-inclusion-diversity-pluralism/> accessed 24 May 2018.

counterspeech',[18] and that the risk of banning hate speech is that 'the ban becomes bigger than the counterspeech'.[19] The Dangerous Speech Project provides 'how-to' guides on its website for counteracting dangerous speech.[20] Public commentary on free speech controversies routinely suggests speaking back as an appropriate response to disputes. For example, in response to controversies around providing platforms to speakers on university campuses, former US President Barack Obama stated, 'the strongest weapon against hateful speech is not repression; it is more speech—the voices of tolerance that rally against bigotry'.[21] In response to white supremacy activities in the United States, and in a media conversation, Professor Richard Epstein opined that, '[c]ounterspeech is the appropriate "remedy" under these circumstances; suppressing speech is not'.[22] Facebook, in a suite of measures designed to counteract the risk of extremism, is partnering with non-government and community organizations to 'empower voices' by training them in how to counter hate speech.[23] In Germany, a closed Facebook group called #ichbinhier engages in speaking back by confronting trolls and seeking to restore civility to online communication.[24] European Digital Rights has cautioned that automated algorithms designed to remove unwanted content from the Internet 'may actually hinder counter-speech'.[25] An academic project called Free Speech Debate, based at Oxford University, takes the position that 'hate speech should best be fought with good speech'.[26] And as the American Civil Liberties Union (ACLU) puts it, 'if there's one cardinal rule in America, it's that we err on the side of counter-speech, not censorship, when we hear things we don't like',[27] and 'the best way to combat hateful speech is

---

[18] Julia Farrington, 'Police Involvement in the Cancellation This Week of a National Youth Theatre Production Highlights Again the Difficult Legal Challenges for Arts Organizations Putting on Contentious Work' (*Index on Censorship*, 7 August 2015) <https://www.indexoncensorship.org/the-arts-the-law-and-freedom-of-speech/> accessed 24 May 2018.

[19] Padraid Reidy, 'Kicking Anti-Semitism off Social Media Won't Solve the Problem' (*Index on Censorship*, 12 February 2015) <https://www.indexoncensorship.org/2015/02/padraig-reidy-running-the-risk-that-the-ban-becomes-bigger-than-the-counterspeech/> accessed 24 May 2018.

[20] 'Counterspeech' (Dangerous Speech Project) <https://dangerousspeech.org/counterspeech/> accessed 6 June 2018.

[21] Nadine Strossen, 'Don't Silence Graduation Speakers: Fight Hate Speech with More Speech' (*USA Today*, 1 May 2018) <https://www.usatoday.com/story/opinion/2018/05/01/censorship-hate-speech-freedom-first-amendment-column/564868002/> accessed 14 January 2019.

[22] Tunku Vardarajan, 'The Weekend Interview with Richard Epstein' *Wall Street Journal* (26 August 2017).

[23] Monica Bickert and Brian Fishman, 'Hard Questions: How We Counter Terrorism' (Facebook, 15 June 2017) <https://newsroom.fb.com/news/2017/06/how-we-counter-terrorism/> accessed 24 May 2018.

[24] Jefferson Chase, 'German Anti-Hate Speech Group Counters Facebook Trolls' (*Deutsche Welle*, 9 April 2017) <https://www.dw.com/en/german-anti-hate-speech-group-counters-facebook-trolls/a-38358671> accessed 14 January 2019.

[25] Amar Toor, 'Automated Systems Fight ISIS Propaganda, But At What Cost?' (*The Verge*, 6 September 2016) <https://www.theverge.com/2016/9/6/12811680/isis-propaganda-algorithm-facebook-twitter-google> accessed 24 May 2018.

[26] 'Rae Langton on Counter-speech' (Free Speech Debate, 15 June 2015) <http://freespeechdebate.com/media/rae-langton-on-counter-speech/> accessed 24 May 2018.

[27] Gabe Rottman, 'The Business of Financing Hate Groups: Legal to Censor, but Unwise' (ACLU, 12 August 2013) <www.aclu.org/blog/free-speech/business-financing-hate-groups-legal-censor-unwise> accessed 22 May 2018.

through counter-speech, vigorous and creative protest, and debate, not threats of violence or censorship'.[28]

The idea of speaking back is therefore widely shared, easily understood, and frequently advocated as the preferred response to difficult speech. It is, in its best form, speech enhancing. I move now to examine and critique some of the assumptions underpinning the conception of speaking back.

14.2 Speaking Back in Context

As a concept, speaking back buttresses the idea that speech ought to be free to the greatest extent possible, and advocates engagement in speech by those who may disagree with, or find abhorrent, another's speech. Perhaps the most central assumption underpinning the conception of speaking back as just outlined is that the arena within which people speak is contextually agnostic. By this I mean that it is thought of as not necessarily more, or less, onerous for any single individual to speak than for another individual to speak. Correlatively, it can be presumed that the speech that occurs in the sphere of discourse does not, to a degree meaningful or significant enough to warrant policy concern, limit or restrict others' ability to speak. The sphere in which public debate occurs is conceptually a level playing field. In this contextually agnostic arena, any individual confronted with speech they dislike, disagree with, or disapprove of, can respond in kind by answering back to, contradicting, or arguing against the earlier speaker.

This premise persists across different theoretical perspectives as to why freedom of speech is important. For example, Jonathan Rauch asserts in an argument in favour of liberal principles of liberty and scientific enquiry that those who feel criticized ought to remain cognizant of the fact that, '[c]riticism, however unpleasant, is not violence', and that '[w]e must all be sensitive...to our obligations to liberal science; specifically, the obligation to put up with criticism...When we do become offended, as we all will, we must settle for responding with criticism or contempt'.[29] David Richards argues on the basis of individual self-realization that, 'protest in one's own voice...is epistemologically important...for it is hearing one's own voice in such protest, on the basis of the principle of free speech, that enables one to hear one's self as a moral person, not as a stereotype'.[30] Joseph Magnet frames counter-speech in the context of the argument from democracy; 'democratic societies need more speech, not less, to nourish the self-government premise of our political systems...free discussion and airing of misunderstandings...are more likely to promote positive intergroup relations'.[31] In all these

---

[28] 'ACLU Statement on Ann Coulter Speech' (ACLU, 26 April 2017) <www.aclu.org/news/aclu-statement-ann-coulter-speech> accessed 18 May 2018.
[29] Jonathan Rauch, *Kindly Inquisitors: The New Attacks on Free Thought* (U Chicago P 1993) 159.
[30] David AJ Richards, *Free Speech and the Politics of Identity* (OUP1999) 135.
[31] Joseph Magnet, 'Hate Propaganda in Canada' in WJ Waluchow (ed), *Free Expression: Essays in Law and Philosophy* (Clarendon P 1994) 248.

conceptions, the exhortation to engage in speaking back is posited as the best response to disagreeable speech.

There are consequences to this view that are not always rendered visible. The first relates to the question of which types of speech ought to generate a speaking back response, and relatedly where the line can be drawn on speech that warrants a legal remedy. Advocates of counter-speech tend to proffer it as the preferred remedy, regardless of the nature of the speech being discussed. It is immaterial whether the speech requiring a response is simply false, as referred to by Justice Brandeis, or something else entirely. Possibilities of the types of speech which might warrant a response in the form of speaking back include (and are not limited to) misleading, detrimental,[32] offensive,[33] insulting,[34] hurtful, malicious, demeaning,[35] vituperative,[36] negative stereotyping or stigmatizing,[37] defamatory, obscene, harassing,[38] persecutory,[39] poisonous,[40] odious,[41] oppressive,[42] vilifying,[43] hateful,[44] assaultive,[45] toxic,[46] discriminatory,[47] destructive[48] or in other ways harmful[49] speech.

---

[32] Adam Welle, 'Campaign Counterspeech: A New Strategy to Control Sham Issue Advocacy in the Wake of *FEC v. Wisconsin Right to Life*' (2008) *Wis L Rev* 795, 797.

[33] Laura Beth Nielsen, 'Power in Public: Reactions, Responses, and Resistance to Offensive Public Speech' in Ishani Maitra and Mary Kate McGowan (eds), *Speech and Harm: Controversies Over Free Speech* (OUP 2012) 148.

[34] Adrienne Stone, 'Freedom of Speech and Insult in the High Court of Australia' (2006) 4 *Int'l J Const L* 677.

[35] James Weinstein, 'Hate Speech Bans, Democracy and Political Legitimacy' (2017) 32 *Const Comment* 527.

[36] Ibid.

[37] Alexander Brown, *Hate Speech Law: A Philosophical Examination* (Routledge 2015) 21–3.

[38] Alexander Tsesis, 'Campus Speech and Harassment' (2017) 101 *Minn L Rev* 1863.

[39] Mari J Matsuda, 'Public Response to Racist Speech: Considering the Victim's Story' in Mari J Matsuda and others (eds), *Words that Wound: Critical Race Theory, Assaultive Speech, and the First Amendment* (Westview P 1993).

[40] Miklos Haraszti, 'Foreword: Hate Speech and the Coming Death of the International Standard Before It Was Born' in Michael Herz and Peter Molnar (eds), *The Content and Context of Hate Speech: Rethinking Regulation and Responses* (CUP 2012).

[41] Engy Abdelkader, 'Savagery in the Subways: Anti-Muslim Ads, the First Amendment, and the Efficacy of Counterspeech' (2014) 21 *Asian Am LJ* 43, 46.

[42] Mary Kate McGowan, 'Oppressive Speech' (2009) 87 *Australian J Phil* 389.

[43] Katharine Gelber and Luke J McNamara, 'Freedom of Speech and Racial Vilification in Australia: "The Bolt Case" in Public Discourse' (2013) 48 *Australian J Pol Sci* 470.

[44] LW Sumner, *The Hateful and the Obscene: Studies in the Limits of Free Expression* (U Toronto P 2004).

[45] Charles R Lawrence III, 'If He Hollers Let Him Go: Regulating Racist Speech on Campus' in Mari J Matsuda and others (eds), *Words That Wound: Critical Race Theory, Assaultive Speech, and the First Amendment* (Westview P 1993).

[46] Lynne Tirrell, 'Toxic Speech: Toward an Epidemiology of Discursive Harm' (2017) 45 *Phil Topics* 139.

[47] Mary Kate McGowan, 'On "Whites Only" Signs and Racist Hate Speech: Verbal Acts of Racial Discrimination' in Ishani Maitra and Mary Kate McGowan (eds), *Speech and Harm: Controversies over Free Speech* (OUP 2012).

[48] Alexander Tsesis, *Destructive Messages: How Hate Speech Paves the Way* (NYU P 2002).

[49] Jeremy Waldron, *The Harm in Hate Speech* (Harvard UP 2012).

Although there is no room here to define all of these types of speech, they clearly cover a spectrum of conduct, ranging from moderate disagreement with a speaker, to personally having one's feelings hurt by another speaker, to being offended, and on to more tangible harms such as discrimination and exclusion. It is notable that some of the types of speech at the harmful end of the spectrum are, in fact, remedial under the law even in countries with strong free speech protections such as the United States. This includes defamatory speech and some obscene speech. In many countries around the world, although not in the United States, 'hate speech' that constitutes discriminatory speech, or speech that incites violence or discrimination against its targets, is also remedial in either or both the criminal and the civil law.[50]

So, to what type of speech ought the speaking back remedy be applied? It seems entirely logical and appropriate that speaking back ought to be applied as a remedy to the less disagreeable end of the scale of types of speech. This is because engaging in speaking back would likely have the best capacity to 'undo' any falsities on the part of a speaker, or offence or hurt feelings on the part of a listener. When listeners speak back, they are countering the messages contained in the original speaker's utterance, and by engaging in the practice of speaking they are empowering themselves, exercising freedom of thought and expression, and developing their own capacities for self-governance. Engaging in speech is likely to be by far the best remedy to disagreeable, but not harmful, types of speech, because it empowers citizens to engage in public debate. Additionally, freedom of speech is too important to be limited in law or policy in response to these kinds of non-harmful types of speech.

However, clearly there is a point on the scale at which the remedy tips to a legal one, both practically and normatively. In practice different countries define this tipping point in very different ways, but the fact that all democratic polities define this tipping point at some point or another suggests that speaking back is not the best, or most appropriate, remedy to *all* speech which one finds disagreeable or intolerable.

Where ought the tipping point to be from a normative point of view? For the sake of the argument here, I will focus on hate speech as an exemplar of a type of speech that is most controversial in the speaking back debate. This is because it is a type of speech that some people argue is appropriately remedied with counter-speech, yet others argue is best remedied in law and policy. Why is there such fundamental disagreement over the appropriate remedy for hate speech? It is a type of speech which some view as sufficiently harmful to warrant a legal response, yet others view either as insufficiently harmful, or as nevertheless requiring protection in accordance with a free speech principle even when the degree of harm it incurs can be accepted.

---

[50] For example, hate speech is remediable under civil and criminal law in Australia and Canada, and under criminal law in other countries such as Germany. See, eg, Katharine Gelber and Luke J McNamara, 'The Effects of Civil Hate Speech Laws: Lessons from Australia' (2015) 49 *L & Soc'y Rev* 631. See also Luke J McNamara, *Human Rights Controversies: The Impact of Legal Reform* (Routledge-Cavendish 2007) 159–250; Erik Bleich, *The Freedom to be Racist? How the United States and Europe Struggle to Preserve Freedom and Combat Racism* (OUP 2011).

In considering this case, it is important to outline what I mean by hate speech, since it is a term that is used in such a wide variety of contexts and with such a broad range of meanings.[51] Indeed, Alexander Brown shows the wide range of contexts within which it is used and suggests that we should view it as 'not admit[ting] of definition'.[52] Stanley Fish describes it as a concept in search of a definition.[53] Such difficulties notwithstanding, hate speech laws are justifiable only on the basis that the speech in question is sufficiently harmful to warrant its regulation by government. Governments routinely regulate all kinds of harms, including speech-based harms such as defamation and incitement to commit a crime.

There is a significant body of scholarly work in which it is argued that the problem with hate speech is not that it merely offends someone or hurts their feelings; rather, hate speech is capable of harming its targets. The particular harm occasioned by hate speech is its silencing and subordinating effect.[54] Hate speech discursively enacts discrimination against its targets in such a way that it is capable of silencing its targets and subordinating them. There is a variety of ways in which hate speech is argued to silence, including literally by rendering listeners incapable of speaking in direct response to speech targeted at them, due to fear or intimidation, indirectly by rendering their voices marginal to public discourse so that their voices are not considered a valid or important component of public debate, and constitutively by establishing and perpetuating a context within which their utterances simply do not count for the utterances that they intend them to be.[55] This means targets can say, 'no' or 'stop' or 'that's not fair', but these utterances do not have their desired effect of stopping unwanted conduct directed at them, because the speech acts of the targets fail to do the job the speaker intends them to do—to convince or persuade someone of their rights to respect, dignity, and equal treatment. The reason for this failure is not lack of fluency or language skills; the failure occurs due to structural inequality which is perpetuated, in part, by hate speech.

When understood in these ways, hate speech is a discursive act of discrimination; it is speech that harms its targets in much the same way as other discriminatory harms (such

---

[51] Sandra Coliver (ed), *Striking a Balance: Hate Speech, Freedom of Expression and Non-Discrimination* (Article 19, International Center Against Censorship 1992); Brown, *Hate Speech Law* (n 37) 19–48; Alexander Brown, 'The "Who" Question in the Hate Speech Debate: Part 1: Consistency, Practical and Formal Approaches' (2016) 29 *Canadian JL & Jurisprudence* 275; Alexander Brown, 'What is Hate Speech? Part 1: The Myth of Hate' (2017) 36 *L & Phil* 419.

[52] Brown, 'What Is Hate Speech? Part 1' (n 51) 5; Alexander Brown, 'What Is Hate Speech? Part 2: Family Resemblances' (2017) 36 *L & Phil* 561.

[53] Stanley Fish, 'Going in Circles With Hate Speech' (*New York Times*, 12 November 2012) <https://opinionator.blogs.nytimes.com/2012/11/12/going-in-circles-with-hate-speech/> accessed 15 January 2019.

[54] Rae Langton, 'Speech Acts and Unspeakable Acts' (1993) 22 *Phil & Pub Aff* 293.

[55] McGowan, 'Oppressive Speech' (n 42); Catharine MacKinnon, 'Foreword' in Ishani Maitra and Mary Kate McGowan (eds), *Speech and Harm: Controversies over Free Speech* (OUP 2012); Rae Langton, 'Beyond Belief: Pragmatics in Hate Speech and Pornography' in Ishani Maitra and Mary Kate McGowan (eds), *Speech and Harm: Controversies over Free Speech* (OUP 2012); McGowan, 'On "Whites Only" Signs and Racist Hate Speech' (n 47). Note also that a hate speech utterance need not incur each of these harms on every occasion for it still to be the case that hate speech is capable of harming in these ways.

as denying someone a job on the ground of their race, or denying someone housing on the ground on their sexuality). By extension, the harm occasioned to the targets also harms their allies, who may become fearful of being targeted for similar harms, and who may develop a fear of associating with people subjected to such harms. By further extension, the harm occasioned to targets and their allies also harms broader public discourse, because it removes some voices from general debate, and marginalizes and renders invalid some who do attempt to have their voices heard. This impoverishes public debate, and therefore processes of self-governance and democratic legitimation.

Understanding hate speech in this way suggests that a counter-speech response can be considered inadequate in several ways. First, if the nature of hate speech is such that it is capable of silencing its targets and their allies, then exhorting people to speak back fails to take the lack of opportunity to speak, and to speak with dignity, force, and validity, into account. The likely result will be that speaking back does not occur, or that if it does it will be ineffectual. This would mean that hate speakers are able to engage in their own speech unchallenged. Second, speaking back places the burden of responding to speech with which one disagrees on those listeners who feel this way—which can mean those who disagree with it,[56] but which in practice is most likely to mean those listeners who are targeted by the speech at issue. Where the speech is harmful, a speaking back remedy expects that the very same targets whose ability to speak back is restricted and constrained by the hate speech itself ought to be the ones responsible for engaging in a counter-speech response. Targets whose ability to speak back may be affected by the speech of others are being exhorted to engage in an activity, the pursuit of which has been rendered more difficult by the speech which ought to be responded to.[57]

In spite of these difficulties, the idea of speaking back has been encouraged by many in the literature and in public debate in response to a very wide variety of types of speech, including speech that is allegedly harmful to its targets' ability to speak back. This renders this conception unrealistic to the extent that it assumes a level playing field for engagement in speech. It also renders it unfair to the extent that it places the burden of bearing the costs of harmful speech by targets, who experience these harms from speech that others in the community do not, while simultaneously expecting those same targets to bear the burden of engaging in the requisite speaking back to challenge the claims made by others.

---

[56] There is arguably an obligation on the part of all who disagree with an utterance to engage in it. 'Interview with Nadine Strossen' in Michael Herz and Peter Molnar (eds), *The Content and Context of Hate Speech* (CUP 2012) 380, 385; 'Interview with Theodore Shaw', in Michael Herz and Peter Molnar (eds), *The Content and Context of Hate Speech* (CUP 2012) 406–7. However, in practice it is intuitively those who are targeted by hurtful or harmful speech who would sense and understand the need for a response.

[57] There are other conceptions of speaking back that respond to these challenges, which I will discuss in the next section below.

14.3 THE EFFECTIVENESS OF SPEAKING BACK

What of the effectiveness of speaking back as a remedy for bad speech? Given the ubiquity of the idea of counter-speech, it is perhaps surprising that there is remarkably little empirical analysis of its effectiveness. Nor is there a clear idea of how to measure the effectiveness of speaking back. Could effectiveness be measured by whether or not there has been an increase in the quantum of speech being engaged in on a particular topic? If so, how could this be measured? Could effectiveness be measured by whether or not the counter-speech effectively put forward persuasive arguments that countered the claims of the person or persons to whom they were responding? Again, it is unclear how the level of persuasion would be measured, or if it would need to be to establish effectiveness. Perhaps the simple act of portraying a contrary view publicly suffices for an effective attempt at speaking back. Or should effectiveness be measured by whether the harms of the speech—which could include silencing and marginalization—are remedied by the speaking back that occurs? In this last case, the fact that speaking back in response to harmful speech is unlikely to occur means this remedy is unlikely to be achieved.

The paucity of literature evaluating instances of speaking back reflects these difficulties of measuring its effectiveness. There are few studies that attempt to measure the effectiveness of speaking back, and those that do assert its effectiveness tend to do so based on a descriptive assessment of the simple fact that the counter-speech puts forward alternative viewpoints in public debate, and not other factors. They are therefore limited in their scope for assessing 'effectiveness'. Others do not attempt to assess effectiveness; they merely advocate speaking back as the appropriate alternative when regulation is found to be incoherent, inconsistent with free speech values, or constitutionally invalid.[58]

Studies that have attempted to examine effectiveness include one investigating anti-Muslim advertisements placed in public transport systems in several sites across the United States.[59] The author noted a context of social prejudice against Muslims, and investigated attempts by the transit authorities to decline advertisements, attempts which were mostly found to be unconstitutional, content-based restrictions on freedom of speech. She details non-legal responses that were pursued instead. Predominant among these was speaking back in the form of public statements by the transit authorities, counter-advertisements on public transport, twitter campaigns by Muslims, and

---

[58] See, eg, David Locke, 'Counterspeech as an Alternative to Prohibition: Proposed Federal Regulation of Tobacco Promotion in American Motorsport' (1995) 70 *Ind LJ* 217; Helen Konrad, 'Eliminating Distinctions Between Commercial and Political Speech: Replacing Regulation with Government Counterspeech' (1990) 47 *Wash & Lee L Rev* 1129; Welle (n 32). Added to this is a new argument emerging that the flood of public speech occurring in the social-media-driven world today, including bot-driven fake news, makes it much harder for speaking back to be effective, which there is no room to examine here. See Richard L Hasen, 'Cheap Speech and What It Has Done (to American Democracy)' (2017) 16 *First Amendment L Rev* 200, 222.

[59] Abdelkader (n 41).

statements of support for Muslims by other faith based non-government organizations. The article describes such counter-speech as the 'preferred self-help remedy of first instance' for those who disagreed with the advertisements.

Another article on the topic examines a selection of case studies, and argues that '[w]hen used wisely, counter-speech may prove to be a very effective solution for harmful or threatening expression'.[60] However, effectiveness is not really assessed; the preference for speaking back is simply conveyed. The article examines five instances of speaking back. In the first, some citizens' attempts to chop down an adopt-a-highway sign by the Ku Klux Klan is unfavourably compared with an alternative response by civil rights activists who erected their own sign in proximity to the offending one, and obtained media coverage which extended their counter-speech beyond those who saw the signs by the highway. The four others were: a public relations campaign by a food manufacturer subjected to a critical television broadcast; the proactive release of an unedited interview tape by a diet company that was accused of using components that risked public health; a tobacco case court settlement that provided money for a comprehensive, public anti-smoking campaign; and protesters appearing outside an art exhibition containing works offensive to Christians. While these are no doubt examples of speaking back occurring, the alleged harms of the speech in question differ widely—from racist speech, to providing medical information about consumables to the public, to publicizing the established health risks of smoking, and a religiously controversial art exhibition. The variety of types of speech discussed in this study makes comparisons of effectiveness difficult, unless one adopts the view from the outset that speaking back is the appropriate response to *all* instances of speech with which anyone disagrees.

Where scholars have focused on the specific case of hate speech, arguments both for and against speaking back as a remedy for hate speech persist, and scholars still express disagreement as to its effectiveness. Richard Delgado and David Yun, for example, have argued that the view that more speech is the best solution to hate speech is 'seriously flawed', because it is 'rarely a realistic possibility for the victim of hate speech'.[61] They argue it is propounded by those whose social world permits them to believe that asserting things makes them true, but that racist utterances occur in contexts in which its targets do not have that power, or in which speaking back is impossible because the racist speech occurs anonymously, scrawled on a wall or poster.[62] Urging targets to speak back can risk their personal safety, and unfairly burden them with the responsibility of educating others.[63]

Charles Calleros has disagreed with this assessment, arguing to the contrary that a more elaborate version of the speaking back argument need not display these

---

[60] Robert D Richards and Clay Calvert, 'Counterspeech 2000: A New Look at the Old Remedy for "Bad" Speech' (2000) *BYU L Rev* 553, 555.
[61] Richard Delgado and David H Yun, 'Pressure Valves and Bloodied Chickens: An Analysis of Paternalistic Objections to Hate-Speech Regulation' (1994) 82 *Cal L Rev* 871, 877, 883.
[62] Ibid 884.   [63] Ibid 885.

weaknesses.[64] Counter-speech need not be immediate and in the same circumstances as the hate speech, nor should targets be required to be the ones who speak back. Rather, effective speaking back could mobilize a broad range of people to engage in discussion and public debate to counter the original messages. In support of his argument, Calleros cites two examples of successful speaking back on university campuses,[65] in which targets of racist hate speech were supported, and a majority of participants condemned bigotry. Delgado and Yun replied to Calleros, agreeing that speaking back can work, but noting that it does burden the targets with educating others about racism, and that not all settings are as conducive to counter-speech as those Calleros cited.[66]

Rae Langton is another scholar who continues to view counter-speech as an 'inspiring but implausible' refrain. Good speech does not always win, she notes, and speakers cannot always speak.[67] Empirical studies of the experiences of targets of hate speech confirm these theoretical and hypothesized suspicions about the difficulties targets experience in speaking back, either individually or collectively. Laura Beth Nielsen, for example, reports that, 'for reasons that are entirely credible, targets of some sorts of problematic public speech do not in fact "talk back" because, for example, they fear violence or even government intervention on behalf of the harasser'.[68] A separate study of the experiences of 101 members of communities targeted by hate speech in Australia reported that all respondents experienced the harms that the hate speech literature alleges occur, including disempowerment from responding, withdrawal from expressive opportunities, silencing, exclusion, and loss of associative freedoms.[69]

14.4 Broader Conceptions of Speaking Back

In part in response to these kinds of criticisms, some scholars have argued for broader conceptions of speaking back that are able to address the limitations and weaknesses I have outlined. Some of these responses, like Calleros's above, call for the promotion of counter-speech as an alternative to regulation, and hint that it might be necessary to provide some support in order for effective speaking back to happen but without developing the idea further. Another example of this is Human Rights Watch, which

---

[64] Charles R Calleros, 'Paternalism, Counterspeech, and Campus Hate-Speech Codes: A Reply to Delgado and Yun' (1995) 27 *Ariz St LJ* 1249, 1257.
[65] Ibid 1259–62.
[66] Richard Delgado and David Yun, 'The Speech We Hate: First Amendment Totalism, the ACLU, and the Principle of Dialogic Politics' (1995) 27 *Ariz St LJ* 1281.
[67] Rae Langton, 'Blocking as Counter-Speech' in Daniel Fogal, Daniel Harris, and Matt Moss (eds), *New Work on Speech Acts* (OUP 2018).
[68] Nielsen (n 33) 149, 155–66.
[69] Katharine Gelber and Luke J McNamara, 'Evidencing the Harms of Hate Speech' (2016) 22 *Soc Identities* 324, 333–5.

in a discussion on Internet freedoms, argues that '[r]estrictions should apply to the fewest people and the fewest rights possible for the shortest period. And we have to consider whether some issues... are better addressed... by enabling and promoting counter-speech'.[70]

Philosophers have sought to deepen conceptions of counter-speech. Rae Langton advocates blocking as a type of counter-speech that challenges a speaker's presumed or implied authority.[71] Mary Kate McGowan has advocated counter-speech that addresses the norms inherent in the hate speech, rather than its content, as a way of addressing the norm-enactment embodied in the hate speech event.[72] Maxime Lepoutre recommends 'positive' counter-speech that 'affirms a... vision of the world that is inconsistent' with the hate speech, and does not directly engage with the hate speaker's claims.[73]

Others acknowledge that speaking back can work better when enabled by government. Owen Fiss, for example, critiques the view that the state is necessarily always an enemy of freedom and suggests that a democratic theory of speech ought to incorporate the premise that fostering full and open debate is a permissible role for government.[74] The state could play a role in furthering 'the robustness of political debate' in situations where otherwise some voices might not be able to be heard.[75] Corey Brettschneider argues in favour of 'democratic persuasion', by which he means that the state should be enjoined to use its considerable expressive power to criticize, condemn, and de-fund hate speakers and their organizations.[76] The state should choose whom to condemn in this way by assessing whether its acts of speaking back instantiate the goals of free and equal citizenship. In this way, the burden of responding does not fall on individual targets and their allies, and the response is authoritative.[77]

Similarly, I have elsewhere defended a broader conception of speaking back that also suggests that state support should be provided to targets and their communities to speak back to harmful speech.[78] My approach differs from others to the extent that, drawing

---

[70] Dinah PoKempner, 'The Internet Is Not the Enemy: As Rights Move Online, Human Rights Standards Move With Them' (*Human Rights Watch*, 2017) <https://www.hrw.org/world-report/2017/country-chapters/the-internet-is-not-the-enemy> accessed 24 May 2018.

[71] Langton (n 67).

[72] Mary Kate McGowan, 'Responding to Harmful Speech: The More Speech Response, Counter Speech, and the Complexity of Language Use' in Casey Rebecca Johnson (ed), *Voicing Dissent: The Ethics and Epistemology of Making Disagreement Public* (Routledge 2018).

[73] Maxime Lepoutre, 'Can More Speech Counter Ignorant Speech' (2020) 16 *J Ethics & Soc Phil* 155, 167.

[74] Owen Fiss, *The Irony of Free Speech* (Harvard UP 1996) 17.

[75] Ibid 4; Owen Fiss, *Liberalism Divided: Freedom of Speech and the Many Uses of State Power* (Westview P 1996).

[76] Corey Brettschneider, *When the State Speaks, What Should It Say? How Democracies Can Protect Expression and Promote Equality* (Princeton UP 2012).

[77] See, however, a critical analysis of state-based counter-speech in Maxime Lepoutre, 'Hate Speech in Public Discourse: A Pessimistic Defense of Counterspeech' (2017) 43 *Soc Theo & Pract* 851.

[78] Katharine Gelber and Susan Brison, 'Digital Dualism and the "Speech as Thought" Paradox' in Susan J Brison and Katharine Gelber (eds), *Free Speech in the Digital Age* (OUP 2019).

from the often implicit role of speech in Nussbaumian capabilities approach,[79] it considers the contribution that engaging in speech makes to fostering individuals' capabilities to choose how to live and function well. Its underlying premise is that free speech is a core component of the central political liberties needed for individuals to be able to participate meaningfully in the activities that will develop their central human functional capabilities, and thereby enable them to choose how to live and function well. It is the responsibility of policymakers in this framework to provide an entire set of conditions that will enable individuals to become capable of choosing how to live well, and who to be.[80]

Freedom of speech conceived in this way mandates that the state provide institutional, educational, and material support to targets of hate speech in order to enable targets to speak back. This would enable targets to contradict the messages contained within the hate speech, and provide the requisite resources for them to be able to speak back and thus counteract the silencing and marginalizing effects of the speech. The kinds of support that could be provided include resources to generate a community awareness campaign or advertisements; the production of newsletters, pamphlets, or posters; the development of anti-racism awareness campaigns in workplaces; subsidizing community art projects; or assistance to create a media item for broadcasting and dissemination within the community where the hate speech occurred.[81]

In this 'much enlarged'[82] conception of speaking back, freedom of speech becomes not merely an 'opportunity', but an 'exercise'.[83] Freedom of speech, and speaking back, become meaningful when individuals are truly able to exercise their capacity to speak. These alternative conceptions of free speech and counter-speech are positive.[84] In these positive conceptions, the problem of context that can render speaking back difficult, or at times even impossible, is recognized and dealt with. In these positive conceptions, the importance of free speech is conceptualized as a *practice* that as many citizens as possible ought to be empowered to participate in, in order to benefit from it individually and collectively. Thought of in this way, the weaknesses and difficulties associated with counter-speech outlined above can be overcome.

---

[79] Martha C Nussbaum, *Sex and Social Justice* (OUP 1999); Martha Nussbaum, 'Aristotelian Social Democracy', in R Douglass, Gerald M Mara, and Henry S Richardson (eds), *Liberalism and the Good* (Routledge 1990); Martha Nussbaum, 'Women's Capabilities and Social Justice' (2000) 1 *J Hum Dev* 219; Martha C Nussbaum, 'Capabilities as Fundamental Entitlements: Sen and Social Justice' (2003) 9 *Feminist Econ* 33.

[80] Martha C Nussbaum, *Frontiers of Justice: Disability, Nationality, Species Membership* (Belknap P 2006) 7, 70.

[81] Gelber, *Speaking Back* (n 12); Gelber, 'Reconceptualizing Counterspeech' (n 12) 214; Katharine Gelber, 'Freedom of Political Speech, Hate Speech and the Argument from Democracy: The Transformative Contribution of Capabilities Theory' (2010) 9 *Contemp Pol Theo* 304.

[82] Gelber, 'Reconceptualizing Counterspeech' (n 12) 214.

[83] Quentin Skinner, 'The Idea of Negative Liberty: Philosophical and Historical Perspectives' in Richard Rorty, JB Schneewind, and Quentin Skinner (eds), *Philosophy in History: Essays on the Historiography of Philosophy* (CUP 1984) 196.

[84] See Chapter 12 of this volume.

14.5 Conclusion

The idea of speaking back is powerful. Rightly, it has had a central place in free speech theory and doctrine for as long as ideas about freedom of speech have been articulated. The discussion in this chapter has sought to unpack elements of the conception as elucidated by different theorists, to highlight both its strengths and its weaknesses. The strengths of the concept lie in its consistency with the free speech principle, and its consistency with a range of theoretical justifications for the protection of freedom of speech including its role in self-realization, the search for truth, and democratic participation. It prioritizes the use of words to resolve disputes, which lies at the heart of civic duty, public engagement, and democratic deliberation.

The concept can also be applied, however, in ways that expose underlying assumptions that do not reflect the realities of speech practices. The idea of speaking back can be used in a way that suggests that public discourse occurs in a contextually agnostic arena. It can also be used to apply to all types of speech and in all situations, thus rendering invisible important differences between types of speech. The most pertinent of these is the question of whether the speech requiring a response merely hurts someone's feelings or disagrees with them, compared with speech that materially harms. Since it is recognized in law and policy that some speech can harm to a sufficient degree to warrant regulation, speaking back cannot *always* be the remedy of choice. Further, when speaking back is relied on as the remedy in all situations, the burden of responding to speech tends to fall disproportionately on the targets of harmful speech, even in cases where the speech in question may impair their ability to respond.

On the question of the effectiveness of counter-speech, the evidence is murky. It seems to be the case that those who prefer speaking back as the remedy of first instance tend to declare its effectiveness, and to measure effectiveness in the simple term of whether contrary viewpoints were aired. When this happens, the harms of some speech, which can include silencing and marginalization from debate, can be overlooked.

The chapter concluded by investigating proposals to broaden the concept of speaking back, by recognizing and, indeed, mandating a role for the state in enabling speech. This can occur either at the individual level of targets and their allies engaging in speaking back, or through the state deliberately using its power and resources to speak back on behalf of targeted communities. These broader conceptions appear to be capable of responding to the potential weaknesses of speaking back as earlier conceptualized.

Broader conceptions of counter-speech rest on positive conceptions of freedom of speech. It is to be noted that a positive view of freedom of speech is not dominant either in the scholarly literature or in free speech doctrine and jurisprudence. Rather, both the scholarly literature and free speech doctrine and jurisprudence are dominated by a negative conception that assumes free speech is a liberty that flourishes best when it is free from government interference. Indeed, a negative conception of free speech is regarded by some as the 'best'[85] way of understanding the freedom. This is in part due to the notion that governments are not to be trusted to differentiate between whose speech to support and whose not to support; a not-unfounded suspicion persists that government would err and inevitably protect the speech of the powerful against the relatively powerless. Government neutrality, while not perfect, is therefore preferable to the distortion that would occur if government were granted such regulatory power.[86]

By contrast, a positive view of freedom of speech rests on the idea that freedom of speech enjoins government to provide resources to support the exercise of freedom of speech. This would necessarily involve governments deciding whose speech to support. However, as long as such support were restricted to instances of demonstrably harmful speech, understood and defined in narrow and careful ways[87] related to the silencing, marginalization and discrimination which are of concern in the context of speaking back, then it ought to be possible to develop policy which would support speaking back in some specific circumstances without risking government tyranny.

Speaking back remains a powerful idea, but it ought not to be considered the only appropriate remedy, or to be necessarily applied to all types of speech. In some circumstances, especially those without sufficient support for targets, the idea of speaking back can be fanciful at best, and harmful at worst. This issue has never been more pressing. As free speech debates continue to gain currency in public discourse, the potential role of speaking back is more vital than ever. At times it can seem as though these debates are becoming more polarized, more hostile, and less open to the exchange of ideas. If, and to the extent that, this is the case then more, and more constructive, dialogue is needed, not less. This means that speaking back has a more vital role than ever to play in helping people navigate the vicissitudes of everyday politics, by encouraging as many people as possible to air their differences through constructive discourse and debate.

---

[85] Frederick Schauer, *Free Speech: A Philosophical Inquiry* (CUP 1982) 129, cited in Eric Barendt, *Freedom of Speech* (2nd edn, OUP 2007) 104.

[86] Schauer, *Free Speech* (n 85) 33–4, cited in Adrienne Stone, 'How to Think about the Problem of Hate Speech: Understanding a Comparative Debate' in Katharine Gelber and Adrienne Stone (eds), *Hate Speech and Freedom of Speech in Australia* (Federation P 2007) 71.

[87] Katharine Gelber, 'Differentiating Hate Speech: A Systemic Discrimination Approach' *Critical Rev Int'l Soc & Pol Phil*, <https://doi.org/10.1080/13698230.2019.1576006>.

PART III

CONTROVERSIES AND CONTEXTS

CHAPTER 15

DEFAMATION LAW, *SULLIVAN*, AND THE SHAPE OF FREE SPEECH

ANDREW T KENYON

15.1 INTRODUCTION

WHEN thinking about defamation law and free speech, it can be difficult *not* to consider the classic US case of *New York Times v Sullivan*.[1] The decision substantially changed how US defamation law treats political speech,[2] and has resonated widely in other jurisdictions. *Sullivan* began the constitutional reform of the US law, sending it into 'a different orbit'[3] from common law and civilian traditions. The case increased the burdens facing public officials who sue in defamation, making it far more difficult for them to succeed. The aim was to create greater 'breathing space'[4] for speech and, in very large measure, US law has done just that. The US approach has been extensively examined, but how and why the reforms were made and their relationship with communicative freedom still warrants attention.[5] There is 'importance, breadth, and...boldness' in the

---

[1] *New York Times v Sullivan*, 376 US 254 (1964).
[2] The decision was far from a forgone conclusion and the newspaper had to be talked out of settling before reaching the Supreme Court: Christopher W Schmidt, '*New York Times v Sullivan* and the Attack on the Civil Rights Movement' (2014) 66 Ala L Rev 293, 329; Anthony Lewis, *Make No Law: The Sullivan Case and the First Amendment* (Random House 1991) 107.
[3] David Partlett, '*New York Times v Sullivan*: The Great American Case' in David Rolph (ed), *Landmark Cases in Defamation Law* (Hart 2019) 125, 128.
[4] *Sullivan* (n 1) 272.
[5] I use terms such as free speech, freedom of expression, and communicative freedom interchangeably in this chapter. Communicative freedom is not used in the sense adopted by Jürgen Habermas: see, eg, Jürgen Habermas, *Between Facts and Norms: Contributions to a Discourse Theory of Law and Democracy* (William Rehg tr, Polity 1996) 119–20.

approach that repays further consideration.[6] Here, I draw out two broad issues from *Sullivan* and subsequent decisions, which I think have relevance for understanding defamation and free speech more generally, especially democratic aspects of freedom of expression.

Before considering those issues, it is worth noting at least three ways in which the reform of defamation law could better protect free speech. First, legal doctrine could be reformed. Higher burdens could be placed on plaintiffs, as in US law, or stronger defences could protect public interest speech, as has happened more recently in many other jurisdictions.[7] Second, remedies could be altered to reduce the chill of defamation law. This could involve limiting damages or developing alternative remedies. Damages have traditionally been presumed and 'at large' in common law defamation. This has made them difficult to predict and, sometimes, far larger than other actions such as those for personal injury. The unpredictability and size of defamation damages has done much to complicate the law,[8] and various reforms have attempted to reduce presumed damages in defamation to relatively little effect.[9] (The reform of damages was also expressly, but unsuccessfully, argued for in *Sullivan*.[10]) Alternative remedies have been sought in the literature for decades, generally without success. Proposals have included 'discursive remedies' or declarations of falsity that could be sought by aggrieved plaintiffs.[11] Such reforms are notable for the possibility they offer of better protecting reputational interests as well as free speech, and there is renewed interest in them with the development of Internet communications. Third, and perhaps less often recognized, the *effective* degree of freedom of speech provided under any given defamation law depends greatly on litigation practice. Reforming defamation litigation has been tried in many

---

[6] Paul Horwitz, 'Institutional Actors in *New York Times Co v Sullivan*' (2014) 48 *Ga L Rev* 809, 814.

[7] See, eg, Adrienne Stone and George Williams, 'Freedom of Speech and Defamation: Developments in the Common Law World' (2000) 26 *Monash U L Rev* 362; Kyu Ho Youm, 'The "Actual Malice" of *New York Times Co v Sullivan*: A Free Speech Touchstone in a Global Century' (2014) 19 *Comm L & Pol'y* 185; Charles J Glasser Jr (ed), *International Libel and Privacy Handbook* (LexisNexis 2016); Lyombe Eko, 'Globalization and the Diffusion of Media Policy in Africa: The Case of Defamation of Public Officials' (2017) 12 *Harv Afr Pol'y J* 17. Care should be taken with some comparative defamation analyses which can overestimate the degree to which *Sullivan*-style protections exist in other jurisdictions or suggest that wherever greater protection for public interest speech exists *Sullivan* has been 'adopted' in some manner or other. As discussed later in this chapter, the position is more complex.

[8] In simple terms, unpredictable and potentially large damages appear to lead to more technical legal appeals which, over time, add to the complexity of the 'monster' that is defamation law in many common law jurisdictions. The term monster comes from one of the English-speaking world's leading observers of comparative defamation law and practice: Matthew Collins, *Collins on Defamation* (OUP 2014) ix.

[9] Examples include caps on damages for non-economic loss, and damages being assessed by judge rather than jury; see, eg, Defamation Act 2005 (NSW) ss 22, 34, 35. Broadly parallel reforms can be seen in some other Commonwealth jurisdictions.

[10] See, eg, David A Anderson, 'Wechsler's Triumph' (2014) 66 *Ala L Rev* 229, 240.

[11] See, eg, John G Fleming, 'Retraction and Reply: Alternative Remedies for Defamation' (1978) 12 *U Brit Colum L Rev* 15; New South Wales Law Reform Commission, *Defamation* (NSW L Ref Com No 75, 1995); Dario Milo, *Defamation and Freedom of Speech* (OUP 2013) ch 8, 256–79; Alistair Mullis and Andrew Scott, 'Reframing Libel: Taking (All) Rights Seriously and Where It Leads' (2012) 63 *Northern Ireland Legal Q* 3.

jurisdictions—at times with relative success—and there have long been proposals for larger reforms such as developing alternative dispute resolution methods and venues for defamation claims.[12] It is also worth noting jurisdictions such as Sweden where protection of media speech (but not individual speech) resembles US protection in its strength, in large part due to procedural protections that limit the bringing of actions.[13]

It can be useful to think about these three interrelated factors—doctrine, remedies, and procedure—as three strands in defamation law's relationship to free speech. *Sullivan* is sometimes thought to involve the doctrinal strand alone, but it is relevant to all three. As well as its doctrinal changes, the decision illustrates the frequent lack of engagement with remedial reform in defamation law, and many of *Sullivan*'s most significant effects link with its procedural requirements. In this chapter, I examine aspects of *Sullivan* and later decisions focusing on the first and third of these three strands. As in *Sullivan* itself, doing this leaves aside important questions of remedies. I also leave aside questions about how the 'institutional' aspects of the US cases, and the later Commonwealth decisions which were also crafted with an eye to journalism, might be reconsidered in light of changed practices of public speech.[14]

For my purposes, two passages from Justice Brennan's opinion in *Sullivan* are particularly notable. They have become classic reference points:

> [W]e consider this case against the background of a profound national commitment to the principle that debate on public issues should be uninhibited, robust, and wide-open, and that it may well include vehement, caustic, and sometimes unpleasantly sharp attacks on government and public officials.[15]

---

[12] See, eg, New South Wales Law Reform Commission (n 11); Law Commission of Ontario, *Defamation in the Internet Age* (Law Com Ontario CP 2017) ch 8, 'Alternative Dispute Resolution in the Internet Era'.

[13] Protections include a constitutional chain of responsibility and the role of the Chancellor of Justice who is required, to the greatest extent possible, not to infringe unduly on free speech: Andrew T Kenyon, Eva-Maria Svensson, and Maria Edström, 'Building and Sustaining Freedom of Expression: Considering Sweden' (2017) 38 *Nordicom Rev* 31, 35–8. A substantial analysis of seven Western jurisdictions concluded Swedish defamation law as it affects media speech is closest to the US position: Thomas Bull, Appendix 8 to Part 2 of SOU 2006:96: Sverige. Tryck- och yttrandefrihetsberedningen, *Ett nytt grundlagsskydd för tryck- och yttrandefriheten?: Tryck- och yttrandefrihetsberedningen inbjuder till debatt: delbetänkande* [*A New Constitutional Protection for Freedom of the Press and Freedom of Expression: The Review Committee Invites Debate*] (Fritze 2006) 335–40.

[14] US and Commonwealth reforms were both shaped with a (sometimes implicit) focus on journalists and institutional media, even if not only media publications benefit from them. On the US example, see, eg Paul Horwitz, 'Institutional Actors in *New York Times Co v Sullivan*' (2014) 48 *Ga L Rev* 809. Public speech is now more open to 'unreasonable speakers' online; see, eg, Lyrissa Barnett Lidsky and RonNell Andersen Jones, 'Of Reasonable Readers and Unreasonable Speakers: Libel Law in a Networked World' (2016) 23 *Va J Soc Pol'y & L* 155.

[15] *Sullivan* (n 1) 270. It appears Brennan was not the original author of these words, but they have become synonymous with his articulation of the First Amendment. These 'most widely cited words' were written by Stephen Bartlett, who was then Brennan's clerk. Bartlett later became a law professor at Berkeley and had a notable role in convincing Brennan to take his first female law clerk: see Seth Stern and Stephen Wermiel, *Justice Brennan: Liberal Champion* (Houghton Mifflin Harcourt 2010) 224 (Barnett's authorship), 399–401 (female law clerk).

> A rule compelling the critic of official conduct to guarantee the truth of all...factual assertions—and to do so on pain of libel judgments virtually unlimited in amount—leads to...'self-censorship'...Under such a rule, would-be critics of official conduct may be deterred from voicing their criticism, even though it is believed to be true and even though it is in fact true, because of doubt whether it can be proved in court or fear of the expense of having to do so...The rule thus dampens the vigor and limits the variety of public debate.[16]

The first extract proclaims US law's commitment to *uninhibited, robust and wide-open public debate*; the second underlines the *chilling effect of traditional defamation law* and notes it dampens the vigour of public debate. These two points capture much of the transformation begun by *Sullivan*. Clearly, the decision was also influenced by the civil rights context in which it arose.[17] The extent of reform that it made—the way in which *Sullivan* did not rest on narrower appeal points but made such far-ranging changes[18]— may well be traced to that context. Much followed from the Supreme Court's apparent determination that Alabama courts should not be able to reconsider the case and determine the publication met whatever new test the Supreme Court established. Beyond that context, however, the reasoning in *Sullivan* took on a broader life through decades of later defamation decisions far removed from those battles over civil rights.

The result is that a public official or public figure who sues in US defamation law must establish with clear and convincing evidence that a defamatory fact about them was published by the defendant who knew it was false or recklessly disregarded the possibility. To recklessly disregard requires a 'high degree of awareness' of the material's 'probable falsity',[19] or 'sufficient evidence to permit the conclusion that the defendant in fact entertained serious doubts' about its truth.[20] This knowledge of falsity requirement is labelled 'actual malice' but it is quite different to malice in other parts of defamation law.[21] This point bears emphasis because references to actual malice outside the United States often mean malice in the common law sense, not the US constitutional form of malice. Since *Sullivan*, actual malice is a distinct requirement arising from the First Amendment. In effect, public officials and public figures must establish that publishers lied, and they must do so to a standard of proof much higher than the balance of probabilities. While oversimplifying things a little, that is a common way of encapsulating the US approach.[22] There is a legal limit on debate about public officials and public

---

[16] *Sullivan* (n 1) 279.
[17] See, eg, Kermit L Hall and Melvin I Urofsky, *New York Times v Sullivan: Civil Rights, Libel Law, and the Free Press* (U P Kansas 2011); Partlett (n 3).
[18] Eg, the Supreme Court could have simply held that Sullivan was not identified by the publication: see n 35.
[19] *Garrison v Louisiana*, 379 US 64, 74 (1964).
[20] *St Amant v Thompson*, 390 US 727, 731 (1968).
[21] See nn 137–8 and accompanying text.
[22] See, eg, Robert D Sack, 'New York Times Co v Sullivan: 50-Year Afterwords' (2014) 66 Ala L Rev 273, 284, citing the statement in *Garrison* (n 19) 75 that 'the use of the known lie as a tool is at once at odds with the premises of democratic government'.

figures: the limit is 'do not lie'. It is a very different limit than traditional defamation law which, as discussed below, often requires defendants to prove the truth of their defamatory speech.

The change in US law has been referenced in countless academic analyses, and *Sullivan* has influenced case law in other jurisdictions, more often by way of general inspiration or foil than direct adoption.[23] So much has been written about *Sullivan* that 'few aspects of the case ... have been insufficiently remarked',[24] but two broad issues warrant examination here. They have particular relevance for comparative understanding of the US law, and for questions of how free speech interacts with defamation law.

First, *Sullivan* needs to be understood comprehensively: it is not just the 1964 decision. Rather, *Sullivan* began a series of Supreme Court decisions which have developed a set of rules affecting defamation procedure as well as doctrine. The rules emerging through all these decisions, and the importance of procedural aspects within them, deserve greater recognition internationally. It is the combination of decisions and their procedural effects that so strongly protect defamatory speech under US law. Simply requiring defamation plaintiffs to prove falsity and fault would not have the same effect as the *Sullivan* rules.

Second, *Sullivan* highlights how the meaning of free speech differs under different defamation laws. One way of capturing this point is to note that many non-US courts have recognized traditional defamation law as having an unwarranted chilling effect on public speech—explicitly or implicitly drawing from *Sullivan* in doing so—but they have generally not embraced the importance of uninhibited, robust, and wide-open public debate. The chilling effect they recognize is not a chill on robust public debate; the freedom of speech envisaged by these decisions is different. This is significant for understanding the frequent references to *Sullivan* internationally alongside the case's often limited influence on formal law. Defamation law is conventionally described as seeking to reconcile the protection of reputation and freedom of speech, and it might be thought that what varies most in US and non-US defamation laws is how they understand and value reputation. The legal weight given to reputation undoubtedly varies across jurisdictions and explains some differences in defamation laws.[25] Equally, however, free speech is open to varying analyses which are also relevant to varied defamation laws. The strong protection of public speech under US law may well relate to the comparatively 'thin' legal approach to reputation; there is, for example, no US constitutional protection for reputation or dignity. But the protection created through the *Sullivan*

---

[23] See, eg, Youm (n 7) 206: 'The value of the *Sullivan* actual malice to freedom of speech and the press globally might be more inspirational than practical'. However, there has been some more substantial adoption of *Sullivan* in the Philippines and Argentina: see Youm (n 7) 192, and 193–5, respectively.

[24] David A Anderson, 'Wechsler's Triumph' (2014) 66 *Ala L Rev* 229, 230.

[25] Reputation in relation to defamation law has a reasonably extensive literature, including the classic US examination in Robert C Post, 'The Social Foundations of Defamation Law: Reputation and the Constitution' (1986) 74 *Cal L Rev* 691. See also Lawrence McNamara, *Reputation and Defamation* (OUP 2007); David Rolph, *Reputation, Celebrity and Defamation Law* (Ashgate 2008).

rules also reveals something about the shape of free speech—and the idea of public debate—recognized by the law.

15.2 THE *SULLIVAN* RULES, NOT THE *SULLIVAN* DECISION

US defamation law has been reshaped by a set of rules created through decades of First Amendment rulings by the Supreme Court.[26] The Amendment reads 'Congress shall make no law...abridging the freedom of speech, or of the press' and, for much of its history, the First Amendment was said to have no effect on traditional defamation law. Defences of truth, fair comment, and privilege were said to protect free speech sufficiently. No more was needed from the Constitution. Since *Sullivan*, however, the Amendment's words have created a dramatically different defamation law. The constitutional arguments were not entirely new in 1964. As Justice Brennan stated in *Sullivan*, somewhat similar developments existed in a minority of US states. They provided a privilege for good faith publication on some matters of public interest, and were based on broadly consistent free speech arguments even if they were not nearly as strong as *Sullivan*.[27] Arguments to reform defamation law and increase protection for public interest or political speech were also raised in commentary and made in Supreme Court argument during the two decades preceding *Sullivan*.[28] But *Sullivan* was the start of national legal reform.

Describing US law in terms of the *Sullivan* rules is useful for at least three reasons.[29] First, it underlines that multiple Supreme Court decisions are involved in understanding US defamation law. Non-US courts have tended to focus on the *Sullivan* decision alone, without addressing later decisions.[30] Second, the label of 'rules' also underlines that the cases do not establish a defence, rather they place extra burdens on public plaintiffs.[31] This differs from many developments outside the United States, where greater protection for free speech has often involved stronger defamation defences. Under the

---

[26] Beyond *Sullivan*, see, eg, *Curtis Publishing v Butts*, 388 US 130 (1967); *Gertz v Robert Welch*, 418 US 323 (1974); *Bose Corporation v Consumers Union of United States*, 466 US 485 (1984); *Anderson v Liberty Lobby*, 477 US 242 (1986); *Philadelphia Newspapers v Hepps*, 475 US 767 (1986); *Milkovich v Lorain Journal*, 497 US 1 (1990).

[27] *Sullivan*, 280. See also nn 136–8 and accompanying text.

[28] See *Schenectady Union Publishing v Sweeney*, 316 US 642 (1942); Norman Rosenberg, 'Taking a Look at "The Distorted Shape of an Ugly Tree": Efforts at Policy-Surgery on the Law of Libel During the Decade of the 1940s' (1988) 15 N Ky L Rev 11.

[29] I take the term *Sullivan* rules from Michael Chesterman, *Freedom of Speech in Australian Law: A Delicate Plant* (Ashgate 2000) 155.

[30] For example, Mark Tushnet, '*New York Times v Sullivan* Around the World' (2014) 66 Ala L Rev 337, 347.

[31] Plaintiffs have become claimants in the UK (and other terms are also used in some other jurisdictions). The single term, plaintiffs, is used here for convenience.

Sullivan rules, the burden is on those who sue, not on those who speak. And it is almost always a substantial burden. Third, using the term rules aims to encompass procedural rules as much as doctrine. The *Sullivan* rules illustrate how procedure can be as important to free speech as substantive law.

Differences between the *Sullivan* rules and traditional law can be stated briefly here. Under traditional defamation law, plaintiffs need prove relatively little because much is presumed in their favour. That approach applied in many US states prior to *Sullivan*, and much of it still applies in Commonwealth jurisdictions such as England and Wales, Australia, Canada, India, Kenya, Malaysia, New Zealand, and Singapore.[32] First, it must be proven the defendant published material. This merely means the material was received by someone other than the plaintiff,[33] as is invariably true for media publications and, indeed, all public speech. Second, the material must identify the plaintiff. This might be through expressly naming them, but the law asks merely whether someone who knows the plaintiff would think they have been identified, so quite oblique or inadvertent references can amount to identification.[34] Identification is rarely an issue under traditional law, but the plaintiff in *Sullivan* actually should have failed on this element.[35] Third, the plaintiff must prove the material conveys a defamatory meaning; that is, it could be expected to harm reputation and would make the material's ordinary recipients think less of the plaintiff.[36] This is not a difficult test to meet. Material that is critical will usually meet the legal test of what is defamatory.[37] And opinion, not only factual statements, can be defamatory under traditional law.

Plaintiffs need only establish publication, identification, and defamatory meaning. Traditionally, it is unnecessary to prove that publication was careless, false, or caused harm to the plaintiff. Thus, important reasons for traditional defamation law being said to chill speech are that it takes relatively little for something to be defamatory, harm is

---

[32] Of course, how those rules operate varies with domestic legal interpretations, as well as questions of media independence and diversity, and the strength and style of civil society and political opposition: see, eg, Andrew T Kenyon, 'Investigating Chilling Effects: News Media and Public Speech in Malaysia, Singapore and Australia' (2010) 4 *Int'l J Comm* 440.

[33] See, eg, *Byrne v Deane* [1937] 1 KB 818; *Dow Jones v Gutnick* (2002) 210 CLR 575.

[34] See, eg, *Cassidy v Daily Mirror* [1929] 2 KB 331.

[35] The advertisement at issue in *Sullivan* did not name him, but Sullivan successfully argued police misconduct described in it would be attributed to him because he was the public official in charge of police. The Supreme Court disagreed; Sullivan was not identified by the publication at all. The decision could simply have stated that and ended. Instead, the point is noted briefly after most of the decision's substance: *Sullivan* (n 1) 288–9.

[36] See, eg, *Parmiter v Coupland* (1840) 151 ER 340; *Scott v Sampson* (1882) 8 QBD 491; *Sim v Stretch* [1936] 2 All ER 1237.

[37] There are two common uses of the word 'defamatory' in cases and analysis. The first, more precise usage is followed here. It identifies a publication that would make ordinary recipients think less of the plaintiff; that publication conveys a *defamatory* meaning. The second uses defamatory as a shorthand for *actionable* publications; that is, where the plaintiff's case is established and no defence exists.

then presumed, and the potential damages have been unconstrained. The traditional approach does not understand speech as a 'preferred value' within law.[38]

Under the traditional approach, publishers are liable unless they establish a defence. Apart from defences such as privileges for fair reports of proceedings in parliament or court,[39] the main defences for media publications have required proving a publication is true,[40] or proving it is honest opinion or comment.[41] Significantly, opinion or comment must be based on facts that are proven true or privileged.[42] Thus, establishing the truth underlying the publication is a central requirement in practice. Defendants often face liability if they cannot prove publications true by evidence admissible in court. The development of wider defences in many jurisdictions has changed the situation somewhat, as discussed below. Now public interest material can be defended if publication was made 'reasonably' or 'responsibly' even if the allegations are not proven true. But the change is not nearly to the level of US law.

Beyond that summary comparison, five aspects of US defamation law underline how the *Sullivan* rules differ from what came before.[43] They concern public plaintiffs, private plaintiffs, the treatment of opinion, pre-trial dismissal of defamation claims, and the strict appellate review applied to public defamation claims. An initial caveat is warranted: US defamation law is a complex mix of constitutional and non-constitutional law, at state and federal levels (with no federal common law).[44] This means aspects of defamation doctrine that are not subject to the US Constitution can vary, sometimes markedly, state by state.

First, US defamation law *classifies plaintiffs more than it classifies speech*, placing burdens on public plaintiffs rather than providing defences for public interest speech.[45] *Sullivan* began the process with public officials, requiring them to prove actual malice to a clear and convincing standard. The aim was to enlarge the legal space for public debate about government. The US legal commitment is to 'uninhibited, robust, and wide-open' debate; the belief is that requiring publishers to prove the truth of all defamatory facts would chill valuable speech. The requirements were soon extended beyond public officials to public figures who 'often play an influential role in ordering society' with

---

[38] See Frederick Schauer, 'Fear, Risk and the First Amendment: Unravelling the "Chilling Effect"' (1978) 58 *BU L Rev* 685, 732.

[39] See, eg, Defamation Act 1996 (UK), s 15, sch 1; Defamation Act 2013 (UK), s 7.

[40] Under the defence of justification, see, eg, *Sutherland v Stopes* [1925] AC 47 and Defamation Act 1952 (UK), s 5.

[41] Under the defence of fair comment, see, eg, *Tse Wai Chun Paul v Albert Cheng* [2001] EMLR 31 and now Defamation Act 2013 (UK), s 3. As to the way that deductions or inferences (which may appear to be facts) are treated in the defence, see, eg, Jason Bosland, Andrew T Kenyon and Sophie Walker, 'Protecting Inferences of Fact in Defamation Law: Fair Comment and Honest Opinion' (2015) 74 *Cal LJ* 234.

[42] See, eg, *Merivale v Carson* (1887) 20 QBD 275.

[43] For a more detailed analysis, also drawing on interview-based material about US litigation practice, see 'US Defamation Law and Practice' in Andrew T Kenyon, *Comparative Defamation Law and Practice* (UCL Press/Routledge 2006) 239–80.

[44] *Erie Railroad v Tomkins*, 304 US 64 (1938).

[45] However, private plaintiffs whose suits do not involve speech of public concern are not subject to the *Sullivan* rules and can pursue their claims under state law.

'uninhibited debate about their involvement in public issues and events' being 'as crucial' as debate about public officials.[46] The possibility of reformulating the rules to cover, in express terms, speech of public concern rather than speech about public plaintiffs was raised but rejected by the Supreme Court.[47] In effect, US law assumes that speech of public concern will most often relate to public figures, and that it is easier for speakers to identify public figures in advance than deciding whether something speakers want to say is of public concern. In that way, the rule is believed to lessen a chilling effect that would exist in the public concern approach. Evaluating the assumption is difficult, but overall it appears less significant a difference than the very strong level of protection the *Sullivan* rules establish. Within each approach—classifying plaintiffs or classifying speech—there is broad agreement on the speech worth protecting. It is the extent of protection that varies so markedly between US and Commonwealth approaches. Even so, classifying plaintiffs has not removed all uncertainty. While elected officials, candidates, and senior appointed officials will come within the *Sullivan* rules, the treatment of lower-level public officials varies under state law; even more variation exists for public figures, including the complications of limited-purpose and involuntary public figures.[48]

Second, *many private plaintiffs also face higher hurdles* in US defamation suits than under traditional law. With the *Sullivan* rules, when private plaintiffs sue media over matters of public concern, they must prove falsity[49] and some degree of fault[50] in the publication. The degree of fault is a question of state law, but it must be at least negligence. Gross negligence or even actual malice can be required in some states.[51] In addition, unless actual malice is proven, damages can only compensate 'actual injury'. The damages requirement is less restrictive than non-US readers might think. Actual damages exclude presumed and punitive damages, but they are not limited to proven economic loss. Rather, they encompass damage to reputation and mental distress.

Courts almost always treat media content as being of public concern. *Sullivan* clearly has an institutional aspect—the rules were established with an eye to media as it operated then—and US courts routinely defer to media judgments about newsworthiness and public concern.[52] The result is three broad approaches exist in US defamation law: public plaintiffs must always establish actual malice; private plaintiffs suing the media will almost invariably need to establish falsity and fault in the published defamatory allegations; private plaintiffs suing over matters that are not of public concern are not subject to these requirements.[53] In the third instance, state law applies in its standard

---

[46] *Curtis Publishing v Butts*, 388 US 130, 164 (1967).
[47] *Rosenbloom v Metromedia*, 403 US 29 (1971); *Gertz* (n 26).
[48] See, eg, Nat Stern, 'Unresolved Antitheses of the Limited Public Figure Doctrine' (1996) 33 *Hous L Rev* 1027; W Wat Hopkins, 'The Involuntary Public Figure: Not So Dead after All' (2003) 21 *Cardozo Arts & Ent LJ* 1.
[49] *Philadelphia Newspapers v Hepps*, 475 US 767, 777 (1986).
[50] *Gertz* (n 26).
[51] For gross negligence in New York, see, eg, *Chapadeau v Utica Observer-Dispatch*, 38 NY 2d 196 (1975); for actual malice in Indiana, see, eg, *Journal-Gazette v Bandido's*, 712 NE 2d 446 (1999).
[52] See, eg, Paul Horwitz, *First Amendment Institutions* (Harvard UP 2013) 213.
[53] *Dun & Bradstreet v Greenmoss Builders*, 472 US 749 (1985).

form (which may closely resemble traditional English defamation law). The differentiated quality of the US approach resembles various scholarly calls for greater differentiation in non-US defamation law to increase protection for publicly valuable speech.[54]

Third, *opinion is treated very differently* from traditional law because of the obligation to prove falsity under the *Sullivan* rules. In *Gertz v Robert Welch*, the Supreme Court set out what was treated as an absolute constitutional protection for opinion. Powell J stated:

> We begin with the common ground. Under the First Amendment there is no such thing as a false idea. However pernicious an opinion may seem, we depend for its correction not on the conscience of judges and juries, but on the competition of other ideas.[55]

The requirement was later reformulated so that defamation must involve statements of fact capable of being proven false,[56] but the protection's substance did not change. One result is that exaggerated speech, hyperbole and parodies are not usually held to convey any facts under US law, providing far greater protection than traditional law. For example, writing of a lawyer that 'history reveals that he will say or do just about anything to win, typically at the expense of the truth' was treated as opinion. As 'rhetorical hyperbole', it could not found a defamation action.[57] While such a publication *may* be defensible as fair comment under traditional law, that defence has long been subject to criticism for its complexity and unpredictability.[58] In practice, the same statement may well be undefended under traditional law, rather than being treated as not even actionable.

Fourth, *common steps in US defamation litigation operate quite differently* than in Commonwealth jurisdictions. One difference is the far more frequent pre-trial dismissal of US defamation cases,[59] due in large part to free speech concerns. Two avenues are particularly important in defamation: motions to dismiss and motions for summary judgment.[60] Motions to dismiss occur before discovery, which under US law includes the potentially extensive deposition process. The motions argue the plaintiff has failed to state a sufficient

---

[54] See, eg, Bob Tarantino, 'Chasing Reputation: The Argument for Differential Treatment of "Public Figures" in Canadian Defamation Law' (2010) 48 *Osgoode Hall LJ* 595; Randall Stephenson, *A Crisis of Democratic Accountability: Public Libel Law and the Checking Function of the Press* (Hart 2018).

[55] *Gertz* (n 26) 339–40.

[56] *Milkovich* (n 26).

[57] *Cochran v NYP Holdings*, 58 F Supp 2d 1113, 1115, 1124 (1998); affirmed on appeal, 210 F 3d 1036 (9th Cir, 2000).

[58] See, eg, Bosland and others (n 41).

[59] In much Commonwealth litigation, pre-trial hearings are very influential in shaping the dispute's boundary, especially regarding the meanings that a publication is capable of conveying which is often central what defences can plausibly be argued. The hearings can encourage settlement but are a far more complex and less effective measure in ending litigation than US defamation law in general. See, eg, Kenyon (n 43) 382.

[60] A third motion has great significance in some states: motions to strike defamation claims under legislation against 'SLAPP' suits (strategic lawsuits against public participation): see, eg, George W Pring and Penelope Canan, *SLAPPs: Getting Sued for Speaking Out* (Temple UP 1996).

legal claim, perhaps because the publication does not identify the plaintiff or does not convey any facts. These motions have long been common in US defamation litigation and have become easier to obtain in federal courts after the Supreme Court reinforced pleading requirements. Pleadings must contain 'enough facts' to make the claim 'plausible on its face'.[61] As Robert Sack has observed, it 'may be painfully difficult to plead "plausibly" facts that would establish a defendant's actual malice at least without first taking the deposition of the defendant'.[62] But the Supreme Court has held the action may be dismissed before depositions, indeed dismissal is the correct course if the pleadings fail that test.

Summary judgment is the second important motion. It is difficult to obtain where facts are in dispute, but only if the disputed facts would affect the claim overall. Thus, defendants can obtain summary judgment if public plaintiffs are unable to prove actual malice because of certain undisputed facts, even if other facts remain in dispute. In US defamation litigation, summary judgment is very prevalent, in large part due to the Supreme Court decision in *Anderson v Liberty Lobby*.[63] Under federal procedure, public plaintiffs must now establish actual malice with convincing clarity to avoid summary judgment. Convincing clarity is not just a matter for trial; it applies at the summary judgment stage in federal courts. *Anderson* is a crucial decision for comparative analysis, underlining the procedural protections that flow from US concern for speech.[64] Defamation defendants 'have been particularly successful' before trial judges since the decision,[65] and the case has markedly reduced US defamation law's chill in the last three decades.

Fifth, *judges play a greater role than might be expected* in US defamation litigation, given constitutional rights to jury trial.[66] In part, this follows from the points just noted—motions to dismiss, summary judgment, and *Anderson v Liberty Lobby*. But it also follows from *Sullivan* itself. One 'core' of *Sullivan* is the requirement for clear and convincing evidence. This underpins its demanding standard of appellate review.[67] The Supreme Court requires appellate courts to review the facts in public defamation cases to ensure constitutional standards are met. '[I]ndependent examination of the whole record' is required to ensure 'the judgment does not constitute a forbidden intrusion on the field of free expression'.[68] This 'distinctly intrusive form of judicial

---

[61] *Bell Atlantic v Twombly*, 550 US 544, 570 (2007).
[62] Sack (n 22) 289. He also cites *Ashcroft v Iqbal*, 556 US 662 (2009).
[63] *Anderson v Liberty Lobby*, 477 US 242 (1986).
[64] For a background on the case, see, eg, Lee Levine and Stephen Wermiel, *The Progeny: Justice William J Brennan's Fight to Preserve the Legacy of New York Times v Sullivan* (ABA Publishing 2014) 237–45. For other US analyses examining the importance of defamation procedure in protecting free speech in general, see, eg, Scott M Matheson Jr, 'Procedure in Public Person Defamation Cases: The Impact of the First Amendment' (1987) 66 *Texas L Rev* 215; Susan M Gilles, 'Taking First Amendment Procedure Seriously: An Analysis of Process in Libel Litigation' (1998) 58 *Ohio State LJ* 1753; for commentary on summary judgment in particular, see Schauer (n 38) 710–12.
[65] Levine and Wermiel, *The Progeny* (n 64) 245.
[66] See, eg, US Const amend VII: 'In suits at common law, where the value in controversy shall exceed twenty dollars, the right of trial by jury shall be preserved, and no fact tried by a jury, shall be otherwise re-examined in any court of the United States, than according to the rules of the common law'.
[67] See, eg, Sack (n 22) 286–8.
[68] *Sullivan* (n 1), 286.

supervision'[69] is central to making the *Sullivan* rules so powerful. Requiring proof of falsity and fault may not have had substantial effects on the US law without also requiring strict appellate supervision:

> What assured a decisive break with the English tradition was the court's demonstrated willingness to supervise the administration of state libel law, to make sure that the preference for 'wide-open, robust debate' was observed in practice as well as in theory.[70]

This point is important for comparative analysis. The *Sullivan* rules are not just a requirement to prove falsity, and they are not just a requirement to prove fault. They are not even just a requirement to prove falsity *and* fault. Instead, they require clear and convincing evidence of falsity and fault—with the fault standard being extremely demanding for public plaintiffs, and a meaningful hurdle for private plaintiffs who sue over matters of public concern—*and* the result is subject to the most exacting judicial review. The *Sullivan* rules illustrate how free speech protection can depend substantially on matters of legal procedure and practice. It is a point that deserves greater recognition in the law elsewhere.

There is a further point to note about the *Sullivan* rules and the chain of decisions that established them: *Sullivan* was *not* unquestioned in the Supreme Court until more than two decades after its delivery. The reform took time to become secure, something which is not unknown in later Commonwealth developments.[71] During the 1980s, voices on the Supreme Court still doubted *Sullivan*'s actual malice rule,[72] but the issue was settled in the rule's favour,[73] and the decision has gained an 'unchallenged authority'.[74] Perhaps one should now state that *Sullivan*'s authority is unchallenged *as yet*, given subsequent changes in US law, the Supreme Court, and public communication.

15.3 THE SHAPE OF FREE SPEECH

The second general issue to consider from *Sullivan* is the way it suggests that free speech's meaning differs under different defamation laws. There are many reasons why the approach to free speech is different under US defamation law. Mark Tushnet has

---

[69] Chesterman (n 29) 165.

[70] David A Anderson, 'An American Perspective' in Simon Deakin, Angus Johnston, and Basil Markesinis, *Markesinis and Deakin's Tort Law* (5th edn, Clarendon P 2003) 721, 725.

[71] See, eg, in Australia *Theophanous v Herald & Weekly Times* (1994) 182 CLR 104 (with strong dissents on final appeal); *Lange v Australian Broadcasting Corporation* (1997) 189 CLR 520 (unanimous judgment on final appeal).

[72] See, eg, *Dun & Bradstreet* (n 53) 764 (Burger CJ) and 765–74 (White J) (1985); Lee Levine and Stephen Wermiel, 'The Landmark That Wasn't: A First Amendment Play in Five Acts' (2013) 88 *Wash L Rev* 1.

[73] See *Hustler Magazine v Falwell*, 485 US 46 (1988).

[74] A Epstein, *Torts* (Aspen 1999) 515.

succinctly outlined some, including the general US preference for 'rules' rather than 'standards' to protect constitutional rights; US cultural and institutional differences, including the Supreme Court's inability to rule on common law; and the lack of any explicit US constitutional protection for reputation or dignity, unlike many other constitutions.[75] All this is true. But here I suggest an additional reason for the difference, which is evident in the reception in many Commonwealth countries of the two quotations from *Sullivan* noted at the outset: what is meant by free speech differs under US and much other defamation law. The difference is perhaps an example of wider aspects of free speech in which US law appears as an outlier,[76] with its very strong protection of negative dimensions of the freedom and weak (but not non-existent) support for some positive dimensions.[77]

With the decision in *Sullivan*, US defamation law began to depart substantially from traditional common law. There was no immediate response from other jurisdictions following that tradition, and for decades their general position was to deny the applicability of *Sullivan* or deny its desirability. Since the 1990s, however, developments have occurred in many countries with the English model of defamation law. In those jurisdictions, there is now generally a defence for publications of *public or political interest* that are made *responsibly or reasonably*, even where publication is widespread such as media publication. The wording of the defence varies, but for simplicity here I call the approach a 'reasonable publication defence'.[78]

On paper, the change made by the reasonable publication defence is significant. Public interest material can be defended if publication is proven to be reasonable without being proven true. However, the change is not nearly to the level of US law's protection of defamatory speech. In each Commonwealth instance, the change has been by way of contrast with *Sullivan*, along with implicit support for one of its central ideas—that traditional defamation law is overly restrictive of public speech—but less support for the second aspect of *Sullivan* noted above; namely, the commitment to vigorous and varied public debate.

For many years, responses often just stated that *Sullivan* does not apply outside the US Constitution. For example, an influential Australian defamation judge simply commented in the 1980s that Australia 'does not have the "public figure" defence afforded by the First Amendment'.[79] Others went further and said *Sullivan* is not wanted; it is not needed. For example, a 1990s Canadian decision rejected the US approach because of the importance of reputation and the way in which *Sullivan* largely deprived people in

---

[75] See Tushnet, 'New York Times v Sullivan' (n 30).

[76] See, eg, the seemingly endless debates on the legitimate treatment of hate speech under a democratic constitution: Michael Herz and Peter Molnar (eds), *The Content and Context of Hate Speech: Rethinking Regulation and Responses* (CUP 2012); James Weinstein, 'Hate Speech Bans, Democracy, and Political Legitimacy' (2017) 32 *Const Comment* 527.

[77] See, eg, Mark Tushnet, *Advanced Introduction to Freedom of Expression* (Edward Elgar 2018) 103.

[78] Broad similarities could also be made with civil law traditions in which a commonplace defence involves showing that publication was made in good faith, involving fact-sensitive evaluation of the circumstances of publication.

[79] *Chappell v TCN Channel Nine* (1988) 14 NSWLR 153, 165 (Hunt J).

public life from legal recourse for defamation.[80] In 1970s England, an official review similarly rejected *Sullivan* because it would have changed the traditional defamation law balance between speech and reputation.[81] Likewise, Australian law reform reports tended to reject *Sullivan*. For example, a review from Australia's three most populous states considered defamation reform in 1990 and observed:

> [We] stand by [the] view that the public figure test has not led to any significant decrease in litigation by public figures in the United States, and what is required is protection for publication of information on matters of legitimate public interest, provided that reasonable steps have been taken to ascertain the truth of the statement and that the publisher is not acting recklessly, or in bad faith.[82]

In fact, US defamation litigation appears to have dropped dramatically under the *Sullivan* rules, although that was perhaps only (or mainly) after the effects of *Anderson v Liberty Lobby*, which occurred only a few years before the above quotation. The prediction of what was required by way of reform, however, accords with the form of defence that emerged in many Commonwealth jurisdictions.

Even after these repeated rejections, *Sullivan* remained a frequent reference point in law reform debates and case law. It stood as a contrasting, and apparently effective, model of protecting public speech. Then, in the last few decades, *Sullivan* began to have greater effects; the case began to 'bite' in Commonwealth laws. Perhaps the most important instance is the unanimous 1993 decision of the House of Lords in *Derbyshire County Council v Times Newspapers*.[83] The decision ended the ability of local government bodies to sue in defamation.[84] The House of Lords 'was greatly influenced' by *Sullivan*,[85]

---

[80] *Westbank Indian Band v Tomat* [1992] 2 WWR 724, [69] (Hinds JA), but the chilling effect of large damages was noted at [70]: 'it would, in my view, be wrong of this court to ignore the significance of the so-called "chilling effect" which large damage awards in defamation cases can have on the freedom of expression'.

[81] Committee on Defamation, *Report of the Committee on Defamation* (Cmd 5909, 1975) (commonly known as the Faulks Committee).

[82] Attorneys-General of Queensland, New South Wales and Victoria, *Reform of Defamation Laws* (DP No 2, 1990) 16–17. See also, eg, Australian Capital Territory Law Reform Commission, *Defamation* (ACT L Ref Com No 10, 1995).

[83] *Derbyshire County Council v Times Newspapers* [1993] AC 534.

[84] The case perhaps had more direct parallels to seditious libel than even *Sullivan*, where an equation was drawn between public officials suing in defamation and state prosecution for seditious libel. In *Derbyshire*, ibid 539, defence counsel raised similar arguments, but they were not directly engaged with by the House of Lords. Counsel argued: 'The plaintiffs seek to extend the tort of libel well beyond the ambit of the criminal offence of seditious libel, which is designed to protect the government and the public against scurrilous and extreme attacks upon the Crown or government institutions… The development of a tort of government libel, much more draconian than the crime of seditious libel, would have a chilling effect upon… freedom of expression'.

[85] *Ballina Shire Council v Ringland* (1994) 33 NSWLR 680, 698 (Kirby P noted the House of Lords was also influenced by an older South African decision, *Die Spoorbond v South African Railways*, 1946 AD 999). The Australian *Ballina* decision took the same approach as *Derbyshire* and prevented local government bodies suing in defamation.

with Lord Keith stating that requiring defendants to prove truth imposed (at least for public speech about local authorities) too great a chill on speech:

> [While *Sullivan* and other decisions] related most directly to the provisions of the American Constitution concerned with securing freedom of speech, *the public interest considerations which underlaid them are no less valid in this country*. What has been described as *'the chilling effect' induced by the threat of civil actions for libel is very important*. Quite often the facts which would justify a defamatory publication are known to be true, but admissible evidence capable of proving those facts is not available. This may prevent the publication of matters which it is very desirable to make public.[86]

Here was express judicial recognition in a leading Commonwealth court that traditional defamation law's chilling effect prevents some valuable true speech being published. Even though I will return to just what was meant by the chilling effect in that statement, larger reforms to defamation law were logically needed after the recognition. Changes followed in a host of countries. As to the changes, for reasons of space I will use just the English example here. But broadly similar developments occurred to varying degrees in many common law jurisdictions,[87] including Australia,[88] Brunei,[89] Canada,[90] Hong Kong,[91] India,[92] Ireland,[93] Kenya,[94] Malaysia,[95] New Zealand,[96] and South Africa.[97] Elsewhere, there has also been more direct recourse to *Sullivan*.[98]

The 1999 House of Lords' decision in *Reynolds v Times Newspapers* developed what was initially known as *Reynolds* privilege.[99] (As addressed in the conclusion below, the *Reynolds* defence has been replaced by a statutory public interest defence under the Defamation Act 2013 (UK).) In *Reynolds*, free speech was clearly linked to the European

---

[86] *Derbyshire* (n 84) 547 (emphasis added).

[87] See, eg, Stone and Williams (n 7).

[88] *Theophanous* (n 71); *Lange* (n 71). See now the statutory defence in Australia's largely uniform national defamation legislation, which unlike *Lange* is not limited to 'political communication', eg Defamation Act 2005 (NSW), s 30.

[89] *Rifli bin Asli v New Straits Times Press (Malaysia) Berhad* [2001] Brunei LR 251 and [2002] Brunei LR 300.

[90] *Grant v Torstar* 2009 SCC 61; (2009) 79 CPR (4th) 407.

[91] *Abdul Razzak Yaqoob v Asia Times Online* [2008] 3 HKC 589.

[92] *Rajagopal v State of Tamil Nadu* [1995] AIR (SC) 264.

[93] *Hunter v Gerald Duckworth & Co* [2003] IEHC 81; see also the subsequent Defamation Act 2009 (Ire), s 26.

[94] Eg, *Mwangi Kiunjuri v Wangethi Mwangi* [2008] eKLR (3 Oct 2008); *Mwangi Kiunjuri v Wangethi Mwangi* [2016] eKLR (15 April 2016) (an approach following *Reynolds* although also largely equating it to *Sullivan*).

[95] *Dato'Seri Anwar Ibrahim v Dato' Seri Dr Mahathir Mohamad* [2001] 2 MLJ 65; *Irene Fernandez v Utusan Melayu (M) Sdn Bhd* [2008] 2 CLJ 814.

[96] *Lange v Atkinson* [2001] NZLR 257; and the reformulated defence which is no longer confined to political issues but applies to responsible communication on matters of public interest: *Durie v Gardiner* [2018] NZCA 278.

[97] *National Media v Bogoshi* [1999] 1 BCLR 1.   [98] See n 23.

[99] *Reynolds v Times Newspapers* [2001] 2 AC 127. For a detailed review see Hilary Young, '*Reynolds v Times Newspapers Ltd*' in Rolph (n 3) 195.

Convention of Human Rights (ECHR),[100] but *Sullivan* was also considered. For example, Lord Steyn quoted at length the passage reproduced at the outset of this chapter on traditional defamation law's chilling effect, including the way in which it dampens vigorous and varied public debate.[101] He then stated: 'The argument for addressing the chilling effect of our defamation law on political speech and for striking a better balance between freedom of speech and defamation is strong'.[102] The new defence aimed to protect public interest material published in a 'responsible' fashion. In *Reynolds*, Lord Nicholls set out ten illustrative factors for assessing responsible publication,[103] including the publication's importance, urgency, and tone, as well as the information's source and any attempts by the publisher to verify the information pre-publication. It also became clear that a 'reportage' defence could protect publications that reported some allegations made by others, without any attempt at verification.[104] The reportage defence is an interesting example of English law being *more protective* of speech than US law's approach to 'neutral reportage'.[105]

Case law after *Reynolds* suggested the defence would be difficult to establish where publications were sensational,[106] used unreliable sources,[107] or had not contacted plaintiffs (unless plaintiffs could be expected to lack relevant information).[108] Final appellate courts emphasized the defence should be applied in 'a practical and flexible manner'[109] with deference given to editorial discretion; that is, the defence should protect more speech than lower courts had often found it to protect. This point was returned to repeatedly in the highest court.[110] However, even applied generously, *Reynolds* did not allow publishers to ask themselves the simple question that summarizes US law: 'do I know, or do I have real suspicions, that I am publishing a lie about a public official or public figure'? Instead, the factors in *Reynolds* bring to mind something like the speech in scholarly publications or the 'perpetual seminar' of John Stuart Mill's free speech writing.[111] It was

---

[100] At the time of the decision, art 10 of the ECHR was about to enter into UK domestic law via the Human Rights Act 1998 (UK).

[101] *Reynolds* (n 99) 208–9.   [102] Ibid 210.   [103] Ibid 205.

[104] Eg, *Al-Fagih v H H Saudi Research & Marketing UK* [2001] EWCA Civ 1634; [2002] EMLR 13; *Roberts v Gable* [2007] EWCA Civ 721; [2008] QB 502; see also *Jameel (Mohammed) v Wall Street Journal Europe* [2007] 1 AC 359, [62]; *Flood v Times Newspapers* [2012] 2 AC 273. See now Defamation Act 2013 (UK), s 4(3). See also Jason Bosland, 'Republication of Defamation under the Doctrine of Reportage: The Evolution of Common Law Qualified Privilege in England and Wales' (2011) 31 *Oxford J Legal Stud* 89; Eric Barendt, 'Balancing Freedom of Expression and the Right to Reputation: Reflections on Reynolds and Reportage' (2012) 63 *Northern Ireland Legal Q* 59.

[105] See, eg, David McCraw, 'The Right to Republish Libel: Neutral Reportage and the Reasonable Reader' (1991) 25 *Akron L Rev* 335.

[106] Eg, *Grobelaar v News Group Newspapers* [2001] EWCA Civ 33; [2001] 2 All ER 437; *Galloway v Telegraph Group* [2006] EMLR 11.

[107] Eg, *James Gilbert v MGN* [2000] EMLR 680.

[108] Cf *Galloway* (n 106) and *Jameel (Mohammed)* (n 104).

[109] *Bonnick v Morris* [2003] 1 AC 300, [24].

[110] See in particular *Jameel (Mohammed)* (n 104) and *Flood* (n 104).

[111] Eric Barendt, *Freedom of Speech* (2nd edn, OUP 2005) 12, describing Mill's approach as assuming there will be 'a lively discussion of rival views, as if society were conducting a perpetual seminar'.

'neutral, investigative journalism' including book-length journalism,[112] or even 'seriously dull' journalism in the words of one judge,[113] that *Reynolds* aimed to protect and encourage. It was not robust public debate. And the same is true of the reasonable publication defences elsewhere.

This is a simple but important point in understanding how free speech is being treated. In many Commonwealth jurisdictions, there are now statements explicitly recognizing the chilling effect of traditional defamation law but not the value in robust and wide-open public debate. The reforms that have followed that partial recognition of the chilling effect aim to protect reasonable publication, not varied and vigorous debate. Thus, reformed Commonwealth defamation law is much more 'conversational' in its conception of public speech than the robust debate that is the model in US defamation law.[114]

The approach taken by civil law systems to free speech in defamation law could also be considered, although recourse to *Sullivan* has been less common there. While there are many differences,[115] one relevant similarity is the civil law's good faith defence. But the similarity is more to the reasonable publication defence than to the US law: good faith defences involve closely investigating the publisher's conduct in a manner resembling the Commonwealth developments. Issues include the legitimacy of the goal pursued (for example, did the publication contribute to public debate), any ill-will held by the publisher, what pre-publication inquiries were made, and the care used in choosing the published words.[116] In addition, civil law regimes can protect opinion almost as strongly as US law, and at times for similar free speech reasons. Under German law, for example, opinion published in public debate can be protected even where its factual basis is not published, and even where the opinion is vitriolic (but not merely abuse of the person concerned). The law guards against too strong a requirement to prove the truth of factual material linked with opinions. There is otherwise a danger of 'choking',[117] 'crippling', or 'paralyzing' the freedom.[118] As Eric Barendt has noted, the German court's language closely resembles the chilling effect.[119]

---

[112] See *Jameel (Mohammed)* (n 104) [35] (Lord Bingham); *Charman v Orion Publishing* [2008] 1 All ER 750.

[113] *Jameel (Mohammed)* (n 104) [150] (Baroness Hale).

[114] See Andrew T Kenyon, 'What Conversation? Free Speech and Defamation Law' (2010) 73 *Mod L Rev* 697.

[115] Under civil law, defamation is generally criminal as well as civil; the breadth of what is protected can extend beyond 'reputation' as understood in common law systems; and rules often limit who can be sued in relation to media publications. For brief discussion see, eg, Andrew T Kenyon, 'Libel and Defamation in Journalism' in Jon F Nussbaum, *Oxford Research Encyclopedia of Communication* (OUP 2019).

[116] See, eg, Emmanuel Derieux and Agnès Granchet, *Droit Des Médias* (7th edn, LGDJ 2015) 441–3 summarising the French good faith defence in those terms.

[117] *Bayer Pharmaceutical Case* [1991] BVerfGE 85. The translation comes from Barendt, *Freedom of Speech* (n 111) 218; it could also be termed 'strangling' or 'constricting'.

[118] *Bayer Pharmaceutical Case* [1991] BVerfGE 85. 'Crippling' comes from the translated judgment available at (*University of Texas*, 19 July 2019) <https://law.utexas.edu/transnational/foreign-law-translations/german/case.php?id=625> accessed 19 July 2019. An alternative would be 'paralyzing'.

[119] Barendt, *Freedom of Speech* (n 111) 218.

It is not just the approach to reputation that varies across defamation jurisdictions, it is also the legal understanding of free speech. This prompts a question about just what is being recognized of the chilling effect in defamation law reforms outside the United States: what speech do they envisage as being inappropriately chilled? One of the more detailed analyses of the chilling effect dates from 1978, when Frederick Schauer examined the concept's meaning in US law.[120] The study examines a range of legal areas including defamation; the chilling effect does not only concern defamation law, even if defamation law has probably seen the most use of the term outside the US.[121] As Schauer explains, the chilling effect combines two basic ideas: the legal system is permeated by uncertainty and error, and laws which limit the errors made 'against' speech are to be preferred. The First Amendment preference is for erroneously allowed speech rather than erroneously penalized speech. Speech is the 'transcendent value'.[122] The chilling effect requires 'that legal rules be formulated so as to allocate the risk of error away from the preferred value' which is speech.[123]

This could suggest an absolute protection for speech, like arguments in *Sullivan* that equated the plaintiff's claim with prosecution for seditious libel.[124] But US defamation law does not provide an absolute protection for speech; rather it imposes a limit of 'do not lie' about public plaintiffs. In that way, US defamation law still seeks to balance free speech and reputation, but the balance arises through the actual malice rules. It is not a balance determined in each particular case.[125] US case law does not closely examine why the *Sullivan* rules, and not another standard such as negligence, are the appropriate point of balance for public plaintiffs.[126] In considering the chilling effect, Schauer notes the 'essence' of *Sullivan* 'is that no newspaper can realistically be expected to bear the burden of verifying all the factual statements appearing in each of its editions',[127] which traditional law often required. The same could be said of the 'essence' of the reasonable publication defences that have emerged in recent decades. The chilling effect of requiring publishers to prove the truth of defamatory facts was recognized in those reforms too, but the reasonable publication defences that resulted are quite different from the *Sullivan* rules.

This is where the two quotations which began the chapter may be useful. In *Sullivan*, the Supreme Court recognized the self-censorship that follows from traditional defamation law. It also recognized the US commitment to uninhibited, robust and wide-open public debate that can include vehement and caustic attacks. Both points are central to the *Sullivan* rules. Together, they suggest a very strong protection for public speech

---

[120] Schauer (n 38).
[121] See, eg, Eric Barendt, Laurence Lustgarten, Kenneth Norrie, and Hugh Stephenson, *Libel and the Media: The Chilling Effect* (Clarendon P 1997).
[122] *Speiser v Randall*, 357 US 513, 526 (1958) (Brennan J) and see discussion in Schauer (n 38) 701–2.
[123] Schauer (n 38) 705.
[124] See, eg, Anderson (n 24) 239.
[125] Schauer (n 38) 710.
[126] See, eg, Sack (n 22) 284; Stephenson (n 54) 32.
[127] Schauer (n 38) 707.

against defamation, and they suggest something important for comparative analysis; namely, US law has a different understanding of the chilling effect than seen in the more recent Commonwealth defences. The Supreme Court stated in *Sullivan* that traditional defamation liability dampens vigorous and varied public debate. What needs to be protected against being chilled—the freedom of speech that is valued—is exactly that form of public debate. That goes quite some way to explaining why the appropriate point of balance would be actual malice (in defamation actions seeking damages at least).[128] Free speech, as understood through the chilling effect, is robust and uninhibited and even caustic. This element of the chilling effect has not been addressed in the reasonable publication defences. In *Reynolds*, for example, the words from *Sullivan* about self-censorship and dampening vigorous public debate were quoted,[129] but the latter aspect was not engaged with. Reasonable or responsible publication is protected under the defences not vigorous debate. The default position is not speech. And, to date, uncertainty over what will be found to be reasonable weighs on publishers,[130] perhaps especially those without substantial resources.

A similar point can be seen in analyses of reputation in defamation law and the understanding of public discourse they suggest. For example, specifically addressing *Sullivan*, Kermit Hall notes the 'competing visions of public discourse' that were at play in the case.[131] In his analysis, a different sense of reputation in northern and southern states influenced the result. Drawing on the work of Robert Post,[132] Hall contrasts a property-based sense of reputation in northern states and dignity and honour in the south. Reputation in the form of dignity and honour produces a very different vision of 'civic discourse',[133] one which was dismissed by the Supreme Court in *Sullivan*. Ideas of 'deference to political authority', the authority which 'sustained racial inequality' in the south, were judged 'antique' in *Sullivan*.[134]

Post has long focused on the way in which the US constitutional understanding of free speech relates to the idea of public discourse. In reviewing Norman Rosenberg's history of US defamation law,[135] Post provides a concise version of his analysis as it relates to defamation. Prior to *Sullivan*, defamation law in most US states—and, one could add,

---

[128] Many other possible reforms might be examined if damages were not the sole or major focus; see, eg, Marc A Franklin, 'A Declaratory Judgment Alternative to Current Libel Law' (1986) 74 *Cal L Rev* 809; Rodney A Smolla and Michael J Gaertner, 'The Annenberg Libel Reform Proposal: The Case for Enactment' (1989) 31 *Wm & Mary L Rev* 25; New South Wales Law Reform Commission (n 11). See also outline of selected Commonwealth and US reform proposals in Andrew T Kenyon, 'Protecting Speech in Defamation Law: Beyond *Reynolds*-Style Defences' (2014) 6 *J Media L* 21, 31–3.

[129] *Reynolds* (n 99).

[130] See, eg, Eric Barendt, '*Reynolds* Privilege and Reports of Police Investigations' (2012) 4 *J Media L* 1, 10.

[131] Quoted in Kermit L Hall and Melvin I Urofsky, *New York Times v Sullivan: Civil Rights, Libel Law, and the Free Press* (UP Kansas 2011) 3.

[132] Post, 'The Social Foundations of Defamation Law' (n 25).

[133] Schauer Hall and Urofsky (n 131) 206.

[134] Ibid 203.

[135] Robert C Post, 'Defaming Public Officials: On Doctrine and Legal History' [1987] *Am Bar Found Res J* 539 (review essay of Norman L Rosenberg, *Protecting the Best Men: An Interpretive History of the Law of Libel* (U North Carolina P 1986)).

defamation law in the English tradition—had 'a strong normative sense' of how public debate should be conducted. Some US states had developed a qualified privilege for good faith publications about politicians and candidates, famously *Coleman v MacLennan* which was later adapted (and altered) by Brennan J in *Sullivan*.[136] However, this good faith defence could be defeated by common law malice. That is the *actual* meaning of actual malice in the older US cases.[137] Actual malice is not the same in the *Sullivan* rules—it is 'substantially more demanding than good faith'[138]—and it provides a quite different style of protection for public speech. Post argues the effect of *Sullivan* 'was to mark off a separate arena of public discussion in which the ordinary rules of civility, as defined and enforced by common law defamation, were suspended.'[139] Under the older law, '[m]alice marked the line of demarcation between approved and disapproved forms of political participation.'[140] I would suggest it still does in the form of actual malice under *Sullivan* and, in doing so, it has changed the 'shape' of the communicative freedom recognized in US law. It is not that varied ideas of reputation are irrelevant here; rather, the point is that different understandings of free speech are also influential in defamation law. And they remain a marked—even if not sufficiently recognized, analysed, and justified—difference between defamation law in the US and many other places.

15.4 CONCLUSION

I have outlined two general aspects of how *Sullivan* and subsequent decisions relate to free speech. The first is that *Sullivan* itself is only one element of a more complex protection of defamatory speech. The US approach classifies plaintiffs rather than speech, operates not as a defence but by imposing greater burdens on the vast majority of plaintiffs (including private plaintiffs suing over media publications), and provides markedly stronger protection for opinion and comment than the traditional law. Further, pre-trial motions are frequently made and effective in ending US defamation claims, and judges (particularly appellate judges) have a major role in seeking to ensure the 'breathing space' of the *Sullivan* rules is protected in practice. All this means there is much more than requirements to prove falsity and fault in US defamation law's extremely strong protection of public speech.

---

[136] *Coleman v MacLennan*, 78 Kan 711; 98 P 281 (1908).

[137] The malice is described as 'actual' in the older cases in contrast to the malice traditionally presumed in making a defamatory publication. The good faith defence countered this presumption of malice, but the defence could then be defeated by showing the publisher acted with actual malice, in the form of ill-will or an improper purpose in the occasion of publication.

[138] Anderson (n 24) 242 (note omitted).

[139] Post, 'Defaming Public Officials' (n 135) 552.

[140] Ibid 553.

The second aspect is that the chilling effect relied on in the *Sullivan* rules has received greater recognition in many other jurisdictions in recent decades. However, the recognition most often focuses on 'chilling' the publication of material that is factually true or believed to be true. It tends to overlook the parallel US commitment to vigorous and varied public debate. Instead, the recognition of *Sullivan* and subsequent decisions is linked to the idea of measured public debate. The protection is for reasonable publication, not robust debate. This provides a different shape to freedom of speech, one that is more conversational than is arguably warranted in the treatment of public speech.

In some ways each of the above aspects also offers a cautionary example of some of the challenges of comparative analysis. The challenges are worth noting given the prevalence of comparative research in defamation and free speech law—a prevalence that is quite understandable with the issues' importance and changes in communication, both in terms of communicating legal material and in terms of changing public speech. Outside the United States, the complexities of the *Sullivan* rules are often reduced to the single decision with which they began. While an understandable shorthand, the approach can miss the *combination* of elements in the rules that are significant to the very different operation and effects of US defamation law. As to the law's operation and effects on public speech, a substantial amount of empirically-informed research into defamation law and litigation, media practices and media content supports the conclusion that traditional defamation law does chill speech and the US law does so less.[141] The law is one notable element in a very different model of free speech under the First Amendment.

Comparative analysis also carries the risk of understanding reforms in one legal system in terms of another (such as the author's own legal system) perhaps more than is warranted. This is seen in some foreign analyses of Commonwealth reasonable publication defences. One example is worth noting here: the replacement of the *Reynolds* defence with a statutory public interest defence in the Defamation Act 2013 (UK). As noted above, *Reynolds* included a list of factors for a judge to draw from in determining whether the publication at issue amounted to 'responsible journalism'. The list was often restrictively interpreted, limiting speakers' ability to rely on it *predictably* and thus limiting the degree to which *Reynolds* reduced defamation law's chilling effect. This is not to say *Reynolds* had no effect; it allowed media outlets with sufficient resources to publish some allegations that would probably not have been published previously.[142] Serious news reporting and investigations gained some benefit from the defence, at least for publishers with the resources to fund legal advice before publication and run cases all the way to appeal. This context of limited benefit to some categories of speaker was the context in which appellate decisions emphasized the need to apply the test more generously to speakers. Promoting a more generous trial-level application of the test is exactly what the statutory reform aimed to do.

---

[141] See, eg, Barendt and others (n 121); Ursula Cheer, 'Myths and Realities about the Chilling Effect: The New Zealand Media's Experience of Defamation Law' (2005) 13 *Torts LJ* 259; Kenyon (n 43) 16–17.

[142] Russell Weaver, Andrew T Kenyon, David F Partlett, and Clive P Walker, *The Right to Speak Ill: Defamation, Reputation and Free Speech* (Carolina Academic P 2006) 240–2.

At least, the parliamentary intention was to apply the defence more generously. And the wording chosen offers some potential for a more robust defence to develop through judicial decisions.[143] The statutory defence requires that the publication's content is of public interest and 'the defendant reasonably believed that publishing the statement complained of was in the public interest'. The court is to make allowance for editorial judgment as it considers appropriate and have regard to all the circumstances of the case.[144] It is easy to imagine how that wording could be interpreted as providing a very strong protection for speech: the focus has become the defendant's belief. But to date, the defence remains within a model of free speech that protects reasonable publication more than one that protects robust debate. Making allowance for editorial judgment has not generally operated as it tends to under the First Amendment. And caution is needed in suggesting English defamation has 'moved from a judicially developed law that rejected...*Sullivan* because it was too generous to publishers to a legislatively enacted statute that rejects...*Sullivan* because it is not generous enough to publishers'.[145] I can well understand how such a reading arises, but it is unlikely that English courts will find publication was 'reasonably believed' to be in the public interest if a publisher had what would amount to 'actual malice' in US law. Rather, the statutory reference to 'all the circumstances of the case' is more commonly understood to direct courts to the sorts of matters considered under *Reynolds* (whether appropriate inquiries were made before publication, comment was sought, and so forth). All this means the public interest defence is most likely to be an incremental reform, not a revolutionary one.

What may be more interesting about *Reynolds*' replacement with the public interest defence is that it illustrates an ongoing search to find a more appropriate protection for speech within at least some Commonwealth defamation laws. It may mark a second generation of change, joined more recently by a relatively modest judicial reworking of the similar defence in New Zealand.[146] In any such efforts, it could be useful to pay closer attention to just what is meant by the chilling effect in the context of US defamation law. That does not mean reform elsewhere would take the same approach—the consideration of reputation, perhaps in part through developing new remedies, may provide alternative reform paths—but the substance of the US analysis deserves greater recognition and engagement. Doing that might lead to apparently modest reforms to the public interest defence that could have marked effects. For example, the UK defence could be reformed through statutory presumptions of public interest and reasonable belief that would require clear and convincing evidence to defeat.[147] Where publishers

---

[143] See, eg, Gavin Phillipson 'The "Global Pariah", the Defamation Bill and the Human Rights Act' (2012) 63 *Northern Ireland Legal Q* 149.

[144] Defamation Act 2013 (UK), s 4. Section 4(3) also confirms the reportage defence. Where the defendant publishes an 'accurate and impartial account of a dispute' involving the plaintiff, the court must disregard any omission by the defendant to take steps to verify the statement at issue.

[145] Tushnet (n 30) 355–6.

[146] *Durie v Gardiner* [2018] NZCA 278.

[147] See, eg, Stephenson (n 54) 6.

of public interest speech had such a defence available, the shape of communicative freedom would have come quite a bit closer to that envisaged by the *Sullivan* rules.

Innumerable factors influence the space that exists for public speech. Laws affecting freedom of speech are just one influence on public discourse, and defamation law just one example of the many forms of law that are relevant. One can well speak of an infrastructure of public speech.[148] Even so, defamation law can illustrate something of a jurisdiction's understanding of free speech and of the public discourse that the communicative freedom seeks to support. Defamation laws differ across jurisdictions in part because what is meant by free speech differs. Traditional common law defamation contains an understanding of free speech, but one that is constrained. In short, the burden and risks lie on speakers. They have chosen to act and therefore must defend their speech if it criticizes another. The default state in such an understanding is not speech but silence. Or, at least, it is speech only in sanctioned places such as parliament, or to sanctioned people, such as reporting suspected crimes to police. It is almost always not speech directed to the public. It is not vigorous and varied public debate.

---

[148] See, eg, Jack M Balkin, 'Digital Speech and Democratic Culture: A Theory of Freedom of Expression for the Information Society' (2004) 79 *NYU L Rev* 1; Jack M Balkin 'Old-School/New-School Speech Regulation' (2014) 127 *Harv L Rev* 2296.

CHAPTER 16

PRIVACY AND SPEECH

IOANNA TOURKOCHORITI

16.1 Introduction

Freedom of speech is a liberty the exercise of which can cause harm. It is a liberty constitutive of autonomy, which can harm another liberty that is also constitutive of autonomy, privacy. Free speech and privacy can be equally justified in reference to the unconditional respect that every human being is entitled to. Privacy helps a person form her personality by deciding to what extent what concerns her will be communicated to others. The response to the question what should be the just limits of freedom of speech in relation to the protection of other values like privacy and human dignity is different across legal systems.

Cases of conflict between freedom of expression and other values are hard cases. They necessitate arguments of principle as well as arguments of consequence. The former focus on a principled rights-based defence and the latter on the effects of the exercise of freedom of expression. A deontological conception can help protect a hard core of freedom of expression. Consequentialist arguments can help evaluate the consequences of the exercise of freedom of expression in concrete cases, weighing its importance in reference to other values. Judges usually engage in a reasoning that has the form of a back and forth movement. They consider principles and the consequences of applying them and the other way around. Judges engage in a spiral reasoning in order to arrive at a 'reflective equilibrium' between deontological arguments that protect a core of a right and consequentialist arguments that evaluate the concrete consequences of the exercise of a right. They weigh competing individual and social interests. In order to decide the grey area in the periphery of the two rights' exercise, judges propose criteria such as 'newsworthiness' or 'legitimate public interest'.

Expressive interests win out in the balance with privacy interests in the United States, whereas it is the other way around in many other countries. Courts interpret the concept broadly in the United States and more narrowly in France and other European states.

This chapter discusses the concept of privacy and case law which shows the different approaches between Europe and the United States concerning the balancing of freedom of speech when it conflicts with other rights. Judges and scholars also refer to the concept of human dignity in this area. The concept of dignity serves in the United States as the foundation for freedom of expression, whereas in Europe it serves to limit freedom of expression. In the United States the reference to human dignity is associated with a conception of negative liberty. This conception prevents limitations to the negative aspect of freedom of expression. The requirement for government transparency creates a presumption in favour of protecting expression. Public debate should be 'robust, uninhibited and wide open'.[1] The requirement for a lively public debate is also present in Europe. The extended interpretation of 'privacy' in the law of many European states means depriving the public debate from information that would be crucial to a well-informed electorate. The dangers of erring on both sides are equally worthy of consideration.

This chapter further discusses the intermediate concepts that judges have come up with in order to balance the exercise of rights in conflict. Those criteria concern the periphery of the activities that are to be protected by the right to privacy. It discusses hard cases and legal criteria which have emerged in cases from Europe and the United States. And it discusses various institutional considerations which affect the outcomes of legal decisions in this area. The chapter ends with a discussion of the right to be forgotten.

16.2 THE CONCEPT OF PRIVACY

Many notions, inclusive and interdependent, have been used as a point of reference in order to define privacy in various contexts and cultures. Privacy is considered as the sphere par excellence of the manifestation of the autonomy of the person. In this sense, privacy means the ability of the individual to make choices on the most important elements that define their personality. Privacy is associated with the psychic and intellectual needs of man. The expression 'privacy' is used to mean many different things, like freedom of thought, the control on personal information, the protection against intrusions in one's domicile, freedom against surveillance.

The definition of the concept 'privacy' necessitates always in time and in space a latent normative choice, on its meaning among the scope of possible meanings of the term. This right is founded on the notion of autonomy and the dignity of the human person, of the respect that human beings owe each other to keep in distance from one another, on the basis of their only quality of being human, transcending any geographical limitation and cultural differentiation. Even if there is consensus upon a solid foundation of a core of the right to privacy, differences persist in social rules concerning the facets and the

---

[1] *New York Times v Sullivan*, 376 US 254, 270.

particular manifestations, which are protected by the law. The periphery of the concept finds its foundation in the conventions and the way of life of every society.[2] In this sense, privacy is a protean concept.[3] It is a notion which depends on the historical and geographical relativity of needs and human conventions. According to a pragmatic approach to the conceptualization of privacy, this notion must be understood in terms of practices; it finds its origins in the activities, the customs, the norms, and traditions which are a product of the history of a culture.

The association of the notion of autonomy with the one of privacy in the legal texts aims at indicating the freedom of action, which must be allowed to the individual concerning her fundamental decisions. The criterion of control, associated with the idea of autonomy defines the right to privacy as the right to control a territory of information, that a person or a group does not want to make known to others and whose content is submitted to socially determined variability dependent on the context and the character of the social occasion. The criterion concerns also the control of who will have access to a person's physical body, and under what circumstances, since physical existence is constitutive itself of information on one's personality.

Privacy denotes the need to protect a condition of being apart from others, which favours the development of mental activities. Emotional vulnerability is a foundation for the protection of privacy. Isolation from others favours psychological ends like peace and mental health. It allows a margin against the pressure to conform to the expectations of society, allowing the individual to define her existence.[4] The impossibility to control one's appearance towards others can have negative effects upon the conception of the self. The impossibility to define and control our public persona can result in a loss of the self. Privacy is considered a condition in view of arriving to autonomy, as the extent of the social and legal space left to the individual, so that they can develop the emotional, cognitive, spiritual, and moral powers of an autonomous agent. It constitutes the sphere par excellence inside which is developed the relation that every individual maintains with themselves. The right to privacy is equivalent to the protection of this core of the existence of the person, which is crucial to our understanding of ourselves as persons capable of having a conception of the good and of devoting ourselves to activities, which are dictated by this conception.[5] In relation to intellectual freedom, privacy can be a right that allows the possibility for free speech as well. Free speech is not a value that is always in conflict with privacy. There are cases where the protection of privacy is

---

[2] Frederick Schauer, 'Free Speech and the Social Construction of Privacy' (2001) 68 *Soc Res* 221.

[3] For the difficulties in defining privacy see Hyman Gross, 'The Concept of Privacy' (1967) 42 *NYU L Rev* 34; Raymond Wacks, 'The Poverty of "Privacy"' (1980) 96 *L Q Rev* 73; WA Parent, 'A New Definition of Privacy for the Law' (1983) 2 *L & Phil* 305; Judith Wagner DeCew, 'The Scope of Privacy in Law and Ethics' (1986) 5 *L & Phil* 145; Jack Hirshleifer, 'Privacy: Its Origin, Function and Future', (1980) *J Legal Stud* 649; HJ McCloskey, 'The Political Ideal of Privacy' (1971) *Phil Q* 303; Richard Epstein, 'A Taste for Privacy? Evolution and the Emergence of a Naturalistic Ethic' (1980) *J Legal Stud* 665.

[4] Sidney M Jourard, 'Some Psychological Aspects of Privacy' (1996) 31 *L & Contemp Probl* 307, 308.

[5] Sissela Bok, *Secrets, On The Ethics of Concealment and Revelation* (OUP 1982) n 15; Michael A Weinstein, 'The Uses of Privacy in the Good Life' in J Roland Pennock and JW Chapman (eds), *Privacy: Nomos XIII* (Atherton P 1971) 88.

important for the protection of free speech itself. A person should be allowed to speak freely in private in order for her to be able to develop her intellectual faculties. India's Supreme Court discussed the importance of privacy for artistic and more generally creative expression in an important decision on biometric data which discusses explicitly this point.[6]

Another aspect of privacy is the one associated with the protection of information, which allows us to maintain degrees of intimacy. The legal recognition of the possibility of the person to control who will have access to information which concerns them, associated with their aptitude to develop various types of interpersonal relations—according to the quantity and the type of information that they decide to make known to others—is associated with the idea of the variety of the social contexts of communication.[7] The social frames of communication can be defined like concentric spheres, to which correspond spheres of privacy and which include successively the intimate interpersonal relations, the institutional and social relations, the public at large, and the press.[8] According to another conception, the spheres of privacy and thus the elements which are submitted to informational self-disposition are not concentric, but only overlap in some respects.[9]

Courts also refer to the concept of human dignity in association with the right to privacy. The concept of 'dignity' is also very elusive. It has been associated with a variety of meanings in the course of the history of ideas.[10] Alan Gewirth proposes two categories for the meanings, which were attributed to the concept, an empirical and a moral.[11] According to the first, it is associated with some degree 'of gravity or decorum or composure or self-respect or self-confidence together with various good qualities, which can justify these attitudes'.[12] In this sense, dignity is context dependent. It is associated with the social recognition of these individual qualities. This conception is very close to the Roman conception.[13] According to the moral meaning of the term, 'dignity' is associated with the intrinsic value of each individual, which belongs to her by virtue of being human. It is a permanent characteristic, which constitutes the foundation of all rights. Used in association with the concept of privacy, the concept of dignity refers to the social status of the person. Some moral elements are built in there as well to the extent that the

---

[6] *Justice KS Puttaswamy (Retd) v Union of India* (2017) 10 SCC 1, 244–5.
[7] James Rachels, 'Why Privacy is Important' (1975) 4 *Phil & Pub Aff* 323.
[8] Rodney A Smolla, *Free Speech in an Open Society* (Vintage Books 1993) 130; Louis Hodges, 'The Journalist and Privacy' (1994) 9 *J Mass Media Ethics* 197, 199.
[9] Ferdinand D Schoeman, *Privacy and Social Freedom* (CUP 1992) 142.
[10] Ernst Bloch, *Droit Naturel et Dignité Humaine* (Denis Authier and Jean Lacoste trs, Payot 2002); Catherine Lecomte, 'Des Dignités à la Dignité' in Jérôme Ferrand and Hugues Petit (eds) *Fondations et Naissances des Droits de l'Homme* (L'Harmattan 2003) vol 1, 159.
[11] Alan Gewirth, 'Human Dignity as the Basis of Rights' in Michael J Meyer and William A Parent (eds), *The Constitution of Rights, Human Dignity and American Values* (Cornell UP 1992) 12.
[12] The 'empirical' conception of dignity associates it to the rituals and to the external aspect of manifestation of magnanimity.
[13] Panayotis *Kondilis*, 'Würde' in '*Historisches Lexicon zur politisch-sozialen Sprache in Deutschland Geschichliche Grundbegriffe* (Band 6, Stuttgart, Klett-Cotta 1984).

right to control elements that define one's personality is associated both with human dignity and privacy.

The reference to human dignity serves in some parts of the world, for example France, in view of protecting the social status of the person from violations coming from freedom of expression. The concept of dignity serves in France as a necessary justification in view of limiting freedom of expression, whereas in the United States it serves as a justification necessary in view of protecting freedom of expression. The concept of dignity is associated with an understanding of the concept of liberty. In a legal system which is centred on the protection of the negative aspect of liberty, as is the case in the US legal order, dignity serves as the concept matrix of the philosophical justification of negative liberties.

16.3 NEWSWORTHINESS

Courts have developed the concept of 'newsworthiness'[14]—or 'legitimate public interest' in cases concerning the conflict between the two rights as a criterion to strike the right balance. Across jurisdictions, courts have elaborated a variety of understandings of what makes a publication newsworthy. 'Newsworthiness' is a standard they have developed in this respect. Its role is 'to confront the legal technique... to the social interests, interpreted by the judge'.[15] In determining what is a matter of legitimate public interest, courts take account of the customs and conventions of the community. Newsworthiness is a matter of community mores. Courts interpret the concept broadly in the United States and they reject almost any action in favour of freedom of the press. Courts interpret the same concept narrowly in European case law. They have elaborated additional criteria such as 'direct' and 'strict association' with the needs for free-flowing information to justify any violation of privacy. The legal reasoning of European Courts is conditioned by the primacy of the protection of privacy. In the United States an inverse ex ante understanding is dominant;[16] freedom of expression and newsworthiness condition the construction of the premises of the legal reasoning. This means that French courts find intrusion of privacy in the majority of cases almost automatically. US plaintiffs must prove that the publication is not newsworthy. This is justified by the

---

[14] Linda N Woito and Patrick McNulty, 'The Privacy Disclosure Tort and the First Amendment: Should the Community Decide Newsworthiness?' (1979) 64 *Iowa L Rev* 185; Robert Post, 'The Social Foundations of Privacy: Community and Self in the Common Law Tort' (1989) 77 *Cal L Rev* 957.

[15] Stéphane Rials, 'Les Standards, Notions Critiques du Droit', in Chaïm Perelman and Raymond Vander Elst (eds), *Les Notions à Contenu Variable en Droit* (Bruyland 1984) 42; Stéphane Rials, *Le Juge Administratif Français et la Technique du Standard: Essai sur le Traitement Juridictionnel de l'Idée de Normalité* (LGDJ 1980).

[16] I refer here to Hans Georg Gadamer's use of the term 'ex ante understanding' in *Truth and Method* (first published 1960, J Weinshemere and DG Marshall tr, Continuum 2004).

special value that free speech has in the US legal order and the fear that the requirement of proving newsworthiness could have a chilling effect upon the press.[17]

According to the American Restatement (Second) of Torts:

> For the determination of what constitutes a question of legitimate public interest we must take into consideration the customs and conventions of the community; and in the last analysis, what is appropriate becomes a question of the mores of the community. The line must be drawn to the point where publicity stops to provide information to which the public has a right, and becomes a morbid and sensational indiscretion on the privacy for its own sake, which was of no interest for a reasonable member of the public with reasonable standards.[18]

The US Supreme Court does not accept the criterion of referencing the sensibility of the 'reasonable man' as sufficient justification to hold the directors of the publication accountable.[19] A category of speech, which is shocking for some, can be important and is thus protected under the First Amendment to the US Constitution. The Court considers that 'offence' is a subjective criterion which can only be evaluated in a political and social context. It would allow a jury to find liability on the basis of its subjective opinions and tastes or on the basis of their disapproval of speech. Similarly, the Supreme Court has held that 'outrageousness' is a highly subjective standard that would allow a civil jury to impose liability on the basis of their tastes or views.[20] Public debate should be 'robust, uninhibited and wide open'.[21] This is equivalent to accepting a privilege of the press to define newsworthiness. The Supreme Court ruled in *Cox Broadcasting v Cohn*[22] that the notion of 'newsworthiness' has constitutional value.

The protection of privacy is relevant concerning public figures and newsworthy persons. Seeing the First Amendment as a tool to protect against the danger of excessive government intervention within civil society led the Supreme Court to accept a high standard of responsibility for defamatory falsehood that concerns public figures.[23] The standard adopted in *New York Times v Sullivan* is 'reckless disregard' as to the falsity of the information. The Supreme Court accepts that the media can presuppose that public figures have voluntarily exposed themselves to increased risk, a presumption which does not apply to private individuals.[24] For these reasons, the Court has held that states must retain substantial latitude in their efforts to enforce legal remedies for defamatory falsehood, which can damage the reputation of a private individual, provided that they do not impose liability without fault.[25]

---

[17] *Diaz v Oakland Tribune Inc*, 139 Cal App 3d 118 (1983).
[18] (The American Law Institute, 1977) s 652D.
[19] *Cox Broadcasting Corp v Cohn*, 420 US 469, 496 (1975).
[20] *Snyder v Phelps*, 562 US 443, 448 (2011) (quoting *Hustler Magazine Inc v Falwell*, 485 US 46, 55 (1988)).
[21] *Sullivan* (n 1) 270.   [22] *Cox* (n 19).
[23] Frederick Schauer, 'Public Figures' (1984) 25 Wm & Mary L Rev 905.
[24] *Gertz v Robert Welch Inc*, 418 US 323 (1974).   [25] Ibid.

The US Supreme Court has rejected a right to respond to a publication which compromises the honour and reputation of a person.[26] French law foresees the possibility of a similar right.[27] The right can be exercised within a deadline of three months following publication and by the same medium of communication. The right to respond can be enforced through preliminary injunction.

16.4 THE DIFFICULTY IN BALANCING PRIVACY RIGHTS AGAINST FREE SPEECH

Courts across the world differ in their approaches to balancing the right to free speech and the right to privacy. The case law of the European Court of Human Rights (ECtHR) is interesting in this respect as the same Court is a quasi-constitutional jurisdiction, which expresses the constitutional ideology dominant in Europe. The European Convention on Human Rights (ECHR) protects freedom of expression in the clause of Article 10 which foresees 'duties and responsibilities' for the exercise of this liberty.[28]

---

[26] *Miami Herald Publishing Co v Tornillo*, 418 US 241 (1974). The Supreme Court held that a law of the state of Florida protecting the right to respond violates the First Amendment for, among others, the following reasons: '(b) the statute operates as a command by a State in the same sense as a statute or regulation forbidding appellant to publish specified matter' (at 256); '(c) the statute exacts a penalty on the basis of the content of a newspaper by imposing additional printing, composing, and materials costs and by taking up space that could be devoted to other material the newspaper may have preferred to print' (at 256–7); '(d) […] the statute still fails to clear the First Amendment's barriers because of its intrusion into the function of editors in choosing what material goes into a newspaper and in deciding on the size and content of the paper and the treatment of public issues and officials' (at 258).

[27] Code civil [Civil Code] art 6; Michel Friedman, *Les Droits de Réponse* (CPJ 1994); Yves Mayaud, 'L'Abus de Droit en Matière de Droit de Réponse' in Jean-Yves Dupeux et Alain Lacabarats (eds), *Liberté de la Presse et Droits de la Personne* (Dalloz 1997) 5, Martine Coisne et Jean Collin, 'Le Droit de Réponse dans la Communication Audiovisuelle' in Jean-Yves Dupeux et Alain Lacabarats (eds), *Liberté de la Presse et Droits de la Personne* (Dalloz 1997) 17, Jean-Paul Levy, 'Pratique du Droit de Réponse dans la Presse Écrite et la Communication Audiovisuelle' in Jean-Yves Dupeux et Alain Lacabarats (eds), *Liberté de la Presse et Droits de la Personne* (Dalloz 1997) 31.

[28] art 10 (2) of the ECHR provides that freedom of speech 'carries with it duties and responsibilities, [and] may be subject to such formalities, conditions, restrictions or penalties as are prescribed by law and are necessary in a democratic society, in the interests of national security, territorial integrity or public safety, for the prevention of disorder or crime, for the protection of health or morals, for the protection of the reputation or rights of others, for preventing the disclosure of information received in confidence, or for maintaining the authority and impartiality of the judiciary'. See Jean-François Flauss, 'La Cour Européenne des droits de l'homme et la Liberté d'expression' in Elisabeth Zoller (ed), *La Liberté d'expression aux Etats-Unis et en Europe* (Dalloz 2008) 97; F Tulkens, 'Report' in *La liberté d'expression et le droit au respect de la vie privée* (Council of Europe, DH-MM, 2000) 19; Council of Europe, *Freedom of Expression in Europe, Case-Law Concerning Article 10 of the European Convention on Human Rights* (Council of Europe 2007).

Privacy is protected by Article 8 of this same convention.[29] The ECtHR interprets broadly the right to privacy compared to the US Supreme Court. The ECtHR rendered the standards of free speech versus privacy dominant in France applicable throughout Europe. For the ECtHR, the privacy of a member of the family of one of the European monarchies is protected, even when the person is in a public place in an activity which is not in direct relation with public life; the Court held that Germany had violated Article 8 of the Convention for not providing to the applicant the protection of private life that she would have enjoyed in France.[30]

The case law of the ECtHR on issues that involve balancing freedom of expression and privacy moves towards protecting freedom of expression under the influence of the case law of the US Supreme Court. For instance, the ECtHR held that under Article 10 of the ECHR, the publication of a discussion on a topic of public interest obtained through interception by persons other than those who gave publicity is protected.[31] The ECtHR followed, in this case, the *Bartnicki v Vopper*[32] decision of the US Supreme Court, which held that the First Amendment protects the transmission of a discussion obtained by interception in violation of federal and state law on a question of public interest. Despite this influence, a strict regime of privacy protection is still dominant in Europe.

The right to privacy is protected in many European legal systems under the general category of 'personality rights', formed in order to protect elements of the personality of the subject—natural and moral, individual and social.[33] Continental civil law accepts an ontological unity between the person and their body.[34] French courts protect under the right to 'privacy' a person's health, sexual preference,[35] nudity,[36] maternity,[37] and death.[38] They also protect family life, the psychological or affective relation that the

---

[29] Which foresees in art 10(2) that: 'There shall be no interference by a public authority with the exercise of this right except such as is in accordance with the law and is necessary in a democratic society in the interests of national security, public safety or the economic well-being of the country, for the prevention of disorder or crime, for the protection of health or morals, or for the protection of the rights and freedoms of others'.

[30] *Von Hannover v Germany* (2005) 40 EHRR 1, concerning the publication of pictures of a member of a royal family in public places during activities, which according to the Court are 'private'.

[31] *Radio Twist v Slovakia* App no 62207/00 (ECtHR, 19 December 2006).

[32] *Bartnicki v Vopper*, 532 US 514 (2001). See also Jesse A Mudd, 'Right to Privacy v Freedom of Speech: A Review and Analysis of *Bartnicki v Vopper*' (2002) 41 Brandeis LJ 179. Previous famous cases are *Pearson v Dodd*, 410 F 2d 710, 133 (DC Cir 1969); *McNally v Pulitzer Publishing Co*, 532 F 2d 69, 79, n 14 (8th Cir 1976).

[33] In France, see Jean Dabin, *Le Droit Subjectif* (LGDJ 2007) 170–1.

[34] In relation to French law, see generally Jean Carbonnier, *Droit Civil I; Les Personnes: Personnalité, Incapacités, Personnes Morales* (PUF 2000).

[35] Tribunal de grande instance Paris, 14 June 1985, D 1991; JCP 1991, II, 21724, soc, 447, obs by A Sériaux.

[36] Cour d'appel Paris, 14 May 1976, D 1976, JCP 1976, 291.

[37] Tribunal de grande instance Paris, 27 Feb 1981, D 1981, 457, com by R Lindon.

[38] Tribunal de grande instance Paris, 13 Jan 1997, D 1998, com 255, obs B Beigner (Fr).

person maintains with their family, whether legitimate or natural,[39] and the personal problems between a married couple.[40] Reporting judiciary proceedings relative to divorce actions and publishing any information from their files is forbidden.[41] Emotional life,[42] religious convictions,[43] holiday, and leisure[44] are equally protected. Publication of a picture of one's residence without authorization constitutes invasion of privacy.[45] The image, a constitutive element of the person, occupies a privileged position in the protection of privacy in French law in reference to the 'moral interests of the person'.[46] In French law, the public's right to know concerning public officials covers only the private facts which relate to their public office.[47] Information must be 'strictly' related to public office. In a series of decisions, French courts held that the protection of medical confidentiality and the right to privacy outweighs the public interest in the health status of a former president of the republic, even if the revelations relating to his health prove that the official lied about his health status.[48] In an appeal before the ECtHR on the grounds of violation of freedom of speech by the ban in the circulation of a book by the president's doctor after his death, the court found that there had been no violation of the right to free speech by the early decisions close to the president's death.[49] For the Court, the distribution soon after the president's death of a book which depicted him as having consciously lied to the French people about the existence and duration of his illness, and

---

[39] Cour de cassation 2e civ, 22 May 1996, D 1996 inf rap 196 (concerning the illicit revelation of the existence of a natural child by the father shortly before his death); Cour de cassation [supreme court for judicial matters] 1e civ, 25 Feb 1997, Bull civ I, No 141 (Fr).

[40] Tribunal de grande instance Paris, 3 Oct 1986, D 1987 inf rap 137.

[41] loi du 29 juillet 1881 sur la liberté de la presse, Journal Officiel de la République Française, 29 July 29 1881, art 39.

[42] Cour d'appel Paris, 5 Mar 1969, JCP 1969, II, 15894.

[43] Crim, 28 fevrier 1874, S 1874, 233 (comment by E Naquet: The protection covers acts of worship of a person inside their home and in a public place).

[44] Tribunal de grande instance Paris, 29 May 1996, Légipresse 1996 135 I, 122 (apart from newsworthy information, narrowly conceived, and independently of whether the person is a public figure); Tribunal de grande instance, Paris, 2 Aug 1996, Légipresse, no. 137-I, 155 (Fr) (whether the person is in a public place or not.); Tribunal de grande instance, Nanterre, 10 Sept 1997, Légipresse 1998 148 I, 10 (if the information at stake concerns her holiday, it constitutes violation of privacy).

[45] Tribunal de grande instance Seine, 1 Apr 1965, JCP 1966, II, 14572 (F).

[46] Emmanuel Dreyer, 'L'Image de la Personne' in Henri Blin, Albert Chavanne, and Roland Drago (eds), Traité du Droit de la Presse (Librairies Techniques 1969) 303.

[47] For a detailed analysis of privacy cases, where the divergence between France and the United States is clearer, see Ioanna Tourkochoriti, 'Speech, Privacy and Dignity in France and the USA: A Comparative Analysis' (2016) 38 Loy LA Int'l & Comp L Rev 217.

[48] TGI Paris, 1re ch, 23 Oct 1996, Cts Mitterrand c/Gubler et a, La Semaine Juridique, JCP, Ed G, no 21, 22844, 1997, 237, com. by Em. Derieux, Dalloz, Sommaires Commentés, 1998, 85-6. com by Thierry Massis. The Paris Court of Appeal upheld the judgment CA Paris, 1re ch A, 27 May 1997, Editions Plon et autres c/Cts Mitterrand, Dalloz, Sommaires Commentés, 1998, pp 85-6. com by Thierry Massis. The Court of Cassation dismissed an appeal on points of law Cour de Cassation, 1re Chambre Civile, 14 December 1999, O.Orban et Société des Editions Plon, Légipresse, n° 169, March 2000, III Cours et Tribunaux, 27-8, note by ED. For a presentation of the case, see the contribution of Arnaud de Raulin in Gilles Lebreton, (ed), Les Droits Fondamentaux de la Personne Humaine en 1995 et 1996 (L'Harmattan 1998) 115-26.

[49] Editions Plon v France (2006) 42 EHRR 36.

which constituted a prima facie breach of medical confidentiality, could only have intensified the grief of the president's heirs. Considerations related to his privacy and that of the family outweighed the public interest. Similarly, the damages French courts ordered the publisher to pay to the president's family were not incompatible with Article 10. The same Court considered that later decisions maintaining the ban on the book no longer met a pressing social need. As time elapsed, public interest prevailed. In addition, the book was already widely known to the public.

The US Supreme Court is predisposed in favour of finding any conceivable justification to refuse media responsibility.[50] The high value attributed to freedom of speech and the precedent of *New York Times v Sullivan*[51] prevent recovery of compensatory damages by public officials for publication of private facts.[52] The case, by imposing stringent, almost impossible to meet, requirements of fault, marked the 'denigration' of the defamation tort for public officials in the United States.[53] It held that a public official cannot recover damages for a defamatory falsehood relating to his official conduct unless he proves that the statement was made with 'actual malice'—that is, with knowledge that it was false or with reckless disregard of whether it was false or not. In this general frame, the question of relevance of the information concerning public figures is likely to be framed as a content-based distinction, and to be presumed suspicious in relation to the values protected by the First Amendment to the Constitution.

16.4.1 Privacy at the Periphery

The difference in the protection of the two rights is visible on the periphery of the two rights. In France the right to privacy is protected by article 9 of the French Civil Code and by articles 226 of the French Penal Code. Article 9 of the civil code foresees civil responsibility for violations of the right[54] and refers to privacy as a 'notion-frame'. Articles 226-1 to 226-9 of the French Penal Code criminalize the gathering, recording, and transmission of confidential speech and the image of a person that is in a private space and any relevant publication.[55] In the United States, the right is protected by common law and the legislation of the various states. In tort law there are four kinds of action, which correspond to four kinds of violation of privacy: unreasonable publicity given to private facts, intrusion upon seclusion, false light privacy and appropriation of one's image for commercial purposes.[56] Some states maintain legislation criminalizing

---

[50] Paul Gewirtz, 'Privacy and Speech' [2001] *Sup Ct Rev* 139, 140.   [51] *Sullivan* (n 1) 254.
[52] Ibid 279.
[53] Harry Kalven Jr, 'The New York Times Case: A Note on 'The Central Meaning of the First Amendment' [1964] *Sup Ct Rev* 191, 205.
[54] According to which: 'Everyone has a right to respect of their privacy. The judges can prescribe all measures, apart from the reparation of the harm done, such as sequestration, seizure, and others appropriate to prevent or stop a violation to the intimacy of privacy: these measures can if there is an emergence be ordered by preliminary injunction'.
[55] Available at: <https://www.legifrance.gouv.fr/content/location/1740> accessed 15 October 2020.
[56] *Cox Broadcasting Corp v Cohn*, 420 US 469, 496 (1975) div 6Ach 28A s 652f.

intrusion upon seclusion. Nevertheless, in some US states there appear to be no holdings related to the common law tort.

16.4.2 Hard Cases

A series of hard cases concerning the balancing of the right to freedom of expression and the protection of privacy relate to the publication of elements of identification of persons participating in newsworthy events. Regarding the publication of elements of identification of the persons involved in judicial proceedings, minor delinquents, and victims of sexual aggressions, there is a difference between European states and the United States. In France, a regime of strict protection of the personality rights of newsworthy persons applies. Law 2000-516, 'Strengthening the protection of the presumption of innocence and victims' rights', prohibits the publication of any element of identification of victims of sexual aggressions and minor delinquents in France.[57] The same law criminalizes the publication of images related to suspects and to victims of crimes, as well as 'the transmission by any medium of the reproduction of the circumstances of a crime or an offence, when this reproduction violates the dignity of the victim'.[58] The law, reflecting long case law on the same topic, maintains the necessity of the consent of the person, for publication of these elements.[59] Publicizing elements of a sexual assault victim's identity, images of a person accused in a criminal proceeding that has not yet been condemned,[60] of a minor victim[61] or author of an offence,[62] incurs criminal liability. As an exception to the general rule of criminal trial transparency,[63] trials against minors may not be made public.[64] The ECtHR has held that there is a violation of the right to privacy in the publication of photos of persons arrested or under criminal prosecution unless the person is a public figure.[65] For instance, the publication of the photo of a teacher prosecuted for irregularities in the management of the school where she taught was considered to be a violation of the right to privacy.[66] So too was the

---

[57] loi n° 2000–516 du 15 juin 2000 renforçant la protection de la présomption d'innocence et les droits des victimes, Journal Officiel de la République Française, 16 juin 2000, 9038.

[58] Ibid.

[59] loi n° 2000–516 du 15 juin 2000 renforçant la protection de la présomption d'innocence et les droits des victimes.

[60] Ibid, art 35.3. ('Wearing handcuffs or being in a provisory detention'. The same article criminalizes the realization or publication or commentary of an opinion poll or any other consultation concerning the culpability of a person involved in a criminal proceeding or on the punishment likely to be imposed on them.).

[61] Ibid, art 39.2.   [62] Ibid, art 39.   [63] Code Pénal, art 306.   [64] Ibid.

[65] Österreichischer Rundfunk v Austria App no 35841/02 (ECtHR, 7 December 2006) (related to the publication of the photo of the deputy head of a neo-Nazi organization convicted under the National Socialist Prohibition Act); Verlagsgruppe News GmbH v Austria (No 2) App 10520/02 (ECtHR, 14 December 2006) (related to the publication of reports on investigations against a businessman including his photo).

[66] Sciacca v Italy (2016) 43 EHRR 20.

publication of the photo of a person charged with kidnapping and torture,[67] and the photo of a defendant in a criminal trial in which that person was identifiable.[68] Even the publication of the photo of a person convicted of having committed a criminal offence is a violation of the right to privacy.[69]

According to the US Supreme Court, however, information in public files, such as judiciary files, is in the public domain, and can thus be reported by the media, provided it has been lawfully obtained.[70] The US Supreme Court has held in a number of cases that the press's publication of the identity of a minor who is the victim of a sexual assault, or a delinquent minor's identity, is constitutional. State laws prohibiting this type of publication were not upheld under the First Amendment.[71] In *Cox Broadcasting Corp v Cohn*,[72] the Court held, in a narrow ruling, that a Georgia law prohibiting the publication of the name or identity of a victim of sexual aggression was unconstitutional. The protection of her privacy did not outweigh the press's freedom of expression, as the information was obtained from a public record—the indictments available for inspection in the courtroom.[73] The Court stressed the legitimate interest of the public in a newsworthy criminal event and the resulting legal process.[74] It referred to the responsibility of the press to report the operations of government, associated with the Madisonian concept of self-government and to the public benefit resulting from receiving information on the actions of government.

In *Florida Star v BJF*,[75] concerning again the publication of the identity of a victim of a sexual aggression, the Court held that freedom of the press outweighs the victim's interest in privacy, since the information published was true and had been lawfully obtained. The journalist had obtained the name of the victim from a police report in the pressroom of the Florida Police Department.[76] Florida had enacted a law, similar in many respects to the one valid in France, making it unlawful to publish the name of a sexual offence victim.[77] The Court recognized that the law served significant interests like the protection of privacy, physical security of victims facing potential retaliation, and encouraging the reporting of crime without fear of exposure. However, the Court considered that holding the publisher liable would be contrary to the First Amendment as, among other reasons, the information was already in the public sphere, in a report

---

[67] *Khuzhin and Others v Russia* App no 13470/02 (ECtHR 23 October 2008).
[68] *Axel Springer SE and RTL Television GmbH v Germany* App no 51405/12 (21 September 2017).
[69] *Egeland and Hanseid v Norway* (2010) 50 EHRR 2.
[70] *Cox* (n 19); *Florida Star v BJF*, 491 US 524, 524 (1989).
[71] See, generally, *Cox* (n 19); *Smith v Daily Mail Publishing Co*, 443 US 97, 108–9 (1979); *Globe Newspaper v Superior Court*, 457 US 596, 607–8 (1982); *Florida Star* (n 70) 524.
[72] *Cox* (n 19) 495–6.   [73] Ibid 496–7.   [74] Ibid 493–5.   [75] *Florida Star* (n 70) 524.
[76] Ibid 535–6.
[77] 1987 Fla Stat s 794.03 provides in its entirety: 'Unlawful to publish or broadcast information identifying sexual offense victim. No person shall print, publish, or broadcast, or cause or allow to be printed, published, or broadcast, in any instrument of mass communication the name, address, or other identifying fact or information of the victim of any sexual offense within this chapter. An offense under this section shall constitute a misdemeanor of the second degree, punishable as provided in s 775.083, or s 775.084'.

available to everyone in the police department's pressroom.⁷⁸ A second problem with Florida's law was that it established a wide scope of the negligence per se standard applied under the civil cause of action. For the Court 'on the basis of the negligence per se standard, the publication per se was enough to hold the editors liable, without taking into consideration other factors such as whether the identity of the victim was already known in the community, whether the victim had voluntarily attracted public attention on the aggression, or whether the identity of the victim had otherwise become a subject of public interest'.⁷⁹ The French law banning the publication of elements of identification of the victims of sexual aggressions is phrased in such a way that the editor is held directly liable for the publication.⁸⁰

In *Globe Newspaper v Superior Court*,⁸¹ the Supreme Court held that the interest in protecting minor victims of sexual aggression from further trauma and embarrassment does not justify a mandatory closure rule in trial, but only a requirement that the trial court, on a case-by-case basis, determine whether the State's legitimate concern for the minor victim's well-being necessitates closure. The Massachusetts law foreseeing a general closure of the proceedings⁸² from the public violates the First Amendment and the necessity to assure an informed 'discussion of governmental affairs'.⁸³

Although the US Supreme Court attributes some weight to the protection of minor victims of sexual aggressions from trauma or embarrassment, it attributes even less weight to the rehabilitation of minor delinquents.⁸⁴ In *Oklahoma Publishing Co v District Court*,⁸⁵ it held that a state court injunction prohibiting the publication of the name and the picture of a minor tried before a juvenile court was contrary to the First and Fourth Amendments, since the elements of identification of the minor had been taken during the instruction of the young delinquent, when the members of the press were present, without any objection on behalf of the judge, the prosecutor or his defence counsel. The name and the picture of the young delinquent had been published in a report concerning judiciary proceedings against the crime.⁸⁶ In *Smith v Daily Mail Publishing Co*,⁸⁷ the Court once again held contrary to the First and Fourteenth Amendments of the Federal Constitution, the criminalization by a West Virginia Statute

---

⁷⁸ *Florida Star* (n 70) 524.
⁷⁹ Ibid 540 (This requirement of the law was not in conformity to the common law tort of invasion of privacy which requires case-by-case findings that the disclosure of a fact about a person's private life was one that a reasonable person would find highly offensive).
⁸⁰ Ordinance 45–174 2 février 1945, art 14.   ⁸¹ *Globe Newspaper* (n 71) 607–8.
⁸² Mass Gen Laws Ann, ch 278 s 16A, provides in pertinent part: 'At the trial of a complaint or indictment for rape, incest, carnal abuse or other crime involving sex, where a minor under eighteen years of age is the person upon, with or against whom the crime is alleged to have been committed… the presiding justice shall exclude the general public from the court room, admitting only such persons as may have a direct interest in the case'.
⁸³ *Globe Newspaper* (n 71) 604–5.   ⁸⁴ Ibid 608–9.
⁸⁵ *Oklahoma Publishing Co* 430 US 308, 310–11 (1977).   ⁸⁶ Ibid 311.
⁸⁷ *Smith* (n 71) 108–9.

of the publication of the name of a minor delinquent accused of murder,[88] when the information was 'lawfully' obtained by the press. The Court held that, regardless of whether the law operated as a prior restraint or as a penal sanction, only an imperative interest could justify criminal sanctions on a newspaper for the truthful publication of an alleged juvenile delinquent's name that was lawfully obtained.[89] The State's asserted interests in protecting the anonymity of juvenile offenders to further their rehabilitation—since publication may encourage antisocial conduct and may cause the juvenile to lose further employment or suffer other consequences—were not sufficient to justify criminal sanctions.[90] Juvenile proceedings may be open to the media and the information collected from them considered 'lawfully obtained'; by contrast in France, there is a general prohibition against public access to juvenile proceedings and to the publication of any information concerning them.[91] In the state of California, publication of the names of minor delinquents accused of crimes is protected, since the media 'has a statutory right to attend the hearing and a constitutional right to say what transpires'.[92]

Unlike in France, the publication of pictures of persons arrested by police wearing handcuffs is protected in the United States, and innocent bystanders at a police raid erroneously implicated are not entitled to relief.[93] Courts impose the actual malice standard for matters of public concern; mere negligence is not enough.[94]

Another category of newsworthy persons concerns participants in newsworthy events. The French Conseil Superieur de l'Audiovisuel issued a warning to public broadcasting corporations for broadcasting images of victims of the terrorist attack in Nice in July 2016 that were contrary to 'human dignity'.[95] The ECtHR has also held that limitations on the publication of the photo of a public official who was the victim of a terrorist attack are not a violation of the right to freedom of speech.[96]

---

[88] The challenged West Virginia statute, W Va Code s 49-7-3 (1976), provided: '[Nor] shall the name of any child, in connection with any proceedings under this chapter, be published in any newspaper without a written order of the court'. See also W Va Code s 49-7-20 (1976) ('A person who violates...a provision of this chapter for which punishment has not been specifically provided, shall be guilty of a misdemeanor, and upon conviction shall be fined not less than ten nor more than one hundred dollars, or confined in jail not less than five days nor more than six months, or both such fine and imprisonment').
[89] Smith (n 71) 102.   [90] Ibid 104.   [91] Ibid 106 (Rehnquist J, concurring).
[92] KGTV Channel 10 v Superior Court, 26 Cal App 4th 1673, 1675 (1994).
[93] Williams v KCMO Broadcasting Division Meredith Corp, 472 SW 2d 1 (Mo Ct App 1971) (news broadcast showing person arrested by mistake is newsworthy and thus protected).
[94] Pfannenstiel v Osborne Publishing Co, 939 F Supp 1497, 1497, 1502 (D Kan 1996) (similarly, a private individual whose photograph was mistakenly published in a newspaper as that of a convicted mentally ill murderer cannot recover for false-light invasion of privacy, unless a reckless or intentional act is proven rather than mere negligence). See also Colbert v World Pub Co, 747 P 2d 286, 290 (Okla 1987).
[95] See Margaut Lacroux, 'Attentat de Nice: de possibles sanctions pour France 2', Libération, 29 juillet 2016 <http://www.liberation.fr/futurs/2016/07/29/attentat-de-nice-de-possibles-sanctions-pour-france-2_1469304> accessed 26 April 2019.
[96] Hachette Filipacchi Associates v France (2009) 49 EHRR 23.

16.4.3 The Spatial Criterion

Some legal systems follow the spatial criterion in order to define legal responsibility. Privacy should be protected independently of whether a person is in a private or public place. French case law considers as a violation of privacy the publication of photos focusing on a person, whether they are in a public or a private place.[97] The French *Cour de Cassation* has referred to article 9 of the Civil Code as the legal basis to protect the right to one's image, considering that the right is protected whether the person is in a public or a private place.[98] The ECtHR has held that the spatial criterion is valid under the ECHR.[99] In the US legal system, it is permissible to publish a photo of a person taken in a public place, independently of whether the person consents or not. Consent is presumed the moment that the person is in a public place.[100]

16.4.4 Institutional Considerations and Aspects of Privacy

In general, privacy in the United States is protected against violations by the government and less against violations coming from civil society.[101] US law protects a core of privacy in association with autonomy in the area of the most important decisions that concern the self. The Supreme Court read a right to privacy in the US Constitution in *Griswold v Connecticut*[102] in relation to contraception. Justice Douglas famously noted that 'specific guarantees in the Bill of Rights have penumbras, formed by emanations from those guarantees that help give them life and substance... Various guarantees create zones of privacy'.[103] Justice Goldberg proposes as a foundation of the right to privacy the Ninth Amendment according to which '[t]he enumeration in the Constitution, of certain rights, shall not be construed to deny or disparage others retained by the people'. As he notes, it was conceived by James Madison 'to quiet express fears that a bill of specifically enumerated rights could not be sufficiently broad to cover all essential rights and that the specific mention of certain rights would be interpreted as a denial that others were protected'.[104] US Supreme Court cases contain a strong rhetoric in favour of 'choices

---

[97] Jacques Ravanas, *La Protection Des Personnes Contre La Réalisation Et La Publication De Leur Image* (LJDG 1978).

[98] Cour de Cassation 1e civ, 12 Dec 2000, Bull civ I, no 98-17521 (Fr) (which ruled that the publication of the image of a child 'isolated from the manifestation, during which the picture was taken' without the authorization of the parents constitutes a violation of the right to privacy).

[99] *Peck v the United Kingdom* (2003) 36 EHRR 41.

[100] *Gill v Hearst Pub Co*, 40 Cal 2d 224 (1953), *Stessman v Am Black Hawk Broadcasting*, 416 N W 2d 685 (Iowa 1987).

[101] See James Q Whitman, 'The Two Western Cultures of Privacy: Dignity Versus Liberty' (2004) 113 Yale LJ 1151, 1178.

[102] *Griswold v Connecticut*, 381 US 479, 486 (1965).   [103] Ibid 484.

[104] Ibid 488–9.

central to personal dignity and autonomy'.[105] The same court has held that there is a reasonable expectation of privacy in a telephone booth, in an office,[106] the apartment of a friend,[107] a taxi,[108] and a vehicle more generally.[109] The Court has also held that the warrantless search and seizure of the contents of a cell phone is unconstitutional.[110]

The tendency in the judgments of the Court in the cases it had to adjudicate balancing the right to information and privacy is to favour the protection of the former to the detriment of the latter. Structural differences between the United States and European countries are also important.[111] European countries apply the protection of constitutional rights against both private and public actors. This means that the constitutional protection of privacy can be invoked against private actors like the press. In the United States, the protection of constitutional rights applies only against the state. The concern to protect liberty against limitations coming by the state and the distrust towards government intervention in civil society is expressed by the state action doctrine.[112] The case law of the US Supreme Court focuses on the protection of negative liberty. It does not accept what is considered in Europe as the horizontal effect of the protection of rights ('effet tiers' in French, 'Drittenwirkung' in German). It is not legitimate for the state to intervene in private relations to enforce the respect of the constitutional rights by civil society actors. These structural reasons indicate the culture of distrust dominant in the United States against state intervention within civil society.

16.4.5 A Closer Look at Speech and Data Privacy

The recent history of the protection of free speech under the First Amendment in the United States shows that it has served as a 'powerful engine of constitutional deregulation'[113] in many areas where government regulation is accepted in Europe. Informational privacy is not considered a value significant enough to mobilize state coercion in the United States. The government cannot legitimately intervene within civil society and limit the collection of data by private actors. Academics debate whether data should be submitted to economic liberty, an argument that would facilitate their protection, or

---

[105] *Planned Parenthood v Casey*, 505 US 833 (1992) (joint opinion), *Lawrence v Texas*, 539 US 558 (2003).
[106] *Silverthorne Lumber Co v United States*, 251 US 385 (1920).
[107] *Jones v United States*, 362 US 257 (1960). [108] *Rios v United States*, 364 US 253 (1960).
[109] *United States v Jones*, 565 US 400 (2012). [110] *Riley v California*, 573 US (2014).
[111] See Ronald J Krotoszynski Jr, *Privacy Revisited, A Global Perspective on the Right to be Left Alone* (OUP 2016) 8.
[112] Charles L Black Jr, 'Foreword: State Action, Equal Protection, and California's Proposition' (1967) 81 Harv L Rev 69; Robert J Glennon Jr and John E Nowak, 'A Functional Analysis of the Fourteenth Amendment "State Action" Requirement' [1976] Sup Ct Rev 221; Louis Michael Seidman and Mark Tushnet, *Remnants of Belief, Contemporary Constitutional Issues* (OUP 1996) ch 3, 49; Mark Tushnet, 'The Issue of State Action/Horizontal Effect in Comparative Constitutional Law' (2003) 1 Int'l J Const Law 79.
[113] Robert Post and Amanda Shanor, 'Adam Smith's First Amendment' (2015) 128 Harv L Rev F 165.

whether they should be excluded from such a protection.[114] Although some think that data collection should be regulated, US law treats the protection of data privacy on a case-by-case basis.[115] The Supreme Court struck down a Vermont law that barred pharmacies from disclosing information to 'data miners'.[116] The creation, assemblage, and communication of information are seen to be in the core of the First Amendment. It is an expressive activity, which should be protected over the rights of the persons concerned.[117] The protective regulation of the state would be an unjustifiable limit to speech.

The United States maintains legislation that secures privacy rights in limited contexts. For instance, the Health Insurance Portability and Accountability Act[118] protects the confidentiality of a patient's medical records. As Ronald Krotoszynski has noted,[119] in practice medical care providers ask their patients to waive a substantial portion of their rights under the law so that the providers may communicate with medical insurance companies and others to obtain benefits. This means that in practice privacy protection is circumscribed almost as a rule. What is more, Congress passed legislation in 2008, which gave retroactive immunity to telephone companies that facilitated the domestic programme that allowed the government to wiretap telephone calls between US residents and citizens of another nation. On the contrary, the Court of Justice of the European Union (CJEU) invalidated an EU Directive on Data Retention for counterterrorism purposes.[120] Data privacy raises concerns related to threats coming from private actors and the government. US government reluctance to intervene in civil society means that it hesitates to intervene in order to protect individuals from violations of their rights both against civil society and the government. In the area of data privacy, the government collects data for counterterrorism purposes from civil society actors. The reluctance to regulate the data private actors collect enables the government to collect data too.

---

[114] Neil M Richards, 'Reconciling Data Privacy and the First Amendment' (2005) 52 *UCLA L Rev* 1149, 1216.

[115] Jeffrey Rosen's book *The Unwanted Gaze, the Destruction of Privacy in America* (Vintage 2001) presents a cases of violation of privacy by private actors showing the reluctance and the delay with which the state reacts to these violations. See also Paul M Schwartz, 'The EU-US Privacy Collision: A Turn to Institutions and Procedures' (2013) 126 *Harv L Rev* 1966, 1978–9 (discussing the US approach that is largely unregulated, giving companies freedom to 'try new kinds of data processing'); Ioanna Tourkochoriti, 'The Transatlantic Flow of Data and the National Security Exception in the European Data Privacy Regulation: In Search for Legal Protection against Surveillance' (2014) 36 *U Penn J Int'l Law* 459; Paul M Schwartz and Daniel J Solove, 'Reconciling Personal Information in the United States and European Union' (2014) 102 *Cal L Rev* 877, 880.

[116] *Sorrel v IMS Health Inc*, 564 US 552 (2011).

[117] Eugene Volokh, 'Freedom of Speech and Information Privacy: The Troubling Implications of a Right to Stop People from Speaking about You' (2000) 52 *Stan L Rev* 1049; A Michael Froomkin, 'The Death of Privacy?' (2000) 52 *Stan L Rev* 1461.

[118] Health Insurance Portability and Accountability Act of 1996, Pub L No 104–91, 110 Stat 1936 (42 USC s 1301ff).

[119] Krotoszynski (n 111) 56.

[120] Case C-293/12 *Digital Rights Ireland Ltd v Minister for Communications, Marine and Natural Resources* [2014] WLR 1607.

In Europe, the right to privacy against the private sector is protected by Articles 7[121] and 8[122] of the European Union Charter of Rights[123] and by secondary legislation. The European Union General Data Privacy Regulation 2016/679 (GDPR)[124] enhances the system of data protection existing in the EU under Directive 95/46/EC,[125] and creates the obligation on Member States to take measures protecting personal data 'revealing racial or ethnic origin, political opinions, religious or philosophical beliefs, trade union membership, and the processing of data concerning health or sex life'.[126] The Directive allows the states to foresee derogations or exemptions for the processing of personal data 'carried out solely for journalistic purposes or the purpose of artistic or literary expression only if they are necessary to reconcile the right to privacy with the rules governing freedom of expression'.[127] In parallel, Directive 2002/58/EC of the European Parliament and of the Council of 12 July 2002 concerning the processing of personal data and the protection of privacy in the electronic communications sector contains detailed provisions for the protection of the right to privacy.

The difference in the legal protection of data privacy between the US and Europe, has given occasion for a rich transatlantic debate. The CJEU has elaborated important case law on the protection of data privacy related to transatlantic data transfers. It invalidated the EU Data Retention Directive,[128] which enabled telephone companies to retain metadata concerning phone communications for two years.[129] For the same court, the Directive did not foresee where the data would be kept, allowing for outsourcing to the United States where it would not be protected. The CJEU invalidated the Commission Decision 2000/520/EC of 26 July 2000 pursuant to Directive 95/46 on the adequacy of the protection provided by the safe harbour privacy principles issued by the US Department of Commerce.[130] On the basis of this decision, US-based companies offering their services to EU citizens were able to transfer data outside the EU. According to the Court, the national security exception in the safe harbour privacy principles was too

---

[121] According to which: 'Everyone has the right to respect for his or her private and family life, home and communications'.

[122] According to which: '1. Everyone has the right to the protection of personal data concerning him or her. 2. Such data must be processed fairly for specified purposes and on the basis of the consent of the person concerned or some other legitimate basis laid down by law. Everyone has the right of access to data, which has been collected concerning him or her, and the right to have it rectified. 3. Compliance with these rules shall be subject to control by an independent authority'.

[123] For an analysis of the various EU Directives protecting privacy and the differences with the US protection in the same area, see Ioanna Tourkochoriti, 'The Snowden Revelations, the Transatlantic Trade and Investment Partnership and the US–EU Divide in Data Privacy Protection' (2014) 36 U Ark Little Rock L Rev 161. See also Tourkochoriti, 'The Transatlantic Flow of Data' (n 115).

[124] 'On the protection of natural persons with regard to the processing of personal data and on the free movement of such data' and repealing Directive 95/46/EC: [2016] OJ L 119/1.

[125] Of the Parliament and the Council of 24 October 1995, 'On the protection of individuals with regard to the processing of personal data and on the free movement of such data': [1995] OJ L 281/31–50.

[126] art 8(1).   [127] art 9.

[128] Directive 2006/24/EC of the European Parliament and of the Council of 15 March 2006 [2016] OJ L 105/54.

[129] *Digital Rights Ireland Ltd* (n 120).

[130] Case C-362/14 *Schrems v Data Protection Commissioner* [2016] 2 WLR 873.

broad. Both decisions showed concern to protect data privacy for EU citizens against the collection of US authorities. Following the invalidation by the CJEU of the safe harbour agreement, the EU and the United States elaborated a new 'Privacy Shield agreement' on data transfers between the EU and the United States, which applies to the commercial sector.[131] The agreement arguably raised the standards of protection of data of citizens in the United States as well. Nevertheless, the CJEU found for a second time that the protection afforded by the US legal system was not equivalent to that guaranteed by the GDPR read in light of the European Charter of Rights.[132] For the CJEU, the agreement contained a derogation from the protection of privacy for national security which did not meet the requirement of proportionality foreseen by the European Charter of Rights (article 52(1)). US legislation on the national security exception (section 702 of the FISA and Executive Order 12333) does not indicate any limitations on the powers it confers to surveillance programmes for the purposes of foreign intelligence or the existence of guarantees for non-US persons potentially targeted by those programmes. It does not grant data subjects enforceable rights before the courts against the US authorities. Neither does it offer effective legal remedies. In the area of law enforcement, the United States and the EU have elaborated a new 'Umbrella Agreement'.[133] The agreement covers all personal data exchanged between the EU and the US for the purpose of the prevention, detection, investigation and prosecution of criminal offences, including terrorism.

16.4.6 The Right to Be Forgotten

The French and many other European legal systems recognize a 'right to be forgotten'.[134] Giving publicity to past criminal convictions, disciplinary measures, and forfeitures of rights to which amnesty has been given entails criminal responsibility.[135] Courts have ordered the suppression of scenes in a film about a criminal convict, describing real life events, for the protection of the privacy of the convict's partner.[136] They have also accepted the seizure of a book through preliminary injunction that presented facts about a minor already known to the public, as it provided a new combination of disparate

---

[131] See 'Commercial Sector: EU–US Privacy Shield' <https://ec.europa.eu/info/law/law-topic/data-protection/international-dimension-data-protection/eu-us-data-transfers_en> accessed 15 October 2020.

[132] Case C-311/18 *Data Protection Commissioner v Facebook Ireland and Maximilian Schrems* (CJEU, 16 July 2020).

[133] See 'Law Enforcement: EU – US Umbrella Agreement' <https://ec.europa.eu/info/law/law-topic/data-protection/international-dimension-data-protection/eu-us-data-transfers_en#law-enforcement-cooperation-eu-us-umbrella-agreement> accessed 26 July 2020.

[134] Cour de Cassation Civile 2nd Chamber, 4 July 1973, application no 72-12123 (publication of the identity of the father of the child of public figure constitutes violation of privacy, even if already revealed, and led to liability of newspapers). Cour de cassation Civile 2nd Chamber, 14 Nov 1975, application n° 72-12123. See also Roseline Letteron, 'Le Droit à l'Oubli' [1996] Revue du Droit Public 385.

[135] See Letteron (n 134) pt 1(2)(c)(i).

[136] Cour de Cassation Civile 1st Chamber, 13 Feb 1985, application n° 72-12123. Cour de cassation Civile 1st Chamber, 3 Dec 1980, application n° 72-12123 (suppression of scenes depicting the reaction of victim's parents in a film on murder convict to the death penalty was not sufficiently justified by court of appeals as constituting violation of privacy).

information 'in a synthesis which provided to the event a new intensity'.[137] The right to be forgotten does not cover the narration of historical events in a book known to the public from reports on judicial proceedings.[138] In the spirit of accepting a strong protection for privacy, the CJEU reaffirmed the protection of a right to be forgotten. The decision in *Google v Spain*[139] posed the principle that a person has the right, under Articles 7 and 8 of the EU Charter of Rights, to have information concerning them removed from results that search engines make available to the public. In the context of speech, US courts are less willing to recognize a right to be forgotten.[140]

16.5 Conclusion

Judges in different parts of the world disagree on the coverage of the concept of privacy. Depending on their ex ante understanding of the notion inspired by a philosophical conception of 'privacy', they decide if some manifestation of human life should be protected in reference to the notion. It is a point where the philosophy of law overlaps with moral philosophy. The legal concept of privacy is dependent on the moral, philosophical concept of the same notion. In the US legal system, which places emphasis on freedom of speech, there is reluctance to protect privacy interests when the two are in conflict. More generally, informational privacy is not a value considered important enough to justify state coercion. In parallel, the concept of human dignity, associated with the concept of privacy, can serve in the United States to protect freedom of expression. In the case law of the ECtHR and many European states like France, it serves as a limit to freedom of speech. This reflects that in Europe it is legitimate for the government to intervene in order to protect privacy and the social status of a person when it is violated by speech. In the United States, the distrust towards the government leads to protecting freedom of expression, even to the detriment of the protection of privacy and human dignity. In Europe, it is legitimate for the government to intervene in order to assure that dignity as social status is protected. Although these jurisdictions influence one another, and the concept of newsworthiness progressively becomes broader, a firm doctrine in favour of protecting privacy persists in Europe. Technological developments and transatlantic data transfers pose additional challenges to the geographical variability in the protection of privacy. The efforts of European institutions to maintain the regime of strong protection also persist.

---

[137] Cour de cassation Civile 1st Chamber 18 May 1972, application n° 72–12123 (Rossi, case concerning the relation of a teacher with her minor student).

[138] Cour de cassation Civile 1st Chamber, 20 Nov 1990, application n° 72–12123. The case has stirred debate as to what extent the 'right to be forgotten' is still protected, see Catherine Costaz, 'Le Droit à l'Oubli' [1995] Gazette du Palais, Doctrine 961.

[139] Case C-131/12 Google Spain SL, *Google Inc. v. Agencia Española de Protección de Datos* (AEPD), 2014 EUR-Lex CELEX LEXIS 317 (May 13, 2014), s 28 <http://curia.europa.eu/juris/document/document.jsf?text=&docid=152065&pageIndex=0&doclang=EN&mode=lls&dir=&occ=first&part=1&cid=103833> accessed 26 April 2019.

[140] See *Sidis v F-R Publi'g Corp*, 113 F 2d 806 (2d Cir 1940).

CHAPTER 17

FREE SPEECH AND ELECTIONS

JOO-CHEONG THAM AND KD EWING[*]

17.1

ELECTIONS give rise to special problems relating to speech. It is at this moment that speech should be most uninhibited, and debate at its most vigorous. Candidates and political parties are seeking a mandate for office based on a programme for government presented to the electors. If successful, that mandate will authorize the candidates or parties in question to govern the lives of their fellow citizens for periods of four or five years. Not only do the programmes of the rival parties and candidates need to be heard, but they also need to be carefully scrutinized. The latter is a process that invites input from not only rival candidates and parties, but also third parties who have an interest in the outcome of the election. In the choice of government and governors, speech thus needs to be lively and robust, which is not to say of course that speech should be unconstrained.

Indeed, the paradox of elections is that they need both freedom *and* restraint if electoral purposes are to be served. The standards international treaties (to the extent that they deal with the matter) insist upon are that elections be 'free *and* fair', standards designed for and expected to accommodate different ideological positions.[1] The requirement of fairness of course begs many questions. But it does nevertheless put us on notice that an election is not a licence for offence or defamation, nor an opportunity for the unconstrained flaunting of private wealth. Elections also raise other questions not always encountered in contests where free speech is disputed. Thus, in the context between candidates and parties, who else should be permitted to speak, and what if anything should they be prohibited from saying?

---

[*] The authors wish to acknowledge their debt to Chris Kaias for invaluable support.

[1] See International IDEA, *International Obligations for Elections: Guidelines for Legal Frameworks* (International Institute for Democracy and Electoral Assistance 2014).

In the context of elections, however, what has become a bigger concern in modern liberal democracies is not (1) who may speak, and (2) what can they say; but (3) what means can they use, (4) what opportunities and restrictions are to apply to the means used, and (5) how much can be spent in projecting electoral messages? These latter questions do not address the content of speech so much as its volume, but they are urgent questions in light of the exponential increase in the sums spent by candidates, parties, and others in seeking to influence electoral outcomes. Candidates and parties at the US elections in 2016, for example, spent collectively an eye-watering US$6.5 billion in a country with 160,000,000 registered voters.[2] These non-content based restrictions form the primary focus of this chapter, though we also address two notably controversial content-based restraints.

17.2

In *Animal Defenders International*,[3] the European Court of Human Rights (ECtHR) was confronted with British legislation that banned all forms of political advertising on radio and television. In considering whether the legislation was compatible with European Convention on Human Rights (ECHR) rights the Court made an important reference to different visions of democracy to explain that questions of this kind could legitimately be resolved in different ways throughout the Council of Europe.[4] But if there are different visions of democracy within Europe, leading to different solutions to knotty free speech problems, so there are different visions between Europe and other parts of the world, calculated to produce, if not a wider range of solutions, then a variation on rationales for possible outcomes. So while the ECtHR could reflect at length on the ban, and divide 9–8 in upholding it, it is simply inconceivable that such a ban would be worth even trying to defend in the US Supreme Court.

This is simply to say that within the genus of western liberal democracies there are different ways by which questions of free speech in elections are thought about and addressed. These differences are reflected in constitutional texts, which instantly sets the United States apart. The First Amendment provides unequivocally that Congress shall make no law abridging freedom of speech. Period. Of course, it does not mean that there can be *no* abridgement of *any* kind, the Supreme Court having developed a substantial jurisprudence to the effect that limits can be imposed where there is a substantial

---

[2] Spending on the presidential election alone was US$2,386,876,712 and the congressional elections was US$4,124,304,874 for a total of US$6,511,181,587: 'Cost of Election' (OpenSecrets.org—Center for Responsive Politics, 2018) <https://www.opensecrets.org/overview/cost.php> accessed 21 February 2019.

[3] *Animal Defenders International v United Kingdom* (2013) 57 EHRR 21. For discussion, see Jacob Rowbottom, 'Political Advertising and the Broadcast Media' (2008) 67 *Cal LJ* 450; Jacob Rowbottom, '*Animal Defenders International*: Speech, Spending, and a Change of Direction in Strasbourg' (2013) 5 *J Media L* 1.

[4] *Animal Defenders International* (n 3) [111]: 'there is a wealth of historical, cultural and political differences within Europe so that it is for each State to mould its own democratic vision'. See also [123], referring to 'the wealth of differences in historical development, cultural diversity, political thought and, consequently, democratic vision of those States'.

government interest,⁵ which in the context of elections might include the risk of corruption.⁶ This contrasts sharply with the ECHR which protects not only the right to freedom of expression but also the right to impart and receive ideas (art 10(1)). To that extent formally it goes beyond the First Amendment. That said, however, the ECHR also constrains the right to freedom of expression by expressly permitting restrictions that are:

> prescribed by law and…necessary in a democratic society, in the interests of national security, territorial integrity or public safety, for the prevention of disorder or crime, for the protection of health or morals, for the protection of the reputation or rights of others, for preventing the disclosure of information received in confidence, or for maintaining the authority and impartiality of the judiciary (art 10(2)).

In the European context, the right to freedom of expression may thus be restricted by a wide range of public interest considerations, including the 'rights of others'. There is thus no sense in which free speech is trumps. The same is true of other Convention rights (including private life, religion and belief, and assembly and association). But to reinforce the point about the equivocal nature of free speech in the European system (especially when compared with the US system), Article 10 of the ECHR, dealing with freedom of expression, is the most heavily qualified of all Convention articles. There is no place for free speech fundamentalism in the European model, and indeed it is striking how free speech considerations can sometimes seem casually to be under-estimated if not casually overlooked. It is striking too that in determining how the balance is to be struck between free speech and other considerations, the European courts are much more willing than their US counterparts to defer to the wisdom of legislators.⁷

So when the ECHR says that restrictions may be imposed where they are 'necessary', in the hands of judges it does not mean necessary any more than in the United States 'no abridgement' does not mean no abridgement. Necessary for the purposes of Article 10 means proportionate, and in deciding what is proportionate, deference is shown to legislators, the degree of deference in election/political campaigning restrictions being surprisingly profound.⁸ This applies to cases which not only impose restrictions on the quantity of speech, prohibit certain means of communication, but also censor the

---

⁵ Some of these permitted restrictions are discussed in *Buckley v Valeo*, 424 US 1 (1976); *Citizens United v Federal Electoral Commission*, 558 US 310 (2010).

⁶ *Buckley* (n 5); *Citizens United* (n 5).

⁷ See especially *Animal Defenders International* (n 3) for a thorough account this issue by parliamentary and non-parliamentary official bodies.

⁸ In *R (Pro-Life Alliance) v British Broadcasting Corporation* [2003] UKHL 23, [2004] 1 AC 185, however, Lord Hoffmann was careful to point out, at [75], that: 'although the word "deference" is now very popular in describing the relationship between the judicial and the other branches of government, I do not think that its overtones of servility, or perhaps gracious concession, are appropriate to describe what is happening. In a society based upon the rule of law and the separation of powers, it is necessary to decide which branch of government has in any particular instance the decision-making power and what the legal limits of that power are. That is a question of law and must therefore be decided by the courts'.

message, again in ways simply inconceivable in the United States. This reflects not only a wide range of permissible limits, but also a relatively low threshold for their justification. It also reflects an understanding of the kind displayed by Justice White in *Buckley v Valeo*, where in dissent he said that:

> The congressional judgment, which I would also accept, was that other steps must be taken to counter the corrosive effects of money in federal election campaigns. One of these steps is § 608 (e), which, aside from those funds that are given to the candidate or spent at his request or with his approval or cooperation, limits what a contributor may independently spend in support or denigration of one running for federal office. Congress was plainly of the view that these expenditures also have corruptive potential; but the Court strikes down the provision, strangely enough claiming more insight as to what may improperly influence candidates than is possessed by the majority of Congress that passed this bill and the President who signed it. Those supporting the bill undeniably included many seasoned professionals who have been deeply involved in elective processes and who have viewed them at close range over many years.[9]

17.3

Textual drafting and judicial deference help to explain the differences of approach between the United States and other jurisdictions in relation to free speech in elections. But they are by no means the whole explanation for the primacy of speech in the United States and its subordination to a range of considerations in Europe and other common law jurisdictions. Although very much in the minority for these purposes, the US position is nevertheless important for the rest of world, not only because it is the model of what they do not want to be.[10] US scholars dominate the international debates with what is a national rather than an international problem, and the US jurisprudence is considered by courts in other parts of the world (even though the courtesy is not returned).[11] Moreover, the United States sets standards that those protected by the First Amendment might expect to see respected when they operate overseas. In other words, there is constant pressure to export First Amendment values, which although initially successful in election law have since been rebuffed, at least for the time being.[12]

---

[9] *Buckley* (n 5) 260–1; cf *Animal Defenders International* (n 3).

[10] As expressed most vividly in *R (Animal Defenders International) v Secretary of State for Culture, Media and Sport* [2998] UKHL 15, [2008] 1 AC 1312, [47] (Baroness Hale).

[11] But see *Brotherhood of Railway Clerks v Allen*, 373 US 113 (1963), where strictly foreign law (British legislation on use of union dues for political purposes) was considered, rather than foreign jurisprudence. It seems nevertheless to have been influential.

[12] See KD Ewing, 'The Repudiation of *Buckley v Valeo*', in Eugen D Mazo and Timothy K Kuhner (eds), *Democracy by the People* (CUP 2018).

What then are the distinguishing features of the US liberal constitutional model (using the term liberal in the traditional rather than the modern US sense)? We would suggest that:

- It begins with the focus of the election on the electors, not candidates or parties. This tilts the balance uncontrollably in the direction of liberty and away from equality.
- As such, electors are consumers entitled to receive information from as many and diverse sources as possible; the contrasting need of candidates and parties for a fair opportunity to reach these electors is rejected.
- If the focus is on information, there is a need for more not less. Everyone must be allowed to speak without restraint as to the identity of the speaker, regardless of their connection with the election.
- This is particularly true of those who may be affected by the outcome of the election, regardless of their status as electors, or legal status generally. Global corporations are free to promote economic interests in the political arena. Why not?

The embrace of the market is thus more than metaphorical: the election is a marketplace; electors are commodities (to be persuaded rather than bought and sold); and money is the currency of this as other markets.[13]

The other feature of the US liberal constitutional model is the constitutional protection of private power, as revealed in *Citizens United v Federal Electoral Commission*,[14] where it was held by tortuous logic that:

- Restrictions on the right of corporations and labor unions to speak at an election could not be justified on the ground of 'anti-distortion' because the restrictions in question contained an exemption for the print and broadcast media; but
- It would not be possible to impose such limits on the print and broadcast media, the Court holding that 'there is simply no support for the view that the First Amendment, as originally understood, would permit the suppression of political speech by media corporations'.[15]

According to the Court in relation to the latter point, 'television networks and major newspapers owned by media corporations have become the most important means of mass communication in modern times. The First Amendment was certainly not understood to condone the suppression of political speech in society's most salient media'.[16]

---

[13] Stanley Ingber, 'The Marketplace of Ideas: A Legitimizing Myth' (1984) *Duke LJ* 1, 51–55. For an empirical study, see Daniel E Ho and Frederick Schauer, 'Testing the Marketplace of Ideas' (2015) 90 *NYU L Rev* 1160.
[14] *Citizens United v Federal Electoral Commission*, 558 US 310 (2010).
[15] Ibid 353.   [16] Ibid.

Because it was not possible to ban media corporations, it was therefore not possible to prohibit (or to use the inflated rhetoric of the court 'censor') other corporations.[17]

This contrasts with the position operating in European jurisdictions and other countries which have adopted similar regimes. Here the focus of social democratic or social liberal models is on the electoral process as a whole, including to a greater extent the position of the candidates and parties, and crucially the movements they represent.[18] But they are also informed by European constitutional values which place a premium on equality as well as liberty. The point is well made by the United Kingdom's Joint Committee on Human Rights, where it is said by way of justification of the legislation that was subsequently challenged unsuccessfully in *Animal Defenders International*:

> There is a different tradition in the USA and Australia which gives greater weight to the interest in fostering as much political expression as possible. But the European tradition seems to us to be preferable, in that it gives what we consider to be appropriate weight to the legitimate objective of securing equality of opportunity for political expression, at any rate in the broadcast media. In our view, this justifies restrictions on the freedom to buy advertising time for political purposes.[19]

This different tradition is to be seen in jurisprudence which, in upholding restrictions on speech, does so on the basis that it promoted a legitimate objective which was 'to contribute towards securing equality between candidates'.[20] Moreover, 'it promoted fairness between competing candidates for election by preventing wealthy third parties from campaigning for or against a particular candidate or issuing material which necessitated the devotion of part of a candidate's election budget, which was limited by law ... to a response'.[21]

As suggested, the same approach is to be seen also in those other jurisdictions which have decisively repudiated the US position, to reflect a more socially liberal or a weak social democratic model of elections. These are hugely important developments which enable electorates to retain the space to contest and contain the political influence of economic power. In Canada it is now widely accepted that political equality will require governmental regulation of political speech, particularly of those who have greater political resources. As the Canadian Supreme Court observed in *Attorney-General of Canada v Harper*, 'the egalitarian model promotes an electoral process that requires the wealthy to be prevented from controlling the electoral process to the detriment of others

---

[17] According to the Supreme Court, 'there is no precedent supporting laws that attempt to distinguish between corporations which are deemed to be exempt as media corporations and those which are not': ibid 352.
[18] This is acknowledged explicitly in the EU Charter of Fundamental Rights, which provides that 'every citizen of the Union has the right to vote and to stand as a candidate at elections to the European Parliament in the Member State in which he or she resides, under the same conditions as nationals of that State' (art 39).
[19] Joint Committee on Human Rights, Draft Communications Bill (2001–2, HL 149, HC 1102) [23] (citations omitted). *Buckley* (n 5) is referred to in this report. See n 23 below for the more recent Australian jurisprudence.
[20] *Bowman v United Kingdom* (1998) 26 EHRR 1, [38].   [21] Ibid [36].

with less economic power'.²² We also see the same in the recent Australian jurisprudence, though it is true that the cases are concerned principally with donation curbs. But the judgments are nevertheless rich in analysis generally about the nature of Australia's democracy, the role of elections, and the role of regulation. According to the High Court of Australia, '[t]he risk to equal participation posed by the uncontrolled use of wealth may warrant legislative action to ensure, *or even enhance*, the practical enjoyment of popular sovereignty'.²³

Although all are members of the same family of western liberal democracies, there are thus sharp ideological differences which may better help to explain the difference of approach, which is tolerant of prohibition, restraint and even censorship outside the United States. These ideological differences are best seen on a scale with the ultra-liberal US jurisprudence at the right-hand end, and the social democratic European states at the left hand of the axis. These ideological differences are reflected in the values expressed in the jurisprudence about the nature of the electoral process and the interests it serves. This is reflected in turn in the theoretical framework constructed by the courts and in the way in which the balance is struck between different participants in the process. With that in mind, we venture to suggest that the ultra-liberalism of the US jurisprudence reflects the economic liberalism which it also underpins. To this end, it is not only the decision but also the rhetoric of the US Supreme Court in *Citizens United* about the political freedoms of corporations that tell us a great deal about the values currently underpinning the First Amendment.²⁴ Neo-liberalism without political freedom for its key actors would be difficult to sustain, and indeed we suspect that a different economic model would produce a different constitutional outcome.

17.4

In his classic work on free speech, Alexander Meiklejohn perhaps unwittingly reinforces some of the claims made above when he wrote that:

> In that method of political self-government, *the point of ultimate interest is not the words of the speakers, but the minds of the hearers.* The final aim of the meeting is the voting of wise decisions. The voters, therefore, must be made as wise as possible. The welfare of the community requires that those who decide issues shall understand them. And this, in turn, requires that so far as time allows, *all facts and interests relevant to the problem shall be fully and fairly presented to the meeting.* Both facts and interests shall be given in such a way that all the alternative lines of action can be wisely measured in relation to one another.²⁵

---

[22] *Attorney-General of Canada v Harper* [2004] 1 SCR 827, 868 (citations omitted).
[23] *McCloy v New South Wales* (2015) 257 CLR 178, 207 [45] (emphasis added).
[24] *Citizens United* (n 5) 352–3.
[25] Alexander Meiklejohn, *Free Speech and its Relation to Self-Government* (Harper Brothers 1948) 25 (emphasis added).

This did not mean, however, that there should not be governmental regulation in relation to political speech, Meiklejohn arguing that the US First Amendment 'does not forbid the abridging of speech [b]ut...it does forbid the abridging of the freedom of speech'.[26] This was based on his analogy with US town hall meetings where '[t]he basic principle is that freedom of speech shall be unabridged' and 'yet the meeting cannot even be opened unless, by common consent, speech is abridged'.[27]

The latter was so, according to Meiklejohn, because rules were necessary for these meetings in terms of who chairs the meeting, the questions to be decided by the meeting, the order of speakers and the relevance of their speech to the meeting.[28] In his words, '[t]he town meeting, as it seeks for freedom of public discussion of public problems, would be wholly ineffectual unless speech were thus abridged'.[29] Similarly with the First Amendment, it is not, according to Meiklejohn, 'the guardian of unregulated talkativeness'[30]—it does not guarantee that 'every individual has an unalienable right to speak whenever, wherever, however he chooses'.[31] What it protects is 'equality of status in the *field of ideas*'.[32] For Meiklejohn, there was thus a distinction between the abridgement of speech, which was not protected from government regulation (through the First Amendment), and the abridgement of freedom of speech, which was. Yet one does not have to accept this (troublesome) distinction to appreciate the point that democratic deliberation requires both the absence and presence of government regulation.

There is thus a tension in Meiklejohn's desire that matter should be 'fully and fairly' presented. Each cannot happen without compromising the other. Fairness means that all views must be heard, but that those representing major strands of opinion should be heard in equal measure, so that electors have an opportunity to assess the quality and the quantity of the message. Space must be created to enable the small fry to squeeze through, and to ensure that the debate is not dominated in advance by those with the biggest mouths or the deepest pockets. Yet this is precisely what the US system does not permit, revealing Meiklejohn's 'fairness' to be a chimera. *Buckley v Valeo* struck the balance in favour of fullness rather than fairness, and in the course of doing so required the First Amendment's protection of free speech to be used to reinforce economic inequality in the political sphere. The case was concerned with a whole suite of campaign financing reform, including spending limitations on candidates. These were defended by the government on a number of grounds, including the ancillary ground that it promoted equality between candidates, to which the Court replied that:

> the concept that government may restrict the speech of some elements of our society in order to enhance the relative voice of others is wholly foreign to the First Amendment, which was designed 'to secure "the widest possible dissemination of information from diverse and antagonistic sources,"' and '"to assure unfettered interchange of ideas for the bringing about of political and social changes desired by the people."' *New York Times Co. v. Sullivan, supra* at 266, 269, quoting *Associated Press v. United States*, 326 U.S. 1, 20 (1945), and *Roth v. United States*, 354 U.S. at 484. The First Amendment's protection against governmental abridgment of free expression

---

[26] Ibid 19. [27] Ibid 22. [28] Ibid 22–3. [29] Ibid 23. [30] Ibid 25.
[31] Ibid 24. [32] Ibid 26 (emphasis added).

cannot properly be made to depend on a person's financial ability to engage in public discussion. *Cf. Eastern R. Conf. v. Noerr Motors,* 365 U.S. 127, 13 (1961).³³

In this way, free speech reinforces the influence of economic power (and economic inequality) in the political process. It also reinforces the role of economic actors in the political process, including, in particular, economic actors such as corporations which—as offspring of the political process—have no legitimate claim to be treated as core participants. But like Mary Shelley's imaginary creation, free speech has transformed a creature that can no longer be contained. The point of course is demonstrated most forcefully by *Citizens United* where, as we have seen, the Supreme Court very controversially struck down a prohibition on electoral speech by corporate entities of different forms.³⁴ Such a prohibition had been upheld by the Court earlier 'as a means to prevent corporations from obtaining "an unfair advantage in the political marketplace" by using "resources amassed in the economic marketplace".³⁵ But in taking a new approach that would lift all restraints on corporate free speech, the Court held quite unpersuasively by focusing again on the audience rather than the speaker that:

> Quite apart from the purpose or effect of regulating content, moreover, the Government may commit a constitutional wrong when by law it identifies certain preferred speakers. By taking the right to speak from some and giving it to others, the Government deprives the disadvantaged person or class of the right to use speech to strive to establish worth, standing, and respect for the speaker's voice. *The Government may not by these means deprive the public of the right and privilege to determine for itself what speech and speakers are worthy of consideration.* The First Amendment protects speech and speaker, and the ideas that flow from each.³⁶

It is impossible now not to be struck by the naïveté of Meiklejohn's work, in what reads like an allegorical account of modern US democracy. It is true that Meiklejohn refers to the need for 'all facts and interests relevant to the problem [to] be fully and fairly presented to the meeting'.³⁷ It is true also that Meiklejohn wrote about the US constitutional system as 'a voluntary compact among political equals';³⁸ and self-government as 'a group of free and equal men, cooperating in a common enterprise, and using for that enterprise responsible and regulated discussion'.³⁹ But although political equality underpins his understanding of free speech, with participants in US town hall deliberations 'meet[ing] as political equals',⁴⁰ the political equality to which he refers is formal only. It is formal in

---

³³ *Buckley* (n 5) 48–9 (citations omitted).
³⁴ The literature on *Citizens United* is voluminous and includes Robert C Post, *Citizens Divided: Campaign Finance Reform and the Constitution* (Harvard UP 2014); Richard L Hasen, *Plutocrats United: Campaign Money, the Supreme Court and the Distortion of American Elections* (Yale UP 2016). For a particularly compelling account, see Timothy K Kuhner, *Capitalism v Democracy: Money in Politics and the Free Market Constitution* (Stanford UP 2014).
³⁵ *Citizens United* (n 5) 350, quoting *Austin v Michigan Chamber of Commerce,* 494 US 652, 659 (1990) and *Federal Election Commission v Massachusetts Citizens for Life, Inc,* 479 US 238, 257 (1986).
³⁶ *Citizens United* (n 5) 340–1 (emphasis added).
³⁷ Meiklejohn (n 25) 26.   ³⁸ Ibid 11.   ³⁹ Ibid 23.   ⁴⁰ Ibid 22.

the sense that when we go to the ballot box, we do so as political equals and engage in what is the only event in our lives in which we are all of the same political rank regardless of our social station or our economic means. But this is not the equality of the citizens who participate in Rousseau's similar meetings in a small town in Switzerland around the same time as the allegorical New England equivalent, where it is assumed that that there must be an equality between citizens for democracy to be meaningful.

The absence of such equality can be addressed (but not removed) by laws that build on the equality of the elector at the ballot box, by enhancing the equality of the means used by candidates and parties to persuade citizens when they are deciding how to cast their vote. But although Meiklejohn accepts the need for regulation, this appears to be confined to the administration of the process, but not the content of what is being said (though surely there must be rules about irrelevant and off the point content). What is not so clear is the extent to which there is scope for regulation based on the identity of the speaker, the lack of diversity in points made, and the volume of the speech. More importantly, however, Meiklejohn does not tell us about the dangers of citizens coming to the meeting with their minds closed because of the strongly expressed opinions they heard from respected or powerful figures in the community in advance. They may also have read something in the local newspaper which circulates in their community, providing a pulpit for the views of the local entrepreneur who owns the newspaper in question. The meeting does not take place in a laboratory, any more than does a contemporary election, which invariably owes more to Hobbes than Mill.

17.5

It is a striking feature of *Citizens United* (and other cases) that the approach to the First Amendment is justified as being '[p]remised on mistrust of governmental power',[41] the US Supreme Court unable, it seems, to get past the reason why the State was founded in the first place (distrust of the British being referred to in the same case).[42] There is an obvious tragedy that in a democracy purporting to represent citizens' views, this should be the attitude to government that apparently prevails. As such, it says a great deal about the failure of the electoral system and the approach to free speech if after three hundred years such views continue to dominate. The Supreme Court is nevertheless also asking a lot if it is asking citizens to be trusting of private power and its aggressive pursuit of self-interest and self-aggrandizement. Is this really to be preferred to that of representative and electorally accountable government? These, paradoxically, are the structures that law based on a distrust of government has helped to create.

The European social democratic/social liberal based heritage is different, not only because government is viewed less negatively but, as already suggested, because

---

[41] *Citizens United* (n 5) 340.
[42] Ibid 353, 429.

elections are viewed differently, as are the values informing elections. To this end, a good starting point is the vision of government portrayed by Rousseau, whose Geneva provides us with a different allegorical account of the conduct of elections. In place of Meiklejohn's town meeting, Rousseau wrote of the 'happiest people in the world', namely 'bands of peasants regulating the affairs of state under an oak tree', 'always acting wisely'.[43] As explained by Cranston, on this model, '*every* citizen was a legislator'.[44] But as *The Social Contract* develops, attention turns from direct to representative democracy, despite 'feeling a certain contempt for the refinements of other nations, which employ so much skill and mystery to make themselves at once illustrious and wretched'.[45] It is true of course that Rousseau famously thought that elections were unnecessary, and that in a well-functioning democracy representatives would be chosen, where necessary by lot.[46]

But as Rousseau reluctantly acknowledged, 'no true democracy exists',[47] and the question arises about the principles by which these elections would be conducted. This is a question which Rousseau avoids, but he leaves us with enough insight to know what the clear preconditions are. The first is equality, by which he meant 'a large measure of equality in social rank and fortune, without which equality in rights and authority will not last long'.[48] In modern liberal society this is aspirational and apparently unsustainable, though Rousseau reminds us that inequality of social rank and fortune should not be permitted to translate into political inequality, or that political inequality should not prevent the attainment of a democracy based on equality of social rank and fortune by democratic means. This is the principle of equality as the foundation of a just electoral system that stands in direct contrast to the principles informing the US Supreme Court, but which underpins the jurisprudence of the ECtHR in addressing a world albeit more brutal than that contemplated by Rousseau.

These cases include *Animal Defenders International* where the aim was not simply to avoid the dangers of *Buckley v Valeo*, but more positively to promote equality and to prevent domination of the process by the rich. If the pursuit of equality could be achieved only by prohibition rather than regulation, then so be it. In that case, prohibition of the use of the broadcast media for all political advertising, including electoral advertising, would be:

> a balanced and proportionate response to the problem: [the applicants] can seek to put their case across in any other way, but not the one which so greatly risks distorting the public debate in favour of the rich. There has to be the same rule for the same kind of advertising, whatever the cause for which it campaigns and whatever the resources of the campaigners. We must not distinguish between causes of which we

---

[43] Jean-Jacques Rousseau, *The Social Contract* (Maurice Cranston tr, Penguin 1976) 149.
[44] Maurice Cranston, 'Introduction to Rousseau' in ibid 20 (emphasis in original).
[45] Rousseau (n 43) 149.
[46] Ibid 156. Election by lot 'would have few disadvantages in a true democracy'. This is because 'where all men were equal in character and talent as well as principles and fortune, it would hardly matter who was chosen': ibid.
[47] Ibid 112.   [48] Ibid 113.

approve and causes of which we disapprove. Nor in practice can we distinguish between small organisations which have to fight for every penny and rich ones with access to massive sums. Capping or rationing will not work.[49]

If prohibition is permitted in the interests of equality, so too are restrictions, the same Court having made clear some fifteen years earlier in *Bowman v United Kingdom* that a cap on third-party election spending served a legitimate purpose, which was 'to contribute towards securing equality between candidates'.[50]

But of course third-party spending limits serve another purpose identified by Rousseau, namely the influence of 'private interests', contrary to Rousseau's concern that '[n]othing is more dangerous in public affairs than the influence of private interests', which in his view leads to the 'corruption of the legislator'.[51] *Bowman* was an unlikely case to lead to the corruption of the legislator, Bowman being a nuisance rather than a threat. The case was concerned with third-party spending limits that had been introduced to complement limits on candidate expenditure. However, the limits on third parties were so tight (£5 per third party) as to constitute a de facto prohibition, as revealed in *Bowman* where the complainant was prosecuted for distributing handbills setting out the views of rival candidates on the questions of abortion and related matters. But the issue was not Bowman herself, so much as the people in the queue behind her, ready to exploit any loosening of the restrictions at a time when Parliament was planning to extend them in other directions:

> Free elections and freedom of expression, particularly freedom of political debate, together form the bedrock of any democratic system. The two rights are interrelated and operate to reinforce each other: for example, as the Court has observed in the past, freedom of expression is one of the 'conditions' necessary to 'ensure the free expression of the opinion of the people in the choice of the legislature'. For this reason, it is particularly important in the period preceding an election that opinions and information of all kinds are permitted to circulate freely.
>
> Nonetheless, in certain circumstances the two rights may come into conflict and it may be considered necessary, in the period preceding or during an election, to place certain restrictions, of a type which would not usually be acceptable, on freedom of expression, in order to secure the 'free expression of the opinion of the people in the choice of the legislature'. The Court recognises that, in striking the balance between these two rights, the Contracting States have a margin of appreciation, as they do generally with regard to the organisation of their electoral systems.[52]

For First Amendment scholars this would be utterly perverse. Quite apart from the respect for the status of candidates and by the parties, the priority given to equality as a justification,

---

[49] *Animal Defenders International* (n 3) [51].
[50] *Bowman* (n 20) [38]. For discussion, see Jane Marriott, 'Alarmist or Relaxed? Election Expenditure Limits and Free Speech' [2005] *Pub L* 764.
[51] Rousseau (n 43) 112.
[52] *Bowman* (n 20) [42]–[43] (citations omitted).

the willingness to contain the influence of third parties, and the equanimity in entertaining restrictions, the ECtHR is arguing that the holding of an election is a reason for—rather than against—controls on speech. In doing so, it is nevertheless wholly consistent with a Rousseau-esque view of the world. It is of course pointless trying to speculate about how Rousseau would have answered the questions of free speech in elections in the modern era. In his ideal world of direct democracy under the village oak tree, there would be no problems of the kind we anticipated in the case of Meiklejohn's town meeting, for the simple reason that this would be a meeting of equals in a 'frugal' community. If anyone had been corrupted in advance it would not be because of their economic vulnerability. In the case of representative democracy, while the scale of modern society would be beyond the scale of Rousseau's contemplation, his assumption of equality and his denigration of 'special interests' point to very different outcomes than those evolving in the United States, even if Mrs Bowman was an implausible cause for concern.

17.6

The foregoing has considered what are effectively non-content based prohibitions and restrictions relating to (1) the quantity of speech on the one hand, and (2) the identity of the speaker on the other, with Europe and the United States divided by a different history, different legal texts, and different ideological traditions. The other question of electoral speech to consider here relates to prohibitions or restrictions on (3) the content of speech, a matter which also seems to divide legislators and judges in Europe and the United States, the latter again taking a more fundamentalist position than the former. Indeed, one of the arguments for caution in relation to non-content based prohibitions and restrictions is that they would lead inexorably to content-based prohibitions and restrictions, which for First Amendment scholars seems to be wholly anathema. Yet here too there is a danger of being too squeamish about content-based restrictions, for the fact that an election is taking place ought to be no excuse to license speech that would be unacceptable outside the election period, whether because it was racist, defamatory, or offensive. Indeed, this is a matter of growing urgency in the wake of 'fake news' allegations.

That said, the problem is a long-standing one, as revealed by *R (Pro-Life Alliance) v British Broadcasting Corporation*,[53] which concerned a proposed election broadcast of the Alliance to include 'prolonged and graphic images of the product of suction abortion: aborted foetuses in a mangled and mutilated state, tiny limbs, a separated head, and the like. Unquestionably the pictures are deeply disturbing. Unquestionably many people would find them distressing, even harrowing'.[54] In the UK, the BBC does not carry commercial advertisements (other than to market its own products), and as we have seen, by

---

[53] *Pro-Life Alliance* (n 8).   [54] Ibid [3].

British law political advertising is banned on commercial television.[55] Instead, political parties are provided with free air time for party election broadcasts, the time being distributed mainly to the larger political parties with significant parliamentary representation.[56] Small parties are not completely cut out, and may be given a free slot provided they contest a minimum of seats either nationally or sub-nationally. In 2001, the Pro-Life Alliance qualified for one broadcast of five minutes' duration in Wales.[57]

That apart, there are a number of legal duties imposed on broadcasters, as in the case of the BBC a duty not to 'include anything which offends against good taste or decency or is likely to encourage or incite to crime or lead to disorder or to be offensive to public feeling'.[58] In *Pro-Life Alliance*, the BBC refused to carry a broadcast by the Pro-Life Alliance on the ground that '"shots of aborted foetuses and of mutilated foetuses" did not comply with the BBC Guidelines',[59] taking the view that some of the 'images are unacceptable in themselves because they are likely to be offensive to public feeling, in particular the images of aborted foetuses mostly in "a mangled and mutilated state"'.[60] In addressing the question, the court was fully mindful of freedom of expression requirements, Lord Nicholls of Birkenhead acknowledging that:

> Freedom of political speech is a freedom of the very highest importance in any country which lays claim to being a democracy. Restrictions on this freedom need to be examined rigorously by all concerned, not least the courts. The courts, as independent and impartial bodies, are charged with a vital supervisory role. Under the Human Rights Act 1998 they must decide whether legislation, and the conduct of public authorities, are compatible with Convention rights and fundamental freedoms. Where there is incompatibility the courts must grant appropriate remedial relief.[61]

Nevertheless, giving what was effectively the leading speech in the House of Lords (in what was a 4–1 decision upholding the ban), Lord Hoffmann held that taste and decency requirements were legitimate restrictions, that there was no reason to exclude them from the party election broadcasts, and that there was no reason to challenge the way in which the standards were applied in this case. In a striking conclusion, Lord Hoffmann said that:

> Public opinion in these matters is often diverse, sometimes unexpected and in constant flux. Generally accepted standards on these questions are not a matter of intuition on the part of elderly male judges. The researches into public opinion by the BSC and the broadcasters would be superfluous if this were the case. And I attach

---

[55] There is a full discussion of the legislation and its history in *Animal Defenders International* (n 3).
[56] See HF Rawlings, *Law and the Electoral Process* (Sweet and Maxwell 1988).
[57] *Pro-Life Alliance* (n 8) [2].
[58] Ibid [89]. The duty of the BBC arose by virtue of its Royal Charter, the corresponding duties on commercial broadcasters arising by virtue of legislation.
[59] *Pro-Life Alliance* (n 8) [43].   [60] Ibid [44].
[61] Ibid [6].

some importance to the fact that Mrs Sloman, who was the principal decision-maker for the BBC, and Mrs Richards, the Controller of BBC Wales, are women. In deciding which members of the public would be likely to find the images offensive, I would imagine that one constituency the broadcasters would have had in mind was the 200,000 women who, for one reason or another, according to the Alliance evidence, have abortions every year. Although people often speak of 'abortion on demand', having an abortion is something which few women undertake lightly. It is often a traumatic emotional experience. I would therefore hesitate a good deal before saying that the broadcasters must have been wrong in saying, as they did, that the images would be offensive to very large numbers of viewers.[62]

In upholding what was in effect the censoring of the broadcast, the House of Lords reversed a unanimous Court of Appeal which had taken a more robust free speech line in what was a far from straightforward case.[63] That said, the activities of the Pro-Life Alliance look like a calculated way of beating the political advertising ban by putting up candidates in a minimum number of seats. It is not without cost, in the sense that election candidates must pay an election deposit which is forfeited unless the candidate in question attracts a minimum number of votes. This is designed to discourage frivolous candidates such as those representing the Pro-Life Alliance who are guaranteed to lose all their deposits. For such groups, this nevertheless may be seen as an acceptable cost of access to a medium from which—along with other interest groups advocating political causes—they would normally be excluded. They are not serious electoral players, and abortion is not even a marginal election issue in the United Kingdom, where pro-choice legislation is long-established and fairly settled, with a broad consensus of approval. The Pro-Life Alliance is a pressure group metamorphosing into a single-issue political party for the purposes of the election, to force onto the agenda an issue of marginal concern, using the election as an opportunity for this purpose.[64]

While free speech scholars may eschew judgment about the content of the Alliance's speech, it is nevertheless important that we are cognizant about the context. For the price of fifty electoral deposits, it would be possible for all interest groups to beat the political advertising ban at election time to convey material of little interest in the election. Assuming that the political broadcast ban was itself lawful (which was subsequently held to be the case), this may have been a more acceptable way of responding to the multiple issues raised by *Pro-Life Alliance*. The House of Lords, however, was required by the presentation of the case to address the matter head on and to conclude that the broadcasters were entitled to censor the message. Yet it is difficult to think of a more blatant example of prior restraint at election time in the modern age, all the more so for the fact that the restraint was imposed by a public body with statutory authority and judicial approval. But it is equally difficult to find many commentators critical of the

---

[62] Ibid [80].   [63] [2002] 3 WLR 1080 (CA).
[64] The six Pro-Life Alliance candidates in Wales obtained a total of 1,609 votes, representing 0.117% of the votes cast.

power,[65] the manner of its exercise in this case, or the House of Lords decision in upholding the BBC.[66] It is also difficult to believe that such messages would be carried with equanimity by public or commercial broadcasters elsewhere.[67] In the end the Alliance got its broadcast, albeit in the form of 'a blank screen bearing the word "censored"'.[68]

17.7

'Fake news', better understood as disinformation ('false, inaccurate, or misleading information designed, presented, and promoted to intentionally cause public harm or for profit'[69]), starkly illustrates the paradox of elections. Freedom of speech in relation to truth and falsity is clearly imperative. For Frederick Schauer, '[i]nherent in the ideal of self-government is the proposition that it is for the people alone to distinguish between truth and falsity in matters relating to broad questions of government policy';[70] for Meiklejohn, citizens 'may not be barred [from speaking] because their views are thought to be false or dangerous'.[71] There are also particular dangers with regulating electoral speech, not only because of the risk of partisan laws and their administration, but also the difficulties of distinguishing between truth and falsity in the context of robust election debates, and the even greater difficulty of doing so during the election campaign period in a way that does not unfairly favour those alleging falsity or those denying it—which are most likely to be the principal contenders in the elections.[72]

At the same time, the fact that new and emerging forms of digital media are largely an 'unregulated sphere'[73] poses clear risks to the integrity of elections due to disinformation, a form of manipulation of voters.[74] Consider, for example, the efforts of the Russian

---

[65] That said, the Court of Appeal took a different view from the House of Lords, where Lord Walker gave a very robust speech in dissent, alluding to the demands of a 'mature democracy'.

[66] Indeed, the most persuasive and influential piece was written in critical response to the Court of Appeal, cited with approval by the House of Lords. See Andrew Geddis, 'What Future for Political Advertising on the United Kingdom's Television Screens?' [2002] *Pub L* 615.

[67] Lord Hoffmann notably cited *Federal Communications Commission v Pacifica Foundation*, 438 US 426 (1978).

[68] *Pro-Life Alliance* (n 8) [4]: 'The blank screen was accompanied by a sound track describing the images shown on the banned pictures'.

[69] European Commission, *A Multi-Dimensional Approach to Disinformation: Report of the Independent High Level Group on Fake News and Online Disinformation* (Report of the Independent High Level Group on Fake News and Online Disinformation 2018) 3.

[70] Frederick Schauer, *Free Speech: A Philosophical Inquiry* (CUP 1982) 7–8; Eric Barendt, *Freedom of Speech* (2nd edn, OUP 2007) 39.

[71] Meiklejohn (n 25) 26.

[72] Jacob Rowbottom, 'Lies, Manipulation and Elections: Controlling False Campaign Statement' (2012) 32 *Oxford J Legal Stud* 507, 525; N Stephanopoulos, 'Liable Lies' (2018) 8 *Const Ct Rev* 1, 3–8.

[73] Digital, Culture, Media and Sport Committee, *Disinformation and 'Fake News': Interim Report* (5th Report 2017–19, HC 383) 10.

[74] Rowbottom, 'Lies, Manipulation and Elections' (n 72) 512–15.

government to influence the US elections in 2016. These efforts, which included extensive use of social media 'to undermine confidence in the election and sow fear and division in American society',[75] were said by a US Congressional Committee to have 'achieved its primary goal of inciting division and discord among Americans'.[76] The consequence, according to this report, was that '[t]he reliability of the democratic vote—the bedrock of the US republic—was widely and repeatedly questioned'.[77] In meeting what seems to be an existential threat to its democracy, the United States is, however, hamstrung by its First Amendment jurisprudence. The Supreme Court has so far wilfully refused to consider 'whether the Government has a compelling interest in preventing foreign individuals or associations from influencing our Nation's political process'.[78]

Otherwise, at its *widest*, regulation of electoral disinformation is constitutionally permissible only if there is actual malice, as understood in New York Times v Sullivan ('knowledge that the statement was false or with reckless disregard of whether it was false or not'[79]). The First Amendment constraint on regulating electoral disinformation may, indeed, be more severe. A strong strand of State appellate court decisions has further required that the false statements be defamatory.[80] Illustrative is the plurality decision of the Washington State Supreme Court in *State of Washington v 119 Vote No! Committee*,[81] which struck down legislation that prohibited any person from sponsoring, with actual malice, a political advertisement containing a false statement of material fact. The essence of the plurality's decision is found in a quote it relied upon: '[i]n political campaigns the grossest misstatements, deceptions, and defamations are immune from legal sanction unless they violate private rights that is, unless individuals are defamed'.[82] As the legislation in question did not require the statements to be defamatory, it was unconstitutional, according to the plurality, as it served no compelling state interest—'the State does not possess an independent right to determine truth and falsity in public issues'.[83]

Under the First Amendment then, regulation of the following types of electoral disinformation would not be permissible: false statements negligently made; misleading statements (whether made intentionally or negligently); and arguably, false statements that are non-defamatory. Constitutional protection of free speech need not, however, exclude the possibility of restrictions on false speech as an aid to democracy itself. The point is highlighted by the UK, where it is an offence to make 'false statement of fact in relation to the candidate's personal character

---

[75] House Permanent Select Committee on Intelligence, Report on Russian Active Measures, HR Doc 115–1110, 2 (2018).
[76] Ibid 1.   [77] Ibid.   [78] *Citizens United* (n 5) 362.
[79] *New York Times v Sullivan*, 376 US 254, 279–80 (1964).
[80] For the conflicting State appellate court decisions, see Daniel Hays Lowenstein and others, *Election Law: Cases and Materials* (6th edn, Carolina Academic P 2017) 689–97.
[81] *State of Washington v 119 Vote No! Committee*, 957 P 2d 691 (1998).
[82] Ibid 697, citing Charles Fried, 'The New First Amendment Jurisprudence: A Threat to Liberty' (1992) 59 *U Chi L Rev* 225, 238.
[83] Ibid 698.

or conduct'.[84] In *R (Woolas) v Parliamentary Election Court*, these restrictions were held not only to be consistent with the right to freedom of expression, but were also used to annul an election in which the incumbent had won by only 107 votes.[85] In the course of its decision, the court provided a strong defence of the legislation under which Woolas was convicted and disqualified from holding office:

> We can think of no reason why Parliament cannot have intended that where a statement was made about the personal character or conduct of a candidate, it did not intend due care to be exercised. Freedom of political debate must allow for the fact that statements are made which attack the political character of a candidate which are false but which are made carelessly. Such statements may also suggest an attack on aspects of his character by implying he is a hypocrite. Again, imposing a criminal penalty on a person who fails to exercise care when making statements in respect of a candidate's political position or character that by implication suggest he is a hypocrite would very significantly curtail the freedom of political debate so essential to a democracy. It could not be justified as representing the intention of Parliament. However imposing such a penalty where care is not taken in making a statement that goes beyond this and is a statement in relation to the personal character of a candidate can only enhance the standard of political debate and thus strengthen the way in which a democratic legislature is elected.[86]

17.8

Woolas thus indicates that competing rights may limit the scope of electoral speech. So far as dishonest statements are concerned, these were said to be aimed at the destruction of 'the rights of the public to free elections (Article 3 of the First Protocol to the Convention) and the right of each candidate to his reputation: Article 8(1)'.[87] As a result, '[t]he right to freedom of expression under article 10 does not extend to a right to be dishonest and tell lies'.[88] While mandating a 'strict approach',[89] the prohibition as to negligent false statements concerning candidates' personal character or conduct was not considered to be incompatible with the free speech guarantee in Article 10 of the ECHR. This is consistent with the European jurisprudence generally, which as we have seen is much more tolerant of prohibitions and restrictions of both content and non-content based speech than is that of the US courts.

As suggested above, there are a number of possible explanations for this difference of approach, including the textual differences, with few constitutional or human rights

---

[84] Representation of the People Act 1983, s 106(1). See also, for Australia, Graeme Orr, *The Law of Politics* (Federation P 2010) 143–50.
[85] *R (Woolas) v Parliamentary Election Court* [2010] EWHC 3169 (Admin), [2012] QB 1 (unsuccessful judicial review of Election Court decision in *Watkins v Woolas* [2010] EWHC 2702 (QB)).
[86] Ibid [124].
[87] Ibid [105]. [88] Ibid [106]. [89] Ibid [92].

texts as unequivocal as the First Amendment. Beyond that, however, there are ideological and cultural differences in terms of a commitment to liberty over equality and a distrust of, and alienation from, government not evident on the US scale in European jurisprudence. There are also different perceptions about the nature of the electoral process, which inform the extent to which regulation is acceptable. The right of the elector to hear speech is given much more weight in US jurisprudence than in its European equivalent, without any consideration as to whether the elector wishes to receive the information, or to do so in the manner or on the scale distributed.

As a result, there is a much greater willingness in the European jurisprudence to entertain a much broader range of justifications for restraints on speech, most of which are located in a sense of electoral fairness. This is a matter consciously rejected in *Citizens United*, and to the extent that 'money is speech' it would be hard to argue that US elections are either free or fair as a result. It remains to be seen whether the US Supreme Court will be as suspicious of regulation in light of the challenges now presented by social media. Beyond the need to protect the integrity of the election process, a compelling concern is now with the privacy of the citizen and protection from unsolicited, unwanted, and manipulative messages, rather than the free speech rights of the messenger. Indeed, part of the case for control is that many of the purveyors of falsehood have no legitimate claim to speak in the first place, with alleged foreign interference likely to be a severe test for the First Amendment.

CHAPTER 18

WHEN IS SPEECH THAT CAUSES UNLAWFUL CONDUCT PROTECTED BY FREEDOM OF SPEECH? THE CASE OF THE FIRST AMENDMENT?

GEOFFREY R STONE[*]

SHOULD speech that causes others to violate the law be protected by the freedom of speech? If those who violate the law can be punished, why not also punish those who cause them to violate the law? For more than two centuries, this question has played a central role in the evolution of First Amendment jurisprudence in the United States. Because the issue has arisen most often in the United States in time of war, I will briefly review the US experience with this question during the 'Half War' with France in 1798, the Civil War, World War I, the Cold War, and over the course of the last half-century. I will then offer some concluding observations.

18.1 THE 'HALF WAR' WITH FRANCE

The period from 1789 to 1801 was a critical era in US history. In an atmosphere of fear, suspicion, and intrigue, the nation's new Constitution was put to a test of its very survival. Sharp internal conflicts buffeted the new nation, which also found itself embroiled in a

---

[*] For a fuller analysis of this subject, see Geoffrey R Stone, *Perilous Times: Free Speech in Wartime from the Sedition Act of 1798 to the War on Terrorism* (WW Norton 2004).

fierce international struggle between Europe's two great powers: the French Republic and Imperial Britain. It was a time of bitter party warfare and rampant hysteria.

By 1798, many of the ideas generated by the French Revolution aroused deep fear and hostility in segments of the US population. A rancorous political and philosophical debate raged between the Federalists, then in power, and the Republicans. The Federalists feared that the sympathy of the Republicans for the French Revolution indicated a willingness to plunge the United States into a similar period of violent upheaval. The Republicans feared that the Federalist sympathy for England denoted a desire to restore aristocratic forms and class distinctions in the United States.

As the international situation deteriorated, President John Adams sent John Marshall to Paris to negotiate a treaty to guarantee the immunity of US shipping from attacks by French corsairs. When this effort failed because the French demanded 'tribute' to help finance their war with England, the Adams administration initiated a series of defence measures that carried the United States into a state of undeclared war with France. The Republicans fiercely criticized these measures, leading President Adams to declare that the Republicans 'would sink the glory of our country and prostrate her liberties at the feet of France'. Such persons, he declared, deserve only our 'contempt and abhorrence'.[1] The Federalists attempted to discredit the Republicans by attacking their loyalty, their ideology, and their morality.

Against this background, the Federalists enacted the Sedition Act of 1798, which prohibited the publication of 'any false, scandalous, and malicious writing' against the US government, Congress, or the president, with intent to bring them into 'contempt or disrepute'.[2] In response to Republican objections that the Act violated the First Amendment, Federalist congressman Long John Allen responded that the First Amendment 'was never understood to give the right...of exciting sedition, insurrection, and slaughter with impunity'. The Act was necessary, he maintained, because a treasonable conspiracy of Republican speakers and editors was attempting to incite the people to 'insurrection'.[3]

In this legislation, the US government declared war on dissent. The Sedition Act was vigorously enforced, but only against supporters of the Republican Party. Prosecutions were brought against the leading Republican newspapers and the most vocal critics of the Adams administration. The Act proved an effective weapon for the suppression of dissent.

Consider, for example, the plight of Matthew Lyon, a Republican congressman from Vermont. During his re-election campaign, Lyon published an article in which he asserted that under President Adams 'every consideration of the public welfare [was]

---

[1] Letter from John Adams to the Inhabitants of Arlington and Bandgate, Vermont, 25 June 1798 in Charles Francis Adams (ed), *The Works of John Adams* (Little, Brown 1854) vol 9, 202; John Adams, 'To the Inhabitant of Chester County in the South of Pennsylvania', *Claypoole's American Daily Advertiser* (Philadelphia, 29 May 1798).

[2] See An Act for the Punishment of Certain Crimes against the United States, 5th Cong, 2d Sess in 1 Public Statutes at Large 596–7.

[3] *Annals of Congr.* 5th Cong, 2d Sess 2097 (5 July 1798).

swallowed up in a continual grasp for power, in an unbounded thirst for ridiculous pomp, foolish adulation, and selfish avarice'.[4] Because this statement clearly brought the president into 'disrepute', Lyon was convicted and sentenced to prison. In all, the Federalists arrested twenty-five Republicans under the Act. At least fifteen of these arrests resulted in indictments. Ten cases went to trial, all resulting in convictions before openly hostile Federalist judges and juries.

The US Supreme Court did not have occasion to rule on the constitutionality of the Sedition Act at the time, and the Act expired by its own terms on the last day of Adams's term of office. President Thomas Jefferson thereafter pardoned all those who had been convicted under the Act, and in 1840 Congress repaid all the fines. The Sedition Act was a critical factor in the demise of the Federalist Party, and the Supreme Court has never missed an opportunity in the years since to remind us that the Sedition Act of 1798 has been judged unconstitutional in the 'court of history'.[5]

18.2 THE CIVIL WAR

During the Civil War, the United States faced perhaps its most severe challenge. As in most civil wars, there were sharply divided loyalties, fluid military and political boundaries, and easy opportunities for espionage and sabotage. Moreover, the nation had to cope with the stresses of slavery, emancipation, conscription, and staggering casualty lists, all of which triggered deep division and even violent protest. Faced with these tensions, President Abraham Lincoln had to balance the conflicting interests of military security and individual liberty, including the freedom to criticize the government.

As a Republican, Lincoln was politically committed to the principle of free speech. Republicans had tied themselves to this position in the decades leading up to the Civil War, when a fierce battle raged over the free speech rights of abolitionists. Southern states equated the advocacy of abolition with incitement to slave revolt. From its founding in 1854, the Republican Party maintained that such laws violated the right of free expression.

The depth of the Republicans' commitment to free speech was severely tested, however, during the Civil War. Critics of the administration attacked Lincoln as repressive and autocratic, and furiously protested Lincoln's suspensions of the writ of habeas corpus, the institution of the draft, the conduct of the war, and Lincoln's issuance of the Emancipation Proclamation. Like the Federalists in 1798, some Republicans demanded that the government suppress 'disloyal' dissent and shut down 'treasonable' newspapers.

Of those who were arrested for disloyal speech, some were persons of influence. The most prominent example was Clement Vallandigham, a former Ohio congressman who was the most forceful spokesman of the Copperheads, who vehemently opposed the

---

[4] Francis Wharton, *State Trials of the United States During the Administrations of Washington and Adams* (Carey and Hart 1849) 333.
[5] *New York Times v Sullivan*, 376 US 254, 276 (1964).

Civil War. Vallandigham was convicted by a military tribunal and exiled by Lincoln for making a speech in Ohio in which he described the Civil War as 'wicked, cruel, and unnecessary' and depicted it as 'a war for the freedom of the blacks and the enslavement of the whites'.[6] In defending Vallandigham's arrest, Lincoln maintained that it was justified because, in Lincoln's understanding, Vallandigham 'was laboring, with some effect, to prevent the raising of troops [and] to encourage desertions from the army'. Lincoln added, '[m]ust I shoot a simple-minded soldier boy who deserts, while I must not touch a hair of a wily agitator who induces him to desert?... I think that in such a case to silence the agitator, and save the boy is not only constitutional, but withal a great mercy'.[7]

Although Vallandigham was a major political figure, most of those arrested for disloyal expression during the Civil War were men of obscurity, whose outbursts were hardly threatening to the war effort. David Lyon of Illinois, for example, was arrested for saying that 'anyone who enlists is a God Damn fool', William Palmer of Ohio was arrested for writing that 'not fifty soldiers will fight to free Negroes', and Jacob Wright of New Jersey was arrested for saying that anyone who enlists is 'no better than a goddamned nigger'.[8] Moreover, during the Civil War as many as 300 opposition newspapers were suspended because of their alleged 'disloyalty' to the Union cause and because that disloyalty would cause individuals to refuse induction in the military, to be insubordinate or to desert if they were already in the military, or to participate in otherwise unlawful activity. Throughout all of this, no one seriously maintained that these actions on the part of the government violated the First Amendment.

18.3 WORLD WAR I

The story of free speech during World War I is an even more disturbing chapter in US history. When the United States entered the war in April 1917, there was strong opposition to both the war and the draft. Many citizens believed that the US's goal was not to 'make the world safe for democracy', as President Woodrow Wilson had declared, but to protect the investments of the wealthy. Many German-Americans, Irish-Americans, socialists, pacifists, and anarchists were sharply critical of the Wilson administration, and such compelling figures as Jane Addams, Eugene Debs, and Emma Goldman all vehemently opposed the war and the draft. During Congress's debate on the war

---

[6] Frank L Klement, *The Limits of Dissent: Clement L Vallandigham and the Civil War* (UP of Kentucky 1970) 154; Michael Kent Curtis, *Free Speech, 'The People's Darling Privilege': Struggles for Freedom of Expression in American History* (Duke UP 2000) 310.

[7] Letter from Abraham Lincoln to Erastus Corning and Others, 12 June 1863 in *Abraham Lincoln: Speeches and Writings, 1859–1865* (Library of America 1989) 462.

[8] See Mark E Neely Jr, *The Fate of Liberty: Abraham Lincoln and Civil Liberties* (OUP 1991) 58–61.

resolution, Senator James Reed warned that the reinstitution of the draft 'will have the streets of our American cities running red with blood'.[9]

President Wilson had little patience for such dissent. After the sinking of the *Lusitania*, he warned that disloyalty 'must be crushed out' of existence,[10] and in calling for the first federal legislation against disloyal expression since the Sedition Act of 1798, he insisted that disloyalty 'was...not a subject on which there was room for...debate', for disloyal individuals 'had sacrificed their right to civil liberties'.[11] In these and similar pronouncements, Wilson set the tone for what was to follow.

Shortly after the United States entered the war, Congress enacted the Espionage Act of 1917. Although the Act dealt primarily with espionage and sabotage, several provisions had serious consequences for the freedom of speech. Specifically, the Act made it a crime for any person willfully to 'cause or attempt to cause insubordination, disloyalty, or refusal of duty in the military forces of the United States' or willfully to 'obstruct the recruiting or enlistment service of the United States'.[12]

Although the congressional debate makes clear that the 1917 Act was not intended to suppress dissent generally, but to address very specific concerns relating directly to the operation of the military, aggressive federal prosecutors, and compliant federal judges soon transformed the Act into a full-scale prohibition of seditious utterance. The administration's intent in this regard was made evident in November 1917 when Attorney-General Charles Gregory, referring to war dissenters, declared: '[m]ay God have mercy on them, for they need expect none from an outraged people and an avenging government'.[13]

In fact, the federal government worked strenuously to create an 'outraged people'. Because there had been no direct attack on the United States, and no direct threat to its national security, the administration found it necessary to generate a sense of urgency and a mood of anger in order to exhort Americans to enlist, to contribute money, and to make the many sacrifices that war demands.

To this end, President Wilson established the Committee for Public Information (CPI), under the direction of George Creel, whose charge was to promote support for the war. The CPI produced a flood of inflammatory and often misleading pamphlets, news releases, speeches, editorials, and motion pictures, all designed to instil a hatred of all things German and of all persons whose loyalty was open to doubt. In a fervour whipped up by the federal government, vigilantes ransacked the homes of German-Americans and attacked those who questioned the war. In Texas, six farmers were

---

[9] Quoted in Edward M Coffman, *The War to End All Wars: The American Military Experience in World War I* (OUP 1968) 25.

[10] Woodrow Wilson, 'Third Annual Message to Congress' quoted in David M Kennedy, *Over Here: The First World War and American Society* (OUP 1980) 24.

[11] Quoted in Paul L Murphy, *World War I and the Origin of Civil Liberties in the United States* (WW Norton 1979) 53.

[12] Act of 15 June 1917, ch 30, tit I, § 3, 40 Stat 219.

[13] *New York Times* (New York City, 21 Nov 1917) 3. See also Robert Justin Goldstein, *Political Repression in Modern America: From 1870 to the Present* (Schenkman 1978) 108.

horsewhipped because they declined to contribute to the American Red Cross; in Oklahoma, a former minister who opposed the sale of Liberty Bonds was tarred-and-feathered; and in Illinois, an angry mob wrapped an individual suspected of disloyalty in a US flag and then murdered him on a public street.

It was in this atmosphere that federal judges were called upon to enforce the Espionage Act of 1917. In this environment, and in the absence of any clear judicial precedents protecting the freedom of speech, it was unlikely that many judges would stand up to the pressures for suppression and, indeed, most did not. A few judges, though, did take a strong stand in support of civil liberties. In particular, federal district judges George Bourquin of Montana, Charles Amidon of North Dakota, and Learned Hand of New York stood fast against the tide. Judges Bourquin and Amidon insisted that in order to sustain a prosecution under the Espionage Act, the government had to offer convincing evidence that the defendant had specifically intended to cause others to interfere with the war effort and that the speech was likely to have that effect.[14]

Judge Hand embraced a different approach. In his opinion in *Masses Publishing Co v Patten*,[15] Hand argued that speech did not violate the Espionage Act unless the speaker *expressly* urged others to do something unlawful. 'If that not be the test', he cautioned, 'I can see no escape from the conclusion that under this [Act] every political agitation...is illegal'. This distinction, he emphasized, 'is not a scholastic subterfuge, but a hard-bought acquisition in the fight for freedom'.[16]

But few other judges displayed the wisdom—or courage—of Judges Bourquin, Amidon, and Hand. During the course of the war, the Department of Justice prosecuted more than 2,000 individuals for allegedly seditious expression, and in an atmosphere of fear, hysteria, and clamour, most judges were quick to mete out severe punishments to those deemed disloyal. The prevailing approach in the lower federal courts is well-illustrated by the decision of the US Court of Appeals in *Shaffer v United States*.[17] In *Shaffer*, the defendant was charged with possessing and mailing copies of a book, *The Finished Mystery*, in violation of the Espionage Act. The book contained the following passage: 'The war itself is wrong...There is not a question raised, an issue involved, a cause at stake, which is worth the life of one blue-jacket on the sea or one khaki-coat in the trenches'.[18]

Shaffer was convicted, and the US Court of Appeals affirmed the conviction, with the following reasoning:[19]

> [T]he question [is] whether the natural and probable tendency and effect of [Shaffer's] words [might be] to produce the result condemned by the statute. [To] teach that [the] war against Germany was wrong [has the natural tendency to

---

[14] See *United States v Hall*, reported in 65th Cong, 2d Sess in Cong Rec S 4559–60 (4 April 1918); *United States v Schutte*, 252 F 212 (D ND 1918). See Geoffrey R Stone, 'The Origins of the "Bad Tendency Test"': Free Speech in Wartime' [2003] Sup Ct Rev 411.
[15] *Masses Publishing Co v Patten*, 244 F 535 (SD NY 1917). [16] Ibid 540.
[17] *Shaffer v United States*, 255 F 886 (9th Cir 1919). [18] Ibid 887. [19] Ibid 887–9.

encourage individuals to refuse military service. Even if Shaffer did not specifically intend] to cause such unlawful conduct, [he] must be presumed to have intended the natural and probable consequences of [his words].

This approach was embraced by almost every federal court that interpreted the Espionage Act during the course of World War I. The result, as Judge Hand had feared, was the suppression of virtually all criticism of the war. In 1919, Assistant Attorney-General John Lord O'Brian explained that the Espionage Act 'was not directed against disloyal utterances'. Rather, its 'sole aim' was 'to protect the process of raising and maintaining our armed forces'.[20] In practice, however, the Act became an efficient tool for the blanket suppression of all 'disloyal utterances'. Professor Zechariah Chafee later concluded that under the 'bad tendency' interpretation of the Act, all 'genuine discussion among civilians of the justice and wisdom of continuing a war...becomes perilous'.[21]

But even this was not enough. Angered by the rulings of Judges Bourquin, Amidon, and Hand, and determined to ensure that no similar decisions would be possible, Congress enacted the Sedition Act of 1918, which made it criminal, among other things, for any person to utter, print, write, or publish any disloyal, profane, scurrilous, or abusive language intended to cause contempt or scorn for the form of US government, the constitution, or the flag, or to utter any words supporting the cause of any country at war with the United States or opposing the cause of the United States.[22]

Even the signing of the Armistice did not bring this era to a close. The Russian Revolution had generated deep anxiety in the United States, and a series of violent strikes and spectacular bombings triggered the period of intense public paranoia that became known as the 'Red Scare' of 1919–20. Attorney-General A Mitchell Palmer announced that the bombings were an 'attempt on the part of radical elements to rule the country'.[23] The *New York Times* proclaimed: 'Red Peril Here!'[24]

Palmer established the 'General Intelligence Division' (GID) within the Bureau of Investigation and appointed J Edgar Hoover to gather and co-ordinate information about radical activities. The GID unleashed a horde of undercover agents and confidential informants to infiltrate radical organizations. From November 1919 to January 1920, the GID conducted a series of stunning raids in thirty-three cities. More than 5,000 people were arrested on suspicion of radicalism. The GID aggressively fed the Red Scare by publicly disseminating sensational and often unwarranted charges that communists and other dissidents had instigated violent strikes and race riots. The public was ecstatic. The *Washington Post* proclaimed that 'there is no time to waste on hairsplitting over any supposed infringements of liberty'.[25]

---

[20] John Lord O'Brian, 'Civil Liberty in War Time' 62 *Rep NY St Bar Assn* 275, 299–300 (17 Jan 1919).
[21] See Zechariah Chafee Jr, *Freedom of Speech* (Harvard UP 1941) 52.
[22] Act of 16 May 1918, ch 75, § 1, 40 Stat 553.
[23] Quoted in Robert K Murray, *Red Scare: A Study in National Hysteria, 1919–1920* (McGraw-Hill 1955) 9.
[24] *New York Times* (New York City, 11 Mar 1919).
[25] *Washington Post* (Washington, DC, 4 Jan 1920) 4.

And where was the US Supreme Court in all this? In a series of decisions in 1919 and 1920—*Schenck v United States, Frohwerk v United States, Debs v United States, Abrams v United States, Schaefer v United States, Pierce v United States*, and *Gilbert v United States*—the Court, embracing the bad tendency standard illustrated by the *Shaffer* opinion, consistently upheld the convictions of individuals who had agitated against the war and the draft—individuals as obscure as Mollie Steimer, a Russian-Jewish émigré who had distributed anti-war leaflets in Yiddish on the Lower East Side of New York, and as prominent as Eugene V Debs, who had received almost a million votes as the Socialist Party candidate for president in 1916.[26] In short, the Court held that speech that has even the tendency to cause others to engage in unlawful behaviour is not protected by the First Amendment.

In the fall of 1919, however, Justices Oliver Wendell Holmes Jr and Louis Brandeis began to dissent from this position. In his landmark dissenting opinion in *Abrams*, for example, Holmes declared that 'we should be eternally vigilant against attempts to check the expression of opinions that we loathe and believe to be fraught with death, unless they so imminently threaten immediate interference with the lawful and pressing purposes of the law that an immediate check is required to save the country'. Holmes explained that this should be the test, rather than mere bad tendency, because 'the ultimate good desired is better reached by free trade in ideas', and because 'the best test of truth is the power of the thought to get itself accepted in the competition of the market'.[27] Thus, except in extraordinary circumstances, even speech that is likely to spur others to engage in unlawful conduct is protected by the constitution.

Several years later, in the mid-1920s, the Supreme Court considered the constitutionality of state laws making it a crime for any individual or organization to advocate the use of force or violence to bring about political change. Although the Court upheld the constitutionality of these laws, and of the convictions under them, Justices Holmes and Brandeis continued to adhere to their own understanding of the First Amendment. In his dissenting opinion in *Gitlow v New York*, for example, Holmes maintained that the critical question should be whether the speech creates 'a clear and present danger', and in his separate opinion in *Whitney v California*, Brandeis insisted that even express advocacy of law violation 'is not a justification for denying free speech' unless the government can demonstrate that 'the advocacy would be immediately acted on'. This was so, Brandeis argued, because 'if there be time [to] avert the evil' by the processes of debate and discussion, then 'the remedy to be applied is more speech, not enforced silence'. Indeed, Brandeis concluded, 'only an emergency can justify repression'.[28] This was not, however, the law.

---

[26] *Schenck v United States*, 249 US 47 (1919); *Frohwerk v United States*, 249 US 204 (1919); *Debs v United States*, 249 US 211 (1919); *Abrams v United States*, 250 US 616 (1919); *Schaefer v United States*, 251 US 466 (1920); *Pierce v United States*, 252 US 239 (1920); *Gilbert v Minnesota*, 254 US 325 (1920).

[27] *Abrams* (n 26) 630–1.

[28] *Gitlow v New York*, 268 US 652 (1925) (Holmes J, dissenting); *Whitney v California*, 274 US 357, 377 (1927) (Brandeis J, concurring).

18.4 The Cold War

Over the next several decades, the Supreme Court began to give somewhat greater protection to free speech, moving at least tentatively in the direction of the Holmes–Brandeis approach. In 1940, for example, in *Cantwell v Connecticut*, the Court held that an individual could not constitutionally be punished for engaging in speech that might so offend others that they might respond with violence unless the speech created 'a clear and present danger to a substantial interest of the State'.[29] At the same time, though, the Court did not expressly call into question the continuing authority of its decisions from the prior era.

During World War II, the Supreme Court faced no major challenges to its overall approach to these issues. Unlike the situation during the Civil War and World War I, few Americans directly challenged the nation's position during World War II. As World War II drew to a close, though, the nation moved almost seamlessly into what came to be known as the Cold War. As the glow of the nation's wartime alliance with the Soviet Union evaporated, fears over national security once again generated wide-ranging federal and state restrictions on 'dangerous' speech. These restrictions included extensive loyalty programmes, emergency detention programmes, attempts to outlaw the Communist Party, requirements that all so-called communist-front and communist-action organizations register with the government, and extensive state and federal legislative investigations of suspected 'subversives'.

In 1947, President Harry Truman's Secretary of Labor demanded that the Communist Party be outlawed. 'Why', he asked, 'should they be able to elect people to public office?' Attorney-General Tom Clark ordered individuals arrested because they 'had been making speeches around the country that were derogatory to our way of life'. President Truman himself proclaimed: 'I want you to get this straight. I hate Communism'.[30]

The Supreme Court's first major encounter with the free speech issues in this era, *Dennis v United States*,[31] involved the prosecution under the federal Smith Act of the leaders of the US Communist Party. The Smith Act made it 'unlawful for any person to knowingly or willfully advocate, abet, advise, or teach the duty, necessity, desirability, or propriety of overthrowing or destroying any government in the United States by force or violence'.[32]

In a six-to-two decision in 1951, the Court held that the convictions did not violate the First Amendment. In a plurality opinion, Chief Justice Vinson declared that although the Court had never 'expressly overruled the majority opinions' in its World War I decisions on the meaning of the First Amendment, 'there is little doubt that subsequent

---

[29] *Cantwell v Connecticut*, 310 US 296, 311 (1940).
[30] Quoted in David Caute, *The Great Fear: The Anti-Communist Purge under Truman and Eisenhower* (Simon and Schuster 1978) 27, 28, 33.
[31] *Dennis v United States*, 341 US 494 (1951).   [32] 54 Stat 670–1 (1940) 18 USC § 2385.

opinions have inclined toward the Holmes–Brandies' approach.[33] In other words, by 1951, the underground tradition of Justices Holmes and Brandeis had become more persuasive precedent than the opinions from which they had dissented.

But that still left Vinson with the task of deciding precisely what the phrase 'clear and present danger' means. Rather than applying the test in the way Holmes and Brandeis understood it, and thus invalidating the convictions, as Justices Hugo Black and William O Douglas argued for in dissent, Vinson diluted the Holmes–Brandeis version of the standard and held that, because the violent overthrow of government is such a grave harm, the danger need neither be clear nor present to justify suppression. In effect, Vinson reasoned, the true meaning of clear and present danger is that in each case the court 'must ask whether the gravity of the "evil", discounted by its improbability, justifies such invasion of free speech as is necessary to avoid the danger'. In this case, he explained, the formation by the defendants of a 'highly organized conspiracy, with rigidly disciplined members', combined with the 'inflammable nature of world conditions, similar uprisings in other countries, and the touch-and-go nature of our relations with countries with whom petitioners were in the very least ideologically attuned', persuade 'us that their convictions were justified'.[34]

In a highly prescient dissenting opinion, Justice Black observed that '[p]ublic opinion being what it now is, few will protest the conviction of these' communists. 'There is hope', he added, 'that in calmer times, when present pressures, passions and fears subside, this…Court will restore the First Amendment liberties to the…place where they belong in a free society'.[35]

Over the next several years, in a series of decisions premised on *Dennis*, the Court upheld the constitutionality of far-reaching legislative investigations of 'subversive' organizations and individuals, and affirmed the power of government to exclude from the bar, the ballot, and public employment any person who had been a member of any organization that advocated the violent overthrow of government.[36]

Towards the end of the decade, however, as the hysteria over the Red Menace began to abate, and with changes in the Supreme Court's composition and perspective, the Court began to take a fresh look at the issue. In 1957, for example, in *Yates v United States*, the Court, in an opinion by Justice John Marshall Harlan, adopted a narrow interpretation of the Smith Act. In effect, the Court drew a sharp distinction between advocacy of unlawful action 'as an abstract principle', and 'advocacy directed' to 'promoting unlawful action'. Thus, the Court held that 'mere doctrinal justification of forceable overthrow', even 'if engaged in with the intent to accomplish overthrow', was not punishable under the Smith Act because such advocacy was 'too remote from concrete action'. At the same time, though, the Court did not insist that the danger must be imminent in order for speech to be punished. Rather, it declared that for speech to be punishable under the Act it must advocate specific, concrete action 'now or in the future'. *Yates* was a puzzling

---

[33] *Dennis* (n 31) 507.   [34] Ibid 510–11.   [35] Ibid 581 (Black J, dissenting).
[36] See, eg, *Barenblatt v United States*, 360 US 109 (1959); *Adler v Board of Education*, 342 US 485 (1952); *Communist Party v Subversive Activities Control Board*, 367 US 1 (1961).

decision, especially because Harlan insisted that the Court had interpreted the Act in that way in order 'to disregard a constitutional danger zone so clearly marked'.[37] *Yates* thus left unclear precisely what the First Amendment *requires* when an individual is prosecuted for speech that might cause others to engage in unlawful conduct.

Over the next decade, though, building upon *Yates*, the Court constrained the power of legislative committees to investigate political beliefs, invalidated restrictions on the mailing of communist political propaganda, limited the circumstances in which an individual could constitutionally be denied public employment because of their political beliefs or associations, and restricted the authority of a state to deny membership in the bar to individuals because of their past communist affiliations.[38] Although the Court proceeded in fits and starts during this decade, in the end it played an important role in helping to bring the Red Scare to a close.

18.5 THE VIETNAM WAR

In the Vietnam War, as in the Civil War and World War I, there was substantial, often bitter, opposition both to the war and the draft in the United States. Lest we forget the stresses of those years, it is useful to recall Theodore White's eyewitness account of the 1968 Democratic Convention:

> On Wednesday, the Democratic Convention defeated the peace plank by a close margin, while in Grant Park the National Guard had arrived in force, to join the police. The National Guard fired tear-gas grenades at the demonstrators on Michigan Avenue, while triple ranks of picket lines of Chicago policemen in blue helmets and carrying billy-clubs block the Michigan Avenue bridges. The demonstrators chant 'Peace Now, Peace Now' and as they approach the Chicago police picket-lines they chant to the police 'Hey, Hey, Go Away'...
>
> Then, like a fist jolting, like a piston extending from its chamber, comes a hurtling column of police... As the scene clears, there are police clubbing youngsters, police dragging youngsters, police rushing them by the elbows, their heels dragging, to patrol wagons... It is a scene from... the Russian Revolution. Gas grenades explode, the police lift a yellow barricade and carrying it like a battering ram they rush the crowd again. There are splotches of blood... Demonstrators in the front rank kneel, with arms folded across their breasts, and begin singing American the Beautiful. Those behind them chant 'Peace Now, Peace Now'. Violence bursts again. A commotion explodes in the front rank; one sees the clubs coming down. There is much blood now. The chants change to 'The Whole World is Watching'.[39]

---

[37] *Yates v United States*, 354 US 298, 318–19, 321, 324–5 (1957).
[38] See, eg, *Schware v Board of Bar Examiners of New Mexico*, 353 US 232 (1957); *Konigsberg v State Bar of California*, 366 US 36 (1961); *Gibson v Florida Legislative Investigating Committee*, 372 US 539 (1963); *Lamont v Postmaster General*, 381 US 301 (1965); *Elfbrandt v Russell*, 384 US 11 (1966); *Keyishian v Board of Regents*, 385 US 589 (1967); *United States v Robel*, 389 US 258 (1967).
[39] Theodore H White, *The Making of the President 1968* (Atheneum 1969) 369–73.

Over the next several years, the United States suffered through a period of intense and often violent struggle. After President Nixon announced the US 'incursion' into Cambodia, student strikes closed a hundred campuses. Governor Ronald Reagan, asked about campus militants, replied: 'If it takes a bloodbath, let's get it over with'.[40] On 4 May, National Guardsmen at Kent State University responded to taunts and rocks by firing their M-1 rifles into a crowd of students, killing four and wounding nine others. Protests and strikes exploded at more than twelve hundred of the nation's colleges and universities. Thirty ROTC buildings were burned or bombed in the first week of May. The National Guard was mobilized in sixteen states. As Henry Kissinger put it later, 'the very fabric of government was falling apart'.[41]

Despite all this, there was no systematic effort during the Vietnam War to prosecute individuals for their opposition to the war. As Todd Gitlin has rightly observed, in comparison to World War I, 'the repression of the late Sixties and early Seventies was mild'.[42] There are many reasons for this, including, of course, the compelling fact that most of the dissenters in this era were the sons and daughters of the middle class, and thus could not so easily be targeted as the 'Other'. But the courts, and especially the Supreme Court, played a key role in this period.

In 1969, the Court, in *Brandenburg v Ohio*,[43] overruled *Dennis* and held that even advocacy of unlawful conduct cannot be punished unless it is likely to incite 'imminent lawless action'. The Court had come a long way in the fifty years since World War I.[44] However, the Court did not rest there. In other decisions it held that the Georgia House of Representatives could not deny Julian Bond his seat because of his express opposition to the draft;[45] that a public university could not deny recognition to the SDS because it advocated a philosophy of violence;[46] that school children had a right to protest the war even on school premises;[47] that the government could not punish an individual for treating the US flag with contempt;[48] that the government could not conduct national security wiretaps without prior judicial approval;[49] and that the government could not constitutionally enjoin publication of the Pentagon Papers, even though the Defense Department claimed that publication would endanger national security.[50]

This is not to say that the government did not find other ways to impede dissent. The most significant of these was the FBI's extensive effort to infiltrate and to 'expose, disrupt and otherwise neutralize' allegedly 'subversive' organizations, ranging from civil rights

---

[40] *San Francisco Chronicle* (San Francisco, 8 April 1970) 1.
[41] Henry Kissinger, *White House Years* (Little, Brown 1979) 513.
[42] Todd Gitlin, *The Sixties: Years of Hope, Days of Rage* (Bantam Books 1987) 415.
[43] *Brandenburg v Ohio*, 395 US 444 (1969).
[44] See Frank R Strong, 'Fifty Years of "Clear and Present Danger": From Schenck to Brandenburg—And Beyond' [1969] Sup Ct Rev 41.
[45] See *Bond v Floyd*, 385 US 116 (1966). [46] See *Healy v James*, 408 US 169 (1972).
[47] See *Tinker v Des Moines School District*, 393 US 503 (1969).
[48] See *Smith v Goguen*, 415 US 566 (1974).
[49] See *United States v United States District Court*, 407 US 297 (1972).
[50] See *New York Times v United States*, 403 US 713 (1971).

groups to the various factions of the anti-war movement. In this COINTELPRO operation, the FBI compiled political dossiers on more than half-a-million Americans.

Although Attorney-General Stone had ended the FBI's surveillance of political radicals in 1924, twelve years later President Roosevelt secretly authorized J Edgar Hoover to resume the FBI's investigation of suspected fascists and communists. The Bureau promptly re-established an aggressive informer programme and a massive classification system. In a 1938 memorandum, Hoover stressed the need to preserve the 'utmost degree of secrecy in order to avoid criticism'. Conceding that such undercover activities were 'repugnant to the American people', he explained that it would be unwise to seek special legislation that might focus attention on the government's plan to develop a programme of such magnitude.[51]

The outbreak of the war in Europe forced the FBI's actions into the open, and in January 1940, Hoover revealed to a House subcommittee that the FBI had revived the GID.[52] Upon learning of this development, Senator Norris of Nebraska fumed that the FBI 'exists only to investigate violations of law', not to gather information about political dissidents. He warned that these activities 'are going to bring into disrepute the methods of our entire system of jurisprudence'.[53] Defending the Department of Justice against this accusation, Attorney-General Robert Jackson replied that 'one of the first steps which I took upon assuming office was to review the activities and attitude of the Federal Bureau of Investigation' and to reaffirm 'the principles which Attorney-General Stone laid down in 1924'. He assured Congress that Director Hoover agreed with these principles and that he and Hoover fully understood that the 'usefulness of the Bureau depends upon a faithful adherence to those limitations'.[54] Little did he know.

Several years later, Attorney-General Biddle informed Hoover that there was 'no statutory authorization or other justification for keeping a "custodial detention" list of citizens', that the classification system used by the FBI was 'inherently unreliable' and that Hoover's list should 'not be used for any purpose whatsoever'. Hoover, however, simply renamed the project 'Security Matter' rather than 'Custodial Detention' and directed FBI agents to continue their work. He cautioned that this programme 'should at no time be mentioned or alluded to in investigative reports discussed with agencies or individuals outside the Bureau'.[55]

By the late 1950s, after the Supreme Court began to embrace restrictive interpretations of the Smith Act and other anti-communist legislation, Hoover decided to take matters into his own hands. Not content merely to compile extensive files on organizations

---

[51] Athan G Theoharis, *Spying on Americans: Political Surveillance from Hoover to the Huston Plan* (Temple UP 1978) 71; Frank J Donner, *The Age of Surveillance: The Aims and Methods of America's Political Intelligence System* (Knopf 1980) 56 (quoting a memorandum written by J Edgar Hoover on 10 October 1938).

[52] Goldstein (n 13) 247.

[53] 76th Cong, 3d Sess in 86 Cong Rec S 5642 (7 May 1940) (reading into the record a 22 February 1940 letter from Senator Norris to Robert Jackson).

[54] 76th Cong, 3d Sess in 86 Cong Rec S 5643 (7 May 1940) (reading into the record a 1 March 1940 reply from Robert Jackson to Senator Norris).

[55] Goldstein (n 13) 248; Theoharis (n 51) 40–4.

and individuals he viewed as dangerous to the national security, Hoover launched COINTELPRO in 1956. This programme reflected a systematic effort to harass dissident organizations, sow dissension within their ranks and inform public and private employers of the political beliefs and activities of dissenters. Targeted initially at the Communist Party, the programme gradually expanded to include Socialist, White Hate, Black Nationalist, civil rights, anti-war and New Left groups as well. COINTELPRO was launched without any executive or legislative authorization, and its existence was a closely guarded secret, shielded from public view by a carefully crafted system of multiple filings.[56]

When these activities finally came to light they were sharply condemned by congressional committees. In 1976, the Senate Select Committee to Study Government Operations with Respect to Intelligence Activities made the following findings:

> The Government has often undertaken the secret surveillance of citizens on the basis of their political beliefs, even when those beliefs posed no threat of violence or illegal acts...The Government, operating primarily through secret informants, [has] swept in vast amounts of information about the personal lives, views, and associations of American citizens. Investigations of groups...have continued for decades, despite the fact that those groups did not engage in unlawful activity. [FBI] headquarters alone has developed over 500,000 domestic intelligence files. [The] targets of intelligence activity have including political adherents of the right and the left, ranging from activist to casual supporters.[57]

Following the example of Attorney-General Stone after the Red Scare, Attorney-General Edward Levi declared that such practices were incompatible with US values and, in 1976, instituted a series of guidelines designed to sharply restrict FBI surveillance of political and religious organizations' activities.

18.6 'The Secret of Liberty'

What can Americans learn from this history? I would like to offer six observations.

First, there is now consensus on two key propositions: that the Constitution applies in time of war, but that the special demands of war may affect the application of the Constitution. Americans have thus rejected the more extreme positions—that the Constitution is irrelevant in wartime, and that wartime is irrelevant to the application of the Constitution. What this means in practice is that in applying the relevant constitutional standard in any particular area of the law, whether it be clear and present danger,

---

[56] See Theoharis (n 51) 133–52; Donner (n 51) 178–84.
[57] Senate Select Committee to Study Governmental Operations with Respect to Intelligence Activities, Final Report, Intelligence Activities and the Rights of Americans, Book II, S Doc No 13133-4, 94th Cong, 2d Sess 5–9 (1976).

compelling governmental interest, probable cause, or whatever, it is appropriate to take the special circumstances of wartime into account in determining whether the government has sufficient justification to limit the constitutional right at issue. What it does *not* mean, however, is that courts should abdicate their responsibilities in the face of assertions of national security or military necessity.

Second, Americans have a long history of overreacting to the perceived dangers of wartime. Time after time, the United States has allowed fears to get the better of it. Although each of these six episodes presented markedly different challenges, in each the United States went too far in restricting civil liberties. Of course, this proposition cannot be proved with the exactitude of a mathematical formula. Nor can it be proved merely by looking back and blithely inferring that because each of these crises ended well, the restrictions of civil liberties were unwarranted. The fallacy of that logic is too patent to require explication. As with any counter-factual, we cannot know for certain what would have happened if Lincoln had not suspended the writ of habeas corpus, or Wilson had not prosecuted those who protested the war, or Roosevelt had not interned Japanese-Americans. Perhaps the South would have succeeded, perhaps the United States would have lost World War I, perhaps Japanese-Americans would have sabotaged the Pacific Coast, perhaps the Berlin Wall would still be standing. Perhaps. But it is difficult to believe, with the benefit of hindsight,[58] that any of these consequences would have resulted.

Because it is impossible to know the counter-factual for certain, we have to rely to some degree on reasoning by inference. Certainly, we know that in every one of these episodes Americans came after-the-fact to regret their actions, and to understand them, in part, as excessive responses due largely to public hysteria and government manipulation. Certainly, we know that it is human nature to be risk-averse in the face of danger, especially when we can mitigate the danger to ourselves by disadvantaging 'others'— whether they be suspected Jacobins, secessionists, anarchists, Japanese-Americans, communists, or 'hippies'. This response enables us both to secure our own safety and to vent our anger and frustration at those we already view with contempt. Certainly, we know that the actual motivations for the restriction of civil liberties in many of these episodes were more complex than the government let on, and that they frequently involved a range of political as well as military considerations. All of these factors help to explain and to ratify the after-the-fact conviction that in each of these instances the United States *unnecessarily* sacrificed the constitutional rights of others.

Third, it is often argued that given the sacrifices the United States asks individuals (especially soldiers) to make in time of war, it is small price to ask others to surrender some of their peacetime freedoms to help the war effort. As members of Congress argued in defence of the Sedition Act of 1918, surely people can restrain their criticism of the government in order to maintain the national unity that is essential to the war

---

[58] On the problems of hindsight, see Jeffrey J Rachlinski, 'A Positive Psychological Theory of Judging in Hindsight' (1998) 65 *U Chi L Rev* 571.

effort.[59] And as the Court argued in *Korematsu v United States*, 'hardships are part of war, and war is an aggregation of hardships'.[60]

This is a seductive, but dangerous argument. To fight a war successfully, it is necessary for soldiers to risk their lives. But it is not necessarily also 'necessary' for others to surrender their freedoms. That necessity must be convincingly demonstrated, not merely presumed. And this is especially true when, as is almost always the case, the individuals whose rights are sacrificed are not those who make the laws, but minorities, dissidents, and non-citizens. In those circumstances, 'we' are making a decision to sacrifice 'their' rights—not a very prudent way to balance the competing interests.

It is also worth noting that this argument is particularly insidious when the freedom of speech is at issue. A critical function of free expression in wartime is to help us make wise decisions about how to conduct the war, whether our leaders are leading well, whether to end the war, and so on. Those questions cannot be put in suspension during a war. The freedom of speech in this context is not merely a right of the individual, but a fundamental national interest that is essential to the very existence of democratic decision-making in wartime.

Fourth, the Supreme Court matters. It is often said that presidents do what they please in wartime. Attorney-General Biddle once observed that 'the Constitution has not greatly bothered any wartime President',[61] and Chief Justice Rehnquist, in his book on this subject, concluded that 'there is no reason to think that future wartime presidents will act differently from Lincoln, Wilson, or Roosevelt'.[62]

The record, however, is more complex than this might suggest. Although presidents may think of themselves as bound more by political than by constitutional constraints in time of war, the two are linked. Lincoln did not propose a Sedition Act, Wilson rejected calls to suspend the writ of habeas corpus. The fact is that even during wartime, presidents have not attempted to restrict civil liberties in the face of settled Supreme Court precedent. Although presidents often push the envelope where the law is unclear, they do not defy established constitutional doctrine.

Perhaps this is because they respect the law. Perhaps it is because they do not want to pick a fight with the Supreme Court in the midst of a war. But whatever the explanation,

---

[59] In support of the Sedition Act of 1918, Senator Borah argued that 'if our soldiers are...in France for the purpose of maintaining and protecting...our form of government, our Constitution and our flag', then 'is it too much to ask complete devotion upon the part of those who remain at home to the things for which our boys are fighting and dying upon the western front?' Senator Poindexter expressed exasperation 'that, regardless of its effect upon the war', some men 'attached so much more importance to the right of free speech, while at the same time we take men's bodies, conscript them into the Army,...subject them to the dangers of the firing line' and commandeer their property to 'subject it to the purposes of the war'. 'I should like to know', he asked, 'what distinction there is...while we are taking their bodies and their property if we also take away from them somewhat of this license of speech which is so much defended?' See Cong Rec, 65th Cong 2d Sess 4633, 4637 (5 April 1918).
[60] *Korematsu v United States*, 323 US 214, 219.
[61] Francis Biddle, *In Brief Authority* (Doubleday 1962) 219.
[62] William H Rehnquist, *All the Laws But One: Civil Liberties in Wartime* (Knopf 1998) 224.

the phenomenon is unmistakable and it is important. The Supreme Court is not powerless to influence these matters. As Chief Justice Rehnquist noted, a decision 'in favor of civil liberty will stand as a precedent to regulate future actions of Congress and the Executive branch in future wars'.[63] The record bears this out.

What this suggests is that in periods of relative calm, the Court should consciously construct constitutional doctrines that will provide firm and unequivocal guidance for later periods of stress. Clear constitutional rules that are not easily circumvented or manipulated by prosecutors, jurors, presidents and even Supreme Court Justices are essential if the United States is to preserve civil liberties in the face of wartime fear and hysteria. Malleable principles, open-ended balances, and vague standards may serve us well in periods of tranquility, but are likely to fail us when we need the Constitution most.[64]

Fifth, it is often said that the Supreme Court will not decide a case against the government on an issue of military security during a period of national emergency. The decisions most often cited in support of this proposition are *Korematsu* and *Dennis*. Clinton Rossiter once observed that 'the government of the United States, in the case of military necessity', can be 'just as much a dictatorship, after its own fashion, as any other government on earth'. The Supreme Court, he added, 'will not and cannot be expected to get in the way of this power'.[65]

In fact, however, this does not give the Court its due. There are many counter-examples. During World War II, for instance, the Court consistently upheld the constitutional rights of US fascists and other dissidents in a series of criminal prosecutions and denaturalization proceedings. In 1943, the Court held in *Schneiderman v United States*[66] that the government could not denaturalize a US citizen because of their membership in the Communist Party unless it could prove by 'clear, unequivocal and convincing evidence' that they had personally endorsed the use of 'present violent action which creates a clear and present danger of public disorder or other substantive evil'.[67] The following year, in *Baumgartner v United States*,[68] the Court held that an individual could not be denaturalized for making even 'sinister-sounding' statements 'which native-born citizens utter with impunity'.[69] *Baumgartner* effectively ended the government's programme to denaturalize former members of the German-American Bund.[70]

---

[63] Ibid 222.
[64] See Vincent Blasi, 'The Pathological Perspective and the First Amendment' (1985) 85 *Colum L Rev* 449.
[65] Clinton L Rossiter, *The Supreme Court and the Commander-in-Chief* (Cornell UP 1951) 54.
[66] *Schneiderman v United States*, 320 US 118 (1943).   [67] Ibid 157–8.
[68] *Baumgartner v United States*, 322 US 665 (1944).   [69] Ibid 677.
[70] For a full discussion of the denaturalization cases, see Harry Kalven, *A Worthy Tradition: Freedom of Speech in America* (Harper & Row 1988) 423–36. The Court also overturned the decision to deport labour leader Harry Bridges, ruling in 1945 that there was no evidence showing that Bridges had any connection with any organization advocating illegal overthrow of the government, except in wholly lawful activities. *Bridges v Wixon*, 326 US 135 (1945).

In *Taylor v Mississippi*,[71] an individual was prosecuted for stating that 'it was wrong for our President to send our boys... [to be] shot down for no purpose at all'. The Court held that even in wartime 'criminal sanctions cannot be imposed for such communication'.[72] In *Hartzel v United States*,[73] the defendant was convicted for distributing pamphlets that depicted the war as a 'gross betrayal of America', denounced 'our English allies and the Jews' and assailed the 'patriotism of the President'. Although the case was in many respects a re-run of *Schenck*, the Court reversed Hartzel's conviction because the government failed to prove that he had specifically intended to obstruct the draft. The Court added that 'an American citizen has the right to discuss these matters either by temperate reasoning or by immoderate and vicious invective without running afoul' of the law.[74] This decision went a long way towards ending government efforts to prosecute anti-war dissent during World War II.[75]

In 1943, at the height of the war, the Court held in *West Virginia State Board of Education v Barnette*[76] that the government cannot not require children in the public schools to pledge allegiance to the US flag, explaining that '[i]f there is any fixed star in our constitutional constellation, it is that no official, high or petty, can prescribe what shall be orthodox in politics, nationalism, religion, or other matters of opinion'.[77] Less than a year after Pearl Harbor, the Court held that civilians in Hawaii could not be tried by military tribunals.[78] And in 1944, the Court held that Executive Order 9066 did not authorize the detention of individuals of Japanese ancestry who had been found to be loyal US citizens, effectively marking the end of the Japanese-American internment.[79]

During the Cold War, the Court rejected President Truman's effort to seize the steel industry[80] and, as I have already indicated, helped end the era of McCarthyism. And during the Vietnam War, the Court repeatedly rejected national security claims by the Executive. So, although it is true that the Court must be careful not to overstep its bounds, it is also true that the Court has a long record of fulfilling its constitutional responsibility to protect individual liberties—even in time of war.

Sixth, the United States had made great progress over time in its protection of civil liberties. This is true not only when it is at peace, but when it is at war as well. Almost all of the major restrictions of civil liberties that I have discussed would be less thinkable today than they were in 1789, 1861, 1918, 1942, 1950, or 1968. This is a profound constitutional achievement, and one Americans should not take for granted.

It is, of course, much easier to look back on past crises and find our predecessors wanting, than it is to make wise judgments when we ourselves are in the eye of the storm.

---

[71] *Taylor v Mississippi*, 319 US 583 (1943).   [72] Ibid 586, 590.
[73] *Hartzel v United States* 322 US 680 (1944).
[74] Ibid 683, 689. See also *Keegan v United States*, 325 US 478 (1945) (overturning the convictions of twenty-four members of the Bund who had been charged with advocating draft evasion).
[75] See Paul L Murphy, *The Constitution in Crisis Times, 1918–1969* (Harper & Row 1972) 227; Kalven (n 70) 185–7.
[76] *West Virginia State Board of Education v Barnette*, 319 US 624 (1943).   [77] Ibid 642.
[78] *Duncan v Kahanamoku*, 327 US 304 (1946).   [79] *Ex parte Endo*, 323 US 283 (1944).
[80] *Youngstown Sheet & Tube Co v Sawyer*, 343 US 579 (1952).

That challenge falls to Americans today. As Justice Brandeis once observed, 'those who won our independence...knew that...fear breeds repression' and that 'courage is the secret of liberty'.[81] Those, I think, are the two most fundamental insights for Americans to bear in mind.

To strike the right balance in this time, the United States needs political leaders who know right from wrong; federal judges who will stand fast against the furies of their age; members of the bar and the academy who will help us see ourselves clearly; an informed and tolerant public who will value not only their own liberties, but the liberties of others; and, most of all, Justices of the Supreme Court with the wisdom to know excess when they see it and the courage to preserve liberty when it is imperiled.

---

[81] *Whitney* (n 28) 375 (1927) (Brandeis J, concurring).

Chapter 19

The Internet and Social Media

Gregory P Magarian

Theorists and law-makers often posit essential characteristics of human communication to ground free speech principles and protections. New technologies, however, can change communication paradigms in ways that destabilize those principles and protections. This chapter surveys the distinctive free speech problems raised by the Internet and social media. It discusses the most pressing, prominent issues around Internet speech regulation, with attention to variations across legal systems. It assesses the present state of a constantly changing media sector, emphasizing the issues that appear likeliest to matter for the future.

The chapter first briefly describes the Internet's communicative architecture. It then discusses structural concerns that have limited online free speech or prompted regulatory attention in the Internet Age. These include inequalities of access; power relationships among governments, private speech intermediaries, and Internet users; and the ways the Internet's architecture complicates effective regulation. Finally, the chapter discusses key substantive issues for online communication, including hate speech, privacy, intellectual property, and the credibility and influence of online news sources.

19.1 The Internet as a Free Speech Medium

The Internet's technological architecture frames any discussion of Internet free speech problems.[1] In the simplest terms, the Internet is an interconnected worldwide network of computer networks, voluntarily interconnected and bound by the use of

---

[1] Lawrence Lessig, *Code and Other Laws of Cyberspace, Version 2.0* (Basic Books 2006).

shared technical standards. Any user of the Internet can make content available to any other user, either selectively (one-to-one communication) or more broadly (one-to-many communication).[2] The Internet enables one-to-one communication through messaging platforms such as email, chat, and text services. The dominant vehicle for one-to-many Internet communication is the World Wide Web, which uses hyperlinks to cross-reference content across networks. The Internet can deliver all manner of media content, including text, sound, still and moving pictures, and executable programmes. No central authority controls the Internet's infrastructure or the flow of information online.[3] As of 2018, more than four billion people worldwide communicated on the Internet.[4]

Social media platforms such as Facebook, Twitter, and Instagram add to the Internet's utility by letting users form online communities for sharing text, pictures, video, and links to Web content.[5] Different social media platforms enable different models of community formation. A speaker on an asymmetric social network, such as Twitter, can make messages generally available to whomever chooses to access them. Speakers on a symmetric social network, such as Facebook, choose to associate as 'friends', and a speaker can choose to send messages either to all or a subset of their friends. More than three billion people worldwide used social media as of 2018, a 13 per cent increase over the prior year.[6] Social media platforms' increasing prominence has made their functions and characteristics crucial in determining the scope and forms of Internet speech regulation.

The advent of smartphones–wireless hand-held devices that allow portable Internet connectivity—has substantially augmented Internet communication. The ability to carry the Internet's expressive capacities wherever the user goes has made smartphones an increasingly important vehicle for online communication.[7] The practical utility of smartphones and the communal function of social media complement and enhance one another.

Given unrestricted access to the Internet, anyone can view news and information from the other side of the world as easily as local content. This transnational scope has powerful implications for the utility and freedom of Internet speech. Online communications of all sorts can reach across national and cultural divides. Content providers can

---

[2] For a discussion of the development and structure of the Internet's architecture, see Manuel Castells, *The Internet Galaxy: Reflections on the Internet, Business, and Society* (OUP 2001) 9–33.

[3] The Internet requires some institutional co-ordination, for example in the assignment and maintenance of domain names. See 'Domain Name Registration Process' (*ICANN WHOIS*, July 2017) <https://whois.icann.org/en/domain-name-registration-process> accessed 28 August 2018.

[4] Simon Kemp, 'Digital in 2018: World's Internet Users Pass the 4 Billion Mark' (*We Are Social*, 30 January 2018) <https://wearesocial.com/blog/2018/01/global-digital-report-2018> accessed 28 August 2018.

[5] For a general description and discussion of social media, see Andreas M Kaplan and Michael Haenlein, 'Users of the World, Unite! The Challenges and Opportunities of Social Media' (2010) 53 *Business Horizons* 59.

[6] Kemp (n 4).

[7] The US Supreme Court, for example, has applied constitutional protections against warrantless searches to the digital contents of mobile phones. *Riley v California* 134 S Ct 2473 (2014).

evade direct regulations by hosting information in low-regulation jurisdictions. The Internet's transnational reach makes the problems of Internet free speech transnational as well.

The freedom of Internet speech matters deeply, at a normative level, because the Internet offers unprecedented opportunities for realizing the social benefits of free speech.[8] The United Nations has passed a resolution that calls on member states to protect the right to access and disseminate information on the Internet.[9] The US Supreme Court, in its first encounter with an effort to regulate the Internet, extolled the Internet's 'vast democratic forums', where anyone formerly limited to passive receipt of information can now speak to the world.[10] Canada's telecommunications regulator has similarly stated that 'fixed and mobile wireless broadband Internet access services are catalysts for innovation and underpin a vibrant, creative, interactive world'.[11] Online communication has made powerful contributions to political dynamism and dissent around the world, especially in countries with authoritarian governments.[12] To take one vivid example, political dissidents in Arab nations centrally used social media in early 2011 to organize and spread the wave of mass political protests known as the Arab Spring.[13] Beyond politics, the Internet promotes and stimulates artistic creativity, scientific inquiry, and commercial exchange.

Just as the Internet enhances the benefits of speech, it enhances the harms that speech can cause and that governments may seek to curb. The Internet creates new ways for both governments and wealthy private institutions to aggrandize power over people and communities. Social media occupy a massive cultural space while arguably promoting limited modes of social interaction that crowd out other forms of human connection. Liberal protections for free speech online must take account of the Internet's hazards as well as its promise.

19.2 STRUCTURAL FREE SPEECH PROBLEMS

How well any mass medium facilitates free speech depends on the medium's political, economic, and technical structures. Who owns, operates, and benefits from the medium's infrastructure? Who can use the medium, and what conditions affect access to it?

---

[8] At the same time, personal communication in the physical world retains distinctive value that the Internet cannot replace. See Timothy Zick, Chapter 20 in this volume.

[9] Office of the High Commissioner for Human Rights (OHCHR), 'The Promotion, Protection and Enjoyment of Human Rights on the Internet' (7 April 2018) UN Doc A/HRC/38/L.10/Rev.1.

[10] *Reno v American Civil Liberties Union*, 521 US 844, 868 (1997).

[11] Telecom Regulatory Policy CRTC 2016–496 (*Canadian Radio-Television and Telecommunications Commission*, 21 December 2016) <https://crtc.gc.ca/eng/archive/2016/2016-496.htm> accessed 28 August 2018.

[12] Kris Ruijgrok, 'From the Web to the Streets: Internet and Protests under Authoritarian Regimes' (2017) 24 *Democratization* 498.

[13] Sarah Joseph, 'Social Media, Political Change, and Human Rights' (2012) 35 *BC Int,l & Comp L Rev* 145.

What methods can governments use to restrict speech on the medium? The Internet's distinctive architecture presents a set of interconnected structural free speech problems.

19.2.1 Inequalities of Access to the Internet

The freedom of speech includes an important dimension of distributive justice.[14] The most basic structural determinant of a communication medium's effectiveness is the medium's accessibility to users. In pre-Internet mass media, scarcity of resources, from printing paper to the broadcast spectrum, created a sharp divide between providers and consumers of information. The Internet's decentralized, many-to-many communication architecture largely obviates that sort of resource concern as to online speech. The Internet has drastically reduced the cost of making information available to a mass audience.[15] Two important resource problems, however, still restrict opportunities to communicate online.

First, many people around the world cannot access the Internet at all. Poorer nations, and poorer people within affluent nations, often cannot afford the keys to the Internet's kingdom. A 2016 report by the International Telecommunications Union found a stark divide in 'Internet penetration': the percentages of different nations' residents who have Internet access. Developed countries, on average, have about 70 per cent penetration rates, while developing countries have only about 15 per cent penetration. Europe leads the world, with Internet access for more than 80 per cent of its residents. Several European nations (Iceland, Luxembourg, Norway) have penetration rates over 95 per cent. In contrast, Asian nations and the Arab states have penetration rates of only about 40 per cent. Africa trails the world with a penetration rate of only 10 per cent. At least ten African nations have penetration rates below 7 per cent.[16] People without Internet access are disproportionately less educated, rural, elderly, and female. The cost of Internet access is a serious factor in the penetration disparity: in the developing world, a fixed broadband connection can cost a large percentage of a family's household income.[17]

Second, even as the Internet has lowered the cost of entry into mass communication, the cost for speakers to actually reach a mass audience remains high. The Internet's flood of information has exposed the importance of a communication resource long taken for

---

[14] Jerome A Barron, 'Access to the Press: A New First Amendment Right' (1967) 80 *Harv L Rev* 1641; Kenneth L Karst, 'Equality as a Central Principle in the First Amendment' (1975) 43 *U Chi L Rev* 20; Owen M. Fiss, 'Free Speech and Social Structure' (1986) 71 *Iowa L Rev* 1405.

[15] Eugene Volokh, 'Cheap Speech and What It Will Do' (1995) 104 *Yale LJ* 1805.

[16] 'Measuring the Information Society Report' (2016) International Telecommunications Union <https://www.itu.int/en/ITU-D/Statistics/Documents/publications/misr2016/MISR2016-w4.pdf> accessed 28 August 2018.

[17] Ibid.

granted: human attention.[18] No one can process all the information the Internet makes available on any given subject. People must choose from among the vast array of information sources online, a reality that places a great premium on content providers' capacity to influence and steer audience choices. The pivotal value of audience attention creates advantages for larger, better-financed content providers, which can devote more resources to capturing audience attention. Thus, even though audiences have myriad options for finding information online, limited numbers of content providers dominate important online information environments, much like large media companies were able to do in the pre-Internet era.[19]

19.2.2 Concentrations of Private Power

Freedom from government regulation does not guarantee a lived experience of expressive freedom. Private speech intermediaries—most notably Internet Service Providers (ISPs), search engines, and social media platforms—largely dictate how information flows among Internet users. All of these entities exist not to promote free speech values but rather to make money. Private intermediaries, while generally lacking governments' political motives and accountability, strongly influence the social and political valences of online speech.[20] Authoritarian regimes and even some democratic governments enlist intermediaries to restrict the public's access to disfavoured speech.[21] More commonly, the nature and power of Internet speech intermediaries exacerbate a difficult, long-standing problem for free speech theory: whether and to what extent governments may and should regulate intermediaries to promote free speech.

Governments have often sought to avoid this problem through commercial regulations that limit intermediaries' ability to control communication. Such *structural regulation* constrains not the content of speech but the commercial mechanisms by which private intermediaries control and channel information. Constitutional speech protections generally do not constrain governments from regulating these structural features of communications media.[22] As long as governments do not regulate with the purpose or effect of stifling particular ideas, they generally do not breach free speech barriers. Thus, in the pre-Internet era, governments often restricted, for example, the number of newspapers or broadcast stations that any person or company could own.[23]

---

[18] Tim Wu, 'Is the First Amendment Obsolete?' (*Knight First Amendment Institute*, September 2017) <https://knightcolumbia.org/content/tim-wu-first-amendment-obsolete> accessed 28 August 2018.

[19] Gregory P Magarian, 'Forward into the Past: Speech Intermediaries in the Television and Internet Ages' (2018) 71 *Okla L Rev* 237.

[20] For a discussion of one important example, see Safiya Umoja Noble, *Algorithms of Oppression: How Search Engines Reinforce Racism* (NYU P 2018).

[21] Lyombe Eko, 'Google This: The Great Firewall of China, the It Wheel of India, Google Inc., and Internet Regulation' (2011) 15 *J Internet L* 3.

[22] See Dieter Grimm, 'Freedom of Media', Chapter 29 in this volume.

[23] C Edwin Baker, *Media Concentration and Democracy: Why Ownership Matters* (CUP 2007) 163–89 (discussing a range of actual and proposed policies for dispersal of media ownership).

The most prominent issue for structural regulation of Internet speech has been net neutrality. ISPs want the latitude to deliver different online content for different prices and at different speeds. 'Net neutrality' means a legal mandate that ISPs deliver service without discriminating, in pricing or terms, among sources or contents of speech. Advocates see net neutrality as essential for realizing the democratic promise of the Internet. They point out that, without net neutrality, ISPs can discriminate against content providers whose messages the ISPs disfavour and can marginalize content providers unable to pay premium prices for higher speed or higher volume services.[24] Opponents of net neutrality most commonly argue that letting ISPs set prices and terms of service will create the most efficient conditions for Internet communication.[25]

Governments around the world have enacted net neutrality mandates. Chile in 2010 became the first nation to adopt net neutrality.[26] The European Union maintains net neutrality regulations, enforced by a transnational regulator.[27] Canada protects net neutrality under its Telecommunications Act, which treats ISPs as utilities.[28] Critics, however, have complained that loopholes and exceptions frequently undermine net neutrality regimes. For example, Canadian regulators have allowed ISPs to impose differential charges for residential Internet service based on usage rates.[29] Such controversies underscore the difficulty of setting and enforcing a baseline of 'neutrality' in any legal setting, let alone a setting as complex and fluid as Internet speech.

Perhaps the most contentious battle over the legality and wisdom of net neutrality has played out in the United States. The Obama administration in 2015 imposed a net neutrality mandate through federal regulations, but the Trump administration in 2017 rescinded those regulations.[30] Legal arguments about net neutrality in the United States are taking on an increasingly constitutional cast. Some advocates for net neutrality have argued that the First Amendment's free speech protections require non-discriminatory access to information and audiences and thus compel net neutrality.[31] Conversely, net neutrality opponents including the recently appointed US Supreme Court Justice Brett Kavanaugh argue that net neutrality violates the First Amendment by restricting ISPs'

---

[24] Dawn C Nunziato, *Virtual Freedom: Net Neutrality and Free Speech in the Internet Age* (Stanford Law Books 2009).

[25] Christopher S Yoo, 'Network Neutrality and the Economics of Congestion' (2006) 94 *Geo LJ* 1847.

[26] Law no 20,453 (Biblioteca del Congreso Nacional de Chile, 26 August 2010) <https://www.leychile.cl/Navegar?idNorma=1016570> accessed 28 August 2018.

[27] Regulation (EU) 2015/2020; 'All You Need to Know about Net Neutrality Rules in the EU' (*Body of European Regulators for Electronic Communications*) <https://berec.europa.eu/eng/netneutrality/> accessed 28 August 2018.

[28] Telecommunications Act, SC 1993, c 38.

[29] *Telecom Decision CRTC 2011-44*, Canadian Radio-Television and Telecommunications Commission (25 January 2011).

[30] Cecelia Kang, 'FCC Repeals Net Neutrality Rules' (*New York Times*, 14 December 2017) <https://www.nytimes.com/2017/12/14/technology/net-neutrality-repeal-vote.html> accessed 28 August 2018.

[31] Moran Yemini, 'Mandated Network Neutrality and the First Amendment: Lessons From *Turner* and a New Approach' (2008) 13 *Va J L & Tech* 1.

editorial autonomy to channel content as they see fit.[32] The success of First Amendment arguments either for requiring or for barring net neutrality would represent a major paradigm shift in what US courts so far have treated as a non-constitutional question of structural regulation.

19.2.3 Practical Problems of Content Regulation

A final set of structural issues for Internet free speech, which interact with some of the substantive issues discussed below, concerns the conceptual and logistical challenges that Internet technology presents when governments seek to regulate the content of speech.

A difficult baseline question about substantive regulation is whether, and to what extent, data on the Internet counts as speech that deserves constitutional protection. The Internet can produce and transmit speech in ways that differ from prior media. Substantial aspects of the Internet's processes for generating data, notably autonomous and semi-autonomous algorithms, do not depend on the direct control by human beings that ordinarily characterizes constitutionally protected speech, and much raw online data does not convey ideas in any conventional sense.[33] In the United States, First Amendment law provides very strong protections for speech but has not fully theorized what counts as speech.[34] Scholars disagree about the extent to which information transmitted online deserves First Amendment protection.[35] The US Supreme Court has suggested but not decided that the First Amendment protects online data flows.[36] Given the importance of US-based intermediaries for Internet communication, US law's resolution of the data-as-speech question may carry great significance for the nature and extent of Internet speech regulations.

Where a government can justify a given regulation of Internet content, what sort of regulation is logistically possible? Direct regulation of online speech is often difficult. The transnational character of online communication means that online speakers can frequently elude national regulatory regimes. The enormous volume of online speech can make content regulation very expensive. To take one example, an attempt in the United States to directly restrict 'indecent' online content failed constitutional review in part because the Internet's architecture compelled regulators to cast a very wide net and still

---

[32] *US Telecom Ass'n v Fed Communications Comm'n* No 15–1063 (DC Cir 1 May 2017) (Kavanaugh J, dissenting from denial of rehearing en banc).

[33] Stuart Minor Benjamin, 'Algorithms and Speech' (2013) 161 *U Penn L Rev* 1445.

[34] Frederick Schauer, 'The Boundaries of the First Amendment: A Preliminary Exploration of Constitutional Salience' (2004) 117 *Harv L Rev* 1765, 1770–1.

[35] Compare Ashutosh Bhagwat, '*Sorrell v IMS Health*: Details, Detailing, and the Death of Privacy' (2012) 36 *Vt L Rev* 855 (arguing against generally treating data flows as protected speech) with Jane Bambauer, 'Is Data Speech?' (2014) 66 *Stan L Rev* 57 (arguing in favor of generally treating data flows as protected speech).

[36] *Sorrell v IMS Health, Inc*, 564 US 552, 570 (2011).

created major impediments to the regulations' effectiveness.[37] Totalitarian and authoritarian regimes can, and often do, stifle disfavoured content by imposing blanket controls on Internet access.[38] Democratic governments have sought to constrain online speech through indirect regulation, using incentives and penalties to make private speech intermediaries regulate content. Critics have called this approach 'soft censorship'.[39] The discussion of substantive Internet speech problems below shows how democratic governments have used indirect regulation to curb hate speech, protect privacy, and secure intellectual property.

The difficulty of directly regulating online content and the greater ease of indirectly regulating speech intermediaries strongly influence how law and public policy interact to promote and restrain Internet speech. Online intermediaries have some characteristics of content providers or editors and other characteristics of mere speech conduits. Search engines use proprietary algorithms, as distinct from human editors, to organize and present information about content that third parties have created.[40] Social media platforms likewise use proprietary algorithms to direct users towards particular content created by other users. In general, a claim for free speech protection from government regulation depends on the premise that the claimant is creating content or at least exercising substantial editorial discretion. Conversely, a party's control over the content of speech can justify making the party liable for harms the speech causes. Thus, the stronger an intermediary's case for free speech protection, the stronger may be the government's motivation to impose speech restrictions.[41] This paradox gets more complicated for online intermediaries whose functions and methods muddy the distinction between speakers/editors and conduits. Sorting out intermediaries' amenability to regulation becomes especially important when the intermediaries' pursuit of their self-interests arguably compromises the free speech interests of Internet users.

19.3 SUBSTANTIVE FREE SPEECH PROBLEMS

In contrast to the structural regulations discussed above, *substantive regulations* deliberately target the content of speech in order to achieve some regulatory goal. Authoritarian regimes regularly impose sweeping substantive restrictions on Internet speech.[42] Democratic political systems' constitutional speech protections generally bar substantive

---

[37] *Reno v American Civil Liberties Union*, 521 US 844 (1997).
[38] Evgeny Morozov, *The Net Delusion: The Dark Side of Internet Freedom* (Public Affairs 2011).
[39] Derek E Bambauer, 'Orwell's Armchair' (2012) 79 *U Chi L Rev* 863.
[40] Nunziato (n 24) 110–13.
[41] Rebecca Tushnet, 'Power Without Responsibility: Intermediaries and the First Amendment' (2008) 76 *Geo Wash L Rev* 986.
[42] 'Freedom on the Net 2017: Manipulating Social Media to Undermine Democracy' (2017) Freedom House <https://freedomhouse.org/report/freedom-net/freedom-net-2017> accessed 28 August 2018 (documenting suppression of Internet speech rights in numerous countries).

speech regulations, subject to varying rules for balancing speech interests against regulatory priorities. Indirect regulatory strategies, under which governments induce private speech intermediaries to restrict online speech, may avoid constitutional bars on substantive regulation while still presenting serious threats to free speech norms and to expressive freedom in practice.

This section discusses several substantive free speech problems with high salience for Internet speech. The problems this section will discuss—hateful and defamatory speech, the interaction of speech and privacy interests, intellectual property, and concerns about the democratic effectiveness of the news media—have long figured heavily in free speech law and theory. The increased speed and scope of Internet communications exacerbate the harms that speech can cause and that governments therefore may seek to ameliorate. The Internet also increases the potential benefits of speech, increasing the urgency of robust constitutional speech protections.

19.3.1 Hateful and Defamatory Speech

The Internet's capacity to give any speaker access to a large audience has had the damaging consequence of propagating harmful and socially corrosive speech. Prominent among the harmful sorts of speech the Internet has amplified are both defamation of individuals' reputations and 'hate speech': denigration of groups' identities. Attacks on individual reputations and group identities can do much greater damage online, because of the speed at which the attacks can take hold with large audiences. The Internet has become a tool for all manner of hate groups, from white supremacists and neo-Nazis to jihadists, to spread their venom and recruit members.[43] Democratic societies have dealt with these problems in divergent ways. The United States, while allowing substantial liability for speech that defames individuals, has a strong First Amendment bar against restricting hateful or derogatory speech.[44] Other democratic governments balance free speech rights against contrary societal and dignitary interests, creating space to regulate Internet hate speech.

The European Union Charter of Fundamental Rights, for example, sets rights of expression and information,[45] as well as assembly and association,[46] alongside, and not above, rights of individual dignity,[47] personal and data privacy,[48] and equality.[49] That juxtaposition of rights creates space for restricting hate speech in order to protect dignitary and equality interests. The EU, seeking to address Internet hate speech through

---

[43] John Herrman, 'How Hate Groups Forced Online Platforms to Reveal Their True Nature' (*New York Times Magazine*, 21 August 2017) <https://www.nytimes.com/2017/08/21/magazine/how-hate-groups-forced-online-platforms-to-reveal-their-true-nature.html> accessed 28 August 2018.

[44] *Matal v Tam*, 137 S Ct 1744 (2017) (striking down a prohibition on federal registration of derogatory trademarks).

[45] Charter of Fundamental Rights of the European Union [2012] OJ 326, title II, art 11.

[46] Ibid, title II, art 12.   [47] Ibid, title I, art 1.   [48] Ibid, title II, arts 7, 8.

[49] Ibid, title III.

indirect regulation, has persuaded ISPs and other providers of access for online speech to enter into an agreement that requires the companies to remove hateful speech, defined by reference to the laws of member states, posted on the companies' platforms.[50] Among EU member states, Germany has taken the most aggressive legal approach to hate speech, specifically targeting social media. A German statute requires social media companies to police their platforms and remove hate speech, in some cases within twenty-four hours. Non-compliance can trigger fines of up to €50 million.[51] European states have also used intermediary regulation to remedy speech that defames individuals. For example, the Italian Supreme Court held the director of a website hosting company criminally liable for defamatory statements posted on a site the company hosted.[52]

Other democratic systems impose direct legal liability on Internet users who post hate speech. In Australia, criminal law prohibits the use of a telecommunications carriage service to deliver menacing, harassing, or offensive messages.[53] Citizens may also bring civil actions to remedy hate speech.[54] Based on such civil suits, the Federal Court of Australia has mandated the removal from the Internet of posts that denied the Holocaust[55] and has ordered a newspaper to publish corrective notices for posts that maligned the ethnic identities of fairer-skinned Aboriginal Australians.[56] In Canada, statutory prohibitions of hate propaganda have supported legal judgments against online hate speech. The Canadian Human Rights Tribunal has imposed sanctions against Internet posters for harshly attacking Jews, Afro-Canadians, and other minority groups[57] and for posting denials of the Holocaust.[58] The Canadian Supreme Court, in a case involving a provincial restriction on non-Internet speech, validated those Tribunal decisions when it substantially reaffirmed the constitutionality of the legal standard that forms the prevalent model for Canadian hate speech prohibitions.[59]

Both protection and restriction of online hate speech present problems. On one hand, the United States has seen a strong increase in hate group activity, much of which reflects the effectiveness of the Internet as a propaganda medium.[60] On the other hand, restrictions on hate speech raise questions about how far the category of prohibited hate speech

---

[50] European Commission Press Release IP/16/1937: European Commission and IT Companies Announce Code of Conduct on Illegal Online Hate Speech (*European Commission*, 31 May 2016) <http://europa.eu/rapid/press-release_IP-16-1937_en.htm> accessed 28 August 2018.
[51] Act to Improve Enforcement of the Law in Social Networks (Network Enforcement Act) 2017.
[52] *Public Prosecutor v Maffais*, case no 54946/2016 (27 December 2016).
[53] Criminal Code Act 1995 (Cth) sch 1 pt 10.6 div 474.17.
[54] Racial Discrimination Act 1975 (Cth) s 18C.   [55] *Jones v Toben* (2002) 71 ALD 629.
[56] *Eatock v Bolt* (2011) 197 FCR 261.
[57] *Warman v Winnicki* (2006) CarswellNat 6178; *Warman v Northern Alliance* (2009) CarswellNat 581.
[58] *Citron v Zundel* (2002) CarswellNat 4364.
[59] *Whatcott v Saskatchewan Human Rights Tribunal* [2013] 1 SCR 467.
[60] 'The Year in Hate: Trump Buoyed White Supremacists in 2017, Sparking Backlash among Black Nationalist Groups' (Southern Poverty Law Center, 21 February 2018) <https://www.splcenter.org/news/2018/02/21/year-hate-trump-buoyed-white-supremacists-2017-sparking-backlash-among-black-nationalist> accessed 28 August 2018. The Southern Poverty Law Center study includes a section, 'How Tech Supports Hate', which lists payment, hosting, and advertising services that Internet companies provide to specific hate groups. See <https://www.splcenter.org/hate-and-tech>.

should extend. Some prominent topics of public discussion, notably immigration and religious extremism, inspire irrational hatred among some members of the public while generating serious public policy discussion among others. The European approach of indirectly regulating hate speech limits public denigration of groups without imposing government censorship. However, indirect regulation empowers private intermediaries, which owe no duty to the public and operate under no free speech mandate, to resolve socially fraught collisions between free speech and equality values. Intermediaries' interest in avoiding liability gives them strong incentives to err on the side of censorship.[61] Canada's and Australia's direct prohibitions on speakers may encourage self-censorship, excessively limiting the scope of online discourse.

19.3.2 Speech and Privacy

Free speech rights frequently interact with privacy interests. The Internet has given rise to at least two sorts of problems that connect speech with privacy. One sort of problem arises when governments compromise privacy in ways that may degrade free speech. The other sort of problem arises when governments seek to safeguard privacy in ways that may threaten free speech.

19.3.2.1 *The Internet as Government Surveillance Tool*

Governments have long invoked national security concerns to justify constraints on civil and political rights, especially the right to free speech. The Internet exacerbates that threat to rights by enabling government surveillance of private communications on a scale never before possible. The Internet lets governments gather troves of data from anyone and everyone who communicates online. Mass Internet surveillance threatens free speech online in at least two ways. First, the mere fact of surveillance casts a shadow of potential government sanction over whatever people say or hear. The ability to think and communicate outside public view stimulates thought and communication.[62] Research shows that fear of government surveillance deters people from entering controversial terms in search engines[63] and from posting controversial political messages on social media.[64] Second, the grim counterpoint to social media's positive role in the Arab Spring is governments' use of the Internet to monitor, repress, and counteract dis-

---

[61] Diana Lee, 'Germany's NetzDG and the Threat to Online Free Speech' (*Media Freedom & Information Access Clinic*, 10 October 2017) <https://law.yale.edu/mfia/case-disclosed/germanys-netzdg-and-threat-online-free-speech> accessed 28 August 2018.

[62] Neil Richards, *Intellectual Privacy: Rethinking Civil Liberties in the Digital Age* (OUP 2015).

[63] Alex Mathews and Catherine Tucker, 'Government Surveillance and Internet Search Behavior' (29 April 2015) <https://www.sebastianwendt.de/wp-content/uploads/2015/06/Government-Surveillance-and-Internet-Search-Behavior.pdf> accessed 28 August 2018.

[64] Elizabeth Stoycheff, 'Under Surveillance: Examining Facebook's Spiral of Silence Effects in the Wake of NSA Internet Monitoring' (2016) 93 *Journalism and Mass Comm Q* 296.

sent. Authoritarian governments commonly track online activity to identify and punish political dissidents.[65]

Democratic governments, though more restrained, still use the Internet heavily for domestic surveillance. A British government programme called Optic Nerve, operating over at least a four-year period, indiscriminately captured millions of Web camera images from Yahoo users. The government used the images for facial recognition experiments and monitoring intelligence targets, although it suspected virtually no one whose image it captured of any wrong-doing.[66] The British also helped other European governments ramp up mass surveillance of their own populations.[67] The Canadian government used free Wi-Fi service at airports to spy on travellers.[68] The US government following the 2001 terrorist attacks vastly increased its spying on citizens.[69] In 2013, journalists revealed that a secret US government programme called Prism had for years been gathering data on Internet users directly from the servers of the world's leading technology companies and speech intermediaries, including Apple, Google, and Facebook.[70]

Threats to privacy from mass surveillance do not begin and end with government action. Private companies often use the Internet and social media platforms to gather information about users, in order to target advertising and other messages. During the 2016 US national election, for example, a right-wing data analytics firm called Cambridge Analytica gathered tens of millions of Facebook profiles in order to help target political appeals to sympathetic audiences.[71]

The need to balance free speech values against legitimate security interests poses a critical challenge for ensuring open, uninhibited communication online. As with other free speech issues, the transnational character of Internet communication complicates the issue of mass surveillance, as one country's surveillance will inevitably sweep in

---

[65] For one example, describing Tunisia's use of Internet surveillance to punish political dissent, see Katherine Maher and Jillian C York, 'Origins of the Tunisian Internet' in Muzammil M Hussain and Philip N Howard (eds), *State Power 2.0: Authoritarian Entrenchment and Political Engagement Worldwide* (Routledge 2016).

[66] Spencer Ackerman and James Ball, 'Optic Nerve: Millions of Webcam Images Intercepted by GCHQ' (*The Guardian*, 28 February 2014) <https://www.theguardian.com/world/2014/feb/27/gchq-nsa-webcam-images-internet-yahoo> accessed 28 August 2018.

[67] Julian Borger, 'GCHQ and European Spy Agencies Worked Together on Mass Surveillance' (*The Guardian*, 1 November 2013) <https://www.theguardian.com/uk-news/2013/nov/01/gchq-europe-spy-agencies-mass-surveillance-snowden> accessed 28 August 2018.

[68] Greg Weston, 'CSEC Used Airport Wi-Fi to Track Canadian Travellers: Edward Snowden Documents' (*CBC*, 30 January 2014) <http://www.cbc.ca/news/politics/csec-used-airport-wi-fi-to-track-canadian-travellers-edward-snowden-documents-1.2517881> accessed 28 August 2018.

[69] Timothy H Edgar, *Beyond Snowden: Privacy, Mass Surveillance, and the Struggle to Reform the NSA* (Brookings Institution P 2017).

[70] Glenn Greenwald and Ewen MacAskill, 'NSA Prism Program Taps in to User Data of Apple, Google and Others' (*The Guardian*, 7 June 2013) <https://www.theguardian.com/world/2013/jun/06/us-tech-giants-nsa-data> accessed 28 August 2018.

[71] Carol Cadwalladr and Emma Graham-Harrison, 'Revealed: 50 Million Facebook Profiles Harvested for Cambridge Analytica in Major Data Breach' (*The Guardian*, 17 March 2018) <https://www.theguardian.com/news/2018/mar/17/cambridge-analytica-facebook-influence-us-election> accessed 28 August 2018.

other countries' citizens and may well violate other countries' laws.[72] In addition, the complicated matter of when and how online intermediaries, predominantly based in the United States and thus subject to US law, share information with other countries' law enforcement agencies has important implications for the freedom of online speech.[73]

19.3.2.2 *The Right to Be Forgotten*

A different sort of conflict between Internet speech and privacy arises from the availability online of personal information. As with other Internet free speech issues, the problem has its roots in the Internet's vast scope and wide reach. More information about individuals is available on the Internet than on any prior medium. A quick online search can collect personal data from many sources at once, and online information generally stays fresh and accessible in perpetuity. The idea of 'the right to be forgotten' holds that personal privacy interests should give people legal authority to have information about them expunged once the information is no longer socially useful.[74] What makes the right to be forgotten practically feasible is the central role in Internet communication of search engines, especially Google. Search engines have centralized the function of accessing information to an extent unimaginable in earlier mass media. Expunging information from search engines can make the information, as a practical matter, disappear from public view.

The EU has staked out a strong commitment to the right to be forgotten. As with hate speech, the EU approach focuses on enlisting intermediaries, in this case search engines, to remove offending information posted by others. In *Google Spain SL v Agencia de Protección de Datos*,[75] the European Court of Justice (ECJ) held that search engines are 'data controllers' under applicable EU directives. That characterization makes search engines susceptible to national authorities' demands to remove personal information. The Court further held that national authorities could properly compel Google to remove search information despite the fact that the company processed the search data in the United States, not in Europe. Underscoring the Internet's distinctive stakes for privacy interests, the Court rejected the privacy claimant's parallel demand that a newspaper remove articles that referred to his past activities. *Google Spain* establishes two broad premises that support a robust right to be forgotten. First, the public's interest in access to information about an individual's past activities should yield, over time, to the individual's interest in having the information expunged. Second, the importance of personal privacy interests justifies imposing a duty on search engines to manage data in ways that comport with privacy rights.

---

[72] Didier Bigo and others, 'Mass Surveillance of Personal Data by EU Member States and Its Compatibility With EU Law' (2013) CEPS Paper in Liberty and Security in Europe <https://www.ceps.eu/publications/mass-surveillance-personal-data-eu-member-states-and-its-compatibility-eu-law> accessed 28 August 2018.

[73] Stephen P Mulligan, 'Cross-Border Data Sharing Under the CLOUD Act' (2018) Congressional Research Service <https://fas.org/sgp/crs/misc/R45173.pdf> accessed 28 August 2018.

[74] Meg Leta Jones, *Ctrl + Z: The Right to Be Forgotten* (NYU P 2016).

[75] Case C-131/12, ECLI:EU:C:2014:317 [13 May 2014].

Unlike the matter of hate speech, where the United States stands largely alone among Western democracies in strongly prioritizing free speech over competing interests, an aversion to the right to be forgotten largely unites common law jurisdictions, notably including Canada and the United Kingdom as well as the United States.[76] One factor in the divergence between these states and Europe may be the differing constitutional status of privacy rights. Whereas the EU Charter of Fundamental Rights includes explicit textual protections for privacy, neither the US Constitution nor the Canadian Charter of Rights and Freedoms contains privacy language. Instead, privacy rights in the United States and Canada have developed through judicial extrapolations from other rights. The UK stands in a complicated position. Legally and culturally, the UK resembles the US and Canada in its prioritization of free speech over personal privacy interests. However, the UK as an EU member state was bound by the broad principles of *Google Spain*. The UK's departure from the EU creates a possibility for the UK to disavow the right to be forgotten. However, EU trade and other regulations that mandate respect for rights recognized by the EU may sustain the UK's commitment to the right to be forgotten.[77]

The right to be forgotten, as recognized in the EU, is far from absolute. Google has rejected more requests to remove information than it has granted, reflecting an understanding that the proper balance of privacy against free speech varies with the circumstances of particular disputes.[78] Still, the right to be forgotten can undercut free speech in important ways. First, successful invocations of the right to be forgotten can have worldwide sweep. France, for instance, has sought to make Google remove offending information not just from its domestic search engine but from any search results accessible in France.[79] Second, as with the European arrangement for private speech intermediaries to police hate speech, the *Google Spain* framework gives private speech intermediaries power over free speech and incentives to prioritize privacy over free speech in order to avoid liability. Third, the free speech cost of the right to be forgotten—unavailability of information—is diffuse and may be invisible, while the right's privacy benefits are concentrated and palpable. This dynamic encourages overprioritizing privacy interests.

19.3.3 Free Speech versus Intellectual Property

The speed and scope of information delivery on the Internet, along with online speakers' capacity to recontextualize and recombine information, have made the Internet a rich engine for cultural production and creativity.[80] Those same qualities give rise to a

---

[76] Michael J Kelly and David Satolam, 'The Right to Be Forgotten' (2017) *U Ill L Rev* 1, 38–9.
[77] Ibid 34–8.   [78] Ibid 17–20.
[79] Edward Lee, 'The Right to Be Forgotten v Free Speech' (2015) 12 *I/S: A J Law & Pol'y Inform Soc'y* 85, 85–7.
[80] Jack M Balkin, 'Digital Speech and Democratic Culture: A Theory of Freedom of Expression for the Information Society' (2004) 79 *NYU L Rev* 1.

range of intellectual property issues.[81] In particular, the ease of downloading digital files enables large-scale violations of intellectual property laws, often across national borders. For the present discussion, intellectual property rights on the Internet matter to the extent they complicate or undermine rights to free expression, particularly the right of access to information. Not all creators of online content seek strong intellectual property protections. Indeed, through Creative Commons licences and other sharing initiatives, the Internet has dramatically increased the amount and variety of information freely available to the public.[82] However, in democratic societies that generally resist government censorship of the Internet, intellectual property's status as a private right and its grounding in liberal ideology make intellectual property rights a formidable antagonist to the freedom of online speech.

Experience in several democratic societies shows how intellectual property rights can mark an outer boundary of Internet free speech. US statutory law grants online speech intermediaries broad immunity from liability for harm from speech they post.[83] However, a different statute requires private Internet intermediaries to remove content from their services when copyright holders allege that the content violates their intellectual property rights.[84] This 'notice and takedown' system represents the apex in US law of indirect regulation as a means of imposing substantive limits on Internet speech.[85] Australia imposes a similar statutory requirement for intermediaries to remove content posted overseas with the 'primary purpose' of infringing intellectual property rights.[86] Elsewhere, judicial decisions have imposed obligations on Internet speech intermediaries to protect intellectual property rights. In a potentially wide-ranging case, Canada's Supreme Court imposed liability on Google when the company refused to exclude from its search results the entire online domain of a company that had unlawfully copied and marketed a competitor's products.[87] All of these restrictions on Internet speech reflect how the speed and scope of Internet communications intensify intellectual property concerns.

The Internet's distinctive means of conveying and presenting information deepen the tension between free speech and intellectual property rights. When you view content on the Internet, your computer displays a visible copy of the content and often creates and stores a cached copy. Does making those copies infringe the rights of copyright holders? In the landmark 2014 decision *Public Relations Consulting Ltd v Newspaper Licensing Agency*,[88] the ECJ held that routine reproduction of copyrighted material in the course

---

[81] Jessica Litman, *Digital Copyright: Protecting Intellectual Property on the Internet* (Prometheus Books 2000).
[82] See Creative Commons <https://creativecommons.org/> accessed 28 August 2018.
[83] Communications Decency Act 47 USC § 230(c)(1) (1996).
[84] Digital Millennium Copyright Act 17 USC § 512 (2012).
[85] The US government's restriction of online speech to protect copyright, as distinct from other countervailing regulatory interests, reflects the US Supreme Court's categorical view that copyright protections do not violate the First Amendment. See *Eldred v Ashcroft*, 537 US 186 (2003).
[86] Copyright Amendment (Online Infringement) Act 2015 (Cth).
[87] *Google Inc v Equustek Solutions Inc* [2017] 1 SCR 824.
[88] Case C-360/13 [2014] ECLI:EU:C:2014:1195 [5 June 2014].

of Internet browsing falls outside the limits of copyright protection as recognized by EU law. A finding that ordinary Web browsing violated the law whenever a search or link led to copyrighted material would have dwarfed hate speech regulations or the right to be forgotten as a restriction on Internet speech. Although the ECJ did not rest its holding on the Charter's protections for expressive freedom, the case shows the crucial role of legal institutions in preserving open public access to online information.

Much of the Internet's value for free speech lies in its openness, the ease with which it connects people to information, and its transcendence of national borders and legal systems. All of those qualities push against conventional regimes of intellectual property protection, which use state authority to restrict the reach and availability of information. The moral rights recognized in some European systems have a deeper normative grounding than economic rights and thus may create an even stronger tension with Internet norms.[89] The conceptual disconnect between Internet communication and intellectual property regimes may ultimately compel liberal societies to reconsider whether, or to what extent, a property model can effectively balance content creators' profit incentives and moral interests against the public's interest in access to information.

19.3.4 The Reliability and Influence of Internet News Sources

One important consequence of the Internet's growth has been a profound change in how people get news about matters of public concern. The Internet has largely wiped out old models of news distribution, under which a relatively small number of television and radio stations, daily newspapers, and magazines dominated the news landscape.[90] Those news outlets depended for their market dominance on the high cost of reaching large audiences. The Internet, by slashing the cost of communication, has changed the production and distribution of news in ways that create both opportunities and problems for democratic societies.

On the positive side, the Internet has fostered a new generation of citizen journalists and commentators on current events.[91] Old systems of news distribution often presented only a narrow range of methodologies and viewpoints, especially in societies that valued news companies' profits more than their social benefits.[92] The Internet opens journalism to people and groups, such as women in some religiously conservative societies, who lack opportunities to speak through established mass media.[93] Anyone can

---

[89] Thomas F Cotter, 'Pragmatism, Economics, and the Droit Moral' (1997) 76 NC L Rev 1.
[90] Ben H Bagdikian, *The New Media Monopoly* (Beacon P 2004).
[91] Stuart Allan and Einar Thorsen (eds), *Citizen Journalism: Global Perspectives* (Peter Lang 2009); Melissa Wall (ed), *Citizen Journalism: Valuable, Useless, or Dangerous?* (International Debate Education Association 2012).
[92] Magarian (n 19).
[93] Courtney C Radsch, 'Unveiling the Revolutionaries: Cyberactivism and the Role of Women in the Arab' Uprisings (2012) James A. Baker III Institute for Public Policy, Rice University <https://www.bakerinstitute.org/media/files/news/130a8d9a/ITP-pub-CyberactivismAndWomen-051712.pdf> accessed 28 August 2018.

now perform the basic journalistic functions of gathering, analysing, and disseminating information of interest to the general public. Large numbers of independent sources can cover important news events, and the low cost of posting information online gives audiences access to all of those sources. In addition, citizen journalists may challenge established norms of what constitutes an important news story.[94] Professional journalists can benefit from the work of citizen journalists by using citizen journalism as raw material, yielding a greater variety of inputs and reflecting a wider range of perspectives. Citizen journalism at its best can break down rigid barriers between producers and consumers of news.[95]

Two characteristics of Internet news, however, create serious hazards for journalism. The first is the loss of professional standards that has attended the decline of the old news media. Journalists in the pre-Internet era routinely had professional training, and news outlets often operated under published standards for competence and ethics.[96] These credentials and standards served to promote public trust in news outlets, at least within broad normative boundaries. Even the most conscientious citizen journalists generally lack formal training and professional structures. They may not check facts as thoroughly as professional journalists do, and they may not observe professional journalistic norms such as requirements of multiple sources for factual claims.[97] Larger online news companies may simply ignore those norms as irrelevant to maximizing profits. The challenge that Internet news poses to established systems of credibility can be liberating and democratizing. However, the dizzying variety of news outlets online, combined with most of those outlets' failure to meet professional standards of journalistic reliability, can leave audiences uncertain about which if any news they can trust. The rise of social media has deepened the problem. Facebook and Twitter have become dominant engines of news delivery.[98] The ease of access to social media means that online audiences sometimes get the worst of both news worlds: reports that combine the market penetration of pre-Internet news behemoths with the ethical commitments of, at best, amateur bloggers or, at worst, wilful propagandists.

The second problem the Internet creates for journalism is the fragmentation of audience attention. The Internet can provide every user with customized, personally tailored

---

[94] 'The Uneven State of Poverty Coverage Over the Last Decade' (*Spotlight on Poverty and Opportunity*) <https://tfreedmanconsulting.com/wp-content/uploads/2017/10/Spotlight_The-Uneven-State-of-Poverty-Coverage-Over-the-Past-Decade_Final_20171023.pdf> accessed 28 August 2018 (study by an online poverty news site, documenting and criticizing the mainstream US media's limited coverage of poverty-related news).

[95] Luke Goode, 'Social News, Citizen Journalism, and Democracy' (2009) 11 New Media & Soc'y 1287.

[96] Blake D Morant, 'Democracy, Choice, and the Importance of Voice in Contemporary Media' (2004) 53 *DePaul L Rev* 943, 951 n 23 (compiling ethical codes from US news outlets).

[97] Wall (n 91).

[98] Alexis C Madrigal, 'What Facebook Did to American Democracy' (*The Atlantic*, 12 October 2017) <https://www.theatlantic.com/technology/archive/2017/10/what-facebook-did/542502/> accessed 28 August 2018.

information.[99] This capacity both enhances individual autonomy and facilitates the creation of virtual communities that promote all manner of collective social goals.[100] At the same time, the Internet's customization of information, especially as to news about matters of public concern, threatens social cohesion by tying distinct communities to divergent sources of information. Social media platforms strongly exacerbate this threat by allowing users to build insular communities in which members reinforce one another's beliefs and biases.[101] As a result, post-modern conceptions of radical uncertainty about truth have become directly relevant for day-to-day social reality.[102] For news in particular, the decline of consensus around basic premises means that democratic citizens can get information through filters that comport with their ideological biases and the biases of their communal enclaves. To take two vivid examples, social media news polarization strongly influenced UK voters' positions on the 2016 European Union referendum[103] and US voters' political views in the run-up to the 2016 national election.[104] At the extreme, virtual echo chambers can become fertile ground for extremist political movements to isolate and radicalize vulnerable and alienated individuals.

The combination of diminished professional standards and splintered audience perceptions of reality creates dangerous opportunities for using news reports to manipulate public opinion. In totalitarian and authoritarian societies, governments brazenly manipulate the Internet and social media to spread propaganda and undermine democracy at home and abroad.[105] In democratic societies, unscrupulous actors use the Internet and social media to covertly promote their political agendas. The most notorious instance is the Russian government's secret use of Facebook and Twitter to influence the 2016 US presidential election in favour of the eventual narrow winner, Donald Trump.[106] The self-interest of social media platforms raises further concerns about the quality of information those platforms make available to audiences. For example, YouTube enhances its advertising revenues by demonetizing less popular channels and

---

[99] Cass R Sunstein, *Republic.com 2.0* (Princeton UP 2007) 1–18 (describing and critiquing the phenomenon of the 'Daily Me').

[100] Felicia Wu Song, *Virtual Communities: Bowling Alone, Online Together* (Peter Lang 2009).

[101] Eli Pariser, *The Filter Bubble: How the New Personalized Web Is Changing What We Read and How We Think* (Penguin 2011).

[102] Joshua Landy, 'Can We Have Our Truth Back, Please?' (*Philosophy Talk*, 10 September 2017) <https://www.philosophytalk.org/blog/can-we-have-our-truth-back-please> accessed 28 August 2018.

[103] Michela Del Vicario and others, 'Mapping Social Dynamics on Facebook: The Brexit Debate' (2017) 50 *Soc Networks* 6 (showing social media's polarizing effect on UK voters' views of the Brexit referendum).

[104] John Keegan, 'Blue Feed, Red Feed' (*The Wall Street Journal*, 18 May 2016) <http://graphics.wsj.com/blue-feed-red-feed/> accessed 28 August 2018 (showing stark differences in US social media users' exposure to information depending on their ideological identities).

[105] Morozov (n 38); 'Freedom on the Net 2017' (n 42) (identifying social media disinformation campaigns by Russia, China, and other governments).

[106] Sheera Frenkel and Katie Benner, 'To Stir Discord in 2016, Russians Turned Most Often to Facebook' (*The New York Times*, 17 February 2018) <https://www.nytimes.com/2018/02/17/technology/indictment-russian-tech-facebook.html> accessed 28 August 2018.

steering users towards more sensational videos.[107] A similar problem of reliability arises when search engines seek to profit by rigging search results.[108]

The Internet's fractured news environment raises difficult questions about whether and how democratic governments can or should try to exert control over news intermediaries in order to promote the public good. Both EU[109] and US[110] regulators have proposed requiring social media platforms to tell users more about the sources of information in their feeds. Further approaches might include public subsidies to promote investigative journalism; structural regulations to promote economic competition among online intermediaries; and indirect content regulations, like the European approach to hate speech and the US approach to intellectual property, which would require major news intermediaries, including social media platforms, to monitor the content they propagate and to remove false or misleading information. All of those approaches present problems. Public subsidies raise worries that government might try to influence news content. Structural regulation may not be feasible for online intermediary functions like search engines and social media, which have tended towards market dominance by one or a few companies. Indirect regulation of news content would, as in other settings, empower private intermediaries to make important decisions about social life. That problem would be especially worrisome as to news, which plays a crucial role in facilitating democratic self-government.

19.4 CONCLUSION

The Internet has emerged as our dominant medium of communication, and it never stops evolving. Efforts to address the online free speech problems discussed in this chapter, from private power and inequality to hate speech and the credibility of news sources, have only just begun. More than ever, different legal regimes' divergent approaches to free speech problems may serve as laboratories of democracy, especially as the Internet's transcendence of national boundaries brings those approaches into direct conflict. The Internet increases both the good and the harm that speech can do. It therefore intensifies the challenges of protecting free speech while also finding regulatory strategies, consistent with the values of liberal democracy, to address damaging speech.

---

[107] Paul Lewis, '"Fiction Is Outperforming Reality": How YouTube's Algorithm Distorts Truth' (*The Guardian*, 2 February 2018) <https://www.theguardian.com/technology/2018/feb/02/how-youtubes-algorithm-distorts-truth> accessed 28 August 2018.

[108] Jennifer A Chandler, 'A Right to Reach an Audience: An Approach to Intermediary Bias on the Internet' (2007) 35 *Hofstra L Rev* 1095, 1112–5; Nunziato (n 24) 12–17.

[109] Jennifer Rankin, 'Tech Firms Could Face New EU Regulations over Fake News' (*The Guardian*, 24 April 2018) <https://www.theguardian.com/media/2018/apr/24/eu-to-warn-social-media-firms-over-fake-news-and-data-mining> accessed 28 August 2018.

[110] Steven T Dennis, 'Senators Propose Social-Media Ad Rules after Months of Russia Probes' (*Bloomberg*, 19 October 2017) <https://www.bloomberg.com/news/articles/2017-10-19/russia-probes-spur-lawmakers-on-election-security-social-media> accessed 28 August 2018.

CHAPTER 20

PARADES, PICKETING, AND DEMONSTRATIONS

TIMOTHY ZICK

20.1 Collective Expression

THE concept of an assembly—a gathering of individuals engaged in communicating and sharing ideas—has ancient origins. In the Agora of ancient Greece, free-born citizens would gather to hear civic announcements and discuss politics. Parades, pickets, and demonstrations are special types of assemblies that occur in the modern Agora.[1] They are forms of civic engagement that communicate aspirations, ideas and, quite often, dissenting opinions to fellow citizens, governments, and broader audiences.[2] For many, gathering together, in public, in these and similar forms, is a cathartic act of self-fulfilment and a demonstration of solidarity. Collective acts excite, entertain, and motivate. They are forms of cultural identification, acts of resistance, and core forms of political contention in a democracy.

Collective action in the form of public gatherings is an integral part of any system of communicative freedom. Rights to peaceably assemble and associate are widely recognized in human rights instruments, including the United Nations Universal Declaration of Human Rights (UDHR), as well as in national constitutions.[3] In the United States, in addition to the freedom of speech, rights to 'peaceably assemble' and to 'petition the Government for a redress of grievances' are explicitly provided for in the First Amendment to the Constitution.[4] The US Supreme Court's explicit recognition, in the 1950s, of a right to 'associate' for expressive purposes provides additional support for the idea that collective endeavours are critically important to a system of free expression.[5]

---

[1] John D Inazu, *Liberty's Refuge: The Forgotten Freedom of Assembly* (Yale UP 2012) 21.
[2] Ibid (noting the 'three themes of assembly: the dissenting, the political, and the expressive').
[3] UDHR (adopted 10 December 1948) UNGA Res 217 A(III) Arts 21, 22.
[4] US Const amend I.   [5] *NAACP v Alabama*, 357 US 449 (1958).

Unlike the spoken or printed word, the modes of collective action discussed in this chapter all rely on some kind of action—assembling, marching, standing, waving banners or placards, and so on—in order to communicate. Although First Amendment jurisprudence has drawn a somewhat tenuous line between covered speech and uncovered conduct,[6] in these instances the conduct does not remove these forms from First Amendment coverage. Indeed, the collective action is intertwined with, and essential to, their effectiveness as modes of expression.

Thus, as the US Supreme Court has observed with regard to parades:

> If there were no reason for a group of people to march from here to there except to reach a destination, they could make the trip without expressing any message beyond the fact of the march itself. Some people might call such a procession a parade, but it would not be much of one.[7]

Rather, the Court concluded, a parade is 'a form of expression, not just motion'.[8] Parade participants are making a collective point, both to one another and to broader audiences. As one historian explained: 'Parades are public dramas of social relations, and in them performers define who can be a social actor and what subjects and ideas are available for communication and consideration'.[9]

Similarly, through the act of assembling with others, typically although not always at a place of business, pickets make the collective point that the target audience's behaviour is objectionable and should be altered. As I explain below, while the First Amendment status of the labour picket remains somewhat uncertain, picketing in a more general sense has been recognized as a form of collective expression under the First Amendment. To take just one example, governments cannot ban pro-life picketers from gathering near the residences of abortion providers or on the public sidewalks next to abortion clinics.[10]

Finally, public demonstrations are clearly expressive events. Quintessentially, one can think of a political protest against racial segregation such as the August 1963 March on Washington for Jobs and Freedom, at which 250,000 people gathered at the Lincoln Memorial in Washington, DC. More recently, one can point to the 2011 wave of demonstrations that constituted the 'Arab Spring'. Demonstrations come in many shapes and sizes, from small gatherings to mass protest events. As the Supreme Court has observed, the political demonstration is the exercise of expressive rights 'in their most pristine and classic form'.[11]

---

[6] See, eg, *US v O'Brien*, 391 US 367 (1968). Concerning free speech boundaries and 'coverage' concerns, see generally Frederick Schauer, 'The Boundaries of the First Amendment: A Preliminary Exploration of Constitutional Salience' (2004) 117 Harv L Rev 1764.

[7] *Hurley v Irish-American Gay, Lesbian, and Bisexual Group of Boston*, 515 US 557, 568 (1995).

[8] Ibid.

[9] Susan G Davis, *Parades and Power: Street Theatre in Nineteenth-Century Philadelphia* (U California P 1986) 6.

[10] *Frisby v Schultz*, 487 US 474 (1988); *Madsen v Women's Health Center Inc*, 512 US 753 (1994).

[11] *Edwards v South Carolina*, 372 US 229, 235 (1963).

Parades, pickets, and demonstrations all further basic expressive values relating to self-governance, the search for truth, and individual autonomy.[12] Organizing and assembling with others in a parade procession is an act of self-fulfilment. Political pickets, protests, and demonstrations are all vital to self-governance. And like publications, speeches, and political advertisements, parades, boycotts, pickets, demonstrations, and protests contribute to the search for truth on a variety of matters of public concern.

Collective expression in these and other forms has been a central aspect of US and world political and constitutional history. Assembling with others for the purpose of communicating dissent or dissatisfaction with regard to political rights, taxes, economic conditions, discriminatory laws, and other matters propelled the American Revolution, the nation's Founding, the abolition of slavery and post–Civil War reconstruction, and a host of modern civil rights movements.[13] Collective contention or 'speech out of doors' has been a vital means of asserting political sovereignty, facilitating constitutional discourse, and advancing civil rights.[14]

Nevertheless, as discussed below, Americans (and others around the world) seeking to engage in collective modes of expression face a variety of doctrinal, legal, social, and political challenges. The US experience has demonstrated the character and weight of these challenges. Owing to their nature, parades, demonstrations, and the like require the provision of adequate public and private space. Yet access to public and private properties has been restricted or denied. Even after basic access rights to some public places, including streets and parks, were formally recognized by the Supreme Court, governments adopted an array of regulations designed to channel and control collective forms of expression. First Amendment doctrines governing access to and expression within public places have contributed to, and in some cases exacerbated, limits on collective expression. Privatization and other changes to the built environment have further limited the public space available for collective expression. Public policing methods in the United States and in other Western democracies have restricted or suppressed even peaceful and orderly forms of collective expression. Add to all of this the fact that rights of assembly and petition, which are explicitly guaranteed by the First Amendment, have been collapsed into the freedom of speech, while the right of 'association' has been interpreted to cover only gatherings that communicate some discernible message.[15] Finally, as noted, under US law certain types of picketing have been treated as illegal conduct.

Despite these limits and challenges, groups continue to engage in collective expression. They assemble in diverse civic, religious, political, and economic associations and challenge restrictions on collective expression. Today, a brief glance at any major media

---

[12] See generally Frederick F Schauer, *Free Speech: A Philosophical Enquiry* (CUP 1982).

[13] Gordon S Wood, *The Radicalism of the American Revolution* (Vintage 1991). See also Pauline Maier, *From Resistance to Revolution: Colonial Radicals and the Development of American Opposition to Britain, 1765–1776* (WW Norton & Co 1972); Timothy Zick, *Speech out of Doors: Preserving First Amendment Liberties in Public Places* (CUP 2009).

[14] Wood (n 13) 231.

[15] Timothy Zick, *The Dynamic Free Speech Clause: Freedom of Speech and Its Relation to Other Constitutional Rights* (OUP 2018) ch 3.

outlet confirms that people across the globe continue to rely on parades, pickets, and demonstrations to communicate dissent and other sentiments on a variety of subjects.

There is a tendency, in some quarters, to dismiss traditional forms of collective expression as archaic, inefficient, and ineffective. After all, as the US Supreme Court has observed, in the digital era, anyone with an Internet connection can become a 'town crier' capable of reaching audiences beyond those available to the ordinary soapbox orator or demonstration participant.[16] More recently, the Court characterized social media and the Internet as a whole as 'the most important places (in a spatial sense) for the exchange of views'.[17] Who needs demonstrations and other traditional forms of public expression when the new town square is at one's fingertips?

Yet despite access barriers and other restrictions, people living in the digital era continue to gather, march, celebrate, debate, and protest in public places. In recent years, the US experience has included anti-war protests, immigrant rights marches, the Occupy Wall Street movement, Black Lives Matter demonstrations, and Million Women events. Citizens of other nations are even more likely to gather in public and participate in marches, demonstrations, and other acts of collective expression. Countless lower-profile pickets, parades, and other gatherings confirm the people's continuing desire to express themselves in collective forms. This phenomenon is present around the world, including in nations where there is no long history of public contention and dissent. For example, the Arab Spring protests in North Africa and the Middle East in 2011 highlighted both the power and perils of demonstrating and marching in the streets to gain recognition for political and human rights.

Digital connectivity has not eradicated more traditional forms of collective expression. Instead, it has facilitated expressive opportunities by connecting individuals and supporting new forms of associational activity. Political dissidents involved in anti-war protests in the United States and street demonstrations during the Arab Spring have used social media to organize and publicize mass protests. The digitization of communication has not extinguished the fundamental desire to, nor the collective values of, gathering with others in public places to communicate identities, ideas, and viewpoints. Rather, the modern Agora has expanded to include digital fora for assembly and other forms of collective expression.

20.2 THE DEMOCRATIZATION OF PUBLIC DISCOURSE AND DISSENT

The US experience highlights the importance of diverse forms of expression to democratic self-governance. American colonists used a variety of individual methods of communication to engage with one another, their representatives, and the British

---

[16] *Reno v ACLU*, 521 US 844, 870 (1999).
[17] *Packingham v North Carolina*, 137 S Ct 1730 (2017).

parliament. Forms of dissent and expression were remarkably diverse. They included broadsides, pamphlets, letters, songs, paintings, pageants, and plays.[18]

In addition, colonists participated in more collective forms of expression and contention. They frequently engaged in public demonstrations, parades, marches, and boycotts.[19] Colonial Americans gathered in streets and town squares, often around Liberty Trees and Liberty Poles, to protest taxation and other perceived abuses of British authority. These events typically involved chanting, marching, and hanging or burning political figures in effigy.[20] Colonial demonstrations sometimes veered into lawlessness, as when assembled crowds destroyed the personal property of tax collectors. However, in the main, these events were peaceful, if spirited, forms of collective dissent.

Collective displays were early aspects of American political discourse and freedom of expression. They democratized public discourse and expression by involving members of the public who could not afford to print or purchase pamphlets and broadsides, or perhaps had difficulty following the sometimes complex arguments presented in those forms.[21] Early parades, pickets, boycotts, and demonstrations expanded and magnified the voice of the people. Through pageantry and political theatre, they significantly expanded the sphere of public discourse in the American colonies. In this way, public assemblies created broad channels of self-governance in which citizens of all trades and backgrounds could effectively participate.

Public demonstrations and other events also established a new and efficacious means of political resistance and dissent. They were critical to the ultimate defeat of measures including the infamous Stamp Act, which required that colonists use only paper approved by parliament to memorialize contracts and conduct commerce. Assemblies in the streets of New York City, Boston, and other population centres, sent a strong message to local and British authorities that taxation without representation would not be tolerated.[22]

In some respects, insofar as authorities were concerned, reports of mass demonstrations were of even greater concern than the explosion of broadsides and newspaper editorials. The latter forms of expression communicated elite concerns to educated audiences. By contrast, demonstrations and parades communicated a degree of mass discontent. And they did so in visual and symbolic ways that newspaper columns and pamphlets could not replicate.

In important respects, demonstrations and other forms of collective expression facilitated and propelled the American Revolution. The early lessons in mass democracy were not lost on subsequent generations. Thus, public demonstrations and parades were significant aspects of outdoor politics for both supporters and opponents of the proposed Constitution, and later for proponents and opponents of the abolition of

---

[18] Stephen D Solomon, *Revolutionary Dissent: How the Founding Generation Created the Freedom of Speech* (St Martin's P 2016) 8.
[19] Gordon S Wood, *The Creation of the American Public, 1776–1787* (U North Carolina P 1969) 320.
[20] Ibid.   [21] Solomon (n 18) 99–100.   [22] Ibid 123–4.

slavery.[23] These democratic modes of dissent were also a central aspect of post-Founding politics. In the nineteenth century, a variety of ethnic, religious, labour, and other assemblies used demonstrations, parades, and pickets to advance their causes.[24] Workers, the poor, racial minorities, and a variety of social movements relied on collective forms of expression to force policymakers and the public at large to give them a hearing.

Evidence suggests that nineteenth-century Americans were generally supportive of these public displays.[25] Although the First Amendment's protections for freedom of speech, assembly, and petition had not yet been applied against state and local governments, Americans vigorously asserted rights to gather and speak in public places. They participated in festivals, parades, and other collective activities. To be sure, not all Americans had equal access to the streets for such purposes. Thus, some jurisdictions enacted and enforced religious and racial restrictions on outdoor assemblies. In general, however, the people had broad access to the streets and other public places for the purposes of demonstrating, marching, and engaging in outdoor discourse and dissent.

Notably, at this time there were generally no permit requirements or other bureaucratic restrictions on parades and similar assemblies. Officials were empowered to suppress unlawful assemblies, and to prevent and punish non-peaceable assemblies, including violent riots. However, during most of the nineteenth century, the threshold for official intervention was relatively high. This afforded marchers, demonstrators, and protesters considerable latitude in terms of both occupying public places and engaging in contentious but non-violent behaviours.[26]

Like their colonial forebears, antebellum Americans generally considered demonstrations and other collective displays to be an effective means of political expression. Being only a generation removed from the American Revolution's experience with such forms, the public appeared to view rights of public speech and assembly as fundamental—even if the courts had not yet formally reached that conclusion. In due course, the Supreme Court would recognize and formalize rights of collective expression. However, by the early twentieth century, both public attitudes and legal latitude respecting these forms had begun to change.

20.3 THE BATTLE FOR ACCESS TO THE PUBLIC FORUM

To be effective, demonstrations, protests, parades, and the like require that participants have access to ample and adequate public space. Early Americans asserted a right to access public places and exercised their rights to collective expression, generally with

---

[23] See, eg, Inazu (n 1) 34–5.
[24] Tabatha Abu El-Haj, 'All Assemble: Order and Disorder in Law, Politics, and Culture' (2014) 16 *U Penn J Const L* 949.
[25] Ibid 969.   [26] Ibid 969–70.

minimal interference, so long as they did not act unlawfully or violently. However, increased concerns about violence, disorder, and disruption, including those stemming from the nation's experience with the Civil War era and other nineteenth-century public riots, contributed to greater restrictions on access to public streets, parks, and other areas critical to effective collective expression. As the United States entered the twentieth century, the battle over access to these places reached a critical juncture.

The battle focused initially on access to public streets and involved labour-related agitation. During the early twentieth century, members of the International Workers of the World (IWW), popularly known as 'the Wobblies', provoked 'free speech fights' by asserting rights to speak and assemble on street corners and in other public places.[27] In particular, they challenged the use of designated 'free speech zones', which limited and confined speakers in order to control their movements, activities, and communications. While the 'fights' were generally peaceful, some involved unlawful and violent conduct.

Long before the Supreme Court applied the provisions of the First Amendment against state and local authorities, the Wobblies asserted a 'First Amendment right' to assemble and communicate in the streets. The Wobblies did not prevail on their constitutional arguments. However, the conflicts they helped generate highlighted the importance of public places to collective forms of expression. Their 'free speech fights' also exposed a central fault line with respect to early conceptions of civil liberties. Despite the United States's long history of public demonstrations, parades, and other forms of collective expression, during the twentieth century public officials and courts began to exert greater control over the public's access to streets and other places needed for collective forms of expression. In particular, permit requirements, which required speakers and assemblies to obtain the permission of government officials prior to being granted access to public streets and parks, became far more common. Some local authorities asserted and exercised the power to deny access for any reason whatsoever, including based on the content of the assembly's message.

By the dawn of the twentieth century, the notion that governments *owned* public places, and thus had a right, like any private owner, to deny access to them, had begun to gain a measure of official acceptance. Thus, in 1897, the Supreme Court affirmed the conviction of a preacher who had made a public address on Boston Common without first obtaining the permission of the city's mayor.[28] The Court affirmed the reasoning of then-Supreme Judicial Court Justice Oliver Wendell Holmes Jr, that the city, as a property owner, had the *absolute* power to deny access to Boston Common. The Court's decision did not prevent labour protesters, religious assemblies, suffragists, and others from gathering and communicating in public places. However, its reasoning provided states, localities, and lower courts with grounds for adopting and upholding measures limiting, and in some cases denying, access by speakers and assemblies to streets, parks, and other public properties. In sum, access to public places for the purpose of assembling and

---

[27] David M Rabban, *Free Speech in Its Forgotten Years, 1870–1920* (CUP 1997) ch 2.
[28] *Davis v Massachusetts*, 167 US 43 (1897).

communicating became more a matter of official discretion, rather than an established social custom or presumptive right.

The Supreme Court did not explicitly apply the First Amendment's guarantees to states and localities until the 1930s. During that same decade, the Court suggested that its initial judgment with regard to public properties—that public officials had the same right to exclude exercised by private property owners—may have been in error. In *Hague v Committee for Industrial Organization*, the Supreme Court invalidated a city ordinance that forbade labour meetings from taking place in public.[29] The Court opined in dictum: 'Wherever the title of streets and parks may rest, they have immemorially been held in trust for the use of the public and, time out of mind, have been used for purposes of assembly, communicating thoughts between citizens, and discussing public questions'.[30]

Hague connected the United States's history of collective expression with what would ultimately become a right of access to certain public properties for the purpose of exercising First Amendment speech, assembly, and petition rights. The Court suggested that by 'immemorially' asserting and exercising expressive rights in public places, Americans had preserved a basic right of access to the public streets and parks. However, *Hague* did not resolve the nature or extent of this access right. Rather, the Court's decision merely suggested that officials lacked an absolute power to exclude individuals or assemblies from accessing public properties that had traditionally been used for expressive purposes.

Over the next several decades, the Supreme Court would build out the First Amendment's 'expressive topography'—the places where speakers and assemblies were permitted to engage in expressive activities.[31] The concept of the 'public forum' was a central aspect of this construction.[32] The Supreme Court would use public forum principles, which are rooted in *Hague*'s recognition of a public 'trust' with regard to public properties, to establish access rights to certain types or categories of places.[33] Public forum doctrine would also ultimately determine the scope of such rights, primarily by articulating the standards under which access restrictions were to be reviewed by courts.

Thus, the modern expressive topography gradually took shape through the categorization of public places and the development of a doctrine that authorized officials to regulate the time, place, and manner of expression in public places.[34] As this happened, public streets, parks, and other properties again became central battlegrounds. Like the Wobblies before them, the Jehovah's Witnesses and other early twentieth-century speakers challenged access and other restrictions that limited their ability to reach

---

[29] *Hague v Committee for Industrial Organization*, 307 US 496 (1939).   [30] Ibid 515.
[31] Zick (n 13) ch 2.
[32] Harry Kalven Jr, 'The Concept of the Public Forum: *Cox v Louisiana*' [1965] *Sup Ct Rev* 1, 11–12.
[33] *Perry Educ Ass'n v Perry Local Educators' Ass'n*, 460 US 37, 45–6 (1983).
[34] *Ward v Rock Against Racism*, 491 US 781 (1989).

public audiences.³⁵ The resulting precedents helped to establish the scope of First Amendment rights in public places and, more generally, the modern US culture of public contention. Labour agitators, suffragists, civil rights activists, and anti-war dissidents have all benefitted from recognition of rights to access public properties for the purpose of assembling, demonstrating, and communicating with public audiences.

Looking back, the Civil Rights Movement of the 1950s and 1960s was a high-water mark for collective expression in the United States. The Supreme Court recognized and enforced First Amendment rights that facilitated peaceful demonstrations, marches, boycotts, and sit-ins. These events were critically important to the movement's progress. In the courts, the NAACP mounted an aggressive and brilliant campaign that challenged various restrictions on collective expression.³⁶ Although civil rights plaintiffs did not win all of these cases, they prosecuted successful challenges to breach of peace, disorderly conduct, and other laws that were being used to restrict public discourse and contention. Their efforts transformed the 'trust' recognized in *Hague* into an enforceable First Amendment right to access and even 'commandeer' the 'public forum'. As the First Amendment scholar Harry Kalven Jr wrote during the Civil Rights Movement:

> In an open democratic society the streets, the parks, and other public places are an important facility for public discussion and political process. They are in brief a public forum that the citizen can commandeer; the generosity and empathy with which such facilities are made available is an index of freedom.³⁷

Professor Kalven recognized the need for 'some commitment to order and etiquette'.³⁸ However, he advocated minimal governmental regulation in the public forum.³⁹ Recognition of a First Amendment 'easement' with respect to certain public places, along with the right to 'commandeer' those places for the purpose of parading, demonstrating, and marching with others, seemed to reinvigorate a US tradition of collective expression.⁴⁰ That tradition encouraged public discourse and tolerated disruption short of actual violence.

Along with the formal recognition of a First Amendment 'easement' in the public forum, the Supreme Court also recognized a First Amendment right to 'associate' with others for the purpose of engaging in political advocacy and other expressive activity.⁴¹ As the Court observed: 'Effective advocacy of both public and private points of view, particularly controversial ones, is undeniably enhanced by group association, as this Court has more than once recognized by remarking upon the close nexus between the

---

[35] For discussion of early cases involving restrictions on the expressive rights of Jehovah's Witnesses, see Daniel Hildebrand, 'Free Speech and Constitutional Transformation' (1993) 10 *Const Comment* 133, 150–9; Stephen Matthew Feldman, 'The Theory and Politics of First Amendment Protections: Why Does the Supreme Court Favor Free Expression over Religious Freedom?' (2006) 8 *U Penn J Const L* 431, 443–51.

[36] Harry Kalven Jr, *The Negro and the First Amendment* (U Chicago P 1956).
[37] Kalven, 'The Concept of the Public Forum' (n 32) 11–12.   [38] Ibid 23.   [39] Ibid.
[40] Ibid 13.   [41] *NAACP v Alabama ex rel Patterson*, 357 US 449 (1958).

freedoms of speech and assembly'.[42] Rooted in First Amendment assembly and free speech rights, the 'right of association' shielded groups from laws and regulations that threatened to undermine or suppress a wide range of collective organization and expression.

Rejection of the private property metaphor, along with judicial recognition of rights to assemble and associate with others in expressive endeavours, greatly facilitated collective rights to communicate, assemble, and organize for political and other purposes. They highlighted and empowered the collective dimension of the First Amendment, which has been vitally important to the continued viability of parades, pickets, and demonstrations as forms of public discourse and contention.

20.4 MODERN CHALLENGES FOR COLLECTIVE FORMS OF EXPRESSION

The Supreme Court's public forum and associational rights decisions empowered demonstrators, parade participants, and labour picketers to raise First Amendment challenges to limits on public dissent and expression. However, these decisions were only the beginning of a lengthy, and perpetual, contest over the nature and extent of rights to communicate and assemble in public places. Under the public forum and time, place, and manner doctrines, governments can still impose significant limits on public expression. In addition, a variety of social, political, and law enforcement factors affect significantly people's ability to demonstrate and otherwise communicate collectively in public places.

Public forum doctrine categorizes the places that are open to collective and other forms of expression.[43] In the United States, speakers have a right of access to public streets, parks, and other properties that have traditionally been open to expressive uses. This category has effectively been limited to public streets and parks. In order to maintain safety, order, tranquillity, and even aesthetic appeal, governments are generally permitted to impose time, place, and manner regulations in these places so long as they do not target the content of expression. In the rare instance in which public officials designate public properties as generally open to a diversity of speakers and expressive activities, the same access and regulatory rules apply in these places. In other places, sometimes referred to as 'limited' public fora, some expressive activity is allowed, but government can limit access to certain speakers or restrict discussion to certain topics. With regard to *private* property, the First Amendment does not require owners to provide speakers with any access.[44]

---

[42] Ibid 460.   [43] *Perry* (n 33) 45–6.
[44] See *Hudgens v NLRB*, 424 US 507 (1976) (no First Amendment right to access private shopping malls).

These doctrines prohibit the sort of unbridled discretion nineteenth-century officials exercised with regard to public expression. They prevent the kind of exercises of autocratic power over collective forms of expression that are common in dictatorships and repressive regimes. Thus, officials cannot deny access to public streets and parks based on the content of what a speaker or assembly wishes to communicate. In all properties that qualify as public fora, officials are prohibited from discriminating based on the speaker's point of view.[45] Further, First Amendment rules ensure that any expressive restrictions are tailored to serve important public interests and leave open adequate alternative avenues of communication. These are all important limitations on government power. They also establish basic 'Roberts Rules of Order' for public discourse and contention, thereby ensuring that access will be distributed and order maintained.[46]

Although its rejection of the private property metaphor has benefitted a diversity of public speakers and assemblies, the Supreme Court's public forum doctrine has been roundly criticized for imposing a rigid and confusing categorization that ultimately diminishes First Amendment rights.[47] The categorization of fora results in relatively limited access rights. Many places where assemblies seek out an increasingly mobile citizenry—municipal airports, private shopping centres and mega-malls, state fairgrounds, and plazas abutting buildings constructed with public funds but without any expressive 'tradition'—are not considered public fora for First Amendment purposes. Thus, small or large groups wishing to parade, demonstrate, or otherwise engage public audiences in these places do not have any First Amendment access rights.

These doctrinal limits have been exacerbated by a variety of social, political, legal, and law enforcement factors that have affected collective expression in the United States and elsewhere. Privatization of public properties, the construction of 'business enterprise zones' in city centres, the proliferation of gated communities, the erection of security barriers around public buildings, and the closing of public parks have all negatively affected the ability of groups to locate and use open public spaces for expressive purposes.[48] In sum, First Amendment doctrines apply in a world characterized by the gradual shrinkage of the public space available for collective forms of expression.[49]

In the remaining spaces, the deference often granted to public officials, including the authority to value not just order and safety but commerce and even aesthetics over the exercise of First Amendment rights, allows for further restrictions on collective expression. Collective forms of expression undoubtedly create unique risks in terms of public safety and order. As the Supreme Court once observed, 'such united and joint action involves even greater danger to the public peace and security than the isolated utterances

---

[45] *Perry* (n 33) 45–6.   [46] Kalven, *The Negro and the First Amendment* (n 36) 12.
[47] See Robert Post, *Constitutional Domains* (Harvard UP 1995) 199 (contending that public forum doctrine is 'virtually impermeable to common sense' and has received 'nearly universal condemnation from commentators').
[48] Zick (n 13) 36–43.
[49] Ibid 25 ('The surface area of our expressive topography—the amount of public space that is available for and actually facilitates the exercise of First Amendment liberties—has been drastically shrinking for many decades').

and acts of individuals'.[50] However, as the Court has also made clear, undifferentiated fear of mob violence is not a valid basis for suppressing collective expression. The challenge facing officials is to maintain the public peace while protecting the people's right to engage in public discourse and contention.

This balance has often been struck in ways that disfavour collective expression. Even in places that are amenable to expressive activity, First Amendment rights have been sharply circumscribed pursuant to time, place, and manner rules. These rules allow officials to restrict, divert, and displace speakers and assemblies in ways that can significantly diminish the effectiveness of public speech and assembly.[51] For example, detailed permit requirements, which include restrictions on various aspects of collective expression, are a common feature of modern public forum management. Today, even small groups seeking to stage a demonstration or protest must sometimes navigate a gauntlet of permit regulations, advance notice requirements, fees, route restrictions, time and size limits, and conduct proscriptions.

Further, governments can control collective expression and public contention through a variety of spatial and other tactics.[52] For example, in the United States and other nations, officials have established 'free speech zones'—areas in which demonstrators and speakers are authorized to assemble and communicate. Expressive zoning has become a widely used spatial tactic around the globe. Zoning has been utilized at major political party conventions, during summits of world leaders, at anti-war demonstrations, and on college and university campuses.

Free speech zones significantly circumscribe movement, which is a critical component of parades and other demonstrations. Zoning displaces speakers, sometimes even moving them beyond sight and sound of intended audiences. Further, it marginalizes dissent by forcing those assembled to use pens and other structures that have been pre-approved by government officials. Zoning sends the message that protest and dissent are a threat to public safety. Finally, zoning and other limits on the place of collective expression diminish the *vocality* of place—as, for example, when speakers or assemblies are displaced from symbolically potent buildings and target audiences such as world leaders.[53] Despite these concerns, US courts have generally upheld the government's authority to regulate collective and other forms of public expression through zoning and other spatial restrictions. Although permit requirements, zoning, and other restrictions may be 'content-neutral', such regulations impose restrictions on public expression that are as or even more problematic than measures aimed directly at a speaker or group's message.[54]

Policing methods also significantly affect collective forms of expression. Protest policing methods vary across nations, depending on social, political, historical, and

---

[50] *Whitney v California*, 274 US 357, 372 (1927).
[51] Zick, *Speech out of Doors* (n 13) 21 ('Speakers like abortion clinic sidewalk counselors, petition gatherers, solicitors, and beggars seek the critical expressive benefits of proximity and immediacy that inhere in such places').
[52] Timothy Zick, 'Speech and Spatial Tactics' (2006) 84 *Tex L Rev* 581, 636.
[53] Zick, *Speech out of Doors* (n 13) ch 4.
[54] Geoffrey R Stone, 'Content Regulation and the First Amendment' (1983) 25 *Wm & Mary L Rev* 189.

institutional variables.[55] In some nations, police forces are relatively tolerant of disruption and engage in softer management styles, while in others police tactics tend to be stricter and more militarized. In most cases, protest policing methods have changed in response to social and political circumstances.

As noted earlier, during most of the nineteenth century, US law enforcement officials generally intervened only when there was a significant threat of imminent violence. Police (and the public) often tolerated the disruption associated with public events. However, partly in response to public riots and other instances of unlawful activity, public policing methods gradually changed. In the United States, during the twentieth century, police more commonly used what political sociologists have called 'escalated force' policing.[56] As discussed, permit requirements and licensing schemes became far more common. On the streets, police interactions with protesters and demonstrators also changed dramatically. Police forces used methods designed to intimidate participants. Officers ordered crowds to disperse. If they refused, police immediately turned to physical force and violence. In the United States, escalated force policing was used against labour agitators, civil rights protesters, anti-Vietnam war activists, and political protesters at events including the 1968 Democratic National Convention. Police forces in other nations reacted in similar ways to certain forms of mass public contention.

By the 1970s, like police forces in other nations, some US police forces had adopted a 'negotiated management' approach to public demonstrations and other events.[57] Under this softer approach, participants and police representatives discuss the details of public events in advance—their location or route, the number of participants, the manner of visual displays, and even arrest logistics for those who violate laws and ordinances. From the perspective of police forces, negotiated management reduces the chances that public events will cause significant disruption or become violent. It provides police with advance notice of the location and size of events, which facilitates planning and improves safety. Although participants may be physically safer under a negotiated management system, compliance can negatively affect collective expression. It can reduce mobility, eliminate spontaneity, and distort messages—particularly those intended to convey opposition to authority. In sum, negotiated management *institutionalizes* protest and contention.[58]

Although many US police departments have aspired to use negotiated management methods, in some high-profile instances—anti-war demonstrations, summits of world leaders, and immigration protests—they have increasingly relied on more forceful and repressive approaches. Starting before but in a pronounced way after the September 11,

---

[55] For discussions of protest policing outside the United States, see generally Donatella della Porta and Herbert Reiter (eds), *Policing Protest: The Control of Mass Demonstrations in Western Democracies* (U Minnesota P 1998). See also Clarke McPhail, David Schweingruber and John McCarthy, 'Policing Protest in the United States: 1960–1995' in Donatella della Porta and Herbert Reiter (eds), *Policing Protest: The Control of Mass Demonstrations in Western Democracies* (U Minnesota P 1998); and Luis A Fernandez, *Policing Dissent: Social Control and the Anti-Globalization Movement* (Rutgers UP 2008).

[56] John D McCarthy and Clarke McPhail, 'The Institutionalization of Protest in the United States' in David S Meyer and Sidney Tarrow (eds), *The Social Movement Society* (Rowman & Littlefield 1988).

[57] Ibid 96–100.   [58] Ibid.

2001 terrorist attacks, US authorities turned to a 'command and control' approach to public policing that is more aggressive and invasive than negotiated management. Command and control emphasizes 'the micromanagement of all aspects of demonstrations' including the use of restrictive permitting processes; efforts to control public space through the use of barricades, police lines, and other mechanisms to surround, subdivide, and direct the flow of protesters; and 'a willingness to use force against even minor violations of the law'.[59] Police dress in riot gear, use military vehicles and weapons, and engage in surveillance of organizations prior to planned demonstrations and other events. As a policing method, command and control is more intimidating, repressive, and dangerous to public event participants than negotiated management. In addition, within and beyond such general approaches, police have broad discretion to arrest participants for minor crimes and to take other actions that restrict public contention.[60] It is these actions, rather than First Amendment doctrines, which often determine the scope of demonstrators' and protesters' rights.

States and localities continue to propose new limits on public demonstrations and other expressive events. In response to recent public demonstrations, a number of US states proposed bills to increase penalties for public order offences, apply 'racketeering' laws to peaceful assemblies, and provide legal immunity to drivers who unintentionally collide with protesters.[61] These proposals were condemned by domestic civil liberties advocates and by the United Nations, which warned that they might constitute violations of human rights.

Despite its long and venerable history of speech out of doors and collective expression, the United States continues to struggle with the balance between public contention and public order. Demonstrations, parades, and other public displays are formally protected by First Amendment speech, assembly, and petition rights. However, the exercise of collective expressive rights is significantly challenged by a combination of First Amendment doctrines that bureaucratize public place, social and legal architectures that limit the expressive topography, and public policing methods.

20.5 THE STRANGE, BUT INSTRUCTIVE, CASE OF THE LABOUR PICKET

Like parades, demonstrations, and protests, pickets combine aspects of speech and assembly. Picketers typically congregate outside a home, a government building, or a place of business, often in an attempt to dissuade others from engaging in some

---

[59] Edward R Maguire, 'New Directions in Protest Policing' (2015) 35 *St Louis U Pub L Rev* 67, 83 (quoting Alex S Vitale, 'The Command and Control and Miami Models at the 2004 Republican National Convention: New Forms of Policing Protests' (2007) 12 *Mobilization* 403, 404, 406.

[60] See John Inazu, 'Unlawful Assembly as Social Control' (2017) 64 *UCLA L Rev* 2 (examining use of unlawful assembly arrests to restrict assemblies).

[61] Christopher Ingraham, 'Republican Lawmakers Introduce Bills to Curb Protesting in at Least 18 States' *Washington Post* (Washington, 24 February 2017).

behaviour or activity. Pickets can also be used to draw attention to broader social causes or political movements. Like parades and demonstrations, pickets are content-diverse.

Despite these attributes and values, in constitutional, political, and cultural terms, picketing has long enjoyed a somewhat diminished status in the United States. The labour picket, in particular, has been singled out as a form of uncovered expression. This is so despite the fact that economic boycotts and pickets have been part of the American expressive repertoire since the colonists used these methods to protest British laws.

The Supreme Court has recognized that labour organizing is covered by the First Amendment's free speech and peaceable assembly guarantees.[62] However, the coverage is neither firm nor robust. In a series of cases decided in the 1940s and 1950s, the Court held that labour picketing can be restricted or enjoined as a form of illegal conduct.[63] Indeed, the Court characterized picketing as a form of intimidation:

> It is idle to talk of peaceful communication in such a place and under such conditions. The numbers of the pickets in the groups constituted intimidation. The name 'picket' indicated a militant purpose, inconsistent with peaceable persuasion. The crowds they drew made the passage of the employees to and from the place of work, one of running the gauntlet.[64]

The Court thus characterized labour picketing as 'a course of conduct' or as speech 'brigaded with illegal action'.[65] It described the labour picket as 'more than free speech, since it involves patrol of a particular locality and since the very presence of a picket line may induce action of one kind or another, quite irrespective of the nature of the ideas which are being disseminated'.[66]

---

[62] *Thornhill v Alabama*, 310 US 88, 106 (1940) (overturning, on First Amendment free speech grounds, conviction of union president for violating ant-picketing statute); *Thomas v Collins*, 323 US 516, 543 (1943) (invalidating, on First Amendment assembly and free speech grounds, a Texas law that required all labour organizers to register with the state).

[63] *Truax v Corrigan*, 257 US 312 (1921) (upholding injunction on picketing on ground it caused economic harms through psychological and moral coercion); *American Steel Foundries v Tri-City Central Trades Council*, 257 US 184 (1921) (enjoining picketers from approaching people in groups); *Giboney v Empire Storage & Ice Co*, 336 US 490 (1949) (enjoining peaceful picketing where its purpose was to compel the employer to violate anti-trust laws); *Building Serv Emps Int'l Union Local 262 v Gazzam*, 339 US 532 (1950) (enjoining peaceful picketing where union's goal of obtaining a union shop agreement ran afoul of state law prohibiting employer coercion of employees' choice of bargaining agent); *Hughes v Superior Court*, 339 US 460 (1950) (enjoining peaceful picketing in support of a group's demand for racially proportional employment where the law did not forbid voluntary adoption of a quota system, but pressure to impose one contravened state public policy); *Int'l Bhd of Teamsters v Hanke*, 339 US 470 (1950) (enjoining peaceful picketing by union of single-owner shop with no employees for purpose of maintaining union standards at union shops where such picketing contravened state public policy). See also *Dennis v United States*, 341 US 494, 529–30 (1951) (Frankfurter J, concurring) (reasoning that picketing should be less constitutionally protected because 'the loyalties and responses evoked and exacted by picket lines differentiate this form of expression from other modes of communication'); *Cox v Louisiana*, 379 US 536, 578 (1965) (Black J, concurring in part and dissenting in part) ('Picketing, though it may be utilized to communicate ideas, is not speech, and therefore is not of itself protected by the First Amendment').

[64] *American Steel Foundries* (n 63) 205.

[65] *Giboney* (n 63) 502. See also *Garrison v Louisiana*, 379 US 64, 82 (1964) (Douglas J, concurring).

[66] *Giboney* (n 63) 503, n 6.

Prominent First Amendment scholars have long noted that the Court has treated the labour picket as distinct from other forms of collective expression.[67] As the Court's descriptions of labour picketing suggest, part of the reason for this disparate treatment relates to the fact that in the early days of American labour activism violence was not uncommon.[68] The Wobblies, whose 'free speech fights' were discussed earlier, contributed to the perception that labour activism was associated with anarchy and violence. Unionism also invoked nativism, fear of socialism, and concerns about market disruption. Thus, during the nineteenth and early twentieth centuries, employers and managers resorted to the labour injunction to restrict collective action by labour activists. Many courts treated pickets, strikes, and other means of unionizing as inherently coercive and threatening activities. As scholars have observed, the early history of violence helped create a judicial caricature of labour pickets and strikes, one that characterized such actions as forms of illegal conduct rather than exercises of speech and assembly rights.[69]

Nineteenth-century courts routinely enjoined worker boycotts, pickets, and other forms of collective activism.[70] Federal and state legislatures enacted restrictions on picketing, striking, and unionizing activities. Although some of these restrictions were repealed, amended, or interpreted narrowly, courts continued to issue injunctions against labour pickets, boycotts, and other collective acts. Today, US labour laws still limit and enjoin certain forms of collective labour activism.[71] In fact, in response to recent strikes, pickets, and protests by US workers, employers and management organizations invoked a wide variety of labour, public order, and racketeering laws to suppress or restrict pickets and other forms of collective action.[72]

The plight of the labour picketer highlights some of the challenges experienced by other participants in collective expression. As noted earlier, those who parade, demonstrate, and picket rely on marching and other conduct to communicate collective messages. Owing to their numbers and methods, these events might be viewed as disruptive or intimidating. For the same reasons, a parade or demonstration might seem more likely to result in violence than a speech by a single soapbox orator. Yet in most contexts, courts have recognized the expressive aspects of such assemblies. By contrast, in the case of the labour picket, this connection has been clouded by social and political attitudes about organized labour and by the history of violence associated with labour agitation. However, labour picketing is undeniably expressive. As one labour scholar has explained:

> Picket lines communicated the issues in a labor dispute to employees and other workers entering and leaving the employer's place of business. The act of joining a picket line was a public demonstration of loyalty to the union or sympathy with the union's goals. By the same token, crossing the picket line, whether by an employee

---

[67] See, eg, Thomas I Emerson, *The System of Freedom of Expression* (Random House 1970) 446.
[68] Marion Cain and John Inazu, 'Re-Assembling Labor' [2015] *U Ill L Rev* 1791, 1796 (observing that 'violent worker uprisings were common in the early days of American labor unionism').
[69] Ibid 1792.   [70] Ibid 1812–5.   [71] Ibid 1825–7.   [72] Ibid 1793–6.

strikebreaker or by another worker delivering goods or supplies, was a public admission of disloyalty to the union, or more, of contempt. Thus, the very existence of the pickets—the public identification of who was for the union and who was against it—was itself a form of moral persuasion. To the community at large, picket lines were a dramatic way of publicizing the labor dispute, as well as involving members of that community—family, friends, neighbors—in conducting the 'patrol' itself. Finally, the number of people in the picket line and supporting it, its organization, its persistence day after day, was an indication to the employer and the strikebreakers of the strength and cohesiveness of the union.[73]

As is true of parades and demonstrations, the non-communicative aspects of labour picketing—for example, conduct that blocks ingress to a particular business, or disruptive noises—are subject to regulation. However, under First Amendment precedents, the communicative aspects of the labour picket cannot be enjoined based upon the message they convey.[74] Among other reasons, this has led some First Amendment scholars to conclude that the Court's categorical treatment of labour picketing as an unprotected form of conduct cannot be squared with modern free speech doctrine.[75] Picketing and economic boycotts were treated as forms of protected expression during the Civil Rights era.[76] Characterizing the same method of expression as uncovered conduct owing solely to its focus on labour relations violates the First Amendment's presumptive ban on content discrimination.

Another problem with the labour picketing precedents is that they utterly ignore First Amendment protection for the right to peaceably assemble.[77] This criticism can be levelled more generally against the Supreme Court's treatment of collective forms of expression. The Court has collapsed the assembly right (along with aspects of the free press right and the right to petition) into the First Amendment's free speech clause.[78] As scholars have observed, freedom of speech and assembly are related, but distinct, rights.[79] The Court's treatment of labour picketing reflects a general neglect of 'the collective and relational dimensions of labor unionism'.[80] Like parades, demonstrations, and protests, pickets are a mode of collective expression by which individuals join together for the purpose of conveying dissent and challenging entrenched power.

---

[73] Dianne Avery, 'Images of Violence in Labor Jurisprudence: The Regulation of Picketing and Boycotts, 1894–1921' (1989) 37 *Buff L Rev* 1, 89.

[74] Eugene Volokh, 'Speech as Conduct: Generally Applicable Laws, Illegal Courses of Conduct, "Situation-Altering Utterances", and the Uncharted Zones' (2005) 90 *Cornell L Rev* 1277, 1319–20 ('Peaceful picketing, it seems to me, should be treated no differently than any other kind of behavior used to communicate a message. It should be restrictable to the extent that its noncommunicative elements cause harm—for instance if it is too loud or blocks the entrance to a building—but not restrictable based on its message (again, unless the message falls within an exception to protection)').

[75] Ibid 1326.

[76] The Court has extended full First Amendment protection to picketing on matters of public concern. See *Carey v Brown*, 477 US 455 (1980); *NAACP v Claiborne Hardware Co*, 458 US 886 (1982); *US v Grace*, 461 US 171 (1983); *Boos v Barry*, 485 US 312 (1988).

[77] Cain and Inazu (n 68).

[78] Inazu (n 1).   [79] Cain and Inazu (n 68) 1829.   [80] Ibid.

Thus, some general lessons in the history and jurisprudence of the labour picket apply more generally to other forms of collective expression. The twentieth-century treatment of collective labour activism in the United States—as a presumptive threat to safety and order—tracks more diffuse political and social attitudes towards collective expression. As noted earlier, starting in the twentieth century, public gatherings were subject to detailed permit schemes and various other methods of bureaucratic control. This shift was partly owing to episodes of violence during public demonstrations and protests. However, in a more general sense, public and official attitudes towards collective expression changed. Public gatherings became potential mobs and public events potential riots. The lack of coverage for labour pickets has been more explicit. Lower courts openly characterized this form of expression as a form of coercion and violent conduct, and a line of Supreme Court precedents rejected First Amendment challenges to restrictions on labour picketing. However, the fear of, or lack of tolerance for, certain forms of disruption has been a constant theme cutting across methods of collective expression. Even though normally covered by the First Amendment and other legal provisions, these modes of expression have been subject to special burdens in the United States and in other nations across the world. Treatment of the labour picket is a reminder of the need to recall the lessons of history and the reasons why laws must protect the diverse array of forms of collective expression.

20.6 THE DIGITAL REVOLUTION AND THE FUTURE OF COLLECTIVE EXPRESSION

Given the rise and remarkable spread of digital communications technologies, some have questioned the continued relevance and vitality of more traditional forms of expression such as those discussed in this chapter. People have indeed migrated from physical places to cyber fora. Indeed, although it acknowledged that the public streets and parks remain important to modern public discourse, the Supreme Court recently observed that social media platforms are clearly the 'modern public square'.[81]

The Internet has significantly changed the expressive culture. It has made speech cheaper and hence easier to broadcast.[82] Digitization and social media have expanded the potential reach of communications—at least those that go viral—to even global audiences. However, these changes have also created an environment in which speech is more isolated and individualistic. Speakers in silos, posting and retweeting, are not actively engaged in political discourse. Indeed, they could be speaking primarily to themselves or like-minded individuals.

As invaluable as they are to modern-day free expression, digital platforms and cyberplaces have not completely replaced more traditional public discourse venues. As the

---

[81] *Packingham* (n 17) 1737.
[82] See Gregory P Magarian, 'The Internet and Social Media', Chapter 19 of this volume.

Supreme Court has recognized, '[e]ven in the modern era, these places are still essential venues for public gatherings to celebrate some views, to protest others, or simply to learn and inquire'.[83] Consistent with that view, even in the digital era the tradition of collective expression continues. Despite online migration, or perhaps in part because of it, speech out of doors remains vital to politics and public discourse. People continue to engage in bursts of collective expression and public dissent. In the United States, they did so recently in connection with social movements including Occupy Wall Street and Black Lives Matter. In other nations, the people have flooded the streets in response to gun violence, immigration policies, environmental concerns, gender equality, economic policies, and a host of other issues. At these public events, determined groups of activists have paraded, protested, picketed, and demonstrated—despite the availability of online alternatives, and despite the limitations and restrictions on collective expression discussed earlier.

There are a variety of possible reasons for the continued resort to traditional forms of collective expression. The basic values associated with these forms—solidarity, identity, expression, and projection—have helped to preserve parades, pickets, and demonstrations as forms of public discourse across the world. There is social and political power in acts of assembly, movement, and collective display. More pragmatically, people likely appreciate that a retweet or Facebook post, or even an online petition or protest, cannot communicate grievances to policymakers and other audiences in the same manner as a public event featuring a handful, hundreds, or even thousands of participants. In democratic nations, as noted, freedoms of speech and assembly are fundamental human and international rights. They support a robust public culture of collective expression, in both digital and real-space fora.

In autocratic societies, advocates for democratic rights are more dependent on public contention to communicate dissent and advocate for changes to governmental forms and leadership. Further, given the persistent digital divide, not all activists have recourse to social media and other forms of cyber-expression.[84] The Arab Spring and similar mass uprisings have demonstrated both the power and peril of resorting to speech out of doors to achieve basic democratic objectives. The people were able to communicate political dissent on a mass scale. In response, governments used repressive and violent means to squelch dissent.

Insofar as the future of collective expression is concerned, traditional means of participation and technology are not at odds with one another. Indeed, they are complementary. The Internet has enabled individuals to form new online associations or 'virtual assemblies'.[85] In addition to having independent value, cyber-associations help support and sustain the kind of bonds that are critical to physical forms of collective expression. Moreover, on the ground, technology has facilitated the organization and execution of effective demonstrations. Access to social media and other platforms has allowed demonstrators and assemblies to counteract regulations and policing methods

---

[83] *Packingham* (n 17) 1735.
[84] Magarian (n 82).   [85] John D Inazu, 'Virtual Assembly' (2013) 98 *Cornell L Rev* 1093.

that otherwise limit the effectiveness of public contention.[86] In these respects, the 'old' town square and the 'modern' town square intersect with one another.

Although we have not witnessed the demise of more traditional forms of collective expression in the United States or elsewhere, as this chapter has discussed these forms face a variety of obstacles and challenges. As we venture deeper into the twenty-first century, three of these ought to be the focus of significant attention.

First, at the level of constitutional interpretation, courts and scholars must continue to highlight the significance of assembly, petition, and mobility rights to collective democratic values. In the United States, for example, these rights, along with the right of 'association', have largely been collapsed into the free speech clause.[87] Important scholarly efforts are underway to correct this problem.[88] Assembly, association, and petition are, and ought to be recognized as, independent rights.

Second, as discussed earlier, governments and courts must continue to ensure that adequate public space is available for collective expression. For a variety of reasons, in the modern era activists have seen the expressive topography—the space available for collective expression—shrink in ways that have left fewer and less effective places for communication. Deference to property owners and managers, under the auspices of principles underlying time, place, and manner and other doctrines, has left collective expression vulnerable to asserted governmental interests in safety, order, and even aesthetics. At this stage, it is not likely that these deeply-rooted doctrines will be abandoned. However, courts can and ought to be more sceptical of the use of burdensome permit schemes, spatial tactics, and other means by which governments can effectively suppress traditional forms of collective expression.

Third, we must recognize that aggressive methods of protest policing, including the rise of 'command and control' regimes and the militarization of public places, are serious threats to the continued vitality of collective forms of expression. Aggressive policing methods, with their zero tolerance for disruption and repressive approach to dissent, render public contention more dangerous for participants and bystanders alike. These methods are also inconsistent with the democratic history of public resistance and reliance on speech out of doors as a means of political change.

As they always have, government officials must balance public interests in order and safety with their obligation to preserve expressive rights. New challenges, including the threat of terrorism, hostile audience reactions to certain demonstrators, and in the United States at least, the presence of openly armed protesters will further complicate this balance.[89] As history shows, whenever groups of speakers and agitators gather, there is a possibility of disruption, disorder, and perhaps even violence. However, if the people are to continue their history and tradition of collective expression in public places, officials will have to calibrate the balance in ways that facilitate and protect parades, demonstrations, pickets, and other democratizing forms of public discourse and dissent.

---

[86] Zick (n 13) ch 9.   [87] Zick (n 15) ch 3.
[88] See, eg, Inazu (n 1); Ronald J Krotoszynski Jr, *Reclaiming the Petition Clause: Seditious Libel, 'Offensive' Protest, and the Right to Petition the Government for a Redress of Grievances* (Yale UP 2012); Ashutosh Bhagwat, 'The Democratic First Amendment' (2016) 110 *Nw U L Rev* 1097.
[89] Timothy Zick, 'Arming Public Protests' (2018) 104 *Iowa L Rev* 223.

CHAPTER 21

INSULT OF PUBLIC OFFICIALS

CHRISTOPH BEZEMEK

21.1 Introducing Walter Chaplinsky

It was 'a busy Saturday afternoon'[1] in April 1940, when Walter Chaplinsky, a member of Jehovah's Witnesses, set out to preach 'the true facts of the situation of the bible to the people'[2] on the town square of Rochester, New Hampshire. He had done so before and had been warned accordingly by local authorities not to cause disturbance and to cut back on the zeal employed to spread his message.[3] Evidently, he did not heed this warning; that is at least what the facts as presented by Justice Murphy writing for a unanimous US Supreme Court revisiting the case in 1941 would suggest: according to the facts so presented, after the good citizens of Rochester complained to the city marshal 'that Chaplinsky was denouncing all religion as a racket', said marshal 'warned Chaplinsky that the crowd was getting restless. Some time later, a disturbance occurred and the traffic officer on duty at the busy intersection started with Chaplinsky for the police station'. On their way, so the summary continues, they encountered the marshal who, upon repeating his prior warning, reportedly was addressed by Chaplinsky as 'a God damned racketeer' and 'a damned Fascist and the whole government of Rochester [as] Fascists or agents of Fascists'.[4]

History tells a different story;[5] a story that neither casts a positive light on Murphy's summary of the facts nor on his statement that '[t]here [wa]s no substantial dispute over

---

[1] *Chaplinsky v New Hampshire*, 315 US 568, 570 (1942).
[2] *State v Chaplinsky*, 18 A 2d 754, 314 (NH 1941).
[3] Shawn Francis Peters, 'Re-Hearing "Fighting Words": *Chaplinsky v New Hampshire* in Retrospect' (2011) 24 *J Sup Ct Hist* 282, 286.
[4] *Chaplinsky v New Hampshire* (n 1) 570.
[5] Vincent Blasi and Seana V Shiffrin, '*West Virginia State Board of Education v Barnette*: The Pledge of Allegiance and the Freedom of Thought' in Michael C Dorf (ed), *Constitutional Law Stories* (2nd edn, Foundations P 2009) 410, 420.

the[m]'.⁶ After all, already the judgment of the Supreme Court of New Hampshire had indicated that before Chaplinsky was escorted to the police station, 'the crowd got out of hand and treated Chaplinsky with some violence'.⁷ Still, this may prove to be an understatement: in fact, Chaplinsky, after refusing to salute the flag,⁸ was assaulted by a veteran with a flagpole and severely beaten by a mob, instigated perhaps less by Chaplinsky's zealous preaching than by his lack of patriotic demeanour. Only after the crowd had left the scene, Chaplinsky indeed was escorted back to the police station, being physically and verbally abused by the officers on the way. It was then, as Chaplinsky himself admitted (who kept denying having invoked 'the name of the Deity'⁹), that the words in question were uttered to the marshal.¹⁰

Subsequently, Chaplinsky was arrested and found guilty of violating a New Hampshire statute prohibiting offensive speech.¹¹ Another conviction in a *de novo* jury trial in the Superior Court was affirmed by the Supreme Court of New Hampshire. The US Supreme Court found no reason to rule otherwise. Still, Murphy's 'examination' of the statute in question made First Amendment history in holding that:

> There are certain well-defined and narrowly limited classes of speech, the prevention and punishment of which have never been thought to raise any Constitutional problem. These include the lewd and obscene, the profane, the libelous, and the insulting or "fighting" words—those which by their very utterance inflict injury or tend to incite an immediate breach of the peace.¹²

This passage became a testament to the US Supreme Court's categorical approach to the First Amendment.¹³ It also gave birth to the 'fighting words' doctrine, banning direct insults and epithets uttered face-to-face from the First Amendment's scope. Thus, the case seems to suggest itself as a starting point for a chapter dedicated to the insult of public officials. After all, even if based on bad facts, *Chaplinsky* still remains good law.¹⁴ And yet, discussing whether and to what extent 'insults' enjoy protection under free speech clauses is necessary but not sufficient to meet the task ahead: Walter Chaplinsky *happened* to insult a public official on a busy Saturday afternoon. The addressee's status,

---

⁶ *Chaplinsky v New Hampshire* (n 1) 569.   ⁷ *State v Chaplinsky* (n 2) 313.
⁸ A refusal which, in itself, was at the centre of important free speech cases—see for the US case law, Supreme *Minersville School District v Gobitis*, 310 US 586 (1940); *West Virginia State Board of Education v Barnette*, 319 US (1943) 624; and for the corresponding European Court of Human Rights case law, *Efstratiou v Greece* App no 24095/94 (ECtHR, 18 December 1996); *Valsamis v Greece* (1997) 24 EHRR 294 (identical cases delivered on the same day).
⁹ *Chaplinsky v New Hampshire* (n 1) 570.   ¹⁰ Peters (n 3) 286.
¹¹ The statute involved is NH Pub L, c 378, s 2 ('No person shall address any offensive, derisive or annoying word to any other person who is lawfully in any street or other public place, nor call him by any offensive or derisive name, nor make any noise or exclamation in his presence and hearing with intent to deride, offend or annoy him, or to prevent him from pursuing his lawful business or occupation').
¹² *Chaplinsky v New Hampshire* (n 1) 569.
¹³ See, eg, Daniel Farber, 'The Categorical Approach to Protecting Speech in American Constitutional Law' (2009) 84 *Ind LJ* 917.
¹⁴ *United States v Stevens*, 559 US 460 (2010); *United States v Alvarez*, 567 US 709 (2012) (Kennedy J (plurality).

however, was of no particular importance. The rationale underlying the case, thus, does not specifically restrict the individual's capacity to speak truth to power; rather it decrees how to make true use of the power of speech.

An adequate understanding of the topic at hand, therefore, requires us to take a step back and to assess the ways in which laws designated as 'insult of public officials', broadly understood,[15] affect an individual's ability to submit grievances, express criticism, and to even mock the conduct of those in a position of authority. This, of course, will require a discussion of how and to what extent such laws affect public discourse in general. At the same time, it will require a discussion of the aims considered legitimate to restrict speech in order to shield members of executive, judicial, and legislative bodies and the means employed to pursue them. However, to meaningfully do so will require, finally, addressing the status of a 'public official' from a free speech perspective.

The specific answers to these questions and their implications for individual cases will, of course, differ in individual cases according to whether they are given on the universal level of international human rights law, on a regional, or on a domestic level. To point this out is to state the obvious. Still, few areas may illustrate just how much the analytical framework employed by courts and human rights bodies in these various jurisdictions relies on common properties. Before, however, attending to these common properties, it is necessary to distinguish two approaches to the problem at hand. This, again, requires turning back to Walter Chaplinsky and to the doctrine developed based on his case.

21.2 Anatomy of an Insult

21.2.1 Paradigm Based on the White Male Point of View

The 'fighting words' doctrine would typically not rank among the favourite subjects of free speech scholars. This has many reasons. One of these reasons is that it does not necessarily exude doctrinal accuracy: Eric Barendt, for example, assessing Chaplinsky, states candidly that:

> It is unclear whether 'fighting words' fall outside the first amendment only when they endanger public order, or alternatively whether some extreme insults may be proscribed, irrespective of their tendency to lead to a breach of peace.[16]

---

[15] The term 'insult' is fuzzy (particularly addressing the multifaceted character of the concept. See Adrienne Stone and Simon Evans, 'Freedom of Speech and Insult in the High Court of Australia' (2006) 4 *Int'l J Const L* 677, 684). Its use in scholarship meanders between fact-related and merely derogatory remarks (see, most recently, Amal Clooney and Philippa Webb, 'The Right to Insult in International Law' (2017) 48 *Colum Hum Rts L Rev* 1). And even to apply this rough classification to a specific case will itself depend on the context of the case in question. While, of course, granting precedence to Andrew Kenyon's chapter on 'Defamation' in this volume, Chapter 15, the following remarks will take both instances into account.

[16] Eric Barendt, *Freedom of Speech* (2nd edn, OUP 2005) 295. Some commentators have come up with still more possible readings of the doctrine: see Burton Caine, 'The Trouble with "Fighting Words": *Chaplinsky v New Hampshire* is a Threat to First Amendment Values and Should Be Overruled' (2004) 88 *Marq L Rev* 441, 450.

Another, and obviously weightier, reason for the 'fighting words' doctrine's depauperated popularity may be found in its insinuated tendency to 'inherently discriminate ... against victims', in particular that it would fail to safeguard 'the interests of women, people of color, gay men, lesbians, bisexuals, or transgendered people' as '[t]he effect of focusing on potential violence [was] that the same words become regulable when directed at someone who would be likely to react violently to a verbal assault, but not regulable when directed at someone who would be unlikely to react violently'.[17]

Both concerns indeed seem troubling. Still, closer scrutiny proves them to be unwarranted: as the analysis below shows, the 'fighting words' doctrine neither features independent prongs that would allow to apply either alternative separately,[18] nor does it reaffirm a 'paradigm based on a white male point of view'.[19]

The latter allegation turns out to be unfounded as the doctrine, from the very outset, does not employ a standard that would take the addressee's specific properties into account: a point clearly indicated by the many judgments that—just as *Chaplinsky*— explicitly rely on the 'average person'[20] or 'the ordinary citizen'.[21] Any concerns that the 'fighting words' doctrine would give 'more license to insult Mother Teresa than Sean Penn just because she is not likely to throw a punch',[22] therefore, are hardly justified. Quite on the contrary, the standard thus defined brings about a 'principle of "equalization of victims"'[23] that allows the specific properties of the addressee to fade and, thus, offers protection to those individuals and groups who are (typically) not expected to react violently to a derogatory remark.[24]

Of course, to qualify as 'insulting or "fighting" words' it would not suffice if the remarks in question were directed at the general public.[25] An appellant's negative attitude towards conscription expressed by the words 'fuck the draft' printed on a T-shirt, thus, was considered protected speech. After all: 'one man's vulgarity is another's lyric'.[26] And while 'the four-letter word displayed [was] not uncommonly employed in a

---

[17] Wendy B Reilly, 'Fighting the Fighting Words Standard: A Call for Its Destruction' (2000) 52 *Rutgers L Rev* 947, 947–8.

[18] See also Melody L Hurdle, '*RAV v City of St Paul*: The Continuing Confusion of the Fighting Words Doctrine' (1994) 47 *Vand L Rev* 1143, 1148–9.

[19] Charles R Lawrence III, 'If He Hollers Let Him Go: Regulating Racist Speech on Campus' (1990) *Duke LJ* 431, 453–4.

[20] *Chaplinsky v New Hampshire* (n 1) 574; verbatim referring to *Chaplinsky*: *Street v New York*, 394 US 576, 592 (1969); *Bachellar v Maryland*, 397 US 564, 567 (1970).

[21] *Cohen v California*, 403 US 15, 20 (1971); *Virginia v Black*, 538 US 343, 359 (2003).

[22] Kathleen Sullivan, 'First Amendment Wars' *The New Republic* (New York 28 September 1992) 35, 40.

[23] Kent Greenawalt, 'Insults and Epithets: Are They Protected Speech?' (1990) *Rutgers L Rev* 287, 297.

[24] For the context sensitive assessment to be made, see Stephen W Gard, 'Fighting Words as Free Speech' (1980) 58 *Wash U L Q* (1980) 531, 556.

[25] A point also emphasized in *Gooding v Wilson*, 405 US 518, 523, 524 (1972). See also Thomas F Shea, '"Don't Bother to Smile When You Call Me That": Fighting Words and the First Amendment' (1975) 63 *Ky LJ* 1, 14; Fran-Linda Kobel, 'The Fighting Words Doctrine: Is There a Clear and Present Danger to the Standard?' (1979) 84 *Dick L Rev* 77, 88; Franklyn S Haiman, '*Speech Acts*' *and the First Amendment* (Southern Illinois UP 1993) 22; Steven G Gey, 'The Nuremberg Files and the First Amendment Value of Threats' (2000) 78 *Tex L Rev* 541, 594.

[26] *Cohen* (n 21) 25.

personally provocative fashion, in [the] instance [in question] it was clearly not "directed to the person of the hearer" '.[27]

The importance for a distinction thus made cannot be overstated for a chapter dedicated to the question of insults from a free speech perspective: it 'intimate[s] strongly that the offensiveness of language alone cannot be the basis for a general prohibition'.[28] Much rather, only remarks 'directed to any person or group in particular'[29] are to be considered insulting or 'fighting words', bereft of free speech protection, in the first place. This again allows to separate 'fighting words' from 'public expression of ideas [which] may not be prohibited merely because the ideas are themselves offensive to some of their hearers'.[30]

'Resort to epithets or personal abuse', when directed to the person of the hearer, had in contrast, been perceived to be outside the scope of the First Amendment's protection even before *Chaplinsky*: already in *Cantwell v Connecticut*, a case decided two years earlier, the Supreme Court considered them not to be 'in any proper sense communication of information or opinion safeguarded by the Constitution';[31] an assertion affirmed in *Chaplinsky*.[32]

21.2.2 Fighting Back

It is important to see against that background, that the utterances deemed 'fighting words', contrary to some accounts,[33] are not to be equated with speech prompting violence; rather they must themselves amount to 'personally abusive epithets'.[34] The Supreme Court's subsequent case law underlined that on more than just a few occasions: 'fighting words' are first and foremost 'personally abusive epithets... when addressed to the ordinary citizen... *inherently* likely to provoke violent reaction'.[35] It needs a 'personal insult' to determine 'that... speech amounted to fighting words'.[36]

The 'fighting words' doctrine, thus, hardly proves to be a 'hopeless anachronism that mimics the macho code of barroom brawls'.[37] Rather, the standard thus developed, in bringing about an 'equalization of victims', specifically protects those subjected to verbal attacks who are not presumed to react to abuse by resorting to violent means. Differing

---

[27] Ibid 20.   [28] Kent Greenawalt, *Speech, Crime and the Uses of Language* (OUP 1989) 298.
[29] *Hess v Indiana*, 414 US 105, 107 (1973).
[30] *Street* (n 20) 592. See also Eugene Volokh, 'Speech as Conduct: Generally Applicable Laws, Illegal Courses of Conduct, "Situation-Altering Utterances" and the Uncharted Zones' (2005) 90 *Cornell L Rev* 1277, 1323.
[31] *Cantwell v Connecticut*, 310 US 296, 309–10 (1940).
[32] *Chaplinsky v New Hampshire* (n 1) 572.   [33] See Lawrence (n 19) 454.
[34] Gard (n 24) 537.   [35] *Cohen* (n 21) 20 (emphasis added).
[36] See also *Hess* (n 29) 107.
[37] Sullivan (n 22) 40.

from the standard developed in *Brandenburg v Ohio*,[38] the concrete danger of action taken pursuant to speech is not of prime importance. The 'fighting words' standard 'implicitly recognizes the legitimacy of protecting against deep hurt',[39] it perceives interest in internal emotional order [to be] analogous to the external condition of order which is the source of the interest in prevention of violence'[40] and it, thereby, recognizes both prongs of the 'fighting words' doctrine as equivalent hypotheses when it comes to the effect of the utterance in question.

The phrase 'insulting or fighting words ... which by their very utterance inflict injury or tend to incite an immediate breach of the peace', thus, does not refer to separate phenomena.[41] The question raised above: 'whether "fighting words" fall outside the first amendment only when they endanger public order, or alternatively whether some extreme insults may be proscribed, irrespective of their tendency to lead to a breach of peace'[42] turns out to be moot. Rather, the 'fighting words' doctrine unfolds as a coherent category in which the standard set ('likely to provoke the average person to retaliation') serves at the same time as the 'measure of the intensity of hurt'.[43] According to this, it is to be determined[44] whether the remarks in question are to be perceived as 'personally abusive epithet' or a 'direct personal insult',[45] 'which by their very utterance inflict injury'.[46]

The definition of 'fighting words' as 'those personally abusive epithets which, when addressed to the ordinary citizen, are, as a matter of common knowledge, inherently likely to provoke violent reaction',[47] thus, serves as a 'test for whether remarks have passed the boundaries of what innocent citizens should expect to tolerate';[48] in particular in situations in which physical altercation is not to be expected.

'Words of this type', as Chafee put it, 'offer little opportunity for the usual process of counter-argument. The harm is done as soon as they are communicated, or is liable to follow almost immediately in the form of retaliatory violence'.[49] For this reason, as Scalia stated for the majority in *RAV v St Paul*, 'for purposes of that Amendment, the unprotected features of [insulting or "fighting"] words are, despite their verbal character, essentially a "nonspeech" element of communication'.[50]

---

[38] *Brandenburg v Ohio*, 395 US 444 (1969). For an extensive discussion of the problems related to 'incitement' from a free speech perspective see Chapter 18 by Geoffrey Stone in this volume.

[39] Greenawalt, 'Insults and Epithets' (n 23) 299.

[40] Mark C Rutzick, 'Offensive Language and the Evolution of First Amendment Protection' (1974) 9 *Harv CR-CL L Rev* 1, 7.

[41] The Court of Appeals for the Seventh Circuit was right in emphasizing: 'the "inflict-injury" subset of the fighting words definition has never stood on its own' (*Purtell v Mason*, 527 F 3d 615, 625).

[42] Barendt (n 16) 295.   [43] Greenawalt, *Speech, Crime & the Uses of Language* (n 28) 297.

[44] Rutzick (n 40) 7.   [45] See Section 21.2.1 in this chapter.

[46] *Chaplinsky v New Hampshire* (n 1) 572.

[47] *Black* (n 21) 359. See also *Cohen* (n 21).

[48] Greenawalt, 'Insults and Epithets' (n 23) 299.

[49] Zechariah Chafee, *Free Speech in the United States* (first published 1941, Harvard UP 1946) 150.

[50] *RAV v St Paul*, 505 US 377, 386 (1991).

Directed to the person of the hearer, 'insulting or fighting words . . . which by their very utterance inflict injury [are much more] equivalent to a physical assault'.[51] Fighting words, thus, are denied First Amendment protection not 'because of some intrinsic property of words as words',[52] but because of their structure:

> The reason why fighting words are categorically excluded from the protection of the First Amendment is not that their content communicates any particular [even if despicable] idea, but that their content embodies a particularly intolerable (and socially unnecessary) mode of expressing whatever idea the speaker wishes to convey.[53]

'Fighting words' themselves are like a slap in the face,[54] the first punch, likely to provoke the average person to retaliation';[55] to fight back—even if by different means.

In the end, this was just what Walter Chaplinsky did when insulting the marshal of Rochester, New Hampshire: he fought back; thus, quite literally, 'adding insult to injury'. Just as the injury, this insult, however, as any insult of comparable gravity 'directed to the person of the hearer', be they a public official or not,[56] was delivered outside the scope of the First Amendment.[57]

21.3 THE SOLE INTENT OF THE OFFENSIVE STATEMENT IS TO INSULT

21.3.1 Insulting to Particular Individuals

Compared to the US Supreme Court's long-standing (even if academically contested) tradition, explicitly denying First Amendment protection to severe insults directed to a specific addressee for the structural reasons outlined above, the European Court of

---

[51] Geoffrey R Stone, 'Sex, Violence, and the First Amendment' (2007) 64 *U Chi L Rev* 1857, 1864. See also Frederick Lawrence, 'Resolving the Hate Crimes/Hate Speech Paradox: Punishing Bias Crimes and Protecting Racist Speech' (1993) 68 *Notre Dame L Rev* 673, 711.
[52] Frederick Schauer, 'Harm(s) and the First Amendment' [2011] *Sup Ct Rev* 81, 86ff.
[53] *RAV* (n 50) 393 (original emphasis).
[54] See William Irvine, *A Slap in the Face: Why Insults Hurt, and Why They Shouldn't* (OUP 2013) for an in-depth analysis.
[55] *Chaplinsky v New Hampshire* (n 1) 574; *Street* (n 20) 592; *Bachellar* (n 20) 567.
[56] Statutes or ordinances prohibiting abusive language directed to public officials (specifically: police officers) beyond fighting words have been regularly found to be 'overbroad' and, thus, to violate the First Amendment—cf, in particular, *Lewis v City of New Orleans*, 415 US 130 (1974); *City of Houston v Hill*, 482 US 451 (1987); *Seals v McBee*, 898 F 3d 587 (5th Cir 2018).
[57] Or any free speech clause for that matter if one was to share the result of the structural analysis pursued by the US Supreme Court.

Human Rights (ECtHR) indicated as much only recently. Although the Court had suggested on several occasions in dicta that 'concrete expressions constituting hate speech, which may be insulting to particular individuals or groups, are not protected by Article 10 of the Convention',[58] such statements typically were only a shorthand description for a sweeping application of Article 17 of the European Convention on Human Rights (ECHR), the Convention's abuse clause, in hate speech cases.[59] And while hate speech is deeply hurtful and disturbing to the groups or individuals affected by it,[60] its regulation in accordance with the prerequisites of Article 17 and Article 10 ECHR is based on the content of the statement in question (and the dangers inherent to it), not on the structure of the remark.[61]

Starting from 2011,[62] however, the Court changed its tone. Based on an earlier ruling that—even if only briefly—touched on a distinction to 'be made between criticism and insult',[63] the ECtHR started to emphasize in a whole line of cases:

> that offensive language may fall outside the protection of freedom of expression if it amounts to wanton denigration, for example where the sole intent of the offensive statement is to insult.

Still, at the same time, the Court, all in line with the US Supreme Court's reasoning in *Cohen*,[64] is eager to point out in this context that 'the use of vulgar phrases in itself is not decisive in the assessment of an offensive expression as it may well serve merely stylistic purposes.'[65]

21.3.2 Chaplinsky Goes to Strasbourg?

It is tempting, against this backdrop, to conclude that the structural assessment underlying the US Supreme Court's 'fighting words' doctrine has finally arrived in Europe. And yet, closer analysis suggests that this temptation ought to be resisted: in none of the cases cited above does the ECtHR make an effort to deny the protection of Article 10 to

---

[58] *Gündüz v Türkey* (2005) EHRR 5. See also *Jersild v Denmark* (1995) 19 EHRR 1, [35] ('There can be no doubt that the remarks in respect of which the Greenjackets were convicted... were more than insulting to members of the targeted groups and did not enjoy the protection of Article 10').

[59] See Christoph Bezemek, 'Abuse of Human Rights' in Michael Potacs and Lubos Tichý (eds), *Abuse of Law* (Univerzita Karlova 2017) 340–2.

[60] Still, whether or not it should be subject to regulation due to these properties is regularly disputed on the meta level of academic debate. Among the more recent accounts, see Timothy Garton Ash, *Free Speech: Ten Principles for a Connected World* (Atlantic 2016).

[61] For the various free speech problems posed by 'hate speech', see Chapter 25 by Alon Harel in this volume.

[62] *UJ v Hungary* (2016) 62 EHRR 30 [20].   [63] *Skałka v Poland* (2004) 38 EHRR 1 [34].

[64] See Section 23.2.1 of this chapter.

[65] *Tuşalp v Turkey* App no 32131/08 (ECHR, 21 February 2012) [48]; *Mengi v Turkey* App no 13471/05 (ECHR, 27 November 2012) [58]; *Grebneva and Alisimchik v Russia* App no 8918/05 (ECHR, 22 November 2016) [52]; *Savva Terentyev v Russia* App no 10692/09 (ECHR, 28 August 2018) [68].

grossly offensive speech from the very outset for structural reasons. Rather, ever since taking an explicitly robust stand on insulting speech, the ECtHR would conclude its formula dedicated to the question by complacently adding that '[f]or the Court, style constitutes part of the communication as the form of expression and is as such protected together with the content of the expression'.[66]

While this affirmation of the protection offered by Article 10 ECHR to the means employed to communicate a message may be a well-suited formal complement to the substance-related dictum in the famed judgment in *Handyside v United Kingdom*, highlighting that Article 10 was applicable also to 'information' and 'ideas' 'that offend, shock or disturb the State or any sector of the population',[67] it falls short of introducing any sharp distinction as to whether the 'vulgar phrases ... that may well serve merely stylistic purposes' are directed at a specific hearer or at the general public as the US Supreme Court most prominently did in *Cohen*.[68] Rather, the Court gives an overall assessment that anticipates a typical result of a proportionality analysis according to Article 10 s 2 ECHR,[69] culminating in the notion of an utterance amounting to 'wanton denigration'.[70] In short, by holding 'that offensive language may fall outside the protection of freedom of expression', the ECtHR engages in the kind of 'ad hoc balancing' that Chief Justice Roberts so emphatically rejected on behalf of a US Supreme Court majority in *United States v Stevens* a decade ago;[71] a fact that gives a clear indication of the different approaches to the respective free speech clauses in Strasbourg or in Washington, DC, when it comes to the question at hand.[72]

This difference becomes particularly clear in cases that display similar properties as the *Chaplinsky* scenario: while Józef Janowski did not succeed in convincing the ECtHR's Grand Chamber in 1999 that his conviction on the account of 'hooliganism' for calling two municipal guards hassling a street vendor in the Polish town of Zduńska Wola 'oafs' and 'dumb' ('ćwoki' and 'głupki') to their face violated his freedom of expression according to Article 10 ECHR, at no point did the majority contemplate whether the offensive words thus uttered would be within the scope of Article 10 or not. Rather, the Court went on to soberly balance the interests involved, taking into account a multitude of

---

[66] *UJ* (n 62) [20].
[67] *Handyside v United Kingdom* (1979–80) 1 EHRR 737 [49]. Some judgments, like *Tuşalp* (n 65) [48], put particular emphasis on this.
[68] *Cohen* (n 21) 20. Notwithstanding dicta as in *Kubaszewski v Poland* App no 571/04 (ECHR, 22 February 2010) [44].
[69] For a thorough discussion of proportionality and the limitations on free speech, see Grégoire Webber's chapter in this volume (Chapter 10).
[70] See, most recently, *Terentyev* (n 65) [68]. Particularly the Court's earlier case law highlights the balancing approach pursued, stressing verbatim that '[i]f the sole intent of any form of expression is to insult ... an appropriate punishment would not, in principle, constitute a violation of Article 10 § 2 [!] of the Convention' *Skałka* (n 63) [34].
[71] *Stevens* (n 14). See also *Alvarez* (n 14) (Kennedy J, plurality).
[72] Not only when it comes to the question at hand, of course: see Frederick Schauer, 'Categories and the First Amendment: A Play in Three Acts' (1981) 34 *Vand L Rev* 265; Farber (n 13).

factors, such as the guards' status as civil servants acting in an official capacity, the specific context of the utterance, the issue whether the applicant acted in his professional capacity as a journalist and, finally, the question whether he contributed to an open discussion on matters of public concern.[73]

The analysis will turn to these factors in the next section.

21.4 Uninhibited, Robust, and Wide-Open

21.4.1 Vehement, Caustic, and Sometimes Unpleasantly Sharp Attacks

When the US Supreme Court rendered its landmark *New York Times v Sullivan* judgment in March 1964, initiating the 'constitutionalization of libel law',[74] Justice Brennan, writing for a unanimous Court, famously emphasized a 'profound national commitment to the principle that debate on public issues should be uninhibited, robust, and wide-open' on which the decision was based, indicating at the same time, that this 'may well include vehement, caustic, and sometimes unpleasantly sharp attacks on government and public officials'.[75]

Just how profound this commitment was would be demonstrated only nine months later, when the reach of the standard developed in *Sullivan* was extended from civil law to criminal law: '[w]e held in New York Times that a public official might be allowed the civil remedy only if he establishes that the utterance was false, and that it was made with knowledge of its falsity or in reckless disregard of whether it was false or true', Brennan, again writing for an unanimous Court, stated, and '[t]he reasons which led us so to hold in New York Times', he concluded, 'apply with no less force merely because the remedy is criminal'.[76]

In *Garrison*, the US Supreme Court 'effectively abolished the crime of seditious libel in the United States'.[77] 'The *New York Times* rule', Brennan reasoned, 'is not rendered inapplicable merely because an official's private reputation, as well as his public reputation, is harmed. The public official rule protects the paramount public interest in a free flow of information to the people concerning public officials, their servants. To this end, anything which might touch on an official's fitness for office is relevant'.[78]

---

[73] *Janowski v Poland* (2000) 29 EHRR 705 [31]–[34].
[74] Elena Kagan, 'A Libel Story: *Sullivan* Then and Now' (1993) 18 *L & Soc Inq* 197, 214.
[75] *New York Times v Sullivan*, 376 US 254, 270 (1964).
[76] *Garrison v Louisiana*, 379 US 64, 74 (1964).
[77] Russel Weaver, 'Defamation and Democracy' in Andrew T Kenyon (ed), *Comparative Defamation and Privacy Law* (CUP 2016) 86.
[78] *Garrison* (n 76) 77.

It hardly is a well-kept secret that this 'national commitment' may indeed be exceptionally 'profound' in the United States when it comes to free speech in general,[79] and to defamation cases involving public officials in particular.[80] Still, the principle underlying the landmark cases in this area went on to become common global property; as did its implications for the 'vehement, caustic, and sometimes unpleasantly sharp attacks on government and public officials'. This, of course, is not to say that a uniform standard was applied (or even accepted) on the universal, regional, or domestic level of free speech protection when it comes to the boundaries of permissible (defamatory or otherwise insulting) criticism of public officials.[81] It is to say, however, (and it is fair to say) that the factors taken into account by universal, regional, and national bodies entrusted with safeguarding freedom of speech in cases involving alleged insults of public officials bear a clear resemblance, as matter of principle.

This hardly comes as a surprise given that 'freedom to think as you will and to speak as you think are means indispensable to the discovery and spread of political truth'.[82] After all, even Robert Bork's infamously narrow concept of speech dedicated to such a 'discovery and spread of political truth' would readily (and particularly) encompass speech 'concerned with governmental behavior, policy or personnel',[83] or, in short, speech concerned with the conduct (broadly speaking) of public officials. And to be sure, '[c]alling a public official a "racketeer" and a "damned fascist" contains an idea and a political idea at that'.[84]

Thus, any court of law fulfilling its function within a democratic system would, when concerned with questions of free speech and criticism of public officials, necessarily have to develop criteria that allow it to assess the interplay of the respective status of the speaker and the addressee, the forum in which the exchange takes place and the message conveyed; and any court would have to do so against the backdrop of the particular importance of open and robust debate for the democratic system as a whole.[85] As with the 'fighting words' doctrine, the approach the US Supreme Court developed to address

---

[79] See Frederick Schauer, 'The Exceptional First Amendment' in Michael Ignatieff (ed), *American Exceptionalism and Human Rights* (Princeton UP 2005) 29.

[80] For a comprehensive discussion of the defamation standards applicable to cases brought by public officials developed in the First Amendment case law of the US Supreme Court, see Andrew Kenyon's Chapter 15 in this volume.

[81] See Barendt (n 16) 205–30.

[82] *Whitney v California*, 274 US 357, 375 (1927) (Brandeis J, concurring). For an extensive account of the interdependence of free speech and democracy, see Chapter 5 in this volume, by James Weinstein and Ashutosh Bhagwat.

[83] Robert H Bork, 'Neutral Principles and Some First Amendment Problems' (1971) 47 *Ind LJ* 1, 27–8.

[84] Frederick Schauer, 'Speech and "Speech", Obscenity and "Obscenity": An Exercise in the Interpretation of Constitutional Language' (1979) 67 *Geo LJ* 899, 920, n 123. See also James Q Whitman, 'Enforcing Civility and Respect: Three Societies' (2000) 109 *Yale LJ* 1270, 1380.

[85] For a general assessment as to this extent, see Barendt (n 16) 18–21. For select national perspectives and experiences, see Aharon Barak, Freedom of Speech in Israel: The Impact of the American Constitution, 8 *Tel Aviv U Stud L* 241 (1988) 242–4 and Stone and Evans (n 15) 681–8. See also *Lohé Issa Konaté* App no 4/2013 (ACtHPR, 4 October 2013) [145]–[149], specifically emphasizing the coherence of the general framework governing the assessment of the questions at hand.

these questions, while taking all of these criteria into account, follows an idiosyncratic structure;[86] in particular when compared to international human rights tribunals.[87]

In an effort to cut across single jurisdictions, the following remarks will focus specifically on the framework developed on the regional and on the universal level in addressing questions concerning insults of public officials from a free speech perspective; contrasting it with US Supreme Court case law time and again. In doing so, particular attention will be paid to how the aforementioned criteria factor in the balancing exercise typically employed by human rights tribunals to determine whether (and which) sanctions for utterances regarded as insulting to public officials were to be reconciled with freedom of speech.

21.4.2 Insult of Public Officials and Its Relation to Self-Government

'[I]f men are to be their own rulers', Alexander Meiklejohn famously stated in 1948, it is imperative 'that whatever truth may become available shall be placed at the disposal of all the citizens' so they would understand 'the issues which bear upon our common life'. Thus, 'no idea, no opinion, no doubt, no belief, no counterbelief, no relevant information may be kept from them' in order for 'men ... not [to] be governed by others [but to] govern themselves'.[88] Today, seventy years later, Meiklejohn's position and similar arguments as to the importance of free speech for democratic government has grown not only to be 'the most fashionable free speech theory in Western democracies'[89] but also the foundation for courts and human rights tribunals to answer how the dependence of any democratic system on free speech affects whether and to what extent deference towards public officials may be decreed by law.

On the universal level, the UN Human Rights Committee (UNHRC) has long since started to identify 'the freedoms of information and of expression [as] cornerstones in any free and democratic society[and] its citizens [as decision-makers that] must be allowed to inform themselves about alternatives to the political system/parties in power, and that ... may criticise or openly and publicly evaluate their Governments without fear of interference or punishment'.[90] Thus, the Committee emphasizes, when it comes to public debate 'concerning figures in the political domain, the value placed by the

---

[86] Melville B Nimmer, 'The Right to Speak from Times to Time: First Amendment Theory Applied to Libel and Misapplied to Privacy' (1968) 56 *Cal L Rev* 935.
[87] See Section 21.3 of this chapter.
[88] Alexander Meiklejohn, *Free Speech and Its Relation to Self-Government* (Lawbook Exchange 1948) 88–9.
[89] Barendt (n 16) 18.
[90] UNHRC, *Views: Communications No 422/1990, 423/1990 and 424/1990* (12 July 1996) UN Docs CCPR/C/51/D/422/1990, CCPR/C/51/D/423/1990, CCPR/C/51/D/424/1990 (*Aduayom, Diasso and Dobou and others v Togo*) [7.4]. See generally Chapter 11 by Michael Hamilton in this volume.

Covenant upon uninhibited expression is particularly high'.[91] Consistently, General Comment No 34 (dedicated to Article 19 of the International Covenant on Civil and Political Rights [ICCPR]) explicitly identifies all public figures, including those exercising the highest political authority [to be] legitimately subject to criticism and political opposition [while considering] the mere fact that forms of expression are considered insulting to a public figure... [is] not sufficient to justify the imposition of penalties'.[92]

Taking it a step further, the African Court on Human and Peoples' Rights (ACtHPR), in its landmark judgment *Konaté v Burkina Faso*, emphasized 'that freedom of expression in a democratic society must be the subject of a lesser degree of interference when it occurs in the context of public debate relating to public figures';[93] thereby relying on a prior decision of the African Commission that 'people who assume highly visible public roles must necessarily face a higher degree of criticism than private citizens; otherwise public debate may be stifled altogether'.[94]

While relying on a broader concept of the 'public figure' than its European pendant,[95] the ACtHPR, thus, employs the same rationale that formed the basis for the ECtHR's important 1986 judgment, *Lingens v Austria*: here the court held, relying on the essential distinction between facts (the existence of which could be demonstrated) and value-judgments (not susceptible of proof),[96] that:

> The limits of acceptable criticism are ... wider as regards a politician as such than as regards a private individual. Unlike the latter, the former inevitably and knowingly lays himself open to close scrutiny of his every word and deed by both journalists and the public at large, and he must consequently display a greater degree of tolerance.[97]

Likewise, the Inter-American Court of Human Rights (IACtHR) regards it as 'logical and appropriate that statements concerning public officials and other individuals who exercise functions of a public nature should be accorded ... a certain latitude in the

---

[91] See UNHRC, *Views: Communication No 1180/2003* (31 October 2005) UN Doc CCPR/C/85/D/1180/2003 (*Bodrožic v Serbia and Montenegro*) [7.2].

[92] UNHRC, 'General Comment 34—Article 19: Freedom of Opinion and Expression' (12 September 2011) UN Doc CCPR/C/GC/34 [10] (General Comment 34), referring to UNHRC, *Views: Communication No 1128/2002* (29 March 2005) UN Doc CCPR/C/83/D/1128/2002 (*de Morais v Angola*); Bodrožic (n 91).

[93] *Lohé Issa Konaté* (n 85) §155.

[94] *Media Rights Agenda v Nigeria* (2000) AHRLR 200 [74]. On this case, see Christof Heyns, 'Civil and Political Rights in the African Charter' in Malcolm D Evans and Rachel Murray (eds), *The African Charter on Human and Peoples' Rights: The System in Practice, 1986-2000* (CUP 2008) 165.

[95] And, of course, the US Supreme Court for that matter. See Section 21.4.3 below.

[96] *Lingens v Austria* (1986) 8 EHRR 47 [46] (accordingly the expressions 'the basest opportunism', 'immoral' and 'undignified' used to refer to the attitude of the Federal chancellor were not to be considered statements of facts but as value judgments). More recently see, eg, *Tuşalp* (n 65) [43]–[45]. For the IACtHR's adoption of this standard, see *Kimel v Argentina* (2 May 2008) [93]. On the importance of the distinction of facts and value-judgments in defamation law, see Chapter 15 by Andrew Kenyon in this volume.

[97] *Lingens* (n 96) [42]. See also, eg, *MAC TV SRO v Slovakia* App no 13466/12 (ECtHR 28 November 2017) [44].

broad debate on matters of public interest that is essential for the functioning of a truly democratic system'.[98] A 'different honor protection standard', the Court would conclude in this context, 'is justified by the fact that public officials voluntarily expose themselves to control by society, which results in a greater risk of having their honor affected'.[99]

Along this line of reasoning, as the ECtHR specifically emphasizes, '[c]ivil servants acting in an official capacity are, like politicians, subject to wider limits of acceptable criticism than private individuals'.[100] Still, the Court would add an important caveat, as it:

> cannot be said . . . that civil servants knowingly lay themselves open to close scrutiny of their every word and deed to the extent to which politicians do and should therefore be treated on an equal footing with the latter when it comes to criticism of their actions'.[101]

After all, 'those who act in an official capacity must enjoy public confidence in conditions free of undue perturbation if they are to be successful in performing their tasks'.[102] Therefore, it may prove necessary 'to protect them from offensive verbal attacks when on duty' as well as from 'defamatory allegations concerning acts performed in the exercise of their duties'.[103]

Still, as the Court would highlight, '[i]t would be going too far to extend [this] principle . . . without reservation to all persons who are employed by the State, in any capacity whatsoever'.[104] Thus, the Court pointed out, such a principle would certainly refer to 'law-enforcement officers' or 'prosecutors' but not necessarily to 'all persons employed by . . . state-owned companies'.[105]

21.4.3 Public Officials, Politicians, and Public Figures

The previous account suggests that while all of the tribunals referred to above seem to lean into the same direction when it comes to the limits of criticism, degradation, or abuse to be endured by those acting on the public's behalf or in the public limelight, they

---

[98] *Herrera-Ulloa v Costa Rica* (IACtHR, 2 July 2004) [128]. See also, eg, *Canese v Paraguay* (IACtHR, 31 August 2004) [98]; *Fontevecchia and D'Amico v Argentinia* (IACtHR, 29 November 2011) [47].

[99] *Donoso v Panamá* (IACtHR 27 January 2009) [122].

[100] See, eg, *Thoma v Luxembourg* (2003) 36 EHRR 21 [47]; or, more recently, *Cheltsova v Russia* App no 44294/06 (ECHR, 13 June 2017) [77]. See also, putting the standard differently, *Nikula v Finland* (2004) 38 EHRR 45 [48]; or, more recently, *Čeferin v Slovenia* App no 40975/08 (ECtHR 16 January 2018) [56] ('The limits of acceptable criticism may in some circumstances be wider with regard to civil servants exercising their powers than in relation to private individuals').

[101] See *Janowski* (n 73) [33], compare and contrast *Oberschlick v Austria (No 2)* (1998) 25 EHRR 357 [29].

[102] *Fürst-Pfeifer v Austria* App no 33677/10 (17 May 2016) [47]. Focused on the task of the judiciary, see *Prager and Oberschlick v Austria* (1996) 21 EHRR 1 [34].

[103] *Mamère v France* (2009) 49 EHRR 39 [27], referring to *Busuioc v Moldova* (2006) 42 EHRR 14 [64], where the standard is, however, put differently ('it may be necessary to protect public servants from offensive, abusive and defamatory attacks which are calculated to affect them in the performance of their duties and to damage public confidence in them and the office they hold').

[104] *Mamère* (n 103) [27].   [105] *Busuioc* (n 103) [64].

do so based on more or less nuanced conceptions of the class of persons thus designated: the UNHRC,[106] just as the ACtHPR,[107] relies on a rather broad notion of 'public figures', that covers those acting in an official capacity just as well as those who entered the arena of public deliberation on their own account.

Such a concept, of course, does not correspond to the one originally shaped in the case law of the US Supreme Court, which defined a 'public figure' as an 'individual [who] voluntarily injects himself or is drawn into a particular public controversy',[108] and therefore, by extending the *Sullivan* standard is 'dumped into the same legal hopper as public officials';[109] a 'designation [which] applies, at the very least, to those among the hierarchy of government employees who have, or appear to the public to have, substantial responsibility for or control over the conduct of governmental affairs'.[110] The IACtHR again follows along these lines.[111] At the same time, the Court refers explicitly to the *Lingens* standard, introduced by the ECtHR,[112] to underline that also those who do not hold but seek public office are necessarily subject not only to greater public scrutiny but also in danger of greater public vilification.[113] The ECtHR, finally, aside from applying a nuanced standard to civil servants and an elevated standard to politicians,[114] holds public officials,[115] as defined in the case law of the US Supreme Court, to yet a stricter standard:

> The limits of permissible criticism are wider with regard to the Government than in relation to a private citizen, or even a politician. In a democratic system the actions or omissions of the Government must be subject to the close scrutiny not only of the legislative and judicial authorities but also of the press and public opinion.[116]

---

[106] See Michael O'Flaherty, 'Freedom of Expression: Article 19 of the International Covenant on Civil and Political Rights and the Human Rights Committee's General Comment No 34' (2012) 12 *Hum Rts L Rev* 627, 640.

[107] See Lyombe Eko, 'Globalization and the Diffusion of Media Policy in Africa: The Case of Defamation of Public Officials' (2016) 11 *Afr Pol'y J* 17, 33–4.

[108] *Gertz v Robert Welch Inc*, 418 US 323 (1974) 351.

[109] Frederick Schauer, 'Public Figures' (1984) 25 *Wm & Mary L Rev* 905, 908.

[110] *Rosenblatt v Baer*, 383 US 75, 85 (1966).   [111] See *Canese* (n 98) [101], [103].

[112] *Lingens* (n 96) [42]. See Section 21.4.2 above.

[113] *Canese* (n 98) [102]. For a closer analysis, see Eduardo Andrés Bertoni, 'The Inter-American Court of Human Rights and the European Court of Human Rights: A Dialogue on Freedom of Expression Standards' [2009] EHRLR 332, 341–2.

[114] While the ECtHR's case law at times (in particular when balancing free speech and the right to privacy) introduces analytically even more nuanced 'category[ies]' of persons such as politicians, public officials, public figures or others who belonged to the public sphere by dint of their activities or high earnings... or their position [which] inevitably and knowingly lay themselves open to close scrutiny by both journalists and the public at large' (see *Satakunnan Markkinapörssi Oy v Finland* (2018) 66 EHRR 8 [180] with further references), it will suffice for the purpose at hand to stick with the classification introduced above. For a closer analysis of the interrelation of free speech and privacy, see Chapter 16 by Ioanna Tourkochoriti, in this volume.

[115] However, the Court's case law does not consistently distinguish between officials and politicians in the sense of a distinction between those seeking and those holding political office: see, eg, *Ziembiński v Poland (No 2)* App no 1799/07 (ECHR, 5 July 2016) referring to the 'mayor of the district [as] an elected local politician and official'.

[116] *Castells v Spain* (1992) 14 EHRR 45 [46]; *Stomakhin v Russia* App no 52273/07 (ECHR, 9 May 2018) [89].

The fine line along which public officials, politicians, and civil servants may be distinguished (and the free speech standard thus applied) is, however, only to be drawn against the backdrop of the national political system in question: whether or not a public prosecutor, for example, is to be considered a civil servant[117] or a political actor[118] (and thus either as public official, public figure, or politician) will, also and in particular, depend on whether the position in question is held by a career bureaucrat or an elected official. To adjust the free speech standard accordingly is hardly inconsistent; just as long as such an adjustment ensures that those acting in an official capacity—irrespective of their status—may be, in principle, subjected to the scrutiny of public opinion no matter which branch of government is concerned.[119] Consistently, according to the ECtHR's case law, the limits of permissible criticism are—again—to be considered wider in those cases where not the individuals serving in a government institution but the institution itself is subject to criticism.[120]

21.4.4 Public Watchdogs, Public Concern, and Precluded Replies

The 'limits of permissible criticism' thus understood are, of course, not exclusively determined by the addressee but also by the speaker and by what is spoken.

The press and its members have traditionally been awarded strong free speech protection in pursuing their task to serve as a 'public watchdog'[121] by universal and regional human rights tribunals;[122] in particular, in cases concerning the question this chapter is dedicated to.[123] Still, the important changes brought about by the 'fourth revolution'[124] affected the status of traditional mass media in more than one way:[125] as the role of the 'public watchdog' is being administered increasingly not by members of the press (broadly understood) but by members of the civil society, the task thus seized provoked a transition from an institutionalist[126] towards a functionalist understanding of the

---

[117] *Nikula* (n 100) [48]–[50]; or, more recently, *Čeferin* (n 100) [56]–[57].

[118] *Lohé Issa Konaté* (n 85) [155]–[156].

[119] See art 10 ECHR; Christoph Grabenwarter, *European Convention on Human Rights: Commentary* (Hart 2014); Eko, (n 107) 30–2, Thomas M Antkowiak and Alejandra Gonza, *The American Convention on Human Rights* (OUP 2017) 249–57 with further references.

[120] See, eg, *Terentyev* (n 65) [76]; *Gazeta and Milashina v Russia* App no 45083/06 (ECtHR 3 October 2017) [62].

[121] See the seminal ECtHR judgment *Barthold v Germany* (1985) 7 EHRR 383. See also, in the given context, in particular, *Pedersen v Denmark* (2006) 42 EHRR 24.

[122] For a more thorough examination of the topic, see Chapter 29 by Dieter Grimm, in this volume.

[123] See, eg, for the weight given to this distinction, *Janowski* (n 73) [32]; *Łopuch v Poland* App no 43587/09 (ECHR, 24 July 2012) [60]; compare and contrast *Lohé Issa Konaté* (n 85) [164] *Fontevecchia and D'Amico v Argentinia* (IACtHR, 29 November 2011) 46.

[124] Luciano Floridi, *The Fourth Revolution* (OUP 2014).

[125] For a closer analysis, see Chapter 19 by Gregory Magarian, in this volume.

[126] See for a classical, even if not particularly influential, account Potter Stewart, 'Or of the Press' (1975) 26 *Hastings LJ* 631.

robust standard of protection to be allotted to those watching over the community.[127] Such a functionalist understanding, however, necessarily needs to rely on a more or less clear perception of what is 'common' to the 'community'.

While this is not the place to reflect deeply upon 'matters of public concern'[128] or 'questions of public interest'[129] at the core of a concept of public discourse as sum of those 'communicative processes necessary for the formation of public opinion, whether or not that opinion is directed toward specific government personnel, decisions, or policies',[130] it is the place to emphasize that actions undertaken by 'government personnel, decisions, or policies' is to be subjected to '[d]emocratic control exercised by society through public opinion [to encourage] the transparency of State activities and [to promote] the accountability of public officials'.[131] And it is the place to emphasize that 'questions of public interest' or 'matters of public concern', speech entitled to particularly robust protection, are not only typically (and oftentimes inextricably) intertwined but also that 'persons taking part in a public debate on a matter of general concern ... are allowed to have recourse to a degree of exaggeration or even provocation, or in other words to make somewhat immoderate statements'.[132]

From the perspective of this interrelation, as the IACtHR specifically emphasizes, the:

> different threshold of protection [which] should be applied, [is not, or at least: not only] based on the nature of the subject, but on the characteristic of public interest inherent in the activities or acts of a specific individual. Those individuals who have an influence on matters of public interest have laid themselves open voluntarily to a

---

[127] For the relevant ECtHR case law, see *Magyar Helsinki Bizottság v Hungary* App no 18030/11 (ECHR, 8 November 2016) [168] ('the Court considers that an important consideration is whether the person seeking access to the information in question does so with a view to informing the public in the capacity of a public "watchdog". This does not mean, however, that a right of access to information ought to apply exclusively to NGOs and the press. It reiterates that a high level of protection also extends to academic researchers ... and authors of literature on matters of public concern ... The Court would also note that given the important role played by the Internet in enhancing the public's access to news and facilitating the dissemination of information ... the function of bloggers and popular users of the social media may be also assimilated to that of "public watchdogs" in so far as the protection afforded by Article 10 is concerned'). For the global level, see General Comment 34 (n 92) [44] ('Journalism is a function shared by a wide range of actors, including professional full-time reporters and analysts, as well as bloggers and others who engage in forms of self-publication in print, on the internet or elsewhere ... Limited accreditation schemes are permissible only where necessary to provide journalists with privileged access to certain places and/or events [and] should be applied in a manner that is non-discriminatory ... based on objective criteria and taking into account that journalism is a function shared by a wide range of actors').

[128] For the US Supreme Court's more recent case law, see *Snyder v Phelps*, 131 S Ct 1207, 1216–18 (2011). For a closer analysis, see Clay Calvert, 'Defining "Public Concern" after *Snyder v Phelps*: A Pliable Standard Mingles with Media Complicity' (2012) 19 *Vill Sports & Ent LJ* 39, 50ff.

[129] See, eg, *Animal Defenders International v United Kingdom* (2013) 57 EHRR 21 [102]; or, more recently, *Iskra v Russia* App no 42911/08 (ECHR, 21 February 2017) [107].

[130] Robert C Post, 'Racist Speech, Democracy and the First Amendment' (1991) 32 *Wm & Mary L Rev* 267, 288.

[131] *Herrera-Ulloa v Costa Rica* (IACtHR 2 July 2004) [128].

[132] *Maciejewski v Poland* App no 34447/05 (ECHR, 12 January 2015) [79] with further references.

more intense public scrutiny and, consequently, in this domain, they are subject to a higher risk of being criticized, because their activities go beyond the private sphere and belong to the realm of public debate.[133]

And above all, '[t]hose individuals who have an influence on matters of public interest', typically also command the means to prove it. Just as the US Supreme Court emphasized in *Gertz v Welch*:[134]

> Public officials and public figures usually enjoy significantly greater access to the channels of effective communication, and hence have a more realistic opportunity to counteract false statements than private individuals normally enjoy.

International human rights tribunals, such as the IACtHR, take this imbalance into account, considering public officials to typically command 'greater social influence and easy access to the media to provide explanations or to account for any events in which they take part'.[135]

On the other hand, certain positions in public service—rather than extending an individual's capacity to counter offence and falsehood or to give a personal account of a certain set of facts—would typically restrict the ability to do so. Judges, the ECtHR would emphasize, 'are subject to a duty of discretion that precludes them from replying'.[136] Still, this qualification would not apply necessarily to high ranking members of the judiciary 'as the President of the Supreme Court of Justice cannot be considered to be in the same position as any other judge'.[137] Again, thus, a line is to be drawn between various individuals acting in a public capacity;[138] even if at this time the line determines an official's capacity to 'speak back'.[139]

21.5 BETWEEN CRITICISM AND INSULT

It is against this backdrop that criticism and insult are to be distinguished.[140] This distinction is of cardinal importance, after all, as the ECtHR emphasizes: 'the latter may, in principle, justify sanctions'.[141] To decide whether a particular remark would 'amount to

---

[133] *Herrera-Ulloa v Costa Rica* (IACtHR, 2 July 2004) [129]; *Fontevecchia and D'Amico v Argentinia* (IACtHR, 29 November 2011) [47].

[134] *Gertz* (n 108) 344.   [135] *Donoso* (n 99) 122.

[136] *Prager* (n 102) [34]; and, more recently, *Mustafa Erdoğan v Turkey* App no 346/04 (ECHR, 27 May 2014) [42].

[137] *Fernandes v Portugal* App no 31566/13 (ECHR, 17 January 2017) [63].

[138] See Section 21.4.3 of this chapter.

[139] For a closer analysis, see Chapter 14 by Katharine Gelber, in this volume.

[140] See Section 21.3.1 of this chapter.   [141] *Sánchez v Spain* (2012) 54 EHRR 24 [67].

wanton denigration',[142] which to sanction met a 'pressing social need'[143] in a proportionate manner, all the factors discussed above are to be taken into account; even if—as international human rights tribunals agree—criminal sanctions are to be reserved for the most severe cases:[144]

> pondering the extreme seriousness of the conduct of the individual who expressed the opinion, his actual malice, the characteristics of the unfair damage caused, and other information which shows the absolute necessity to resort to criminal proceedings as an exception.[145]

Thus, in particular, according to the ECtHR's long-standing case law:

> a prison sentence in defamation cases will be compatible with the freedom of expression as guaranteed by Article 10 of the Convention only in exceptional circumstances, notably where other fundamental rights have been seriously impaired, as, for example, in the case of hate speech or incitement to violence.[146]

Even if 'only by a careful examination of the context in which the offending, insulting or aggressive words appear . . . a meaningful distinction [is to be drawn] between shocking and offensive language which is protected by [free speech] and that which forfeits its right to tolerance in a democratic society',[147] this examination would be governed by a framework that offers guidance on the limits of speech deemed to be insulting to public officials in the respective context. While these limits may not be as clear-cut as those delineated by the US Supreme Court's approach to the First Amendment, this framework ensures that the balancing test employed to explore them by international human rights tribunals is hardly 'free-floating'[148] but rather determined by a set of differently weighed criteria that need to be taken into account.

This abets the rationality of judicial decision-making just as it abets the rationalization of judicial decisions. It makes us understand why, even absent structural considerations as pursued by the US Supreme Court in *Chaplinsky* and its aftermath,[149] Józef Janowski, while a journalist by profession, was not successful in relying on the ECHR's free speech clause when fighting his fine for insulting two municipal guards on duty.[150]

---

[142] See Section 21.3.2 of this chapter.
[143] See, eg, *Grebneva and Alisimchik* (n 65) [53]–[66] on a newspaper satire concerning a regional prosecutor depicted as a 'prostitute werewolf'; compare and contrast from a First Amendment perspective, *Hustler Magazine Inc v Falwell*, 485 US 46 (1988).
[144] *Lohé Issa Konaté* (n 85) [157]–[165] with further references. See also General Comment 34 (n 92) [47].
[145] *Donoso* (n 99) [120].
[146] *Paraskevopoulos v Greece* App no 64184/11 (ECHR, 28 June 2018) [42]. For the Court's prior case law see, in particular, *Cumpănă v Romania* (2005) 41 EHRR 14 [115]. For a more thorough discussion of these topics see Chapter 18 by Geoffrey Stone and Chapter 25 by Alon Harel, in this volume.
[147] *Terentyev* (n 65) [68]. [148] Cf *Stevens* (n 14). See Section 21.3 of this chapter.
[149] See Section 21.2.1 of this chapter. [150] See Section 21.3.2 of this chapter.

Just as it makes us understand why Maciej Ziembiński, acting in his professional capacity as a journalist, did engage in protected speech in referring to the district mayor and one official as 'dull bosses' and to another official as 'a numbskull', 'a dim-witted official' and 'a poser'.[151] It makes us understand, how the immediacy of face-to-face insults directed at officials in pursuit of their duties differs from criticism of their actions conveyed by blogs or mass media.[152] Just as it makes us understand how speech may be restricted when it effectively impedes the administration of said duties by civil servants, undermining 'public confidence' in a branch of government,[153] but must not be restricted when it questions or ridicules the actions or the demeanour of the state's highest representatives,[154] foreign just as domestic,[155] in a republic just as in a monarchy:[156] be it by wielding derogatory messages on a placard to the president's motorcade,[157] or by burning a photograph of the royal couple at the occasion of the king's visit to the region.[158]

By mapping the path that leads from demeaning personal encounters to the essential task fulfilled by public watchdogs in shaping an open discourse that monitors the conduct of those serving the community on to the criticism of those who, as heads of state, symbolize the community as a whole, the framework described above provides a cross-section of the different layers of free speech problems between the quasi-factual 'slap in the face' and the symbolically charged uproar directed against those representing what is 'common' to the community. Hardly any case displays these different layers more vividly than that of Walter Chaplinsky, who was abused for disrespecting the flag as a symbol of the wider community and who answered this by resorting to abuse himself, calling a community official 'a damned Fascist and the whole government of Rochester Fascists or agents of Fascists'.[159]

Chaplinsky's case may prove to be an apt example for the marks along the path that leads from prohibited insult to protected criticism. A doctrinal discussion as attempted here, contrasting different approaches to cases similar to Walter Chaplinsky's, should, however, not hide the fact, that in many countries this (or in any case: a similar) path has yet to be trod.[160] An analytical framework as the one described above may provide guidance when it comes to remedying that. Still, a framework—notwithstanding its extensive reach—is not a substitute for the effective free speech protection we find lacking regularly (also and in particular) when it comes to speech considered defamatory of or

---

[151] *Ziembiński* (n 115).   [152] See Section 21.4.4 of this chapter.
[153] *Prager and Oberschlick v Austria* (n 102) [34].   [154] See Section 21.4.2 of this chapter.
[155] *Colombani v France* App no 51278/99 (ECHR, 25 June 2002) [68]; *Güvener v Turquie* App no 75510/01 (ECHR, 26 June 2007) [31].
[156] *Eon v France* App no 26118/10 (ECHR, 14 March 2013); *Taulats and Capellera v Spain* App no 51168/15 (ECHR, 12 March 2018).
[157] *Eon* (n 156).   [158] *Taulats* (n 156).   [159] *Chaplinsky v New Hampshire* (n 1) 570.
[160] See Clooney and Webb (n 15) 1, with numerous examples. Focusing an OSCE member states, compare Scott Griffen, *Defamation and Insult Laws in the OSCE Region: A Comparative Study* (OSCE Representative of Freedom on the Media, 2017).

'insulting' to public officials.[161] Such restrictions, oftentimes reinforced by means of criminal law rather than being dedicated to the 'true use of the power of speech', significantly curtail the possibility 'to speak truth to power'.[162] Whether they exist in a given political community and how they are enforced will tell a lot about the general state of public discourse, as it will tell a lot about whether or not such public discourse may rightfully claim to be 'uninhibited, robust, and wide-open'.

---

[161] *Criminal Defamation and 'Insult' Laws in the OSCE Region* (Helsinki Commission Report, 2017).
[162] See Section 21.1 of this chapter.

CHAPTER 22

FREEDOM OF EXPRESSION IN THE WORKPLACE

CYNTHIA ESTLUND

The workplace is a distinctive expressive domain because the 'censor' and the speaker are typically bound together by an employment contract that affords the former a large measure of hierarchical control over the latter. The employer, having hired the employee to do a job, has legitimate interests in regulating some employee speech. The employee is typically dependent on the employer for their livelihood, and vulnerable to the employer's overreaching beyond those legitimate interests. Those features of the employment relationship give rise to a distinct set of questions about the value and limits of free speech in the workplace setting, public or private. This chapter will focus on how US law—primarily constitutional law but also non-constitutional law—has dealt with those questions.

The United States—an outlier among Western democracies in many respects—obviously has its own distinctive history and constitutional make-up. Two features of US constitutionalism are especially relevant here. The first is the famously robust commitment to freedom of expression relative to other political values with which it can sometimes conflict. A second feature cuts in the opposite direction: the 'state action' doctrine blocks the entry of constitutional free speech principles into 'horizontal' relations among citizens, including the employment relations through which most individuals derive their livelihood.

Beyond those distinctive features of US constitutionalism, the US law of work is distinguished by the persistence of 'employment-at-will'—the presumptive right of both parties to terminate employment at any time and for any reason or no reason at all. That principle potentially empowers employers to censor, suppress, or punish employees' speech and associations—on-duty or off-duty—on pain of dismissal. In the private sector that power is unconstrained by the Constitution, though it has come to be constrained by a variety of narrower non-constitutional speech protections. In the public sector, employer action is state action that is at least potentially constrained by the First Amendment—though not, as it turns out, by the famously robust First Amendment principles that govern in the public square, but by a weaker workplace-specific version of those principles. The employment relationship between the speaker and the censor sharply inflects the former's free speech rights and the latter's power to control speech.

While the US law governing freedom of expression in the workplace is unique in some ways, the problems it addresses will arise in any society that both recognizes the value of freedom of expression and channels labour into the production of goods and services largely through the institution of employment. In particular, clashes between employees' freedom of speech and association and employers' claimed prerogatives may arise as to expression that is either at work or off-duty and outside the workplace; expression whose content is either related or wholly unrelated to the employment; or expression that is actually part of the employee's job. Several of the many possible permutations have arisen in US Supreme Court decisions on the First Amendment rights of public employees. The answers the Court has given in those decisions might be instructive, whether or not they are persuasive, both in the US private sector and in other societies grappling with these issues.

As a preface to those doctrinal matters, however, we should begin by asking whether and why we should care about freedom of expression in the workplace. From that preface, the chapter will turn to the free speech rights of public employees under the First Amendment, and then more briefly to the non-constitutional free speech rights of employees in the private sector, before concluding.[1]

22.1 Why Freedom of Expression in the Workplace Matters

As a way into the question of why we should care about free speech in the workplace, imagine a society with none of it. Specifically, imagine an electoral democracy with free speech protections against the sovereign, and with pure employment-at-will: both employers and employees are free to end the employment relationship at any time and for any reason or no reason. In that system, employers could freely dictate their employees' associations and expression, on and off the job, and could enforce those dictates by the threat of discharge. Employees would be free to quit, but the employer's commands would effectively be binding on employees up to the limits of their economic dependence on the employer.

In that imagined world, the employer could prohibit employees from speaking out contrary to the employer's interests and views—from disclosing dangerous and illegal

---

[1] The focus here on employees' free speech rights vis-à-vis their employers leaves aside, among other things, the historically freighted issue of state regulation of collective expression by workers and their unions.

activities of the employer, or opposing the employer's favoured political views and candidates—all on pain of discharge. Indeed, the employer could compel employees to actively support the employer's political preferences. And unless we import into this imagined world the secret ballot (which gained currency in the United States only in the late nineteenth century), employers could dictate their employees' actual votes if they chose to do so. Employees could be dragooned—to whatever extent they needed or wanted to keep their job—into amplifying the political voices of their employers and of the monied classes instead of expressing and promoting their own opinions and interests.

If we extend these conditions into government employment, it would mean that incumbent elected officials and their appointees could prescribe whatever conditions they wished on public employment. The employer could demand employees' silence about political matters and abstention from political activity, both off-duty and on-duty, or they could demand employees' strict loyalty to and active political support of the officials or party in power, in either case backed by the threat of discharge. Incumbents could thus entrench their own power and insulate themselves from electoral challenge—not absolutely but by a margin that would grow with the public payroll. And much information and informed opinion about the operations of government, and about corruption, deception, or abuse of power, could be bottled up inside government offices by a code of silence.

In this imagined world, employees would still be formally free to speak their minds and vote their own preferences—as long as they were willing to quit or court dismissal. That freedom would be largely illusory, however, for those who lacked the resources to survive without a job and who could not readily find another employer that did not impose the same restrictions. Not all employers would exploit their power over employees; but the latters' freedom and political independence would be tenuous and subject to their employers' whims. Political equality among citizens would be a formalist fiction. At least if a large share of the citizenry were economically dependent on employment, it is debatable whether this imagined society could fairly call itself either free or democratic.

Is the problem of employee unfreedom in this imagined society dissolved by the fact that it arises within a voluntary contractual relationship that the employee freely enters and can freely leave?[2] On a traditional liberal understanding of political freedom, one might be untroubled by non-state restrictions to which one has consented in the contractual sense; after all, the freedom of contract is itself an essential aspect of liberal freedom.[3] For others in the republican tradition, the problem of employer domination is more serious; a free and self-governing society must ensure citizens' freedom from

---

[2] Armen A Alchian and Harold Demsetz, 'Production, Information Costs, and Economic Organization' (1972) 62 *Am Econ Rev* 777, 777.

[3] Samuel Freeman, 'Capitalism in the Classical and High Liberal Traditions' (2011) 28 *Soc Phil and Pol'y* 19, 20–2; Elizabeth Anderson, *Private Government: How Employers Rule Our Lives (and Why We Don't Talk about It)* (Princeton UP 2017) 53–8.

domination by others, not just the state.[4] Neo-republicans, like their forebears, are more sensitive than classical liberals to the problem of domination within non-state or 'horizontal' relationships, and less beguiled by the magic of contractual consent. But thoughtful liberals and republicans alike would be concerned by the spillover effects of employer domination in our imagined system of public discourse, political equality, and democratic accountability.

One need not simply imagine such a system, for something much like it prevailed in the United States for much of its history. It was against that background that the modern US law of employee speech rights evolved. In that evolution one can discern a gradual and partial shift from a starkly liberal conception towards a more republican conception of what kind of freedom matters in a democratic society. Let us turn first to the highly articulated body of law that evolved in public sector employment under the First Amendment.

22.2 Public Employee Speech Rights under the First Amendment

Until the late 1920s, the First Amendment did not amount to much, at least in the courts. It did not even entail a right to speak in the public square, for that was the government's property to govern as it wished.[5] By 1940, the Supreme Court had begun deploying the First Amendment to open up public spaces for expression and to limit the power of the government-as-sovereign to regulate citizens' speech. For several more decades, however, the government-as-employer remained unconstrained by the First Amendment. Although action by a government employer was 'state action', the so-called 'rights-privileges' doctrine blocked employees' constitutional claims: public employment was not a right but a privilege that the government could withhold or withdraw at its whim—for good reason, bad reason, or no reason at all.[6] Nothing in the Constitution thus constrained government censorship or punishment of its employees' speech and associations. As Justice Holmes memorably put it: '[t]he petitioner may have a constitutional right to talk politics, but he has no constitutional right to be a policeman'.[7]

In the constitutional vacuum created by the rights-privileges doctrine, various government bodies pursued diametrically opposed conceptions of the proper relationship between public employment and partisan electoral politics. Where political patronage,

---

[4] Philip Pettit, *Republicanism: A Theory of Freedom and Government* (OUP 1999); Quentin Skinner, 'Freedom as the Absence of Arbitrary Power' in Cécile Laborde and John Maynor (eds), *Republicanism and Political Theory* (Blackwell 2008); Frank Lovett, *A General Theory of Domination and Justice* (OUP 2010).

[5] Stewart Jay, 'The Creation of the First Amendment Right to Free Expression: from the Eighteenth Century to the Mid-Twentieth Century' (2007) 34 *Wm Mitchell L Rev* 773, 821.

[6] William W Van Alstyne, 'The Demise of the Right-Privilege Distinction in Constitutional Law' (1968) 81 *Harv L Rev* 1439, 1439–41.

[7] *McAuliffe v New Bedford*, 29 NE 517, 517 (Mass 1892).

or the 'spoils system', held sway, public employees could get or keep their jobs only by joining and actively supporting the party in power. Elsewhere, and especially in the federal government, a progressive movement in favour of merit-based civil service reached its apotheosis with the Hatch Act, which prohibited most federal employees from actively participating in partisan politics. Both systems deprived public employees of political freedoms that the First Amendment guaranteed to other citizens, but both were constitutionally permissible conditions on the 'privilege' of public employment.

The rights-privileges distinction came under growing pressure during the 1950s as the hydra-headed anti-communist crusade gained steam. Legal elites, including those on the Supreme Court, came to recognize that the government could command ideological conformity and quash dissent, not only by exercising its coercive powers as sovereign but also by conditioning citizens' access to professional licences, public contracts, public employment, and other economic goods that the government controlled. Accordingly, rights-privileges gave way to the doctrine of 'unconstitutional conditions',[8] and some government entitlements, including some jobs, were deemed 'property' protected by due process.[9] Under those doctrines, even if the government is not required to grant individuals professional licences, jobs, or welfare benefits, it may not deny those valuable benefits for unconstitutional reasons (or in some cases without due process of law). That reframing of the nature of government employment teed up the question whether the government may condition a job on the sacrifice of the freedom of speech protected by the First Amendment. In other words, could the government fire Holmes's policeman for talking politics?

In the public sector, First Amendment questions might arise either over the discharge or discipline of an individual employee based on expressive activity or over broad policies restricting public employees' beliefs, associations, and expression (like the Hatch Act). Individual personnel actions have generated the bulk of the litigation and a body of doctrine that has exercised a certain gravitational pull on the Court's treatment of systemic policies that regulate the speech of large groups of public employees.[10]

22.2.1 The First Amendment in Individual Disciplinary Decisions

The First Amendment made its official debut within public employment in *Pickering v Board of Education*,[11] which overturned the discharge of a teacher who had written a letter to the editor criticizing the school board's budgeting process and its allocation of

---

[8] *Perry v Sinderman*, 408 US 593 (1972).
[9] *Board of Regents v Roth*, 408 US 564 (1972). The classic article is Charles A Reich, 'The New Property' (1964) 73 *Yale LJ* 733.
[10] More extended treatment of these cases may be found in Cynthia Estlund, 'Harmonizing Work and Citizenship: A Due Process Solution to a First Amendment Problem' [2006] *Sup Ct Rev* 115; Cynthia Estlund, 'Free Speech Rights That Work at Work: From the First Amendment to Due Process' (2007) 54 *UCLA L Rev* 1463.
[11] *Pickering v Board of Education*, 391 US 563 (1968).

funds between educational and athletic programmes. The Court emphasized that the subject of Pickering's letter was 'a matter of legitimate public concern' as to which 'free and open debate is vital to informed decision-making by the electorate'.[12] Because teachers like Pickering were especially 'likely to have informed and definite opinions' on such matters within the educational system, it was 'essential that they be able to speak out freely on such questions'.[13] The interest of the public in hearing what they had to say thus bolstered public employees' interest in speaking freely in the public sphere.

In opening up government workplaces to First Amendment scrutiny, *Pickering* opened up a raft of questions about how that would work. One thing was clear from the outset: the Court had no intention of importing into government workplaces the 'uninhibited, robust, and wide-open' debate of the press and the public square.[14] As the Court explained in *Pickering*:

> the State has interests as an employer in regulating the speech of its employees that differ significantly from those it possesses in connection with regulation of the speech of the citizenry in general. The problem in any case is to arrive at a *balance between the interests of the teacher, as a citizen, in commenting upon matters of public concern and the interest of the State, as an employer, in promoting the efficiency of the public services it performs through its employees.*[15]

Thus was born the *Pickering* balancing test, which seemed capable of handling the full gamut of free speech controversies that could arise out of public employment. Yet the sheer number of potential controversies, coupled with the indeterminacy of the test, seemed to ensure a steady flow of those claims into the federal courts.

The Supreme Court tightened the spigot on those claims in *Connick v Myers*.[16] Sheila Myers had been fired for circulating a questionnaire among her co-workers on issues such as employees' morale, confidence in supervisors, and fairness in transfer and promotion decisions. Averring that 'government offices could not function if every employment decision became a constitutional matter',[17] the Court held that only speech on 'matters of public concern' was protected under *Pickering*.[18] *Connick* picked up the key phrase from *Pickering*, where it appeared to function as one dimension of the overall balancing test, and promoted it to a threshold test. Although it had long been clear that expression on public issues was at the core of First Amendment values, *Connick* broke new ground in requiring the speaker to bring her speech within that core as a threshold

---

[12] Ibid 571–2. [13] Ibid 572. [14] *New York Times Co v Sullivan*, 376 US 254, 270 (1964).
[15] *Pickering* (n 11) 568 (emphasis added). [16] *Connick v Myers*, 461 US 138 (1983).
[17] Ibid 143.
[18] Ibid 154. The Court held that one of Myers' questions—on whether employees felt pressured to work on political campaigns—did touch on matters of public concern, and did trigger the balancing test. In applying that test, the Court seemed to tip the scales towards the government by allowing it to rely on predictions about the impact of speech versus its actual impact. The employer's fear that Myers' speech might trigger a 'mini-insurrection' in the office thus outweighed her free speech interests. See *Connick* (n 16) 150–4.

matter.[19] Was it not for the public to decide what it was concerned about? Now it was for the courts to define the contours of the category of speech on matters of public concern. And it did not generally include speech on 'internal office affairs even within an important public office'.[20]

What was now the two-step *Connick–Pickering* test cut out a good deal of what employees might want to talk about with each other. But what about 'water-cooler' speech among co-workers on other topics? That scenario might test the joints of *Pickering*'s rationale, for casual conversations among co-workers are of no immediate value to voters. Yet those conversations surely play a role in the formation of public opinion; they may also contribute more diffusely to civic life by cultivating bonds across lines of identity that separate citizens in most social settings.[21] And individuals' freedom to converse with their co-workers during the work day is surely an aspect of personal liberty.

The Court gave at least a tacit nod to those free speech values when the water-cooler scenario arose in *Rankin v McPherson*.[22] McPherson, a clerical employee in a county sheriff's office, had been overheard chatting with a co-worker about the assassination attempt on President Reagan; she was fired for saying, 'If they go for him again, I hope they get him'. The Court held that the comment was on matters of public concern given its context—a conversation about Reagan's policies and their impact on racial minorities—despite its provocative tinge.[23] Proceeding to the balancing test, the Court held that McPherson's interest in freely speaking on such matters at work outweighed the negligible impact of her comment on legitimate managerial interests.[24] *Rankin* represented a qualified victory for the freedom of speech among co-workers, albeit only as to speech on public issues.

Until the mid-2000s, the key public employee speech cases in the Supreme Court involved speech that either took place at work (as in *Rankin*), or was about the employer (as in *Pickering*), or both (as in *Connick*). The full spectrum of public employee speech controversies included speech that was either more or less connected to their work—speech that was either part of the employee's job, or was wholly unrelated to the job. Those scenarios probed the scope of the *Connick–Pickering* test.

The Court confronted the problem of speech-that-is-the-job in *Garcetti v Ceballos*.[25] Assistant district attorney Ceballos claimed that he had suffered reprisals after opining in a memo, and later testifying, that an arresting police officer may have lied in an affidavit that was the basis for an arrest warrant. Ceballos believed he was legally and professionally obligated to disclose exculpatory information about possible police misconduct. But the Supreme Court held that the First Amendment offered him no refuge because

---

[19] Cynthia L Estlund, 'Speech on Matters of Public Concern: The Perils of an Emerging First Amendment Category' (1990) 59 *Geo Wash L Rev* 1, 3.

[20] *Connick* (n 16) 149.

[21] Cynthia Estlund, *Working Together: How Workplace Bonds Strengthen a Diverse Democracy* (OUP 2003).

[22] *Rankin v McPherson*, 483 US 378 (1987).   [23] Ibid 386.   [24] Ibid 388–9.

[25] *Garcetti v Ceballos*, 547 US 410 (2006).

the memo and the testimony were within his job duties as supervising attorney in the underlying prosecution:

> We hold that when public employees make statements pursuant to their official duties, the employees are not speaking as citizens for First Amendment purposes, and the Constitution does not insulate their communications from employer discipline.[26]

Recall *Pickering*'s reference to 'the interests of the [employee], *as a citizen*, in commenting upon matters of public concern'. Just as *Connick* transformed the last phrase into the threshold 'public concern' test, *Garcetti* gave independent threshold significance to the phrase 'as a citizen'. So while Ceballos had plainly spoken on matters of public concern, he lost because he 'did not act as a citizen when he went about conducting his daily professional activities, such as supervising attorneys, investigating charges, and preparing filings'.[27] In effect, the speech through which an employee performs the job belongs to the government employer, and is subject to its plenary control. If the legislature or the agency decides to protect employees who report official mistakes, misconduct, or abuse, (for example, through a 'whistle-blower' statute), so be it. But the employer is otherwise free to punish the employee without any burden of justification.

The problem of speech-that-is-the-job poses a serious dilemma. Much of the actual work of public employees is performed through speech or writing; and much of that expression is inescapably on matters of public concern, sometimes including official misconduct. No doubt it would be a difficult and sensitive judicial task to balance the individual and public interests in airing crucial matters of public concern against managers' ability to evaluate employees' job performance without judicial second-guessing. Perhaps the employee should have to make some heightened showing of the public importance and accuracy of the speech.[28] Or perhaps the solution lies in the environs of 'First Amendment due process'.[29] But *Garcetti* gave a categorical verdict in favour of managerial freedom, however unjustified, over employee freedom of expression, however valuable.

At the opposite end of the spectrum of job relatedness—that is, off-duty speech that is unrelated to the job or agency—one might look for a similarly categorical approach, this time favouring free speech interests. That is one reading of *United States v National Treasury Employees' Union (NTEU)*,[30] which struck down a statutory ban on federal employees' accepting any compensation for off-duty speeches or writings, even those with no connection to the employee's official duties. The opinion was a bit opaque about why the speech was protected: was it because it all fell within the 'protected category of citizen comment on matters of public concern', or because it was off-duty and 'unrelated to the employment'?[31] We will return to *NTEU* for its analysis of broad policies

---

[26] Ibid 421.   [27] Ibid 422.   [28] Ibid 434–6 (Souter J, dissenting).
[29] Cynthia Estlund, 'Free Speech Rights that Work at Work' (n 10) 1472–3.
[30] *NTEU*, 513 US 454 (1995).   [31] Ibid 466.

restricting employee speech; but its import was unclear for challenges to individual discharge or discipline based on expression that was unrelated to the work.[32]

That issue seemed to arise in *City of San Diego Police Department v Roe*,[33] which upheld the discharge of a police officer for making and selling sexually explicit videos in which he appeared in (and then partly out of) a generic police uniform while issuing and revoking traffic tickets. *City of San Diego*, a *per curiam* decision, delivered both good news and bad news for public employee speech rights. The good news lay in the Court's reading of *NTEU* on a crucial point: an employee's speech that is unrelated to the employment—that is, unrelated in time (off-duty), place (outside the workplace), and subject matter—enjoys stronger First Amendment protection than is afforded by *Connick* and *Pickering*. In short, when the nexus between the speech and the work becomes too attenuated, the government's heightened power to regulate its employees' speech runs out, and employees recover something like their full freedom as a citizen vis-à-vis the government. That good news for public employees is tempered, however, by the Court's narrow view of what speech counted as 'unrelated to the employment'. It did not include Roe's pornographic videos because his use of a generic police uniform 'brought the mission of the employer and the professionalism of its officers into serious disrepute'.[34] Roe was thus relegated to the *Connick–Pickering* test, which he failed at the threshold: His videos were not on matters of public concern.[35]

As the doctrine now stands, individual public employee speech cases fall into four categories, as depicted in Figure 22.1. '*Garcetti* speech' that is part of the employee's job performance is wholly unprotected by the First Amendment. Speech that is not part of the job itself but is somehow related to the employment (in time, place, or subject matter) comes in two flavours: '*Pickering* speech' on matters of public concern, protected under a balancing test, and '*Connick* speech' that is *not* on matters of public concern, and

Speech is ... → ↓	least ← —————— Job-Relatedness —————— → most		
	unrelated to job/work	related to the work (at or about work)	*part of* the work/ Job Performance
On Matters of Public Concern	'*NTEU* Speech' More PROTECTED	'*Pickering* Speech': BALANCE	'*Garcetti* Speech': UNPROTECTED
Not on Matters of Public Concern		'*Connick* Speech': UNPROTECTED	

FIGURE 22.1 A Map of Public Employees' Free Speech Rights

---

[32] It was unclear whether the speech had to pass *Connick*'s threshold test, and whether *Pickering*'s deferential balancing test applied if the speech *was* on a matter of public concern.
[33] *City of San Diego Police Department v Roe*, 543 US 77 (2004). [34] Ibid 81. [35] Ibid 84.

is unprotected. Speech that is 'unrelated to the employment' in time, place, and subject matter (call it '*NTEU* speech') is constitutionally protected to some greater but still-uncertain degree, whether or not it is not on matters of public concern.

One question, to which I will shortly turn, is whether this doctrinal matrix, developed to resolve quotidian conflicts between government managers and individual employees, applies to broader rules and policies affecting public employee speech rights. The former tend to fall into recurring patterns, while the latter are more likely to be *sui generis*. Moreover, some of the concerns that shadow individual disputes—concerns about micro-managing government offices and unleashing a flood of litigation—fall away in the context of large-scale rules and policies. Indeed, in that context, some of the arguments for affording the government greater power to control the speech of its employees than the speech of citizens at large might be misplaced.

Consider the Supreme Court's own answer to this question: '[w]hat is it about the government's role as employer that gives it a freer hand in regulating the speech of its employees than it has in regulating the speech of the public at large?':[36]

> Government agencies are charged by law with doing particular tasks. Agencies hire employees to help do those tasks as effectively and efficiently as possible. When someone who is paid a salary so that she will contribute to an agency's effective operation begins to do or say things that detract from the agency's effective operation, the government employer must have some power to restrain her.[37]

This explanation meshes well with the *Pickering* balancing test, though somewhat less well with *Connick* and *Garcetti*, which allow the government employer to restrain some employee speech with no showing that it 'detract[ed] from the agency's effective operation'. All in all, however, the *Waters* explanation seems keyed to the quotidian context of personnel management. And it hints at the larger stakes in those controversies for democratic governance.

Clearly democracy requires informed public debate about public affairs, the performance of public officials, and the workings of government; and public employees are crucial sources of information and informed opinions on these matters. But free public discourse and democratic processes for electing officials and expressing policy preferences do not translate into democratic governance unless elected officials can actually implement those policies. And they can do that only by effectively managing government workplaces and public employees. Democratic governance depends on *both* open and informed public debate about governance *and* public officials' ability to manage employees and evaluate their performance. That is the central dilemma at the heart of the doctrine governing public employee speech rights. But that dilemma comes into play quite differently, if at all, when the government enacts broad speech-restrictive rules for its employees. Let us now turn to that branch of public employee speech doctrine.

---

[36] *Waters v Churchill*, 511 US 661, 671 (1994). [37] Ibid 674–5.

22.2.2 Systemic Regulation of Public Employee Speech and Association

The entry of the First Amendment into public employment put at risk some deeply entrenched systemic features of public employment that had grown up in the era of rights-privileges. In particular, the First Amendment now cast a shadow over both the Hatch Act ban on partisan political activity by civil service employees and the still-extant state and local patronage systems that compelled partisan activity by public employees. But the two systems met different fates in the immediate wake of *Pickering*.

The Hatch Act ban on active partisan involvement in political campaigns survived its post-*Pickering* test in *Civil Service Commission v National Association of Letter Carriers*.[38] The Act plainly banned forms of political expression that are normally highly protected under the First Amendment. Citing *Pickering*'s paeon to balancing of interests, the Court turned to the arguments on the other side. First, the Court agreed with the Act's supporters that, paradoxically, it actually protected most employees' political freedom—that *prohibiting* employees from engaging in partisan activity was necessary to protect them from being *coerced* to do so by their bosses.[39] But the main defence of the Act was on systemic political process grounds: Congress had long ago determined that 'the rapidly expanding Government workforce should not be employed to build a powerful, invincible, and perhaps corrupt political machine'.[40] Beyond concerns about corruption and entrenchment of incumbents, Congress feared that a bureaucracy staffed with partisans entailed 'hazards to fair and effective government', including the risk of 'political justice'.[41] The Court found in these arguments a powerful justification for the Act's infringement on public employees' rights to participate actively in partisan politics.[42]

Letter Carriers and its disquisition on the evils of political patronage cast a shadow over the patronage systems still in place in state and local governments. The Court took the next step in *Elrod v Burns*, overturning the dismissal of several Cook County sheriff's employees 'solely because of their partisan political affiliation or nonaffiliation'.[43] The decision was straightforward as a matter of First Amendment doctrine: 'The right to associate with the political party of one's choice is an integral part of this basic constitutional freedom'.[44] But the Court also reprised the political process arguments that had won the day in *Letter Carriers*: political patronage impairs the 'free functioning of the electoral process', 'starve[s] political opposition by commanding partisan support', and 'tips the electoral process in favor of the incumbent party'.[45]

The defenders of patronage had their own political process argument: political patronage helped to support the vitality of political parties and thus of the democratic process. According to the *Elrod* petitioners, 'we have contrived no system for the

---

[38] *Civil Service Commission v National Association of Letter Carriers*, 413 US 548 (1973).
[39] Ibid 566.   [40] Ibid 565.   [41] Ibid.
[42] The Hatch Act was significantly narrowed in 2012, largely freeing employees to engage in off-duty partisan politicking that bore no imprint of official power or authority. 5 USC ss 1501–8, ss 7321–6 (2012).
[43] *Elrod v Burns*, 427 US 347, 349 (1976).   [44] Ibid 357.   [45] Ibid 356.

support of party that does not place considerable reliance on patronage. The party organization makes a democratic government work and charges a price for its services'.[46] The Court demurred, for while patronage supplied a dubious economic motivation for partisan involvement of a kind, it also impeded individuals' more genuine support for political parties without jobs to distribute.[47]

Letter Carriers and *Elrod* together put a strong stamp of judicial approval on a particular conception of the proper relationship between public employment and partisan politics: non-partisan merit-based selection for public employees, but for a handful of politically-accountable policy-making officials. Good-government reformers had made headway over the last century in promoting the civil service system over the political spoils system. There is much to be said for that system, including the incidental protection of freedom of expression off the job that follows from requiring a job-related basis for discipline and discharge. Now the First Amendment was squarely on the side of the reformers, and in the hands of judges who were notably distant from, if not disdainful of, the grubby world of partisan politics. The subsequent collapse of the major political parties as grassroots organizations and orchestrators of electoral politics might suggest that there was something in the petitioners' warning after all.[48] Still, it is hard to see how the practice of assigning rank-and-file jobs based on party membership and participation could survive once the First Amendment had entered the scene.

Although both *Letter Carriers* and *Elrod* reviewed broad policies affecting public employee speech rights, it was only later in *NTEU* that the Court explicitly addressed the distinction between individual disciplinary actions based on speech and 'a sweeping statutory impediment to speech'. Recall that *NTEU* struck down a statute banning federal employees' acceptance of outside compensation, or honoraria, for nearly all speeches and writings, including those with no 'connection with the employee's official duties'.[49] On the one hand, the Court observed, legislative, and especially congressional, policy judgments were generally entitled to greater deference than 'an individual executive's disciplinary action'.[50] On the other hand, 'the widespread impact' of the statutory ban, along with its tendency to 'chill[] potential speech before it happens' cut in favour of closer scrutiny.[51] The Court held that the *Pickering* balancing test still applied to the ban, but that 'the Government's burden is greater ... than with respect to an isolated disciplinary action'. Specifically:

> The Government must show that the interests of both potential audiences and a vast group of present and future employees in a broad range of present and future expression are outweighed by that expression's 'necessary impact on the actual operation' of the Government.[52]

The government failed to meet that burden with regard to the honoraria ban.

---

[46] Ibid 368.   [47] Ibid 369–71.
[48] Samuel Issacharoff, 'Outsourcing Politics: The Hostile Takeover of Our Hollowed Out Political Parties' (2017) 54 *Hous L Rev* 845.
[49] *NTEU* (n 30) 457.   [50] Ibid 468.   [51] Ibid.   [52] Ibid.

NTEU suggested a possible template—a more speech-protective version of *Pickering*—for First Amendment review of broad policies regulating public employees' speech, or at least their off-duty speech unrelated to the employment. The *NTEU* version of *Pickering* still recognized that the government's 'interests as an employer in regulating the speech of its employees' differed from its interests as sovereign in 'regulat[ing] the speech of the citizenry in general'. But the difference appears to be narrower, and the protection of speech greater, when the government is exercising regulatory authority across broad swaths of its workforce than when it is making individual personnel decisions based on speech with some bearing on the job.

22.2.3 Janus *and the Double-Edged First Amendment*

The latest First Amendment challenge to systemic policies governing public employees was *Janus v AFSCME*, which overturned a long line of cases on the constitutionality of compulsory union fees in the public sector. *Janus* requires a brief detour into the field of labour law.

Under US collective bargaining statutes, public and private, a union chosen by a majority of employees in a bargaining unit is the 'exclusive' representative of all employees, and is duty-bound to fairly represent all of them, whether union members or not. Inherent in such systems is a serious free rider problem: if employees get the benefit of union representation without paying for it through union dues, then union members must pay higher dues to subsidize the representation of non-members, which might lead some members to quit and become free riders. Accordingly, unions have long bargained for 'union security' provisions to compel all employees to pay dues or fees to the union as a condition of employment. To unions' opponents, requiring individuals to pay money to an organization they oppose is a form of compelled speech; and when the state is doing the compelling, it violates the First Amendment. That claim has fuelled a tireless and well-funded battle against union security provisions on multiple fronts, political and judicial, since the New Deal.[53]

Over forty years ago in *Abood v Detroit Board of Education*,[54] the Supreme Court established a compromise on the constitutionality of compulsory union fees in the public sector: individuals could not be compelled to support the political and ideological activities of unions, but they could be compelled to bear their fair share of the costs of negotiating and administering the collective agreement through a reduced 'agency fee'. Although the latter 'has an impact upon [objectors'] First Amendment interests',[55] the impact was modest:

> A public employee who believes that a union representing him is urging a course that is unwise as a matter of public policy is not barred from expressing his view-

---

[53] See Sophia Z Lee, *The Workplace Constitution from the New Deal to the New Right* (CUP 2014) 5–6.
[54] *Abood v Detroit Board of Education*, 431 US 209 (1977).   [55] Ibid 222.

point. Besides voting in accordance with his convictions, every public employee is largely free to express his views, in public or private, orally or in writing.[56]

That modest burden was outweighed by the government's interest in maintaining a system of exclusive representation—versus 'the confusion and conflict that could arise if rival...unions, holding quite different views [about terms and conditions of employment] each sought to obtain the employer's agreement'[57]—and the obvious risk of free riding in that system. The *Abood* compromise was repeatedly reaffirmed in succeeding decades.

Janus reversed *Abood*. For the *Janus* majority, the exaction of agency fees was no minor imposition on free speech; it was akin to 'compelling individuals to mouth support for views they find objectionable'.[58] From that tendentious premise, it followed that agency fees must be subjected to 'exacting scrutiny'.[59] And while the majority grudgingly accepted the government's interest in a system of exclusive representation, it denied that agency fees were necessary to support that system. The free rider problem attending exclusive union representation was no more serious, opined the majority, than that facing any other 'private groups [that] speak out with the objective of obtaining government action that will have the effect of benefiting non-members',[60] and could not justify the burden on objectors' free speech rights.

Janus is willfully obtuse about the distinctive free rider problem facing unions under US labour laws.[61] Moreover, by forcing union members to subsidize the representation of anti-union (or merely opportunistic) free riders, *Janus* arguably creates a compelled speech problem much like the one it purports to solve.[62] But the linchpin of *Janus* is the disingenuous equation of the compelled payment of small sums of money with the compelled expression of views.[63] *Abood* and its precursors had opened that door by characterizing mandatory fees as a form of compelled speech; but that characterization was tempered by the recognition that the agency fee does nothing to impair the right of 'every public employee...to express his views, in public or private, orally or in writing', and to oppose positions taken by the union in politics or collective bargaining. *Abood*'s disapproval of compelled financial support for unions' ideological activities was one half of a compromise that sought to respect both the free speech interests of objectors and the practical imperatives of a system of exclusive representation. But the *Abood* compromise proved to be highly vulnerable to the uncompromising version of the First Amendment wielded by the *Janus* majority.

---

[56] Ibid 229.   [57] Ibid 224.   [58] *Janus v AFSCME, Council 31*, 138 S Ct 2448, 2463 (2018).
[59] Ibid 2477.   [60] Ibid 2466.
[61] See Ibid 2488–91 (Kagan, J, dissenting). The free rider problem reflects the two-sided (*Janus*-faced?) nature of unions, which has implications for a range of constitutional claims by and against unions. See Cynthia Estlund, 'Are Unions a Constitutional Anomaly?' (2015) 114 *Mich L Rev* 170.
[62] Catherine L Fisk and Margaux Poueymirou, '*Harris v Quinn* and the Contradictions of Compelled Speech' (2015) 48 *Loy LA L Rev* 439.
[63] See William Baude and Eugene Volokh, 'Compelled Subsidies and the First Amendment' (2018) 132 *Harv L Rev* 171. (forthcoming)

The main rationale of *Janus* is grounded not in the jurisprudence of public employee speech rights surveyed above, but in a libertarian strain of First Amendment law that is becoming a useful bludgeon against the regulatory state.[64] Justice Kagan in dissent called out the majority for 'weaponizing the First Amendment, in a way that unleashes judges... to intervene in economic and regulatory policy'.[65] The First Amendment is a protean weapon in that regard because much of the activity that modern states regulate—indeed, much regulation itself—can be portrayed as expressing something, verbally or otherwise. That includes the conduct of business or labour relations, the payment of health insurance premiums, and cake-baking.[66] Merely complying with duly-enacted laws that one opposes, or paying fees to a duly-elected union that one opposes as in *Janus*, may be seen as compelled speech triggering 'exacting' First Amendment scrutiny.

The body blow that *Janus* struck against public sector unions is of a piece with the larger campaign against the regulatory state, for *Janus* depicts public sector unions as leading culprits in the growth of government and state budgets.[67] More than was necessary to uphold the rights of objectors, the majority thus signalled its agreement with their opposition to public sector unions. Barely off-stage is public sector unions' role in the electoral arena. *Abood* long ago ended objectors' forced contribution to unions' partisan electoral activities. But at least for anti-union activists, it was a more-than-incidental benefit of *Janus* that unions would now be strapped for cash, and less able to participate in electoral politics. Unions will have to spend more of their members' dues representing a growing number of non-members, and perhaps redirecting some of the money those members would have chosen to spend on advancing their own shared political views through the union. That is another free speech problem that *Janus* creates.[68]

While the majority conspicuously ignored the jurisprudence of public employee free speech rights in its main argument, it managed to unsettle some of that jurisprudence in addressing what it called the 'alternative justifications' for *Abood*. *Abood*'s defenders had argued that the line it drew between unions' political activities and their collective bargaining activities was compatible with *Connick*'s line between speech on matters of public concern and speech on ordinary terms and conditions of employment. Just as actual speech on the latter was unprotected, they argued, 'compelled speech' on such matters in the form of the agency fee raised no First Amendment concerns. But even if collective-bargaining related speech was on matters of public concern, its compelled support, like its suppression, should be subject to *Pickering*-type balancing, in which the government's

---

[64] Robert Post and Amanda Shanor, 'Adam Smith's First Amendment' (2015) 128 *Harv L Rev F* 165; Amanda Shanor, 'The New *Lochner*' [2016] *Wis L Rev* 133.

[65] *Janus* (n 58) 2501 (Kagan J, dissenting).

[66] *Masterpiece Cakeshop Ltd v Colorado Civil Rights Commission*, 584 US ___, 138 S Ct 1719 (2018); *Burwell v Hobby Lobby Stores Inc*, 573 US ___, 134 S Ct 2751 (2014).

[67] *Janus* (n 58) 2474–5.

[68] See Catherine L Fisk and Erwin Chemerinsky, 'Political Speech and Association Rights after *Knox v. SEIU, Local 1000*' (2015) 98 *Cornell L Rev* 1023.

interest in defending exclusive representation from the threat of free riding should outweigh the limited burden of the agency fee on dissenters' free speech interests. The *Janus* majority rejected every part of that argument, and in the process reconfigured some of its doctrinal elements.

First, the majority cast doubt on whether *Pickering* was applicable at all to 'general rules that affect broad categories of employees', and denied its relevance to 'compel[led] speech or speech subsidies'.[69] The paradoxical upshot is that the outright suppression or punishment of public employees' speech on matters of public concern appears to trigger a lower level of scrutiny than does the exaction of a small fee for representational services that one opposes.

Second, in applying the law of public employee speech, *arguendo* as it were, the Court recast the *Connick* category of speech on matters of public concern: a single employee's demand for 'a 5% raise...would likely constitute a matter of only private concern...But a public-sector union's demand for a 5% raise for the many thousands of employees it represents would be another matter entirely', given its impact on the public fisc.[70] Of course, the first might lead to the second; that is how speech works. But the Court deemed it obvious that, '[w]hen a large number of employees speak through their union, the category of speech that is of public concern is greatly enlarged, and the category of speech that is of only private concern is substantially shrunk'.[71] That sounds right—and it even sounds like potential good news for employee speech rights.[72] *Janus*'s 'enlarged' view of public concern speech could work in favour of unions and their members in future cases—for example, in challenging restrictions on union organizing or bargaining rights. It might even unsettle the disfavoured constitutional treatment of labour picketing versus picketing on 'public issues'.[73] Then again, maybe not, for *Janus* suggests that actual state suppression of speech is not as bad as state-compelled financial support of speech—once the latter is equated to forcing employees to 'recite words with which they disagree'.[74] Chances are slim, at least while this majority holds sway, that either *Janus*'s higher level of scrutiny for broad policies affecting employee speech or its expansion of the category of speech on matters of public concern will end up protecting the actual speech of either individual employees or unions.[75]

The Court sought support from elsewhere in the public employee speech canon, albeit only in the course of refuting the *stare decisis* argument: '[b]y overruling *Abood*, we end the oddity of privileging compelled union support over compelled party support', struck down in *Elrod*.[76] The 'oddity' was not so odd, however, given some crucial

---

[69] *Janus* (n 58) 2472–3.   [70] Ibid 2473.   [71] Ibid.

[72] Estlund, 'Are Unions a Constitutional Anomaly?' (n 61) 186–9.

[73] James Gray Pope, 'Labor and the Constitution: from Abolition to Deindustrialization' (1987) 65 *Tex L Rev* 1071, 1114–5; Cynthia L Estlund, 'Speech on Matters of Public Concern: The Perils of an Emerging First Amendment Category' (1990) 59 *Geo Wash L Rev* 1, 15–16, n 85.

[74] *Janus* (n 58) 2473.

[75] As Justice Kagan said in dissent, 'I would wager a small fortune that the next time a general rule governing public employee speech comes before us, we will dust off *Pickering*': *Janus* (n 58) 2494 (Kagan J, dissenting).

[76] Ibid 2484.

differences between political patronage and the agency fee: First, patronage compelled actual party membership and active involvement in party activities; the agency fee compels neither union membership nor union activity. Second, political patronage required support of partisan political speech; agency fees require support of only unions' representational functions. Third, the union speech supported by agency fees yields tangible economic gains to employees that nearly always exceed the burden of the agency fee by a large margin; there was no parallel in the patronage context. Fourth, political patronage strongly discouraged individuals from joining or supporting competing organizations or causes; the agency fee does nothing of the sort.

In one sense, however, the analogy to *Elrod* holds: like *Elrod*, though for far flimsier reasons, *Janus* rejects a considered state policy judgment about the appropriate relationship between the government and its employees. Agency fees are one component of the policy of allowing public employees, by majority rule, to choose collective representation and bargaining on behalf of shared goals. In undercutting both the state policy and the collective choice of employees, *Janus* is doubly anti-democratic. To be sure, democratic self-governance is often in tension with individual liberty, and that makes the First Amendment a potential double-edged sword for public employees. *Janus* sharpened the edge that cuts against those who seek to amplify their collective voice in both the workplace and the political process through democratic institutions. Although *Janus*'s blow against public sector unionism is less dispositive than *Elrod*'s rejection of political patronage, it may lead to much the same end as individuals take up the invitation to exit from collective institutions that they no longer have to pay for.

22.3 Non-Constitutional Speech Rights in the Private Sector Workplace

For public employees, the First Amendment has become a weapon—double-edged and of fluctuating efficacy—against state policies, managerial judgments, and collective decisions that impinge on individual freedom of expression. Free speech claims in private employment have followed a very different course, for the state action barrier continues to block constitutional claims against private sector employers. Indeed, in the hands of the *Lochner* Court, the Constitution forbade the legislature from protecting employee speech and associations—specifically, union activity and membership—against employer reprisals: Any legislative restriction on employers' freedom to fire employees was fatally at odds with the constitutional 'liberty of contract'.[77] But once the *Lochner* era gave way to the New Deal, law-makers began to carve out exceptions to employment-at-will and to restrain employer power over employee speech.

---

[77] *Adair v United States*, 208 US 161, 174 (1908).

First and still foremost, the National Labor Relations Act (NLRA) of 1935 prohibits employers from interfering with employees' union activity and 'other concerted activity for... mutual aid or protection'.[78] Even with no union in sight, employers are generally barred from punishing employees for joining together to protest poor working conditions or unfair employer actions (even if they protest by walking off the job),[79] or for discussing their salaries with each other,[80] or for publicly airing shared work-related complaints.[81] Employees have the right to communicate with their co-workers about such matters at the workplace during non-work time as well as off-duty and on social media.[82]

The NLRA creates a rudimentary analogue to the First Amendment for the private sector workplace, complete with its own 'public forum' doctrine.[83] But its protections are in some ways the reverse of the actual First Amendment in public sector employment. The NLRA protects speech about working conditions, but *not* speech on matters of public concern unrelated to the interests of employees as such. That is not because the values underlying the NLRA are at odds with the First Amendment values of freedom, democracy, and active citizenship; it is because the NLRA sought to pursue those values within the polity of the workplace. It aimed to empower workers vis-à-vis employer sovereignty, to render them citizens versus mere subjects of the workplace, and to bring a measure of democracy to the private sector workplace.

The NLRA protected employees' freedom of speech and association both for its intrinsic value and for its role in promoting 'industrial democracy' in the form of union representation and collective bargaining. In that respect federal labour law mirrored central goals of the First Amendment within the larger polity. Indeed, the First Amendment might have been put to the service of those goals of workplace democracy within the public sector workplace. But as we have seen, the doctrine has gone in quite the opposite direction: *Connick* denied First Amendment protection in the public sector for speech on shared workplace concerns that would have been protected by the NLRA in the private sector. And then *Janus* turned the First Amendment into a cudgel against the collective bargaining systems, modelled on the NLRA, by which legislatures have sought to enhance public employees' voice at work. Anti-union advocates are surely plotting to extend *Janus* into the private sector, though that effort faces a formidable state action hurdle.[84]

---

[78] 29 USC s 157 (2012).
[79] *National Labor Relations Board v Washington Aluminum Co*, 370 US 9 (1962).
[80] *Quicken Loans Inc v National Labor Relations Board*, 830 F 3d 542 (DC Cir 2016); *Banner Health System v National Labor Relations Board*, 851 F 3d 35 (DC Cir 2017).
[81] *Triple Play Sports Bar*, 361 NLRB 308 (2014), affirmed in *Three D LLC v National Labor Relations Board*, 629 F Appx 33 (2d Cir 2015); *North West Rural Electric Co-op*, 366 NLRB 132 (2018).
[82] *Republic Aviation Corp v National Labor Relations Board*, 324 US 793 (1945); *Eastex Inc v National Labor Relations Board*, 437 US 556 (1978).
[83] Cynthia Estlund, *Regoverning the Workplace: From Self-Regulation to Co-Regulation* (Yale UP 2010) 27–9.
[84] See *Janus* (n 58) 2479, n 24.

The NLRA protects a wide swathe of private sector employee speech in and about the private sector workplace.[85] But it fails to protect much valuable speech, including speech on matters of public concern other than workplace issues and purely individual speech that has no element of 'concerted activity'. Some of that speech finds refuge under a motley patchwork of federal, state, and local statutes and state common law doctrines that is impossible to summarize and synthesize here. But it is worth noting one important strain of that law, which protects 'whistle-blowers'—employees who disclose harmful or illegal activity within the organization to the public, the government, or sometimes higher-ups in the organization.[86] Crucially, whistle-blower laws are widespread in the public sector, where they supplement the First Amendment, and fill some of its gaps. But in the private sector, there is no constitutional protection to supplement; whistle-blower protections are islands of protection in a sea of employer discretion.

In some ways, whistle-blower protections track the First Amendment as it operates in public sector employment; but the divergences are revealing. For example, most whistle-blower laws protect employees only when they report or complain of statutory violations.[87] In some ways that is narrower than *Connick*'s category of speech on matters of public concern. But in other ways it is broader, for many laws regulate terms and conditions of employment, and prohibit employer retaliation against employees who report or complain about violations. For another example, some early common law decisions denied protection to those who reported wrong-doing internally as part of their job.[88] Increasingly, however, such reporting is within the zone of protected activity, contra *Garcetti*.[89]

Obviously, there is nothing shady or surprising in the fact that statutory and common law doctrines protect some speech that the Constitution does not. While *Connick* and *Garcetti* deny First Amendment protection to some public employee speech, they do not preclude legislatures or state courts from protecting that speech (as some public sector labour laws and whistle-blower laws do). And while the state action doctrine blocks constitutional claims against employer censorship and punishment of speech in the private sector, it poses no hurdle to legislation or common law doctrine that protects that speech. Still, it is noteworthy that legislatures and common law courts have often discerned significant value in employee speech that the Supreme Court has excluded from First Amendment protection even in the public sector.

What this very short and partial survey of private sector speech protections has left out thus far are the spaces in between those protections—spaces that, under the

---

[85] At least as a formal matter. The NLRA's protections are backed by limited administrative remedies that fail to deter or wholly remedy employer violations.

[86] For an overview of the statutory provisions protecting employee complaints or whistle-blowing against reprisals, see Richard Moberly, 'The Supreme Court's Antiretaliation Principle' (2010) 61 *Case W Res L Rev* 375.

[87] Richard Moberly, 'Protecting Whistleblowers by Contract' (2008) 79 *U Colo L Rev* 975, 983–7.

[88] Orly Lobel, 'Citizenship, Organizational Citizenship, and the Laws of Overlapping Obligations' (2009) 97 *Cal L Rev* 433, 444–55.

[89] Richard Moberly, 'Sarbanes-Oxley's Whistleblower Provisions: Ten Years Later' (2012) 64 *SC L Rev* 1, 18.

background rule of employment-at-will, are subject to plenary managerial power. Even relative to the limited First Amendment protection of public employee speech, the non-constitutional protection of employee speech in the private sector is spotty and sparse.[90] Private sector employees are largely unprotected in their 'water-cooler speech' (except for that which is covered by the NLRA), in their off-duty political associations and expression, and in their refusal to support the employer's political agenda.[91] If there is any such thing as an exception that proves the rule, it might be the Third Circuit's singular decision in *Novosel v Nationwide Insurance Co*.[92] *Novosel* held that an employee who was fired for refusing to support his employer's lobbying position had stated a claim in tort for wrongful discharge in violation of public policy—that is, the public policy embodied in the First Amendment. The case is widely admired by employment law scholars, but widely criticized or ignored in the courts.[93]

In the few remaining outposts of job security in the private sector, mostly in the small and shrinking domain of union representation, the employer's burden of justifying discharge and serious discipline provides indirect protection of speech.[94] Such 'just-cause' protections are pervasive elsewhere in the developed world.[95] But in the at-will world in which most US employees work, that indirect protection of speech is lacking, too. What is left is employees' right of exit, and whatever reputational pressures might face an employer that sought too openly to dictate or suppress employees' off-duty, non-work related speech. That is not nothing, but it is nothing like what public employees, and most employees in the rest of the developed world, enjoy by way of freedom from employer censorship and repression of speech.

22.4 CONCLUSION

Woven through US history is an abiding attachment to the liberal idea that the freedom to choose whether to enter or exit an employment relationship was all the freedom employees needed vis-à-vis their employer. Over the last century, US courts and legislatures have carved employee rights, including free speech rights, out of the broad power

---

[90] Anderson (n 2) 39–41. Anderson echoes (and will hopefully amplify) decades of criticism of employment at will in the legal literature. See Cynthia Estlund, 'Book Review: Rethinking Autocracy at Work' (2018) 131 *Harv L Rev* 795, 802–6.

[91] Hence the upsurge in employer recruitment of employees to support their political agenda. See Alexander Hertel-Fernandez, *Politics at Work: How Companies Turn Their Workers into Lobbyists* (OUP 2018).

[92] *Novosel v Nationwide Insurance Co*, 721 F2d 894 (3d Cir 1983).

[93] Matthew T Bodie, 'The Best Way Out Is Always Through: Changing the Employment At-Will Default Rule to Protect Personal Autonomy' (2017) 217 *U Ill L Rev* 223, 250–2.

[94] Cynthia L Estlund, 'Wrongful Discharge Protections in an At-Will World' (1996) 74 *Tex L Rev* 1655, 1684–5.

[95] 'Detailed Description of Employment Protection Legislation, 2012–2013, OECD Countries' (OECD, 2013) <https://www.oecd.org/els/emp/All.pdf> accessed 26 August 2018.

that employers otherwise wield under their side of employment-at-will, that is, their power over continued employment. Even today, employment-at-will is the norm, and employee rights and freedoms—beyond the right to refuse or quit employment—are exceptional. There are by now quite a lot of exceptions, and together they carry the whiff of a competing idea—one that resonates with neo-republican thought—that a free society should protect employees from employer domination beyond ensuring their freedom to exit the employment relationship.[96] That includes a measure of protection for employees' freedom of expression.

But how much and what kind of protection? Specifically, how much and what kind of freedom of expression is compatible with the control that employers need (or demand) over those they hire to do a job? The Supreme Court set out to answer a version of that question for government employers and employees under the First Amendment. The resulting body of law might have offered a model for how legislatures and common law courts should balance free speech rights and employer needs in the private sector as well. But it has not turned out that way. As a descriptive matter, a comparison between the two bodies of law reveals as many paradoxes as parallels. The main currents of the law of private employee speech rights, far from tracking the Court's First Amendment doctrines in the public sector, protect both more and less speech, and very different kinds of speech, than the latter. As a normative matter, neither body of law responds adequately to the problem that employer domination poses for employees' freedom of expression in a democratic and capitalist society.

In the public sector, the doctrine's categorical exclusions from the First Amendment leave employees vulnerable to unjustified employer domination, and leave a great deal of valuable speech unprotected. But a combination of statutory speech protections and civil service protections have done much to supplement those constitutional protections. In the private sector, employees are relegated to an incoherent collection of statutory and common law protections that leave too much room for employers to leverage their economic power into power over employees' speech and associations. Perhaps employers have been too successful in persuading law-makers and judges of the necessity of managerial discretion and the adequacy of exit in curbing abuse. One way or another, the beguiling promise of consent through contract continues to exercise a strong gravitational pull on the law of employee speech rights.

---

[96] Others in the neo-republican camp would argue that genuine freedom to exit is the best protection against domination: Robert S Taylor, *Exit Left: Markets and Mobility in Republican Thought* (OUP 2017). Still others would argue that an intolerable level of employer domination is inherent in capitalism, in which a relative few own and control the means of production from which others derive their livelihood: Alex Gourevitch, 'Labor Republicanism and the Transformation of Work' (2013) 41 *Pol Theo* 591.

CHAPTER 23

MUSIC AND ART

MARK TUSHNET

23.1 INTRODUCTION

POLITICAL theorist Alexander Meiklejohn argued for a theory of free expression defined with reference to democratic self-governance. In his initial presentation Meiklejohn appeared to limit the theory's coverage to 'governance-relevant' speech—roughly, speech dealing with politics and public affairs.[1] Responding to criticism that such a limitation was 'shocking' in part because it excluded 'scholarship…art and literature',[2] Meiklejohn modified his account to include within the theory's coverage 'forms of thought and expression within the range of human communication from which the voter derives the…knowledge, intelligence…and sensitivity to human values'. 'Literature and the arts' were now explicitly within his theory's coverage.[3] Critics such as Robert Bork then observed that many activities other than 'thought and expression' contributed to the development of the governance-relevant capacities that, according to the revised accounted, explained the theory's coverage.[4]

Meiklejohn's difficulties exemplify a more general problem within the theory of free expression. One either develops accounts of that theory's foundations which exclude arts and music from its coverage, or one develops accounts which, though including those topics, would extend coverage to a far wider range of human activities. And yet most theorists of free expression agree with Zachariah Chafee that excluding arts and music from a theory of free expression is 'shocking' or at least highly questionable.[5] How then can we incorporate music and art within the coverage of freedom of expression? Because theorists almost universally agree that music and art are covered by the theory

---

[1] Alexander Meiklejohn, *Free Speech and Its Relation to Self-Government* (Harper Brothers 1948).
[2] Zechariah Chafee Jr, 'Book Review' (1949) 62 *Harv L Rev* 891, 900.
[3] Alexander Meiklejohn, 'The First Amendment Is an Absolute' [1961] *Sup Ct Rev* 245.
[4] Robert H Bork, 'Neutral Principles and Some First Amendment Problems' (1971) 47 *Ind LJ* 1.
[5] Bork is an exception.

of free expression, rather little analytic work has been done to provide what nearly all agree is the obvious answer.[6]

Further, determining whether music and art are covered by a theory of free expression has little practical relevance. Democratic governments rarely attempt to coercively regulate art and music. Typically such attempts are readily handled in one of two ways. We can deploy doctrines aimed at specific problems of regulation of expression whose extension to music and art does not threaten a similar extension to wider swathes of human activity. Or doctrines of minimal rationality that can apply to regulation of human activity generally can be invoked; those doctrines rarely prohibit regulation but might be useful for the rare efforts to regulate music and art. Still, the effort to account for music and art within a theory of free expression may illuminate something about the structure of such theories more generally.

A more practical concern arises in connection with the possible limits free expression places on government subsidies. Many governments subsidize music and art, encouraged as we will see by constitutional mandates, but they also do so selectively, supporting some activities and not others. Bringing music and art within a theory of free expression—and thereby imposing some distinctive free expression limits on government action—may have some practical pay-off.

23.2 Defining the Scope of the Issue

An account of freedom of *speech* can deal with many aspects of music and art. Obviously such an account would cover regulations aimed at the lyrics of a musical composition. That remains true even if, as many musicians would contend, the music enhances the meaning and impact of the lyrics. Such enhancement is indistinguishable from the boost spoken words get from a speaker's eloquence or from the especially powerful rhetorical form in which an argument is put. Perhaps accounts of freedom of speech should or do take eloquence into account. For example, US Supreme Court Justice Oliver Wendell Holmes, Jr voted to grant free expression protection to pamphlets flung from the top of an apartment building by a defendant he called 'puny anonymities', while upholding the conviction of Eugene V Debs, a major leader of the Socialist Party and a powerful speaker; the power of rhetoric might have played some role in his decisions. Whatever role eloquence and rhetoric play in an account of free speech, the same role can be played by similar enhancements from music.

A similar approach can be taken to regulation of some forms of representational art and even music. Sometimes pictorial or even musical representations stand in for verbal arguments. In the United States, political cartoons use donkeys and elephants as symbolic stand-ins for the Democratic and Republican parties. During World War II, the

---

[6] For an overview, see Mark V Tushnet, Alan Chen, and Joseph Blocher, *Free Speech Beyond Words: The Surprising Reach of the First Amendment* (NYU Press 2017).

first four notes of Beethoven's Fifth Symphony were used to signal 'Victory' because they could readily be heard as the components of the letter 'V' in Morse code. Marianne's cap became a symbol of democracy. Examples could be multiplied.

One can imagine situations in which governments might seek to regulate or suppress these nonverbal symbols. Yet, ordinary free speech analysis has the resources with which to deal with such attempts. When a person uses a nonverbal symbol with the intent that it communicate a message which could be translated into words—as the notes can be translated into 'V for Victory'—and when a significant portion of the audience for the symbol understands what the symbol is intended to communicate (when there is 'uptake'), then the law should treat the regulation of the symbol as a regulation of the intended-and-received message.

Contrast the foregoing analysis of lyrics with a different argument, that the rhythmic qualities of hip-hop music, independent of the accompanying words, reduce listeners' inhibitions on violence. Here any regulation would be aimed at the music itself, nonverbal material not reasonably described as speech. When they have not taken on symbolic meaning, musical notes alone are part of the domain of interest here.

So is non-representational art and much representational art, with a similar qualification. Art critics can write about what a representation 'means', and even what a piece of non-representational art means. If one account of a particular work's meaning comes to be widely shared, perhaps it will become a symbol. Otherwise, accounts of freedom of speech cannot be applied directly to non-representational art, much representational art, and music understood as 'notes', tonal qualities, and the like. As a shorthand, this chapter will refer to the domain of interest simply as 'music and art', omitting the qualifications.

As already noted, democratic governments rarely attempt to regulate music and art as such. Non-democratic ones have done so, with the National Socialist regime's campaign against degenerate art and the Stalinist promotion of socialist realism and disparagement of modern non-representational art as the classic examples. The better analysis of regulations of music and art by non-democratic regimes focuses on the undemocratic features of the regime that generate the regulations, not on the regulations themselves.

Still, one can devise not unreasonable hypothetical cases, often bearing some similarity to real ones, in which democratic governments would attempt to regulate non-representational art. Consider the case of a building owner who chooses to place a large piece of abstract sculpture at the building's entrance—on its own property but readily visible to the passing public. The city government might seek to force the sculpture's removal on the ground that it was so ugly—or so attractive—that it distracted drivers and caused collisions, or on the ground that the public congregated to view the sculpture and thereby disrupted the pedestrian flow nearby.

If music and art are not covered by a constitutional principle of free speech, the analysis is straightforward. The only question is whether the regulation serves a permissible government goal. The term 'serve' is used to capture the idea that the regulation advances the goal to some degree—the formulation used in legal systems where proportionality doctrine prevails—or that it is a minimally rational means of advancing the goal, in the terms used in US law. If music and art are covered by some constitutional principle akin to freedom of speech, though, government regulation would be permissible only if it satisfied some more stringent requirement. As suggested below, music and art might fall into an intermediate category, with their regulation requiring more than merely rational justification but less than a compelling one.

One might think that we could assimilate music and art to speech by encompassing them within a larger category of expression. Some difficulties with doing so should be noted. As the next section shows, constitutional texts vary in the verbal formulation of the constitutional provision. Some do use the word 'expression', but others use only 'speech', and sometimes do so in an overall constitutional context that strongly indicates that 'speech' is different from 'expression' or similar terms.

In addition, many forms of human activity can readily be characterized as expression, particularly if one treats the recognition or promotion of human autonomy as a value underlying constitutional protection for speech as a form of expression. Running a small business may be the way a person expresses herself, for example. We might think, though, that regulations of small businesses should not trigger the requirement that a somewhat stringent standard of review be satisfied. The solution to this difficulty, if there is one, lies in coming up with an account of why music and art are particularly 'speech-like' in ways that other forms of expression are not.

With the domain of interest now defined, we can examine how constitutional texts deal with speech, music, and art.

23.3 CONSTITUTIONAL TEXTS

Constitutional provisions dealing with speech, expression, music, and the arts fall into several groups.[7] Differences in constitutional language *support* but do not *require* that the constitutional tests for determining whether a regulation violates the protected activity differ as between speech on the one hand and music and art on the other.

First, some constitutions refer to speech only, leaving the coverage of music and art to interpretation. The classic example is the early US First Amendment ('Congress shall make no law... abridging the freedom of speech').

Second, some constitutions protect speech and then use terms encompassing (or potentially encompassing) music and the arts in another provision. Article 5 of the German Basic Law is an example. Its first clause provides, 'Every person shall have the right freely to express and disseminate his opinions in speech, writing, and pictures'. Then comes the second clause: 'Art and scholarship, research, and teaching shall be free'. Kenya's constitution guarantees 'the right to freedom of expression', which is then

---

[7] The discussion here is based upon a selective survey of constitutional provisions.

specified to include, separately, 'freedom to seek, receive or impart information or ideas' and 'freedom of artistic creativity'.[8]

That music and art are separately specified opens up the possibility that the legal tests for determining when a regulation violates freedom of speech differ from those for determining when a regulation violates the protected freedom with respect to music and art.[9] A similar possibility arises from the possibility that freedom with respect to music and art might be protected by a constitutional provision not referring to them at all. Here the most notable example is the German Basic Law's protection for the 'free development of personality'. No interpretive contortions are needed to establish that musical and artistic expression is within the scope of the free development of personality. And yet, it seems obvious that—precisely because of the broad scope of the personality-development principle—the constitutional test for determining when that right has been violated must be more generous towards regulation than the test for determining when a right of free speech has been violated.

The first clause in the German Basic Law protecting 'the right freely to express opinions in speech...and pictures' exemplifies a third set of constitutional provisions. These provisions protect 'expression', which can be broader than 'speech', but protect it only in connection with additional terms such as 'opinions' or 'ideas'.[10] The European Convention on Human Rights (ECHR), for example, provides that 'everyone has the right to freedom of expression', which 'shall include freedom to hold opinions and to receive and impart information and ideas'. Of course, the word 'include' might imply that 'opinions' and 'information' are illustrations of what is encompassed within 'expression'. Against that might be set the general interpretive principle *expressio unius est exclusio alteris*.

Other examples are France ('The free communication of ideas and opinions is one of the most precious rights of man. Any citizen may therefore speak, write and publish freely'), Canada ('freedom of thought, belief, opinion and expression'), Ireland ('The right of the citizens to express freely their convictions and opinions'), and Mexico ('Expression of ideas shall not be subject to judicial or administrative inquiry'). Variants refer to 'thoughts' rather than 'opinions' (Denmark, Guatemala, Honduras, Iceland). And, like the German provision, Portugal's refers explicitly to 'images': 'Everyone shall possess the right to freely express and publicise his thoughts in words, images or by any other means'.

Provisions that refer to 'ideas' and 'opinions' might not cover the domain of music and art considered in this chapter. As Section 23.2 argues, much music and art cannot

---

[8] The parallel provision in South Africa's Constitution similarly has four subclauses specifying what is included in 'the right to freedom of expression'.

[9] I use the term 'violation' here, because it seems straightforward to use the same test for determining 'infringement', no matter whether speech or music and art are at stake.

[10] A cautionary note about the use of translations as the basis for comparisons: doing so is necessary for the material to be accessible to a wide range of scholars, but translations might not capture connotations. In the present context, the words translated here as 'opinions' and 'ideas' might in their original languages have broader connotations than they do in English.

easily be described as conveying ideas, opinions, or information. Again, residual clauses such as personality-development might be invoked where constitutions refer to expression specified as including ideas and opinions.

A fourth group of constitutional provisions, in contrast, is comprehensive, either expressly or by plain implication covering music and art. In Brazil, 'expression of intellectual, artistic, scientific, and communication activity is free, independent of any censorship or license'.[11] Other examples are Armenia ('Everyone shall have the freedom of literary, fine arts, scientific, and technical creation') and Sweden ('freedom of expression: that is, the freedom to communicate information and express thoughts, opinions and sentiments, whether orally, pictorially, in writing, or in any other way').

Finally, and with different constitutional implications, there are provisions asserting government responsibility for supporting the arts. So, in Bulgaria, 'The State shall establish conditions conducive to the free development of science, education, and the arts', and in Bahrain, 'The State sponsors the sciences, humanities and the arts'. Notably, other provisions specifically referring to the arts sometimes also refer to the citizenry and thereby could support the idea that citizens have rights with respect to their own artistic activity. So, for example, in Slovenia, 'The freedom of scientific and artistic endeavour shall be guaranteed', and in Korea, 'All citizens shall enjoy freedom of learning and the arts'.

State support for the arts obviously can include subsidies. A mandate to support the arts is sometimes linked to a similar mandate with respect to national culture (Afghanistan: 'The state shall devise effective programs for fostering knowledge, culture, literature and the arts'; 'Indonesia: 'Every person shall have the right...to benefit from science and technology, arts and culture, for the purpose of improving the quality of his/her life and for the welfare of the human race'). These formulations suggest, though of course they do not require, that the mandate might not extend to works aimed at transforming the culture, or standing in opposition to it.

Further, some of these provisions read as if they are concerned at least in significant part with a government duty to ensure protection of artists' copyrights or moral rights. Examples are Montenegro ('The freedom to publish works of science and arts, scientific discoveries and technical inventions shall be guaranteed, and their authors shall be guaranteed the moral and property rights') and Nicaragua ('The State promotes and protects the free creation, research, and diffusion of the sciences, technology, the arts and letters, and guarantees and protects intellectual property').

This examination of constitutional texts dealing with speech, music, and art suggests a small but not unimportant conclusion: constitution-writers have devoted little attention to the special problems that music and art pose for a theory of free speech (and, perhaps a bit less so, for a theory of free expression). The reason may be one alluded to earlier: regulation of music and art independent of the occasions when they clearly communicate meaning is rare. Further, to the extent that the question comes to their attention, constitution-writers may assume, and perhaps not unreasonably, that the

---

[11] India's provision lies on the border between the 'limited expression' and comprehensive ones, protecting 'freedom of speech and expression'.

principles used to determine the law of free speech (or expression) could readily be adapted to deal with whatever problems might arise in connection with regulation of music and art.

23.4 Regulatory Principles for Music and Art

As already noted, there is near unanimity among scholars who have devoted attention to the question whether music and art, even within the narrowed domain identified in Section 23.2, deserves protection via constitutional provisions dealing with speech and expression. The reason is not that any specific account of constitutional protection for speech and expression—individual autonomy, self-governance, the discovery of truth, suspicion of government's ability to regulate within acceptable limits—fully justifies giving music and art constitutional protection. Rather, the reason is that music and art have characteristics that overlap with the characteristics of expression and speech that the standard accounts single out as the basis for constitutional protection. Those various overlaps give music and art a family resemblance to standard expression and speech, and it is the resemblance that explains the widespread agreement that music and art are constitutionally protected.

A preliminary note on doctrinal structure: in any liberal society, all government regulations, whether of speech, music, or anything else, must satisfy a requirement of minimal rationality—they must do something to advance a permissible government objective. The reason is that for liberals all restrictions on freedom must be justified.

Beyond minimal rationality, there are two categorical possibilities, which have their analogues in proportionality analysis. Some restrictions impair interests like those captured in constitutional provisions dealing with free development of personality. Such restrictions require moderate or strong justifications (under varying doctrinal formulations). Other restrictions impair interests typically described as fundamental, including the interests protected by freedom of expression. These restrictions require very strong or compelling justifications (again, under varying doctrinal formulations). In proportionality analysis, these distinctions can be described using Alexy's three tiers of analysis, though the edges of the categories are blurrier when one does such an analysis than when one uses the more categorical approach favoured by US law.

Foundational theories of free expression include those focusing on individual autonomy, the marketplace of ideas, democratic self-governance, and a historically grounded suspicion of the ability of governments to regulate only that expression that can permissibly be regulated according to other foundational theories. None of these are entirely suitable with respect to music and art.

With respect to autonomy-based theories, as C Edwin Baker wrote, 'all aesthetic experiences... can affect who a person is [and] how she sees the world'. Yet, he continued, this does not 'distinguish them from, say, hiking in a wilderness area [or] cooperation in a barn raising'.[12] This may be true even of expression outside the domains of music and art of interest here, but it seems clearly true with respect to those domains. The observation suggests that constitutional provisions dealing with free development of the personality provide a better foundation for protection of music and art.

Seanna Shiffrin offers an autonomy-based account that she argues appropriately limits it to freedom of expression:

> Communication of the contents of one's mind...uniquely furthers the interest in in being known by others. It thereby also makes possible complex forms of social life... [and] helps to develop some of the capacities prerequisite to moral agency because communication demands having a sense of what others are in a position to know and understand.[13]

Music and art, she continues, should be protected because 'they also represent the externalization of mental contents...that may not be accurately or well-captured through linguistic means'.[14]

Some of the work here is done by 'uniquely', and that characterization is perhaps questionable. A person's manner of 'being in the world', as it might be put, also furthers the interest in being known by others, for example. Consider here the choices people make about the clothing they wear, from choices about head coverings to choices about 'baggy pants'. Again, it might be better to lodge these interests' protection in rights other than free expression, the former in a right of free exercise of religion, the latter in a right to free development of personality.

Further, it may be inapt even to describe music and art (again, in the domain of interest) with reference to 'linguistic means'. Some abstract sculptures may be best described as nothing more than efforts to explore the relation between material and the space that surrounds it. The 'mental content' is perhaps the effort itself, but then it seems a bit off to describe the art work as an externalization of that content. It is almost certainly inaccurate to describe the work as a unique externalization of that effort, and that is probably what matters were the work to be subject to regulation: the government might reasonably ask, 'why explore the relation between material and space in *that* way rather than in some other way about which we would have no concern?' Again, consider the distractingly ugly sculpture.

With respect to the marketplace-of-ideas account, we have already seen how difficult it is to characterize music and art as vehicles for ideas, much less competing ideas whose truth can be tested in the marketplace. Indeed, one might take the history of music and art to show that markets produce a succession of dominant forms, with none having any

---

[12] C Edwin Baker, 'Autonomy and Free Speech' (2011) 27 *Const Comment* 251, 271–2.
[13] Seanna Valentine Shiffrin, 'A Thinker-Based Approach to Freedom of Speech' (2011) 27 *Const Comment* 283, 291–2.
[14] Ibid 295. It might be more precise to say that music and art externalize mental contents no less accurately than words do.

plausible claim to 'truth': baroque art, romanticism, expressionism, neo-expressionism, and so on through an indefinite list of artistic styles.

As noted in Section 23.1, Meiklejohn attempted to connect music and art to democratic self-governance, an attempt now largely viewed as strained. Perhaps better, the links he drew connect nearly every human activity to democratic self-governance and so are unsuitable for an account for something distinctive about music and art as forms of expression.

Robert Post has offered a variant of Meiklejohn's account, one located more in political sociology than in political theory.[15] On Post's account, freedom of expression covers activities that are widely understood to contribute to public discourse. Here, it is the belief or understanding rather than the reality that matters. For Post, the very fact that there is nearly unanimous agreement that music and art are covered by free expression in itself establishes that they are so covered. And, conversely, the very fact that some activities that political theorists might say are rationally indistinguishable from music and art with respect to public discourse are nearly universally agreed not to be covered establishes that they are not.

Post's description of social understandings seems accurate enough. One might wonder, though, whether those understandings exist precisely because they have not come under pressure. That is, people agree that music and art are covered because they have not seen attempts to regulate music and art which have some plausible justification—as they have seen such attempts with respect to hiking in a wilderness area, to use Baker's example. We have no way of knowing whether the facts about social understandings would be stable were people to confront regulations of music or art which they believed were (1) minimally rational (if the regulations are not minimally rational, one needs no special account of protection for music and art), (2) appropriate regulations with respect to free development of personality (surviving the degree of scrutiny applied to determine whether that right is violated), and (3) *not* justified when the tests applicable to verbal expressions and ideas are applied.

Suspicion-of-government accounts of free expression rely heavily on historical examples. The justifications governments have offered for regulation of expression are understood in retrospect to have been inadequate, despite what contemporaries thought. That leads to suspicion of the justifications offered today for regulations of expression.

Here the historical evidence points in diametrically opposite directions. Supporting the view that music and art should receive special protection are the Soviet campaign for socialist realism in art and the Nazi attack on degenerate art. Yet, as noted earlier, those examples may be inapt when we try to understand the scope of free expression in reasonably well-functioning though imperfect democratic societies. Supporting the view that music and art should receive no special protection is the fact that governments have rarely attempted to regulate them. We have no basis in experience to be suspicious of justifications offered today for whatever regulation the government offers.

---

[15] Robert Post, 'Participatory Democracy as a Theory of Free Speech' (2011) 97 *Va L Rev* 477.

Though none of the foundational accounts of free expression is fully satisfactory—either for free expression generally, or for music and art specifically—pieces of most do contribute to an account of free expression that would cover music and art. The autonomous artist celebrated by the romantic tradition has affinities to the autonomous author writing in the garret. Meiklejohn correctly saw that producing and appreciating music and art contributed something to people's civic capacities. Rather than an overlapping consensus in which each account converges to support inclusion of music and art within an account of free expression, two alternative images seem better: a jigsaw puzzle assembled out of parts of each foundational account, or a family resemblance between features on each account and music and art.

There is one final point. Legal rules are always imperfect reflections of their underlying justifications. Sometimes they encompass matters as to which the rules' rationales are inapplicable. The reason lies in the limitations of language coupled with difficulties of implementation by real-world institutions such as courts. The inclusion of music and art within the coverage of free expression may be an example. Language might in principle be available to deal with the exclusion of those topics; indeed, the burden of Section 23.2 of this chapter is to lay out—in words—the domain of interest. Yet, embodying that understanding in a judicially articulated rule which legislatures and executives can administer might be difficult. Further, the effort might not be worth it given both the possibility of difficulties at the domain's margin (an innovative cartoon not using established symbols to make an obviously political point, for example) and the infrequency of troublesome attempts to regulate material within the domain.

23.5 Government Subsidies for Music and Art

Government subsidies for music and art are sometimes controversial. Most controversies arise because of direct or indirect concern about viewpoint. Several US senators objected (after the fact) to a grant from the government's agency for supporting the arts to Andres Serrano, who used the grant to produce 'Piss Christ', a photograph of a small crucifix submerged in a tank of Serrano's urine. The objection was that the artwork was offensive to Christians. In principle, this is no different from an objection to a public subsidy to a play such as Clifford Odets's 'Waiting for Lefty' on the ground that it expresses sympathy for socially disruptive labour strikes. Objections to public subsidies for music or art based upon the message the works are thought to convey do not implicate the distinctive domain of music and art within free expression theory. Whatever account we have of the permissible limits on denying public subsidies to written works applies in full force to denials of public subsidies to artworks based upon their messages. Had Serrano been denied a grant to create 'Piss Christ' or penalized in future competitions for grants, we would analyse it in exactly the same way we would analyse any denial based upon viewpoint of a subsidy to written or oral material.

A controversy contemporaneous to that over 'Piss Christ' presents a slight variant on the foregoing problem. Chris Ofili constructed an artwork, 'The Holy Virgin Mary', out of materials including elephant dung. When the work was displayed in a city-supported museum, New York's mayor objected, citing as offensive the juxtaposition of the Virgin Mary and elephant dung—an objection based upon the work's viewpoint, asserted to be disparagement of the Virgin Mary. Ofili and his defenders responded that he had used the material as part of his general project as an artist of exploring the textural qualities of different materials. Here the artist's intention and the viewer's interpretation come apart: the intention is unrelated to viewpoint while the uptake is so related.[16] Had Ofili's work been taken down—had the subsidy been withdrawn—we would focus on the reasons for the withdrawal, that is, on the uptake rather than the intention. And, again, the analysis would reproduce whatever we would say about withdrawing a subsidy to a written work.

Selective subsidies to music and the arts do sometimes present questions different from the ones already described.[17] Consider a government programme implementing a constitutional commitment to foster culture. The government chooses to provide grants to artists working in the traditional arts but not those engaged in modern art, even modern art framed as adaptations of traditional arts to contemporary conditions. Or, it chooses to subsidize those who perform classical music but not jazz (or the reverse). Its reason might be that traditional arts and classical music are under greater pressure than modern art and jazz: modern art and jazz have their private patrons, whereas traditional art and classical music do not.

The distinctions the government draws are subject matter-based but not viewpoint-based. Intuition and widespread practice suggest rather strongly that selective subsidies aimed at offsetting failures in the private markets for supporting music and art should be permitted. One classical basis for concern about selective subsidies is that they might communicate government disparagement of the unsubsidized activities. But reacting to 'market failures' does not seem to convey that sort of disparagement.

The government's policy is certainly reasonable. Does the policy satisfy a more stringent standard—a requirement that the goal be important or compelling, for example? If it does not, the conclusion is that selective subsidies based upon subject matter are consistent with principles of free expression if there is a reasonable basis for distinguishing between the activities subsidized and those left to contend in the market on their own.

Should the analysis change if the government's reason for choosing to subsidize one rather than another form of art or music is openly normative? Suppose it views traditional arts and classical music as contributing more to human well-being and the like than modern art and jazz. Here the concern about disparagement might come into play.

---

[16] Serrano eventually offered a similar account of 'Piss Christ' as an exploration of colour and light.
[17] The questions raised in the text can arise in connection with subsidies to speech and written work as well.

Yet, consider a selective subsidy programme clearly implicating 'speech' in an uncontroversial sense: the government supports novelists but not poets, because in its view novels are a better form of expression than poetry. The programme disparages poetry (and poets!), but one is hard-pressed to work up outrage at the government's normative preference. The choice seems well within the range of ordinary policy choice we give governments.

The conclusion is that subject matter-based selective subsidies should be permitted if the government has a reasonable basis for the distinctions it draws. This is not to say, though, that the government's choices are unconstrained, but only that they are not constrained by principles of free expression. In a reasonably well-functioning democracy political considerations will place some limits on what the government in power can do. Selective subsidies that threaten to limit the distribution of too wide a range of views are likely to face opposition.

That opposition is likely to grow the more apparent it is that subsidizing some but not other subject matters is likely to have a disparate impact on the opposition. If it is widely known, for example, that musicians working in a particular genre tend to be politically liberal (or conservative), conservatives (or liberals) will oppose a system that subsidizes that genre but not others. Some selective subject-matter subsidies might have a modest disparate political impact, but it is not obvious that we could design a doctrine that targeted such subsidies, without making constitutionally problematic a large number of subsidies that ought to be accepted.

Music and art criticism of a particular sort does raise broad questions about selective subject-matter subsidies. The criticism is that certain genres have an inherent political valence: traditional music validating tradition over innovation, or jazz as validating innovation over tradition; romanticism in the arts validating individualism, or atonal music as validating disruption. Such criticism might be thought to throw into doubt the possibility of selective subject-matter subsidies, for the reasons that selective subsidies based on content are questionable: Government action through subsidies would tilt the 'discursive'—or in the present context the pre-discursive (see Section 23.4)—playing field in favour of the values implicit in the chosen genres.

We can be agnostic about the accuracy of this sort of criticism, thereby conceding the possibility that it (or some forms of it) are correct, without concluding that it has implications for constitutional doctrine. The reason is, roughly, institutional: We have little to no reason to believe that lawyers and judges will be at all facile in determining whether this sort of criticism is valid, or if so which of many variants is correct. As Justice Holmes put it in a related context, '[i]t would be a dangerous undertaking for persons trained only to the law to constitute themselves final judges of the worth of [expression]...outside of the narrowest and most obvious limits'.[18]

---

[18] *Bleistein v Donaldson Lithographing Co*, 188 US 239, 251 (1903). The case dealt with whether advertising could be an 'art' within the meaning of copyright law.

23.6 Conclusion

Constitution-writers and scholars of free expression agree that music and art are covered by principles of free expression. Exactly why they are is a bit unclear, but the unclarity has few practical implications. Examination of the coverage of music and art, though, may tell us something about free expression theory. It may show that that theory deals with subjects sharing a family resemblance rather than resting upon 'foundations'. If so, the examination has significant theoretical implications—and almost no practical ones.

CHAPTER 24

FREE SPEECH AND COMMERCIAL ADVERTISING

FREDERICK SCHAUER

24.1 INTRODUCTION AND A DEFINITIONAL PRELIMINARY

IN the contemporary world, a substantial percentage of the universe of public communication—public speech—consists of advertising. Speech offering to sell goods and services, typically with inducements to purchase, and often including the price and other conditions of the proposed sale, is a ubiquitous part of modern life. An important question in the theory and practice of freedom of speech is the extent to which, if at all, such communications should be protected against government regulation.

Given that the United States is something of a protective outlier on free speech questions generally, even when compared to other liberal industrialized democracies,[1] it is not surprising that free speech protection for commercial advertising is more robust in US law than it is anywhere else in the world. But the question has arisen in many other countries that profess to take the freedom of speech seriously, and thus this entry will deal with the question of free speech protection for commercial advertising of some sort and to some degree as a question with worldwide implications, and with both theoretical and doctrinal dimensions.

It is common in much of the relevant literature to refer to the topic under discussion as 'commercial speech', but that phrase is potentially misleading. A great deal of political communication, for example, is published by profit-seeking (even if not always

---

[1] See Frederick Schauer, 'The Exceptional First Amendment' in Michael Ignatieff (ed), *American Exceptionalism and Human Rights* (Princeton UP 2005) 29–56.

profit-making) newspapers, magazines, and other publications, but it is rarely suggested that the political commentary such publications offer is entitled to anything less than however much free speech and free press protection some jurisdiction offers to those who offer their political opinions orally or distribute those opinions in the form of free handbills. And so too with art and literature, which again is often produced and sold for monetary gain, but which is seldom for that reason thought less worthy of free speech solicitude. Similarly, to the extent that individuals possess a free speech right to speak out for or against those policies that would affect them, it seems odd to hold that such rights would not be possessed by for-profit business entities speaking out for or against the policies that would affect *them*.[2] Consequently, the focus of this entry will be, more narrowly, on commercial advertising, and to some extent those other forms of speech that, even though not advertising, are themselves integral parts of commercial transactions. These are the forms of speech, in the literal sense of 'speech' that are often thought to be deserving of less or no free speech protection, and it is this subset of the full universe of commercial speech that will be the focus here.[3]

24.2 THE US EXPERIENCE

In 1942, no country in the world believed that principles of freedom of speech, whether those principles be moral, political, legal, or constitutional, extended to unalloyed commercial advertising. And thus when FJ Chrestensen, an individual New York entrepreneur whose business consisted of offering tours of his World War I vintage submarine, claimed a First Amendment immunity from laws regulating hand-billing, his free speech argument was peremptorily dismissed by the Supreme Court. Although acknowledging that Chrestensen had a right to be where he was, and that he would have had as well a right to distribute political or protest matter at that location, the Court with little to no argument asserted that the First Amendment imposed 'no...restraint on government as respects purely commercial advertising'.[4]

Valentine v Chrestensen represented the state of US law until the 1970s, and free speech arguments against the regulation or prohibition of commercial advertising were routinely rebuffed. Things changed in the 1970s, however, first with a decision largely about abortion advertising that was unclear as to whether the basis of the decision was

---

[2] In the United States, see *First National Bank of Boston v Bellotti*, 435 US 765 (1978). In the context of contemporary US debates about expenditures in campaigns and elections, some commentators have defended the position that corporations, possibly excluding media corporations, have only derivative and thus weaker free speech rights. See Robert C Post, *Citizens Divided: Campaign Finance Reform and the Constitution* (Harvard UP 2014). For this author's response, see Frederick Schauer, 'Constitutions of Hope and Fear' (2014) 124 *Yale LJ* 528.

[3] On some of these definitional intricacies, see Steven H Shiffrin, 'The First Amendment and Economic Regulation: Away from a General Theory of the First Amendment' (1983) 78 *Nw U L Rev* 1212. And see also Paul Horwitz, *First Amendment Institutions* (Harvard UP 2013) 243–7.

[4] *Valentine v Chrestensen*, 316 US 52, 54 (1942).

the right to freedom of speech or, instead, the right to an abortion.[5] Shortly thereafter, however, the Supreme Court made it clear that commercial advertising itself—speech that did 'no more than propose a commercial transaction'—was subject to at least some degree of First Amendment protection. In the 1976 decision in *Virginia State Board of Pharmacy v Virginia Citizens Consumer Council, Inc*,[6] the Court relied heavily on the idea that the free speech clause of the First Amendment protected not only the right to speak but also the right to receive information. And thus, for the Supreme Court, the consumer's interest in receiving (accurate) information about goods, services, and their prices was sufficiently great, and sufficiently related to the First Amendment's guarantee of freedom of speech, that commercial advertising could no longer be considered totally outside of the coverage of the First Amendment, as *Valentine v Chrestensen* had earlier concluded.

As discussed at length in the entry in this volume on 'What is Speech? The Question of Coverage'[7], that a form of communication or expression is *covered* by the principle of (or right to) freedom of speech does not necessarily mean that a particular act of communication or expression will wind up being *protected*. What a determination that there is free speech coverage does produce is a heightened threshold of justification for covered conduct, higher than the justification otherwise applicable within some jurisdiction for conduct not covered by a right.[8] So although the Supreme Court in *Virginia Pharmacy* rejected the earlier view, exemplified by *Valentine v Chrestensen*, that commercial advertising remained completely uncovered by the First Amendment, and although the Court thus concluded that any regulation of commercial advertising must meet a higher standard of justification than the minimal 'rational basis' standard applied to government regulation generally,[9] the heightened standard of justification for the regulation of commercial advertising was not nearly as high as the standard of justification applied to political, ideological, artistic, literary, or other speech whose content went beyond simple commercial advertising.[10] In the language of American constitutional law, regulation of commercial advertising was to be subject to 'intermediate scrutiny', a degree of scrutiny higher than 'rational basis' but also lower than the 'strict scrutiny' applicable, in one formulation or another, to the use of race in governmental

---

[5] *Bigelow v Virginia*, 421 US 809 (1975).

[6] *Virginia State Board of Pharmacy v Virginia Citizens Consumer Council, Inc*, 425 US 748 (1976) ('*Virginia Pharmacy*').

[7] See Schauer, Chapter 9 in this volume.

[8] See Thomas Scanlon, 'A Theory of Freedom of Expression' (1972) 1 *Phil & Pub Aff* 204: 'On any very strong version of the doctrine [of freedom of expression] there will be cases where protected acts are held to be immune from restriction despite the fact that they have as consequences harms which would normally be sufficient to justify the imposition of legal sanctions'.

[9] See *Ferguson v Skrupa*, 372 US 726 (1963); *Williamson v Lee Optical of Oklahoma, Inc*, 348 US 483 (1955).

[10] To oversimplify, the heightened scrutiny applied to fully covered expression can be exemplified by the 'clear and present danger' idea first put forward by Justice Oliver Wendell Holmes, Jr, in *Schenck v United States*, 249 US 47 (1919), and now reformulated to have even greater stringency in *Brandenburg v Ohio*, 395 US 444 (1969).

decision-making,[11] to restrictions on rights of privacy and related individual liberties,[12] and to most forms of the speech lying at the core of the First Amendment's concerns.[13]

The Supreme Court formulated this intermediate scrutiny standard four years after *Virginia Pharmacy* in *Central Hudson Gas & Electric Corporation v Public Service Commission of New York*,[14] and as so formulated commercial speech will be protected (1) if it 'concern[s] lawful activity' and is not 'misleading', (2) if the 'asserted governmental intertest' in regulating is 'substantial', (3) if 'the regulation directly advances the governmental interest asserted', and (4) if the regulation is 'not more extensive than is necessary to serve that interest'.[15] And although this test has been slightly reformulated in subsequent cases,[16] the *Central Hudson* test still structures the US approach to the regulation of commercial advertising, and does so in a way that a significant number of what would previously have been considered routine regulations of commercial advertising have been held to be unconstitutional.[17]

Within the United States, the approach to the protection of commercial advertising and related forms of commercial speech that was launched in *Virginia Pharmacy*, and which has an even more robust presence now, has been subject to strong criticism from two opposed directions. In one direction, Supreme Court Justice Clarence Thomas has criticized the lesser protection of commercial speech compared to almost all other forms of communication covered by the First Amendment. For Justice Thomas, the analysis starts not with the historical background of commercial advertising's complete non-coverage, but instead with the fact that commercial speech is speech. And thus, for him, the more deferential standard of *Central Hudson*, compared to the less deferential standards of review applied throughout much of the balance of First Amendment doctrine, cannot be justified:

> [T]here is no "philosophical or historical basis for asserting that 'commercial' speech is of 'lower value' than 'noncommercial' speech." Indeed, I doubt whether it is even possible to draw a coherent distinction between commercial and noncommercial speech.[18]

And Justice Thomas's views about the undesirability and possible impossibility of drawing a distinction between commercial and non-commercial speech are consistent with

---

[11] See *Loving v Virginia*, 388 US 1 (1967).   [12] See *Roe v Wade*, 410 US 113 (1973).
[13] See n 10.
[14] *Central Hudson Gas & Electric Corporation v Public Service Commission of New York*, 447 US 557 (1980) ('*Central Hudson*').
[15] Ibid 566.   [16] See, eg, *Lorillard Tobacco Co v Reilly*, 533 US 525 (2001).
[17] Ibid; *Thompson v Western States Medical Center*, 535 US 357 (2002); *44 Liquormart, Inc v Rhode Island*, 517 US 484 (1996) ('*44 Liqourmart*').
[18] *Lorillard* (n 16) 575 (Thomas J, concurring in part and concurring in the judgment), quoting *44 Liquormart* (n 17) 522–3 (Thomas J, concurring in part and concurring in the judgment). To the same effect, see Martin H Redish, 'Commercial Speech, First Amendment Intuitionism and the Twilight Zone of Viewpoint Discrimination' (2007) 41 *Loy LA L Rev* 67; Martin H Redish and Kyle Voils, 'False Commercial Speech and the First Amendment: Understanding the Implications of the Equivalency Principle' (2017) 25 *Wm & Mary Bill Rts J* 765.

his broader view that distinguishing among the forms or the subjects of speech, even apart from the question of commercial speech, is inconsistent with the underlying premises of the idea of free speech, which for him are essentially about refusing to permit government to decide which forms of speech are more or less valuable.[19]

From exactly the opposite direction, the increase in the degree of free speech protection afforded to commercial speech has been attacked since *Virginia Pharmacy* itself as being both excessive and inconsistent with the traditional reluctance of the courts to interfere with legislative decisions about the appropriate degree of regulation of commercial activities in general. That reluctance—commonly associated in the United States with the rejection, in the 1930s and thereafter, of the Court's 1905 decision in *Lochner v New York*[20]—is now more or less entrenched in contemporary US constitutional law. And thus Justice (later Chief Justice) Rehnquist, dissenting in *Virginia Pharmacy*, objected to the constitutionalization of commercial speech, arguing that doing so was tantamount to an unfortunate revitalization of the *Lochner* regime. The basic claim, elaborated several years after *Virginia Pharmacy* in an important article by Thomas Jackson and John Jeffries,[21] is that objectors to government regulation in general have opportunistically seized on the fact that virtually all regulation is a regulation of language in some form. And thus if almost all regulations are vulnerable to attack on free speech grounds because of the almost coincidental presence of what might literally be described as 'speech', there is a risk that free speech principles will be a back door route to a broad-based deregulatory agenda. The Rehnquist and Jackson/Jeffries argument has in recent years become ubiquitous, with Supreme Court Justice Elena Kagan in another case referring to the 'weaponization' of the First Amendment,[22] and numerous scholars joining in the chorus of objections to the deregulatory uses of the First Amendment,[23] which appear to the objectors far removed from what any sensible conception of the idea of freedom of speech is all about. Such objections, however, have had little effect on the actual development of constitutional doctrine, and the commercial speech 'revolution' that commenced in 1976 with *Virginia Pharmacy* continues apace, and shows all signs of continuing expansion.

---

[19] See *Reed v Town of Gilbert*, 135 S Ct 2218 (2015) (Thomas J, for the Court).

[20] *Lochner v New York*, 198 US 45 (1905). The decline of the *Lochner* approach began with *Nebbia v New York*, 291 US 502 (1934), and *West Coast Hotel Co v Parrish*, 300 US 379 (1937), was canonically reaffirmed in *United States v Carolene Products*, 304 US 144 (1938), and is now exemplified by the cases cited above in n 9.

[21] Thomas H Jackson and John C Jeffries, Jr, 'Commercial Speech: Economic Due Process and the First Amendment' (1979) 65 Va L Rev 1.

[22] *Janus v American Federation of State, County, and Municipal Employees, Council 31*, 138 S Ct 2448 (2018) (Kagan J, dissenting).

[23] See, eg, Tamara Piety, *Brandishing the First Amendment: Commercial Expression in America* (U Michigan P 2012); Leslie Kendrick, 'First Amendment Expansionism' (2015) 56 Wm & Mary L Rev 1199; Frederick Schauer, 'The Politics and Incentives of First Amendment Coverage' (2015) 56 Wm & Mary L Rev 1613; Frederick Schauer, 'First Amendment Opportunism,' in Lee C Bollinger and Geoffrey R Stone (eds), *Eternally Vigilant: Free Speech in the Modern Era* (U Chicago P 2002) 174; Amanda Shanor, 'The New *Lochner*' [2016] Wis L Rev 133.

24.3 Beyond the United States

Not surprisingly, given the incentives that commercial advertisers would have to try to gain some immunity from government regulation, the issue of free speech protection for commercial advertising, or for other forms of solely commercial communication, has arisen in many other countries with strong legal or constitutional protection for freedom of speech. To the extent that a generalization is possible, however, the conclusion would be that such arguments have fared at least somewhat less well in other jurisdictions than they have in the United States.

In some sense, the question is most straightforward in Australia. Because neither freedom of speech nor freedom of the press is explicitly protected in the Australian constitution, what protection does exist is a function of judicial interpretations of those various provisions of the constitution creating a representative democracy.[24] The free speech right is thus limited to 'political discussion' or discussion 'on matter of government and politics', which the High Court and other Australian courts have thus far held does not include commercial advertising.[25] As a result, the kinds of issues that have arisen in the United States have tended not in Australia to be understood in constitutional or 'freedom of political communication' terms.

In some sense, the situation in Canada regarding free speech and commercial advertising has been almost directly opposed, at least as to methodology, to the situation in Australia. The Canadian Charter of Rights and Freedoms explicitly protects the freedom of expression in section 2(b), and then provides that limitations shall be evaluated under Canada's version of the proportionality test, as embodied in Section 1 of the Charter. And although the phrase 'freedom of expression' is sufficiently flexible as to allow the courts to determine that some forms of communication are simply not covered by the Charter, in fact that has not been the Supreme Court of Canada's approach. Rather, the Court has interpreted section 2(b) capaciously, finding virtually all forms of communication to be within that section's initial protection of freedom of expression.[26] As a result, what appears to be a two-step process in theory has devolved into a one-step process in practice, with almost all restrictions on almost all forms of communication— or at least those forms that have generated litigation—being thought covered by section

---

[24] See especially *Australian Capital Television Pty Ltd v Commonwealth* (1992) 177 CLR 106, followed by *Theophanous v Herald & Weekly Times Ltd* (1994) 182 CLR 104, and *Lange v Australian Broadcasting Corporation* (1997) 189 CLR 520. For commentary, see Michael Chesterman, *Freedom of Speech in Australian Law: A Delicate* Plant (Ashgate 2000); Deborah C Cass, 'Through the Looking Glass: The Right to Political Communication' in Tom Campbell and Wojciech Sadurski (eds), *Freedom of Communication* (Dartmouth 1994).

[25] See the joint judgment of Mason CJ, Toohey and Gaudron JJ in *Theophanous* (n 24). Even clearer on the point is *Tobacco Institute of Australia v Australian Federation of Consumer Organisations* (1993) 41 FCR 89.

[26] See especially *Irwin Toy Ltd v Quebec (Attorney General)* [1989] 1 SCR 927.

2(b) and then being tested against the proportionality or reasonableness standard of section 1.

When this one-step process has been applied to commercial advertising, the results have been variable, such that some advertising restrictions have been upheld and others invalidated, with few generalizations or patterns discernable. Writing in 2003, in what remains the most thorough theoretical and doctrinal discussion of free speech and commercial advertising that exists in any country, the Canadian philosopher Roger Shiner concluded that the outcomes in Canada did not differ substantially from those in the United States, despite plain differences in approach.[27] For Shiner, the Canadian courts' application of reasonableness review turned out, even without a canonical 'test', to produce outcomes similar to those produced by US courts in applying the four-part *Central Hudson* test.[28] Sixteen years after Shiner's book, however, there seems to be greater divergence. As US courts, and especially the Supreme Court, have applied what is in practice increasingly close and sceptical scrutiny to restrictions on commercial advertising, including restrictions on tobacco and alcohol advertising, there have been few substantial changes in approach or tone in the Canadian decisions, and it is fair to conclude that as of the date of this writing, the US approach has emerged as far less deferential to government decisions regulating commercial advertising than what now exists in Canada.

Much the same can be said about the situation in the United Kingdom.[29] Unlike Australia, the courts of the United Kingdom have been unwilling to categorically remove commercial advertising from the protection afforded to political, ideological, artistic, scientific, and literary speech. But the courts have been willing to say that commercial advertising is less central to free speech principles, and thus that administrative controls on advertising will be evaluated with substantially greater deference.[30] In theory, the UK courts have been willing to examine advertising restrictions and evaluate their permissibility against the standards of the UK Human Rights Act 1998 and of Article 10 of the European Convention on Human Rights (ECHR), but in practice the explicit acknowledgement of the lesser free speech value of commercial speech has produced a regime largely accepting a range of restrictions on commercial advertising that would not be acceptable for many or even most other forms of public communication.

The experience in Europe, both under the ECHR and for European Union law decisions by the European Court of Justice, bears substantial similarity to the experience in

---

[27] Roger A Shiner, *Freedom of Commercial Expression* (OUP 2003).

[28] See, eg, the similarities between the Canadian case of *RJR-MacDonald Inc v Canada (Attorney General)* [1995] 3 SCR 199 and, in the United States, *Lorillard* (n 16).

[29] See generally Eric Barendt, 'Freedom of Expression in the United Kingdom under the Human Rights Act 1998' (2009) 84 *Ind LJ* 851; Richard Caddell, 'Freedom of Commercial Speech and the UK Courts' (2005) 64 *Cambridge LJ* 274.

[30] See *Boehringer Ingelheim Ltd v Vetplus Ltd.* [2007] EWCA (Civ) 583; *R (on application of British American Tobacco UK Ltd.) v Secretary of State for Health* [2004] EWHC (Admin) 2493; *R (on application of North Cyprus Tourism Centre Ltd) v Transport for London* [2005] EWHC (Admin) 1698.

Canada. This is not surprising, for what the European jurisdictions and Canada have in common is a commitment to proportionality review. And thus both under European law and in Canada, judges have been unwilling to exclude commercial advertising from the ambit of free expression protection, and unwilling, as in the UK, to give such communication categorically lesser protection.[31] Rather, they are essentially deciding whether some restriction on communication is reasonable, a determination made without benefit (or burden) of categorial distinctions among types of speech. As a result, the outcomes are difficult to categorize, especially in light of the doctrine of margin of appreciation, under which European transnational courts are in general willing to defer to national decisions and national variations, including ones which implicitly vary with respect to the degree of protection of commercial advertising. Still, it is probably fair to conclude that in practice commercial advertising restrictions are, under European law, given considerable deference, producing far less protection than in the United States, considerably less protection than in Canada, and a degree of minimal but not non-existent protection roughly similar to that of the UK.[32]

24.4 THE THEORY OF PROTECTION

The theoretical and normative questions about free speech protection for commercial advertising are largely centred on three questions. First, are there grounds for treating commercial advertising, or commercial expression more generally, as a less valuable form of communication than political, ideological, scientific, literary, and artistic expression? Second, are there grounds for regulating the accuracy or truthfulness of commercial expression that do not exist, or exist to a lesser extent, for many other forms of expression? And, third, are regulations on the transmission of accurate commercial information—accurate advertising—illegitimately paternalistic? This section shall take up each of these questions in turn.

With respect to the question of allegedly lesser value, it is impossible to address that question without presupposing an underlying or background justification for the special protection of freedom of speech itself. If that justification, for example, is some form of individual autonomy, or self-expression, or self-realization, then it becomes necessary to distinguish between the advertiser and the recipient of an advertisement. Perhaps recognizing that not very much individual autonomy is implicated by a chain pharmacy's advertisement of the price at which it is willing to sell aspirin or sleeping pills, the US Supreme Court in *Virginia Pharmacy* focused instead, for almost the first time, on the recipient of speech rather than on the speaker. But if presumably accurate price information is related to a potential purchaser's autonomy, it is difficult to see how this form of autonomy is

---

[31] See *Jakubowski v Germany* [1994] 19 EHRR 64; *Cosado Coca v Spain* [1994] 18 EHRR 1; *Markt-Intern Verlag GmbH and Klaus Berman v Germany* [1990] 12 EHRR 161.
[32] See Shiner (n 27) 94–110.

distinct from the autonomy implicated by the decision of what to buy in the first place. And here we encounter a problem that plagues autonomy-based theories of free speech theory generally, and not simply the theory of commercial speech or commercial advertising. And that is the problem of distinguishing autonomous communications, whether from the perspective of the communicator or from the perspective of the recipient of the communication, from autonomous behaviour of any kind.[33] And thus if we think of the recipient interest in the context of commercial advertising as the interest in obtaining information, the problem is then one of attempting to distinguish the information we receive from the propositions uttered by others from the information we obtain just by our experience of living in the world. But if this is so, then it would seem applicable to information on any topic, and not just about potential commercial transactions.

In response, the proponent of an autonomy-based justification for the value of information *simpliciter* would argue that there is an important distinction between getting information and acting on that information. Knowing the price of a pharmaceutical is one thing—deciding to buy it is another. It may be that knowing a price is probabilistically causal of a decision to buy or a decision not to buy, but the information itself is distinguishable from the decision. And if we are concerned that people in the exercise of their autonomy be able to make good decisions for their own well-being, then a free speech interest in information *qua* information can be understood as a relevant foundation for a principle of freedom of speech.

Much the same can be said on both sides of questions about the relationship between free speech as a facilitator of truth and knowledge and the value of the commercial information we receive from advertisements. If we believe that unmediated information flow will over time incline towards truth and incline towards increased knowledge, then there is no reason to suppose that the information that comes from advertising is different in kind from the information we receive from other sources. But on the other side we see the argument, again, that the information we receive from the propositions uttered by others may not be substantially different from the information we receive just from living in the world, and from what we see and hear and do.

This is not the place to explore in full the arguments for and against autonomy-based justifications for a free speech principle.[34] And the same can be said as well about truth- or knowledge-based arguments.[35] But it does appear that the US Supreme Court was correct in thinking that insofar as a principle of freedom of speech can support the inclusion of commercial advertising, then the shift from speaker to listener seems sound. And it seems plausible as well to question whether the information people receive from advertising is different from the information they receive from a vast variety of other sources, much of it equally valuable or equally worthless as the information that people receive from advertising.

---

[33] For a lengthier exploration of many of the issues, see Frederick Schauer, 'On the Distinction between Speech and Action' (2015) 65 *Emory LJ* 427. And see Schauer, Chapter 9 in this volume.

[34] See Mackenzie and Meyerson, Chapter 4 in this volume.

[35] See Marshall, Chapter 3 in this volume.

When we turn to those free speech justifications sounding in democratic theory,[36] however, the inclusion of commercial advertising, as the High Court of Australia concluded, seems at best remote. It is true, of course, that some information relevant to some governmental or democratic decisions might come from advertisements doing nothing more than propose a commercial transaction. But the difficulty in drawing a sharp line is not, in law or in life, a barrier to recognizing substantial differences away from the border. And thus the more a principle of free speech is seen to be based on the relationship between citizen speech and self-government or democracy, the less plausible it is to include pure commercial advertising within the scope of the protection.

The second question alluded to above is the question about the regulation of inaccuracy. In *Virginia Pharmacy*, the US Supreme Court explicitly excluded the regulation of false or misleading advertising from its then-new coverage of commercial advertising within the First Amendment. In the Court's view, such an exclusion was based on its perception that the profit motive made commercial advertising more resistant to excess deterrence—the so-called chilling effect—than speech spoken (or written, or published) for ideological rather than commercial motives. But this surely, as the same court recognized a decade earlier in *New York Times Co v Sullivan*,[37] gets things backwards. The classic ideological speaker is sufficiently committed to the message that they are willing to risk some sanctions in order to get the message out. But commercial speakers, being profit-sensitive, are likely more responsive to sanctions, and thus more easily chilled.

Yet whether the US Supreme Court got it right or wrong, it remains the case that many commercial representations are more easily verified or falsified than most of the representations of political policy, as generations of legal remedies for commercial misrepresentation have made clear. And even if the United States is an international outlier in refusing to sanction even the clearest factual misrepresentations in public debate generally,[38] most other countries are more comfortable with sanctions for at least some harmful factual or historical untruths.[39] And thus it seems safe to conclude that the free speech protection of commercial advertising, where such protection exists, does not include the protection of factually false commercial advertising.

That conclusion brings us to the third and arguably most important issue. If the protection of commercial advertising is not based on its potential to mislead—misleading advertising being excluded at the outset—then what justifies its regulation? Commonly, the answer to that question is that people make bad consumer choices, and more people make more bad consumer choices when advertising induces them, even without plain factual falsity, to do so. People buy cigarettes that endanger their health and lives, they gamble money they cannot afford to lose, they drink more beer and even stronger alcoholic

---

[36] See Bhagwat and Weinstein, Chapter 5 in this volume.
[37] *New York Times Co v Sullivan*, 376 US 254 (1964), holding for the first time that actions for libel were constrained by the First Amendment, and that public officials needed to prove intentional falsity in order to recover in a defamation action.
[38] *United States v Alvarez*, 567 US 709 (2012). See Frederick Schauer, 'Facts and the First Amendment' (2010) 57 *UCLA L Rev* 897.
[39] See Ludovic Hennebel and Thomas Hochman (eds), *Genocide Denials and the Law* (OUP 2011).

beverages than are good for them or the people with whom they interact, and so on almost ad infinitum. So the question arises as to whether regulation designed to decrease demand and to decrease the frequency of poor consumer decisions can be justified.

When put this way, it is clear that the debates about the regulation of commercial advertising are largely debates about paternalism.[40] And although this entry is not the place to rehearse these centuries-old debates, it has become clear that the debates about the protection of commercial advertising have become the platform on which these larger battles are waged. For objectors to paternalism, paternalistic regulation of advertising for tobacco, alcohol, gambling, and much else is objectionable largely because of the paternalistic motives of the regulators. And for those who find paternalism either unobjectionable or positively desirable in the service of keeping people from making bad decisions about their own lives, the regulation of advertising is often seen to be the best way to pursue those goals.

In these debates, it is easy to lose sight of the role that speaking or writing or publishing is playing, and that was the point made by then-Justice Rehnquist in *Virginia Pharmacy* more than forty years ago. Whatever the arguments for and against paternalism, they appear to have little to do with any of the standard or even not-so-standard arguments for a distinct principle of freedom of speech. And even less to do with the presence or absence of something spoken, written, or, most commonly, printed or broadcast. If tobacco paternalism, for example, is wrong, then it is as wrong to deprive people of the cigarettes offered for sale by willing sellers as it is to restrict tobacco advertising. And if tobacco paternalism is desirable, then restricting tobacco advertising seems a weak even if politically necessary remedy compared to simply prohibiting tobacco sales. And on neither side of this debate does speech as such serve very much of a function. If there is a reason for protecting speech when its consequences are equivalent to the consequences of more obviously regulable activities, as Thomas Scanlon aptly put it almost half a century ago,[41] then in the context of commercial advertising there needs to be a reason to protect the advertising of goods and services going beyond the anti-paternalistic arguments for not restricting the harmful good and services themselves. If the free speech arguments are simply opportunistic surrogates for broader arguments and larger battles, it is hard to see what work the principle of free speech is doing at all.

---

[40] The classic objection to paternalism is found in John Stuart Mill, *On Liberty* (David Spitz ed, WW Norton 1975). And a rigorous modern philosophical defence of paternalism is Sarah Conly, *Against Autonomy: Justifying Coercive Paternalism* (CUP 2012). The issues are analysed deeply and rigorously in Gerald Dworkin, 'Paternalism' (*Stanford Encyclopedia of Philosophy*, 6 November 2002) <https://plato.stanford.edu/archives/fall2019/entries/paternalism> accessed 19 December 2019.

[41] See Scanlon (n 8).

CHAPTER 25

HATE SPEECH

ALON HAREL

25.1 INTRODUCTION

HATE speech is abusive speech that targets members of certain groups—typically minority groups—including racial groups, ethnic groups, religious groups, groups defined on the basis of sexual orientation and so on. Most typically, hate speech legislation includes racist, sexist, and homophobic speech. Speech that targets other groups, such as individuals targeted on the basis of class, can also be classified as hate speech.[1] Hate speech can be directed at particular individuals (degrading the religion, ethnic origins, sexual orientation, and so on of a particular individual) or towards a group sharing particular characteristics (degrading the religious or ethnic group or other group as a whole). Most groups protected by hate speech legislation are groups that have been subjected to past discriminatory treatment. But, the restrictions on hate speech legislation have often been expanded and the proper scope of the groups that deserve protection have been subject to a fierce debate.[2]

While much of hate speech can be legitimately prohibited by standard recognized legal exceptions to free speech, such as fighting words or incitement to violence, other forms of hate speech cannot. To address the prevalence of hate speech as such, many legal systems prohibit some forms of hate speech and impose criminal or civil sanctions for violating such prohibitions. Those systems need to address the serious challenge of defining the category of hate speech, draw its boundaries, and determine the sanctions.[3] The primary

---

[1] For a critique of the fact that class-based hate speech is typically ignored by legal theorists, see: Stanley Fish, 'Boutique Multiculturalism, or Why Liberals Are Incapable of Thinking about Hate Speech' (1997) 23 *Crit Inq* 378, 382.

[2] Jen Neller, 'The Need for New Tools to Break the Silos: Identity Categories in Hate Speech Legislation' (2018) 7 *Intl J Crime, Justice & Soc Democracy* 75.

[3] We speak here of a category 'hate speech' as a single category. As some theorists have noted, hate speech consists of many distinct subcategories which may merit differential treatment. See, eg, Caleb Yong, 'Does Freedom of Speech Include Hate Speech' (2011) 17 *Res Publica* 385.

task of this chapter will be to explore the moral and political arguments for and against the legal regulation of hate speech as such or, at least, some subcategories of hate speech.

To do so, Section 25.2 points out that in contrast to other prominent constitutional debates the treatment of hate speech is controversial among liberals. This is because both the concerns raised by proponents and opponents of hate speech restrictions are liberal concerns. More specifically, hate speech legislation touches upon a conflict between liberty and autonomy on the one hand and autonomy, dignity, and equality on the other. Section 25.3 examines some of the more prominent justifications for hate speech legislation, while Section 25.4 examines some of the more compelling arguments against regulating hate speech. Section 25.5 concludes.

While this chapter has little to offer in terms of a conclusive answer whether and, if so, how to regulate hate speech, I wish to convince the reader that much of the existing debate is deficient because it rests upon empirical claims concerning the social and political effects of hate speech and those are too speculative and, further, they often provide superficial rationalizations for more foundational normative convictions. In Section 25.5, I (too) briefly identify what these foundational non-empirical conflicting convictions are.

25.2 Hate Speech and Free Expression

Liberal theorists disagree with respect to the proper treatment of hate speech. Some believe that hate speech ought to be protected while others believe that it ought to be criminalized, or at least be classified as a tort. This disagreement is reflected also in the legal systems. While the United States protects speech stringently, other legal systems often incorporate prohibitions on hate speech.[4] This is a notable phenomenon. Typically, most liberals would oppose restrictions on abortion, support gay sex marriage, oppose capital punishment, and so on. The debates concerning these issues are conducted between liberals and radicals or between liberals and conservatives. In the context of free speech, liberals typically would be inclined to oppose restrictions based on concerns for protecting public order and security. In contrast, in the context of hate speech, liberals are sharply divided.[5] This section explains why this issue is so divisive among liberals. I argue that the disagreement among liberals can be explained by pointing out that both proponents and opponents of hate speech can rest their case in foundational liberal values.

---

[4] See, eg, in the United Kingdom, the Racial and Religious Hatred Act 2006 (UK); in Canada, the Criminal Code 1985 (Can), s 319; in Germany, the Criminal Code 1998, s 130; in Australia, Racial Discrimination Act 1975 (Cth), s 18C; in Israel, the Israeli Criminal Code 1977, s144. For a useful comparison of the regulation of hate speech in different jurisdictions, see Michel Rosenfeld, 'Hate Speech in Constitutional Jurisprudence: A Comparative Analysis' (2001) 24 *Cardozo L Rev* 1523.

[5] David Brink, 'Millian Principles, Freedom of Expression and Hate Speech' (2001) 7 *Legal Theory* 119.

To do so, I first examine the liberal values underlying the opposition to regulation of hate speech. More particularly, I show that prohibitions on hate speech are particularly detrimental to liberal free speech values. Hate speech is often political speech which, as a general rule, is constitutionally privileged. Further, restrictions on hate speech are inevitably content-based restrictions; speech that advocates hatred is sanctioned while speech which opposes hatred or advocates equality is permissible or even condoned. I then examine why other liberals are disposed to regulate hate speech. The prevalence of hate speech may undermine the autonomy of the targets of hatred, their dignity or equality. I conclude by arguing that the hate speech controversy is reminiscent of a much deeper controversy in political theory between foundational liberal values: liberty on the one hand and autonomy, dignity, and equality on the other.

Freedom of speech is among the most cherished right of liberal democracies. It is entrenched in the constitutions of many liberal democracies as well as in international human right treaties. It is understood to be foundational to liberal polities either in the sense that it is a precondition for the existence of a liberal polity and/or in the sense that the protection of speech is conducive to foundational liberal values such as autonomy, and liberty.[6] The traditional liberal values underlying the protection of speech include autonomy[7] and self-realization.[8]

Yet it is evident that freedom of speech is not an absolute right.[9] The scope of what constitutes speech, what speech ought to be protected and the balancing between the value of free speech and conflicting rights, values, and other concerns is controversial.[10] But despite the willingness to restrict speech for the sake of realizing or promoting other important values, the freedom associated with the right to engage in hate speech is particularly central to liberal polities. I will show that traditional constitutional doctrines require an especially stringent protection of hate speech and, further, that these doctrines are grounded in a liberal understanding of the value of freedom.

The legal regulation of hate speech is challenging for liberals for two reasons. First, most liberal political systems differentiate between different categories of speech. Thus, for instance, political speech is stringently protected, while commercial speech is protected to a lesser degree. Political speech is considered to have special status because free

---

[6] Alon Harel, 'Freedom of Speech' in Andrei Marmor (ed), *The Routledge Companion to Philosophy of Law* (Routledge 2012) 599.

[7] Thomas Nagel, 'Personal Rights and Public Space' (1995) 24 *Phil & Public Aff* 83, 86, Thomas Scanlon, 'A Theory of Freedom of Expression' (1972) 1 *Phil & Pub Aff* 204, Susan Brison, 'The Autonomy Defense of Free Speech' (1998) 108 *Ethics* 312.

[8] Eric Barendt, *Freedom of Speech* (2nd edn, OUP 2005) 13; Frederick Schauer, *Free Speech: A Philosophical Enquiry* (CUP 1982) 49. For a comprehensive survey, see David Van Mill, 'Freedom of Speech (*Stanford Encyclopedia of Philosophy*, 1 May 2017) <https://plato.stanford.edu/entries/freedom-speech/> accessed 4 April 2019; Harel (n 6).

[9] Toni Massaro, 'Equality and Freedom of Expression: The Hate Speech Dilemma' (1991) 32 *Wm & Mary L Rev* 211, 233.

[10] Harel (n 6).

political speech is a prerequisite for democracy.[11] Thus in an important case concerning limitations on campaign finance, the US Supreme Court asserted that:[12]

> The Act's contribution and expenditure limitations operate in an area of the most fundamental First Amendment activities. Discussion of public issues and debate on the qualifications of candidates are integral to the operation of the system of government established by our Constitution. The First Amendment affords the broadest protection to such political expression in order 'to assure (the) unfettered interchange of ideas for the bringing about of political and social changes desired by the people'.

Before we examine the implications of this view on hate speech, let us point out a second relevant doctrine which seems to require a special protection of hate speech. In many jurisdictions, constitutional doctrine contains also a special prohibition on viewpoint discrimination. This doctrine, as explained by the US Supreme Court, dictates that:

> Government has no power to restrict expression because of its message, its ideas, its subject matter or its content.[13]

The Court continues and argues:

> [G]overnment may not grant the use of a forum to people whose views it finds acceptable, but deny use to those wishing to express less favored or more controversial views... There is an 'equality of status in the field of ideas,' and government must afford all points of view an equal opportunity to be heard... Selective exclusions from a public forum may not be based on content alone, and may not be justified by reference to content alone.[14]

The privileged status of political speech and the stringent treatment of viewpoint discrimination raise special problems for the regulation of hate speech. As shown below, the regulation of hate speech often implies regulation of both viewpoint-based and political speech.

First, hate speech is often (although not always or necessarily) political.[15] Among the most famous US cases of free speech is the case of *National Socialist Party of America v*

---

[11] Lillian Bevier, 'The First Amendment and Political Speech: An Inquiry into the Substance and Limits of Principle' (1978) 30 *Stan L Rev* 299; Alexander Meiklejohn, *Free Speech and Its Relation to Self-Government* (Harper & Brothers 1948).

[12] *Buckley v Valeo*, 424 US 1, 14 (1976).

[13] *Police Department of City of Chicago v Mosley*, 208 US 92, 95 (1972).

[14] Ibid 96 (citations omitted).

[15] The claim that hate speech is (or even can be) political has been challenged by some on theoretical grounds. Thus Heyman argued that political speech should only contain speech that respects civic participation: Steven Heyman, *Free Speech and Dignity* (Yale UP 2008) 178–9. Heyman argued that:

> To use Meiklejohn's language, hate speech may be regarded as a form of abuse that violates the rules of order that make democratic deliberation possible. In Habermasian terms, one can argue that hate speech is not an instance of 'communicative freedom' oriented towards mutual understanding. Rather, the aim of hate speech is to dominate and subordinate others. In this way it is inconsistent with those 'relations of mutual recognition in which each person can expect to be respected by all as free and equal.

Heyman, however, relies on a non-conventional definition of political speech. Under the conventional characterizations much of hate speech falls clearly under the category of political speech.

Village of Skokie.[16] In this case, it was decided that the displaying of the Nazi swastika is a protected form of speech. In another important US case, *American Booksellers v Hudnut*,[17] a US Court even stated that a prohibition on pornography defined as graphic sexually explicit subordination of women was unconstitutional, precisely because it targets speech that conveys and reinforces certain sexist values, and sexist values are classified by the Court as political; they have social, cultural, and political ramifications. Numerous other decisions proclaim that the regulation of hate speech often infringes upon the protection of political speech, namely speech that is particularly privileged in traditional free speech jurisprudence.

Second, hate speech in its very nature is identified on the basis of its content or even viewpoint.[18] There may be viewpoint-neutral rules against harassment—rules which are independent of the content of the harassing speech. Yet, hate speech is regulated precisely because it reinforces hatred, namely precisely because of the viewpoint contained in it. Speech which praises racial or gender equality is permissible and even condoned while speech which advocates racial or gender hierarchy, hatred, or subordination is prohibited. Restrictions on hate speech are typically not viewpoint neutral.[19]

The privileging of political speech and the strict prohibition on viewpoint discrimination are not mere formal entrenched constitutional doctrines; they reflect foundational liberal convictions. Freedom of political speech is important because it is a prerequisite for sustaining a democratic polity in which citizens deliberate together on matters of public importance. Viewpoint discrimination is particularly detrimental to autonomy as it subjects the deliberation of citizens to the values, interests, and preferences of others. By censoring some viewpoints or reinforcing others the state dominates our deliberative powers. There is no greater threat to liberal freedom than the control that the state may have over what we think or believe to be true. For both reasons, defending the regulation of hate speech is a particularly difficult task for liberals.

If the protection of hate speech is so central to the protection of the most cherished values of liberals: liberty and autonomy, why would liberals ever be prone to regulate hate speech?

Non-liberal theorists, in particular minoritarian voices, point out that hate speech is offensive and its victims are deeply wounded by it.[20] Liberals are unlikely to be moved by considerations that are based on subjective emotions and sensibilities. Speech should not be regulated merely because it is offensive. Instead, liberal advocates of hate speech

---

[16] *National Socialist Party of America v Village of Skokie*, 432 US 43 (1977).
[17] *American Booksellers v Hudnut*, 771 F.2d 323 (7th Cir, 1985).
[18] Andrew Altman, 'Liberalism and Campus Hate Speech: A Philosophical Examination' (1993) 103 *Ethics* 302; Adrienne Stone, 'Viewpoint Discrimination, Hate Speech Laws, and the Double-Sided Nature of Freedom of Speech' (2017) 32 *Const Comment* 687, 690.
[19] In addition, there is a related concern. Some advocates of hate speech differentiate between hate speech directed against minorities and hate speech directed against powerful or privileged majorities: Rosenfeld (n 4) 1527. This proposal seems to pose an even greater threat to the ideal of viewpoint neutrality. Yet as advocates of hate speech regulation argue, not all content-based or viewpoint-based restrictions are unconstitutional: see, eg, *Chaplinsky v New Hampshire*, 315 US 568 (1942); Steven Shiffrin, 'Hate Speech, Legitimacy and the Foundational Principles of Government' (2017) 32 *Const Comment* 675, 676–7; Brink (n 5) 129.
[20] Section 25.3 of this chapter provides some examples.

base their support of hate crimes on three traditionally liberal values: autonomy of the targets of hate speech, the dignity of the targets of the hatred, and equality.

First, hate speech may affect the autonomy of the targets of hate speech. It may lead to the exclusion of minorities from mainstream society. The hostile and unwelcoming environment resulting from hate speech alienates already marginalized members of society and leads them to recede from the active fabric of the social structure and thus deprives them of choices and opportunities and undermines their autonomy.[21] It also violates their autonomy by illegitimately seizing control of their life to other more powerful groups. Hence hate speech legislation protects individuals against being dominated by others.[22]

Second, as many have noted, hate speech may undermine the dignity of the victims.[23] At times, this is associated with psychological feelings such as the negative impact on the individual's feeling of self-worth.[24] Liberals, however, would be disposed to endorse a more objective view of dignity. Jeremy Waldron developed such an argument, which rests on the claim that dignity is a civic status.[25] Such civic status requires assurance in the future protection of justice and rights:

> [i]n a well-ordered society, where people are visibly impressed by the signs of one another's commitment to justice, everyone can enjoy a certain assurance as they go about their business. They can feel secure in the rights that justice defines; they can face social interaction without the elemental risks that such interaction would involve if one could not count on others to act justly.[26]

In addition, it has been argued that the dignity of individuals requires that they be perceived and treated as full-fledged agents whose views count. Hate speech undermines the conditions and the recognition of the targets of the hatred and thereby undermines the recognition that they are full-fledged agents.[27] Hence both Canadian and German jurisprudence of hate speech endorse the view that dignitarian considerations require limitations on hate speech.[28]

Finally, hate speech is perceived by many liberals to be detrimental to equality. Hate speech is not merely offensive to minorities, as it undermines their status in the society,

---

[21] Calvin Massey, 'Hate Speech, Cultural Diversity, and the Foundational Paradigms of Free Expression' (1992) 40 *UCLA L Rev* 103, 156.

[22] Andrew Brown 'What is Hate Speech? Part 2: Family Resemblances' (2017) 36 *Law & Phil* 561, 607.

[23] Robert Simpson, 'Dignity Harm and Hate Speech' (2013) 32 *Law & Phil* 701.

[24] Mari Matsuda, 'Public Responses to Racist Speech: Considering the Victim's Story' in Mari Matsuda and others (eds), *Words that Wound: Critical Race Theory, Assaultive Speech and the First Amendment* (Routledge 2018).

[25] Jeremy Waldron, *The Harm in Hate Speech* (Harvard UP 2012).   [26] Ibid 84.

[27] Heyman (n 15) ch 10.

[28] For Canadian jurisprudence, see *R v Keegstra* [1990] 3 SCR 697. For German sources concerning the relevance of dignity to the regulation of hate speech, see Rosenfeld (n 4) 1548–54; *Lüth* [1958] BVerfGE 7, 198.

affects their life prospects, and is responsible for the entrenchment of stereotypes which result in inequality and subordination. As Toni Massaro has pointed out:

> The central constitutional dilemma is that the Bill of Rights protects both individual autonomy and certain collective goals, like equality... Disagreements regarding the constitutional meaning of equality, the proper role of government in inculcating values, and the constitutional and social significance of group identity versus individual personality further compound these theoretical complexities.[29]

Hence, the conflict between advocates of the legal protection of hate speech and its opponents is an internal conflict between foundational liberal values: autonomy or liberty on the one hand and autonomy, dignity, and equality on the other values.[30] This explains why the debate concerning hate speech is not (only) a debate between liberals and radicals or liberals and conservatives but also an inter-liberal debate between liberals and liberals.

25.3 ARGUMENTS FOR REGULATING HATE SPEECH

There are two primary tactics in justifying the regulation of speech. Under the first, the advocate of regulation challenges the conviction that what is considered to be speech is indeed speech. Philosophers have long analysed the concept of speech acts, namely speech which is used to perform acts such as requests, warnings, invitations, promises apologies, and so on. Perhaps hate speech should not be conceptualized as 'mere' speech but as an act—an act of subordination. Under the second tactic, hate speech is particularly harmful; the harms resulting from hate speech are particularly grave (and perhaps distinct) and therefore they justify its regulation. The special gravity of the harms is therefore what ultimately justifies the regulation of hate speech. The rest of this section investigates these arguments.

25.3.1 Hate Speech Is Not Speech or (at Best) 'Low-Value' Speech

One of the most famous arguments in advocating the regulation of pornography has been the view that pornography is not speech but an act.[31] Under this view, pornography

---

[29] Massaro (n 9) 214.
[30] Owen Fiss, *Liberalism Divided: Freedom of Speech and the Many Uses of State Power* (Westview 1996); Simpson (n 23) 702.
[31] Catherine MacKinnon, *Feminism Unmodified: Discourses on Life and Law* (Harvard UP 1987) 148, 154; Ronald Dworkin, *Freedom's Law: the Moral Reading of the American Constitution* (Harvard UP 1989), ch 10, 'MacKinnon's Words'.

does not simply depict subordination of women or even bring about or cause subordination. Instead, it is in itself an act of subordination! In the anti-pornography ordinance that was passed by Indianapolis City Council in 1984 (but later declared invalid on appeal on the grounds that it violated the right to free speech), pornography was defined as: 'the graphic sexually explicit subordination of women in pictures or words'. I will present this argument in the context of pornography and later apply it to the case of hate speech.

Feminist philosophers defended the claim that pornography is an act of subordination (and not merely depiction of subordination) by using the famous JL Austin speech act theory.[32] Under this theory, words are often used not to depict (truly or falsely) states of affairs but rather to perform acts in the world including warning, promising, and marrying.[33] Austin famously distinguished between three types of acts that can be performed by speech (speech acts): locutionary acts, perlocutionary acts, and illocutionary acts. Locutionary acts are indeed mere descriptions; perlocutionary acts are speech acts that change or affect the world; for example, in the case of pornography it is claimed that pornography causes the perpetuation of subordination or discrimination. Finally, illocutionary speech acts can do things in the world. Thus, for instance, the utterance 'I promise to meet you for lunch' may under the proper circumstances constitute a promise, and the declaration 'I hereby pronounce you husband and wife' may under the proper circumstances constitute marriage. It is this third type of act (illocutionary) which is relevant for our purposes.

Hornsby and Langton suggest that pornography is an illocutionary act of subordination. Precisely as the words 'I promise' do not merely depict a promise but also (under the proper 'felicity conditions') constitute the act of promising, so pornography is not merely a depiction of subordination but also an act that subordinates women. To support the claim, Langton (following MacKinnon) provides a list of other speech acts that subordinate, such as the phrase 'whites only' uttered by an official in South Africa during the apartheid. Langton suggests that speech acts that subordinate fall into two categories of illocutionary acts, labelled by Austin verdictives and excertives. Verdictives include actions of ranking, valuing, and placing, such as 'You are the winner of the race' when uttered by an umpire in a race. Close relatives to verdictives are excertives, namely speech acts that order, permit, prohibit, authorize, and so on. Pornography is an excertive because it is used to 'rank women as sex objects'. It is also a verdictive as it 'sexualizes rape, battery, sexual harassment... and it thereby celebrates, promotes, authorizes and legitimizes' sexual violence.[34] MacKinnon further argues that:

> Pornography participates in its audience's eroticism through creating an accessible sexual object, the possession and consumption of which is male sexuality, as socially constructed; to be consumed and possessed as which, is female sexuality, as socially constructed; pornography is a process that constructs it that way.[35]

---

[32] JL Austin, *How to Do Things with Words: The William James Lectures Delivered at Harvard University* (2nd edn, OUP, 1975).
[33] Jennifer Hornsby, 'Speech Acts and Pornography' in Susan Dwyer (ed), *The Problem of Pornography* (Wadsworth 1995) 220, 223–5; Rae Langton, 'Speech Acts and Unspeakable Acts' in Rae Langton (ed), *Sexual Solipsism: Philosophical Essays on Pornography and Objectification* (OUP 2009) 25, 27–8.
[34] MacKinnon (n 31) 173; Langton (n 33) 40.   [35] MacKinnon (n 31) 173.

These observations may be applicable also to hate speech.[36] According to some theorists, hate speech, or at least some forms of hate speech, should be conceptualized as acts of subordination rather than as mere speech. Some racial sexist or homophobic slurs can certainly be locutionary, namely they may describe what the speaker believes. They can also be perlocutionary, namely affect and change the world by persuading people to discriminate against minorities or even incite people to commit violence. But, most significantly, such slurs can be illocutionary; they can constitute acts of subordination. Under this view, hate speech is not merely speech but an act which wrongs people by treating them as if they were inferior moral beings.[37] Arguably, the constitutional protection of speech does not apply to such acts, as the protection of speech is designed to protect speech or communicative action rather than acts. The speech act argument purporting to justify the exclusion of hate speech from the scope of the right to free speech, on the grounds that it does not constitute speech, rests on the conviction that hate speech constructs the world in certain ways (rather than merely describes the world). It is not merely that hate speech condones subordination or even brings about or causes subordination. Instead, it is claimed that it constructs the social world or produces social reality of subordination.[38]

There are several difficulties in this argument. Larry Alexander argued that hate speech can never subordinate. Austin has pointed out that speech acts depend upon the existence of conventions. Thus, for instance, a certain utterance constitutes a promise, given certain social conventions. Similarly, an oath presupposes the existence of conventions dictating what words constitute an oath. Yet Alexander argues there is 'no recognized convention through which people could be subordinated through speech acts. To be subordinated there must be an alteration of one's legal or moral rights and no such alteration seems to result from speech.'[39]

Second, even if it is correct, this argument provides us little guidance as to what forms of speech are unprotected. Altman differentiates between derisively calling someone 'a faggot' and saying to that person 'you are contemptible for being homosexual'.[40] Altman concedes that both utterances treat the person as inferior but that the former utterance is more powerful. But he himself concedes that no clean and neat distinction can be drawn. At least from an institutional perspective the difficulty in drawing a clear line between speech and conduct in these contexts may ultimately result in over-inclusive prohibitions. It is simply too easy to describe any pernicious and offensive speech as a degrading act.

Note also that the speech act theory does not differentiate between acts which cause significant harms and those which do not. An utterance can be classified as unprotected even if its effects are marginal (if it is an act of subordination), and it can be classified as

---

[36] Ishani Maitra, 'Subordinating Speech' in Ishani Maitra and Mary Kate McGowan (eds), *Speech and Harm: Controversies over Free Speech* (OUP 2012) 94.

[37] Altman (n 18) 311.

[38] Judith Butler, *Excitable Speech: A Politics of the Performative* (Routledge 1997).

[39] Larry Alexander, 'Banning Hate Speech and the Sticks and Stones Defense' (1996) 13 *Const Comment* 71, 88.

[40] Altman (n 18) 310.

protected even in case its causal effects are significant (if it is not an act of subordination).[41] I believe that many opponents of hate speech may be therefore reluctant to endorse these implications.

A somewhat different argument was raised by Brink,[42] who argues that while hate speech is speech, it is a 'low-value' speech—speech which is devoid of the characteristics which justify the prohibition on censorship. What explains the prohibition on censorship is the contribution of speech to our deliberative values. 'So,' Brink argues, 'if hate speech does not advance but retards deliberative values, then it is low-value speech, and hate speech regulation need not satisfy strict scrutiny or similarly demanding standards.'[43]

The claim that hate is speech can be regulated because it is low-value speech that 'does not advance but retards deliberative values' is highly problematic. First, hate speech can be deliberative. Note that Brink distinguishes sharply between false speech and speech that does not advance deliberative values. To the extent that deliberative values are promoted by deliberation even when the deliberation rests on false, or evil premises, hate speech can be conducive to deliberative values.

Brink argues that hate speech typically 'does not articulate the grounds for the speaker's perspective and attitudes, or a proposal for debate and decision'.[44] But unless one excludes deliberation as a definitional matter from the category of hate speech, it is difficult to defend this position. The hate speech speaker may exploit theories of the so-called scientific racism to justify their speech. While these theories have been proven to be false, it is not for lack of deliberation on the part of their inventors or adherents.

25.3.2 The Uniqueness of the Harms of Hate Speech

This section investigates two arguments justifying the regulation of hate speech which rest on the uniqueness of the harms resulting from hate speech. I differentiate below between two types of harm-based arguments: those based on extrinsic harms and those based on intrinsic harms. Proponents of the Critical Race Theory believe that the extrinsic harms resulting from hate speech are particularly grave and consequently should override the benefits of protecting hate speech. Other theorists maintain that hate speech may harm the very same values protected by the right to free speech itself. Failing to regulate hate speech is therefore detrimental to the very same values underlying the protection of speech. Hence these harms are labelled intrinsic harms.

25.3.2.1 *Critical Race Theory: Extrinsic Harms*

An influential group of theorists that characterized themselves as being part of the Critical Race Theory movement justified the regulation of hate speech on the grounds that the harms resulting from these crimes are particularly grave and different in kind

---

[41] Harel (n 6) 612.   [42] Brink (n 5).   [43] Ibid 138.
[44] Ibid 139.

from other types of harms.[45] Mari Matsuda tries to identify the harms resulting from hate speech by listening closely to the victims of hate speech. In her view, there is an outsider and an insider's reaction to hate speech. Outsiders typically regard instances of hate speech as isolated incidents while insiders perceive racism to be endemic to the society. Matsuda argues that:

> From the victim's perspective all of these implements inflict wounds, wounds that are neither random nor isolated. Gutter racism, parlor racism, corporate racism and government racism work in coordination, reinforcing existing conditions of domination.[46]

Matsuda points out that victims of hate crimes are deeply affected by hate messages: they experience emotional distress, fear, post-traumatic distress, nightmares and, at times, psychosis and suicide. Racial stereotypes are deeply ingrained in the culture, such that no one can avoid being influenced by them. Matsuda calls for endorsing the internal perspective of the victim and taking seriously their own experiences.

Matsuda also believes that hate speech is unique and should be treated as a distinct category. She argues:

> racist speech is best treated as a *sui generis* category, presenting an idea so historically untenable, so dangerous, and so tied to perpetuation of violence and degradation of the very classes of human beings who are least equipped to respond that it is properly treated as outside the realm of protected discourse.[47]

To characterize speech which is particularly harmful, Matusda articulates three conditions. First the message of the speech ought to be a message of racial inferiority. Second, it ought to be directed against a historically oppressed group, and third, it is persecutory, hateful, and degrading.[48]

Charles Lawrence emphasizes the fact that hate speech is part of a much grander structural framework of the society.[49] The very effort to separate speech and conduct is bound to fail. The racist acts of millions of people are mutually reinforcing and cumulative. Racist speech should be conceptualized as part of a much broader practice—the practice of discrimination and subordination. Further, the special harms of hate speech result from the fact that discrimination and subordination are so overwhelming. It is the accumulation of discrete acts of discrimination, practices, racist norms, racial stereotypes, and ideas which together result in particularly severe harms. Lawrence believes

---

[45] Matsuda (n 24).
[46] Mari Matsuda, 'Public Response to Racist Speech: Considering the Victim's Story' (1989) 87 *Michigan L Rev* 2320, 2335.
[47] Ibid 2357.
[48] Ibid.
[49] Charles Lawrence, 'If He Hollers Let Him Go: Regulating Racist Speech on Campus' in Mari Matsuda and others (eds), *Words that Wound: Critical Race Theory, Assaultive Speech and the First Amendment* (Routledge 2018).

that these incidents are manifestations of an ubiquitous and deeply ingrained cultural belief system, an American way of life and it is this fact which explains the uniqueness of the harms resulting from hate speech.

To illustrate the particular harms of hate speech, Lawrence compares the experiences of a gay person who is being called 'faggot' to those of a person who is being called a liar and says:[50]

> [H]e realized that any response was inadequate to counter the hundreds of years of societal defamation that one word—'faggot'—carried with it. Like the word 'nigger' and unlike the word 'liar', it is not sufficient to deny the truth of the word's application, to say, 'I am not a faggot'. One must deny the truth of the word's meaning, a meaning shouted from the rooftops by the rest of the world a million times a day. The complex response 'Yes, I am a member of the group you despise and the degraded meaning of the word you use is one that I reject' is not effective in a subway encounter.

Richard Delgado also supports the view that racist speech is unique and deserves a special legal treatment. He believes that:

> The racial insult remains one of the most pervasive channels through which discriminatory attitudes are imparted. Such language injures the dignity and self-regard of the person to whom it is addressed, communicating the message that distinctions of race are distinctions of merit, dignity, status, and personhood.[51]

Critical race theorists argue that members of minorities internalize racial stereotypes and it results in isolation desperation and self-hatred. Racial speech is also harmful to society as a whole and not only to its victims, as it results in inequality alienation and impedes economic, social, and political assimilation of minorities into the society.[52] Delgado also suggests an extensive use of tort law remedies to address the problem of hate speech. All three critical race theorists discussed above emphasize the uniqueness of the harm resulting from hate speech. Its uniqueness rests at least partly upon its prevalence in the society.[53] The mutually reinforcing influence of racial speech and racist practices has grave psychological impact on minorities. They stress the subjective feelings of alienation, desperation, and powerlessness resulting from hate speech.

This view is not uncontroversial. Larry Alexander has argued that what is really painful is not the hate speech itself but the knowledge that other people hate or have contempt for you because of your race or sexual orientation. Hate speech is only an indication of these negative sentiments. Alexander also argues that the same disdain conveyed by hate speech can be easily conveyed in other ways which cannot or ought not be regulated. If indeed what is painful is the knowledge that other people have disdain for you, Alexander asks, should a person have a right to ignorance—a right not to know what other people think of him?[54]

---

[50] Ibid.
[51] Richard Delgado, 'Words That Wound: A Tort Action for Racial Insults, Epithets, and Name Calling' (1982) 17 *Harvard Civil Rights—Civil Liberties L Rev* 133, 135–6.
[52] Matsuda (n 24). [53] Delgado (n 51). [54] Alexander (n 39) 76–85.

The question of whether hate speech has especially grave political, social, and psychological effects can in principle be examined empirically, and indeed there is some social science research examining the harmful effects of hate speech.[55] The opponents of harm-based arguments point out how difficult it is to establish the evidence for these harms and, even if those are established, to demonstrate the effectiveness of hate speech legislation and evaluate its long-term effects. They point out that it is not sufficient to show that hate speech inflicts severe and distinctive harms. In addition, one needs to show that legal regulation of hate speech is an effective means of addressing these harms.[56] It is also necessary to show that such regulation is unlikely to have other hidden costs. Perhaps even effective prohibitions would trigger resentment and thereby increase rather than decrease racial hatred. Perhaps, as Toni Massaro argues, silencing bigots only sends bigotry underground and may give bigots martyr status to boot.[57] Perhaps the pressure to enact such statutes may weaken the pressure to address racial hatred in other ways. Finally, perhaps the prohibitions may increase the visibility of hate speech and, consequently, its impact in the society.[58] These observations illustrate that even if propenents of the Critical Race Theory succeed in illustrating the uniqueness of the harms resulting from hate speech, they may fail to justify the enactment of prohibitions on hate speech—either because such prohibitions are ineffective or because they have unexpected or unaccounted for costs.[59]

Even if these empirical concerns could be addressed, one can still ask whether psychological harms are sufficient to justify restrictions on speech.[60] Liberal theorists in general are hostile to restrictions which rest on psychological sensibilities. Such sensibilities are simply too erratic to provide useful precise guidelines. Once offensiveness or emotional harms and the resulting alienation are in themselves a justification for imposing restrictions on speech the decision what is or what is not sufficiently offensive or harmful becomes manipulable and unpredictable. The famous Serrano photograph labelled 'Piss Christ', which depicts a small plastic crucifix submerged in a small glass tank of the artist's urine, is highly offensive to devout Christians, and yet it seems to be the price to pay in a free society. A free society is a society in which crude, impolite, disrespectful, and offensive statements are tolerated, and those often have an important role in awakening one's awareness to unpopular views. Hence, arguably, even extreme offensiveness (and the resulting alienation) cannot in itself justify the imposition of restrictions on speech.

---

[55] Gloria Cowan and Cyndi Hodge, 'Judgments of Hate Speech: The Effects of Target Group, Publicness, and Behavioral Responses of the Target' (1996) 26 J Appl Psych 355.

[56] Jean Stefancic and Richard Delgado, 'A Shifting Balance: Freedom of Expression and Hate-Speech Restriction' (1993) Iowa L Rev 737, 743–4; Shiffrin (n 19) 684.

[57] Nadine Strossen, 'Regulating Racist Speech on Campus: A Modest Proposal?' [1990] Duke LJ 484, 559–60; Massaro (n 9); Stefancic and Delgado (n 56) 744.

[58] Sally Reid and Russel Smith, 'Regulating Racial Hatred' (1998) Australian Institute of Criminology, Trends and Issues in Crime and Criminal Justice 79/1998. <https://aic.gov.au/publications/tandi/tandi79> accessed 22 April 2019; Stefancic and Delgado (n 56) 744.

[59] Strossen (n 57).   [60] Alexander (n 39) 86.

Last, even if critical race theorists are right in that hate speech is particularly harmful, one may still question whether the gravity of these harms overrides the concerns justifying the protection of speech. This requires a thorough examination of the justifications underlying the protection of speech and their relative strength. Pointing out that there are grave harms resulting from hate speech is not sufficient as, in addition, one needs to establish that these harms outweigh the gravity of the concerns that lead us to protect free speech in the first place.

25.3.2.2 *The Silencing Argument: Intrinsic Harms*

Under the silencing argument, the reason for the special treatment of hate speech is the fact that hate speech 'silences' its targets, and thereby free speech itself requires rather than precludes regulation of hate speech. This argument is particularly compelling as, unlike the discussion in the last subsection, it does not depend on the balancing of free speech with other rights or values such as dignity, equality, or psychological harms. Instead, under this argument, free speech itself requires rather than forbids the restriction of hate speech. The analogy to the treatment of pornography can also be used here. I shall examine this argument in the context of pornography and later show that it is applicable also to hate speech. Then I shall raise some critical concerns.

Catharine MacKinnon propagated the view that pornography 'silences women'. In her view, the anti-pornography legislation is not only not detrimental to free speech values; in fact, it is grounded in the same values as the values underlying the protection of speech itself. Regulation of pornography is necessary to protect women's speech.[61] There are different possible interpretations of this claim. First, the claim can be understood as suggesting that women are less likely to exercise their right to free speech as a result of pornography either because they are intimidated or because their inferior status in society (resulting from the prevalence of pornography) undermines their confidence and results in passivity and subordination. Second, the claim can be understood as suggesting that while women may exercise their right to free speech, they are unlikely to be heard; their speech is silenced, not in the sense that women fail to exercise their right to free speech, but in the sense that their speech fails to persuade or even be heard, or, at least, taken seriously. Women fail to be full-fledged participants in the marketplace of ideas because women speakers are perceived to be of lesser public importance or significance.

This argument has been imported from the context of pornography to the context of hate speech more generally. Thus, for instance, Caroline West suggests to:

> examine the prevailing assumption that the value of freedom of speech is necessarily only or best served by permitting racist hate speech. Racist hate speech could function to undermine freedom of speech, rather than to exemplify or enhance it.[62]

---

[61] MacKinnon (n 31) 164.
[62] Caroline West, 'Words that Silence? Freedom of Expression and Racist Hate Speech in Speech' in Ishani Matra and Mary Kate McGowan (eds), *Speech and Harm: Controversies over Free Speech* (OUP 2012) 222; Kathleen Sullivan, 'Free Speech Wars' (1994) 48 *SMU L Rev* 203.

In attacking this view (in the context of pornography), Ronald Dworkin has argued that the right to free speech does not include 'a right to circumstances that encourage one to speak, and a right that others grasp and respect what one means to say'.[63] In his view, the right to free speech is a negative right designed to remove any state-induced barriers to speech, but it is not designed to provide favourable circumstances for speech or to guarantee a favourable audience.[64] Yet, as has been shown persuasively by rights theorists, this view has some major disadvantages.[65] After all, at least part of the value of the right to free speech is grounded in the fact that many people of different persuasions *exercise* such a right. If some forms of speech intimidate and humiliate in ways which curtail the exercise of the right to free speech, why should we not limit the right in ways that, in the long run, reinforce the willingness to engage in speech; that is, exercise the right?

There are two counter-arguments to the silencing argument. First, institutional concerns, in particular the concern of abuse, may limit our willingness to take the silencing argument into account. Given the impreciseness of the concept of silencing political institutions may be too restrictive and be prone to restrict speech which needs to be protected. Second, the empirical doubts raised earlier are also relevant here. It is quite difficult and speculative to argue that hate speech 'silences' and, further, to measure how much it silences. Perhaps the very existence of hate speech induces minority members to raise their political voice and perhaps it also triggers greater sympathy on the part of the public. This does not mean of course that hate speech ought to be condoned in order to bring about these effects, but it means that it does not silence minorities.

To sum up, there are two types of harm-based arguments. The first rests on claims concerning the special gravity of extrinsic harms resulting from hate speech (eg, alienation and the failure on the part of minorities to integrate into the society). The second argument (the silencing argument) rests on the view that, ironically, the protection of hate speech undermines the values of the right to free speech itself. We have seen that while these arguments are powerful they are not free of difficulties. Most importantly, these arguments rest on certain speculative factual presuppositions concerning the kind of and the gravity of the harms resulting from hate speech. It seems that while much of the debate between proponents and opponents of hate speech legislation is conceptualized in empirical terms, the empirical claims used by both parties are too speculative; perhaps, therefore, something other than empirical claims govern the controversy. We will return to this point later, but first let us examine some of the arguments against the regulation of hate speech.

---

[63] Dworkin (n 31) 232.

[64] Ibid; Charles Fried, 'The New First Amendment Jurisprudence: A Threat to Liberty' (1992) 59 *U Chi L Rev* 225, 226–8.

[65] Charles Taylor, *Philosophy and the Human Sciences: Philosophical Papers 2* (CUP 1985) ch 7, 'Atomism'.

25.4 Arguments against Regulating Hate Speech

Opponents of regulating hate speech provide equally powerful arguments why hate speech should be protected. There is a large overlap between the general arguments used to justify the protection of speech in general and the arguments used to justify the protection of hate speech. It is beyond the scope of this chapter to provide a comprehensive survey of the justifications for free speech. In this section, I will explore only some arguments that have been used or can be used specifically in the context of hate speech legislation.

25.4.1 The Institutional Arguments

One of the standard arguments against the regulation of speech in general and the regulation of hate speech in particular is based on the belief that political and legal institutions are not to be trusted in drawing the boundaries of speech, as they are either too ignorant or too biased to draw the boundaries between speech that ought to be protected and speech that ought to be regulated. Further, as a general rule, we should prefer to err by protecting speech that ought not to be protected than by regulating speech that ought not to be protected. Opponents of regulation of hate speech point out that almost inevitably such prohibitions would depend on institutional discretion.[66] Government often has self-serving incentives to over-regulate speech and it ought not to be trusted. This concern is even greater when private entities (such as entities that host or index content—Internet intermediaries) are required (or able) to monitor hate speech.[67]

One of the most powerful arguments in this context is provided by Daniel Farber, who argues that because information is a public good it is likely to be undervalued both by the private and by the political market. Speech ought to be protected not because it is particularly valuable but because political and perhaps also legal institutions are particularly prone to under-estimate its value and therefore to over-regulate speech.[68] Hence, political institutions ought not be trusted.[69]

There are at least two separate institutional arguments. Some have argued that governments inevitably use hate speech legislation to suppress minorities.[70] One prominent example is the conviction in France of pro-Palestinian activists, who were prosecuted

---

[66] Kathleen Sullivan, 'Free Speech and Unfree Markets' (1995) 42 *UCLA L Rev* 949.

[67] Danielle Keats Citron and Helen Norton, 'Intermediaries and Hate Speech: Fostering Digital Citizenship for Our Information Age' (2011) 91 *BU L Rev* 1435.

[68] Daniel Farber, 'Free Speech Without Romance: Public Choice and the First Amendment' (1991) 105 *Harv L Rev* 554.

[69] Sullivan (n 66).

[70] Glenn Greenwald, 'In Europe Hate Speech Laws are Often Used to Suppress and Punish Left-Wing Viewpoints' (The Intercept, 30 May 2017) <https://theintercept.com/2017/08/29/in-europe-hate-speech-laws-are-often-used-to-suppress-and-punish-left-wing-viewpoints/> accessed 22 April 2019.

for their support of the Boycott, Divestment, Sanctions (BDS) movement against Israel. Others have argued that even if hate speech legislation is not abused, it is subject to the problem of slippery slope, namely a gradual expansion of the scope of hate speech prohibitions.[71] After all, the boundaries between what is hate speech and what is not are blurred and there is a natural disposition to stretch the meaning of hate speech.[72]

Both concerns ought to be taken seriously. Hence, one of the most important considerations in the decision whether to regulate hate speech or not is the question of whether we can draw clear boundaries and thus restrain the disposition of political and legal institutions to over-regulate speech. Further, to establish the soundness of the institutional argument, the fear of over-regulation should be shown to be greater than the fear of under-regulation. Even if the former risk is greater than the latter risk, it needs to be established that narrow and well-defined rules cannot overcome these institutional concerns. This is not an easy or even a feasible task.

25.4.2 The Millian 'Dead Dogma' Argument

In *On Liberty*, John Stuart Mill discusses in great detail the reasons for the protection of speech. Among his many contributions in this book is the 'dead dogma' argument. Mill argues:

> However unwillingly a person who has a strong opinion may admit the possibility that his opinion may be false, he ought to be moved by the consideration that however true it may be, if it is not fully, frequently, and fearlessly discussed, it will be held as a dead dogma, not a living truth. There is a class of persons (happily not quite so numerous as formerly) who think it enough if a person assents undoubtingly to what they think true, though he has no knowledge whatever of the grounds of the opinion, and could not make a tenable defence of it against the most superficial objections.[73]

This is a powerful argument. Mill believes that suppression of speech is not only detrimental when it suppresses valuable speech, but also detrimental when it suppresses prejudices and falsities. The truth need not only be believed or adhered to; in addition, it needs to be debated, challenged, and rethought. As the Talmud says: 'two knives sharpen each other'.[74] To be a 'living truth' rather than a 'dead dogma' the most fundamental beliefs concerning equality and dignity need to be subject to criticisms. Mill's dead dogma metaphor is powerful and, at the same time, could be criticized in this context on the grounds that it is

---

[71] Eugene Volokh, 'The Mechanisms of the Slippery Slope' (2003) 116 *Harv L Rev* 1026.
[72] Michael McConnell, 'You Can't Say That: "The Harm in Hate Speech" by Jeremy Waldron' *New York Times* (22 June 2012) 14; Greenwald (n 70).
[73] JS Mill, *On Liberty and Other Writings* (Stefan Collini ed, CUP 1989) 37.
[74] *Genesis Rabbah: The Judaic Commentary to the Book of Genesis* (Jacob Neusner tr, Brown UP 1985) ch 69.

based on a too idealistic perception of public discourse. Much of hate speech is based on prejudice and the Talmudic metaphor of sharpening knives presupposes some degree of thoughtfulness (or, at least intellectual sharpness) on the part of participants.

Yet, even if we admit that much of hate speech cannot serve to guarantee the status of 'living truth' to the conviction concerning equality and dignity, it may still have an indirect positive role in inducing people to challenge the most foundational convictions and to maintain a degree of scepticism concerning conventional beliefs. Arguably, this can in the long run contribute to a deeper and more intense public discourse as it may reinforce scepticism and, consequently, deliberativeness.

25.4.3 Entrenchment of Differences: The Vices of Identity Politics

Protection of hate speech requires identifying the protected groups. Some theorists argue that by defining the protected groups, the legal system entrenches these categories. Jacobs and Potter speak of balkanization, arguing that hate crime legislation entrenches the perception that individuals belong to well-defined groups and thus reinforces hostility and conflict.[75] This argument can be applied also to hate speech legislation. The identity categories that are used to protect groups tend to perpetuate their distinct existence and to trigger conflicts between these groups and other groups.[76] Moran and Sharpe argue that legal categorization may 'deny multiplicity, complexity and ambiguity'.[77] Further, it is argued that the categories used by the law are not always the most important or significant categories of identity.[78]

Essentializing and entrenchment of difference and its divisive effects is a general problem of laws that use identity categories. The very same difficulties exist also in the context of affirmative action laws and in other contexts. The question to what extent such laws affect, perpetuate, or transform identity or merely reflect pre-existing identity is also in principle an empirical matter. It needs, however, to be conceded that even if hate speech legislation has desirable effects, it may also contribute to the undesirable entrenchment of identity.

25.4.4 Hate Speech and Multiculturalism

Hate speech is, as some have argued, a too broad category. It could be either a part of a valuable comprehensive form of life (eg, religion), or else it could be a relatively isolated expression of hatred. Arguably, hate speech may have redeeming values stemming not

---

[75] James Jacobs and Kimberly Potter, *Hate Crimes: Criminal Law and Identity Politics* (OUP 1998) 8.
[76] Neller (n 2).
[77] Leslie Moran and Andrew Sharpe, 'Violence, Identity and Policing: The Case of Violence against Transgender People' (2004) 4 *Crim Justice* 395.
[78] Neller (n 2).

from its being speech but from its being an integral part of a comprehensive valuable form of life such as religion. This observation demonstrates the relevance of multiculturalism to the proper regulation of hate speech.[79]

Multiculturalists advocate granting special respect and privileges to cultures.[80] This often justifies the protection of traditional non-egalitarian practices, if and when those practices are part of comprehensive forms of life.[81]

A comprehensive form of life is composed of a thick interconnected network of values, beliefs, practices, rituals, and ceremonies. In other words, practices and rituals are perceived as tangible manifestations of values, principles, and beliefs, but beliefs and values are abstract formulations or self-understandings of practices and rituals. There is therefore mutual interdependence between values, beliefs, and practices, which together form a comprehensive form of life. Values justify and rationalize practices, but practices express and convey values, and thus help sustain them. Religions are the most characteristic forms of such comprehensive forms of life. Besides religions, one can identify other long-term ideological and cultural commitments which can be characterized as 'comprehensive forms of life'.

This description enables one to identify several important features of comprehensive forms of life. First, comprehensive forms of life are typically dependent upon the existence of a community. It is difficult and perhaps even conceptually impossible to comprehend an individual developing by themselves or for themselves a comprehensive form of life. Second, a comprehensive form of life typically involves an intensive commitment of individuals—commitment which is required in order to sustain the form of life and develop it. The degree of commitment differs from one person to another, and different comprehensive forms of life may require different forms of commitment. Finally, it seems that comprehensive forms of life provide individuals with a sense of identity and belongingness. It defines what they perceive is essential to their identity.

What is the relevance of these considerations to hate speech? The answer is that often (although not always) hate speech is but an aspect of a comprehensive form of life. The recent Israeli Supreme Court cases concerning hate speech can establish this observation. In one of the leading cases, a distinguished rabbi of a yeshiva located at one of the holy sites published a Halakhic ruling that Jews ought not to rent out apartments to Arabs. He added that Arabs were a major threat to Jews. The identity of the speaker (a rabbi) and the style of discourse which he chose indicate that his speech is part of what he perceived to be the Jewish tradition.

The legal establishment considered the possibility of prosecuting the rabbi and, eventually, the Attorney-General decided not to prosecute. A petition against this decision was submitted and rejected by the Supreme Court (HCJ 9290/10). In contrast, in CA 2831/95 the Supreme Court affirmed the conviction of Rabbi Elba on the grounds

---

[79] Alon Harel 'Hate Speech and Comprehensive Forms of Life' in Michael Herz and Peter Molnar (eds), *The Content and Context of Hate Speech* (CUP 2012) 306.
[80] Will Kymlicka, *Multicultural Citizenship: A Liberal Theory of Minority Rights* (OUP 1996).
[81] Joseph Raz, *Ethics in the Public Domain: Essays in the Morality of Law and Politics* (Clarendon 1995) ch 7, 'Free Expression and Personal Identification'.

that he incited racism. The primary theoretical question we are interested in here is not the doctrinal soundness of these decisions but whether the cultural context of the speech—its being an integral part of a comprehensive form of life—ought to influence its regulation.

John Locke thought that it should not. Locke expressed his conviction that baptizing a child could be adequately perceived by the state as the practice of 'washing an infant with water'. Therefore, it ought to be regulated only if the practice of 'washing infants with water' has a negative effect on their health.[82] Of course, Christianity would reject such a thin description of baptism as an inadequate one. Baptizing, it would be argued, is different than washing an infant with water because it is bound up with numerous beliefs as to its spiritual significance. The political theorist needs to ask whether the state and, in particular, the legal system ought to accept Locke's position and abstract all cultural practices from their immense cultural richness, or whether in deciding whether to regulate these practices, it should take into account their rich significance for its adherents. In the context of hate speech, the question is whether religious-based or cultural-based hate speech deserve to be protected more than hate speech that is not grounded in comprehensive forms of life.

In the case of isolated instances of harmful conduct—ones that are not deeply rooted in particular cultures or religions—censorship or criminal punishment express the (justified) disapproval of the particular act of expression. Its condemnatory force targets the speech and only the speech. In contrast, if the speech is bound up and interconnected with other values and practices, it is the whole tradition which is being condemned by censoring it.

A critic would argue that this claim is false. The state, under this view, prohibits the speech and not the other benign religious practices. The prohibition on hate speech condemns what it prohibits, namely the hate speech, and does not condemn what it does not prohibit, namely other religious practices. Why should such a prohibition be understood as condemning the religion as such?

The answer is that the state cannot determine the social significance of the prohibitions it issues. Of course, the state controls what it prohibits, but it does not control how its prohibitions are understood and/or interpreted by those who are subject to it. Given that harmful behaviour including hate speech is perceived as interconnected with other practices and values, it is inevitable that the prohibition of deeply rooted harmful practices or the censorship of hate speech will be understood as condemning the form of life as such, rather than merely a harmful practice or speech. The social meaning of the state's regulation is not determined exclusively by the state's own intentions; or even by the content of the state's prohibitions. The meaning is constructed in a dialogue between the state and the relevant cultural community, and regulation of hate speech which forms part of comprehensive forms of life is typically understood as a direct condemnation of the form of life and the values it stands

---

[82] John Locke, *Two Treatises of Government and a Letter Concerning Toleration* (Ian Shapiro ed, Yale UP 2003) 233–4.

for. This explains why certain harmful religious practices often give rise to legal exemptions, such as the exemption enjoyed by turban-wearing Sikhs to ride motorcycles without helmets, despite the resulting risks.

To sum up, under this argument, censoring hate speech which constitutes part of comprehensive forms of life is bound to be understood as a public condemnation of the form of life as a whole, and not merely of the expression itself. To prevent such a condemnation of forms of life, hate speech conducted within the frame of such a tradition ought to be tolerated at least in cases in which it does not cause the immediate eruption of violence.

Comprehensive forms of life are composed of interconnected chains of beliefs and practices; they are therefore indivisible wholes. Regulation of deeply rooted hate speech would inevitably be understood as condemnation of a form of life—forms of life which has noble aspects; it is often conducive to the forming of cultural communities and solidarity among members of the community. Hence, the state ought to be particularly cautious in regulating hate speech in these cases.

25.5 CONCLUSION

This chapter does not purport to provide an answer to the question of whether hate speech ought to be regulated and if so, how to do it. The chapter pointed out that hate speech legislation divides not only liberals and conservatives or liberals and radicals. In addition, it divides liberals, as there are foundational liberal values that support as well oppose the regulation of hate speech.

The chapter also contested that many of the arguments concerning hate speech are grounded in speculative empirical conjectures. Theorists ask questions such as what the psychological effects of hate speech are; what the likelihood that they bring about violence; what the likelihood that our political institutions abuse their powers and regulate speech that ought to be regulated or fail to regulate speech that ideally ought to be protected. As I have claimed elsewhere, such arguments are often mere rationalizations for more foundational convictions and sentiments.[83]

What are therefore the underlying foundational convictions dividing the advocates and opponents of hate speech legislation? Needless to say there may be more than one issue dividing the participants in this debate. However, let me raise one important consideration. In the context of the free speech debate some people are disposed to the conviction that individuals can (and should) withstand social pressures and can (and should) grow and flourish despite prevalent social hatred. In their view, too great protection on the part of the state is not only dangerous when the state abuses its powers but also when it acts properly. Individuals should courageously face the burdens resulting from the ignorance and prejudices of others. In contrast, others believe that individuals

[83] Alon Harel, *Why Law Matters* (OUP 2014).

are part of the social fabric of society and hate speech undermines the very ability to lead a flourishing life. The debate concerning hate speech hinges, therefore, on fundamental disagreements concerning the nature of human beings, their ability to resist social pressures, and the degree of protection they need in order to preserve their dignity. It is ultimately these conflicting foundational premises rather than empirical conjectures which should dictate whether and how much to regulate hate speech.

CHAPTER 26

PORNOGRAPHY

CAROLINE WEST

26.1 Introduction

PORNOGRAPHY is often defended on the basis of freedom of speech or expression. Even if some pornography is not just offensive but actively harmful, it is speech; and, as such, enjoys the special protections generally extended to speech in liberal societies.[1] In the United States, pornography even enjoys legal protection under the free speech clause of the First Amendment of the US Constitution.

But is pornography genuinely a form of 'speech' (or 'expression') in the relevant sense, as the traditional defence assumes? And if pornography is a kind of speech, does it really deserve to be protected? Or is (some) pornography so harmful that anti-pornography regulation of some kind may be justified, even if it would interfere with pornographers' free speech? Furthermore, what if—as some prominent feminists argue—pornography 'silences' some speakers, or systematically interferes with their communicative capacities? Could there actually be a free speech argument *against* (some) pornography?

Traditionally, liberals and libertarians defended a moral right to pornography from conservatives who objected to pornography's obscenity and its morally corrupting effect on producers and consumers. Since the 1970s, however, the most powerful arguments for legal restriction of (some) pornography have come from feminists concerned about pornography's (alleged) harms to women. Pornography's feminist opponents share with liberals a commitment to the harm principle: the idea that the state can only legitimately legislate to restrict the choices of consenting adults in order to prevent harm to others. But they disagree with pornography's liberal defenders that pornography—even at its most violent and misogynistic—is just harmless entertainment; or that any harms associated with such pornography are outweighed by greater costs involved in restricting it,

---

[1] For a classic discussion of the distinction between harm and offence, see Joel Feinberg, *Offense to Others* (OUP 1985) chs 11 and 12.

so that it falls entirely to private individuals to do what they can (eg, though protests or boycotts) to counter these harms.

This chapter will critically examine the traditional free speech defence of pornography, as well as prominent feminist arguments for legal regulation of some pornography, before turning to discuss a surprising but increasingly influential free speech based line of argument against pornography. In discussing these matters, my primary focus will be on general issues of political morality, rather than questions of legal (eg, First Amendment) interpretation.

The topic of pornography is important for several reasons. The decades following the emergence of the Internet have seen an explosion in the amount of readily accessible pornography, much of which is explicitly or implicitly violent and misogynistic; and pornography use is rampant among adolescents as well as adults. Contemporary liberal democratic societies, which value equality as well as free speech, therefore face challenging and pressing questions about how best to respond to the proliferation of violent and degrading pornography.

The topic of pornography is also of broader interest for free speech theorists, for contemporary speech act accounts of pornography and silencing engage fundamental questions about the nature and value of speech. How should we understand the meaning of 'speech' in the context of discussions of free speech? Is there more to free speech than simply 'locutionary freedom' of speakers to produce and disseminate meaningful words and their expressive equivalents without government interference? What other linguistic and social conditions undermine (or promote) mental communication? Drawing on philosophy of language, some influential recent work on pornography by feminist philosophers directs attention to previously under-recognized ways in which the speaking capacity of speakers can be curtailed by the speech acts of others—including, perhaps, pornographers.

To begin, let us try to clarify the meaning of 'pornography'.

26.2 On 'Pornography'

'Pornography' is notoriously difficult to define. There are many different types of pornography, catering for many different audiences; and multiple alternate definitions of 'pornography' have been proposed.[2] These conceptions differ, sometimes dramatically, not simply about *what* material is pornographic, and *why*, but also about whether 'pornography' is a purely descriptive term, or whether it has an evaluative component. Different uses of 'pornography' have the potential to lead to confusion

---

[2] For more detailed discussion see, eg, Leslie Green, 'Pornographies' (2000) 8 *J Pol Phil* 27; Michael C Rea 'What is Pornography?' (2001) 35 *Noûs* 118; Caroline West, 'Pornography and Censorship' (*Stanford Encyclopedia of Philosophy*, 5 May 2004) <https://plato.stanford.edu/entries/pornography-censorship/> accessed 23 June 2019, section 1.

and misunderstanding. To avoid this, it is important to be clear about what particular conception is being deployed in any given discussion, and why.

On one common definition, pornography is sexually explicit material (pictures or words) which is primarily designed to produce sexual arousal in viewers. This definition is descriptive because it leaves open whether pornography is in any way morally problematic or harmful. Within the general category of pornography, so defined, distinctions are also drawn between 'hardcore' and 'softcore' pornography; and between 'violent', 'non-violent and degrading', and 'non-violent and non-degrading' pornography. 'Feminist pornography' is a subset of pornography (in this general sense) that aims to subvert traditional gender roles, bodies, and narratives unreflectively endorsed by mainstream heterosexual pornography.

Other definitions of 'pornography' are evaluative or moralized: it is built into the definition that pornography is (somehow) bad. Moralized approaches are common among pornography's critics, who may use the term 'pornography' specifically to single out the particular type of material that possesses the (allegedly) objectionable feature. When used in a moralized way, 'pornography' functions as a semi-technical term with a specific meaning and scope that may depart somewhat from ordinary usage.

One influential moralized approach, which has provided the dominant legal framework for understanding pornography in the United States and the UK, defines pornography in terms of *obscenity*: a work is obscene if an average, reasonable person applying community standards would find the work as a whole to lack any serious literary, artistic, political, or scientific value, and the work describes or depicts in an obvious way offensive sexual conduct.[3] On this conception, which is employed by many of pornography's conservative critics, pornography should be regulated because it transgresses certain (allegedly) shared community standards of morality or decency, and thus counts as obscene.

Many anti-pornography feminist definitions of pornography are also moralized—although in an importantly different way to that of conservatives. Unlike conservatives, who object to pornography's obscenity, anti-pornography feminists have no objection to material that is merely sexually explicit or offensive; rather, feminist concern centres squarely on (alleged) *harms to women*. This focus is reflected in the distinctive way that many anti-pornography feminists define pornography as sexually explicit material that harms women in certain way(s)—for example, which depicts the abuse and degradation of women in such a way as to endorse, encourage, or eroticize it.[4] On some feminist

---

[3] Susan Dwyer (ed), *The Problem of Pornography* (Wadsworth 1995) 242, 245; Catherine Itzin (ed), *Pornography: Women, Violence and Civil Liberties* (OUP 1992). For critical discussion of this approach see Frederick Schauer, *Free Speech: A Philosophical Enquiry* (CUP 1982); Joel Feinberg, *Harm to Others* (OUP 1987); Catharine MacKinnon, *Feminism Unmodified: Discourses on Life and Law* (Harvard UP 1987) chs 13 and 14.

[4] See, eg, Itzin (n 3); Helen Longino, 'Pornography, Oppression, and Freedom: A Closer Look' in Laura Lederer (ed), *Take Back the Night* (William Morrow 1980) 40; Diana Russell, 'Pornography and Rape: A Causal Model' in Drucilla Cornell (ed), *Feminism and Pornography* (OUP 2000); Jennifer Saul, *Feminism: Issues and Arguments* (OUP 2003) ch 3.

definitions, pornography need not even be sexually explicit; material that merely implies certain messages about sex can sometimes count as pornography if it contributes in certain ways to sexualized violence and oppression.

Perhaps the best-known (and most controversial) feminist definition of pornography is provided by Andrea Dworkin and Catharine MacKinnon, who define 'pornography' as the 'graphic sexually explicit subordination of women through pictures and/or words'.[5] This includes women, for example, dehumanized as sexual objects, enjoying humiliation or pain, physically hurt, presented in positions of sexual submission or degradation, or reduced to body parts. This definition allows that material that uses or treats men, transpeople, or children in place of women, may also count as pornography. This definition formed the basis of their well-known Antipornography Civil Rights Ordinance, which was ultimately struck down by US courts as unconstitutional on the grounds that it violated pornographers' First Amendment right to free speech. So defined, pornography is *necessarily* harmful in a particular way (it subordinates women), and objectionable for this reason. On this definition, there is not—indeed, there *could* not be—any such thing as good pornography. Dworkin and MacKinnon distinguish 'pornography', so defined, from harmless sexually explicit 'erotica', which depicts mutually respectful sexual relations between consenting adults. Since the type(s) of sexually explicit material that count as obscene may differ somewhat from those that harm women, conservative and feminist definitions of 'pornography' are not coextensive—in particular, unlike conservatives, anti-pornography feminists have no objection to harmless sexually explicit erotica.

It may seem question-begging to define pornography as material that is somehow harmful, however this is not so. For it is a further substantive question exactly what (if any) types of sexually explicit material are harmful in the relevant ways, and so fall under the extension of the term 'pornography', so defined. This is the subject of ongoing discussion and dispute. Images that endorse brutalization and degradation of women will count in principle, but there is room for debate about whether a particular film or genre really functions in this way. For example, there may be dispute about whether a film that depicts hierarchical sexual relations in order to *subvert* (rather than endorse) traditional sexual hierarchies, actually succeeds in this aim, and thus counts as harmless 'erotica' (rather than 'pornography'), in MacKinnon's sense. This issue is complex because whether a particular film or image is functioning to endorse oppressive sexual hierarchies seems to be context-sensitive; it depends not simply on the intrinsic content of the material, but also on how it is interpreted or used on a particular occasion.[6] The very same material—for example, a graphic documentary film about the sex trade—might count as pornography in one context (eg, if used for masturbation), but not in another (eg, when shown in gender studies class). Likewise, although it may *depict* sexual

---

[5] MacKinnon, *Feminism Unmodified* (n 3) 156. See also Andrea Dworkin, *Pornography: Men Possessing Women* (Women's P 1981); Catharine MacKinnon, *Toward a Feminist Theory of the State* (Harvard UP 1989); Catharine MacKinnon, *Only Words* (Harvard UP 1993).

[6] Mary Kate McGowan, *Just Words: On Speech and Hidden Harm* (OUP 2019) ch 6.

relations of domination and submission, BDSM material may not function to *endorse* hierarchical sexual relations on many or most occasions of use. If so, it would fall in the category of unobjectionable erotica, rather than harmful pornography. Because of this context-sensitivity, attempts to define pornography in terms of a simple content list are likely to be problematic.

I will not attempt here to develop or defend any particular way of defining 'pornography'—in part because I believe that what conception is most useful depends upon one's immediate interests or aims, and these may vary from occasion to occasion. However, when it matters, I will take care to specify which of the many senses of 'pornography' is in play.

26.3 Is Pornography 'Speech'?

The free speech defence of pornography assumes that pornography is speech, in the sense of 'speech' relevant to a free speech principle. This starting assumption has important consequences for debates over regulation of pornography, for the high cultural and legal value that liberal societies place on freedom of speech means that it can be significantly harder to justify regulation of speech than of non-speech conduct: levels of harm that would be sufficient to justify regulation of non-speech conduct may be deemed insufficient when the object of the proposed regulation concerns speech. Hence, while debates about whether pornography should be regulated often focus on whether the harms associated with pornography are sufficient to outweigh a weighty background presumption in favour of free speech, the first question to ask is whether pornography should be treated as a kind of speech at all.

As Frederick Schauer has argued, not all 'speech' in the ordinary conversational sense is or deserves to be covered by a free speech principle.[7] Perjury, insider trading, 'Whites Only' signs, and oral or written fraud are all forms of 'speech' in the ordinary sense, yet their regulation raises no free speech concerns; there is no free speech defence of perjury, for example. It is not that there are free speech considerations in favour of permitting perjury, which then get outweighed by countervailing costs; rather, acts such as perjury are not covered by a free speech principle in the first place.

Conversely, some things that do not satisfy the ordinary definition of 'speech' seem to count as speech in the sense relevant to a free speech principle—for example, silent protest vigils or flag-burning. Thus, 'speech' in the context of a free speech principle seems to function as a semi-technical term that encompasses both somewhat more and less than 'speech' in the ordinary conversational sense.

---

[7] Frederick Schauer, 'The Boundaries of the First Amendment: A Preliminary Explanation of Constitutional Salience' (1972) 117 *Harv L Rev* 1765; Frederick Schauer, 'Speech and "Speech"—Obscenity and "Obscenity": An Exercise in the Interpretation of Constitutional Language' (1979) 67 *Geo LJ* 899; Schauer, *Free Speech* (n 3); see also Schauer, Chapter 9 in this volume.

Is pornography speech in the relevant semi-technical sense? This depends partly on how we should define 'speech' in the context of a free speech principle. This is obviously a large and complex topic that cannot be considered in detail here. One promising approach is to use the underlying rationale(s) for giving special protection to an area of conduct called 'speech' to settle the scope of speech.[8] As Jennifer Hornsby and Rae Langton put it: '[w]hat one ought to mean by "speech", in the context of discussions of free speech, is whatever it is that a correct justification of the right to free speech justifies one in protecting.'[9] An advantage of this approach is that it ensures that our general commitment to a free speech principle is justified—just so long as there actually is some conduct to which we have reasons of the relevant kind to extend special protection.[10]

Exactly what things do or would fall under the extension of 'speech', so determined, is a substantive issue. It is questionable, however, that it includes all pornography. Consider, for example, the classic Millian justification of free speech in terms of its role in promoting truth (or knowledge).[11] As a matter of fact, it is unlikely that the production and consumption of pornography is generally conducive to the discovery of truth or knowledge. As Ronald Dworkin observes, 'most pornography makes no contribution at all to political or intellectual debate: it is preposterous to think that we are more likely to reach truth about anything at all because pornographic videos are available.'[12] Alternatively, consider the justification of free speech in terms of democracy, according to which free speech is valuable because citizens in a democracy need access to information in order to make well-informed political decisions, and to be free from obstruction in making their own views known and having an impact on the political process. Again, it is hard to see how pornography—especially violent and degrading pornography—contributes much to informed political deliberation or effective participation. Of course, there are several other justifications of a free speech principle. All of them, however, locate the value of speech in some good inherent in, or associated with, mental communication. Freedom of speech matters, not because of some intrinsic value possessed by orthographic tokens, but because their production and distribution is the necessary means by which we communicate our thoughts and feelings to each other. Certain types of pornography, however, do not seem to be in the business of communicating ideas, and may even function in ways that impede successful mental communication.

---

[8] See further David Braddon-Mitchell and Caroline West, 'What is Free Speech' (2004) 12 *J PolPhil* 437.

[9] Jennifer Hornsby and Rae Langton, 'Free Speech and Illocution' (1998) 4 *Legal Theory* 21: see also Section 26.5 below.

[10] Cf Stanley Fish, *There's No Such Thing as Free Speech—And It's a Good Thing, Too* (OUP 1994); Larry Alexander, *Is There a Right of Freedom of Expression?* (CUP 2005).

[11] John Stuart Mill, *On Liberty* (Hackett 1978) ch 2; see also Macleod, Chapter 1 in this volume; and Blasi, Chapter 2 in this volume.

[12] Ronald Dworkin, 'Women and Pornography', *New York Review of Books* (New York, 21 October 1993).

In this vein, Schauer argues that hardcore pornography is not 'speech' in the First Amendment sense because it is not in the business of mental communication.[13] Rather, it functions as a purely physical aid to sex, akin to a mechanical sex toy. Just as production and distribution of rubber sex toys cannot plausibly be given a free speech defence, so there is no free speech defence for hardcore pornography—for the reason that hardcore pornography is not 'speech' in the relevant sense. More recently, Ishani Maitra and Mary Kate McGowan have argued that if (some) pornography functions in the way that anti-pornography feminists such as Catharine MacKinnon claim, then it is not covered by the First Amendment.[14] If these scholars are right, pornography cannot legitimately be defended on the ground of free speech, and anti-pornography regulation should not be seen as raising any free speech concerns whatsoever.

26.4 Should Pornography Be Protected?

Suppose, however, for the sake of argument, that pornography is a form of speech. Should it be protected, or is (some) pornography harmful enough to justify anti-pornography legislation—either in the form of criminal liability or civil penalties—even on the assumption that pornography is speech? For, although liberal societies place a high value on speech, freedom of speech is not, and has never been, absolute. Even in the United States, where speech enjoys exceptionally stringent levels of protection by international standards, there are laws against some harmful speech, such as defamation. In a liberal society, whether legal regulation of pornography is justified depends on whether the likely harms associated with regulating pornography (including costs to free speech) outweigh those of permitting it, and whether other, less restrictive means of preventing these harms are available.

If we start from the assumption that pornography is a form of speech, however, then the scales are tipped against regulation from the outset.[15] Precisely how heavily the scales are weighted in favour of free speech depends on how highly free speech should be valued and what is the best way to respond to possible conflicts and trade-offs between free speech and other values. Liberal societies differ somewhat in how they deal with these questions. While most liberal societies outside the United States recognize constraints on free speech imposed by values such as equality and dignity, and on this basis defend regulation of hate speech, US courts (along with many US legal theorists)

---

[13] See Schauer, 'The Boundaries of the First Amendment' (n 7); Schauer, 'Speech and "Speech"' (n 7); Schauer, *Free Speech* (n 3).

[14] Ishani Maitra and Mary Kate McGowan, 'The Limits of Free Speech: Pornography and the Question of Coverage' (2007) 13 *Legal Theory* 41. The view that pornography is not speech should be distinguished from the view that it is 'low-value' speech.

[15] This assumes the traditional libertarian conception of free speech as 'negative locutionary freedom'. On a different conception of free speech, the scales may not be weighted so heavily in favour of pornographers: see further Section 26.5 below.

have often resisted such attempts at 'balancing', holding that the commitment to free speech must remain near 'absolute'. This means that in the United States, arguments for legal regulation of certain types of harmful hate speech and pornography must meet an exceptionally high burden of proof.

Notwithstanding its putative status as speech, it is undisputed (even in the United States) that at least some pornography should be regulated. Child pornography is regulated in order to prevent direct harm to (child) actors. Snuff films, recording actual rape and murder of actors, are (or would be) illegal for a similar reason. (On the other hand, realistic simulations of sexual abuse of women and children remain legal in many liberal jurisdictions.) Strictly speaking then, what is at issue in contemporary debates over regulating pornography is whether legal regulation of *further* types of pornography—such as violent and misogynistic pornography made and used by ostensibly consenting adults in private—is permissible or desirable.

26.4.1 The Traditional Pornography Debate: Liberals versus Conservatives

According to traditional liberal defence of pornography, further regulation of pornography would constitute illegitimate state interference with individual liberty—including, pornographers' freedom of speech—and place us on a dangerous slippery slope to thought control. Liberal defenders of pornography usually concede that if there was reliable evidence that production and consumption of pornography was associated with extremely significant third-party harms, such as a substantial increase in the incidence of violent sexual crime, then regulation of the types of pornography responsible might be justified. However, they claim, there is insufficient evidence to associate violent or misogynistic pornography with significant harm. Insofar as performers are all consenting adults, no one is harmed in the making of pornography; and no one is harmed as a result of the consumption of pornography, for consumers are perfectly well equipped to distinguish pornographic 'fantasy' from reality.[16] Consequently, pornography use has no negative effects on consumers' attitudes and behaviour towards women in the real world.[17] (As will be discussed later, the empirical evidence about pornography's effects is hotly disputed.) Because the production and use of pornography by consenting adults is comparatively harmless, anti-pornography regulation would constitute illegitimate interference with pornographers' freedom of speech. Moreover, given the difficulty of defining pornography, there is a real danger that anti-pornography regulation would be used, intentionally or unintentionally, to threaten further sorts of speech, and would have a more general 'chilling effect' on speech.

---

[16] See Ronald Dworkin, *A Matter of Principle* (1986 Harvard UP), ch 17.

[17] For discussion of how consumption of pornographic 'fiction' could influence user's attitudes to women in the real world, see Rae Langton and Caroline West, 'Scorekeeping in a Pornographic Language Game' (1999) 77 *Australasian J Phil* 303.

The traditional liberal defence is a defence of a *right* to pornography—that is, a negative right of consenting adults not to be prevented by the state from producing and viewing pornography in private—not necessarily a defence of pornography itself, which pornography's liberal defenders may personally disapprove of. Putting up with speech we dislike is the price we must pay for enjoying the freedom to express our opinions— even if it is not 'we' (ie, white male judges) but women who may disproportionately pay this price.[18] Of course, while traditional free speech defenders of pornography have been liberals and libertarians, not all liberals defend a right to pornography. Some liberals argue that pornography—particularly pornography that depicts and endorses sexual violence and degradation—is harmful in ways that justify legal regulation.[19]

Traditionally, liberals' main opponents in debates over pornography have been moral and religious conservatives. According to conservatives, the state should prohibit production and consumption of all pornography on the grounds that it is morally corrupting and indecent, or leads to indecency by promoting promiscuity and other allegedly 'deviant' sexual acts.[20] Conservatives typically include all sexually explicit material primarily intended for sexual gratification within the category of pornography, since conservatives tend to view all such material as obscene. According to conservatives, the state is justified in using its coercive powers to uphold certain community standards ('legal moralism'), and to prevent individuals from harming themselves ('legal paternalism'). This is true even when the individuals concerned are not minors who lack the mental capacities to make informed decisions, but fully consenting mentally competent adults.[21] The state is therefore justified in prohibiting the production, distribution, and consumption of pornography—even by consenting adults in private—in order to prevent moral corruption and indecency.[22]

Liberal defenders of pornography famously disagree, rejecting both legal moralism and legal paternalism—at least where consenting adults are concerned. Avoiding offence may be legitimate grounds for legal restrictions on public display of some pornography (eg, zoning laws); however, the state has no business interfering in the private choices and activities of consenting adults—except to prevent harm to others. John Stuart Mill's 'harm principle' provides the traditional framework for debates over the legitimacy of state regulation of pornography.[23]

---

[18] Susan Brison, '"The Price We Pay?" Pornography and Harm' in Andrew I Cohen and Christopher H Wellman (eds), *Contemporary Debates in Applied Ethics* (Blackwell 2013) 319.

[19] See, eg, David Dyzenhaus, 'John Stuart Mill and the Harm of Pornography' (1992) 102 *Ethics* 534; Danny Scoccia, 'Can Liberals Support a Ban on Violent Pornography?' (1996) 106 *Ethics* 776; Cass Sunstein, 'Pornography and the First Amendment' (1986) *Duke LJ* 589; Jeremy Waldron, *The Harm in Hate Speech* (Harvard UP 2012).

[20] Fred R Berger, 'Pornography, Sex and Censorship' (1977) 4 *Soc Theo & Pract* 183.

[21] Patrick Devlin, *The Enforcement of Morals* (OUP 1968); Michael Sandel, 'Morality and the Liberal Ideal [1984] *New Republic* 15.

[22] Robert Baird and Stuart Rosenbaum (eds), *Pornography: Private Right or Public Menace?* (Prometheus 1991).

[23] 'On Liberty' in John Stuart Mill, *Three Essays* (OUP 1975)) 15; see also Chapters 1 and 2 in this volume.

Mill rejects the idea that the state is entitled to use physical or legal compulsion to restrict the freedom of mentally competent adults, against their will, for their own good. It is, however, perfectly legitimate for third parties to seek to influence individuals' choices through so-called 'non-coercive' or persuasive means.

Applying Mill's 'harm principle' to the case of pornography appears to imply that only if the production and consumption of pornography can be shown to be associated with harm to individuals other than those consenting adults directly involved in its production and use would there be legitimate grounds for legal regulation of pornography. On the assumption that pornography is a form of speech, the associated harms to others would have to be particularly substantial in order for legal regulation to be justified. 'Non-coercive' interference, by contrast, such as public education campaigns to inform citizens of the risks associated with pornography production or use, may be both liberally acceptable and desirable.

An important and contested question concerns the interpretation of 'harm'. 'Harm' may be understood narrowly or broadly. On a narrow conception, a harm must result from a single act and must injure the interests of an identifiable individual. This usually includes economic and psychological, as well as bodily, injury. On a broader conception, a harm can be due to a series of acts, none of which are individually either necessary or sufficient for the harm, and it can injure the interests of a group (as opposed to any identifiable individual). Insofar as liberal societies acknowledge the existence of group-based social harms, such as racial and sexual discrimination, they already utilize this broader conception of harm.

In an influential defence of pornography, Ronald Dworkin echoes Mill's concern by defending pornography partly on the basis of a right to 'moral independence'. People, he says, 'have the right not to suffer disadvantage in the distribution of social goods and opportunities, including disadvantages in the liberties permitted to them by the criminal law, just on the ground that their officials or fellow citizens think that their opinions about the right way for them to lead their own lives are ignoble or wrong'.[24] The fact (if it is one) that a majority of people want pornography banned because they find it offensive is not legitimate grounds for interfering with the personal choices of mentally competent adults: if consenting adults wish to make or view pornography in private then the state has no business interfering. To give moral majorities the power to force everyone to live however the majority judges best would violate the basic right of every individual to be treated with equal concern and respect.

This defence assumes that opposition to pornography centres on its offensiveness, rather than harm to others. Since the 1960s, however, growing opposition to pornography—particularly material that depicts and endorses the brutalization or degradation of women—has come from feminists concerned about the ways in which (some) pornography harms women. Because feminist arguments for regulation of pornography centre on (alleged) harms, as opposed to (mere) offensiveness, they appear to have more promising liberal credentials.[25]

---

[24] Ronald Dworkin, *A Matter of Principle* (Harvard UP 1986) 353; see, generally, ch 17.

[25] For an argument that Dworkin's own premises actually support a case against, rather than for, permitting pornography see Rae Langton, 'Whose Right? Ronald Dworkin, Women, and Pornographers' (1990) 19 *Phil & Pub Aff* 311. Of course, not all feminists object to pornography or support legal restrictions: cf Gayle Rubin, 'Misguided, Dangerous and Wrong: An Analysis of Antipornography Politics' in Alison Assiter and Avedon Carol (eds), *Bad Girls and Dirty Pictures: The Challenge to Reclaim Feminism* (Pluto 1993) 18.

26.4.2 Anti-Pornography Feminism

Anti-pornography feminists reject the claim made by pornography's traditional liberal defenders that pornography—even at its most misogynistic—is harmless entertainment. On the contrary, production and consumption of pornography is associated with significant real-world harms to women, both individually and as a group. (Recall that anti-pornography feminists are employing a restricted use of the term 'pornography' to refer to a specific subset of sexually explicit material that harms women—for example, by depicting and endorsing the brutalization or degradation of women.)

These (alleged) harms can be divided into two categories: (1) direct harms involved in the *production* of pornography; and (2) direct and indirect harms associated with, or resulting from, the *consumption* of pornography.

26.4.2.1 *Production-Based Harms*

Harms directly involved in the production of pornography centre on coercion and exploitation of vulnerable individuals and groups. Catharine MacKinnon famously likens the pornography industry to a practice of 'sexual slavery'.[26] Some high-profile cases seem to warrant this description. In the book *Ordeal*, for example, Linda Machiano (aka Linda Lovelace) tells of being kidnapped, beaten, tortured, and drugged in order to perform her starring role in *Deep Throat*, one of the highest grossing pornographic films of all-time.[27] Although estimates vary, there is evidence that a significant number of women and children are similarly physically coerced into performing in pornography. Several human rights bodies report links between sex trafficking (especially of women and children from poorer nations, who are often tricked and coerced into sex work) and pornography. Of course, since many of these acts are criminal offences in their own right, they can be prosecuted independently of anti-pornography regulation. Nonetheless, the additional profits to be made from selling visual footage of forced sex acts may act as an additional incentive for sex traffickers.

Not all of the women who perform in pornography are overtly physically coerced. However, many (although not all) women who perform in pornography come from underprivileged socio-economic backgrounds and have few alternative options. Some have suffered a history of sexual abuse or have been 'groomed' for sex work from a young age.[28] There are also numerous first-hand reports from actors of psychological manipulation and financial pressure from agents and directors to perform increasingly extreme and painful sex acts.

According to liberal defenders of pornography, however, while it is unfortunate that socio-economic disadvantage leaves people with limited alternatives and vulnerable to manipulation and abuse, this does not provide a rationale to prohibit the production or consumption of pornography—any more than it provides grounds for banning fast food or supermarket chains, who similarly take advantage of a poorly educated workforce

---

[26] MacKinnon, *Feminism Unmodified* (n 3).
[27] Linda Lovelace and Mike McGrady, *Ordeal* (Citadel 2006).
[28] Catharine MacKinnon and Andrea Dworkin, *In Harm's Way: The Pornography Civil Rights Hearings* (Harvard UP 1997).

with few alternative avenues for employment.[29] The solution to exploitation is to address the root causes of socio-economic disadvantage, not to deprive already disadvantaged individuals of yet another opportunity that may be preferred to existing alternatives. This reply assumes that the pornography industry is merely a beneficiary, and not itself a significant contributing cause, of underlying socio-economic disadvantage.

Some female porn actors vigorously reject the idea that they are coerced or exploited by the pornography industry: this suggestion is moralistic and patronizing, denies their agency, and serves only to perpetuate damaging social stigma around sex work. They defend their choice to work in pornography as free, enjoyable, lucrative, and empowering.[30]

Of course, the fact that *some* women make the choice to perform in porn from a range of reasonable alternatives does not mean that this choice is free or rewarding for all or even most of the women who perform in it, many of whom may lack such alternatives. Nor does the fact that some individual women benefit from performing in pornography show that the industry as a whole does not harm women as a group.[31]

26.4.2.2 *Consumption-Based Harms*

Second, anti-pornography feminists point to a range of harms associated with the use of pornography (ie, material that depicts and endorses sexual violence or degradation). These range from direct physical harms to individual women, such as crimes of sexual assault, to broader indirect social and reputational harms to women as group.[32]

The general facts of sexual inequality are well-known and disappointingly persistent. Despite advances in formal equality, women are still disproportionately concentrated in low-status, low-paying, and insecure occupations. The overwhelming majority of people living in poverty are women and children. Women are disproportionately victims of sexual violence and harassment in both the home and workplace. According to anti-pornography feminists, consumption of pornography plays a significant role in creating and/or perpetuating this pattern of systematic violence and discrimination against women: for example, by reproducing and reinforcing the false and pernicious idea that women exist primarily to serve men's sexual needs.

The claim that pornography is a significant cause of sexual violence and discrimination need not be interpreted as the extreme claim that consumption of pornography is

---

[29] Dworkin, 'Women and Pornography' (n 12).

[30] See Anna Arrowsmith, 'My Pornographic Development' in Hans Maes (ed), *Pornographic Art and the Aesthetics of Pornography* (Palgrave Macmillan 2013) 287; Lori Gruen and George Panichas (eds), *Sex, Morality and the Law* (Routledge 1997) ch 3; Wendy McElroy, *XXX: A Woman's Right to Pornography* (St Martin's P 1995) ch 7; Candida Royalle, 'Porn in the USA' in Drucilla Cornell (ed), *Feminism and Pornography* (OUP 2000) 540; Nadine Strossen, *Defending Pornography: Free Speech, Sex, and the Fight for Women's Rights* (NYU P 1995) ch 9.

[31] Brison (n 18).

[32] See Andrea Dworkin, *Pornography* (n 5), MacKinnon, *Feminism Unmodified* (n 3), Sheila Jeffreys, *Anitclimax: A Feminist Perspective on the Sexual Revolution* (NYU P 1990); Susanne Kappeler, *The Pornography of Representation* (Polity P 1986); Rosalind Coward, *Female Desire: Women's Sexuality Today* (Paladin 1984); Carol Smart, *Feminism and the Power of Law* (Routledge 1989) ch 6; Itzin (n 3).

either necessary or sufficient for sexual violence—for example, that consumption of pornography causes previously 'decent chaps' suddenly 'to metamorphose into rapists', as Joel Feinberg suggests.[33] Nor need it be understood as suggesting that production and consumption of pornography is the *sole* cause of women's subordinate social status. Many anti-pornography feminists advocate the more 'sensible' claim that consumption of (inegalitarian) pornography, in combination with other factors (eg, labour and family relations, 'macho' values, etc), causes the subordination of women by significantly increasing the probability of sexual violence and discrimination.[34]

Whether or not this claim is true is an empirical matter that is difficult to confirm (or disconfirm) decisively, since the causes of sexualized violence and discrimination are complex and multifaceted. Particularly disputed is the claim that consumption of violent and misogynistic pornography significantly increases the incidence of sexual violence. In support of this connection, anti-pornography feminists point to a significant body of social science research finding a positive correlation between exposure to violent pornographic images (eg, rape, bondage, mutilation) and positive reactions to rape and other forms of violence against women, in both experimental and non-experimental settings.[35] Studies find, among other things, that exposure to violent pornography can significantly enhance a subject's arousal in response to portrayals of rape, that exposure to films that depict sexual violence against women can act as a stimulus for aggressive acts against women, and that prolonged exposure to degrading pornography (of a violent or non-violent sort) leads to increased callousness towards victims of sexual violence, a greater acceptance of 'rape myths' (eg, that women enjoy being raped and do not mean no when they say 'no'), a greater likelihood of having rape fantasies, and a greater likelihood of reporting that one would rape a woman if one could get away with it. Sceptics, however, point to countries such as Japan that have low reported rates of sexual assault but high rates of pornography consumption as evidence that the connection between pornography consumption and sexual violence is weak.[36] If it could be shown beyond reasonable doubt that some pornography significantly increased the

---

[33] Feinberg (n 1) 153.   [34] AW Eaton, 'A Sensible Antiporn Feminism' (2007) 117 *Ethics* 674.
[35] Edward Donnerstein, Daniel Linz, and Steve Penrod, *The Question of Pornography: Research Findings and Policy Implications* (Free P 1987); Edna Einsiedel, 'The Experimental Research Evidence: Effects of Pornography on the "Average Individual"' in Catherine Itzin (ed), *Pornography: Women, Violence and Civil Liberties* (OUP 1992) 248; Gert Martin Haid, Neil M Malamuth, and Carlin Yuen, 'Pornography and Attitudes Supporting Violence Against Women: Revisiting the Relationship in Nonexperimental Studies' (2010) 36 *Aggressive Behavior* 14; Catherine Itzin, '"Entertainment for Men": What It Is and What It Means' and "Legislating Against Pornography Without Censorship" in Catherine Itzin (ed), *Pornography: Women, Violence and Civil Liberties* (OUP 1992); Thomas Mappes and Jane Zembaty, *Social Ethics: Morality and Social Policy* (7th edn, McGraw-Hill 1997) ch 5; Diana Russell 'Pornography and Rape: A Causal Model' in Drucilla Cornell (ed), *Feminism and Pornography* (OUP 2000); James Weaver, 'The Social Science and Psychological Research Evidence: Perceptual and Behavioural Consequences of Exposure to Pornography' in Catherine Itzin (ed), *Pornography: Women, Violence and Civil Liberties* (OUP 1992); Ray Wyre, 'Pornography and Sexual Violence: Working with Sex Offenders' in Catherine Itzin (ed), *Pornography: Women, Violence and Civil Liberties* (OUP 1992).
[36] See, eg, Lynne Segal, *Sex Exposed: Sexuality and the Pornography Debate* (Rutgers UP 1993); Strossen (n 30).

probability of sexual violence, the case for legal regulation would be strong; as things stand, however, this claim is far from established.

Considerably less controversial is the claim that (inegalitarian) pornography influences user's attitudes towards women—in particular, their views about what women are like, how it is appropriate to treat women sexually, and what sexual activities are enjoyable and erotic. Many critics of pornography are particularly concerned about the influence of readily accessible violent and misogynistic pornography on adolescents, who report viewing pornography partly in order to learn how to have sex. There is strong and disturbing evidence that among this teenage cohort, pornography is playing a significant 'educative' role, helping to create and reinforce damaging inegalitarian norms about women and sex.[37] Since liberal principle permits paternalistic intervention to protect children from harm, there is a strong case both for tightening age-restrictions on access to pornography and attempting to mitigate its harmful effects through public and/or school-based education campaigns.

However, when it comes to consumption of violent and/or misogynistic pornography by consenting adults, liberal defenders resist holding pornographers responsible for attitudinal changes in users, holding that any harm that results from pornography use is the responsibility of hearers, rather than speakers. For—the argument goes—pornography's influence on its mentally competent adult users is 'mentally intermediated': it is determined, not by what speaker's say, but rather by how rationally-competent hearers choose to respond to what is said. The doctrine of mental intermediation has been used by US courts and legal theorists to defend pornography.[38] However, it has been questioned whether pornographic 'speech' is actually mentally intermediated since (among other things) users may not be consciously aware of its message, and this defence has been criticized as resting on false assumptions about how pornographic 'speech' works.[39]

26.4.2.3 *Causal versus Constitutive Anti-Pornography Arguments*

Traditionally, feminist arguments against pornography have posited a *causal* connection between the production and/or consumption of pornography and various harms to women, both as individuals and as a group. According to this causal approach, legal regulation of pornography may be justified or required because the harms that production and/or consumption of pornography *cause* to women outweigh the reasons against regulation. A variety of different causal analyses have been provided, focusing on a range of different harms associated with pornography and offering a variety of different accounts of how pornography may be implicated in bringing about these harms.

---

[37] See Rae Langton, 'Is Pornography Like the Law?' in Mari Mikkola (ed), *Beyond Speech: Pornography and Analytic Feminist Philosophy* (OUP 2017) 32, citing Maddy Coy and others, '*Sex without consent, I suppose that is rape': How Young People in England Understand Sexual Consent* (Office of the Children's Commissioner, November 2013).

[38] See, eg, *American Booksellers Association, Inc v Hudnut*, 771 F2d 323 (1985).

[39] Jennifer Hornsby, 'Free and Equal Speech' (1996) 1 *Imprints* 59.

In the 1980s, a distinctive new line of feminist anti-pornography argument emerged. Due originally to Andrea Dworkin and Catharine MacKinnon, this 'radical' feminist line of argument against pornography maintains that pornography should be regulated because it *constitutes* (as opposed to merely causes) a civil rights violation. Specifically, pornography *subordinates* women, or deprives them of their right to equal civil status; and it *silences* women, or violates their free speech right. The idea that pornography is, in and of itself, an act of sex discrimination is reflected in Dworkin and MacKinnon's well-known definition of pornography *as* the graphic sexually explicit subordination of women.

When initially proposed, this constitutive claim was greeted with considerable scepticism. Critics dismissed the claim as a 'dangerous confusion' and a 'conceptual sleight of hand'.[40] More sympathetic audiences treated the claim as merely 'metaphorical'.[41] Drawing on speech act theory, among other things, contemporary feminist philosophers have sought to defend and develop this constitutive claim.[42]

One influential approach, due (independently) to Jennifer Hornsby and Rae Langton, draws on JL Austin's speech act theory to make sense of how pornography might constitute, as opposed to merely cause, subordination.[43] Austin distinguished three different types of speech acts, or ways that we do things with words: (1) the act of uttering a semantically meaningful sentence, which he called the 'locutionary' act; (2) the act performed *in* saying certain words, which he termed the 'illocutionary' act; and, (3) the later effects achieved *by* the speech, which he termed the 'perlocutionary' act. To use a well-known example: One man says to another, 'shoot her'; this is the locutionary act. 'In saying "shoot her", he *urged* him to shoot her'; this is the illocutionary act. 'By saying "shoot her", he *persuaded* him to shoot her'; this is the perlocutionary act.

According to Langton, in addition to having certain subordinating perlocutionary or causal effects, pornography may be a speech act that has the illocutionary force of subordinating women. To illustrate how a speech act could have the illocutionary force of subordinating members of a social group, Langton offers the following paradigm example:

> Consider this utterance: 'Blacks are not permitted to vote'. Imagine that it is uttered by a legislator in Pretoria in the context of enacting legislation that underpins apartheid. It...makes it the case that blacks are not permitted to vote. It—plausibly—subordinates blacks.[44]

---

[40] Rae Langton, 'Speech Acts and Unspeakable Acts' (1993) 22 *Phil & Pub Aff* 293, citing William Parent, 'A Second Look at Pornography and the Subordination of Women' (1990) 87 *J Phil* 205.

[41] Ibid, citing Frank Michelman, 'Conceptions of Democracy in American Constitutional Argument: The Case of Pornography Regulation' (1989) 56 *Tenn L Rev* 291.

[42] Melinda Vadas, 'A First Look at the Pornography/Civil Rights Ordinance: Could Pornography Be the Subordination of Women?' (1987) 84 *J Phil* 487; Langton 'Speech Acts and Unspeakable Acts' (n 40); Jennifer Hornsby, 'Speech Acts and Pornography' in Susan Dwyer (ed), *The Problem of Pornography* (Wadsworth 1995); Mary Kate McGowan, 'Conversational Exercitives and the Force of Pornography' (2003) 31 *Phil & Pub Aff* 155, 2019; McGowan, *Just Words* (n 6) ch 6.

[43] Langton, 'Speech Acts and Unspeakable Acts' (n 40); Hornsby (n 42).

[44] Langton, 'Speech Acts and Unspeakable Acts' (n 40) 302.

According to Langton, pornography could subordinate women by unfairly *ranking* women as inferior, *legitimating* acts of sex discrimination, and depriving women of important powers (eg, freedom of speech).

Langton's speech act approach has been highly influential; however, it faces several well-known challenges.[45] Many of these difficulties stem from the fact that pornographic speech acts differ from paradigm Austinian speech acts (particularly standard exercitives) in several potentially important ways.[46] Firstly, it is unclear that pornographers have the requisite authority to subordinate women.[47] Unlike the Pretorian legislator in Langton's example, pornographers generally do not occupy any formal position of authority. While this is widely regarded as the most significant challenge to the hypothesis that pornography subordinates women as Langton proposes, recent work by Langton and others goes a considerable way to addressing this concern.[48] Secondly, most pornographic utterances do not take the form of classic Austinian illocutions (eg, 'I hereby authorize you to discriminate'), or explicitly say that women are or should be subordinate.[49] Thirdly, pornographers plausibly do not *intend* to subordinate women by producing pornography, but this intention seems to be required on traditional Austinian speech act theory in order for pornographic speech acts to subordinate. More fundamentally, it is debatable whether pornography is a speech act at all, since much pornography does not seem to operate at the conscious level of communicated intentions characteristic of speech acts; it seems often to influence consumers' attitudes in ways that consumers may be less than fully aware of. Langton attempts to extend the speech act account to accommodate desire, as well as belief change.[50] Other speech act accounts may avoid some of these problems.[51]

26.4.2.4 *Pornography and Silencing*

In addition to constituting subordinating women, pornography is alleged to 'silence' women, or systematically interfere with women's communicative capabilities.[52] MacKinnon writes: 'The free speech of men silences the free speech of women; it's the

---

[45] For criticisms of Langton's approach, see Louise Antony, 'Against Langton's Illocutionary Treatment of Pornography' (2011) 2 *Jurisprudence* 387; Louise Antony, 'Be What I Say' in Mari Mikkola (ed), *Beyond Speech: Pornography and Analytic Feminist Philosophy* (OUP 2017).

[46] See McGowan, *Just Words* (n 6); McGowan, 'Conversational Exercitives and the Force of Pornography' (n 42).

[47] Nancy Bauer, *How to Do Things With Pornography* (Harvard UP 2015); Judith Butler, *Excitable Speech: A Politics of the Performative* (Routledge 1997); Leslie Green, 'Pornographizing, Subordinating and Silencing' in Robert Post (ed), *Censorship and Silencing: Practices of Cultural Regulation* (Getty Research Institute 1998); Leonard W Sumner, *The Hateful and the Obscene: Studies in the Limits of Free Expression* (U Toronto P 2004).

[48] See, eg, Langton 'Is Pornography Like the Law?' (n 37); Ishani Maitra, 'Subordinating Speech' in Ishani Maitra and Mary Kate McGowan (eds), *Speech and Harm: Controversies over Free Speech* (OUP 2012) 94–120.

[49] This concern is addressed in Langton and West (n 17).

[50] Rae Langton, 'Beyond Belief: Pragmatics in Hate Speech and Pornography' in Ishani Maitra and Mary Kate McGowan (eds), *Speech and Harm: Controversies over Free Speech* (OUP 2012).

[51] For a helpful discussion of speech act accounts of pornography and the challenges they face, see McGowan, *Just Words* (n 6) ch 6.

[52] MacKinnon, *Feminism Unmodified* (n 3); MacKinnon, *Only Words* (n 5).

same social goal, just other people'.⁵³ According to the 'silencing argument', as it has come to be known, regulation of pornography may be justified or required in order to protect women's free speech right. MacKinnon herself favours civil (as opposed to criminal) regulation that would enable those harmed in the production or pornography, or as a result of its consumption, to sue pornographers for demonstrable harm. Like MacKinnon's claim about subordination, the claim that pornography silences women has also been taken up and developed in different directions by a number of feminist philosophers, including Langton,⁵⁴ Hornsby and Langton,⁵⁵ and West.⁵⁶

The silencing argument has both theoretical and dialectical significance. At the level of strategy, it recasts debates over pornography as posing a conflict, not simply between freedom of speech and other values (eg, equality), but within free speech itself, between pornographers' freedom of speech and women's freedom of speech in sexual contexts. Since free speech enjoys significant cultural and political capital in liberal societies, this is a politically promising strategy. The silencing argument also has legal significance in the US context, within which MacKinnon originally develops it, where courts have routinely prioritized the First Amendment right to freedom of speech over the Fourteenth Amendment right to equality. In dismissing the Dworkin-MacKinnon anti-pornography ordinance as unconstitutional, Judge Frank Easterbrook of the US Court of Appeals granted that pornography of the sort targeted by the ordinance perpetuates women's subordinate civil status, but views this harm as insufficient to justify interfering with pornographers' freedom of speech. In a striking passage, he writes:

> we accept the premises of this legislation. Depictions of subordination tend to perpetuate subordination. The subordination of women in turn leads to affront and lower pay at work, insult and injury at home, battery and rape on the streets...[T]his simply demonstrates the power of pornography as speech.⁵⁷

In principle, to succeed the silencing argument must establish that (1) women can be silenced in some way(s), (2) pornography can somehow be responsible for this, and (3) such silencing, if it occurred, would interfere with women's free speech interest.⁵⁸ Let us consider these issues in turn.

---

⁵³ MacKinnon, *Feminism Unmodified* (n 3) 156. The claim that pornography silences women has been developed in different ways: see Langton, 'Speech Acts and Unspeakable Acts' (n 40); Hornsby (n 42); Ishani Maitra, 'Silencing Speech' (2009) 39 *Canadian J Phil* 309; Mary Kate McGowan, 'On Multiple Types of Silencing' in Mari Mikkola (ed), *Beyond Speech: Pornography and Analytic Feminist Philosophy* (OUP 2017); McGowan, *Just Words* (n 6).
⁵⁴ Langton, 'Speech Acts and Unspeakable Acts' (n 40); Rae Langton, *Sexual Solipsism: Philosophical Essays on Pornography and Objectification* (OUP 2009).
⁵⁵ Hornsby and Langton (n 9).
⁵⁶ Caroline West, 'The Free Speech Argument Against Pornography' (2003) 33 *Canadian J Phil* 391.
⁵⁷ *American Booksellers Association* (n 38).
⁵⁸ This requires establishing empirical matters that fall to social scientists, rather than philosophers or legal theorists, to investigate.

The first issue concerns the nature of silencing: what might it involve? Multiple possible types of silencing have been distinguished in the literature.[59] For brevity, I will focus on one sense of silencing that has received most discussion in the literature. This type of silencing occurs when there are systematic barriers to audience 'uptake': the speaker produces meaningful sounds or scrawls which are heard by an audience, but communication fails because the audience systematically fails to recognize the speaker's intention in so speaking.[60] In this case, although the speaker is free to make meaningful noises, she is prevented from *doing* certain (illocutionary) things with her words. For example, a woman may say 'no', sincerely intending to refuse sex, but her audience may somehow fail to grasp that she means to refuse him by so speaking. Pornography may contribute to such recognition failure by interfering with the felicity conditions for some of women's speech—for example, by building an expectation that when a woman says 'no' she does not intend to refuse. When such uptake-failure is sufficiently systematic, it constitutes a kind of silencing that Langton calls 'illocutionary disablement'.[61] Although the appropriate noises are produced, the woman is unable to perform the illocutionary act of refusal because her audience is unable to recognize she is attempting to refuse him in so speaking.[62]

Illocutionary disablement contrasts with 'locutionary silence' (where no words are produced at all because speaking out would be costly), and 'perlocutionary frustration', where hearers grasp perfectly well that the speaker intends to refuse, but the speech fails to achieve its intended effects (eg, getting the man to stop). In cases of perlocutionary frustration, communication succeeds, but is ineffective; the audience grasps the woman's intention to refuse, but dismisses or ignores it. In cases of illocutionary disablement, by contrast, communication fails because the audience fails to recognize the speaker's intention to refuse, which is a precondition for successful refusal.

Let us suppose that women sometimes actually experience such illocutionary or communicative disablement: for example, their intention to refuse sex by conventional means (eg, saying 'no') sometimes goes unrecognized; and this is not a one-off idiosyncrasy (eg, due to the man being temporarily distracted, or an incompetent English-speaker), but part of a more systematic pattern. The next question is whether and how pornography could be implicated in this pattern of events.

One possibility is that pornography use leads to recognition failure along the lines previously suggested. Perhaps watching certain sorts of pornography creates and/or reinforces in users the (perhaps implicit) belief that women often feign resistance in order to heighten sexual excitement and anticipation. Someone in the grip of this belief might find it difficult to recognize a woman's (sincere) intention to refuse. However, this is just one possible way that pornography could contribute to uptake

---

[59] For a helpful overview of possible kinds of silencing, see McGowan, *Just Words* (n 6) ch 6.
[60] Langton, 'Speech Acts and Unspeakable Acts' (n 40); Hornsby (n 42).
[61] Mary Kate McGowan, 'On Silencing and Sexual Refusal' (2009) 17 J PolPhil 487: McGowan maintains that although illocution (successful refusal, in this example) does not require uptake, successful *communication* (of refusal) requires uptake.
[62] See West (n 56).

or recognition failure. Other suggestions are that pornography influences attitudes by a process of Pavlovian or operant conditioning,[63] or by triggering unconscious imitation mechanisms[64] or alternatively that pornography might *constitute* (as opposed to merely cause) women's silencing via a mechanism of 'sneaky norm enactment'.[65]

In the end, it is an empirical question exactly how pornography silences women in this way, if it does. For argument's sake, let's suppose—not implausibly—that it does. The third important question concerns what this would mean for women's free speech interest, and how this feeds into arguments for regulation. This, of course, raises a large and complex set of issues that cannot be comprehensively discussed here, but it is worth highlighting some key points and clarifying some possible misunderstandings.

26.5 SILENCING AND FREE SPEECH

MacKinnon famously claims not simply that pornography silences women, but moreover that it does so in such a way as to violate their civil right to free speech.[66] Anti-pornography regulation is justified, or even required, in order to secure women's free speech right. In a review of MacKinnon's 1993 work—the ironically titled, *Only Words*— Ronald Dworkin dismisses the claim that pornography (or its consumption) interferes with women's free speech right as 'absurd' and 'dangerously confused'.[67] Daniel Jacobsen offers a similar criticism,[68] explicitly insisting that 'speech' in 'free speech' means freedom of locution, not illocution.[69] According to Dworkin, the silencing argument is premised on 'an unacceptable proposition: that the right to free speech includes a right to circumstances that encourage one to speak, and a right that others grasp and respect what one means to say'.[70] Dworkin is concerned that (so interpreted) the silencing argument overgeneralizes and entails the 'absurd' result that 'everyone—the bigot and the creationist as well as the social reformer—has a right to whatever respectful attention on the part of others is necessary to encourage him to speak his mind and to guarantee that he will be correctly understood'.[71]

---

[63] Mackinnon, *Feminism Unmodified* (n 3); Scoccia (n 19).
[64] Langton (n 50); Susan Hurley, 'Imitation, Media Violence, and Freedom of Speech' (2004) 117 *Phil Stud* 165.
[65] McGowan, *Just Words* (n 6).   [66] MacKinnon, *Feminism Unmodified* (n 3).
[67] Dworkin, 'Women and Pornography' (n 12).
[68] Daniel Jacobsen, Freedom of Speech Acts? A Response to Langton' (1995) 24 *Phil & Pub Aff* 64.
[69] Ibid; and Alexander Bird, 'Illocutionary Silencing' (2002) 83 *Pacific Phil Q* 1; cf Mari Mikkola, 'Illocution, Silencing and the Act of Refusal' (2011) 92 *Pacific Phil Q* 415; Maitra and McGowan (n 14); and Mary Kate McGowan and others, 'A Partial Defence of Illocutionary Silencing' (2011) 26 *Hypatia* 132.
[70] Dworkin, 'Women and Pornography' (n 12) 38.   [71] Ibid 40.

In fact, however, the silencing argument (as proposed by Hornsby and Langton,[72] among others) does not have this unwelcome implication. The misapprehension that it does is actually due to Dworkin's failure to distinguish silencing (systematic illocutionary disablement) from perlocutionary frustration.[73] The claim that free speech includes illocution does not require a respectful attentive audience, it requires only 'minimal reciprocity': that 'a hearer has a capacity to grasp what communicative act a speaker might be intending to perform'[74]—or at least that uptake is not systematically interfered with by the actions of other agents. The speaker intentions of bigots and creationists are at least grasped, even if not always agreed with; there is no analogous failure of reciprocity in this case.

Not only is the proposal that freedom of speech is freedom of illocution not absurd, something very like seems necessary for speech to possess the kind of value liberals traditionally attach to it. While free speech may not require a sympathetic listening audience, it does seem to require that speech can at least be well enough understood. There are multiple reasons why liberals may place special value on free speech, but on every account what is of value is something associated with *communication*. The theoretical significance of the speech act approach is that it draws attention to the important but neglected fact that freedom of locution is not the same as, and not sufficient for, freedom to communicate. To protect communication, the state must protect the illocutionary as well as the locutionary dimensions of speech—or else what is being protected might as well be gibberish. A society that permitted the distribution of meaningful sounds and scrawls, but somehow managed systematically to prevent those sounds and scrawls from being comprehended by hearers, would be little better as far as free speech values are concerned than a society that simply prevented the distribution of intelligible noise altogether. Insofar as uptake or recognition failure constitutes a systematic form of communicative interference, a case can be made that it constitutes a free speech violation.[75] Perhaps a similar case can be made for some other forms of silencing as well.

A second important insight from the speech act approach to pornography is that significant threats to speaker's communicative capacities may come not only or primarily from the actions of state officials, but also from those of private individuals—including the speech acts of other private individuals, such as pornographers. Communication is a social activity, involving a speaker and an audience. Its success generally depends not simply on the speaker's opportunity to produce words, but also on the audience's ability to grasp the speaker's intention in speaking. Whether this occurs can depend as much on the actions (and inactions) of other speakers, as much as it does on those of government officials.[76]

---

[72] Hornsby and Langton (n 9). [73] Ibid. [74] Ibid 25. [75] See West (n 56).
[76] For further discussion and development of the speech act approach to free speech, see McGowan, *Just Words* (n 6), and Rae Langton, *Accommodating Injustice: The John Locke Lectures 2015* (OUP, forthcoming).

26.6 Non-Legal Remedies

In this chapter, I have focused on the most controversial free speech issue traditionally raised by discussions of pornography: namely, whether—given certain empirical assumptions about the effects of pornography's production and consumption—further legal regulation of pornography can be justified as a matter of political morality. However, as everyone acknowledges, legal regulation is costly. Consequently, if effective but less restrictive measures to prevent or counteract pornography's harms are available, these should obviously be preferred.

By far the most popular alternative to regulation recommends countering 'bad' speech with more 'good' speech. In principle, this might include government sponsored public education campaigns to inform consumers of the harmful effects of consuming violent and misogynistic pornography, and/or to promote a counter-message of sexual equality and respect for women. In practice, however, currently it falls mostly to private speakers to counter pornography's messages about women and sex, unsupported by much in the way of positive assistance or encouragement from government. Even if legal regulation of violent and misogynistic pornography is unwarranted or undesirable, all things considered, such state inaction in the face of pornography's role in endorsing and perpetuating sexism may be indefensible. If pornography (in the restricted feminist sense) is harmful—if it perpetuates and legitimates harmful sexist attitudes and behaviour (quite apart from whether or not it also leads to sexual violence)—then there may be an important role for governments to play in helping to counter harmful sexist messages through explicitly government-backed public education campaigns. Without restricting anyone's speech, such campaigns would lend the epistemic and political authority of the state to private opinion in challenging the kind of misogyny and sexism depicted and endorsed by much mainstream heterosexual pornography. State-backed counter-speech may be especially crucial if private counter-speakers are silenced, so that counter-speech is otherwise liable systematically to be ignored or misunderstood.[77]

In the end, it is an empirical question whether and to what extent counter-speech will be effective in preventing or countering harmful messages conveyed by violent and misogynistic pornography. There are several reasons to think that counter-speech may be less effective than advocates commonly suppose. Firstly, if widespread consumption of pornography restricts the ability of women successfully to communicate certain important thoughts, feelings, and wishes to audiences—that is, if pornography silences women—then counter-speech is not an option, at least for those silenced. Secondly, pornography may affect consumers' attitudes and behaviours in ways that escape their

---

[77] For related discussion of how communications can receive less credibility than is warranted, see Kristie Dotson, 'Tracking Epistemic Violence, Tracking Practices of Silencing' (2011) 26 *Hypatia* 236 on 'testimonial quieting' and Miranda Fricker, *Epistemic Injustice: Power and the Ethics of Knowing* (OUP 2007), for her discussion of testimonial injustice.

conscious notice. It may be going too far to liken consumers of pornography to Pavlov's dogs, but it is not unreasonable to think that much of pornography's influence on viewers' attitudes is considerably less than fully mentally intermediated. (Note that if it turns out that pornography alters consumer's mental states in significantly non-mentally intermediated ways, then the case for defending it as speech is considerably weakened.)[78] For it is difficult to have a discussion about feelings and attitudes that you are not aware of and consequently cannot yourself articulate in conversation; and which, in any case, may not readily be amenable to rational revision through belief change.

26.7 Conclusion

How should liberal societies respond to the proliferation of harmful pornography? This chapter has focused on some central philosophical questions raised by debates over legal regulation of pornography. What are the harms of pornography? Could these harms be significant enough to justify the state legally restricting the freedom of consenting adults to produce, distribute, or consume violent and misogynistic pornography in private? Do considerations of free speech tell for, or against, permitting such pornography? Supposing that legal restrictions on pornography could be justified in principle, would they actually be best, all things considered? Is the most effective preventative to pornography's harms to legislate or educate (or both)? These questions are difficult, but important. The quest to resolve them satisfactorily accounts for ongoing philosophical, legal, and social-scientific interest in the topic of pornography.

---

[78] See Scoccia (n 19).

CHAPTER 27

RELIGIOUS SPEECH

GAUTAM BHATIA

THE tensions between religion and freedom of expression are familiar to most modern democracies. As a wide-ranging system of moral beliefs and commitments—what John Rawls called a 'comprehensive doctrine'[1]—religion, by its very nature, assigns to the freedom of expression a particular place in its hierarchical order of values. In non-theocratic states (to which this chapter limits itself), this may clash with the (higher) normative value accorded to the freedom of expression under the secular order.[2] Moreover, religious claims themselves will often be made from within the constitutional system:[3] that is, the state's own constitutional commitment to protect religious freedom will be invoked to argue that, in certain domains, the secular order must defer to religion's hierarchy of values. This may include—as this chapter shall discuss—the subordination of religious expression to revealed religious truth. Disputes will often also involve contestation over a constellation of other constitutional norms, such as the commitment to maintaining diversity and pluralism, the right to equality and cultural dissent, and not least, the imperatives of public order. Consequently, such disputes raise a host of complex issues. Depending upon the context, the state's adjudicatory authorities must decide whether to attempt an accommodation between the conflicting claims of religion and free speech, or privilege one over the other.

The tension between religion and freedom of expression is not limited to open conflict. There are situations where the state is supportive of religious expression. The conflict here occurs between a perceived proximity between the state and religious speech on the one hand, and the state's own claim to establish a public sphere where all citizens can participate

---

[1] See, eg, John Rawls, *Political Liberalism* (Columbia UP 2005).
[2] It does not address, for example, a constitution such as that of Saudi Arabia, which in express terms equates the constitution with religious law. See, eg, Constitution of Saudi Arabia, 1992, art 1. It does address a constitution like that of Kenya, which expressly declares that 'There shall be no state religion': Constitution of Kenya 2010, art 8. Admittedly, however, there is no bright-line definition. The case of Indonesia, which will be discussed later in this chapter, is an example of a constitutional system that straddles the grey area.
[3] When using terms such as 'constitutional system' or 'constitutional order', I do not limit it to democracies having written constitutions or bills of rights.

equally regardless of religious affiliation. And lastly, sometimes the state can be over-zealous while pursuing the above endeavour, leading to a third kind of conflict: *between* the state and religious expression (the right to which, of course, is a subset of the freedom of expression).

In this chapter, I shall explore the topic of 'religious speech' in the context of these three frameworks. I shall begin with a brief recapitulation of the central importance of freedom of expression (focusing specifically on religious speech) to modern constitutional democracies (Section 27.1). I shall then discuss the role of religion in censorship—that is, censorship of religious (or irreligious) speech, which is often framed in the language of blasphemy, apostasy, or other variants of religious dissent (Section 27.2). I shall go on to discuss the constitutional issues that arise when the state chooses to sanction, endorse, or otherwise ally itself with religious speech by mandating, encouraging, or permitting (for example) religious instruction or religious symbols in state schools (Section 27.3). Next, I shall examine situations in which the state privileges other values over the right to (religious) expression, such as (for example) limiting invocations to religion in an election campaign, curtailing religious expression in public forums, or subordinating religious expression to anti-discrimination laws (Section 27.4). I shall conclude with an argument that, despite the differences in context across the globe, issues around religious speech essentially come down to whether—and the extent to which—constitutional democracies are willing to support genuine pluralism and diversity in forms of life and expression (Section 27.5).

The analysis in this chapter will be comparative and doctrinal (focusing on legal texts and the judgments of appellate or constitutional courts). By way of prelude, I must spell out two caveats. First, the constitutional status of religion in any democracy is the result of centuries of contestation, conflict, negotiation, and accommodation. Legal doctrine is embedded in this history, and makes sense only within it. A chapter of this nature must inevitably sacrifice some historical nuance in favour of breadth.[4] Second, while every democracy has a complex history of the state/religion relationship, not all of them have witnessed it play out in the legal terrain, before courts or tribunals. This chapter is also restricted, therefore, to countries where the issues highlighted above are either explicitly spelt out in legal texts, and/or have become the subject of constitutional adjudication.[5]

27.1 Free Speech as a Political and Constitutional Value

The freedom of speech and expression occupies a foundational place in modern democracies. Free speech guarantees are indispensable elements of the Universal Declaration

---

[4] For recent work dealing with this issue, see Gunther Frankenberg, *Comparative Constitutional Studies: Between Magic and Deceit* (Edward Elgar 2018).

[5] I cover Indonesia, India, Kenya, South Africa, the United Kingdom, Germany, the European Court of Human Rights, Canada, the United States, Colombia, and the work of United Nations bodies.

of Human Rights (UDHR),[6] supranational legal instruments,[7] and national constitutions and bills of rights.[8] Where there is no codified bill of rights, the right to freedom of speech has been held to flow from the democratic form of government itself.[9]

World over, legal scholarship and judicial decisions converge upon three basic justifications for the central importance of the freedom of speech in a democracy. For the purposes of this chapter, I shall briefly summarize them, with the caveat that the arguments are far more nuanced than the following schematic account will allow; readers interested in the details should refer to Part II of this volume. The first justification—originally drawn from the writings of John Milton[10] and John Stuart Mill[11]—holds that free speech is indispensable to the discovery of truth. A variant of argument goes that the 'marketplace of ideas' is always a *better* path to the truth than the state (or any other centralized authority) determining what is true and what isn't.[12] The second justification holds that, as communicative beings, the freedom of expression is fundamental to our sense of self, our identity, and our place in the world.[13] It is through words and expressive conduct that we become fully human. And the third justification holds that the freedom of speech is essential for democracy to function.[14] A political system where the government is chosen *by* the people and is meant to be accountable *to* the people, cannot exist unless channels of communication *between* people, and between the people and the government, are kept open.

Each of the three justifications raises interesting questions when juxtaposed alongside the claims of religion. The truth-based justification is premised on the assumption that—at least in certain domains—the 'truth' is not necessarily known at any given time, and it is through a contest between opposing arguments that we approach the truth. For monotheistic religions in particular, however, the truth is 'revealed', and at least in certain core matters, there can be no (or at best, minimal) debate.[15] As we shall see, this inherent tension between the freedom of speech and religion comes to a head, in particular, when

---

[6] Art 19 UDHR.

[7] ECHR art 10; American Convention on Human Rights, 1144 UNTS 123, 9 ILM 352 (1969) art 13; African Charter on Human and Peoples' Rights (1981) art 9.

[8] Constitution of India, 1950, art 19(1)(a); Constitution of Mexico, 1917, art 17; Constitution of the Republic of the Philippines, 1987, s 4; Constitution of the Republic of South Africa, No 108 of 1996 (1996) s 16.

[9] See, eg, *Australian Capital Television Ltd v Commonwealth* (1992) 199 CLR 106, and subsequent developments.

[10] John Milton, *Areopagitica* (first published 1644).

[11] John Stuart Mill, *On Liberty* (John W Parker 1859).

[12] *Abrams v United States*, 250 US 616 (1919) (Holmes J, dissenting).

[13] C Edwin Baker, 'Scope of the First Amendment Freedom of Speech' (1978) 25 *UCLA L Rev* 964, 966.

[14] Frederick Schauer, 'Free Speech and the Argument from Democracy' (1983) 25 *Nomos* 241.

[15] The distinction is not always clear-cut. For example, hate speech laws *do* commit to the proposition that the values of equality and non-discrimination are beyond challenge (and therefore, not subject to a continuous process of rebuttal through speech). In *American Booksellers v Hudnut*, 771 F 2d 323 (7th Cir 1985), the Court of Appeals for the Seventh Circuit held that it was impermissible for the government *even* to determine 'truth' in the realm of equality and discrimination. The United States is an outlier in this respect, however. Most other jurisdictions agree that the freedom of expression can be regulated in order to preserve certain basic constitutional values (such as equality).

individuals or (dissenting) groups question, attack, or (re)interpret key tenets of religious doctrine.

The argument that speech and expression is central to individual autonomy gives us a particularly strong reason to value *religious* expression. As scholars like Charles Taylor explain, individuals are not atomized beings, but operate within contexts of choice that make their autonomous actions and decisions meaningful.[16] It can scarcely be denied that an individual's religion—and, by extension, religious community—is one of the most important 'contexts of choice' that they will have access to through the course of their life. This, in turn, requires that religious expression be treated with particular solicitude by the state, because the purposes served by religious expression are at the heart of why we prioritize the freedom of expression as a value.

Lastly, the argument from democracy raises its own set of issues: is the democratic sphere committed to communication only of a *certain kind*, and are certain forms of religious speech inconsistent with this commitment? To take an example from a parallel domain: certain democratic countries forbid the existence of political parties that are explicitly anti-democratic.[17] If we understand democracy to include a commitment to equal concern and respect, then how do we address an individual invoking their right to religious expression to deny equal concern and respect to others (for example, by invoking religious faith to claim an exemption from anti-discrimination laws in the marketplace)? How do we respond when—in that most quintessential of democratic activities, the election campaign—an individual or a political party explicitly invokes religious supremacy in a pitch for votes?

It is therefore evident that questions of religious speech in a democracy are intertwined with *why* we value the freedom of speech, *how* we understand the democratic sphere, and *what* it is about religion and religious expression that we deem worthy of respecting and protecting. These are all contested moral questions, and so—as we shall see—it is unsurprising that different democratic countries have addressed them differently.

27.2 Religion as Censor: Blasphemy Laws and Their Variants

27.2.1 The Distinction between Hate Speech and Blasphemy

In this section, I shall consider restrictions upon the freedom of speech that are justified substantially on the grounds of religion. As we shall see, primarily, these restrictions

---

[16] Charles Taylor, *The Ethics of Authenticity* (Harvard UP 1991).
[17] See, eg, the concept of 'militant democracy', expressed through arts 21(2) and (3) of the Basic Law for the Republic of Germany, 1949.

take the form of blasphemy laws, which invariably censor certain kinds of religious expression, or expression about religion.

An initial distinction is important: between religious hate speech and blasphemy (or its variants). The prohibition of hate speech—and, specifically, religious hate speech—is well known both to international human rights instruments, and to domestic laws. For example, Article 20 of the International Covenant for Civil and Political Rights (ICCPR) prohibits 'any advocacy of national, racial or *religious hatred* that constitutes incitement to discrimination, hostility or violence'.[18] The Constitution of South Africa does not extend the freedom of expression to 'advocacy of hatred that is based on race, ethnicity, gender or *religion*, and that constitutes incitement to cause harm'.[19] The underlying justification for prohibiting hate speech—as is often evident from the text of the constitutional provisions themselves—is to prevent discrimination or violence against vulnerable or marginalized people.[20] Religion—like race, or gender, or caste—is a marker of group membership that often serves as the site, or locus, of discrimination or violence. This is why hate speech prohibitions are often framed around group markers. As the Canadian Supreme Court observed, 'hate speech is, at its core, an effort to marginalize individuals based on their membership in a group'.[21] The Court went on to explain that 'hate speech seeks to delegitimize group members in the eyes of the majority, reducing their social standing and acceptance within society'.[22] The end-point of such hate speech, therefore, is social discrimination against the target group, which could, at times, rise to violence. The South African Constitutional Court follows a similar approach towards defining hate speech,[23] and the same approach was acknowledged, as well, by the United Nations Human Rights Committee (UNHRC), when it upheld France's law penalizing Holocaust denial. The UNHRC noted that the purpose of the restriction was to ensure that the Jewish community was able to 'live free from fear in an atmosphere of anti-semitism'.[24]

Hate speech restrictions and blasphemy laws overlap to a certain extent. Both restrict what can be said about members of a religion and (on occasion) about a religion itself. Both occasionally invoke maintaining public order and peace as one of their goals. But that is where the overlap ends. Blasphemy laws are not concerned with the egalitarian commitments of hate speech laws: rather, their purpose is either to protect the *sentiments* of religious believers by preventing an expressive challenges to their religious beliefs, or to protect core religious tenets from challenge by subversive or dissenting views (often, these two objectives are symbiotic). Even when blasphemy laws cite public

---

[18] ICCPR (1966) art 20 (emphasis added).

[19] For other examples, see Uladzislau Belavusau, 'Hate Speech' in Rainer Grote, Frauke Lachenmann, and Rudiger Wolfrum (eds), *The Max Planck Encyclopedia of Comparative Constitutional Law* (OUP 2017) (emphasis added).

[20] For a more detailed examination, see Alon Harel's chapter on hate speech in this volume (Chapter 25).

[21] *Saskatchewan (Human Rights Commission) v Whatcott* [2013] 1 SCR 467 [71].   [22] Ibid.

[23] See, eg, *Afriforum v Malema* 2011 (6) SA 240 (EqC).

[24] *Robert Faurisson v France*, Comm no 550/1993 (8 November 1986, UNHRC).

order as a justification, what they are concerned with is possible violence or disorder that arises as a result of hurt sentiments.

The distinction is often evident from the texts of blasphemy laws. Section 295A of the Indian Penal Code, for example, penalizes 'outraging the *religious feelings* of any class'.[25] In a slight variation, section 138 of the Kenyan Penal Code prohibits 'wounding the *religious feelings*' of any person.[26] While the Indian and Kenyan Penal Codes focus on protecting religious *sentiments*, Article 156(a) of the Indonesian Criminal Code prohibits 'abuse or defamation *of a religion*'[27]—thus focusing on preserving religious tenets from challenge (the rest of the legal provision—as we shall discuss below—makes this clear). Similarly, the Austrian Criminal Code penalizes 'anyone who publicly disparages a person or thing that is the object of worship of a domestic church or religious society, *or a doctrine*'.[28] Notably, these provisions do not speak the language of discrimination, or incitement to cause harm.

27.2.2 The Justifications for Blasphemy Laws

Courts have struggled with how to justify the exalted immunity offered to religion through blasphemy laws. Granting religion—and, by extension, religious believers—an *ipso facto* special status by granting them the unique power of censorship appears to conflict with the fundamental commitments of constitutional democracies to treat all citizens with equal concern and respect. In the reasoning of courts, therefore, we often see attempts at masking: although the text of the law categorically speaks of protecting religious *sentiments* or *feelings* (or protecting the religion itself), this is taken to be merely a shorthand for other, putatively more legitimate, secular goals.

27.2.2.1 *Public Order*

The first of these goals is that of public order. In *Ramji Lal Modi v State of UP*,[29] the Supreme Court of India upheld the constitutional validity of section 295A of the Indian Penal Code on the basis that it was reasonable to assume that a calculated and

---

[25] Indian Penal Code (1860) s 295A (emphasis added).
[26] Kenyan Penal Code (1930) s 138 (emphasis added).
[27] Presidential Decree No 1/PNPS/1965, read with art 156(a) of the Penal Code of Indonesia (1982) (emphasis added).
[28] Austrian Criminal Code (1974), s 188 (emphasis added). It is tellingly titled 'vilification of religious teachings.' See also art 216 of the 2004 Turkish Penal Code ('disrespecting the religious belief of a group'); s 816 of the 2004 Ethiopian Criminal Code ('scoffing' at religion); s 204 of the 1990 Nigerian Criminal Code ('public insult...on religion'); art 208 of the Brazilian Penal Code (1940) ('public vilification'); many common law countries retain the concept of 'blasphemous libel', and Ireland prohibits it as part of its Constitution (art 40.6.1), subject to the outcome of a 2018 referendum. Note, however, that in many of the above examples, the laws in question are rarely—if ever—enforced. In 2015, blasphemy laws were upheld by courts in Poland and Malaysia. For a reasonably comprehensive treatment of jurisdictions with blasphemy laws (or variants), see Library of Congress (Legal Reports), 'Blasphemy and Related Laws', <https://www.loc.gov/law/help/blasphemy/index.php> accessed on 24 August 2018.
[29] *Ramji Lal Modi v State of UP*, AIR 1957 SC 620.

intentional insult to religious sentiments could well trigger public disorder. It was argued before the Court that the statute (which we have seen above) was over-broad, and in criminalizing 'insults' to religious feelings *simpliciter*, bore no relationship to public order. The Court rejected this argument in the terms described above, postulating an almost necessary link between religious insult and public disorder, without inviting the State to provide a factual foundation for it.

Similarly, 'peace and public order' was invoked by the Office of the Attorney-General in Indonesia, as part of the guidelines for when 'preventive action' could be taken against individuals or groups under the Indonesian blasphemy law.[30] Public order (which is a ground for restricting religious freedom under the Indonesian Constitution)—along with its variant, 'national harmony'—was also invoked by the state and religious groups in support of the blasphemy law during proceedings challenging its constitutional validity. And it was an argument that was accepted by the Indonesian Constitutional Court as a significant reason for upholding the law.[31]

The basis of this conflation appears to be that individuals' commitment to religion is so deep and central to their lives (recall John Rawl's account of 'comprehensive doctrines'), that an insult to religious feelings is equivalent, in terms, to undermining an individual's entire world-view and integrity, the consequences of which can often (if not always) lead to public disorder. In this way, constitutional democracy can have its cake and eat it too: religious sentiments are protected not because they are *religious*, but in service of the *secular* goal of preserving public order.

The first problem with this argument, of course, is that it constitutionalizes the heckler's veto.[32] It is not the wounded believers—who actually cause public disorder—that are penalized, but the speaker who inflicted the wound that led to the believers breaching public order. The second problem is that it permanently infantilizes the citizenry when it comes to the issue of religion and religious speech. It is one thing to regulate speech in cases of temporary diminished autonomy—such as shouting 'fire' in a crowded theatre, or inciting an enraged mob to imminent violence. A blanket ban on 'blasphemy' on the basis of public order suggests, however, that religion causes a permanent impairment of autonomy.[33] This is inconsistent with the foundational principles not only of the free speech guarantee but, more generally, of liberal democracy itself.

27.2.2.2 *Offence*

The public order-based justification for blasphemy laws, therefore, involves far-reaching compromises with other fundamental values. Perhaps aware of this, some courts have chosen not to travel down this road. Take, for example, the jurisprudence of the European Court of Human Rights (ECtHR). The ECtHR has accorded a wide 'margin of

---

[30] Melissa A Crouch, 'Law and Religion in Indonesia: The Constitutional Court and the Blasphemy Law' (2012) 7 *Asian J Comp L* 1, 8.
[31] Ibid.   [32] See, eg, Harry Kalven, *The Negro and the First Amendment* (U Chicago P 1966).
[33] For a discussion, see Thomas Scanlon, 'A Theory of Freedom of Expression' (1972) 1 *Phil & Pub Aff* 204, although Scanlon subsequently resiled from these views.

appreciation' to national authorities, on the basis that there exists an 'obligation to avoid as far as possible expressions that are *gratuitously offensive* to others and thus an infringement *of their rights*'.[34] After formulating this proposition in *Otto-Preminger-Institut v Austria*, the ECtHR then refined it in *Wingrove v United Kingdom*, noting that blasphemy laws fall within the category of 'protection…of the rights of others',[35] which is a permissible restriction upon the freedom of speech under the European Convention of Human Rights (ECHR). In these cases, it was effectively held that there existed an enforceable right *not* to be outraged or offended in matters of religious conviction.[36]

A free-standing right not to be offended in matters of religion appears to be extraordinarily broad. It also appears to be rootless—what, precisely, is the *value* upon which it is based? In *Otto-Preminger-Institut*, the dissenting opinion made a passing reference to the idea of 'tolerance', observing that 'tolerance works both ways and the democratic character of a society will be affected if violent and abusive attacks on the reputation of a religious group are allowed'.[37] This justification was elaborated in slightly greater detail by the Supreme Court of India, while upholding a government-imposed book ban upon an allegedly blasphemous text. The Court noted that 'India is [a] country with *vast disparities in language, culture and religion* and unwarranted and malicious criticism or interference in the faith of others cannot be accepted'.[38] The basis of the judgments of both the ECtHR and the Indian Supreme Court appears to be located in the idea of pluralism, and the necessity of preserving the integrity and well-being of communities in a pluralist democracy.

This argument comes close to couching the issue in the language of regulating hate speech. The overlap is visible most clearly in judgments such as the US Supreme Court case of *Beauharnais v Illinois*, where the constitutionality of a statute prohibiting group libel (and therefore couched more in the language of defamation *of* classes—including religious classes—of people) was nonetheless upheld by invoking principles midway between promoting pluralism and controlling the effects of hate speech:

> Illinois did not have to look beyond her own borders or await the tragic experience of *the last three decades* to conclude that wilful purveyors of falsehood concerning racial and religious groups promote strife and tend powerfully to obstruct the *manifold adjustments required for free, ordered life in a metropolitan, polyglot community*.[39]

There remains, however, a crucial distinction. The regulation of religious hate speech is premised upon protecting the *individual* from discrimination, subordination, and violence (all tangible harms), based upon their membership of a certain religious group.

---

[34] *Otto-Preminger Institute v Austria* (1995) 19 EHRR 34 [49] (emphasis added).
[35] *Wingrove v The United Kingdom* (1997) 24 EHRR 1 [48].
[36] See, eg, Joel Feinberg, *Offense to Others* (OUP 1988), discussing the 'offence principle'.
[37] *Otto-Preminger Institute* (n 34) [6] (joint dissenting opinion).
[38] *Baragur Ramachandrappa v State of Karnataka* (2007) 5 SCC 11 [9] (emphasis added).
[39] *Beauharnais v Illinois*, 343 US 250, 259 (1952) (emphasis added).

On the other hand, the defence of blasphemy law based on the claims of pluralism and tolerance either takes the *religious group* itself as the constitutive unit of concern (and aims at preserving group integrity), or takes the individual's membership of the group as a good, and seeks to protect it by penalizing expression that could potentially undermine it.

27.2.2.3 *The Problem of Religious Dissent*

There is, however, one serious problem with the above premises: they are based upon a monolithic and homogenous view of communities and groups. This is a flawed view. As Madhavi Sundar points out in an important article, groups and communities, at all times, are characterized by cultural dissent.[40] Norms that have come to define or characterize the group are not static and eternal; they are both constructed, and under constant challenge, revision, and modification. Sundar argues, therefore, that the law needs to recognize the existence of cultural dissent, lest it become 'complicit in...suppressing internal cultural reform'.[41]

Blasphemy laws are examples par excellence of invoking the power of the state to 'suppress internal cultural reform'. This was most clearly in evidence in the constitutional challenge to blasphemy before the Indonesian Constitutional Court, where orthodox religious groups categorically invoked the problem of controlling dissenting or heterodox sects.[42] Before the Indian Supreme Court as well, the book ban which was challenged was imposed on the basis that a revisionist reading of the biography of a sect's founder insulted true believers.[43] The point should be obvious: religious groups are rarely democratic in character, and in an overwhelming majority of cases, religious norms and proscriptions are imposed from above, without the democratic participation of the members of the community. Religious dissent often represents counter-views to the dominant orthodoxy, and blasphemy laws, in turn, are weaponized by religious gatekeepers to quell or undermine those expressive challenges to the existing norms. The existence of a blasphemy law, therefore, cannot be justified merely by invoking the integrity of communities and groups. Rather, it must be acknowledged that the integrity of groups comes at the cost of placing the state power in service of the status quo, along with existing hierarchies of power and influence within those groups. Blasphemy laws invariably require the state to take sides in an intra-religious dispute, instead of acting as a neutral arbiter.

This point was noted specifically by both by the 2009 Joint Statement by the UN Special Rapporteurs on racism, racial discrimination, xenophobia and related intolerance, freedom of religion or belief, and promotion and protection of the right to freedom of opinion and expression, and in the 2013 Annual Report of the United Nations High Commissioner for Human Rights. The Joint Statement recorded that, inter alia,

---

[40] Madhavi Sundar, 'Cultural Dissent' (2001) 54 *Stan L Rev* 495. See also, James C Scott, *Domination and the Arts of Resistance: Hidden Transcripts* (Yale UP 1992), for an account of how the visible 'public transcript' is always accompanied by a private, hidden, off-stage transcript of resistance and dissent.
[41] Sundar (n 40) 509.   [42] Crouch (n 30).   [43] *Baragur Ramachandrappa* (n 38).

blasphemy laws could result in censure of 'intra-religious criticism'.[44] And the UN High Commissioner observed that blasphemy laws were used to persecute religious dissenters.[45] These observations highlight the inherent tensions and contradictions in justifying blasphemy laws on the touchstone of preserving the integrity of communities in a pluralistic and diverse society, or by invoking the value of 'tolerance'.

27.3 RELIGION, SPEECH, AND THE STATE: INSTRUCTION, SYMBOLS, AND PRAYER

27.3.1 Religious Expression and the Public Sphere

In contemporary political theory, the rise of the modern state has been accompanied by a division between the 'public' and the 'private' spheres.[46] Where—and how—religion fits into this binary has always been deeply contested. At one extreme, we have the picturesque—but ultimately vague—image of a 'wall of separation between Church and State',[47] which—as is well known—has been honoured more in the breach. The idea underlying the 'wall of separation' is that religion and the state occupy different and mutually exclusive spheres. At the other extreme, the public sphere is itself defined and constituted by religious norms, which are upheld and enforced by the state. Between these two extremes, however, there exists a wide spectrum, and courts and legislatures have struggled with the relationship between religion and the public sphere.

One important terrain upon which this struggle has played out is that of religious speech, especially in public forums where there is no viable right of exit, or of avoidance. For example, is it permissible to have religious instruction in state schools?[48] On the one hand, the Indian Constitution explicitly prohibits religious instruction 'in any educational institution wholly maintained out of State funds'.[49] Similarly, the US Supreme Court located this prohibition within the concept of the separation of church and state.[50] On the other hand—despite mandating the separation of church and state—religious

---

[44] Githu Muigai, Asma Jahangir, and Frank La Rue, 'Freedom of Expression and Incitement to Racial or Religious Hatred' (Joint statement, OHCHR side event during the Durban Review Conference, Geneva, 22 April 2009) <https://www2.ohchr.org/English/issues/religion/docs/SRjointstatement22april09.pdf> accessed on 27 August 2018.

[45] United Nations General Assembly, 'Annual Report of the United Nations High Commissioner for Human Rights (Addendum)', Human Rights Council, 22nd Session (2013), A/HRC/22/17/Add 4 [19].

[46] See, eg, Nancy Fraser, 'Rethinking the Public Sphere: A Contribution to a Critique of Actually Existing Democracy' (1990) 25/26 *Soc Text* 56; Seyla Benhabib, *The Claims of Culture: Equality and Diversity in the Global Era* (Princeton UP 2002).

[47] *Everson v Board of Education*, 330 US 1 (1947).

[48] Of course, this debate is not only about the place of religion in the public sphere, but also concerns the rights of parents.

[49] Constitution of India, art 28(1).   [50] *McCollum v Board of Education*, 333 US 203 (1948).

instruction is permitted in Colombian public schools (although non-Catholic religious groups must accede to a specific agreement to be allowed to do so).[51] And the German basic law goes so far as to state that 'religious instruction *shall* form part of the curriculum in state schools'.[52]

In constitutional challenges to religious instruction in schools, some courts have tried to draw a distinction between *indoctrination* (impermissible) and instruction *about* religion (permissible). This has been the route followed, for example, by Canada and by the ECtHR. For example, in *Canadian Civil Liberties Association v Ontario*, the Ontario Court of Appeal noted that:

> The crucial issue in this appeal is whether the purpose and effects of the regulation and the curriculum are to indoctrinate school children in Ontario in *the Christian faith*. If so, the rights to freedom of conscience and religion under s. 2 (a) of the Canadian Charter of Rights and Freedoms and the equality rights guaranteed under s. 15 of the Charter may be infringed. On the other hand, it is conceded that education designed to teach about religion and to foster moral values *without indoctrination in a particular faith* would not be a breach of the Charter.[53]

Similarly, the ECtHR accepted that states were well within their rights to 'impart knowledge...of a religious or philosophical kind' in schools,[54] as long as it did not relapse into sectarianism, or a pursuit of indoctrination. The Court accepted that, given the country's history, even a curriculum devoted to multiple religions may place more importance on one religion (in this case, Christianity)—but that, in itself, would not breach the Convention, as long as the 'information or knowledge included in the curriculum is conveyed in an objective, critical and pluralistic manner'.[55]

Additionally, religious speech in this context is not, of course, limited to religious instruction: the place of religious *symbols* (another form of expression) within public spaces (such as the schoolroom) has been equally debated. In dealing with these issues— in a manner similar to judgments about religious instruction in schools—courts in constitutional democracies broadly accept that the state has a duty of 'neutrality and impartiality' in the public sphere, and cannot therefore specifically endorse *a* religion. For example, in one of its most controversial decisions, the German Constitutional Court found that a Bavarian law mandating that all state schools hang a crucifix in the classroom was unconstitutional.[56] The basis of the Court's decision was that the presence of the crucifix signalled a state endorsement of Catholicism, even though it did not

---

[51] See the discussion in Vicente Prieto, 'Colombia' in *The Routledge International Handbook of Religious Education* (Derek Davis and Elena Mikhailovna eds, Routledge 2013) 84.
[52] Basic Law for the Federal Republic of Germany, art 7(3) (emphasis added).
[53] *Canadian Civil Liberties Assn v Ontario (Minister of Education)* (1990) 71 OR (2d) 341 (ON CA) (emphasis added). For a discussion, see Paul Clarke, 'Religion, Public Education and the Charter: Where Do We Go Now?' (2005) 40 *McGill J Educ* 351.
[54] *Folgero v Norway*, App no 154702/02 (UNHRC, 29 June 2007) [84].
[55] Ibid.
[56] *Crucifix Case* [1995] 32 BVerfGE.

reach the level of *identification* with it.[57] This logic, however, has been divisive. The Romanian High Court, for example, overruled a decision of the Romanian National Council for Combating Discrimination (CNCD), and held that the presence of Romanian Orthodox icons in state schools was permissible.[58] Similarly, in *Lautsi v Italy*, the Grand Chamber of the ECtHR overruled a judgment of the Second Section of the Court, and held that the display of crucifixes in state schools did not violate the ECHR. The Grand Chamber conceded that the crucifix was a Christian symbol, and was accorded 'preponderant visibility' in the classroom.[59] However, it went on to hold that, nonetheless, it was a 'passive symbol',[60] and its presence did not rise to the level of religious indoctrination (thereby remaining consistent with the state's obligations of neutrality and impartiality).

There are cases, however, where religious speech and expression is of a character that cannot, under any circumstances, be described as 'passive'. Take, for example, school prayers (an example of religious speech par excellence). In upholding voluntary school prayers in public schools (despite fears that in a school environment, such action could never be truly voluntary and would brand dissenters as outsiders), the German Constitutional Court hinted, inter alia, at how, as a historical matter, Christianity had always been rooted in German culture[61] (the point, as readers will recognize, is couched in a similar fashion to the ECtHR's analysis of Christianity-skewed school curricula).

Indeed, this argument is at the heart of a further distinction that was proposed by Bavaria in the *Crucifix* case, and has subsequently been accepted by some courts: that is, a distinction between the state endorsing *religion*, and promoting *culture* (of which religion is a part, but is not constitutive). For example, while considering a challenge to a new set of school textbooks on the ground that they brought in religious instruction through the back door, the Indian Supreme Court noted that the constitutional prohibition was upon 'imparting religious instruction or of performing religious worship. There is no prohibition for having study of religious philosophy and culture'.[62] The same distinction is often found in the judgments of the US Supreme Court.[63]

27.3.2 'Religion' and 'Cultural' or 'Civilizational Values': A Critique of the Distinction

In many ways, however, the distinction between (impermissible) religious instruction and (permissible) instruction in cultural (or civilizational) values reproduces the same problems that we saw earlier while examining the issues of cultural dissent and community-based defence of blasphemy laws. Prohibition of overt, state-sanctioned

---

[57] Ibid. [58] See CNCD Decision 323/2006, reversed by the High Court in 2008.
[59] *Lautsi v Italy* (2012) 54 EHRR 3 [71].   [60] Ibid [72].
[61] *School Prayers Case*, BVerfGE 52, 223.
[62] *Aruna Roy v Union of India* (2002) 7 SCC 368 [40].
[63] See, eg, *Lynch v Donnelly*, 465 US 668 (1984), on the subject of a crèche on Christmas Day.

religious expression in spaces such as the schoolroom responds to the concern that religious messaging that carries the state's imprimatur in these public spaces will serve to marginalize unorthodox, dissenting, or plural views. Switching 'religion' with 'culture' does little to address that concern, given how intertwined the two concepts are. It is one thing to argue that—for example—the Sunday holiday may have had its origin in one religion, but has now become so secularized that it no longer carries any religious connotations.[64] It is another thing to argue, however, that symbolism or instruction does carry connotations, but that they speak to culture instead of religion. Questions of impartiality and neutrality with respect to the latter remain troubling ones.

For this reason, contemporary scholarship (and indeed, the jurisprudence of the ECtHR) suggests that—from an international human rights perspective—the correct approach is to ensure that instruction is 'objective', 'plural', 'neutral', and 'critical'.[65] A variant of this approach appears to have been encoded in the South African Constitution, which allows 'religious *observances*' to be conducted at state or state-aided institutions, so long as they were both voluntary, and on an 'equitable basis'.[66] This has been labelled an approach of 'proactive tolerance' of religious expression in public spaces.[67] This has also been the approach adopted by the UNHRC. Its General Comment No 22 permits (mandatory) 'instruction in ... the general history of religions and ethics if it is given in a neutral and objective way'.[68] In *Leirvag v Norway*, the UNHRC found that giving priority to the tenets of one religion over others, requiring actual religious practices, and the subjective experience of objectors, were all contributory factors towards demonstrating that instruction was not neutral or objective.[69] A system of 'partial exemptions' was found to be too burdensome upon both parents and children.

However, while the UNHRC and the ECtHR appear to have laid down markers on what may constitute non-objective or non-neutral instruction (veering towards indoctrination), it is still a challenge to define what constitutes 'objective', 'neutral', and 'critical'. Carolyn Evans argues, for instance, that the Toledo Guidelines—which emphasize a participatory curriculum-framing process and the avoidance of stereotypes—provide a useful marker to examine the character of religious instruction, or instruction about religion.[70] Instead of masking the genuine issues using the cover of culture/civilizational values, it is potentially both more honest—and more effective—to concede the importance of religion in public life, while maintaining an approach that allows the recipients of religious speech a degree of critical distance.

[64] *McGowan v Maryland*, 366 US 420 (1961).
[65] Carolyn Evans, 'Religious Education in Public Schools: An International Human Rights Perspective' (2008) 8 *Hum Rts L Rev* 449.
[66] Constitution of the Republic of South Africa, s 15(2) (emphasis added).
[67] Lourens du Plessis, 'Freedom of or Freedom from Religion? An Overview of Issues Pertinent to the Constitutional Protection of Religious Rights and Freedoms in the "New South Africa"' (2001) 2 *BYU L Rev* 439, 458.
[68] Office of the High Commissioner for Human Rights, General Comment No 22: The Right to Freedom of Thought, Conscience and Religion (art 18) (48th session, 1993) UN Doc CCPR/C/21/Rev 1/Add 4 [6].
[69] *Leirvag v Norway*, App no 1155/2003 (UNHRC, 3 November 2004) [14.3].
[70] Evans (n 65).

27.4 Reconciling Religious Speech with Other Constitutional Values

In the previous section, we discussed the issues that arise when the state appears to sanction, support, or otherwise endorse religious expression in quintessentially public spaces, such as a state-run schoolroom. A different—yet related—set of issues arise when the state seeks to proscribe certain forms of religious expression in the public sphere.

It is important to begin with a conceptual distinction. In this section, I shall not examine cases where the right to religious expression (as a subset of the right to religious practice) runs up against a generally-worded secular legislation (although those situations raise important questions in their own right). For example, we will not be discussing the South African Constitutional Court's decision about whether the use of cannabis for religious purposes could be permitted under the Drug Act,[71] or the US Supreme Court judgment concerning the use of peyote by Native Americans.[72] These cases concerned laws of general application that specifically impacted certain religious communities, whose (expressive) practices went against what was considered 'normal'. On the other hand, the cases that we shall be examining involve targeted proscription of certain kinds of religious speech and expression, on the ground that that particular form of religious expression is inconsistent with other values that the state is committed to maintaining in that particular sphere.

27.4.1 Religious Speech and Elections

The Indian electoral law—the Representation of the People Act—proscribes the soliciting of votes by appeals to religion, during an election campaign. In 2016, a seven-judge bench of the Supreme Court was asked to decide whether—on a true interpretation of the law—electoral candidates were barred only from citing their own religion to voters as a reason to vote for them, or whether they were also barred from invoking the voters' religion. A razor-thin majority of the Court (4–3) held that markers of personal identity (including religion, caste, and so on) could not be the bases of soliciting or receiving votes. Therefore, the law was to be interpreted in a manner in which any form of speech that solicited votes on religious (or other identitarian grounds) was barred.[73] The dissenting judgment, however, invoked precisely the kinds of arguments that we have discussed in the previous two sections: it argued that historically, religion, caste, and so on, had been sites of group discrimination and exclusion. The public sphere presented an

---

[71] *Prince v President of the Law Society of the Cape of Good Hope* 2002 (2) SA 794.
[72] *Employment Division v Smith*, 494 US 872 (1990).
[73] *Abhiram Singh v CD Commachen* (2017) 2 SCC 629.

opportunity for marginalized groups to mobilize and seek equality. Consequently, the dissent argued that any law that sought to curtail identitarian expression in the public sphere ought to be interpreted as narrowly as possible.[74] The dissenting opinion viewed religious speech as potentially *emancipatory*, allowing marginalized groups an opportunity to participate in the public sphere as equals. The majority, on the other hand, operated on the premise that the democratic public sphere simply had no room for expressions of (religious and others) identities, and especially not as part of the quintessentially public act of voting.

The dissenting opinion's concern about the interface between state proscriptions and their disproportionate impact upon dissenting and marginalized groups (something that we have seen before in the context of blasphemy laws and the culture-based justification of religious expression in public spaces such as the schoolroom) was perhaps borne out by history. Two decades before, the Supreme Court had held that appeals to Hinduism or 'Hindutva' (a particular ideological variant) did not breach the Representation of the People Act, because they referred not to religion but to a 'way of life'.[75] The distinction between 'religion' and 'way of life' (in order to get around the secular principle that seeks to keep religion from dominating the public sphere) is, of course, strikingly similar to the distinction between 'religion' and 'cultural' or 'civilizational' values, which we have discussed in the previous section. In both cases—perhaps unsurprisingly—the conflation between religion (impermissible) and 'culture' or 'ways of life' (permissible) is made in the context of the majoritarian ideology. This is unsurprising because it is, after all, the dominant religion that appears *normal* enough to be a part of 'culture' or 'way(s) of life'. It does raise the question, however, whether minority or dissenting groups will be afforded the same leeway.

27.4.2 Religious Expression in the Public Sphere

Indeed, there is good reason to believe the contrary, as another set of circumstances demonstrates. In the previous section, we discussed cases where the state appears to endorse or support religion in public spaces such as schoolrooms. What happens, however, when individuals (within these same spaces) want to engage in religious expression? These controversies have come up repeatedly in European countries, and have gone before the ECtHR.

For example, in *Dahlab v Switzerland*,[76] the ECtHR upheld the prohibition upon a primary school teacher from wearing an Islamic headscarf. The ECtHR reasoned that the headscarf was a 'powerful *external* symbol',[77] whose proselytizing effect was

---

[74] Ibid (Chandrachud J, dissenting).
[75] *Ramesh Yeshwant Prabhoo v Prabhakar Kashinath Kunte* (1996) 1 SCC 130.
[76] *Dahlab v Switzerland*, App no 42393/98 (ECtHR 15 February, 2001).
[77] Ibid (emphasis added).

potentially irreconcilable with other fundamental values such as gender equality, tolerance, and non-discrimination. The Grand Chamber came to a similar conclusion in *Leyla Sahin v Turkey*[78] (involving a prohibition upon wearing a headscarf in the university), and cited *Dahlab* at some length.

It is interesting to note that while the crucifix was considered to be a 'passive symbol' whose impact was minimal, the headscarf was held to be a 'powerful external symbol' that potentially had a 'strong proselytizing effect' (in a manner that was inconsistent with other fundamental values of the Convention, such as gender equality). In two distinct ways, this speaks to the common threads that have been running through this chapter. First, decision-making authorities are invariably embedded within the larger social context, and are therefore likely to treat the claims of dissenting or marginalized communities with greater scepticism or hostility. Indeed, this very point was recognized by the South African Constitutional Court in *MEC v Pillay*, where it found that a school's refusal to allow a Tamil Hindu learner (ie, a religious minority) to wear a nose-ring violated the Equality Act.[79] In considering the legal standards to decide whether or not the learner had been discriminated against, the Langa CJ made the telling observation that:

> The norm embodied by the [Equality] Code is not neutral, but enforces mainstream and historically privileged forms of adornment, such as ear studs which also involve the piercing of a body part, at the expense of minority and historically excluded forms. It thus places a burden on learners who are unable to express themselves fully and must attend school in an environment that does not completely accept them.[80]

In other words, therefore, legal tests (of the manner discussed above) that do not come with embedded minority protections are likely to be interpreted in a manner that (unconsciously) privileges the expression of the dominant religion, or dominant groups within a religious community.

Secondly, the language of 'external symbols' is not neutral. It privileges 'privatized religions' (ie, religions that understand the relationship between human and divine to be a private and personal affair), and disadvantages religions that are constituted by expressive conduct (ie, religious expression in the form of dress or symbols, public prayer, and community experience). In other words, different religions accord different levels of importance to forms of religious speech and expression. Prohibiting 'external symbols'—language that is common to more than one jurisdiction—while framed in neutral terms, nonetheless takes a position on how much, and what manner of, religious expression is 'normal' (or desirable) within the context of religion.

---

[78] *Leyla Sahin v Turkey*, App no 447774/98 (ECtHR 10 November 2005).
[79] *MEC for Education: Kwazulu-Natal v Pillay*, 2008 (2) BCLR 99 (CC).
[80] Ibid [44].

27.4.3 Religious Expression and Anti-Discrimination Norms

The last set of examples pertains to what is commonly perceived to be the private sphere: that is, day-to-day economic transactions between individuals. In the last fifty years, many constitutional democracies have come to understand that formal, legal systems of discrimination have been upheld by a pattern of individual, discriminatory acts. Legislatures have therefore felt it necessary to introduce anti-discrimination norms into the private sphere, through civil rights laws. These laws are premised on the foundation that the constitutional norms of equality must be taken into the private domain, through state action, for equality to have any meaning. Religion, race, sex, sexual orientation etc can no longer, therefore, be grounds for refusing to serve someone in a shot, refusing them housing, or transport, and so on.

In recent years, however, resistance to this has been articulated in the language of religious expression. In both the United States and the United Kingdom, bakers' refusal to serve lesbian, gay, bisexual, and transgender (LGBT) individuals on grounds of religious freedom and freedom of religious expression, has generated high-profile litigation. In the UK, the case involved a Northern Irish baker's refusal to bake a cake with a message that read 'Support gay marriage'. This was, however, held to constitute unlawful discrimination by the Northern Irish court, and the baker's argument that he was required to 'endorse' the message by baking the cake was rejected.[81] One of the key components of the reasoning of the court was that the importance of religious speech and expression was diminished in the commercial sphere:

> The defendants are entitled to continue to hold their genuine and deeply held religious beliefs and to manifest them but, in accordance with the law, not to manifest them in the commercial sphere if it is contrary to the rights of others.[82]

This decision was, however, reversed by the UK Supreme Court, which took the case out of the realm of conflicting religious expression and equality rights altogether, by reasoning there had been no discrimination in the first place; the bakers' refusal was to the *message* on the cake, and not to the buyer of the cake.[83]

In the United States, no actual words were required.[84] However, the baker argued that the act of baking a cake was itself an expressive act, and therefore protected by the free speech and religious freedom clause of the US Constitution. The baker was found liable for discrimination by the Colorado Civil Rights Commission. This decision was reversed on appeal to the Supreme Court; however, the Court decided the case on narrow grounds—finding that the Civil Rights Commission had acted in a biased manner—and left the constitutional questions open.[85]

---

[81] *Lee v Ashers Baking Co* [2015] NICty 2.   [82] Ibid [94].
[83] *Lee v Ashers Baking Co* [2018] UKSC 49.
[84] The UK Supreme Court in *Ashers* expressly distinguished the two factual situations on this basis. Ibid [59–62].
[85] *Masterpiece Cakeshop v Colorado Civil Rights Commission*, 584 US ___ (2018).

At one level, these cases are pitched as clashes between the competing values of religious expression and anti-discrimination, played out in the private sphere. At another level, however, they invoke religious speech—which, by virtue of its *expressive* character, possesses greater constitutional sanctity than religious practice—in order to continue a system of private discrimination that civil rights laws ostensibly exist to proscribe. How the introduction of the principle of freedom of (religious) speech will affect the reconciliation between the competing remains to be determined. An obvious solution is that which is presented by the Northern Irish court, which makes it clear that if the dominant character of the transaction is commercial, then—for constitutional purposes—it cannot be treated as 'speech'. Whether this logic will be accepted by other courts, however, is unclear at the moment.

27.5 Conclusion

This chapter has explored the relationship between individuals, religious communities, and the state, around the axis of religious speech and expression. When considering these issues, it is important to remember that the relationships in question are invariably mediated by inequalities and hierarchies. These hierarchies take many forms. A number of modern states have a dominant majority religion (that has been historically linked with state authority itself), and multiple minority religions. Not only does this lead to potential conflicts regarding the state's role as an arbiter, but it also—invariably—triggers clashes between public, expressive assertions of minority religions and the majority religion-infused public values of the state. Within a religion, there are dominant strands, powerful gatekeepers, and officially sanctioned authorities on the one hand, and dissenters and heterodox streams of thought on the other. And insofar as the state commits itself to protecting forms of religious life and expression, conflicts arise when these conflict with the guaranteed constitutional rights of others. Because of the layered and competing interests involved, each of these issues is fraught with difficulty.

In this chapter, I have suggested that conflicts around religious speech and expression are best understood from the perspective of modern constitutional democracies' commitment to maintaining pluralism, diversity, and both intra- and inter-group equality. This theme runs through the diverse issues that this chapter has explored, across jurisdictions. Blasphemy laws, for example, are often masked in the language of maintaining public order, or protecting the legitimate rights of believers from having their core world-views mocked, vilified, or undermined. At their heart, however, they are invariably about preserving religious status quo—as upheld and maintained by dominant forces within an organized religion—against internal challenge and reform. Blasphemy laws, therefore, act as brakes upon genuine, intra-group pluralism and cultural dissent.

Inter-group pluralism is impacted by the state allying itself with dominant religion, by allowing, endorsing, or mandating religious expression in public spaces. Here again, the justifications have been framed in neutral terms: 'passive' symbolism that does not reach the level of indoctrination, or the substitution of 'culture' for religion. As we have seen, however, the bases of these justifications—not coincidentally—end up favouring the dominant religion, and threatening inter-group parity.

And lastly, questions of breaking down hierarchies in the public sphere arise when the state decides that certain forms of religious expression are incompatible with other public values. When it comes to prohibiting the use of religious expression in certain kinds of public discourse (such as election campaigns), or religiously expressive acts in public spaces (such as dress), once again, policies and laws framed in neutral terms can contribute to upholding hierarchies rather than breaking them down. Of course, this is not always the case: invocation of religious expression can *also* be used to perpetuate hierarchies, as a get-out-of-jail card from complying with the state's anti-discrimination framework of laws.

I therefore suggest that the best way of navigating this terrain is through the lens of pluralism and (what Susanne Baer has described as) the anti-hierarchy principle.[86] Religious expression can both contribute to, and impede, genuine pluralism and individual and group equality in a society. A state that is committed to both values should—based on the context—extend its support to, or carefully regulate—religious speech and expression, depending upon its impact on pluralism, diversity, and equality.

---

[86] See the extensive discussion in Susanne Baer, 'Equality: The Jurisprudence of the German Constitutional Court' (1999) 5 *Colum J Eur L* 249.

CHAPTER 28

GLORIFYING CENSORSHIP? ANTI-TERROR LAW, SPEECH, AND ONLINE REGULATION

ELIZA BECHTOLD AND GAVIN PHILLIPSON

28.1 INTRODUCTION

A group of British Asian university students, after a few drinks at home, dress up as jihadis and brandish an ISIS flag; their friends take pictures and upload them, chortling, to Facebook. They have gone to some trouble with the outfits and flag and, though the flag isn't identical to that used by ISIS, it looks very similar. Their idea is to satirize what they perceive as media-driven exaggerated obsession with terrorism and the Islamophobia it produces. Merely an insensitive prank? Not so: these students would *prima facie* have committed a serious terrorism offence for which they could go to prison. The UK's Counter-Terrorism and Border Security Act 2019[1] amended the Terrorism Act 2000 to create a new offence of publishing an image in circumstances that *arouse a reasonable suspicion* that the person is a member or supporter of a proscribed organization. If arrested, the students would doubtless protest that they were at home and not in public, intended only a satirical stunt, had no thought of being regarded as actual ISIS supporters and that the comments in their Facebook post show no evidence that it encouraged anyone to support ISIS. The police would tell them their protestations

---

[1] Section 2 of the Counter-Terrorism and Border Security Act 2019 amended s 13 of the Terrorism Act 2000 to criminalize the publication by a person of an image (whether still or moving) of an item of clothing or an article (such as a flag) in such a way or in such circumstances as to arouse reasonable suspicion that the person is a member or supporter of a proscribed organization.

are irrelevant: their intention in committing the stunt is not material; because the images were 'published', it is irrelevant that they were recorded in private;[2] the offence doesn't require demonstrating that the publication of the image caused any risk of harm or 'encouragement' to anyone.

Searches of the students' laptops then reveal that one of them, Abdul, had visited a jihadi website that instructs would-be jihadis on how to conduct terrorist operations against the infidels, an offence that carries up to fifteen years in prison. Abdul may protest that he visited the site partly for a drunken 'dare', and partly to make sure 'we got the flag right' and insist his laptop will show that he downloaded nothing, only clicking on a couple of links. One of his friends may say he'd heard that 'you were ok as long as you didn't visit such sites over and over'. The police will tell him that the legislation as passed criminalizes a single visit, regardless of whether any material is downloaded: 'just looking once is all that's needed'.

The above hypothetical illustrates a central theme of this chapter: that many leading Western democracies—and the European Union—are enacting increasingly draconian measures against terrorist-related speech that undermine long-standing free speech principles. In certain instances, such measures are so illiberal that their results are hard to believe. Consider that when the British government introduced the bill containing this offence of visiting a terrorist website, *three* separate visits were required to incur liability in order to ensure the authorities established a 'pattern of behaviour' rather than a deliberate 'one-off action' sparked by mere curiosity.[3] The government changed this to only one required visit during the bill's passage through parliament. Hence, the offence as enacted is shorn of the main protective feature by which it was justified.

The Counter-Terrorism and Border Security Act 2019 also amends other draconian speech-related offences to capture even more attenuated terrorist-related expression. To give just one example, it broadens further the UK's already astonishingly expansive 'encouragement of terrorism' offence.[4] Previously, 'statements that are *likely to be understood* by some or all of the members of the public to whom they are published as a direct or indirect encouragement or other inducement to them to the commission, preparation or instigation of acts of terrorism' were proscribed.[5] 'Encouragement' could constitute merely 'glorifying' terrorism, and the offence required no specific intent[6] or proof that a single person *was* actually encouraged. However, the government was concerned that, if such statements were directed at children or vulnerable adults who were unable to understand the content, liability would not be established. This was for the excellent reason that no actual encouragement *could* take place in such circumstances, given that the audience was incapable of understanding the message. The government, however,

---

[2] Save that a satirical intention that was manifest to the observer of the image would presumably help negate a reasonable suspicion that the person in the image was a member or supporter of ISIS.
[3] Explanatory Notes to the Counter-Terrorism and Border Security Bill 2018, para 37.
[4] Counter-Terrorism and Border Security Act 2019, s 5.
[5] See Terrorism Act 2006, s 1(1).
[6] It could be committed recklessly: Terrorism Act 2006, s 2(1).

determined that the 'encouragement' offence should apply even in such circumstances,[7] and pushed through an amendment so that the offence is now committed if *a reasonable person would* understand the statement as an encouragement or inducement to them to 'the commission, preparation or instigation of acts of terrorism'. This substitutes a hypothetical risk for a real one.

Such draconian offences are not limited to the UK. Both Spain and France have experienced a recent surge in prosecutions of 'glorifying terrorism' offences, which target the 'glorification', 'advocacy', or 'encouragement' of terrorism on the basis that such expression may incite future terrorist acts. Amnesty International reports that those prosecuted under the Spanish offence,[8] under which posting online is an aggravating factor, include artists, rappers supporting communist causes, puppeteers, one student who posted jokes and memes about a Franco-era prime minister, and another who re-tweeted a historical joke about a prime minister killed by the ETA in 1973.[9] A tweet about a dead ETA leader saying the people 'are with' him, 'will always remember', and will 'win for' him, landed the poster a year in prison—this despite the fact that the ETA had declared a permanent ceasefire seven years earlier and had disarmed by the time the conviction was handed down.[10] In a touch of almost surreal irony, a Spanish film-maker making a critical documentary about prosecutions brought for glorification-related offences was himself prosecuted for such an offence.[11]

Meanwhile, France recently adopted harsher penalties for violations of its 'apology of terrorism' offence, which now attracts a sentence of up to seven years in prison and a fine of as much as €100,000.[12] Between 2014 and 2016, the number of persons sentenced for this offence rose by over 1,000 per cent, from 3 to 306; these include a vegan activist who was convicted for a Facebook post applauding the death of a butcher in a terrorist attack.[13] In Germany, under the new NetzDG Law, thousands of pieces of online content are being rapidly removed, often within twenty-four hours of notification, and the EU is legislating to empower Member States to order online platforms to remove terrorist-related content within one hour.[14] Beyond Europe, Australia has created an extraordinarily comprehensive counter-terrorism framework that incorporates glorification-related offences,[15] including legislation requiring that publications, films, or computer games

---

[7] This is made clear in the Explanatory Notes (n 3) paras 41 and 42.

[8] Criminal Code of Spain 1995, art 578.

[9] Amnesty International, 'Tweet...If You Dare: How Counter-Terrorism Laws Restrict Freedom of Expression in Spain' (13 March 2018) <https://www.amnesty.org/download/Documents/EUR4179242018 ENGLISH.PDF> accessed 15 April 2019.

[10] Ibid 7, 15. Amnesty International found the vast majority of glorification prosecutions in Spain relate to disbanded or inactive domestic armed groups.

[11] Ibid 12.

[12] Council of Europe Commissioner for Human Rights, 'Misuse of anti-terror legislation threatens freedom of expression,' (Human Rights Comment, 12 April 2018) <https://www.coe.int/en/web/commissioner/-/misuse-of-anti-terror-legislation-threatens-freedom-of-expression> accessed 1 April 2019.

[13] Ibid.   [14] See n 110 and accompanying text.

[15] See Criminal Code Act 1995 (Cth), div 101.

that 'advocate' the doing of a terrorist act be classified as 'Refused Classification',[16] preventing their commercial release.

The purpose of the above examples is to make an important initial point: all these draconian offences and policies come *not* from authoritarian or non-democratic countries, but rather from leading Western liberal democracies—and the EU, which proudly proclaims its foundations to lie in respect for human rights and the rule of law.[17] Far more draconian laws exist in the non-democratic world.[18] Even in the United States, long an outlier in its constitutional protection of extreme political speech, recent case law suggests that the offence of providing material support to designated foreign terrorist organizations has blown something of a hole in the famous *Brandenburg* principle, which protects even speech intended to incite violence, absent proof that 'imminent lawless action' is likely to occur.[19]

In what follows, having outlined a number of factors that tend towards skewed perceptions of the risks of terrorism, we sketch the rapid spread of laws aimed at terrorist propaganda, noting the unusual role of the UN Security Council in 'directing national legislative practice' in the criminal sphere.[20] We argue that, while there are legitimate arguments for restricting certain types of terrorist material, existing laws and policies tend indiscriminately to lump truly dangerous material (such as bomb-making instructions and direct incitement to violence) together with mere expressions of support or sympathy for groups that use violence, including against despotic regimes, or groups that once, but no longer, used violence to achieve political ends.[21] We contend that skewed perceptions of the threat of terrorism appears to have an almost unique capacity to cause the weakening, if not outright abandonment of the standards that normally provide robust expression to freedom of speech. This may be seen first in the recent proliferation of measures aimed at proscribing or removing terrorist-related speech. But as we seek to show, this tendency is also apparent in two case studies, which examine decisions of the European Court of Human Rights (ECtHR) and of US courts under the First Amendment in turn. Finally, we consider what appears to be the remedy *de jour* for states and supranational authorities concerned about terrorism propaganda: simply removing it from the Internet by way of notice and take-down orders. We argue that this technique poses a threat that is unique in scale and intensity to traditional standards of freedom of expression and the open, public processes that are meant to help uphold them.

---

[16] Classification (Publications, Films, and Computer Games) Act 1995 (Cth), s 9A.
[17] Treaty on European Union (Maastricht Treaty) art 2.   [18] See n 85 and accompanying text.
[19] *Brandenburg v Ohio*, 395 US 444, 447 (1969); see n 90 and accompanying text.
[20] Helen Duffy and Kate Pitcher 'Inciting Terrorism? Crimes of Expression and the Limits of the Law' (2018) Grotius Centre Working Paper No 2018/076-HRL <https://papers.ssrn.com/sol3/papers.cfm?abstract_id=3156210> accessed 20 April 2019, 3.
[21] See n 10 and accompanying text.

28.2 THE ROLE OF THREAT INFLATION AND RISK MISPERCEPTION

The proliferation of measures aimed at terrorist propaganda that this chapter considers are premised on the notion that terrorism poses a major and growing threat to safety and security in the West. Yet, the evidence shows that the public hugely overestimate the threat from terrorism, something doubtless due partly to the massive media coverage given even to low-casualty terrorism attacks. For example, in the period following the 9/11 attacks, the probability of a US citizen dying in the United States as a result of terrorism has remained steady at roughly one in fifty million.[22] Yet, in 2018, 40 per cent of US citizens feared that they or a family member might become a victim of terrorism.[23] In 2017, the statistical probability of an EU inhabitant dying from terrorist violence was 0.0000133 per cent.[24] But a Special Eurobarometer public opinion survey carried out in the 28 EU countries in 2017 found that 95 per cent of respondents regarded security challenges, especially terrorism, as very important.[25] The disconnect between the perceived and actual risks of terrorism can be explained, in large part, by the interplay of two related concepts: risk misperception and threat inflation, to which both media and governments contribute. A number of factors contribute to skewed perceptions of risk: the availability of vivid examples (as after a major attack), the greater impact of risks that seem unfamiliar and difficult to control, and 'probability neglect' (focusing on the terrible consequence should an attack happen rather than the low probability of its occurrence). Hence, 'worst case scenarios have a habit of migrating from the realm of fantasy to the domain of policy deliberation'.[26] Finally there is the phenomena of 'the social amplification of risk,'[27] in particular via the media, a 'major agent of amplification', something that works through 'the volume [of information transmitted and] the extent of

---

[22] John Mueller and Mark G Stewart, 'Public Opinion and Counterterrorism Policy' (*The Cato Institute*, 20 February 2018) <https://www.cato.org/publications/white-paper/public-opinion-counter-terrorism-policy> accessed 5 May 2019.

[23] Ibid.

[24] According to Europol's EU 2018 Terrorism Situation and Trend Report, 68 people died in the EU as a result of terrorist violence in 2017. See European Union Agency for Law Enforcement Cooperation, 'European Union Terrorism and Situation and Trend Report' (*Europol*, 20 June 2018) <https://www.europol.europa.eu/sites/default/files/documents/tesat_2018_1.pdf> accessed 1 May 2019, 9. That same year, the EU's Statistical Office estimated that the EU population was 511.8 million: Eurostat, 'EU Population up to Almost 512 Million at 1 January 2017' (*Eurostat*, 10 July 2017) <https://ec.europa.eu/eurostat/documents/2995521/8102195/3-10072017-AP-EN.pdf/a61ce1ca-1efd-41df-86a2-bb495daabdab> accessed 30 September 2019.

[25] European Commission, 'Special Eurobarometer 464b Report: Europeans' Attitudes toward Security' (*European Commission*, December 2017) <https://ec.europa.eu/commfrontoffice/publicopinion/index.cfm/ResultDoc/download/DocumentKy/80698> accessed 30 September 2019.

[26] Frank Furedi, *Invitation to Terror: The Expanding Empire of the Unknown* (Continuum 2007) 114.

[27] Roger E Kasperson and others, 'The Social Amplification of Risk: A Conceptual Framework' in Paul Slovic (ed) *The Perception of Risk* (Taylor & Francis 2000) 232–45.

dramatization'.[28] Quantitative studies have demonstrated how media coverage tends particularly to amplify the threat of Islamist terrorism; one found that jihadi attacks received 450 per cent more coverage than attacks by non-Muslims.[29] These twin phenomena of threat inflation and risk misperception help explain the blizzard of initiatives against terrorist speech—a factor whose importance in fuelling actual terrorist attacks is itself frequently overstated.[30]

28.3 THE RECENT PROLIFERATION OF GLORIFICATION-RELATED OFFENCES AND POLICIES AT THE NATIONAL, REGIONAL, AND SUPRANATIONAL LEVELS

Since 9/11, the UN Security Council has adopted several resolutions aimed at preventing terrorism. The first of these was Resolution 1373,[31] followed, after the London bombings in 2005, by Resolution 1624,[32] which imposes positive obligations on states to prevent terrorism and condemns 'in the strongest terms the incitement of terrorist acts and *repudiat*[*es*] attempts at the justification or glorification (*apologie*) of terrorist acts that may incite further terrorist acts'. It called on states to 'prohibit by law incitement to commit a terrorist act or acts'; while it adds that they should also ensure the protection of freedom of expression, it provides no clear guidance on how to do so and fails to define either 'terrorist acts' or 'incitement'. Subsequently, Resolution 2178[33] stressed the need for states to act co-operatively to prevent terrorists from exploiting technology, communications, and resources to incite support for terrorist acts, while Resolution 2354[34] repeated the repudiation of attempts at *apologie* or glorification of terrorist acts and stressed 'the urgent need to globally counter the activities of [ISIS, Al-Qaida etc] to incite and recruit to commit terrorist acts'. A recent review of this extraordinary burst of UN norm-making argues that it has resulted in an international, supranational approach that 'prioritises...technical solutions to terrorism without due regard to the constitutionalist values of rights and democratic legitimacy',[35] a description that, as we shall see, also fits many recent European initiatives.

---

[28] Ibid. See also Cass Sunstein, 'The Laws of Fear' (2002) 115 *Harv L Rev* 1119, 1132.
[29] Kimberly A Powell, 'Framing Islam: An Analysis of US Media Coverage of Terrorism Since 9/11' (2011) 62 *Comm Stud* 90, 91.
[30] See n 59 and accompanying text.
[31] UNSC Res 1373 (28 September 2001) UN Doc S/RES/1373.
[32] UNSC Res 1624 (14 September 2005) UN Doc S/RES/1624.
[33] UNSC Res 2178 (24 September 2014) UN Doc S/RES/2178.
[34] UNSC Res 2354 (24 May 2017) UN Doc S/RES/2354.
[35] Fiona de Londras 'The Transnational Counter-Terrorism Order: A Problématique' [2019] *Cur Legal Probl* 1.

Like the UN, the Council of Europe and the EU have taken proactive measures in efforts to prevent terrorism, but have gone even further by calling for proscriptions on *indirect* incitement. The Council of Europe's Convention on the Prevention of Terrorism ('COE Convention'), which entered into force in 2007, instructs that '[e]ach Party shall adopt such measures as may be necessary to establish [intentional] public provocation to commit a terrorist offence... as a criminal offence under its domestic law'. The term 'public provocation to commit a terrorist offence' is defined as 'the distribution, or otherwise making available, of a message to the public, with the intent to incite the commission of a terrorist offence, where such conduct, *whether or not directly advocating terrorist offences*, causes a danger that one or more such offences may be committed'. The EU's principal counter-terrorism legislation[36] requires Member States to punish such messages, defined in almost identical terms, save that it stresses that advocacy of terrorism offences can be direct or indirect, 'such as by the *glorification* of terrorist acts'.[37]

Additionally, the lack of a generally-accepted definition of terrorism in international law provides states with space to incorporate increasingly expansive definitions of terrorism and related offences into counter-terrorism frameworks. Moreover, while international law proscribes incitement to terrorism,[38] both glorification offences and definitions used to allow notice-and-takedown orders typically do not require intent to commit a crime, any direct link with an act of terrorism, or any proof of likelihood that such an act might subsequently occur.[39]

In response to the 'gathering pace' of this 'global trend',[40] a range of bodies—from UN committees to international human rights NGOs[41]—have urgently highlighted the danger to free speech posed by the rapid spread of glorification-related offences throughout Western democracies.[42] The Council of Europe has warned that 'the misuse of anti-terrorism legislation has become one of the most widespread threats to freedom of expression, including media freedom, in Europe'.[43] Amnesty International has warned that '[t]he ever-expanding national security state in Europe reveals how a deluge of laws and amendments passed with break-neck speed is undermining fundamental freedoms

---

[36] Directive (EU) 2017/541 of the European Parliament and of the Council of 15 March 2017 on combating terrorism and replacing Council Framework Decision 2002/475/JHA and amending Council Decision 2005/671/JHA [2017] OJ L88/6.

[37] Ibid art 5 (emphasis added).   [38] UNSC Res 1624 (n 32).

[39] See UNCHR, 'Report on the Special Rapporteur on the Promotion and Protection of Human Rights and Fundamental Freedoms While Countering Terrorism on the Role of Measures to Address Terrorism and Violent Extremism on Closing Civic Space and Violating the Rights of Civil Society Actors and Human Rights Defenders' (18 February 2019) UN Doc A/HRC/40/52.

[40] Duffy and Pitcher (n 20) 2.

[41] See, eg, Amnesty International, 'UN High Level Conference of Heads of Counter-Terrorism Agencies of Member States: Statement of Amnesty International' (Amnesty International, 29 June 2018) <https://www.un.org/counterterrorism/ctitf/sites/www.un.org.counterterrorism.ctitf/files/S4-Amnesty-International.pdf> accessed 15 December 2019.

[42] With the exception of the United States: see n 94 and accompanying text.

[43] See Council of Europe Commissioner for Human Rights (n 12).

and dismantling hard-won human rights protections'.[44] In February 2018, the responsible UN Special Rapporteur cautioned that '[n]ew counter-terrorism laws across the globe that criminalize... views that appear to praise, glorify, support, defend, apologize for or that seek to justify acts defined as "terrorism" under domestic law implicate both serious concerns of legality and limitations on freedom of thought and expression'. She specifically warned that 'such measures frequently target the legitimate activities of human rights defenders, journalists, lawyers, and artists'.[45] The Office of the UN High Commissioner for Human Rights (UNHCHR) has described the trend of proscribing 'statements which may not go so far as to incite or promote the commission of terrorist acts, but might nevertheless applaud past acts' as 'troubling'[46] and stressed the importance of avoiding 'vague terms of an uncertain scope such as glorifying or promoting terrorism' when restricting expression'.[47] The Commissioner for Human Rights for the Council of Europe similarly warned against the use of overly broad and vague terminology in such laws, emphasizing that '[v]iolence and the threat to use violence with the intention to spread fear and provoke terror is the defining component of the concept of terrorism'.[48]

28.4 CATEGORIES OF TERRORIST SPEECH

As a recent UN report reveals, many instances of hate speech—those that incite to violence against particular racial or religious groups—may also be classified as advocacy of terrorism. This is because the killing of members of a group for ideological reasons (political or religious) with the purpose of intimidating sections of the public or governments constitutes terrorism under most definitions of that term. For example, the common jihadi slogan, 'Behead the unbelievers!' is a call for the killing of non-Muslims and as such amounts to religiously-motivated hate speech. Consider further this recent UN summary of material that constitutes both incitement to terrorism and hate speech:

---

[44] Amnesty International, 'EU: Orwellian counter-terrorism laws stripping rights under guise of defending them' (*Amnesty International*, 17 January 2017) <https://www.amnesty.org/en/latest/news/2017/01/eu-orwellian-counter-terrorism-laws-stripping-rights-under-guise-of-defending-them/> accessed 19 April 2019.

[45] See UNCHR 'Report of the Special Rapporteur on the Promotion and Protection of Human Rights and Fundamental Freedoms while Countering Terrorism on the Human Rights Challenge of States of Emergency in the Context of Countering Terrorism' (1 March 2018) UN Doc A/HRC/37/52.

[46] UNHCHR, 'Human Rights, Terrorism and Counter-Terrorism: Fact Sheet No 32' (*Office of the High Commissioner for Human Rights*, July 2008) <https://www.ohchr.org/Documents/Publications/Factsheet32EN.pdf> accessed 15 December 2019.

[47] Ibid (emphasis omitted).

[48] Council of Europe Commissioner for Human Rights (n 12). See also The Representative on Freedom of the Media, *Joint Declaration on Freedom of Expression and Responses to Conflict Situations* (OSCE 2013) <https://www.osce.org/fom/237966?download=true> accessed 13 May 2019.

Asia and the Middle East have seen killings of presidents of the Ahmadiyya community in Pakistan following a television broadcast during which two maulanas stated that the Ahmadiyya community was deserving of death; incitement by a government-appointed imam in Saudi Arabia to eliminate all Shia believers in the world; incitement to and acts of violence against the Sufi community in Sri Lanka.[49]

Aron Harel's chapter in this volume on hate speech presents an extensive survey of the main normative and theoretical arguments in relation to hate speech; many of these apply equally to statements glorifying or supporting terrorism, simply because the protection of such speech may be justified by those arguments advanced against viewpoint-discriminatory laws that are used to contest the legitimacy of hate speech bans.[50] This chapter is intended to complement Harel's focus on theoretical considerations by concentrating on policy and doctrinal issues, and so confines itself to making a few brief observations on the particular complexities raised by bans on terrorism propaganda.

It is important to stress that the kind of terrorism propaganda targeted by the laws we consider actually consists of some very different classes of speech. The proposed new EU Regulation targets expression that may be distilled down to three distinct categories,[51] namely:

1) material that directly or indirectly incites to committing terrorist offences, including 'by the glorification' of terrorist acts, thereby intentionally 'causing a danger' that such offences may be committed;[52]
2) soliciting persons inter alia to 'commit or contribute to the commission of terrorism offences' and/or to 'participate in the activities of a terrorist group, including by supplying information or material resources, or by funding its activities'...in each case intentionally causing a danger that terrorism offences may be committed;[53]
3) material that provides instructions for, inter alia, the 'making or use of explosives, firearms or other weapons or noxious or hazardous substances' for the purpose of committing terrorist offences.[54]

---

[49] UNGA, 'Report of the Special Rapporteur on the Promotion and Protection of the Right to Freedom of Opinion and Expression' (7 September 2012) UN Doc A/67/357, [28].

[50] See Harel, Chapter 25 in this volume. See also Stone, Chapter 18 in this volume. See, generally, Ian Cram 'Countering Terrorism through Limits on Inciteful Speech: Principles and Problems' in Ian Cram (ed), *Extremism, Free Speech and Counter-Terrorism Law and Policy* (Routledge 2019) and Eric Barendt, 'Incitement to, and Glorification of, Terrorism' in Ivan Hare and James Weinstein (eds) *Extreme Speech and Democracy* (OUP 2009).

[51] We use here the definition as amended by the European Parliament: legislative resolution of 17 April 2019 on the proposal for a regulation of the European Parliament and of the Council on preventing the dissemination of terrorist content online (COM(2018) 0640 – C8-0405/2018–2018/0331 (COD)). References to 'terrorism offences' are to those listed in Directive (EU) 2017/541 (above, n 36).

[52] Ibid, Am 53.   [53] Ibid, Ams 54, 55.   [54] Ibid, Am 56.

These three categories raise strikingly different issues in free speech terms. The least problematic is (3)—instructions for the manufacture of explosives and the like. Such speech does not purport to make any contribution to public discourse; it is purely a means to an end—the production of instruments of killing. Restrictions would be based on content but not viewpoint and the link with violence would be explicit and undeniable since the sole purpose of such expression is enabling the building of explosives and other means of killing.[55] Even Eugene Volokh, arch defender of First Amendment freedoms, concedes that such speech may require restriction.[56] Category (2) is more problematic. On the one hand, soliciting such involvement implicates freedom of association as well as speech; however, a narrow restriction on invitations to assist proscribed groups would leave untouched the general sphere of political speech:[57] it would not circumscribe the expression of any general viewpoint and, again, the link with terrorist activity—assuming the group in question was known to be engaged in ongoing violent activity—would be clear and strong.

That leaves the most problematic category: general advocacy or glorification of terrorism. This is so different from bomb-making instructions that it is doubtful whether they can or should go in the same category. First, such offences can catch any praise of any group using political violence anywhere in the world. When such an offence was introduced in the UK, the government was reduced to defending it by arguing that 'there is nowhere in the world today where resort to violence, including violence against property, could be justified as a means of bringing about change'.[58] What is bizarre about this argument is not (just) that it seeks to argue that there is nowhere in the world where violence or serious damage to property could legitimately be used to bring about political change. Rather, it is the fact that it makes anyone who disagrees with this view and expresses support for such violence, for example, against a murderous dictatorship, as in Syria, guilty of a criminal offence. It thus elevates one view of contemporary global politics— essentially a pacifist one—into dogma, the challenge to which is made a criminal offence. Moreover, the general notion of glorification or advocacy of terrorism makes no distinction between material that would clearly also constitute illegal hate speech as commonly defined: for example, calling for violence against a minority racial or religious group, like the Rohingya in Myanmar, and violence against state authorities like the army or police. The former case appears to present a stronger case for criminalization (or least withdrawal of constitutional protection) than the latter, especially if the state in question was an oppressive one. Bans on glorification or advocacy of terrorism are frequently justified on the basis that such speech poses a real danger of radicalizing some hearers sufficiently to stir them into violent action. But here the relative paucity of

---

[55] See further Frederick Schauer 'Recipes, Plans, Instructions and the Free Speech Implications of Words That Are Tools' in Susan J Brison and Katharine Gelber (eds), *Free Speech in the Digital Age* (OUP 2019).

[56] Eugene Volokh 'Crime-Facilitating Speech' (2005) 57 *Stan L Rev* 1095.

[57] As indeed argued by the US Supreme Court in a recent decision: see n 102 and accompanying text.

[58] Joint Committee on Human Rights, *Counter-Terrorism Policy and Human Rights: Terrorism Bill and Related Matters* (2005–6, HL 75-I/HC 56-I) [29].

the evidence forms a jarring mismatch with the sweeping restrictions increasingly being introduced. Thus, as a recent working group found:

> There is evidence that the internet allows terrorists to effectively disseminate their motivations for committing their crimes, but evidence shows that radicalization may as well be caused by consumption of daily news (including coverage of terrorist acts). Available evidence also shows that radicalization tends to occur primarily as a result of offline rather than online dynamics.[59]

The report noted that this 'weak evidence of a causal link' should have led to the targeting of a narrow class of those terrorism materials posing the greatest risk (such as training manuals and instructions) in the proposed measure under consideration, but instead the opposite was the case. This is an observation of general applicability: there is a striking mismatch between the evidential base justifying restrictions on terrorist-related speech and the breadth of the measures implemented. Moreover, as the next section shows, human rights and constitutional courts have failed to match the rhetoric of rigorous review of such measures with reality.

28.5 Case Study One: Strasbourg's Struggles with Pro-Terrorist Speech

We have noted above statements by the Council of Europe setting out strict and demanding requirements that terrorism offences must comply with human rights standards, particularly freedom of expression.[60] Sadly, this kind of rhetoric is not matched by the standards laid down in the actual case law of the ECtHR. The Court has indeed made well-known statements to the effect that the Article 10 right to freedom of expression contained in the European Convention on Human Rights (ECHR)[61] applies 'not only to 'information' or 'ideas' that are favourably received or regarded as inoffensive, but also to those that 'offend, shock or disturb'.[62] However, in cases involving terrorist-related speech, the Court routinely abandons or dilutes such principles. While some judgments set out clear standards, others simply ignore them; moreover, the criteria

---

[59] Joris van Hoboken 'The Proposed EU Terrorism Content Regulation: Analysis and Recommendations with Respect to Freedom of Expression Implications' (3 May 2019) Transatlantic Working Group, First Session of the Transatlantic High Level Working Group on Content Moderation Online and Freedom of Expression, February 27 – March 3 2019, Working Paper 3 <https://www.ivir.nl/publicaties/download/TWG-working-papers-Ditchley-1.pdf> accessed 15 December 2019, 4.

[60] Council of Europe Commissioner for Human Rights (n 12).

[61] Convention for the Protection of Human Rights and Fundamental Freedoms (European Convention on Human Rights, as amended).

[62] *Handyside v United Kingdom* (1979–80) 1 EHRR 737, [49].

enunciated are often so varying and prolix as to frustrate the enterprise of identifying a set of clear and consistent principles governing this area.

In general, the Court applies a contextual approach that involves the weighing and balancing of multiple factors. However, sometimes it shortcuts this process by finding forms of blatantly racist or otherwise hateful speech to fall outside the protection of Article 10 altogether, under Article 17,[63] as inimical to fundamental Convention values.[64] But since there is no clear test for determining when the court will apply Article 17 and when it will stay 'inside' Article 10, this only adds further uncertainty. For example, in cases involving Holocaust denial, the Court sometimes applies one Article and sometimes the other; it has opined that decisions about which Article to apply are 'taken on a case-by-case basis', depending on 'all the circumstances of each individual case'.[65] Since, as noted above, a fair proportion of terrorist propaganda also constitutes hate speech against particular religious or racial groups, this tendency makes the application of Article 10 to certain kinds of terrorist propaganda even more uncertain.

What principles then, *can* we extract from the Court's jurisprudence in this area? Since the Court frequently declares that speech 'deserve[s] little, if any, protection' if its content 'is at odds with the democratic values of the Convention system',[66] it is fairly clear that direct and unequivocal incitement of violence is unprotected. Where the position is less clear-cut, the Court's general approach is to examine a wide range of factors, including the content of the expression, likelihood and seriousness of its consequences,[67] the speaker's intention and position in society, the tone and form of the address and its likely impact on the public'.[68] This all-factors-considered approach is thorough, but makes it difficult to predict results.

A recent case commentary argues that a test of 'clear and imminent danger of violence' is now a well-established aspect of the court's jurisprudence[69] (albeit ignored in the case in question); however this seems hard to reconcile with perhaps the leading decision by the Grand Chamber in *Sürek v Turkey (No 1)*.[70] There, an editor's conviction for publishing letters by readers that accused the 'fascist Turkish' army of 'massacres' in their struggle with the PKK was found to amount to 'stigmatising the other side to the

---

[63] Article 17 provides that the ECHR does not imply a right for any state, group, or person 'to engage in any activity or perform any act aimed at the destruction of any of the rights and freedoms set forth herein or at their limitation to a greater extent than is provided for in the Convention'.

[64] *M'Bala M'Bala v France* App no 25239/13 (ECHR, 10 November 2015).

[65] *Pastörs v Germany* App no 55225/14, [37] (ECHR, 3 October 2019).

[66] Ibid [47].

[67] Stefan Sottiaux, 'Leroy v France: Apology of Terrorism and the Malaise of the European Court of Human Rights' Free Speech Jurisprudence' (2009) 3 *Eur Hum Rts L Rev* 415, 420.

[68] David J Harris and others, *Harris, O'Boyle and Warbrick: Law of the European Convention on Human Rights* (4th edn, OUP 2018) 607.

[69] Ronan Ó Fathaigh and Dirk Voorhoof, 'ECtHR engages in dangerous "triple pirouette" to find criminal prosecution for media coverage of PKK statements did not violate Article 10' (*Strasbourg Observers*, 14 October 2019) <https://strasbourgobservers.com/2019/10/14/ecthr-engages-in-dangerous-triple-pirouette-to-find-criminal-prosecution-for-media-coverage-of-pkk-statements-did-not-violate-article-10/> accessed 15 December 2019.

[70] *Sürek v Turkey (No 1)* ECHR 1999-IV.

conflict' and hence appealing 'to bloody revenge by stirring up base emotions'.[71] On this basis, the publisher's conviction was found *not* to violate Article 10. This seems impossible to reconcile with the Court's decision, around the same time, in *Sürek and Özedmir v Turkey*,[72] in which a newspaper complained of criminal sanctions for publishing an interview with a leading member of the PKK; one of his statements said 'the war will go on until there is only one single individual left on our side',[73] which sounds just as bellicose as the statements condemned by the Court in *Surek*. But, as a leading text notes, the majority 'downplayed the virulent nature of some contested passages' as merely showing 'implacable resolve'[74] and found in this case that Article 10 *was* breached by the editor's conviction. And this decision, in turn, seems impossible to reconcile with a 2019 decision finding no breach of Article 10 where a newspaper editor was convicted purely for carrying statements by a member of a banned group, even though the statements largely welcomed the start of a peace process with the Turkish government, albeit forecasting a return to guerrilla war should the talks fail.[75] The dissenting judge complained bitterly that the courts' judgment 'ignore[d] fundamental aspects' of 'well-established' Article 10 jurisprudence;[76] a commentary laments that the decision 'utterly upended' Article 10 standard of review, by finding no violation even though the national courts wholly failed to 'adduce sufficient reasons justifying the newspaper editor's conviction' and 'did not even attempt to apply standards that were in conformity with Article 10 principles'.[77]

While this decision raises serious free speech concerns, more concerning still is that in *Leroy v France*,[78] in which the Court found no violation of Article 10 in relation to the conviction of a man for publishing a drawing representing the attack on the twin towers of the World Trade Centre with the caption '[w]e all dreamt it…Hamas did it'. The Court suggested that, through his choice of language, the applicant had expressed moral support for the perpetrators of the 9/11 attacks and, in so doing, expressed approval of the violence and diminished the dignity of the victims. The court wholly disregarded his intent, which it admitted played no part in his prosecution or conviction; moreover, there was no evidence that the cartoon increased the risk that any terrorist offences would be committed. Hence, rather than treating praise for terrorist acts as a particular kind of indirect incitement to terrorism, applying its standard incitement test, this decision 'recognises apology as a separate category of unprotected speech'.[79] While the cartoon was undoubtedly extremely offensive, it's not clear that it was calculated, still less likely to incite further attacks, and the writer protested that his intent was merely to express his virulent hostility to the United States.

There appear to be three main reasons that account for the yawning gap between Strasbourg's rhetorical declaration of human rights principles and the actual standards

---

[71] Ibid [61]–[62].
[72] *Sürek and Özedmir v Turkey* Apps no 23927/94 and 24277/94 (ECHR, 8 July 1999).
[73] Ibid [61].   [74] Harris and others (n 68) 606.
[75] See *Gürbüz and Bayar v Turkey* App no 8860/13 (ECHR, 23 July 2019).
[76] Ibid [5]–[7] (Judge Pavli).   [77] Fathaigh and Voorhoof (n 69).
[78] See *Leroy v France* App no 36109/03 (ECHR, 10 February 2008) [43].   [79] Sottiaux (n 67) 425.

applied to particular cases. First, the margin of appreciation doctrine tends to allow states a particularly wide margin of latitude in relation to 'incitement to violence against an individual... public figure or sector of the population'.[80] Second, in seeking to address speech that may incite violence or hatred against another group, any potential for rigour in the Courts' review is undercut by the profoundly illiberal principle it has adopted that, in the field of religious beliefs, statements that are 'gratuitously offensive to others' are 'an infringement of their rights'.[81] This make it impossible for the Court to draw principled lines between expression that is merely provocative and offensive (as in *Leroy*) and that which actually threatens the rights of others, including by inciting violence. Third, the court regards speech directed at fundamental Convention values as outside its protection: this 'militant democracy' approach affords little protection for radical critics of established liberal democracy, especially if they appear to suggest violence as an attractive or justified response to injustice in Western societies or their military interventions abroad.

Our reluctant conclusion is that Strasbourg cannot be relied upon to set out clear and principled lines in its approach to extreme speech inciting or praising violence or terrorism: *Leroy* is the clearest example of the Court wholly failing to distinguish between speech inciting violence and that which merely praises it. However, the jurisprudence overall shows inconsistency, an over-reliance on vague balancing exercises and, hence, a failure to draw consistent and principled lines between protected and unprotected speech.

28.6 Criminalizing Terrorist-Related Speech beyond Europe

Australia's counter-terrorism framework includes a criminal offence of 'advocating'— defined as 'counselling, promoting, encouraging or urging'—the doing of a terrorist act or the commission of a range of terrorism offences.[82] This offence is 'significantly broader than the criminal offences for incitement at the state and federal levels'.[83] Unlike other liberal democracies, alleged violations of Australia's anti-terrorism laws rarely raise concerns regarding compatibility with human rights protections, an inattention likely due to the absence of a human rights instrument at the federal level.[84] Beyond the democratic world, laws in this area are radically broader still. A recent UN report noted

---

[80] See, eg, *Sürek* (n 70) [61].
[81] This is cited as an established principle in the case law by one of the leading texts: Pieter van Dijk and others, *Theory and Practice of the European Convention on Human Rights* (5th edn, Intersentia 2018) 784–5.
[82] See Criminal Code Act 1995 (Cth), s 80.2C.
[83] George Williams, 'The Legal Assault on Australian Democracy' (2016) 16 *QUT Law Rev* 19, 26.
[84] Ibid 24.

with concern the Chinese Cybersecurity Law of 2016, which reinforces vague prohibitions against the spread of 'false' information that disrupts 'social or economic order', national unity or national security; it also requires companies to proactively monitor their networks and report violations to the authorities. Failure to comply has reportedly led to heavy fines for the country's biggest social media platforms.[85]

The one significant counter-trend has been seen in Canada: its recent decision to abolish its problematic glorification-related offence represents a perhaps unique example of a state's willingness to consider and meaningfully respond to the concerns of the human rights community regarding the free speech dangers flowing from glorification-related offences. In 2015, the then Conservative government introduced a new offence of 'advocacy or promotion or the commission of terrorism offences'.[86] This offence was met with immediate criticism from the legal profession and human rights organizations with respect to its over-breadth and implications for free speech.[87] In response, the Trudeau government introduced legislation to replace it with the new offence of 'counselling another person to commit a terrorism offence, whether or not a terrorism offence is committed or a specific terrorism offence is counselled'.[88] Because counselling offences exist in other parts of Canada's criminal law framework, this amendment limits the risk of uncertainty and over-breadth, thereby reducing the likelihood of a chilling effect on speech.[89] Additionally, unlike glorification-related offences, it requires more than the mere expression of support or advocacy for terrorism.

28.7 CASE STUDY TWO: US COURTS AND SPEECH-BASED COORDINATION WITH DESIGNATED FOREIGN TERRORIST ORGANIZATIONS

The United States remains an outlier among liberal democracies in generally prohibiting government proscriptions on speech based on the message, ideas, subject matter, or content.[90] However, even here the peculiar pressures exerted by the fear of terrorism

---

[85] UNGA, 'Report of the Special Rapporteur on the Promotion and Protection of the Right to Freedom of Opinion and Expression' (6 April 2018) UN Doc A/HRC/38/35, [15].

[86] Anti-Terrorism Act 2015, s 16.

[87] See, eg, Canadian Civil Liberties Association, 'Understanding Bill C-51: The Anti-Terrorism Act, 2015' (19 May 2015) <https://ccla.org/understanding-bill-c-51-the-anti-terrorism-act-2015/> accessed 30 September 2019.

[88] See An Act Respecting National Security Matters 2019, s 143. The Act received Royal Assent on 21 June 2019.

[89] Canadian Civil Liberties Association, 'The Terrorist Speech Offence and Bill C-59' (12 September 2018) <https://ccla.org/terrorist-speech-bill-c-59/> accessed 30 September 2019.

[90] See *Ashcroft v American Civil Liberties Union*, 535 US 564, 573 (2002).

have taken their toll. The cornerstone of the US's free speech doctrine is the case of *Brandenburg v Ohio*,[91] in which the Supreme Court struck down legislation that criminalized the advocacy of violence as a means of accomplishing political reform as well as associating with groups that taught or advocated the doctrines of criminal syndicalism.[92] The Court held that only advocacy that is 'directed to inciting or producing imminent lawless action and is likely to incite such action' falls outside of the First Amendment's protection.[93]

Thus, the kind of prohibitions on advocating or encouraging terrorism seen in Europe and Australia would be presumptively unconstitutional in the United States. Indeed, in its response to the United Nations Security Council Counter-Terrorism Committee regarding implementation of Security Council Resolution 1324,[94] the United States emphasized that the First Amendment extends to speech advocating illegal conduct, such that while it could be constitutional to allow for punishment in 'cases where a speaker urges an already "agitated mob" to commit illegal acts...the majority of terrorist propaganda found on the internet could thus not be prosecuted under US criminal law because such advocacy likely lacks (at least without proof of additional facts) the potential to produce imminent lawless action required under the *Brandenburg* exception'.[95]

However, while *Brandenburg* remains good law, its efficacy and applicability in the context of terrorist-related expression has been rendered uncertain following the Supreme Court's 2010 decision in *Holder v Humanitarian Law Project* ('*HLP*').[96] US citizens and domestic organizations interested in providing support for the *lawful* activities of two designated foreign terrorist organizations,[97] including training members how to use international law to resolve disputes peacefully and how to petition the UN and other representative bodies for relief, sought an injunction to prohibit enforcement of a federal statute that criminalized 'knowingly providing material support or resources to a foreign terrorist organization'.[98]

The Court held that the government could prohibit the plaintiffs' proposed activities without violating the First Amendment. Making no mention of *Brandenburg*, the Court rejected the plaintiffs' argument that the statute restricted 'pure political speech' on the grounds that only 'material support' was targeted, that independent advocacy or membership in international terrorist organizations is not prohibited, since the statute was 'drawn to cover only a narrow category of speech to, under the *direction of, or in coordination with* foreign groups that the speaker knows to be terrorist organisations'.[99] Despite the peaceful nature of the plaintiffs' proposed activities, the Court accepted the

---

[91] See n 19. [92] Ibid 448. [93] Ibid 447–8.
[94] UNSC 'Response of the United States of America to the Counter-Terrorism Committee: United States implementation of Security Council resolution 1624 (2005)' (16 June 2006) UN Doc S/2006/397.
[95] Ibid. [96] *Holder v Humanitarian Law Project*, 561 US 1 (2010).
[97] The PKK and the 'Tamil Tigers', which aim to establish independent states for, respectively, Kurds in Turkey and Tamils in Sri Lanka.
[98] 18 USC § 2339B.
[99] *Humanitarian Law Project* (n 96) 21 (emphasis added).

government's conclusion that *all* contributions to foreign terrorist organization, even for ostensibly benign purposes, further terrorist activities.[100] Highlighting the 'sensitive interests in national security and foreign affairs at stake', the Court found that the government met its burden of demonstrating that the statute served the interest of preventing terrorism, even if those providing support intend to promote an organization's nonviolent ends.[101] The Court emphasized that its holding 'in no way suggest[ed] that a regulation of *independent* speech would pass constitutional muster, even if the Government were to show that such speech benefits foreign terrorist organizations'.[102]

While the Court thus stressed the narrowness of its holding in *HLP*, human rights defenders have expressed serious concerns regarding the potential scope of the decision. David Cole, current Legal Director of the American Civil Liberties Union, argues that *HLP* constituted a dramatic retreat from the precedents and principles that have served as the cornerstone of First Amendment doctrine since the 1950s, expanded government authority to suppress political expression and association on the grounds of national security and, for the first time, upheld the criminalization of speech that does not advocate the commission of a crime.[103] He also points out the strange phenomena of the Court going beyond standard deference to Executive national security concerns to expound *its own* justifications for upholding the statute on the government's behalf:

> [T]he Court posited that teaching a group how to bring human rights claims before the United Nations human rights bodies might lead the group to use those tactics "to threaten, manipulate and disrupt", and declared this threat to be "real, not remote," even though the government had never articulated such a concern, much less substantiated it with any evidence. It speculated that the "relief" the PKK might obtain from the UN "could readily include monetary aid," which could then be used for terrorism, even though the government did not suggest as much, and the UN human rights bodies are not authorized to order monetary damages as relief.[104]

Cole's concerns appear to be well-founded: recent arguments by the government in cases involving the material support statute reveal that it is adopting an extremely broad interpretation of the Supreme Court's holding. For example, in *Mehanna v United States*,[105] the government argued that an individual who translated terrorist propaganda for a website, following a call from Al-Qaeda for such work, violated the material support statute, notwithstanding the fact that it presented no evidence that the individual had ever been in contact with Al-Qaeda, that he translated or spoke under Al-Qaeda's direction, or that he acted at Al-Qaeda's request.[106] This argument appears to come close to collapsing the

---

[100] Ibid 31.   [101] Ibid.   [102] Ibid 34 (emphasis added).

[103] David Cole, 'The First Amendment's Borders: The Place of *Holder v Humanitarian Law Project* in First Amendment Doctrine' (2012) 6 *Harv L & Pol'y Rev* 147.

[104] Ibid 154 (citations omitted).

[105] See also *United States v Mehanna* 734 F 3d 32 (1st Cir 2013). The Supreme Court denied the petition for a writ of certiorari.

[106] Brief for the United States in Opposition to Defendant's Petition for Writ of Certiorari to the United States Court of Appeals for the First Circuit, *Mehanna v United States* No 13–1125 (July 2014).

very distinction—between 'free-standing advocacy' and support 'co-ordinated' with a proscribed group—on which the Supreme Court had rested its holding.

While US law's uniquely strong protection of political speech remains largely intact following *HLP*, the degree to which the Supreme Court's decision affects the application of *Brandenburg* in cases involving terrorist-related expression remains unclear. What is clear, however, is that US courts, like those in other liberal democracies, allow sometimes extreme deference to national security interests to lead them to sidestep traditional free speech protections when it comes to some terrorist-related speech. What is more striking is an eerie echo in the US Supreme Court of the way in which European courts and authorities claim to be upholding high and rigorous standards of free speech that promptly disappear in their actual judgments and policy positions. As Cole puts it:

> The Court claimed to be applying the "demanding" scrutiny traditionally triggered by content-based speech regulation. But the Court actually applied an unrecognizably lenient form of that scrutiny...[N]ever before has the Court substituted deference for stringent scrutiny in reviewing a content-based regulation of speech.[107]

28.8 REGULATING TERRORIST-RELATED SPEECH ONLINE: THE 'VOLUNTARY' EUROPEAN FRAMEWORK

Notwithstanding the aggressive use of the criminal law against terrorist speech noted above, the proliferation of terrorist-related content on the Internet appears to have led to concerns that a criminal law response is no longer adequate in the digital age. In response to such concerns, Europe's supranational bodies have adopted a framework of ostensibly co-operative initiatives, under which global platforms including Facebook, YouTube, and Twitter make efforts to detect and remove online terrorist-related expression, including content flagged by EU authorities, under a framework comprised of regulatory and non-regulatory initiatives.[108] In December of 2018, the Commissioners for Migration, Home Affairs and Citizenship and the Security Union issued a statement in which they represented that since the launch of the EU Internet Forum in 2015, over

---

[107] Cole (n 103) 158.
[108] These include the EU Internet Forum and the Commission Work Programme for committing to continue to promote co-operation with social media companies to detect and remove terrorist and other illegal content online.

77,000 pieces of content had been referred to Internet platforms, 84 per cent of which had been removed.[109]

The voluntary framework between the EU and social media companies such as Facebook and YouTube, places extremely powerful levers to control vast amounts of speech in the hands of national and supranational authorities. Indeed, where content is *removed* at the behest of European authorities, rather than being merely geo-blocked, this measure affects online speech worldwide. However, because these measures are not legally binding and are entered into on an ostensibly voluntary basis, they do not formally constitute legal restrictions on speech; hence, they do not trigger constitutional or international free speech protections.

28.9 Rethinking Online Regulation of Terrorist-Related Speech: The Shift to a Compulsory Regime

While the above ostensibly voluntary approach raised serious free speech concerns, in September of 2018, the European Commission published a proposal for a Regulation on preventing the dissemination of terrorist content online[110] ('Proposed Regulation'), which introduces a compulsory framework to prevent the 'misuse' of digital intermediaries to spread terrorist propaganda and incitement to violence. The Commission's proposal places unprecedented obligations on intermediaries including, inter alia, the removal of terrorist content within *one hour* of receiving a removal order from a variety of public authorities,[111] a duty of care obligation to ensure that platforms are not used for the dissemination of terrorist content[112] and, depending on the circumstances, an obligation to take proactive measures to better protect their platforms from hosting such content.[113] Additionally, Member States are obliged to institute financial penalties for failure to comply with removal orders.[114] The definition of 'terrorist content', which applies to removal orders, referrals, and proactive measures is broad, encompassing

---

[109] European Commission, 'Fighting Terrorism Online: Public-private sector cooperation as important as ever at the fourth EU Internet Forum' (*Europa*, 5 December 2018) <https://ec.europa.eu/commission/presscorner/detail/en/STATEMENT_18_6681> accessed 15 December 2019.

[110] Commission, 'Proposal for a Regulation of the European Parliament and of the Council on Preventing the dissemination of terrorist content online' COM (2018) 640.

[111] Ibid art 4.
[112] Ibid art 3.
[113] Ibid art 6.
[114] Ibid art 18.

information 'inciting or advocating, *including by glorifying*, the commission of terrorist offences, thereby causing a danger that such acts be committed'.[115]

To ensure the removal of illegal terrorist content, the Regulation introduces a removal order that may be issued as an administrative or judicial decision by a competent authority in a Member State. In such cases, the hosting service provider is obliged to remove the content or disable access to it within one hour. Article 8 of the Proposed Regulation calls for hosting service providers to set out in their terms and conditions their policy to prevent the dissemination of terrorist content, including, where appropriate, a meaningful explanation of the functioning of proactive measures including the use of automated tools. Overall, the Regulation gives wide and discretionary power to state authorities, and, as we saw above, lumps together a wide range of terrorist-related speech that have very different free speech implications.[116] It has been argued that:

> The clear incentive in this case is to accept the most conservative interpretation of the law as a global standard, in contravention of the EU's reservation of power to Member States to define and enforce their own free expression protections.[117]

The Commission's rationale for the shift from a voluntary to a compulsory system, based on generalized references to its previous recommendations, is that the online dissemination of terrorist-related content represents a particularly egregious threat to regional safety and security that warrants aggressive measures that are not required to adequately address other forms of harmful online expression.[118] Indeed, the Commission justifies the step of allowing derogations from the long-established principle established under the E-Commerce Directive that intermediaries cannot be placed under any general obligation to monitor their sites for unlawful content by citing the 'particularly grave risks associated with the dissemination of terrorist content'[119]—claims that, as seen above, do not appear to be borne out by the available evidence.

The European Union Agency for Fundamental Rights expressed concerns that the Proposed Regulation contained insufficient safeguards with respect to freedom of expression. It highlighted the absence of a guarantee of involvement by an independent judicial authority in the process of executing removal orders and any mechanism whereby the content/hosting service provider may effectively challenge the order

---

[115] Ibid art 2(5)(a) (emphasis added). As this book went to press, the European Parliament had proposed several amendments, whose general effect is to insert more limitations and safeguards into the proposal: above (n 51). However, which if any of these amendments will make it into the final version of the Regulation is currently unknown, especially given that both the Parliament and the Commission have been reconstituted since the Regulation was considered by them.

[116] See n 51 and accompanying text. See also 'Proposal for a Regulation' (n 110), art 2(5). See also Joan Barata, 'New EU Proposal on the Prevention of Terrorist Content Online: an Important Mutation of the E-Commerce Intermediaries Regime' (Center for Internet and Society White Paper, 12 October 2018) 6.

[117] Barata (n 116) 7.

[118] Commission, 'Staff Working Document: Impact Assessment Accompanying the Proposal for a Regulation of the European Parliament and of the Council on preventing the dissemination of terrorist content online' SWD (2018) 408 final, 1–2.

[119] 'Proposal for a Regulation' (n 110).

before the removal is carried out.¹²⁰ The following section considers the significance of this shift away from primary reliance on criminal law to administrative notice-and-takedown orders.

28.10 THE FREE SPEECH DANGERS OF NOTICE-AND-TAKEDOWN PROCEDURES

Before the advent of the Internet, there were no available means for alienated and angry individuals to disseminate pro-terrorist messages—assuming that such expression would be rejected by the mainstream media—other than by proclaiming them in traditional public spaces. But shouting slogans or waving signs in support of terrorists or terrorism in the town square would then expose them to the immediate attention of the police (especially if the call for violence was explicit), as well as potentially hostile counter-demonstrators. In the digital age, in contrast, such persons can instantaneously reach an audience of thousands or even millions via social media—and can do so hidden under a cloak of anonymity. To this fact can be added that the major platforms themselves are owned and operated by US companies, which are shielded from liability for hosting terrorist-related content by the First Amendment and section 230 of the Communications Decency Act 1996,¹²¹ and have resources and influence that dwarf those of many nation states.

Hence, it may be hypothesized that 'the emergence of [these] enormously powerful companies, [which] dominate key online platforms and services' has 'threatened' nation states, who feel a need to rein them in. Moreover, given their size and power, these companies provide 'clear, centralised targets for those seeking to influence the...marketplace of ideas'¹²²: if you control Facebook, you control a truly global platform for online speech. This makes the social media giants tempting not only as platforms for propaganda but as potential censors of such material to be co-opted by national and supranational authorities. While the UN cautions that 'States should not use Internet companies as tools to limit expression that they themselves would be precluded from limiting under international human rights law,'¹²³ the attraction of doing just that to states anxious both about the proliferation of extreme speech online and the immense

---

¹²⁰ European Union, 'Opinion of the European Agency for Fundamental Rights: Proposal for a Regulation on preventing the dissemination of terrorist content online and its fundamental rights implications' FRA Opinion 2/2019 (12 February 2019) <https://fra.europa.eu/sites/default/files/fra_uploads/fra-2019-opinion-online-terrorism-regulation-02-2019_en.pdf> accessed 15 December 2019.

¹²¹ Section 230 provides platforms with immunity from civil and criminal liability for hosting many classes of unlawful content, even when notified of its presence.

¹²² Dinah PoKempner, 'Regulating Online Speech: Keeping Humans, and Human Rights at the Core' in Susan J Brison and Katharine Gelber (eds), *Free Speech in the Digital Age* (OUP 2019).

¹²³ UNGA, 'Report of the Special Rapporteur on the Promotion and Protection of the Right to Freedom of Opinion and Expression' (9 October 2019) UN Doc A/74/486, [29].

power of the social media giants is plain. This, above all, may explain the rapidly growing use of the enormously potent but blunt tool of notice-and-takedown in Europe.

As argued above, misperceptions of the threat posed by terrorism have long inspired over-reaction and hyper-legislation by state and supranational actors including the UN and EU; these actors now possess a powerful new avenue for speech-control that bypasses traditional and long-standing protections for freedom of expression found even in over-broad criminal offences. Criminal law—while very much still with us in the digital age—may nevertheless be considered the paradigm for dealing with unlawful expression in 'old' media, including newspapers, pamphlets, broadcasting, and public demonstrations. While this chapter has cited egregious misuses of criminal law in the context of terrorist-related expression, this has affected a tiny volume of speech and defendants in such cases are availed of several crucial protections, including constitutional and international human rights law protections for freedom of expression and public trials by independent courts. Moreover, even in instances in which oppressive convictions, such as those in Spain, are secured,[124] these at least occur in the full view of the public, allowing for scrutiny of, and public debate about, such uses of criminal law to supress 'dangerous' speech.

Now compare this to the 'new media' remedial paradigm of notice-and-takedown, in which, not only the speaker, but the public in general may not be aware when speech is censored. In human rights law, the familiar 'three pillars'[125] by which the legitimacy of restrictions on speech must be tested are legality, necessity, and proportionality,[126] all of which serve crucial purposes. The *legality* requirement means that the basis for the restriction must be set out in law of sufficient clarity so that speakers can foresee to a reasonable degree of clarity when their speech may be limited. Next, there must be a real *necessity* to limit freedom of speech; this means acting for a 'legitimate aim' that in principle serves the welfare of all (and not just the objectives of the government), such as ensuring public safety where there is a pressing need to further that aim. Finally, under the proportionality principle, measures should be carefully tailored and go no further than truly necessary, and the least intrusive means used, wherever possible. Further, there should be notice and transparency mechanisms in place so that both speakers and the general public are fully aware of when speech is being restricted, as well as having effective means to challenge decisions of the authorities to do so.

It is immediately apparent that the notice-and-takedown procedures that seem to be the tool of choice for public authorities in Europe against terrorist propaganda only very doubtfully satisfy these safeguards. The legal power in an instrument like the Proposed Regulation is broad, vague and extends to expression that lies at the core of political

---

[124] See n 10 and accompanying text.
[125] The phrase is PoKempner's: (n 122) 226.
[126] These three conditions appear in each of the 'limitation' paragraphs of the generally qualified rights in Articles 8–11 ECHR (protecting privacy, and the freedoms of religion, expression, association, and assembly); a similar formulation (though without specifying particular legitimate aims) appears in the general limitations clause of the Canadian Charter of Rights and Freedoms, s 1, Part 1 of the Constitution Act, 1982, being Schedule B to the Canada Act 1982 (UK), 1982, c 11.

speech, via the use of the notoriously slippery notion of 'glorification' of terrorism; it requires neither proof that the speaker engaged in 'explicit' 'intentional' advocacy of violence nor that the speech created an 'imminent risk of... hostility or violence'.[127] Further, the frantic haste with which the mechanism is intended to operate—aiming at removal of flagged material within one hour—completely excludes the possibility of free speech concerns playing a meaningful role in decisions made under this procedure. The kind of dense, contextual enquiry into restrictions on speech that Strasbourg engages in[128] would simply be impossible. As for possible safeguards, speakers may not even be notified when their speech is censored, let alone given adequate means of challenging such censorship: there appears to be no *guarantee* that individual decisions will be subject to proper public scrutiny or judicial review.[129]

The traditional criminal law paradigm—even in instances where the laws themselves, or particular convictions secured under them, are draconian—is at least firmly embedded in the public justice system, with its attendant panoply of procedural, civil, and human rights. In contrast, the new model is bureaucratic, secretive, and often lacking in the traditional protections that human rights law and due process norms and procedures designed to secure. It is, however, extremely cheap. It has been reported that Facebook's content moderators typically receive about two weeks training and are paid around $15 an hour, leading one commentator to observe that such '[c]ensorship on the cheap is unlikely to protect rights'.[130] But of course this is not the primary aim—as far as the platforms are concerned, the exercise of flagging content for removal 'is intended to produce rapid decisions over huge volumes of data in ways that will keep the platform away from controversy and trouble'.[131] Compare this with the extensive resources involved in conducting a criminal trial. Canada's leading hate speech case is *R v Keegstra*.[132] It has been estimated that putting Keegstra on trial cost over a million dollars, in a saga that took a total of fourteen years to complete.[133] As a study of the enforcement of Australia's hate speech laws showed, the process of prosecuting such offences is 'arduous, stressful, time-consuming and expensive'.[134] Compared to this, the attractions to the authorities of the unobtrusive and almost immediate removal of content at minimal cost are obvious.

Routine commitments by European bodies that the removal or restriction of access to terrorist content online 'must be done in full respect for the human rights and fundamental freedoms, the rule of law and democracy, particularly in relation to the principles

---

[127] See UNGA (n 49) 12.
[128] See n 60 ff and accompanying text.
[129] Plainly the position under the proposed Regulation is greatly preferable in this respect as compared to merely voluntary arrangements, which have virtually no safeguards; however, the efficacy of the Regulation in this respect depends in large part upon the success or otherwise of proposed amendments by the European Parliament (n 51) the eventual fate of which is unknown at the time of writing.
[130] PoKempner (n 122) 234.   [131] Ibid.
[132] [1990] 3 SCR 697.
[133] Cram (n 50) 42.
[134] Ibid 43.

and norms relating to the freedom of expression'[135] now look increasingly hollow.[136] But there may be a coming sting in the tale for the EU in its recent proposals to move from a voluntary code to a compulsory scheme. As one human rights advocate has observed, 'press[ing] corporations "to assume the burden of censorship"' has been a 'favourite mode' of regulating online speech; this is partly because, as noted above, the market dominance of giants like Google makes such agreements potent regulatory tools but also because it avoids the need to 'legislate clear requirements that could be put to judicial test'.[137] With the Proposed Regulation, the EU has given itself a powerful new regulatory tool—but given that censorship will now be openly exercised by public authorities acting under EU legislation, legal challenges can be brought, and may be expected. The latest round in the struggle over extreme speech and censorship may be about to start.

---

[135] See Council of Europe, Counter-Terrorism Strategy (2018–2022) CM (2018) 86, [1.1].
[136] UNGA (n 49) [42].   [137] PoKempner (n 122) 232.

CHAPTER 29

FREEDOM OF MEDIA

DIETER GRIMM

29.1 Freedom of Media as Distinct Right

In a number of jurisdictions, freedom of media is treated as a subset of freedom of speech. It is speech amplified by technical means such as print or electromagnetic waves. Like freedom of speech, it is conceived as an individual right of the speakers, regardless of whether they express themselves in a face-to-face situation or address an indefinite number of people via newspapers or magazines, radio or TV. It is also regarded as a right of the owners of media, even if they do not speak themselves, because they may determine what is published and what not. The right is not limited to natural persons, but entitles juristic persons as well. It is a right vis-à-vis the state with negative effect: the state has to omit restrictions that are incompatible with the constitutional guarantee.

However, freedom of media should be regarded as a *distinct* right. Both rights share the quality of communicative rights, but they refer to different types of communication, individual communication there and mass communication here. The difference was already made in the beginning of constitutionalism. While the first modern bill of rights, the Virginian of 1776, guaranteed only 'freedom of the press', the French Declaration of 1789 contained a guarantee of freedom of opinion in article X and called 'the free communication of thoughts and opinions' in article XI 'one of the most precious rights of man', followed by the specification that 'every citizen may therefore speak, write and print freely'. The First Amendment to the US Constitution prohibited laws 'abridging the freedom of speech, or of the press'.

When the early constitutions were adopted, no other means of mass communication than the press existed. Younger constitutions like the German Basic Law of 1949 mention broadcasting next to the press, but did not foresee the emergence of television. Even very recent constitutions remain silent regarding the Internet. However, only an extremely crude textualist or originalist would conclude that media not explicitly mentioned in the constitution are not protected against government intrusion. 'Press' is a subcategory of the broader notion of 'media of mass communication' and thus open for the inclusion of newly emerging media without a constitutional amendment being necessary.

If a constitutionally guaranteed freedom covers several objects, like speech and press in the First Amendment of the US Constitution, this does not mean that all have to be treated alike. The meaning of a constitutional guarantee cannot be determined irrespectively of the segment of reality in which it shall take effect. The aim of constitutional interpretation is to give the norm utmost effect under the prevailing circumstances. Hence, circumstances matter for constitutional interpretation. They are an element among others, such as the text and the purpose of the norm, which determines the meaning at a given time. Differences in the object to which a norm applies may therefore require different interpretations if the norm shall take effect in social reality.

While the text of the norm remains stable as long as the norm is in force, the circumstances to which it applies are in constant flux. This implies that the meaning of a norm may change if the circumstances change in a way or to a degree that the norm, interpreted in the traditional way, would no longer fulfil its purpose. Not all methodological approaches recognize this. Some assume either that the meaning of a constitutional norm is determined once and for all by its authors and cannot be altered by way of interpretation, or that the adaptation of a norm to social change is not the task of the interpreter but the constitution maker. However, both alternatives pay a price in normativity insofar as they are unable to react to new challenges, so that the norm remains confined to problems known at the time of enactment and falls short of the problems that arise later.

29.2 THE ROLE OF MASS COMMUNICATION

What, then, distinguishes individual speech from mass communication? The evident difference is that the latter depends on technology whereas individual speech does not. But technology as such is not sufficient to explain the difference. Technology can also be used for individual communication over distances that cannot be bridged by the human voice, as the telephone, email, or Skype show. Mass communication, to the contrary, is based on a technology that is not interactive, but asymmetric. It is not communication among certain persons, but communication that is addressed to and can be received by an indefinite number of readers, listeners, and viewers but not vice versa. It is unilateral speech from a few to the many. The actors in the media system are the communicators; the general public or a segment of that public is the recipient.

By way of individual communication, the recipients may then communicate among themselves about the products or messages of mass communication, but they cannot interact with the communicators, unless a direct contact is enabled by mass media. But if so, it is a contact with certain selected recipients and usually arranged for the purpose of becoming part of the programme and being transmitted to an audience. The recipient changes roles and becomes for a moment themselves a communicator, albeit to the conditions set by the media. Without such an initiative of a journalist, no recipient gets a chance to appear in mass media.

The asymmetry is reinforced by the preconditions of mass communication. While individual communication depends mainly on natural capabilities, the ability to speak and to listen, and capabilities acquired in elementary school, namely the capacity to write and to read, mass communication usually requires an organizational structure and financial means to establish and maintain a publishing house, a radio station, a TV network. To be sure, everybody may have the right to establish such an enterprise. But only a few will have the means to do that. Similarly, everybody may have the right to choose journalism as a profession. But this right does not include a guarantee to find a position with the mass media.

Disposition of the means of mass communication greatly enhances the impact of speech, not only in terms of the numbers of recipients who can be reached but also in terms of the influence that goes along with it. The specific weight of the influence is determined by the fact that it concerns an essential element of personal and social life, namely information. The sociologist Niklas Luhmann begins his book *The Reality of Mass Media* with the sentence: 'We know what we know about our society and even the world in which we live through mass media'.[1] Mass media provide information about events, facts, actions, beliefs, opinions, and so on, which would not otherwise be obtainable for the recipients.

This is not to say that mass media monopolize the flow of information. There are other institutions that produce knowledge and disseminate information, like schools and universities, and other means that may be used to gather information, like books and lectures. But none of them surpasses the media of mass communication in range and impact. To the contrary, these other institutions or media get wide attention for their products or messages only through mass media reporting and largely depend on their services if they seek influence beyond their immediate audience.

Moreover, if mass media share their role as mediators of information with a number of other institutions, they are unique in establishing, fuelling, and maintaining the public discourse. They disseminate information about events and opinions that, in turn, provoke reactions by others, which are again subject matters for media reporting and so on. They shape the discourse by setting an agenda, keeping an issue on the stage, or no longer pursuing it. If a subject matter gets broad public attention and preoccupies society for a certain time, it is through continuous media reporting. The general public and the public sphere is a product of mass media. They achieve it 'by uniting strangers through common exposure to common texts'[2] and, one should add, images. There would be no public discourse without media.

---

[1] Niklas Luhmann, *Die Realität der Massenmedien* (2nd edn, Westdeutscher Verlag 1986) 1; see also Niklas Luhmann, *The Reality of the Mass Media* (Kathleen Ross tr, Stanford UP 2000) 1.

[2] Robert Post, 'Data Privacy and Dignitary Privacy: *Google Spain*, the Right to be Forgotten, and the Construction of the Public Sphere' (2018) 67 *Duke LJ* 980, 1018.

Yet, the activity of media does not exhaust itself in reporting about events happening in the outside world or transmitting opinions expressed elsewhere. Media intervene actively into the public discourse by producing and sometimes even provoking events for emission and by expressing views and opinions of their own. Media may have an agenda. But even if this is not the case, they are not just neutral conveyors of information but independent actors. As the German Constitutional Court said in its first TV ruling: TV is not only a medium but also a factor.[3]

The impact of media reporting affects all other societal subsystems. The image that the general public has of their performance depends largely on information acquired through the media. Everybody may have insights into various social systems, the educational system, the health system, the judiciary, and so on—from personal experience or perhaps conversations with relatives or neighbours—but not a general view. One can never be sure that what one knows from personal experience or hearsay is just a single case, an exception, even an outlier, for the good or the bad, or the normality. General impressions are based on the information disseminated by mass media.

The impact is particularly strong on the political system, although different in democratic systems on the one hand, and authoritarian or totalitarian systems on the other. Since in democratic states, the success or failure of political leaders and political parties is measured in terms of winning or losing elections, there is a heightened necessity for self-presentation of politicians in the media. They are compelled to convey their programme and their intentions to the general public and need the media for that, but have to succumb to their conditions. Even events controlled by politics like parliamentary debates or committee hearings are staged with media attention in mind. Politics function differently in the presence and in the absence of media.

The image of politicians is largely formed by their appearance in the media. Prominence is a product of media presence. The public learns about the political class, their programmatic views, and their activities through media reporting, and compares candidates and platforms based on media information. Only few people will have the opportunity to compare the media appearance of politicians with their personal impression of them. But politics do not exhaust themselves in periodical elections. They rather culminate in elections. More important than an election campaign is usually the knowledge and trust that is built over time, but again based on the continuous flow of information that media transmit.

Among the media of mass communication, TV has the widest range, whereas the use of print media is declining or shifts to their online services. People devote a considerable part of their daily time to consuming TV programmes. The average German spends 217 minutes per day watching TV. This still surpasses the use of the Internet (196 minutes, 39 per cent of which for media consumption), while the rate for consumption

---

[3] *First Television Case* [1961] 12 BVerfGE 205, 260. For a partial English translation and commentary, see Donald P Kommers and Russell A Miller, *The Constitutional Jurisprudence of the Federal Republic of Germany* (3rd edn, Duke UP 2012) 510 ff.

of radio programmes is 181 minutes.[4] TV is still the foremost source of information for the majority of the population. Newscasts are routinely among the programmes with the highest viewing rate.

This is not contradicted by the fact that most of the output of TV, but also of the radio and the print sector, is not information in the narrower sense of politically and socially relevant information, but entertainment. However, entertainment output, too, produces effects of social and political relevance. World views and convictions are formed or influenced. Values are confirmed or challenged. The evaluation and interpretation of facts is framed. Lifestyles and role models are offered. Standards of behaviour and decency are formed and changed. All these are, in turn, elements that shape the context in which political, social, economic, and cultural questions are treated.

But also in terms of impact, TV surpasses the other media. It owes its attraction largely to the fact that it is able to produce pictures and sounds from events in any part of the world in real time. This is why it develops a specific authenticity and persuasiveness. Reality beyond individual cognizance is largely perceived through TV reporting. However, media reporting about reality is not necessarily identical with reality. There is no reporting about reality without selection. This is true for all media of mass communication, but in TV, because of its omnipresence and actuality, it seems least obvious. The selection is partly imposed by objective constraints, partly guided by subjective choices.

An evident constraint is the space available in a newspaper or the time available in a radio or TV programme. Another constraint flows from the fact that media can only report in a linear manner. Simultaneity cannot be reproduced in the media. Other constraints are inbuilt in the type of media. Each of them has to accept losses of reality. Newspapers are confined to texts. They cannot reproduce sounds and can show images only in static form and they are unable to report in real time. The radio is able to report in real time, but is limited to transmitting sounds. TV can offer all this plus moving images. Yet for TV everything is unattractive that cannot be illustrated by pictures. If pictures are unavailable, it differs from radio only in that one can watch the speaker.

An independent factor is the financial regime under which media operate. A commercial TV network or station that earns money through advertising will favour other subjects and formats than public TV financed by the state budget or viewers' fees. Commercial TV has to create a favourable environment for advertising. This means usually that it tries to promise a wide audience to the economy in order to attract advertising. For this reason it will develop a tendency towards mass entertainment, while a publicly financed TV is freer in producing a programme that features other subjects as well, especially information and culture. Within the private sector, pay TV will develop other priorities than free TV.

All these constraints require decisions as to what is worth being reported and when, where, and how. It also requires prioritization among the subjects that are selected for

---

[4] Data available at: 'Wie lange nutzen die Deutschen Fernsehen, Radio und Internet?'(*NDR*, 9 April 2019) <https://www.ndr.de/der_ndr/daten_und_fakten/Wie-lange-nutzen-die-Deutschen-Fernsehen-Radio-und-Internet-ndrdaten101.html> accessed 10 December 2019.

reporting. The priority is not inherent in the objects of reporting. It is the result of a choice. Which criteria are at work here? Some are systemic. Mass media share the conditions under which societal subsystems in general operate in a functionally divided society. Each has a logic or rationality of its own, a code according to which it functions, communicates internally, measures systemic success and failure, and processes messages from its environment. This restraint is a condition of successful fulfilment of the function. Every system is self-referential. It is primarily interested in itself and in the performance of other systems only insofar as its own operations depend on or are influenced by them.

The code that governs the media system is the distinction between information and non-information, put simply, between new and old.[5] Within the media system, there is competition for the attention of the public or that segment of the public that certain media try to reach. Attention is the scarce good of the media system.[6] This creates an incitement to produce programmes that are likely to get attention. Conflict gets more attention than harmony. Personalized conflicts get more attention than structural conflicts. Extremism gets more attention than normality, and so on. These selection criteria are common to mass media. What differs is the standard of reporting according to the expectation, the horizon, and the educational background of the segment of society that a certain medium addresses or hopes to reach.

Still, the choices imposed by these constraints leave enough room for further selection that is not systemically conditioned. Some choices concern the general orientation of the media. A media owner may decide to publish a conservative newspaper or disseminate a progressive radio programme. Other choices have their reason in subjective preferences of journalists or economic considerations of the publisher. Journalists may decide to suppress certain news that they deem dangerous for society and to emphasize others that they find helpful. A local editor may hesitate to criticize the biggest advertiser in town. The weight that is given to an event or an opinion, and the time span during which it occupies the public are largely determined by such considerations.

And inevitably, the reporting about reality is the product of a certain perception of reality by the media actors, such as the journalist, the photographer, or the camera man. It is rare that the object of reporting carries an obvious meaning with it. Rather, it is given a certain meaning by the journalist. This does not mean that reality in the outside world and the presentation of reality in the mass media are unrelated. After all, it is reporting about something that actually occurred. But the two do not reach congruence. Media reporting is not simply a one-to-one representation of reality, but a certain view of it. Rather, media create a sort of 'second reality'.

Nevertheless, the impression of authenticity and objectivity that especially TV conveys to viewers blurs the difference between the two realities. Unless a product is

---

[5] See Luhmann (n 1) 32 ff.
[6] See Georg Franck, *Die Ökonomie der Aufmerksamkeit* (Hanser 1998); Thomas H Davenport and John C Beck, *The Attention Economy: Understanding the New Currency of Business* (Harvard Business School P 2001).

declared as fiction, people are inclined to take what they read, hear, or see in mass media as reality. Usually, they don't have the means to ascertain the truth or falsehood or even the selectivity of the information. This is even more so if they are used to always tuning into the same station which they trust or which confirms instead of challenges their views. However, based on the information obtained they form their opinion about reality and orient their behaviour accordingly.

The enormous impact that media of mass communication have on people's knowledge, views, and behaviour makes them susceptible to attempts to bring them under control or at least use them for purposes other than genuine journalism. Such attempts may emanate from other subsystems of society whose operations are affected by media coverage. As long as they use the wide range of media to plan events which find media attention or to advertise their products and services, this remains within the boundaries of intersystemic co-operation. But if they use their power to impose their own logic on the functioning of the media system, they compromise the specific contribution of media to society as a whole.

Two systems have particular effective means to exercise control: the political system has the means of law and the monopoly of legitimate force, the economic system the means of money. The tension that arises from this asymmetry is mitigated, but not completely levelled by the mutual interdependence of the systems. But the risk can also emanate from media actors themselves. Owners or journalists may try to privilege their own views or interests by treating them at preferred places or by suppressing or disfavouring alternative views. Attempts like these culminate in measures to establish a monopoly. In this way, media power may easily be transformed into political power and undermine the democratic process.

29.3 Freedom of Media as Functional Right

The meaning of freedom of media must be determined with these characteristics of its object in mind. They suggest a distinction between freedom of media and freedom of speech.[7] While freedom of speech as an essential element of the dignity and autonomy of the individual is a value in itself, independently of the manner in which it is used, freedom of media derives its importance from the role that it plays for individual opinion formation and the communication process of a society. It is not a value in itself, irrespectively of the manner in which it is used by the actors within the media system. Its value lies rather in the service that it renders other values, namely the two fundamental pillars of liberal constitutionalism: individual self-development and collective self-government.

---

[7] For a comparison of various jurisdictions, see Eric Barendt, *Broadcasting Law: A Comparative Study* (Clarendon P 1993).

Both depend on the activity of mass media. There is no individual self-development without free access to information about facts, beliefs, viewpoints, interests, customs, and patterns of behaviour which are current in a society. There is no collective self-government without free elections, and there are no free elections without full information about candidates for public office, the platforms of the competing parties, and the promises and performance of politicians. Media play a key role in enabling access to this information. In this function, they can be supported and complemented, but not replaced by other institutions. However, the media can fulfil it in accordance with the principles of self-development and self-government only if they are themselves free. This is why constitutions of liberal democracies contain a specific guarantee of freedom of media.

However, if media are indispensable for autonomy and democracy, it cannot be irrelevant *how* they fulfil the function. This requires clarity about the purpose behind the constitutional guarantee. Different from freedom of speech that is guaranteed in the interest of the individual bearers of the right, freedom of media does not primarily exist in the interest of the media owners, managers, and journalists. Rather, it exists in the interest of the individual recipients, the general public, and a democratic polity. Therefore, freedom of media is not only a distinct right, distinguishable from freedom of speech, but also a different type of right. Freedom of media is a *functional* right or, in the terminology of the German Constitutional Court, a 'serving freedom'.[8]

The term may sound peculiar. Is a serving freedom still a freedom? Doesn't it rather transform a liberty into a duty? The answer depends on who or what benefits from the service. If it is a certain pre-established truth or ideology or a group of power-holders, it would be difficult to call it a freedom. If, to the contrary, it is in itself a freedom value like individual self-development and collective self-government, the idea of a serving freedom or a functional freedom is not necessarily contradictory. Its meaning is then derived from a more general freedom, as a matter of fact, from the fundamental principles of modern constitutionalism: individual freedom and democratic rule as the type of rule which is best compatible with individual freedom as basis of the whole construction.

The jurisprudence of the German Constitutional Court on freedom of media is grounded in this idea,[9] but is not as alien to the US jurisprudence as one might expect.[10] Already in its early decisions on broadcasting, the US Supreme Court had defended the necessity of licensing by referring to the scarcity of frequencies, which had no parallel in the field of the press. The criterion for the choice between several applicants was the

---

[8] *Third Broadcasting Case* [1981] BVerfGE 57, 295, 320; see also Kommers and Miller (n 3).
[9] The series of decisions is available in English in: Decisions, vol. 2, parts I and II. Excerpts with introduction in Kommers and Miller (n 3) 441 ff; Christian Bumke and Andreas Vosskuhle, *German Constitutional Law: Introduction, Cases, and Principles* (Andrew Hammel tr, rev edn, OUP 2019) 159 ff.
[10] See, in general, Lucas A Powe, *American Broadcasting and the First Amendment*, (U California P 1987); Marc A Franklin, David A Anderson, and Lyrissa B Lidsky, *Mass Media Law: Cases and Materials* (8th edn, Foundation P 2011). Even the term 'serving' appears in US literature, see Owen M Fiss, 'The Censorship of Television' (1999) 93 *Nw U L Rev* 1215, 1224.

public interest, understood as the 'interest of the listening public'.[11] Regulation of broadcasting could therefore not be limited to the technical aspects of broadcasting, but had to include the programme that an applicant intended to offer. Decisive was the 'ability of the licensee to render the best practical service to the community reached by his broadcasts'.[12]

In the *Red Lion* case of 1969,[13] a specific requirement concerning the programme was at stake, namely the duty of a broadcaster to allow free time for response to a person who had been attacked in a broadcast. Together with some other obligations it formed the so-called fairness doctrine. The complaining broadcaster relied on traditional First Amendment arguments, according to which the amendment protected the bearers of the right 'to use their allotted frequencies continuously to broadcast whatever they choose, and to exclude whomever they choose from ever using the frequency'.[14] The broadcaster contended that nobody could be prevented from saying what they deemed right, and nobody was obliged to take the opinions of their adversary into account or even disseminate them.

The Supreme Court rejected this classical free speech argument by insisting on the special conditions of broadcasting, under which not everyone who wished to broadcast could get a licence. The loss that went along with the selection had to be compensated for in the programme of the licensees. The Court justified this with the purpose of the First Amendment. In its view, it does not exhaust itself in individual self-development but also pursues the purpose 'of producing an informed public capable of conducting its own affairs'.[15] The First Amendment, therefore, has not only an individual, but also a collective aspect: 'The people as a whole retain...their collective right to have the medium function consistently with the ends and purposes of the First Amendment'.[16] If this right enters into conflict with the individual right of the broadcaster, it is 'the right of the viewers and listeners, not the right of the broadcaster which is paramount'.[17]

So the Court, in spite of deriving the meaning of freedom of media from the service for the viewers and listeners, ultimately handled the case like a conflict of rights, as occurs frequently, and solved it by giving priority to the right of the people. However, it seems not so easy to conceive of the people as the bearer of an entitlement like freedom of broadcasting. Who should speak in its name? Who should have standing in court? The 'people as a whole' gain agency through the state and its democratically elected or appointed agents. Therefore, it might have been more appropriate to US fundamental rights practice to classify the fairness doctrine as a limitation of the First Amendment, which could, however, be justified by the legitimate government interest in a rich public discourse that supports the people in 'conducting its own affairs'.

The German Court's functional approach is different. It frames freedom of media in a way that society's interest in a free public discourse is neither a collective right of the

---

[11] *National Broadcasting Company, Inc v United States*, 319 US 190, 216 (1943).
[12] *Federal Communications Commission v Sanders Brothers Radio Station*, 309 US 470, 475 (1940).
[13] *Red Lion Broadcasting Corporation v Federal Communications Commission*, 395 US 367 (1969).
[14] Ibid 386.   [15] Ibid 392.   [16] Ibid 390.   [17] Ibid.

people nor an external limitation to the right of the media owners or journalists, but an integral part of its scope. This is reached by developing the understanding of fundamental rights from a one-dimensional to a two-dimensional concept.[18] According to this concept, fundamental rights are first and foremost subjective rights (entitlements) of the individual vis-à-vis the state. They prohibit state acts that would violate the right. But they do not exhaust themselves in this negative aspect. They are also objective principles, even the highest principles of the whole legal order. In this (objective) capacity, fundamental rights transcend individual liberty and protect the general freedom of those institutions of society or areas of social life that are covered by fundamental rights.

This opened the door to include into the scope of media freedom, not only the individual owners, journalists, and the various newspapers and magazines, but also 'the institutional autonomy of the press', and later that of broadcasting (understood as including TV) as social institutions.[19] It is the *media system* that ought to participate in the freedom guarantee of the constitution. The reason for this extension is precisely the indispensable function of media with regard to the more general principles of individual self-development and collective self-government, which presuppose that the media system itself is free. Both are the points of reference of media freedom, not only democracy as US scholars are inclined to assume.

This understanding allows the meaning of the individual side of the right to be defined more precisely. The qualification as a functional right does not reduce it to a mere objective guarantee of a social function and thus deprive it of its quality as an individual entitlement. After all, the social function can only be fulfilled by individuals, and they may invoke it when they fear that media freedom is in danger. But it does not protect them in the way freedom of speech (or some other personal right) is protected, which allows its bearer to use it at will, but also not to use it. The personal right leaves the decision whether and how to use it to the bearer of the right. But it permits the legislature to draw certain limits to the use of the right in the interest of other rights or the rights of others.

To the contrary, functional freedom in its individual aspect is a more limited freedom. But the limits exist in the interest of the more general institutional freedom. It does not give its bearer the right to dispose of the function. Rather, the function is preestablished. Individual freedom of the media actors has its place within the boundaries of the function and may be exercised only in a way compatible with it. Freedom of media, therefore, means that the media actors are free to act according to the specific logic of the media system—that is, according to journalistic criteria—and are not submitted to the logic of other systems that may have an interest in controlling the media and using them for their particular purposes, which are not the purposes of the constitutional guarantee of media freedom.

---

[18] The landmark decision is *Lüth* [1958] BVerfGE 7, 198. See also Kommers and Miller (n 3) 442 ff. See, generally, Dieter Grimm, 'The Role of Fundamental Rights after Sixty-Five Years of Constitutional Jurisprudence in Germany' (2015) 13 *Int'l J Const L* 9.

[19] See *Press Freedom Case* [1959] 10 BVerfGE 118; *First Television Case* (n 3).

Such threats can be external, but also internal. The foremost external threat emanates from government and the political forces behind it. In a democracy, parties and candidates compete for votes. The election decides who may take office and implement their programme. Under these circumstances, it seems natural that politicians have an interest to maximize their own chances and minimize those of their competitors and are therefore tempted to bring mass media under their control. Public TV lends itself more easily to political influence than the private sector. This threat is met by the negative dimension of fundamental rights. However, which political behaviour or influence is regarded as incompatible with media freedom varies greatly from country to country.

But there are also menaces emanating from private actors who attempt to instrumentalize the media of mass communication for their purposes, mostly but not exclusively economic in nature.[20] They, too, have effective means. Usually, private media are more prone to these menaces than the public sector. Media freedom is protected vis-à-vis them by the objective dimension of the right. It compensates the imbalance between the media and other powerful subsystems of society and stabilizes the borderline between the various subsystems of a functionally divided society and guarantees each of them a functioning according to its specific logic.[21]

Finally, there are also internal threats. Owen Fiss calls them 'managerial censorship'.[22] These threats emanate from the media actors themselves as bearers of the individual right. This is the case for example if media actors pursue goals other than those corresponding with the function, so if they succumb to expectations of other systems or try to establish a monopoly that excludes plurality of viewpoints or is used in order to favour certain interests and disfavour others. It occurs if they suppress or distort information systematically, and even more so if they try to build monopolistic structures. In cases like these, media freedom in its capacity as a subjective right of the media actors on the one hand and in its capacity as objective principle on the other enter into conflict and have to be balanced.

Since private actors are entitled, not bound by fundamental rights, freedom of media vis-à-vis these rights can only be furnished by the state. Consequently, in constitutional systems that recognize the twofold dimension of fundamental rights, the state is under a double obligation. It has to refrain from all acts that would unduly limit the freedom of media, but in addition, it has to take action to protect the media against attempts of private actors to impose their own logic on the media system or operate in a dysfunctional way within the media system. The means to reach this end is foremost a prohibition of monopolistic structures and a guarantee of plurality and diversity of subject matters, viewpoints, and so on, either in the media system as a whole or within each unit. Requirements concerning the truthfulness and diversity of the programme of broadcasting and TV stations are not excluded.

---

[20] See C Edwin Baker, *Media, Markets, and Democracy* (CUP 2002).
[21] This is the fundamental insight of Niklas Luhmann, *Grundrechte als Institution: ein Beitrag zur politischen Soziologie* (Duncker & Humblot 1965), to which he reduces the function of fundamental rights in his sociological perspective.
[22] See Fiss (n 10).

Because of this possibility, the concept of media freedom as positive right has been reproached as paternalism. But paternalism it would be only if the regulation concerned the demand side. Yet, it leaves consumers completely free in deciding what they want to watch and what not. It concerns only the supply side. It wants to guarantee individuals and the public in general access to the information that they need to form opinions and participate in the democratic process. However, it starts from the assumption that a pure market system will be unable to furnish a programme that meets the needs of a society, based on the free formation of opinion behind which the fundamental principles of individual self-development and collective self-government stand.[23]

Hence, freedom of media is a round-about freedom. It operates not only in the vertical, but also in the horizontal direction. Both dimensions entail obligations of the state as the addressee of fundamental rights. However, the different dimensions of the right operate in different forms.[24] Freedom of media as negative right with a vertical dimension is fulfilled by abstention. If the obligation has been violated, there is but one reaction: the act is declared unconstitutional. As positive right with horizontal application, freedom of media requires regulation in order to guarantee the institutional freedom of the media system. However, different from the right in its negative capacity, the legislature has a wide range of means. The fundamental right sets the goal but does not prescribe the means to reach it.

At this point, the *Red Lion* doctrine of the US Supreme Court and the jurisprudence of the German Constitutional Court depart. The Supreme Court concludes, from the premise that media freedom is not guaranteed in the interests of the owners or journalists but in the interest of the general public, that Congress *may* regulate broadcasting, whereas the German Court comes to the conclusion that parliament *must* regulate broadcasting in accordance with the purpose of media freedom. It contains a duty to legislate. Between 'may' and 'must' lies the difference between the US and the German (and European) approach.

Consequently, the Supreme Court stopped referring to *Red Lion* when the scarcity of frequencies had come to an end, and did not intervene when the fairness doctrine that it had approved of in *Red Lion* was abolished under Ronald Reagan's presidency.[25] Justice Thomas even denied, in a later case, that there is any protected interest other than the individual right of the broadcasters, and he defined this right in analogy to property.[26] But that case also initiated a certain revitalization of *Red Lion*, which continued in the *Turner II* case.[27] Here, Justice Breyer in his concurring opinion insisted that there are 'important First Amendment interests on both sides of the equation', those of the

---

[23] See Baker (n 20); Fiss (n 10).
[24] See Dieter Grimm, 'The Protective Function of the State' in Georg Nolte (ed), *European and US Constitutionalism* (CUP 2005) 137.
[25] See Victor Pickerd, *America's Battle for Media Democracy* (CUP 2014).
[26] *Denver Area Educational Telecommunication Consortium, Inc v Federal Communications Commission*, 518 US 727 (1996).
[27] *Turner Broadcasting System v Federal Communications Commission*, 520 US 180 (1997) ('*Turner II*'). See the discussion in Fiss (n 10) and Owen M Fiss, *The Irony of Free Speech* (Harvard UP 1996) 5 ff, 69 ff.

broadcasters and those of the public, which, for him, required striking a reasonable balance between speech-restricting and speech-enhancing aspects.[28] In this context, *Red Lion* was cited twice with approval.[29]

He thereby distanced himself from Justice Kennedy who wrote the majority opinion in *Turner II* and tried to solve the case by employing anti-trust instruments. Anti-trust considerations overlap indeed with First Amendment interests insofar as monopolistic structures in the media system are incompatible with freedom of media. However, anti-trust laws have a purpose different from the First Amendment. They are concerned with competition and thus follow a market rationale, whereas the informational purpose of the First Amendment cannot exclusively rely on market mechanisms. It is not only about consumer interests but also about individual self-fulfilment and democracy.

29.4 REPERCUSSIONS ON THE INTERNET

Just as radio and TV were new media in the twentieth century, the Internet and the so-called social media are the new media today. As always with scientific and technological progress, some older problems disappear, some new ones appear. The Internet undermines the difference between individual and mass communication. The asymmetry between communicators and recipients is levelled. Everybody can be communicator and recipient in one person and reach an indefinite number of readers, viewers, and listeners. Professionality of journalism is no longer required. Scarcity of resources is no problem on the Internet. New forms of democratic participation emerge. Because of the transnational character of the medium, state control of content has become more difficult. No central authority exists.

On the other hand, the harm that may go along with speech increases because of the new media. Power-holders obtain new opportunities to control and surveil citizens. Fake news and hate speech get a broader and longer lasting reach. Privacy is more difficult to defend. The filter of journalistic professionalism that traditional media furnish is absent on the Internet. New private power structures emerge, in particular in the form of intermediaries such as search engines, which determine the order and prioritization of messages. All of them operate for profit, not in the interest of free communication. These questions will be treated in a special chapter of this Handbook.[30]

This short outlook is confined to the repercussions of the new media on the old ones that were the topic of the present chapter. Obviously, they come under pressure. Many people no longer fulfil their need for information by reading newspapers or watching TV but by using the Internet instead. The willingness to pay for a service that is seemingly

---

[28] *Turner II* (n 27) 227.   [29] Ibid 227–8.
[30] See Gregory P Magarian, The Internet and Social Media, Chapter 19 in this volume. See also Marion Albers and Ioannis Katsivelas (eds), *Recht & Netz* (Nomos 2018). See, furthermore, the seminal German Constitutional Court decisions: *Right to be Forgotten I* (2019) 152 BVerfGE 152 and *Right to be Forgotten II* (2019) 152 BVerfGE 216.

also available for free is shrinking. This means at the same time that the number of journalists employed with the traditional media diminishes and with them the plurality and authenticity of information. In view of the breadth of the Internet and the loss of trust in professional journalism, the credibility of the traditional media is challenged. The fragmentation of the recipients increases with all its consequences for the public discourse and democracy.

As a result, the meaning of freedom of media has to be reconsidered. After a period of euphoria about the new opportunities, the necessity of speech regulation is meanwhile recognized. The reason is not only the amount of hate speech and pornography on the Internet, but also the power of the intermediaries. On the other hand, regulation has become much more difficult, mainly because of the transnational character of the Internet and the increase of players involved. However, all this is still in the beginning and will pose the most important challenge in the field of media freedom in the near future.[31]

---

[31] But see Jack Balkin, 'Free Speech is a Triangle' (2018) 118 *Colum L Rev* 2011.

Index

A

Abood v Detroit Board of Education (1977) 422–5
Abrams v United States (1919) 38
  Holmes's dissent in 46–7, 54, 57–9
absolute rights, freedoms
  dignity 112–13
  freedom of opinion (Mill) 30–3
  freedom of speech not an absolute right 457
  proportionality analysis 191–2
access to speak 245
accountability, Madison on 26–8
Acheson, David 127
act utilitarianism (Mill) 31–3
Adams, John 25, 332–3
adaptative change in ideas 39–40
Addams, Jane 334–5
adverse selection 129
advertising *see* commercial advertising
African Court on Human and People's Rights (ACtHPR) xxi–xxii, 401
Akerlof, George 119, 128–33, 135
Aleinikoff, T Alexander 174–5, 187
Alexander, Larry 463, 466
Alexy, Robert xix, 181, 183, 186, 190, 242
Allen, Long John 332
Altman, Andrew 463
Alvarez v United States (2012) 48–9, 52
American Booksellers v Hudnut (1985) 458–9
American Civil Liberties Union (ACLU) 252–4
American Civil War 21–2, 331, 333–4, 341
  Battle of Gettysburg (1863) 37
  Copperheads 333–4
  Emancipation Proclamation 333
  Federalists 333
American Convention on Human Rights (ACHR) 204
American Law and Economics Association 119
American Restatement (Second) of Torts 297
Amidon, Charles 336–7
Amnesty International 524–5
Ancient Greek philosophers 20–1, 43, 51
Anderson v Liberty Lobby (1986) 279
animal abuse 47
Animal Defenders International v United Kingdom (2013) 313, 317, 322
anti-discrimination norms, religious expression 515–16
Antipornography Civil Rights Ordinance 480
anti-Semitism 503
Arab Spring (2011) 352, 360–1, 370, 372, 387
Arbel, Yonathan 127
Areopagitica (Milton's polemic against censorship) xiv, 20–4, 46, 51–2, 58–9, 166–7
Aristotle 20–1
Armenian genocide, denying 189
art
  see also music and art
  intellectual property rights 436
  non-representational 433
  protection as free speech 69–70
  representational 433
'art-mobs' 199
Austin, JL 462–3, 491–2
  see also speech acts and speech act theory
Australia
  commercial advertising 449–50
  Constitution 86
  counter-terrorism measures 520–1
  criminal law 256
  defamation law 281–2
  elections and electoral speech 317–18
  freedom of expression 86, 91
  High Court 86, 91, 149–50, 181, 317–18

on primary purpose of freedom of
speech 49
and proportionality analysis 181, 186
Austrian Criminal Code 504
autonomy
agents as autonomous 64
Baker on 67–71
breadth of protection for speech 69–70
capabilities theory (Sen) 79
commercial advertising 452
complexity 61
content-based restrictions incompatible with premise that citizens autonomous 65
as a contested concept 61–2
critique of individualistic focus 71–2
'double-sidedness' 62
and First Amendment 74–5, 77
formal 68–9, 71
versus undermining will of others 69
and freedom of speech xv, 61–80
freedom of thought 72–4
and hate speech 61–2, 69, 71, 78–9, 460
individual xv
and liberal neutrality 77
listener-based approach 66–7, 69, 71–4, 76–7, 80–1
mental 63–7
Millian principle (Scanlon) 63–6, 73
absolutist constraint 65–6
autonomy as side-constraint on exercise of power 64, 78
compared with persuasion principle (Strauss) 66
consequences 65
earlier approach 65–6, 78
false or deceptive advertising, laws against 65–6
hostility to content-based restrictions of speech 65
intuitionist approach 65–6
later approach 65–6, 78
and relational autonomy 77
as moral independence 63–4, 78
and negative liberty 61–2, 78
neglect of background social conditions, alleged 71–2
non-communicative activities 70–1

non-violent, non-coercive expressive activity, immunity of 70–1
obligation not to impair 64
persuasion principle (Strauss)
compared with Millian principle (Scanlon) 66–7
false statements of fact 66–7
government engaging in 'thought control' 66–7
inducement and persuasion 66–7
manipulative speech 67
and relational autonomy 77
and politics 77–8
and privacy 294
as rational self-legislation 78
Raz on 79
relational xv, 63, 71–2, 74–81
respect for, and legitimacy of legal order 67–8
Schauer on 70–1
self-expression and freedom of speech xv, 67–72
as self-realization 78
Sen on 79
as side-constraint on exercise of state power 64, 78
and social relationships 71–80
speaker-based approach 62–4, 67–77, 80–1
speech systems, regulatory control over 63
state duties in respect to 61–2
substantive 61–2, 65–6
versus formal 68
'thinker-based' approach (Shiffrin) 71–4
and thought control 67–8, 73
Strauss on 66–7

B

Baer, Susanne 517
Baker, C Edwin
on autonomy 67–71, 78
commercial speech 69–70
compared with Shiffrin's views 73
critique of views on 71
formal 68–9, 71
harms caused by undermining will of others 69
liberty of speakers 67–72
on legitimating function of freedom of expression 92–3

Baker, C Edwin (*Continued*)
  on music and art 437–8
  and state control of speech 243
balkanization, and hate speech 472
Balkin, Jack 198–9, 241–2
Ballantyne and others v Canada (2004) 198
Barak, Aharon 107, 109–10, 181, 190
Barenblatt v United States (1959) 174
Barendt, Eric 285, 391
Bar-Gill, Oren 127
Bartnicki v Vopper (2001) 299
Baumgartner v United States (1944) 347
behavioural economics 127–8
Berlin, Isaiah 33, 154–5, 232
Big Brother Watch v UK (2018) 202
bigots 252–4, 260–1, 467
  and creationists 495–6
Bill of Rights
  England 97
  United States 25, 28, 113
    dignity absent in 113
Black, Justice Hugo 174–7, 191–2, 340
Black Lives Matter 372, 386–7
Blackmun, Justice Harry 142
blasphemy
  see also hate speech; religious expression
  distinguished from hate speech 502–4
  justification for laws 504–8
    offence 505–7
    public order 504–5
    religious dissent, problem of 507–8
    and state power to suppress cultural reform 507
Blencoe v British Colombia (2000), Canada 107
Blocher, Joseph 47
Bond, Julian 342
Bork, Robert 399, 431
Born, Georgina 236–7, 242
Bourquin, Judge George 336–7
Bowman v United Kingdom (1998), ECtHR 317, 323
Boycott, Divestment, Sanctions (BDS) movement 470–1
Boyron, Sophie 235, 246
Brandeis, Justice Louis 40–3, 249, 251–2, 338
  on civic duties 41–2
  clear-and-present danger test 42
  Holmes–Brandeis approach 339–40
  on individual liberty and majority rule 43
  on popular sovereignty 43
  in *Whitney v California* 40–1
Brandenburg v Ohio (1969) 342, 393–4, 521, 532–3
Brazil 109–10, 436
Brennan, Justice William 149–51, 271, 274, 287–8
Brettschneider, Corey 262
Breyer, Justice Stephen 553–4
Brink, David 456, 464
Brison, Susan xv, 71–2, 79
  'The Autonomy Defense of Free Speech' 78
  critique of autonomy accounts 79
  defining hate speech 78
Buckley v Valeo (1976) 221, 319
Bulgaria 436

C

Calabresi, Judge Guido 119
Calleros, Charles 260–2
Cambridge Analytica (right-wing data analytics firm) 361
Canada
  autonomy case law 79–80
  Charter of Rights and Freedoms (1982) 87, 107, 178–9, 449–50
  commercial advertising 449–51
  criminal law 256, 532
  dignity case law 107, 115–16
  elections and electoral speech 317–18
  freedom of Internet speech 352, 355
  hate speech 50, 460, 503
  Human Rights Tribunal 359
  proportionality analysis 449–50
  spying on travellers 361
  Supreme Court 107, 178–9, 181–2, 184, 186, 189, 219–20, 449–50, 503
  Telecommunications Act 355
Canadian Civil Liberties Association v Ontario (1990), Canada 509
Cantwell v Connecticut (1940) 339, 393
capabilities theory (Sen) 79
Cardozo, Justice Benjamin 240
Carlill v Carbolic Smoke Ball Co (1893), UK 131–2
Catholicism
  Milton on 4, 22–3, 47

religious expression 509–10
censorship
  Areopagitica (Milton's polemic against censorship) xiv, 20–1
  Crown censorship regime 21
  Index on Censorship 252–4
  versus legitimate justifications for restrictions 138–9
  religion as censor 502–8
  risks of 252–4
  self-censorship 149, 272, 286–7, 359–60
Central Hudson Gas & Electric Corpn v Public Service Commsn (1980) 447, 450
CERD *see* Committee on the Elimination of Racial Discrimination (CERD)
certification and licensing 133–4
Chafee, Zechariah 34–5, 337, 431–2
Chaplinsky v New Hampshire (1942) 407–8
  insult of public officials 389–91, 395–8, 408–9
  truth justification for freedom of speech 48–9
Chechen Republic, hate speech 208
child pornography 139–40, 142, 484
chilling effect on speech 296–7, 329, 453, 484, 532
  defamation 276–7, 281–7, 289–91
  and 'warming' effect 132
Chinese Cybersecurity Law (2016) 531–2
Christian theology 51
citizenship responsibilities (Milton) 21
Citizens United v Federal Electoral Commission (2010) xxii, 49, 110, 217
  elections and electoral speech 316, 320–1
City of San Diego PD v Roe (2004) 418
Civil Rights Movement 377
Civil Service Commission v National Association of Letter Carriers (1973) 420–1
Clark, Tom 339
Coase, Ronald 118, 121
coercion 13, 92–4
  compelled speech 70, 74, 126
  employer 383
  interference with agents 13
  labour pickets 384, 386
  political legitimacy 92–5
  and pornography 486
  pornography 487

of public opinion 17
racist speech 71
rights–privileges distinction 414
and scope of right to freedom of speech 197
state, in the US 307–8, 311
vague and value-laden concept 71
Cohen v California (1971) 48, 396–7
COINTELPRO programme (1956) 342–4
Cold War 331, 339–41
Coleman v MacLennan (1908) 287–8
collective expression xx, xxii, 369–88
  see also demonstrations; parades; protests
  access to the public forum xxii, 374–8
  Arab Spring (2011) 352, 360–1, 370, 372, 387
  Civil Rights Movement 377
  concept of assembly 369
  concept of public forum 376
  democratization of public discourse and dissent 372–4
  free speech zones 380
  future of and digital revolution 386–8
  labour pickets 371, 382–6
  means of resistance and dissent 373
  modern challenges 378–82
  negotiated management approach in the US 381
  parades 371, 515
  policing methods 380–1
  private property 378
  public order offences 382, 505–6
  racial segregation 370
  'Roberts Rules of Order' 379
  single-person protests 199
Colombia 217–18, 508–9
command-and-control regulation 118, 381–2, 388
commercial advertising/speech 69–70, 73, 198
  Australia 449–50
  autonomy 452
  Canada 449–51
  chilling effect 453
  in Europe 450–1
  factually false 453
  and freedom of speech xx, 444–54
  beyond the US 449–51
  definitions 444–5
  experience of the US 445–8

commercial advertising/speech (*Continued*)
  paternalism 454
  protection, theory of 451–4
  United Kingdom 450
  Virginia Pharmacy case (1976) 445–8, 451–4
  weaponization critique xxii–xxiii
Committee for Public Information (CPI),
    World War I 335–6
Committee on the Elimination of Racial
    Discrimination (CERD)
  see also International Convention on the
    Elimination of All Forms of Racial
    Discrimination (ICERD)
  General Recommendation No 35 206–7
  incitement to hatred 206, 208
common law, English 25
communication
  individual 352
  role of mass communication 543–8
Communications Decency Act 1996 538
compelled speech 70, 74, 126
Connick v Myers (1983) 415–17, 425, 427–8
Constitution, US
  Bill of Rights 25, 28, 113
    dignity absent in 113
  First Amendment *see* First Amendment of
    American Constitution and free speech
  Fourteenth Amendment 493
  freedom of speech as a political and
    constitutional value 500–2
  immunity from economic regulation not
    codified in 120
  and learning from wartime 344–5
  positive constitutional law, principle
    of xiii, xviii
  religious expression and
    anti-discrimination 515
  speech and debate clause of Article I 97
constitutionalism
  and dignity 106–7
  living constitution 164–5
  workplace, freedom of expression
    in 410–11
constitutional texts on speech, music and
    the arts 434–7
  France 435
  German Basic Law 434–5
  ideas and opinions 435–6
consumption-based harms 488–90

Convention on the Rights of Persons with
    Disabilities (CRPD) 196
Convention on the Rights to the Child
    (CRC) 196
corporate speech 49
Council of Europe
  Commissioner for Human Rights 524–5
  Convention on the Prevention of Terrorism
    (COE Convention) 524
  and counter-terrorism 524
  and national security 209
Council of the European Union
  and national security 209
Counter-Reformation, Catholic 22–3
counter-speech xix–xx, 249–65
  advocates 255
  body politic and democratic
    deliberation 251–2
  broader conceptions 261–5
  context 254–8
  Dangerous Speech Project 252–4
  defining 251–4
  effectiveness of speaking back 259–61, 264
  Free Speech Debate 252–4
  hate speech 258
  'much enlarged' conception of speaking
    back 263
  philosophical perspective 262
  remedy for bad speech 250–1
  type of speech that speaking back remedy
    applied to 256
coverage of the right to free speech 162–8
  see also freedom of speech; right to free
    speech
  distinction between coverage and
    protection 168–71
  examples 162–3
  flexible or purpose-oriented view of legal
    interpretation 165
  invisible questions 164
Cox Broadcasting v Cohn (1975) 297, 303
Cranston, Maurice 321–2
Creel, George 335–6
criminal law
  Australia 256
  blasphemy 504
  Canada 256, 532
  coverage of the right to free speech 162
  German Criminal Code 143–4

Kenyan Penal Code 504
Holocaust denial as a crime 114–16
terrorist-related speech 531–2
traditional paradigm 540
crisis centres, speech provided by 47
Critical Race Theory 464–8
Curran, James 236–7, 242, 246

D
Dahl, Robert 88
Dahlab v Switzerland (2001), ECtHR 513–14
Daly, Erin 110–11
damages 23, 129, 132
  civil 534
  and defamation law 270–1, 275–7, 286–7
Dangerous Speech Project 252–4
Darwin, Charles
  The Origin of Species 39
data privacy 307–10
'dead dogma' argument (Mill) 29, 471–2
Debs, Eugene 334–5
defamation xx, 269–91
  see also libel; slander
  Australia 281–2
  and autonomy 79
  'chilling' and 'warming' effect 132
  counter-speech 256
  damages 270–1, 275–7, 286–7, 301
  defamatory opinion 275
  economic perspectives 127
  England 281–4
    reportage defence 283–4
  Internet, defamatory speech on 358–60
  liability 132
  malice *see* malice
  neutral reportage 283–4
  political speech 269–70, 274, 283–4
  profane speech 48–9
  proof of falsity and fault 279–80
  public interest defence 281–4, 290–1
  reasonable publication defence 281, 284–5
  Reynolds case (UK) 283–7, 289
  shape of freedom of speech 280–8
  Sullivan rules xxi–xxii, 28, 270–4, 281–2
    actual malice *see* malice
    clear and convincing evidence
      requirement 279–80
    compared with previous law 276–7, 280–1
    and electoral disinformation 328
  evaluating 288
  inapplicable outside US
    Constitution 281–4
  and judgment 274–80
  and privacy 297, 301
  traditional US approach versus *Sullivan*
    rules 272, 274–80, 286–7
    burden on plaintiffs 276–7
    common steps in US litigation 278–9
    compared with non-US courts 274–80
    judicial role 279–80
    media content of public concern 277–8
    opinion 278
    private plaintiffs 277
    summary judgment 279
    vehement, caustic and sharp attacks 286–7
Defamation Act 2013, UK 283–4, 289
Delgado, Richard 260–1, 466
deliberative democracy
  versus pluralist 98–100
democracy
  aggregative models 75
  ballot measures 96–8
  complexity 246
  concept/definition 83, 95–6
  core democratic functions of freedom of
      expression 90–5
    informing function xvi, 90–2
    legitimating function xvi, 92–5
  defensive 103–4
  democratic positive free speech 235–8
  direct/participatory versus
      representative xvi, 96–8
  forms 95–104, 233–4
  and freedom of expression xv, 82–105
    core democratic functions of 90–5
    and dignity 110
    essential connection between 83–90
    implications of forms of democracy
      for 95–104
  individual laws xvi
  justification xvi
  libertarian versus militant 103–4
  and media 246–7
  pluralist versus deliberative 98–100
  and popular sovereignty 82–3
    political expression as a necessary
      component of 84–8
  protected and unprotected speech 35–6

democracy (*Continued*)
  public discourse and dissent,
    democratization 372–4
  representative versus direct/participatory
    xvi, 96–8
  self-government, democratic xv
  substantive versus proceduralist xvi, 101–3
  United Kingdom 49
  workplace, freedom of expression in 419
demonstrations xx, xxii, 231–2, 369–73,
    386–7, 515
  see also collective expression; labour pickets;
    parades; protests; public gatherings,
    demonstrations and protests
  anti-war 380–2
  Arab Spring (2011) 352, 360–1, 370, 372, 387
  Black Lives Matter 372, 386–7
  colonial 373
  effective 387–8
  limits on 382
  mass demonstrations 373
  micromanagement 381–2
  negotiated management approach
    in the US 381
  peaceful 377
  planned 381–2
  political 90
  'racketeering' laws 382
  rights of demonstrators 381–2
Dennis v United States (1951) 123–4, 135, 174,
    339, 342
*Derbyshire County Council v Times
  Newspapers* (1993), UK 282–3
Dharmapala, Dhammika 126–7
digital economy xiii, xx, xxiv
  see also Internet
dignity xvi–xvii, 106–17
  absolute 112–13
  of all human beings 108
  anti-totalitarian origins 114
  background/history 106–9
  challenges 109
  and constitutionalism 106–7
    as a constitutional value 107
  daughter-rights 107, 109–10
  defining 107–9, 114
  and equality 50, 116
  as a framework (mother-right) 107, 109–10
  and freedom 108

  and freedom of speech 109–13
    conflict with 112
    limiting 111
    re-enforcing 111
  German approach 50, 106–7, 112
  hard cases 114–17
  and hate speech xvii, 460
  International Covenant on Civil and
    Political Rights (ICCPR) 114
  legal status 107–8
  level of compared with other rights 107, 117
  and privacy 295–6
  as a property of human beings 108
  and proportionality analysis 113
  as a right 107, 117
  subsidiary role 112
  thick notions of 114
  Universal Declaration of Human Rights
    (UDHR) 49, 107
  in the US versus Europe 292–3
  violation of
    abuse of children 116–17
    degrading and dehumanizing 116–17
    and Holocaust denial 114–15
    and pornography 116
Director, Aaron 118, 120–1
direct/participatory democracy
  versus representative xvi, 96–8
discrimination
  see also Committee on the Elimination of
    Racial Discrimination (CERD);
    International Convention on the
    Elimination of All Forms of Racial
    Discrimination (ICERD)
  anti-discrimination laws and norms 94–5,
    515–16
  hate speech 256–8
  against LGBT community 515
  religious 503, 506–7
Dmitriyevskiy v Russia (2017), ECtHR 211
'double-sideness' of freedom of speech xvii,
  xx–xxi
Douglas, Justice William 174, 340
Dworkin, Andrea 480, 493
Dworkin, Ronald 63–4, 78, 469, 486, 495–6

E

Easterbrook, Judge Frank 493
economic perspectives xvii–xviii, 118–36

see also L&E (law and economics) movement
atomistic competition 130
behavioural economics 127–8
cost-benefit statement 123–4, 126–7
critical review of 120–8
economic analysis compared with L&E movement 119
hate speech 126–7
information asymmetry in goods and services market xvii–xviii
libel 122, 126–7
liberty 130–5
mirror-image position 124
new information economics 119, 128–30
opt-in liability 134–5
'prove-me-wrong' offers 132
reputation 129, 133–5
signalling and screening regime 134–5
slander 122, 126–7
used car market 130
'weighted balancing' 123–4
elections and electoral speech xx, 312–30
Australia 317–18
Canada 317–18
in Europe 313–15, 324
fake news (disinformation) 324, 327–8
First Amendment of American Constitution and free speech 313–14
freedom and restraint, need for 312
India 512–13
legitimating function of freedom of expression 93–4
and religious expression 512–13
textual drafting and judicial deference 315
United Kingdom 313, 317, 322–7
United States 314–17, 324
Elrod v Burns (1976) 420–1, 425–6
Emerson, Thomas 51–2, 248
England
see also United Kingdom
Bill of Rights (1689) 97, 159
Civil War 21, 82–3
common law 25, 214–15
defamation law 281–4
reportage defence 283–4
Glorious Revolution (1689) 24
Enlightenment thinking xiv, 88
truth justification for freedom of speech 51, 53

Epstein, Richard 252–4
equality
see also inequality
and dignity 50, 116
and hate speech 460–1
political *see* political equality
racial 220
right to 217–18
of status 91
and truth justification 50
Erasmus 20–1
Espionage Act 1917 34, 38, 335–7
ethics 511
journalism 201–2, 366
utilitarian 31
EU *see* Europe and European Union
Euripides 20–1
European Convention on Human Rights (ECHR)
see also defamation; human rights; privacy rights; Universal Declaration of Human Rights (UDHR)
commercial advertising 450–1
constitutional texts 435
elections and electoral speech 313–15
and human dignity 107
informing function of freedom of expression 90
insult of public officials 395–6
legitimate aim 180–1
privacy 298–9
Protocol 13 107
public order offence 505–6
restrictions on freedom of speech in international law 204
and structure of a right to free speech 221–2
terminology, freedom of speech 160–1
terrorist-related speech 528–9
truth justification for freedom of speech 49
European Court on Human Rights (ECtHR)
blasphemy laws 505–6
elections and electoral speech 313
freedom to seek and receive information 200–1
guarantees of freedom of expression 178
and Holocaust denial 189
and human dignity 107, 115

European Court on Human
    Rights (ECtHR) (*Continued*)
  insult of public officials 395–7, 402, 406–7
  and national security 210–11
  privacy 298–9
  religious expression 509–10
  and structure of a right to free speech 221–2
Europe and European Union
  see also European Convention on Human Rights (ECHR); European Court on Human Rights (ECtHR)
  Agency for Fundamental Rights 537–8
  Brexit referendum and UK withdrawal from the EU 96, 363, 366–7
  Charter of Fundamental Rights 178–9, 358–9
  commercial advertising 450–1
  Commissioners for Migration, Home Affairs and the Security Union 535–6
  counter-terrorism measures 524
  Data Retention Directive 308
  dignity 292–3
  elections and electoral speech 313–15, 324
  newsworthiness concept 296–7
  privacy rights 298–301, 308–11
  right to be forgotten 363
  social-democratic model xxii
  and social media companies 536
European Digital Rights 252–4
European Human Rights Commission 117
Evans, Carolyn 511
evolutionary theory 39
exceptionalism, First Amendment xix, xxi–xxii

F

Facebook *see* social media platforms
factual truth 45, 50–6
  changing of facts 52–3
  the deeper good 56
  harmful truths 56
  narrative defence of truth justification 58
  and opinion 52
  and transcendent truth 56
fake news (disinformation) xvii–xviii, 131, 134–5, 259, 554
  elections and electoral speech 324, 327–8
fallibility, Mill on 5–8, 29
Fallon, Richard H 71

false speech 329, 464
  see also fake news (disinformation)
Farber, Daniel 125–6, 135, 470
FBI (Federal Bureau of Investigation) 342–4
Federal Communications Commission (FCC), US 121
  fairness doctrine 133–4
'fighting words' doctrine xxi–xxii, 48, 156
  see also insult of public officials
  insult of public officials 390–4, 396–7, 399–400
First Amendment of American Constitution
  and free speech xiv, xix, xxi–xxiii, 26, 47, 55, 97–8, 163, 176–7, 180–1
  see also Constitution, US; Madison, James; Supreme Court, US; United States
  and autonomy 74–5, 77, 126
    reliance on liberal conception of autonomy 74–5
    saluting the US flag seen as violation 70
  Citizens United v Federal Electoral Commission xxii
  commercial advertising 445–6
  content-based versus viewpoint-based restrictions 141–2, 146–7
  defamation law 274, 281–2
  deregulatory uses 448
  discovery of improper governmental motives 138
  double-edged 422–6
  elections and electoral speech 313–14, 316–17, 319, 323–4
  exceptionalism xix, xxi–xxii
  fairness doctrine as a limitation of 550
  freedom of discussion (Mill) 15
  and freedom of media 542–3
  Free Speech Clause 147
  free speech zones 380
  individual disciplinary decisions 414–19
  L&E movement and economic perspectives 120, 126, 135
  and labour organizing 383–4
  Madison as principal author 24–5
  political speech 177
  and privacy rights 307–8
  proportionality analysis 174, 176–7
  public employee speech rights under 413–26
  public gatherings, demonstrations and protests 369–70, 375–80

expressive topography 376
ratification of 28
and Sedition Act 25
truth justification for freedom of
    speech 47, 55, 59
and unlawful conduct 331–49
workplace, freedom of expression in 411,
    413–14, 426–8, 430
    double-edged 422–6
    individual disciplinary decisions 414–19
    public employee speech rights
        under 413–26
First Television Case (1961), Germany 222
First World War *see* World War I
Fishkin, James 99
Fiss, Owen 244–5, 262, 552
flags 75–6, 408
    see also symbols
    burning 14–15, 36, 75–6, 94, 160, 481
        bans on 126
    disrespecting 126, 408
    saluting 51–2, 70, 348, 389–90
    terrorist groups 518–19
    and unlawful conduct 335–7, 342
Florida Star v BFJ (1989) 303–4
forgotten, right to be 310–11, 362–3
Fourteenth Amendment of American
    Constitution
    and equality 493
France
    Civil Code 306
    Conseil Superieur de l'Audiovisuel 305
    constitutional texts 435
    Cour de Cassation 306
    dignity 296
    European Constitution referendum 96
    French Declaration of 1789 542
    French Republic 331–2
    'glorifying terrorism' offences 520
    'Half War' with 331–3
    Penal Code 301–2
    penalties for violations of 'apology of
        terrorism' offence 520–1
    privacy rights 298–301, 303–6
    pro-Palestinian activists, conviction 470–1
Frankfurter, Justice Felix 173, 176–8, 191
Frantz, Laurent B 188, 191–2
Fraser, David 115
Freedom of Discussion Principle (Mill) 3–19

see also Harm Principle (Mill); Mill, John
    Stuart; *On Liberty* (Mill)
defining what is freedom from 3
engagement with falsehoods and partial
    truths 8–10, 29
epistemic argument/knowing the
    world 3–12, 14
    discursive engagement with the
        world 4–6
    evidence 5–8
    fallibility 5–8, 29
    sensible engagement with the world 4–5
    evidence 5–8
        interpretation 6–7
        misleading 5–6
        offered by others 6
    false beliefs 8–9
    interference and discussion of
        opinion 12–16
    judgments 6–7
    scope 12–16
    truth-apt propositions 14–16
    unit of reference for comparing costs and
        benefits of communicative acts 31–2
freedom of expression
    see also freedom of speech
    chilling effect *see* chilling effect on speech
    collective expression xx, xxii, 369–72
    contested questions 176–80
    core democratic functions of 90–5
        informing xvi, 90–2
        legitimating xvi, 92–5
    and democracy xv, 82–105
        core democratic functions *see above*
        and dignity 110
        essential connection between 83–90
    European Convention on Human Rights
        (ECHR) 49
    and freedom of speech xiii, 161, 168
    guarantees 176, 178
    and hate speech 456–61
    informing function xvi, 69, 90–2
    legitimating function xvi, 92–5
    necessary component of formal political
        equality argument 88–90
    philosophical literature xv, xvii
    and popular sovereignty *see* popular
        sovereignty
    suspicion-of-government accounts 439

freedom of expression (*Continued*)
  in workplace *see* workplace, freedom of expression in
freedom of speech
  see also freedom of expression; speech
  and advertising *see* advertising
  and autonomy *see* autonomy
  changing context xxiii–xxv
  chilling effect *see* chilling effect on speech
  classic views *see* historical arguments for free speech (1644–1927)
  contexts and controversies xx–xxiii
  coverage of the right to free speech xviii–xix, 162–8
    compared with protection xviii, 168–71
  and dignity 109–13
    conflict with 112
    limiting freedom of speech 111
    re-enforcing freedom of speech 111
    see also dignity
  'double-sideness' of xvii, xx–xxi
  economic analysis 119
    see also economic perspectives
  example of falsely shouting 'Fire'! 40, 65
  and freedom of expression xiii, 161, 168
  fundamental questions/perspectives xiv–xviii
  ideal theory 72
  importance for development as thinkers 73
  individual interests, serving 61
  in international law *see* international law
  as a legal idea xviii–xx
  legitimate aim 180–2
  limitations on, and proportionality analysis 173–92
  Mill on absolute freedom 30–3
  minimal impairment (necessity or least restrictive means) 184–5
  not an absolute right 457
  and personal liberty 161
  as a political and constitutional value 500–2
  political liberalism, central commitment of xiii
  positive constitutional law, principle of xiii, xviii
  preferred limit to (Hand) 36
  and privacy *see* privacy

  public good aspect 125–6
  rational connection (suitability) 183–4
  rationale for protection 44
  as a right and a remedy 42–3
  and silencing 495–6
  societal interests, serving 61
  terminology, development of 159–62
  traditional justifications 61
  unlawful conduct protected by *see* unlawful conduct, protected by freedom of speech
freedom of the press 25, 28
  institutional press 91–2
freedom of thought 72–4
Free Speech Debate 252–4
Fried, Charles 63–4, 189
Funeral Oration of Pericles 41

G

Garcetti v Ceballos (2006) 416–19, 428
Garoupa, Nuno 127
Garrison v Louisiana (1964) 398
General Intelligence Division (GID) 337, 343
Germany
  Basic Law xxiii, 160–1
    constitutional texts 434–5
    freedom of media 542–3
    and human dignity 106–7, 112, 115
    positive free speech 239
    structure of a right to free speech 217–18, 222
  Criminal Code 143–4
  on dignity 50, 106–7, 112
  Federal Constitutional Court 143, 186, 222, 238–42, 246, 545, 549–50, 553
  Federal Republic 143–4
  and freedom of media 550–1
  hate speech 460
  militant democracy 104
  Nazi Party *see* Nazi Party, Germany
  NetzDG Law 520–1
  overthrow of Weimar Republic by Nazi Party 104
  speaking back 252–4
  and state control of speech 245
  viewpoint theory 143–4
Gertz v Welch (1974) 406
Gewirth, Alan 295–6

Gitlin, Todd 342
Globe Newspaper v Superior Court
    (1982) 303–4
Glorious Revolution (1689), England 24
Goldman, Emma 334–5
Google v Spain (2014), CJEU 310–11, 362–3
Gordon, Thomas 82–3
Gregory, Charles 335
Grimm, Dieter xv–xvii, xxiii–xxiv
Griswold v Connecticut (1965) 306–7
guarantees 129

H
Habermas, Jürgen 99, 102
*Hague v Committee for Industrial
    Organization* (1939) 376
Hall, Kermit 287
Hamdani, Assaf 127
Hammer, Peter 123
Hand, Judge Learned 33–7, 123, 336–7
    on authority of the majority 36
    correspondence with Zechariah Chafee 34–5
    on doctrinal safe harbour protecting
        speech 35
    on hostile criticism 33–4, 36
    on *Masses* judgment 34–7
    preferred limit to freedom of speech 36
    on protected and unprotected speech 35–6
Handyside v United Kingdom (1979–80),
        ECtHR 397
harassment, rules against 459
Harlan, Justice John Marshall 176–7, 340–1
harm and harms
    see also Harm Principle (Mill)
    consumption-based harms 488–90
    emotional, speech causing 47
    false beliefs 64
    harm-based restrictions on freedom of
        speech 138–40
    harmful acts performed as a result of
        speech 64
    harm-insensitive restriction 140–1
    hate speech 464–9
        extrinsic harms 464–9
        intrinsic harms 468–9
        isolated instances of harmful conduct 474
        psychological 492–3
        speech act theory 463–4
        uniqueness of 464–9

Holocaust denial 115
    interpretation 486
    isolated instances of harmful
        conduct 474
    pornographic, and debasement of
        women 479–80
        consumption-based 488–90
        misogynistic 489–90
        production-based 487–8
        violent 488–90
    production-based harms 487–8
    and speech 138–41
    undermining will of others 69
Harm Principle (Mill) 3, 17–19, 30
    see also Freedom of Discussion Principle
        (Mill)
    critique of corn-dealers as 'starvers of the
        poor' 15, 31–2
    HLA Hart's restatement 153
    pornography 486
Hart, HLA 153
Hartzel v United States (1944) 348
hate speech xx–xxi, 455–76
    see also discrimination; Holocaust denial;
        religious expression
    arguments against regulating 470–5
        institutional 470–1
        Millian 'dead dogma' argument
            29, 471–2
    arguments for regulating 461–9
    and autonomy 61–2, 69, 71, 78–9, 460
    and balkanization 472
    bigots 252–4, 260–1, 467
    and creationists 495–6
    blasphemy, distinguished from 502–4
    Canada 50, 503
    counter-speech 258
    Critical Race Theory 464–8
    defining 78, 114, 257
    deliberative values 464
    and dignity xvii
    dignity of victims 460
    directed against minorities versus
        majorities 459–61
    discriminatory 256–8
    economic perspectives 126–7
    entrenchment of differences 472
    and equality 460–1
    and freedom of expression 456–61

hate speech (*Continued*)
  Germany 460
  harms 464–9
    extrinsic 464–8
    intrinsic 468–9
    isolated instances of harmful
      conduct 474
    psychological 492–3
    speech act theory 463–4
    uniqueness of 464–9
  homosexuality 463, 466
  identity politics, vices 472
  incitement to hatred 205–6
  on Internet 358–60
  legal regulation 457–8
  liberal view 459–61
  as 'low-value' speech 461–4
  and 'mere' speech 461
  and multiculturalism 472–5
  non-liberal viewpoint 459–60
  offensiveness 260
  as political speech 457–8
  and pornography 461–2, 469
  prevalence 455–6
  questioning whether defined as
    'speech' 116, 461–4
  Rabat Plan of Action (2012) 206–7
  racist 69, 71
  regulation of 50
  separation of speech and conduct 465–6
  silencing argument xix, 468–9
  and subordination 463
  targets, autonomy of 460
  in the United States 456
  unregulated 79
  and viewpoint theory 458
hatred, incitement to 205–9
Health Insurance Portability and
  Accountability Act (1996) 308
heresy 21
Herodotus 20–1
Heyman, Steven 458–9
Hinduism 513–14
historical arguments for free speech
  (1644–1927) xiv
  Learned Hand 33–7
  Louis Brandeis 40–3
  James Madison 24–8
  John Stuart Mill 28–33

John Milton 20–4
Oliver Wendell Holmes 34, 37–40
Holder v Humanitarian Law Project
  (2010) 533–4
Holmes, Justice Oliver Wendell 34, 37–40, 47,
  338, 375–6, 432
  on adaptation 39–40
  Civil War soldier 37, 39
  clear-and-present danger test 40, 42
  The Common Law 38, 40
  dissent, in *Abrams v United States* 46–7,
    54, 57–9
  and distinction between coverage and
    protection 169–70
  and First Amendment 163
  on freedom of speech and other rights 39
  on free speech claims 37–8
  Holmes–Brandeis approach 339–40
  marketplace-of-ideas metaphor 40
  in Supreme Court 37–8
  on truth 45–6
  and rights 37, 40
Holmes, Stephen 149
Holocaust denial 176, 189, 207, 359, 503, 529
  see also hate speech; racist speech
  as a crime 114–16
  and dignity 114–15
  harms 115
  proportionality analysis 176, 189
  terrorist-related speech 529
Hoover, J Edgar 343–4
Hornsby, Jennifer 462, 482, 491–3
hostility-based restrictions on freedom of
  speech 65, 138–9
human dignity *see* dignity
human rights
  dignity *see* dignity
  European Convention on Human Rights
    (ECHR) 49
  Inter-American Court of Human
    Rights xxi–xxii
  International Covenant on Civil and
    Political Rights (ICCPR) 114,
    194–5, 197
  in international law xiii
  terminology, freedom of speech 160–1
  Universal Declaration of Human Rights
    (UDHR) 49–50, 107
Human Rights Act 1998, UK 450

Human Rights Watch 261–2
hunger-strikes 199

I

ICCPR *see* International Covenant on Civil and Political Rights (ICCPR)
identity politics, vices 472
illocutionary speech acts 462–3, 491, 496
  illocutionary disablement 494, 496
improper governmental motives, discovering 138
Independent Press Standards Organisation (IPSO), UK
  certification regime 134
  Editor's Code 134
independent thought, Milton on 22
India
  Constitution 217–18, 508–9
  Penal Code 504–5
  public order 504–5
  Representation of the People Act 512–13
  Supreme Court 506, 512–13
Indonesia
  Constitution 505
  Constitutional Court 505, 507
  Criminal Code 504
inequality 123, 163, 466
  see also equality
  discrimination 501–2
  economic 319–20
  political 322
  racial 287
  sexual 488
  social 74–5, 322
  stereotypes 460–1
  structural 257
information
  asymmetry of in goods and services market xvii–xviii, 130, 136
  Committee for Public Information (CPI), World War I 335–6
  freedom to seek and receive 200–1
  informing function of freedom of expression xvi, 69, 90–2
  and mass media 544
  new information economics 119, 128–30
  and non-information 547
  paternalistic government 77

political 126
privacy protection 295
Instagram *see* social media platforms
insult of public officials xx, 389–409
  see also Chaplinsky v New Hampshire (1942)
  and criticism 406–9
  fighting back 393–5
  'fighting words' doctrine 390–4, 396–7, 399–400
  insulting to particular individuals 395–400
  offensive language 390, 393, 395–8, 402, 407
  proportionality analysis 397
  public concern 405
  public watchdogs 404–5
  and self-government 400–2
  as sole intent of offensive statement 395–8
  vehement, caustic and sharp attacks 398–400
  white male point of view 391–3
intellectual property and freedom of speech 363–5
  violation of copyright 16
Inter-American Court of Human Rights (IACtHR) xxi–xxii, 401–3, 405–6
International Convention on the Elimination of All Forms of Racial Discrimination (ICERD) 205–6, 208
  see also Committee on the Elimination of Racial Discrimination (CERD)
International Convention on the Protection of the Rights of All Migrant Workers and Members of Their Families (ICRMW) 196
International Covenant on Civil and Political Rights (ICCPR) 114
  hate speech 503
  incitement to hatred 205–8
  insult of public officials 400–1
  and international law 194–5, 197, 199, 204
  restrictions on freedom of speech in international law 203
  structure of a right to free speech 219
international law, freedom of speech in 193–212
  freedom to seek and receive information 200–1
  human rights xiii
  restrictions on freedom of speech 203–11
    incitement to hatred 205–9
    national security 209–11
    respect for the reputations of others 205

international law, freedom of
    speech in (*Continued*)
  scope of right 197–203
    'art-mobs' 199
    hunger-strikes 199
    single-person protests 199
    special protection for journalists and
      public watchdogs 201–3
  Treaty protections 195–6
International Telecommunications Union
    (ITU) 353
International Workers of the World (IWW)
    ('Wobblies') 375
Internet
  see also digital economy
  content regulation issues 356–7
  devolved and transnational
      architecture xxiv
  digital revolution and future of collective
      expression 386–8
  freedom of speech on xx, 350–68
    Canada 352, 355
    Internet as a free speech medium 350–2
    offensive speech 359
    social benefits xxiv
    structural platforms 352–7
    substantive problems *see below*
  as government surveillance tool 360–2
  inequalities of access to 353–4
  net neutrality 355–6
  online associations 387–8
  pornography on 478
  private power, concentrations of 354–6
  social media platforms 351, 360–1, 366, 368
  structural regulation 354, 357–8
  substantive free speech problems 357–68
    hateful an defamatory speech 358–60
    intellectual property 363–5
    Internet as government surveillance
        tool 360–2
    news sources, reliability and influence
        of 365–8
    privacy and speech 360–3
    right to be forgotten 362–3
  technological architecture 350–1
  virtual assemblies 387–8
  and World Wide Web 350–1
Internet service providers (ISPs) 355, 358–9

intolerance
  moral reproach arising from xiv–xv
  and paternalism, in freedom of speech
      regulations 147–51
    Prisoner's Dilemma 153–4
    questioning whether intolerance
        worse 151–5
    religious expression 153–4
  in regulation of speech 147–55
ISIS (Islamic State of Iraq and
    Syria) 518–19
Israel
  Boycott, Divestment, Sanctions (BDS)
      movement against 470–1
  and dignity 111
  popular sovereignty, commitment to 87
  Supreme Court 473–4

J

Jackson, Robert 343
Jackson, Thomas 448
Jacobs, James 472
James, William 39
James v Turilli (1971) 131–2
Janus v AFSCME (2018) xxii–xxiii, 422–7
Jefferson, Thomas 25
  Bill for Establishing Religious Freedom 46
Jeffries, John 448
Jestaedt, Matthias 170–1
*Jewish Community of Oslo and others v
    Norway* (2005), UNHRC 208
Jewish people 108–9, 115, 207
  anti-Semitism 503
  and hate speech 471–3
  Holocaust denial *see* Holocaust denial
Jolls, Christine 127–8
journalism
  citizen journalists 365–6
  ethics 201–2, 366
  grave risks 203
  journalistic purposes derogation from data
      protection regulations 201–2
  professionality of 554
  responsible 289
  special protection for journalists and
      public watchdogs 201–3
  status-driven categorizations of
      journalists 201–2

Journal of Law & Economics 121
Judaism and Talmud 471–2
  see also Jewish people

K

Kagan, Justice Elena 138, 448
Kalven, Harry 377
Kavanaugh, Justice Brett 355–6
Kelsen, Hans 85–6
Kennedy, Justice Anthony 146–7, 554
Kenyan Penal Code 504
Kerrouche v Algeria (2016), UNHRC 200
King, Martin Luther 36
Kissinger, Henry 342
Konigsberg v State Bar of California (1961) 174
Korematsu v United States 345–6
Krotoszynski, Ronald 308
Ku Klux Klan 260

L

L&E (law and economics) movement
  see also economic perspectives
  conferences 119
  flourishing of 119
  leanness of literature on free speech 119
  literature on free speech 119, 135
  and marketplace of ideas 118
labour pickets xx, 370, 382–7
Langton, Rae 261–2, 462, 482, 491–4
  see also pornography
Lautsi v Italy (2012) 509–10
Lawrence, Charles 465–6
Learned Hand (federal judge) *see* Hand, Judge Learned
legality principle 214–15
legitimating function of freedom of expression xvi, 92–5
  anti-discrimination laws 94–5
  elections and electoral speech 93–4
  individual laws 94
  legitimate aim 180–2
    means-to-objectives 182
    tobacco objectives 182, 185
  normative legitimacy 92–3
  political legitimacy and coercion 92–5
Leirvag v Norway (2004), UNHRC 511
Lepoutre, Maxime 262
Leroy v France (2008), ECtHR 530–1

Letter Carriers see Civil Service Commission v National Association of Letter Carriers (1973)
Levellers (Puritan group) 82–3
Levi, Edward 344
Levy, Leonard 53–4
LGBT community, discrimination against 515
liability
  defamation 132
  meaning conveyed by speaker's words 34–5
  opt-in liability, signalling and screening 134–5
  and warranties 131–2
libel 176–7, 272
  see also defamation; slander
  blasphemous 504
  civil actions, threat of 283
  economic perspectives 122, 126–7
  First Amendment 453
  group 78–9, 506
  private 15
  seditious 28, 282–3
  state law 280
  truth justification for freedom of speech 48–9
libertarian democracy
  versus militant 103–4
liberty
  see also On Liberty (Mill)
  autonomy, liberty-based approach to 62–3
  economic perspectives 130–5
  and formal autonomy 68
  licensing and certification 133–4
  negative *see* negative liberty
  reputation 133
  signalling and screening 134–5
  of speakers 62–4, 67–77, 80–1
  Trees and Poles 373
  warranties and liability 131–2
licensing
  and certification 133–4
  FCC's regime 121, 133–4
  Milton on 21–2, 24
Lichtenberg, Judith 236
Lincoln, Abraham 333–4, 345–6
Lingens v Austria (1986), ECtHR 401, 403
Lipson, Morris 245

Lochner v New York (1905) 426, 448
Locke, John 27, 51, 474
locutionary speech acts 462, 491
Loewenstein, Karl 104
Luhmann, Niklas
   The Reality of Mass Media 544
Lüth (1958), Germany 240
Lyon, David 334
Lyon, Matthew 25, 332–3

M
McAdams, Richard 126–7
McCrudden, Christopher 109–11
McGowan, Mary Kate 262, 483
Machiano, Linda 487
Machiavelli, Niccolò 20–1, 23–4
McIntyre, Lee 55
MacKinnon, Catherine 462, 468, 480–1, 483, 487, 492–3
   see also pornography
   Only Words 495
Madison, James 24–8
   see also First Amendment of American Constitution and free speech
   on accountability 26–8
   on factions 98
   on meaning of the First Amendment 25
   on natural rights 27
   on popular sovereignty 84
   principal author of the First Amendment 24–5, 28
   on public opinion 85–6
   Report on the Virginia Resolutions 25–6
   on republicanism 28
   as a textualist 26
Magnet, Joseph 254–5
Maitra, Ishani 483
majority rule 36
malice 25, 205, 272–3, 287–8
   actual malice 169–70, 280, 287–8, 328, 407
   defamation law 272–3, 276–80, 286–8, 290
   privacy 301, 303–4
margin of appreciation doctrine 450–1
marketplace-of-ideas metaphor 40
   economic perspectives 118
   music and art 438–9
   truth justification for freedom of speech 48–9, 53–5
Marshall, Justice Thurgood 141–2, 145

Massaro, Toni 460–1, 467
mass communication, role of 543–8
   means 544
   preconditions 544
   role of mass media as mediators of information 544
   television 545–6
Masses Publishing Company v Patten (1917) 34–7
Masterpiece Cakeshop v Colorado Civil Rights Commission (2018) 218
Matsuda, Mari 464–5
MEC v Pillay (2008), South Africa 514
media, freedom of xx, xxiii, 542–55
   breakdown of traditional media xxiv
   credibility issues xxiv
   and democracy 246–7
   as a distinct right 542–3
   diversity of media sectors 236–7
   freedom of the press 25, 28
   as a functional right 548–54
   gatekeeping function of traditional media xxiv
   mass communication, role of 543–8
   mass media 85–6, 198
   mixed media system 246
   pluralism 235–6
   repercussions on the Internet 554–5
Mehanna v United States (2013) 534–5
Meiklejohn, Alexander 145, 165–7, 318–19, 321–2, 400, 431–2, 439–40, 458–9
   Free Speech and its Relationship to Self-Government 90–1
The Metaphysical Club 39
militant democracy
   versus libertarian 103–4
Mill, John Stuart
   see also Freedom of Discussion Principle (Mill); *On Liberty* (Mill)
   on absolute freedom of opinion 30–3
   Autobiography 17
   classic argument for free speech 28–33
   compared with Milton 29–30
   'dead dogma' argument 29, 471–2
   and defamation law 284–5
   Harm Principle 3, 17–19, 30
      critique of corn-dealers as 'starvers of the poor' 15, 31–2
      HLA Hart's restatement 153

liberal theory of freedom of speech
  xiv–xv, 482
  and religious expression 501
  on role of state 486
  on thought and discussion *see On Liberty*
    (Mill)
  on utility/utilitarianism *see* utility/
    utilitarianism (Mill)
Millian principle of autonomy
    (Scanlon) 64–5
  absolutist constraint 65–6
  compared with persuasion principle
    (Strauss) 66–7
  consequences 65
  false or deceptive advertising, laws
    against 65–6
  hostility to content-based restrictions of
    speech 65
  intuitionist approach 65–6
Milton, John xiv–xv, 20–4, 57
  Areopagitica xiv, 20–4, 46, 51–2,
    58–9, 166–7
  and *Chaplinsky* 48–9
  compared with Mill 29–30
  Paradise Lost 20–1
  and religious expression 501
  on truth 45, 51–2
monopolies, speech 198–9
moral reproach xiv–xv, 16
moral rights 436
Moynihan, Daniel Patrick 52
multiculturalism 50, 472–5
Mungan, Murat 127
music and art
  see also art
  and freedom of speech xx, 431–43
    constitutional texts 434–7
    defining the scope of the issue 432–4
    non-propositional expression xiv–xv
    government subsidies for 440–2
    marketplace-of-ideas metaphor 438–9
    regulatory principles for 437–40

N
Nagel, Thomas 63–4
narrative, truth as 57–60
  and factual truth 58
  subject to qualification 58–9
  and transcendent truth 58

National Labor Relations Act (NLRA)
  1935 427–8
national security 209–11
National Socialist Party of America v Skokie
  (1977) 458–9
Nazi Party, Germany 103–4, 143–4, 220
  see also Holocaust denial
  art, regulation of 433
  concentration camps 193
  and human dignity 115
  swastika 458–9
negative liberty
  and autonomy 61–2, 76, 78, 307
  positive free speech 231–2, 234–5, 242
  and privacy rights 292–3, 307
Netherlands, European Constitution
    referendum 96
neutrality
  content-based 8, 48, 142–7, 150, 155
  liberal 76–7
  net neutrality 355–6
  neutral reportage, US 283–4
  state duty of 509–11
  subject-matter 144–5
  viewpoint 8, 138, 143–4, 147, 459
    and subject-matter neutrality 144–5
    US-style 143–4
new information economics 119, 128–30
news sources, reliability and influence
    of 365–8
newsworthiness 292, 296–8, 302–3, 305
New York Times v Sullivan (1964)
  see also defamation
  and commercial advertising 453
  defamation rules xxi–xxii, 28, 270–4, 281–2
    compared with previous law 276–7,
      280–1
  and judgment 274–80
  and electoral disinformation 328
  evaluating 288
  inapplicable outside US
    Constitution 281–4
  insult of public officials 398, 403
  and privacy rights 297, 301
  and seditious libel 28
New Zealand
  Bill of Rights Act 178–9
  viewpoint neutrality 144
Nielsen, Laura Beth 261

Nietzsche, Friedrich 51
Nixon, Richard 342
notice-and-takedown procedures 364, 521, 524, 538–41

O

Obama, Barack 252–4, 355–6
O'Brian, General John 337
Occupy Wall Street movement 372, 386–7
offensiveness
    artworks offensive to Christians 260, 440–1
    cartoons 530
    extreme 467
    gratuitous statements 197–8, 505–6, 530–1
    hate speech 260, 463
    images 325–6
    insult of public officials 390, 393, 395–8, 402, 407
    international law 197–8, 211
    Internet, offensive speech on 359
    'Piss Christ' 440–1
    pornography 477, 486
    prohibiting offensive speech 390
    public feeling 325
    sexual conduct 479
O'Gorman, Daniel 132
Oklahoma Publishing Co v District Court (1977) 304–5
On Liberty (Mill)
    see also Freedom of Discussion Principle (Mill); Mill, John Stuart
    chapter one 17, 30–1
    chapter two ('On the Liberty of Thought and Discussion') 3–19, 28–33
    chapter three ('On Individuality') 30–1
    critique and unanswered questions 33
    'dead dogma' argument 29, 471
    dedicated to defending a single principle 17
    and search for truth 46, 166–7
opinion formation, individual and collective 245–6
Optic Nerve (British surveillance programme) 361
Osborne v Ohio (1990) 142–3
Otto-Preminger Institute v Austria (1995), ECtHR 506
Özgür Gündem v Turkey (2001), ECtHR 221–2

P

Palmer, A Mitchell 337
    General Intelligence Division (GID) 337, 343
Palmer, William 334
parades xxii, 369–71, 385
    see also collective expression; demonstrations; labour pickets; protests
    democratization of public discourse and dissent 373–4
    and pickets 382, 384–5
Pascal, Blaise 57
paternalism and intolerance, in freedom of speech regulations 147–51
    objectionable or tolerable paternalism 154–5
    Prisoner's Dilemma 153–4
    questioning whether intolerance worse 151–5
    religious expression 153–4
Peirce, Charles Sanders 39
PETA Deutschland v Germany (2012), ECtHR 193–4, 208–9
perlocutionary speech acts 462, 491
Perry, Michael 58
personality rights 299–303
persuasion principle of autonomy (Strauss)
    compared with Millian principle (Scanlon) 66–7
    false statements of fact 66–7
    government engaging in 'thought control' 66–7
    and inducement 66–7
    manipulative speech 67
    and relational autonomy 77
Petrarch 20–1
Pickering v Board of Education (1968) 414–17, 419–20, 425
pickets, labour see labour pickets
Plato 51
pluralism
    and Dahl 98
    deliberative versus pluralist democracy 98–100
    limits to sorts of protection of free expression required by 100
    media 235–6
    and religion 516–17

Police Department of Chicago v Mosley
  (1972) 141–2, 145
political equality 83, 93–4, 320–1
  between candidates 317
  elections and electoral speech
    xxii, 323–4
  inter- and intra-group 516
  political expression as a necessary
    component of 88–90
  speaker interests 89–90
  and voting 88–9
political speech 113, 126, 198–9, 220
  see also elections and electoral speech;
    hate speech
  and autonomy 65–6, 73
  constitutional protection and privileged
    status 77–8, 110, 141–2, 146–7, 197, 204,
    328–9, 457–9, 521, 535
  defamation law 269–70, 274, 283–4
  equal treatment of speakers 90
  extreme 526
  and First Amendment 177
  hate speech as 457–8
  and incendiary speech 73
  versus non-political speech 73,
    77–8, 197–9
  patronage 425–6
  prioritization 211
  and terrorism 527, 533–4
popular sovereignty
  accountability and responsibility of
    representatives 86
  audience interests 89
  Brandeis on 43
  commitment to and right of free
    speech 86–7
  and democracy 82–3
  and freedom of expression 84–8
    as a necessary component of
      formal political equality
      argument 88–90
    not a necessary component of popular
      sovereignty argument 87–8
  Israel's commitment to 87
  paradox of power 87
  public opinion, crucial role 85–6
  and voting 88–9
Porat, Ariel 127
pornography xix–xi, 477–98

  as act of subordination 462, 480,
    488–9, 492
  anti-pornography feminism 477–80,
    487–95
  causal versus constitutive
    arguments 490–2
  BDSM material 480–1
  child pornography 139–40, 142, 484
  and coercion 486
  consumption of 487–90
  defending 462, 485, 487–8, 490
  defining 478–9
  feminist 479
  hardcore and softcore 479, 483
  harms, to women 479–80, 487–95
    causal versus constitutive
      arguments 490–2
    consumption-based 488–90
    misogyny 489–90
    production-based 487–8
    violence 488–90
  and hate speech 462, 469
  as illocutionary act 462
  on the Internet 478
  justification for regulation 495
  and legal moralism/paternalism 485
  liberals versus conservatives 484–8
  mental intermediation doctrine 490
  misogynistic 489–90
  moralization among critics 479
  moral right to 477–8, 486
  non-legal remedies 497–8
  obscenity 116, 479
  offensiveness 477, 486
  protection issue 483–95
  questioning whether defined as
    'speech' 116, 477, 481–4
  questioning whether right to 485
  'rape myths' 489–90
  and sexual incquality 488
  sexually explicit material designed to
    produce arousal 479–80
    questioning being defined as 480–1
  and sexual violence 488–90
  and silencing 492–5
  and speech acts 478, 491–2
  traditional debate 484–6
  uses 478–9
  violent 488–90

positive free speech xix
　access to speak 245
　as a democratic freedom 231–48
　democratic media and courts 246–7
　democratic positive 235–8
　free speech as a negative liberty 231–2, 234–5
　German Federal Constitutional Court 238–42
　and law 237
　legal prohibitions versus legal obligations 242
　media pluralism 235–6
　negative and positive free speech rights 220–2
　and negative freedom 234
　negative liberty 231–2, 234–5, 242
　and positive freedom 234–5
　public discourse 243–4
　state control 243–6
　structure of right to free speech 221–2
　sustained plural public speech 235
Posner, Eric 126
Posner, Richard 123–5
　'Dennis' formula 123–4, 135
　Economic Analysis of Law 118
Post, Robert 55, 101–2, 114, 287, 439
　'Equality and Autonomy in First Amendment Jurisprudence' 244–5
　and state control of speech 243–6
Potter, Kimberly 472
press, freedom of 25, 28
Prism (US secret government surveillance programme) 361
privacy xx–xxi, xxiii, 292–311
　and actual malice 301, 303–4
　and autonomy 294
　being apart from others 294–5
　concept of privacy 293–6
　consequentialist arguments 292
　data 307–10
　and dignity 295–6
　in Europe 298–301, 308–11
　and expressive interests, in the US 292–3
　Florida law 303–4
　France 298–301, 303–6
　and freedom of speech
　　difficulty in balancing rights 298–311

　　hard cases 302–5
　　institutional considerations 306–7
　　privacy on the periphery of the two rights 301–2
　　spatial criterion 306
　horizontal application of free speech rights xxiii
　and Internet 360–3
　newsworthiness 292, 296–8, 302–3, 305
　and personality rights 299–303
　Privacy Shield Agreement, US 309–10
　protection of information 295
　right to be forgotten 310–11
　Umbrella Agreement between US and EU 309–10
　victims of sexual aggression 303–5
proceduralist democracy
　versus substantive xvi, 101–3
production-based harms 487–8
profit motive and commercial speech 73
proportionality analysis
　abridgement 180
　balancing test 173–4
　　appeal to US Supreme Court 176
　　outcome of balancing 189
　　proportionality *stricto sensu* (overall balance) 186–91
　Canada 449–50
　and dignity 113
　and distinction between coverage and protection 170–1
　insult of public officials 397
　interests
　　characterization of 187–8
　　comparability of 189–91
　　formulation of 188–9
　　number of 187
　　outcome of balancing 189
　limitation clauses 178–9
　and limitations on freedom of speech 173–92
　necessity xix
　outside the US 170
　proportionality *stricto sensu* (overall balance) 186–91
　　outcome of balancing 189
　structured proportionality xix
　US Supreme Court xxi–xxii

protection, theory of
  commercial advertising 451–4
protests 90, 260, 342, 371, 374, 382–6
  see also Arab Spring (2011); collective
      expression; demonstrations; labour
      pickets; parades
  anti-war 372
  armed 388
  civil rights 381
  immigration 381–2
  labour 375–6
  mass protests 372
  political 381
  single-person 199
public forum doctrine 378
  see also collective expression
  access to the public forum xxii, 374–8
  concept of public forum 376
  management of forums 380
public interest defence
  defamation 281–4, 290–1
public officials
  elections and electoral speech 93–4
  insult of see insult of public officials
  and politicians/public figures 402–4
  public watchdogs 404–5
  right to criticize 82–3
public opinion, crucial role 85–6
public order
  blasphemy laws 504–5
  in India 504–5
  offences 382, 505–6
public reason and freedom of speech xvii,
      137–56
  see also restrictions on freedom
      of speech
  intolerance and paternalism in
      regulations 147–51
    questioning whether intolerance
        worse 151–5
  regulation of speech
    content-based versus viewpoint-based
        restrictions xvii, 141–7, 155–6
  speech and harm 138–41
  viewpoint theory 139–41
    content-based versus viewpoint-based
        restrictions xvii, 141–7, 155–6
*Public Relations Consulting Ltd v Newspaper
    Licensing Agency* (2014), ECJ 364–5

public sphere, and religious expression
      508–10, 513–14
  'religion' and 'cultural' or 'civilizational'
      values, critique of distinction 510–11
public watchdogs, special protection
      for 201–3

R
R (Pro-Life Alliance) v BBC (2003), UK
      314–15, 324–7
Rabat Plan of Action (2012) 206–7
racist speech 69, 71
  see also Holocaust denial
  ant-Muslim 259–60
Ramji Lal Modi v State of UP (1957),
      India 504–5
Rankin v McPherson (1987) 416
Rasmusen, Eric 126
Rauch, Jonathan 254–5
Rawls, John xvii, 137, 499, 505
Raz, Joseph 79
  The Morality of Freedom 248
Reagan, Ronald 342
reason see public reason and freedom of
      speech
Redish, Martin 145–6
Red Lion Broadcasting Corpn v FCC
      (1969) 550, 553–4
reductio ad absurdum strategy 190
Reed, James 334–5
Reformation 21–2
relational autonomy and freedom of
      speech xv, 71–4, 80–1
religion
  see also Catholicism; Jewish people;
      religious expression
  artworks offensive to Christians 260,
      440–1
  as a censor 502–8
    distinction between hate speech and
        blasphemy 502–4
  dominant 516–17
  Hinduism 513–14
  inter-group pluralism 516–17
  Judaism and Talmud 471–2
  myth, role played by 57
  pluralism 516–17
  'religion' and 'cultural' or 'civilizational'
      values, critique of distinction 510–11

religion (*Continued*)
  religious symbols 14–15, 509–10, 513–14, 516–17
  and truth 21, 53
  versus way of life 513
religious expression xx–xxi, 499–517
  see also hate speech; racist speech
  and anti-discrimination norms 515–16
  blasphemy
    distinguished from hate speech 502–4
    justification for laws 504–8
    and state power to suppress cultural reform 507
  Crucifix case (*Lautsi v Italy*) 509–10
  and elections and electoral speech 512–13
  as emancipatory 512–13
  headscarf as symbol 513–14
  Joint Statement by the UN Special Rapporteurs and Annual Report of UN High Commissioner for Human Rights 507–8
  'passive' symbolism 516–17
  paternalism and intolerance, in freedom of speech regulations 153–4
  problem of religious dissent 507–8
  and the public sphere 508–10
    'religion' and 'cultural' or 'civilizational' values, critique of distinction 510–11
  reconciling with other constitutional values 512–16
  symbols 513–14
  Toledo Guidelines 511
representative democracy
  versus direct/participatory xvi, 96–8
republicanism
  Madison on 28
  Milton on 22–3
  'neo-republican' thought in First Amendment xxii
Republican Party, US 333
reputation
  economic perspectives 129, 133–5
  and liberty 133
  respect for the reputations of others 205
restrictions on freedom of speech 203–11
  censorship versus legitimate justifications 138–9
  content-based xvii, 65, 139–47, 155–6
  content-neutral 8, 48, 139, 142–7, 150, 155
  expressing a viewpoint preferred/disliked by government 139
  'gag rules' 149
  harm-based 138–40
  harm-insensitive 140–1
  hostility-based 138–9
  incitement to hatred 205–9
  in international law 203–11
    incitement to hatred 205–9
    national security 209–11
    respect for the reputations of others 205
  intolerance and paternalism in regulations 147–51
    whether paternalism worse 151–5
  motive-based 139, 144–7, 156
  national security 209–11
  respect for the reputations of others 205
  subject-matter regulation 147–50
  viewpoint theory *see* viewpoint theory
Reynolds v Times Newspapers (2001), UK 283–7, 289–91
Richards, David 254–5
Richardson, Eliot 36
right to free speech xviii
  coverage of xviii–xix, 162–8
    compared with protection xviii, 168–71
  expanding to more than an individual right 49
  force of 213–16
  horizontal application xxiii
  judicial enforceability 215–16
  labelling 159–62, 168
  negative and positive 220–2
  object of 213–14, 222
  popular sovereignty, commitment to 86–7
  positive obligations of the state xix, 62
  and proportionality analysis 171
  protecting, comparing with covering 168–71
  scope of 197–203, 213–14, 218–20
  state action doctrine xxiii
  statutory 215–16
  structure of 213–22
  subject of 213–14, 216–18
  super-constitutional 215
  vertical application xxiii

Rodley, Nigel 197
Romanian National Council for Combating Discrimination (CNCD) 509–10
Roosevelt, Franklin D 343, 345–6
Rorty, Richard 54
Rosen, Gary 27
Rosenberg, Norman 287–8
Rosenberger v University of Virginia (1995) 146–7
Rousseau, Jean-Jacques 323–4
  The Social Contract 321–2
Rowbottom, Jacob 244
Rushton, Michael 123
Russian Revolution 337
R v Keegstra (1990), Canada 79–80, 115–16, 540
R v Morgentaler (1988), Canada 107
Rwanda genocide (1994) 208–9

S

Sack, Robert 278–9
Sarpi, Fra Paolo 22–3
Saunders, Kevin 251–2
Scanlon, Thomas 63–6, 77
  see also autonomy
  on autonomy as side-constraint on exercise of power 64, 78
  Millian principle 64, 73
    absolutist constraint 65–6
    compared with persuasion principle (Strauss) 66
    earlier approach 65–6
    exceptions to 65
    false or deceptive advertising, laws against 65–6
    intuitionist approach 65–6
    later approach 65–6, 78
  on reasons for which speech may be legitimately restricted 67–8
  'A Theory of Freedom of Expression' 64
Schauer, Frederick 74–5, 327
  on autonomy 63–4, 70–1, 78
  and popular sovereignty 87
  on pornography 481, 483
  truth justification for freedom of speech 52–3, 56
Schneiderman v United States (1943) 347
Second World War *see* World War II
Sedition Act 1798 25–7
  and wartime 332–3, 335, 346

self-expression and freedom of speech 67–72
  see also autonomy
self-government
  democratic xv
  freedom of expression and contested questions 177–8
Sen, Amartya 79
Senate Select Committee to Study Government Operations with Respect to Intelligence Activities 344
Serrano, Andres
  'Piss Christ' 440–1
Shaffer v United States (1919) 336
Shiffrin, Seana
  and Baker's views on autonomy 73
  and Brison's view of autonomy 78
  and coverage of freedom of speech 167
  on harm-based regulation of speech 140
  on music and art 438
  'thinker-based' approach to autonomy 71–4
signalling and screening 134–5
silencing argument
  fallibility and infallibility 5–6
  and free speech 495–6
  hate speech xix, 468–9
  pornography 492–5
single-person protests 199
Sisyphus, myth of 58
slander 176–7
  see also defamation; libel
  economic perspectives 122, 126–7
Slovenia 436
smartphones 351
Smith, Adam
  Wealth of Nations 120
Smith v Daily Mail Publishing Co (1979) 303–5
social media platforms 351, 360–1, 366, 368, 386
Socrates 51
Souter, Justice David 147
South Africa
  amending Bill of Rights 215
  Bill of Rights (1996) 178–9
  Constitution 219, 503
  Constitutional Court 110, 512
  Final Constitution (1996) 217
  and hate speech 50

religion (Continued)
　hate speech 503
　limitation clauses 184
　post-apartheid 220
South Korea
　transition towards democracy 198–9
sovereignty
　absolute 84
　and flag burning 36
　over own mind 63–4
　parliamentary 82–3
　popular *see* popular sovereignty
　'rational sovereigns,' human beings
　　as 63–4
　theories 25
Spain
　'glorifying terrorism' offences 520
speaking back *see* counter-speech
Special Rapporteur, UN 524–5
speech
　chilling effect *see* chilling effect on speech
　coercive 71
　commercial 69–70, 73, 198
　compelled 70, 74, 126
　corporate 49
　defining 159–72
　freedom of *see* freedom of expression;
　　freedom of speech
　and harm 138–41
　hate speech, questioning whether counting
　　as 'speech' 116, 461–4
　labelling the right to freedom of 159–62, 168
　laissez-faire approach to 118, 126
　and law violation 36
　meaning conveyed by speaker's words 34–5
　offensive *see* offensiveness
　ordinary definition 481
　political versus other forms 73
　pornography, questioning whether
　　counting as 'speech' 116, 477, 481–4
　protected and unprotected 35
　regulation of *see* regulation of speech
　religious *see* religious expression
　restrictions as 'content-neutral' 48
　social activity 251
　source in the self 68
　truth value of certain categories 48
　unfree 136
speech acts and speech act theory 114, 257, 496
　and autonomy 75–6

　conventions 463
　harms, acts causing 463–4
　and hate speech 461–2, 467
　illocutionary speech acts 462–3, 491, 496
　　illocutionary disablement 494, 496
　locutionary speech acts 462, 491
　perlocutionary speech acts 462, 491
　and pornography 478, 491–2
Spence, Michael 119, 129–31
Spinoza, Baruch 82–3
state
　see also autonomy
　autonomy as side-constraint on exercise of
　　power 64, 78
　and blasphemy laws 507
　control of speech 243–6
　and dominant religion 516–17
　duties regarding autonomy 61–2
　　negative duty of non-interference
　　　62, 77
　　positive obligation to act xix, 62
　　reasons for which speech may be
　　　legitimately restricted 67–8
　justification for interferences with
　　expressive activity 71
　libel law 280
　Mill on role of 486
　state action doctrine xxiii
　state coercion in the US 307–8, 311
Stevens, Justice John Paul 110, 142–3, 149
Stiglitz, Joseph 119, 129–31
Stomakhin v Russia (2018), ECtHR 211
Stone, Attorney General Harlan Fiske 343–4
Strauss, David
　Baker's views on autonomy compared
　　with 71
　persuasion principle of autonomy
　　compared with Millian principle
　　(Scanlon) 66–7
　false statements of fact 66–7
　government engaging in 'thought
　　control' 66–7
　and inducement 66–7
　manipulative speech 67
subordination
　hate speech 463
　pornography as act of 462, 480, 488–9, 492
substantive democracy
　versus proceduralist xvi, 101–3
Sullivan, Kathleen 125–6

Sullivan case *see New York Times v Sullivan* (1964)
Sundar, Madhavi 507
Sunstein, Cass 99, 127–8, 251–2
Supreme Court, US
　see also Constitution, US; First Amendment of American Constitution and free speech; United States; *individual cases*
　balancing test, appeal of 176
　and balancing under First Amendment 173–4
　classic statements 235
　and commercial advertising 452
　composition 340–1
　content-based versus viewpoint-based restrictions 146–7
　and First Amendment abridgement 178–9
　freedom of Internet speech 352, 356
　insult of public officials 400, 403
　and labour organizing 383, 385
　libertarian democracy 103–4
　and mass media 549–50
　and privacy law 297–8, 304–7
　proportionality analysis xxi–xxii
　public gatherings, demonstrations and protests 369–70, 378
　religious expression and public sphere 508–9
　and state control of speech 243
　striking down of flag-burning bans 126
　structure of a right to free speech 220
　truth justification for freedom of speech 47–9
　workplace, freedom of expression in 413, 430
Sürek and Özedmir v Turkey (No 1) (1999), ECtHR 529–30
Sürek v Turkey (No 1) (1999), ECtHR 529–30
symbols
　see also flags
　buildings 380
　desecrators and venerators 126, 408
　external 513–14, 516–17
　heads of state 408
　kitemarks 134
　Nazi swastika 458–9
　nonverbal 433
　passive 509–10, 514, 516–17
　religious 14–15, 509–10, 513–14, 516–17

sovereignty 36
speech acts 75–6
truth justification for freedom of speech 57

T

Taylor, Charles 502
Taylor v Mississippi (1943) 348
teleology, utility as ultimate principle of 12
television 545–6
terrorist-related speech xx–xxi, 518–41
　all-factors-considered approach 529
　Al-Qaeda 534–5
　categories 525–8
　'clear and imminent danger of violence' 529–30
　counter-terrorism measures 210, 524
　criminalizing, beyond Europe 531–2
　generally-accepted definition in international law 524
　glorification-related offences and policies at the national, regional and supranational levels 519–20, 523–5, 527–8
　Holocaust denial 529
　notice-and-takedown procedures 521, 524, 538–41
　propaganda 526
　Proposed Regulation 536–8, 540–1
　regulating online 535–6
　　and potential shift to a compulsory regime 536–8
　role of threat inflation and risk misperception 522–3
　skewed perceptions of the risks of terrorism 521
　Strasbourg's struggle with pro-terrorist speech 528–31
　US courts and speech-based coordination with designated foreign terrorist organizations 532–5
　voluntary European framework 536
Thaler, Richard 127–8
theism 54
thick democracy *see* substantive democracy
Thomas, Justice Clarence 447
Thucydides 20–1
　History of the Peloponnesian War 41
totalitarian regimes 106–7
transcendent truth 50–4
　and factual truth 56
　narrative defence of truth justification 58

Trenchard, John 82-3
Tribe, Laurence 140
Truman, Harry 339
truth
    see also truth justification for freedom of speech; truth-seeking
    concept of 44-5
    factual 50-6
    Freedom of Discussion Principle (Mill)
        engagement with falsehoods and partial truths 8-10
        value of truth 11-12
    as an ideal xv
    as knowledge 12
    meaning of and freedom of speech 45
    as narrative xv, 57-60
    partial 8-10
    political 21
    post-truth world 55, 249-50
    realization of 50
    religious 21, 53
    and rights (Holmes) 37, 40
    seeking of 32
    transcendent 50-4
    and utility 12
    value of 11-12
    whole truth, achieving 10
truth justification for freedom of speech xv, 44-60
    see also truth; truth-seeking
    Ancient Greek philosophers 51
    appraising 50-6
    arguments in defence of 45, 50-3
    arguments in opposition to xv, 44-5, 53-6
    background 46-50
    evaluating 57-60
    factual truth 45, 50-6
    First Amendment 47, 55, 59
    and freedom of speech doctrine in the US 47-9
    and freedom of speech doctrine outside the US 49-50
    libel 48-9
    marketplace-of-ideas metaphor 48-9, 53-5
    narrative, truth as 57-60
    non-recognition of 49
    origins 46-7
    and religious expression 501-2
    stolen valour provision 48-9
    subordinate to other values, seen as 50
    transcendent truth 50-4, 56
    and truth-seeking 51-2, 59
    truth value of certain categories of speech 48
truth-seeking 30, 32, 133-4, 166-7
    and truth justification for freedom of speech 51-2, 59
Turner, Piers 5
Tushnet, Mark xiv-xv, xx, 280-1
Twitter *see* social media platforms

U

UN General Assembly
    Third Committee 200
UN High Commissioner on Human Rights (UNHCHR) 206-7, 507-8, 524-5
UNHRC (United Nations Human Rights Committee) 198-200
    Concluding Observations on State Reports 196, 210
    General Comment 34 196-9, 205, 207, 209, 211, 400-1
    General Comment 37 199
    hate speech 503
    insult of public officials 400-1
    and national security 209-10
    respect for the reputations of others 205
    restrictions on freedom of speech in international law 204
    and special protection for journalists and public watchdogs 201
United Kingdom
    see also England
    Brexit referendum and withdrawal from the EU 96, 363, 366-7
    commercial advertising 450
    common law 25
    Counter-Terrorism and Border Security Act 2019 518-20
    Court of Appeal 181
    defamation law
        Defamation Act 2013 283-4, 289
        Reynolds case 283-7, 289-91
    democracy and freedom of speech 49
    elections and electoral speech 313, 317, 322-7
    English Civil War 21, 82-3
    Glorious Revolution (1689), England 24

House of Lords 84
Human Rights Act 1998 450
Imperial Britain 331–2
Independent Press Standards Organisation (IPSO) 134
Joint Committee on Human Rights 317
journalistic protection, Code of Practice 202
LGBT community, discrimination against 515
signalling and screening regime 134–5
Supreme Court 515
United Nations Human Rights Committee *see* UNHRC (United Nations Human Rights Committee)
United States
see also Constitution, US; First Amendment of American Constitution and free speech
advertising and freedom of speech 444–54
beyond the US 449–51
experience of US 445–8
American Civil War 21–2, 331, 333–4
courts and speech-based coordination with designated foreign terrorist organizations 532–5
defamation law *see* defamation
elections and electoral speech 314–17, 324
Espionage Act 1917 34, 38, 335–7
Federal Communications Commission (FCC) 121, 133–4
Food and Drug Administration 126
freedom of speech doctrine in 47–9
freedom of speech doctrine outside 49–50
hate speech 456
Inter-American Court of Human Rights (IACtHR) xxi–xxii, 401–3, 405–6
libertarian democracy 103–4
public gatherings, demonstrations and protests 372
Sedition Act 1798 25–7, 332–3, 335, 346
viewpoint neutrality 143–4
wars and unlawful conduct protected by free speech xx–xxi, 331–49
Americans learning from history 344–9
Civil War 333–4

Cold War 331, 339–41
'Half War' with France 331–3
Vietnam War 341–4
World War I 334–41
United States v National Treasury Employees' Union (1995) 417–19, 421–2
Universal Declaration of Human Rights (UDHR) 49–50, 107
public gatherings 369
religious expression 500–1
terminology, freedom of speech 160–1
unlawful conduct *see* wars and unlawful conduct protected by free speech
UN Security Council (UNSC)
and terrorism 521, 523
Counter-Terrorism Committee 533
utility/utilitarianism (Mill)
rule versus act utilitarianism 31–3
truth and utility 12

V

Valentine v Chrestensen (1942) 445–7
Vallandigham, Clement 333–4
vehement, caustic and sharp attacks
defamation 286–7
insult of public officials 398–400
Venetian republic 22–3
video games, violent 47
Vietnam War 341–4
viewpoint theory 139–41
child pornography 139–40, 142
content-based versus viewpoint-based restrictions xvii, 141–7, 155–6
harm-insensitive restriction 140–1
and hate speech 458
viewpoint neutrality 138, 143–4
harassment, rules against 459
and subject-matter neutrality 144–5
US-style 143–4
Vinson, Justice Frederick 173, 339–40
Virginia Pharmacy Board v Virginia Consumer Council (1976) 445–8, 451–4
Volokh, Eugene 527

W

Waldron, Jeremy 460
warranties 130
and liability 131–2

wars and unlawful conduct protected by free
    speech xx–xxi, 331–49
  American Civil War 331, 333–4, 339, 341
  Americans learning from history 344–9
  Cold War 331, 339–41
  'Half War' with France 331–3
  Vietnam War 341–4
  World War I 331, 334–41, 345
  World War II 339, 348
Waters v Churchill (1994) 419
*West Virginia State Board of Education v
    Barnette* (1943) 70, 74, 348
Whigs 82–3
White, Theodore 341
Whitney v California (1927) 40–1, 249
Wilders, Geert 208
Williams, Susan xv, 242
  on autonomy 71–2, 74–9
Wilson, James 85
Wilson, Woodrow 38, 334–6, 345–6
Wingrove v The United Kingdom (1997),
    ECtHR 506
Wohlschlegel, Ansgar 127
workplace, freedom of expression in xx,
    xxii–xxiii, 410–30
  *see also Civil Service Commission v
    National Association of Letter Carriers
    (1973); Connick v Myers (1983); Elrod v
    Burns (1976); Garcetti v Ceballos
    (2006); Pickering v Board of Education
    (1968); United States v National
    Treasury Employees' Union (1995)*

  First Amendment 411, 413–14, 426–8, 430
    double-edged 422–6
    individual disciplinary
      decisions 414–19
    public employee speech rights
      under 413–26
  importance 411–13
  Janus v AFSCME (2018) 422–7
  National Labor Relations Act (NLRA)
    1935 427–8
  non-constitutional speech rights in the
    private sector 426–9
  rights-privileges doctrine 413–14
  systemic regulation of public employee
    speech and association 420–2
  whistle-blowers 428
World War I 34, 331, 334–8, 341, 345
  Armistice 337
World War II 339, 348
World Wide Web 350–1
Wright, Chauncey 39

X
xenophobia 507–8

Y
Yates v United States (1957) 340–1
Yun, David 260–1

Z
zones, free speech 380

Printed and bound by CPI Group (UK) Ltd, Croydon, CR0 4YY